REASONS AND PERSONS

At last the horizon appears free to us again, even granted that it is not bright; at last our ships may venture out again, venture out to face any danger; all the daring of the lover of knowledge is permitted again; the sea, *our sea*, lies open again; perhaps there has never yet been such an 'open sea'.

NIETZSCHE, p. 448

REASONS AND PERSONS

BY

DEREK PARFIT

CLARENDON PRESS · OXFORD

OXFORD
UNIVERSITY PRESS

Great Clarendon Street, Oxford OX2 6DP

Oxford University Press is a department of the University of Oxford.
It furthers the University's objective of excellence in research, scholarship,
and education by publishing worldwide in

Oxford New York

Auckland Cape Town Dar es Salaam Hong Kong Karachi Kuala Lumpur
Madrid Melbourne Mexico City Nairobi New Delhi Shanghai Taipei Toronto

With offices in

Argentina Austria Brazil Chile Czech Republic France Greece
Guatemala Hungary Italy Japan Poland Portugal Singapore
South Korea Switzerland Thailand Turkey Ukraine Vietnam

Oxford is a registered trade mark of Oxford University Press
in the UK and in certain other countries

Published in the United States
by Oxford University Press Inc., New York

First published 1984
First issued in paperback (with corrections) 1986
Reprinted with further corrections 1987

British Library Cataloguing in Publication Data
Data available

Library of Congress Cataloging in Publication Data
Parfit, Derek.
Reasons and persons.
Includes bibliographical references and index.
1. Ethics 2. Rationalism. 3. Self. I. Title.
BJ1012.P39 1984 170 83–15139

ISBN 978-0-19-824908-5 (pbk)

Printed in Great Britain
on acid-free paper by
CPI Antony Rowe, Chippenham, Wiltshire

To my parents
Drs. Jessie and Norman Parfit
and my sisters
Theodora and Joanna

ACKNOWLEDGEMENTS

SIXTEEN years ago, I travelled to Madrid with Gareth Evans. I hoped to become a philosopher, and as we drove through France I put to him my ideas. His criticisms made me despair. But before we reached Spain, I saw that he was almost as critical of his own ideas. Like many others, I owe much to the intensity of his love of truth, and his extraordinary vitality. I record this debt first because he died when he was 34.

I owe a great deal to my first teachers: Sir Peter Strawson, Sir Alfred Ayer, David Pears, and Richard Hare. I have since learnt from many people. In discussion I have learnt most from Thomas Nagel, Ronald Dworkin, Tim Scanlon, Amartya Sen, Jonathan Glover, James Griffin, Ann Davis, Jefferson McMahan, and Donald Regan. I have learnt much more from reading the writings of these and many other people. Some of my debts I acknowledge in the endnotes to this book. But I am certain that, because of my weak memory and failure to make proper notes, this book presents, as if they were my ideas, many claims or arguments that I ought to attribute to some source. These forgotten sources, if they read this book, will be rightly aggrieved. Though they should be mentioned in the endnotes, I hope that most are at least mentioned in the Bibliography.

Several people helped me to write this book. Before he died two years ago, John Mackie wrote extremely helpful comments on my earlier work. In the last few months I have received many comments on a draft of this book—so many that I have not had time to make all the needed revisions. Here is a randomly ordered list of those who have helped me in this way: Jonathan Glover, Sir Peter Strawson, John McDowell, Susan Hurley, Paul Seabright, John Vickers, Hywel Lewis, Judith Thomson, Samuel Scheffler, Martin Hollis, Thomas Nagel, Robert Nozick, Richard Lindley, Gilbert Harman, Christopher Peacocke, Peter Railton, Annette Baier, Kurt Baier, Richard Swinburne, Michael Tooley, Mark Sainsbury, Wayne Sumner, Jim Stone, Dale Jamieson, Eric Rakowski, James Griffin, Gregory Kavka, Thomas Hurka, Geoffrey Madell, Ralph Walker, Bradford Hooker, Douglas Maclean, Graeme Forbes, Bimal Matilal, Nicholas Dent, Robert Goodin, Andrew Brennan, John Kenyon, James Fishkin, Robert Elliott, Arnold Levison, Simon Blackburn, Ronald Dworkin, Amartya Sen, Peter Unger, Peter Singer, Jennifer Whiting, Michael Smith, David Lyons, Milton

Wachsberg, William Ewald, Galen Strawson, Gordon Cornwall, Richard Sikora, Partha Dasgupta, Dr. Jessie Parfit, and Dr. Charles Whitty.

I learnt something from everyone just named, and from some I learnt a great deal. From a few people I learnt so much that I want to thank them separately. Jonathan Bennett sent me very helpful comments on half of my draft. Bernard Williams sent me extremely helpful comments on a draft of Part Three. Six other people sent me very helpful comments on drafts of the whole book. Four of these were John Leslie, Michael Woodford, Larry Temkin, and Donald Regan. From two other people I learnt even more. John Broome was a Visiting Fellow at my College throughout the academic year at the end of which I write these words. Both in written comments, and in very many discussions, he solved very many of my problems, and suggested many great improvements. If every passage due to John Broome was mentioned in the endnotes, there would be at least thirty of these notes. As the different academic disciplines drift away from their neighbours, it is heartening to find that an economist should be, in his spare time, so good a philosopher. The person from whom I have learnt the most is Shelly Kagan. Kagan's extraordinarily acute and penetrating comments were half as long as my draft, and many of his suggestions are printed, with little change, in this book. If his co-authorship was mentioned in the endnotes, there would be at least sixty of these notes.

I write these words the day before this text goes to the printer. Because I received so many good objections or comments, I could not have revised and produced my text on time without help of other kinds. I have been helped by Patricia Morison, and greatly helped by Susan Hurley and William Ewald. Jefferson and Sally McMahan saved me many days of work in sorting papers, checking references, and compiling the Bibliography. This book is printed from camera-ready copy. Given my slowness in making the needed revisions, the four people who produced this copy have often, uncomplainingly, worked overtime, and late into the night. These generous people are Angela Blackburn, Jane Nunns, Paul Salotti, and, most generous of all, Catherine Griffin.

I am grateful for the help of everyone mentioned above. To those mentioned in the last two paragraphs I record here my extreme gratitude. This book has one author, but is really the joint product of all of these people.

Finally, I record my great gratitude to an entity that is not a person: All Souls College. If I had not had the extraordinary privilege of being a Prize Fellow and then a Research Fellow of this College for the past sixteen years, this book would certainly not exist.

All Souls College, Oxford   D. A. P.
12 September 1983.

INTRODUCTION

Like my cat, I often simply do what I want to do. I am then not using an ability that only persons have. We know that there are reasons for acting, and that some reasons are better or stronger than others. One of the main subjects of this book is a set of questions about what we have reason to do. I shall discuss several theories. Some of these are moral theories, others are theories about rationality.

We are particular people. I have my life to live, you have yours. What do these facts involve? What makes me the same person throughout my life, and a different person from you? And what is the importance of these facts? What is the importance of the unity of each life, and of the distinction between different lives, and different persons? These questions are the other main subject of this book.

My two subjects, reasons and persons, have close connections. I believe that most of us have false beliefs about our own nature, and our identity over time, and that, when we see the truth, we ought to change some of our beliefs about what we have reason to do. We ought to revise our moral theories, and our beliefs about rationality. In the first two parts of the book I give other arguments for similar conclusions.

I shall not describe, in advance, these arguments and conclusions. The List of Contents provides a summary. The book is long, and sometimes complicated. I have therefore separated my arguments into 154 parts, and given each part a descriptive title. I hope that this makes the arguments easier to follow, and shows what the book contains more clearly than an Index of Subjects could. If I had not rearranged the arguments into these separate parts, such an Index would have been too thick with references to be of much use.

Many introductions to books of this kind try to explain the central concepts that are used. Since it would take at least a book to give a helpful explanation, I shall waste no time in doing less than this. My central concepts are few. We have *reasons for acting*. We *ought* to act in certain ways, and some ways of acting are *morally wrong*. Some outcomes are *good* or *bad*, in a sense that has moral relevance: it is bad for example if people become paralyzed, and we ought, if we can, to prevent this. Most of us understand my last three sentences well enough to understand my arguments. I shall also use the concept of what is in someone's *self-interest*, or what would be *best for this person.* I discuss this briefly in Appendix I. My last central concept is that of a *person.* Most of us think we understand what persons are. Part Three claims that we do not.

Many introductions also try to explain how, when discussing morality, we can hope to make progress. Since the best explanation would be provided by *making* progress, this is the only explanation I shall try to give.

Strawson describes two kinds of philosophy, descriptive, and revisionary. Descriptive philosophy gives reasons for what we instinctively assume, and explains and justifies the unchanging central core in our beliefs about ourselves, and the world we inhabit. I have great respect for descriptive philosophy. But, by temperament, I am a revisionist. Except in my dreary Chapter 1, where I cannot avoid repeating what has been shown to be true, I try to challenge what we assume. Philosophers should not only interpret our beliefs; when they are false, they should *change* them.

Note added in 1985:   In this reprinting I have made several corrections. Thus I have withdrawn my support for the Wide Psychological Criterion of personal identity (p. 208 and elsewhere), since this conflicts with my view that we should not try to decide between the different criteria. I have replaced 'bad' with 'worse' in Claim Q (p. 360) and several later sentences. Other minor substantive corrections include those made in Notes 15 to part I and 83 to part III, and pages 66/lines 15–17, 67/19–23, 211/19–25, 312/31–2, and 374/1–2 and 12–13. For some of these corrections I am grateful to the contributors to *Ethics,* July 1986.

Note added in 1987:   In this reprinting I have widened my definition of Reductionism (p. 210), and removed an apparent circularity from the Physical and Psychological Criteria (pp. 204 and 207). Other minor substantive corrections come on pages 72/lines 2–4, 73/5–15, 81/17–24, 82/5–11, 311/40, and Note 59 to Part I. (I have also made several stylistic corrections or revisions.)

CONTENTS

PART ONE · SELF-DEFEATING THEORIES

CHAPTER 1 · THEORIES THAT ARE INDIRECTLY SELF-DEFEATING   3

1	The Self-interest Theory	3
2	How S Can Be Indirectly Self-defeating	5
3	Does S Tell Us to Be Never Self-denying?	7
4	Why S Does Not Fail in Its Own Terms	11
5	Could It Be Rational to Cause Oneself to Act Irrationally?	12
6	How S Implies that We Cannot Avoid Acting Irrationally	13
7	An Argument for Rejecting S When It Conflicts with Morality	17
8	Why This Argument Fails	19
9	How S Might Be Self-Effacing	23
10	How Consequentialism Is Indirectly Self-defeating	24
11	Why C Does Not Fail in Its Own Terms	28
12	The Ethics of Fantasy	29
13	Collective Consequentialism	30
14	Blameless Wrongdoing	31
15	Could It Be Impossible to Avoid Acting Wrongly?	35
16	Could It Be Right to Cause Oneself to Act Wrongly?	37
17	How C Might Be Self-Effacing	40
18	The Objection that Assumes Inflexibility	43
19	Can Being Rational or Moral Be a Mere Means?	45
20	Conclusions	49

CHAPTER 2 · PRACTICAL DILEMMAS   53

21	Why C Cannot Be Directly Self-defeating	53
22	How Theories Can Be Directly Self-defeating	55
23	Prisoner's Dilemmas and Public Goods	56
24	The Practical Problem and its Solutions	62

CHAPTER 3 · FIVE MISTAKES IN MORAL MATHEMATICS   67

25	The Share-of-the-Total View	67
26	Ignoring the Effects of Sets of Acts	70
27	Ignoring Small Chances	73
28	Ignoring Small or Imperceptible Effects	75
29	Can There Be Imperceptible Harms and Benefits?	78
30	Overdetermination	82
31	Rational Altruism	83

CHAPTER 4 · THEORIES THAT ARE DIRECTLY
SELF-DEFEATING   87

  32 In Prisoner's Dilemmas, Does S Fail in Its Own Terms?   88
  33 Another Weak Defence of Morality   91
  34 Intertemporal Dilemmas   92
  35 A Weak Defence of S   93
  36 How Common-Sense Morality Is Directly Self-Defeating   95
  37 The Five Parts of a Moral Theory   98
  38 How We Can Revise Common-Sense Morality so that It Would
        Not Be Self-Defeating   100
  39 Why We Ought to Revise Common-Sense Morality   103
  40 A Simpler Revision   108

CHAPTER 5 · CONCLUSIONS   111

  41 Reducing the Distance between M and C   111
  42 Towards a Unified Theory   112
  43 Work to be Done   113
  44 Another Possibility   114

                    PART TWO · RATIONALITY AND TIME

CHAPTER 6 · THE BEST OBJECTION TO THE
SELF-INTEREST THEORY   117

  45 The Present-aim Theory   117
  46 Can Desires Be Intrinsically Irrational, or Rationally Required? 120
  47 Three Competing Theories   126
  48 Psychological Egoism   127
  49 The Self-interest Theory and Morality   129
  50 My First Argument   130
  51 The S-Theorist's First Reply   132
  52 Why Temporal Neutrality Is Not the Issue Between S and P   133

CHAPTER 7 · THE APPEAL TO FULL RELATIVITY   137

  53 The S-Theorist's Second Reply   137
  54 Sidgwick's Suggestions   137
  55 How S Is Incompletely Relative   140
  56 How Sidgwick Went Astray   141
  57 The Appeal Applied at a Formal Level   142
  58 The Appeal Applied to Other Claims   144

CHAPTER 8 · DIFFERENT ATTITUDES TO TIME   149

  59 Is It Irrational to Give No Weight to One's Past Desires?   149
  60 Desires that Depend on Value Judgements or Ideals   153
  61 Mere Past Desires   156
  62 Is It Irrational To Care Less About One's Further Future?   158
  63 A Suicidal Argument   163
  64 Past or Future Suffering   165
  65 The Direction of Causation   168
  66 Temporal Neutrality   170
  67 Why We Should Not Be Biased towards the Future   174

Contents

xiii

68	Time's Passage	177
69	An Asymmetry	181
70	Conclusions	184

CHAPTER 9 · WHY WE SHOULD REJECT S

187

71	The Appeal to Later Regrets	187
72	Why a Defeat for Proximus is Not a Victory for S	188
73	The Appeal to Inconsistency	189
74	Conclusions	191

PART THREE · PERSONAL IDENTITY

CHAPTER 10 · WHAT WE BELIEVE OURSELVES TO BE

199

75	Simple Teletransportation and the Branch-Line Case	200
76	Qualitative and Numerical Identity	201
77	The Physical Criterion of Personal Identity	202
78	The Psychological Criterion	204
79	The Other Views	209

CHAPTER 11 · HOW WE ARE NOT WHAT WE BELIEVE

219

80	Does Psychological Continuity Presuppose Personal Identity?	219
81	The Subject of Experiences	223
82	How a Non-Reductionist View Might Have Been True	227
→ 83	Williams's Argument against the Psychological Criterion	229
84	The Psychological Spectrum	231
85	The Physical Spectrum	234
86	The Combined Spectrum	236

CHAPTER 12 · WHY OUR IDENTITY IS NOT WHAT MATTERS

245

87	Divided Minds	245
88	What Explains the Unity of Consciousness?	248
89	What Happens When I Divide?	253
90	What Matters When I Divide?	261
91	Why There Is No Criterion of Identity that Can Meet Two Plausible Requirements	266
92	Wittgenstein and Buddha	273
93	Am I Essentially My Brain?	273
94	Is the True View Believable?	274

CHAPTER 13 · WHAT DOES MATTER

281

95	Liberation From the Self	281
96	The Continuity of the Body	282
97	The Branch-Line Case	287
98	Series-Persons	289
99	Am I a Token or a Type?	293
100	Partial Survival	298
101	Successive Selves	302

CHAPTER 14 · PERSONAL IDENTITY AND RATIONALITY

307

| 102 | The Extreme Claim | 307 |
| 103 | A Better Argument against the Self-interest Theory | 312 |

104 The S-Theorist's Counter-Argument   315
105 The Defeat of the Classical Self-Interest Theory   317
106 The Immorality of Imprudence   318

CHAPTER 15 · PERSONAL IDENTITY AND MORALITY   321

107 Autonomy and Paternalism   321
108 The Two Ends of Lives   321
109 Desert   323
110 Commitments   326
111 The Separateness of Persons and Distributive Justice   329
112 Three Explanations of the Utilitarian View   330
113 Changing a Principle's Scope   332
114 Changing a Principle's Weight   334
115 Can It Be Right to Burden Someone Merely to Benefit
        Someone Else?   336
116 An Argument for Giving Less Weight to Equality   339
117 A More Extreme Argument   342
118 Conclusions   345

PART FOUR · FUTURE GENERATIONS

CHAPTER 16 · THE NON-IDENTITY PROBLEM   351

119 How Our Identity in Fact Depends on When We Were Conceived   351
120 The Three Kinds of Choice   355
121 What Weight Should We Give to the Interests of Future People?   356
122 A Young Girl's Child   357
123 How Lowering the Quality of Life Might Be Worse for No One   361
124 Why an Appeal to Rights Cannot Solve the Problem   364
125 Does the Fact of Non-Identity Make a Moral Difference?   366
126 Causing Predictable Catastrophes in the Further Future   371
127 Conclusions   377

CHAPTER 17 · THE REPUGNANT CONCLUSION   381

128 Is It Better If More People Live?   381
129 The Effects of Population Growth on Existing People   382
130 Overpopulation   384
131 The Repugnant Conclusion   387

CHAPTER 18 · THE ABSURD CONCLUSION

132 An Alleged Asymmetry   391
133 Why the Ideal Contractual Method Provides No Solution   391
134 The Narrow Person-Affecting Principle   393
135 Why We Cannot Appeal to this Principle   395
136 The Two Wide Person-Affecting Principles   396
137 Possible Theories   401
138 The Sum of Suffering   406
139 The Appeal to the Valueless Level   412
140 The Lexical View   413
141 Conclusions   414

CHAPTER 19   THE MERE ADDITION PARADOX   419

142   Mere Addition   419
143   Why We Should Reject the Average Principle   420
144   Why We Should Reject the Appeal to Inequality   422
145   The First Version of the Paradox   425
146   Why We Are Not Yet Forced to Accept the Repugnant Conclusion   430
147   The Appeal to the Bad Level   432
148   The Second Version of the Paradox   433
149   The Third Version   438

CONCLUDING CHAPTER   443

150   Impersonality   443
151   Different Kinds of Argument   447
152   Should We Welcome or Regret My Conclusions?   449
153   Moral Scepticism   452
154   How both Human History, and the History of Ethics, May Be
        Just Beginning   453

APPENDICES

A   A World Without Deception   457
B   How My Weaker Conclusion Would in Practice Defeat S   461
C   Rationality and the Different Theories about Self-Interest   464
D   Nagel's Brain   468
E   The Closest Continuer Schema   477
F   The Social Discount Rate   480
G   Whether Causing Someone to Exist can Benefit this Person   487
H   Rawlsian Principles   490
I   What Makes Someone's Life Go Best   493
J   Buddha's View   502

Notes   505
Bibliography   533
Index of Names   541

PART ONE

SELF-DEFEATING THEORIES

1

THEORIES THAT ARE INDIRECTLY
SELF-DEFEATING

WHAT do we have most reason to do? Several theories answer this question. Some of these are moral theories; others are theories about rationality. When applied to some of our decisions, different theories give us different answers. We must then try to decide which is the best theory.

Arguments about these theories are of many kinds. One argument is that a theory is *self-defeating*. This argument, uniquely, needs no assumptions. It claims that a theory fails even in its own terms, and thus condemns itself.

The first part of this book discusses what this argument achieves. As I shall explain, all of the best known theories are in certain ways self-defeating. What does this show? In some cases, nothing. In other cases, what is shown is that a theory must be developed further, or extended. And in other cases what is shown is that a theory must be either rejected or revised. This is what is shown about the moral theories that most of us accept.

I start with the best-known case.

1. THE SELF-INTEREST THEORY

We can describe all theories by saying what they tell us to try to achieve. According to all moral theories, we ought to try to act morally. According to all theories about rationality, we ought to try to act rationally. Call these our *formal* aims. Different moral theories, and different theories about rationality, give us different *substantive* aims.

By 'aim', I shall mean 'substantive aim'. This use of aim is broad. It can describe moral theories that are concerned, not with moral goals, but with rights, or duties. Suppose that, on some theory, five kinds of act are totally forbidden. This theory gives to each of us the aim that he never acts in these five ways.

I shall first discuss the *Self-interest Theory*, or *S*. This is a theory about rationality. S gives to each person this aim: the outcomes that would be best for himself, and that would make his life go, for him, as well as possible.

To apply S, we must ask what would best achieve this aim. Answers to this question I call *theories about self-interest*. As Appendix I explains, there are three plausible theories.

On the *Hedonistic Theory*, what would be best for someone is what would give him most happiness. Different versions of this theory make different claims about what happiness involves, and how it should be measured.

On the *Desire-Fulfilment Theory*, what would be best for someone is what would best fulfil his desires throughout his life. Here again, there are different versions of this theory. Thus the *Success Theory* appeals only to a person's desires about his own life.

On the *Objective List Theory*, certain things are good or bad for us, even if we would not want to have the good things or avoid the bad things. Here again, there are different versions. The good things might include the development of one's abilities, knowledge, and the awareness of true beauty. The bad things might include sadistic pleasure, being deceived, and losing liberty, or dignity.

These three theories partly overlap. On all these theories, happiness and pleasure are at least part of what makes our lives go better for us, and misery and pain are at least part of what makes our lives go worse. These claims would be made by any plausible Objective List Theory. And they are implied by all versions of the Desire-Fulfilment Theory. On all theories, the Hedonistic Theory is at least part of the truth. To save words, this will sometimes be the only part that I discuss.

All these theories also claim that, in deciding what would be best for someone, we should give equal weight to all the parts of this person's future. Later events may be less predictable; and a predictable event should count for less if it is less likely to happen. But it should not count for less merely because, if it happens, it will happen later.

It would take at least a book to decide between the different theories about self-interest. This book discusses some of the differences between these theories, but does not try to decide between them. Much of this book discusses the Self-interest Theory. As I have said, this is not one of the theories about self-interest. It is a theory about rationality. We can discuss S without deciding between the different theories about self-interest. We can make claims that would be true on all of these theories.

It will help to call some aims *ultimate*. Other aims are *instrumental*, mere means to the achievement of some ultimate aim. Thus, for all except misers, being rich is not an ultimate aim. I can now re-state the *central claim* of S. This is

(S1) For each person, there is one supremely rational ultimate aim: that his life go, for him, as well as possible.

As we shall see, S makes several other claims.

There are several objections to S. Some of these I discuss in Parts Two and Three. In what follows I discuss the objection that, like certain other theories, S is self-defeating.

2. HOW S CAN BE INDIRECTLY SELF-DEFEATING

If we call some theory *T*, call the aims that it gives us *our T-given aims*. Call T

indirectly individually self-defeating when it is true that, if someone tries to achieve his T-given aims, these aims will be, on the whole, worse achieved.

On this definition, we do not simply ask whether a theory is self-defeating. We ask whether it is self-defeating when applied to certain people, during certain periods.

My S-given aim is that my life go, for me, as well as possible. It can be true that, if I try to do whatever will be best for me, this will be worse for me. There are two kinds of case:

(a) My attempts may often fail. I may often do what will be worse for me than something else that I could have done.

(b) Even if I never do what, of the acts that are possible for me, will be worse for me, it may be worse for me if I am purely self-interested. It might be better for me if I had some other disposition.

In cases of kind (a), the bad effects come from what I do. Suppose that I steal whenever I believe that I will not be caught. I may be often caught, and punished. Even in self-interested terms, honesty may therefore be the best policy for me. These cases are not worth discussing. If this is the way in which S is self-defeating, this is no objection to S. S is self-defeating here only because of my incompetence in attempting to follow S. This is a fault, not in S, but in me. We might object to some theory that it is too difficult to follow. But this is not true of S.

The cases worth discussing are of kind (b). In these cases it will be worse for me if I am purely self-interested, even if I succeed in never doing what will be worse for me. The bad effects come, not from what I do, but from my disposition, or the fact that I am purely self-interested.

What does this fact involve? I could be purely self-interested without being purely selfish. Suppose that I love my family and friends. On all of the theories about self-interest, my love for these people affects what is in my interests. Much of my happiness comes from knowing about, and helping to cause, the happiness of those I love. On the Desire-Fulfilment Theory, it will be better for me if, as I want, things go well for those I love. What will be best for me may, in these and other ways, largely overlap with what will be best for those I love. But, in some cases, what will be better for me will be worse for those I love. I am self-interested if, in all these cases, I do what will be better for me.

It may be thought that, if I am self-interested, I shall *always* be trying to do whatever will be best for me. But I often act in one of two ways, believing that neither would be better for me. In these cases I am not trying to do what will be best for me; I am acting on a more particular desire. And this may be true even when I am doing what I know will be best for me. Suppose that I know that, if I help you, this will be best for me. I may help you because I love you, not because I want to do what will be best for me. In describing what it would be for me to be self-interested, it is enough to claim that, while I often act on other desires, I *never do what I believe will be worse for me*. If this is true, it will be clearer to call me, not *self-interested*, but *never self-denying*.

I shall now redescribe the interesting way in which, for any individual, S may be indirectly self-defeating. This is true when, if someone is never self-denying, this will be worse for him than it would be if he had some other disposition. Even if someone succeeds in never doing what would be worse for him, it may be worse for him that he is never self-denying. It might be better for him if he had some other disposition. He might then sometimes do what would be worse for him. But the costs to him of acting in this way might be less than the benefits of having this other disposition.

These claims can be true on all of the different theories about self-interest. Hedonists have long known that happiness, when aimed at, is harder to achieve. If my strongest desire is that I be happy, I may be less happy than I would be if I had other desires that were stronger. Thus I might be happier if my strongest desire was that someone else be happy.

Here is another example. *Kate* is a writer. Her strongest desire is that her books be as good as possible. Because she cares so much about the quality of her books, she finds her work rewarding. If her desire to write good books was much weaker, she would find her work boring. She knows this, and she accepts the Hedonistic Theory about self-interest. She therefore believes that it is better for her that her strongest desire is that her books be as good as possible. But, because of the strength of this desire, she often works so hard, and for so long, that she collapses with exhaustion, and is, for a period, very depressed.

Suppose that Kate believes truly that, if she worked less hard, her books would be slightly worse, but she would be happier. She would find her work just as rewarding, and she would avoid these severe depressions. Kate therefore believes that, when she works so hard, she is doing what is worse for her. But how could it become true that she never acts in this way? It may be a fact that she would never act in this way only if she had a much weaker desire that her books be as good as possible. And this would be even worse for her, since she would then find her work boring. On the Hedonistic Theory, it would be worse for Kate if she was never self-denying.[1]

Suppose that we accept not the Hedonistic but the Desire-Fulfilment Theory about self-interest. We may then deny that, in this example, Kate is doing what is worse for her. Her strongest desire is that her books be as good as possible. By working so hard, though she makes herself exhausted and depressed, she makes her books slightly better. She is thereby causing her strongest desire to be better fulfilled. On our theory about self-interest, this may be better for her.

If we are not Hedonists, we need a different example. Suppose that I am driving at midnight through some desert. My car breaks down. You are a stranger, and the only other driver near. I manage to stop you, and I offer you a great reward if you rescue me. I cannot reward you now, but I promise to do so when we reach my home. Suppose next that I am *transparent,* unable to deceive others. I cannot lie convincingly. Either a blush, or my tone of voice, always gives me away. Suppose, finally, that I know myself to be never self-denying. If you drive me to my home, it would be worse for me if I gave you the promised reward. Since I know that I never do what will be worse for me, I know that I shall break my promise. Given my inability to lie convincingly, you know this too. You do not believe my promise, and therefore leave me stranded in the desert. This happens to me because I am never self-denying. It would have been better for me if I had been *trustworthy,* disposed to keep my promises even when doing so would be worse for me. You would then have rescued me.

(It may be objected that, even if I am never self-denying, I could decide to keep my promise, since making this decision would be better for me. If I decided to keep my promise, you would trust me, and would rescue me. This objection can be answered. I know that, after you have driven me home, it would be worse for me if I gave you the promised reward. If I know that I am never self-denying, I know that I shall not keep my promise. And, if I know this, I cannot decide to keep my promise. I cannot decide to do what I know that I shall not do. If I *can* decide to keep my promise, this must be because I believe that I shall not be never self-denying. We can add the assumption that I would not believe this unless it was true. It would then be true that it would be worse for me if I was, and would remain, never self-denying. It would be better for me if I was trustworthy.)

I have described two ways in which it would be worse for someone if he was never self-denying. There are many other ways in which this can be true. It is probably true of most people, during most of their lives. When the Self-interest Theory is applied to these people, it is what I call indirectly individually self-defeating. Does this make S fail in its own terms? Does S condemn itself? This depends on whether S tells these people to be never self-denying.

3. DOES S TELL US TO BE NEVER SELF-DENYING?

It may seem obvious that S tells everyone to be never self-denying. But, as described so far, S claims only that, for each person, there is one supremely rational ultimate aim: that his life go, for him, as well as possible.

When applied to acts, S claims both

(S2) What each of us has[2] most reason to do is whatever would be best for himself, and

(S3) It is irrational for anyone to do what he believes will be worse for himself.

S must also make claims about what we should do when we cannot predict the effects of our acts. We can ignore cases of *uncertainty*, where we have no beliefs about the probabilities of different effects. In *risky* cases, where we do have such beliefs, S claims

(S4) What it would be rational for anyone to do is what will bring him the greatest *expected* benefit.

To calculate the expected benefit from some act, we add together the possible benefits, and subtract the possible costs, with each benefit or cost multiplied by the chance that the act will produce it. Thus, if some act has a chance of nine in ten of bringing me some benefit B, and a chance of one in ten of causing me to lose some benefit that would be twice as great as B, the expected benefit is $B \times 9/10 - 2B \times 1/10$, or seven-tenths of B.

What should S claim about the rationality of desires and dispositions? Since S claims that, for each person, there is one supremely rational ultimate aim, S should clearly claim that the supremely rational desire is the desire that this aim be achieved. S should claim

(S5) The supremely rational desire is that one's life go as well as possible for oneself.

Similarly, S should claim

(S6) The supremely rational disposition is that of someone who is never self-denying.

If someone is never self-denying, though he sometimes acts on other desires, he never acts against the supremely rational desire. He never does what he believes will be worse for him.

To save words, call both desires and dispositions *motives*. There are ways in which, over time, we can cause our motives to change. We can develop habits. If we act in ways that we do not now enjoy, we may come to enjoy them. If we change our work, or where we live, or read certain books, or have children, this may cause predictable changes in our motives. And there are many other ways in which we can cause such changes.

According to (S2), what each person has most reason to do is to cause himself to have, or to allow himself to keep, any of the *best possible sets of motives, in self-interested terms*. These are the sets of motives of which the following is true. There is no other possible set of motives of which it is true that, if this person had these motives, this would be better for him. By 'possible' I mean 'causally possible, given the general facts about human nature, and the particular facts about this person's nature'. It would often be hard to know whether some set of motives would be causally possible for someone, or would be one of the best sets for this person in self-interested terms. But we can ignore these difficulties. There are many cases in which someone knows that it would be better for him if there was some change in his motives. And in many of these cases such a person knows that, in one of the ways described above, he could cause this change. (S3) implies that it would be irrational for this person not to cause this change.

Similar claims apply to our emotions, beliefs, abilities, the colour of our hair, where we live, and anything else that we could change. What each of us has most reason to do is to make any change that would be best for himself. If someone believes that he could make such a change, it would be irrational for him not to do so.

We can now return to my earlier question. We are discussing the people of whom it is true that, if they were never self-denying, this would be worse for them than if they had some other disposition. Suppose that these people know that this is true. Does S tell them to be never self-denying?

S claims the following. If such a person was never self-denying, he would have the disposition that is supremely rational. But it would be irrational for this person to cause himself to have, or to keep, this disposition. It would be rational for him to cause himself to have, or to keep, the other disposition, since this would be better for him.

These claims may seem to give conflicting answers to my question. They may seem to tell this person both to be, and not to be, never self-denying.

This misinterprets S. When S claims that one disposition is supremely rational, it does not tell us to *have* this disposition. Remember the distinction between formal and substantive aims. Like all theories about rationality, S gives to everyone this formal aim: to be rational, and to act rationally. What distinguishes different theories is that they give us different substantive aims. In its central claim, (S1), S gives to each person one substantive aim: that his life go, for him, as well as possible. Does S give to each person *another* substantive aim: to be rational, and to act rationally? It does not. According to S, our formal aim is not a substantive aim.

It may be thought that, in making these claims, I have not described the best version of the Self-interest Theory. But this is the version that would be accepted by most of those who believe this theory. Most of these people would accept (S2) and (S3). Suppose I know that it will be best for me if I make myself irrational. I shall soon describe a case in which this would almost certainly be true. If this is true, (S2) implies that what I have most reason to do is to make myself irrational. (S3) implies that it would be irrational for me *not* to do so. These claims do not give me, as a substantive aim, being rational.

Does this imply that, for S, being rational is a mere means? This depends on what is the best theory about self-interest. On the Hedonistic Theory, S gives to each person this substantive aim: the greatest possible happiness for himself. Being rational is not an essential part of *this* aim. It is a mere means. So is acting rationally, and having rational desires or dispositions. Consider next the Objective List Theory. On some versions of this theory, being rational is one of the things that is good for each person, whatever its effects may be. If this is so, being rational is not a mere means, but part of the substantive aim that S gives to each person. The same would be true, on the Desire-Fulfilment Theory, in the case of those people who want to be rational, whatever the effects may be.

It may be objected: 'Suppose that we accept the Hedonistic Theory. S then tells us that being rational is a mere means. If this is so, why should we try to be rational? Why should we want to know what we have most reason to do? If we accept what S claims, and believe that being rational is a mere means, we shall cease to be interested in the questions that S claims to answer. This must be an objection to S. An acceptable theory about rationality cannot claim that being rational is a mere means.'

We could answer: 'A theory would be unacceptable if it claimed that being rational did not matter. But this is not what S claims. Suppose that I cling to some rock as a mere means of escaping death. Though my act is a mere means, it matters a great deal. The same can be true about being rational.' This may not completely answer this objection. As we shall see, there is a similar objection to certain moral theories. To save words, I discuss these objections at the same time. This discussion is in Section 19.

I can now explain a remark that I made above. According to S, the disposition that is supremely rational is that of someone who is never self-denying. I wrote that, in making this claim, S does not tell us to have this disposition. S gives to each person one substantive aim: that his life go, for him, as well as possible. On some theories about self-interest, being rational would, for some people, be part of this aim. But this would only be because, like being happy, being rational is part of what makes our lives go better. Being rational is not, *as such*, a substantive aim. Nor is having the supremely rational disposition.

In the case of some people, according to S, being rational would *not* be part of what makes their lives go better. These are the people that I am discussing. It is true of these people that, if they were never self-denying, this would be worse for them than if they had some other disposition. Since this is true, being never self-denying would *not* be part of the aim that S gives to these people. S does not tell these people to have what S claims to be the supremely rational disposition: that of someone who is never self-denying. And, if they can change their disposition, S tells these people, if they can, *not* to be never self-denying. Since it would be better for these people if they had some other disposition, S tells them to cause themselves to have, or to keep, this other disposition. If they know that they could act in either of these ways, S claims that it would be irrational for them not to do so. It would be irrational for them to cause themselves to be, or to allow themselves to remain, never self-denying.

4. WHY S DOES NOT FAIL IN ITS OWN TERMS

These claims answer the other question that I asked. When S is applied to these people, it is what I call indirectly self-defeating. Does this make S fail in its own terms? Does S condemn itself?

The answer is No. S is indirectly self-defeating because it would be worse for these people if they were never self-denying. But S does *not* tell these people to be never self-denying, and it tells them, if they can, *not* to be. If these people are never self-denying, this is worse for them. This is a bad effect, in S's terms. But this bad effect is not the result either of their doing what S tells them to do, or of their having a disposition that S tells them to have. Since this is so, S is not failing in its own terms.

It may be objected: 'This bad effect may be the result of these people's *belief* in S. If they believe S, they believe that it would be irrational for them to do what they believe will be worse for them. It may be true that, if they believe that it is irrational to act in this way, they will never do so. If they never act in this way, they are never self-denying. Suppose that, in one of the ways that you described, having this disposition is worse for them. This is a bad effect in S's terms. If belief in S has this effect, S does fail in its own terms.'

In answering this objection, we need to know whether these people can change their disposition. Suppose, first, that they cannot. Why would this be true? If they cannot change their disposition, and they have this disposition *because* they believe S, the explanation must be that they cannot cause themselves to be disposed to do what they believe to be irrational. They could change their disposition only if they believed some other theory about rationality. S would then tell them, if they can, to make themselves believe this other theory. This possibility I discuss in Sections 6 to 8. As I shall argue, even if this is true, S would not be failing in its own terms.

Suppose next that these people can change their disposition, without changing their beliefs about rationality. If these people are never self-denying, this will be worse for them than it would be if they had some other disposition. S tells these people to cause themselves to have this other disposition. The objection given above clearly fails. It may be true that these people are never self-denying because they believe S. But S claims that it is irrational for these people to allow themselves to remain never self-denying. If they do remain never self-denying, this cannot be claimed to be merely 'the result of their belief in S'. It is the result of their failure to do what they could do, and what S tells them to do. This result is worse for them, which is a bad effect in S's terms. But a bad effect which results from *disobeying* S cannot provide an objection to S. If my doctor tells me to move to a healthier climate, he would be open to no criticism if, because I refuse to move, I die.

There is a third possibility. These people may be unable to change either their dispositions, or their beliefs about rationality. Their belief in S is bad for them, which is a bad effect in S's terms. Is this an objection to S? It will be easier to answer this question after I have discussed other theories. My answer is in Section 18.

5. COULD IT BE RATIONAL TO CAUSE ONESELF TO ACT IRRATIONALLY?

I turn now to a new question. A theory may be unacceptable even though it does not fail in its own terms. It is true of many people that it would be worse for them if they were never self-denying. Does this give us independent grounds to reject S?

According to S, it would be rational for each of these people to cause himself to have, or to keep, one of the best possible sets of motives, in self-interested terms. Which these sets are is, in part, a factual question. And the details of the answer would be different for different people in different circumstances. But we know the following, about each of these people. Since it would be worse for him if he was never self-denying, it would be better for him if he was sometimes self-denying. It would be better for him if he was sometimes disposed to do what he believes will be worse for him. S claims that acting in this way is irrational. If such a person believes S, it tells him to cause himself to be disposed to act in a way that S claims to be irrational. Is this a damaging implication? Does it give us any reason to reject S?

Consider

Schelling's Answer to Armed Robbery. A man breaks into my house. He hears me calling the police. But, since the nearest town is far away, the police cannot arrive in less then fifteen minutes. The man orders me to open the safe in which I hoard my gold. He threatens that, unless he gets the gold in the next five minutes, he will start shooting my children, one by one.

What is it rational for me to do? I need the answer fast. I realize that it would not be rational to give this man the gold. The man knows that, if he simply takes the gold, either I or my children could tell the police the make and number of the car in which he drives away. So there is a great risk that, if he gets the gold, he will kill me and my children before he drives away.

Since it would be irrational to give this man the gold, should I ignore his threat? This would also be irrational. There is a great risk that he will kill one of my children, to make me believe his threat that, unless he gets the gold, he will kill my other children.

What should I do? It is very likely that, whether or not I give this man the gold, he will kill us all. I am in a desperate position. Fortunately, I remember reading Schelling's *The Strategy of Conflict.* [3] I also have a special drug, conveniently at hand. This drug causes one to be, for a brief period, very irrational. Before the man can stop me, I reach for the bottle and drink. Within a few seconds, it becomes apparent that I am crazy. Reeling about the room, I say to the man: 'Go ahead. I love my children. So please kill them.' The man tries to get the gold by torturing me. I cry out: 'This is agony. So please go on.'

Given the state that I am in, the man is now powerless. He can do nothing that will induce me to open the safe. Threats and torture cannot force concessions from someone who is so irrational. The man can only flee, hoping to escape the police. And, since I am in this state, he is less likely to believe that I would record the number of his car. He therefore has less reason to kill me.

While I am in this state, I shall act in irrational ways. There is a risk that, before the police arrive, I may harm myself or my children. But, since I have no gun, this risk is small. And making myself irrational is the best way to reduce the great risk that this man will kill us all.

On any plausible theory about rationality, it would be rational for me, in this case, to cause myself to become for a period irrational.[4a] This answers the question that I asked above. S might tell us to cause ourselves to be disposed to act in ways that S claims to be irrational. This is no objection to S. As the case just given shows, an acceptable theory about rationality *can* tell us to cause ourselves to do what, in its own terms, is irrational.

Consider next a general claim that is sometimes made:

> (G1) If there is some motive that it would be both (a) rational for someone to cause himself to have, and (b) irrational for him to cause himself to lose, then (c) it cannot be irrational for this person to act upon this motive.

In the case just described, while this man is still in my house, it would be irrational for me to cause myself to cease to be irrational. During this period, I have a set of motives of which both (a) and (b) are true. But (c) is false. During this period, my acts are irrational. We should therefore reject (G1). We can claim instead that, since it was rational for me to cause myself to be like this, this is a case of *rational* irrationality.

6. HOW S IMPLIES THAT WE CANNOT AVOID ACTING IRRATIONALLY

Remember Kate, who accepts the Hedonistic Theory about self-interest. We may accept some other theory. But on these other theories there could be cases that, in the relevant respects, are like Kate's. And the claims that follow could be restated to cover these cases.

It is best for Kate that her strongest desire is that her books be as good as possible. But, because this is true, she often works very hard, making herself, for a period, exhausted and depressed. Because Kate is a Hedonist, she believes that, when she acts in this way, she is doing what is worse for her. Because she also accepts S, Kate believes that, in these cases, she is acting irrationally. Moreover, these irrational acts are quite voluntary. She acts as she does because, though she cares about her own interests, this is not her strongest desire. She has an even stronger desire that her books be as good as possible. It would be worse for her if this desire became weaker. She is acting on a set of motives that, according to S, it would be irrational for her to cause herself to lose.

It might be claimed that, because Kate is acting on such motives, she cannot be acting irrationally. But this claim assumes (G1), the claim that was shown to be false by the case I called Schelling's Answer to Armed Robbery.

If we share Kate's belief that she is acting irrationally, in a quite voluntary way, we might claim that *she* is irrational. But Kate can deny this. Since she believes S, she can claim: 'When I do what I believe will be worse for me, my *act* is irrational. But, because I am acting on a set of motives that it would be irrational for me to cause myself to lose, *I* am *not* irrational. More precisely, I am *rationally irrational*.'

She can add: 'In acting on my desire to make my books better, I am doing what will be worse for me. This is a bad effect, in self-interested terms. But it is part of a set of effects that is one of the best possible sets. Though I sometimes suffer, because this is my strongest desire, I also benefit. And the benefits are greater than the losses. That I sometimes act irrationally, doing what I know will be worse for me, is the price I have to pay if I am to get these greater benefits. This is a price worth paying.'

It may be objected: 'You do not *have* to pay this price. You *could* work less hard. You could do what would be better for you. You are not compelled to do what you believe to be irrational.'

She could answer: 'This is true. I *could* work less hard. But I only *would* do this if my desire to make my books better was much weaker. And this would be, on the whole, worse for me. It would make my work boring. How could I bring it about that I shall not in the future freely choose, in such cases, to do what I believe to be irrational? I could bring this about only by changing my desires in a way that would be worse for me. This is the sense in which I cannot have the greater benefits without paying the lesser price. I cannot have the desires that are best for me without sometimes freely choosing to act in ways that will be worse for me. This is why, when I act irrationally in these ways, I need not regard *myself* as irrational.'

This reply assumes one view about voluntary acts: *Psychological Determinism*. On this view, our acts are always caused by our desires, beliefs, and other dispositions. Given our actual desires and dispositions, it is not causally possible that we act differently. It may be objected: 'If it is not causally possible that Kate act differently, she should not believe that, to act rationally, she *ought* to act differently. We only *ought* to do what we *can* do.'

A similar objection will arise later when I discuss what we ought morally to do. It will save words if Kate answers both objections. She can say: 'In the doctrine that *ought* implies *can*, the sense of 'can' is compatible with Psychological Determinism. When my act is irrational or wrong, I ought to have acted in some other way. On the doctrine, I ought to have acted in this other way only if I could have done so. If I could *not* have acted in this other way, it cannot be claimed that this is what I ought to have done. The claim (1) that I could not have acted in this other way is not the claim (2) that acting in this way would have been impossible, given my actual desires and dispositions. The claim is rather (3) that acting in this way would have been impossible, even if my desires and dispositions had been different. Acting in this way would have been impossible, whatever my desires and dispositions might have been. If claim (1) was claim (2), Determinists would have to conclude that it is not possible for anyone ever to act wrongly or irrationally. They can justifiably reject this conclusion. They can insist that claim (1) is claim (3).'

Kate could add: 'I am not claiming that *Free Will* is compatible with Determinism. The sense of 'can' required for Free Will may be different from the sense of 'can' in the doctrine that ought implies can. These senses are held to be different by most of those Determinists who believe that Free Will is *not* compatible with Determinism. This is why, though these Determinists do not believe that anyone deserves punishment, they continue to believe that it is possible to act wrongly or irrationally.'

Kate may be wrong to assume Psychological Determinism. I claimed earlier that our beliefs about rationality may affect our acts, because we may want to act rationally. It may objected:

> This misdescribes how these beliefs affect our acts. We do not *explain* why someone has acted rationally by citing his desire to do so. Whenever someone acts rationally, it may be trivially true that he wanted to do so. But he acted as he did because he had a belief, not a belief *and* a desire. He acted as he did simply because he believed that he had a reason to do so. And it is often causally possible for him to act rationally whatever his desires and dispositions are.[4]

Note that this objector cannot claim that it is *always* possible for someone to act rationally, whatever his desires and dispositions are. Even if he denies Determinism, this objector cannot claim that there is *no* connection between our acts and our dispositions.

This objector must also admit that our desires and dispositions may make it *harder* for us to do what we believe to be rational. Suppose that I am suffering from intense thirst, and am given a glass of iced water. And suppose I believe that I have a reason to drink this water slowly, since this would increase my enjoyment. I also have a reason not to spill this water. It is much easier to act upon this second reason than it is, given my intense thirst, to drink this water slowly.

If the objector's claims are true, Kate's reply must be revised. She might say: 'It would be worse for me if my strongest desire was to avoid doing what I believe to be irrational. It is better for me that my strongest desire is that my books be as good as possible. Since this is my strongest desire, I sometimes do what I believe to be irrational. I act in this way because my desire to make my books better is much stronger than my desire not to act irrationally. You claim that I could often avoid acting in this way. By an act of will, I could often avoid doing what I most want to do. If I could avoid acting in this way, I cannot claim that I am in no sense irrational. But, given the strength of my desire to make my books better, it would be *very hard* for me to avoid acting in this way. And it would be irrational for me to change my desires so that it would be easier for me to avoid acting in this way. Given these facts, I am irrational only in a very weak sense.'

Kate might add: 'It is not possible *both* that I have one of the best possible sets of motives, in self-interested terms, *and* that I never do what I believe to be irrational. This is not possible in the relevant sense: it is not possible *whatever* my desires and dispositions are. If I was never self-denying, my ordinary acts would never be irrational. But I would have acted irrationally in causing myself to become, or allowing myself to remain, never self-denying. If instead I cause myself to have one of the best possible sets of motives, I shall sometimes do what I believe to be irrational. If I do not have the *disposition* of someone who is never self-denying, it is not possible that I *always act* like someone with this disposition. Since this is not possible, and it would be irrational for me to cause myself to be never self-denying, I cannot be criticised for sometimes doing what I believe to be irrational.'

It may now be said that, as described by Kate, S lacks one of the essential features of any theory. It may be objected: 'No theory can demand what is impossible. Since Kate cannot always avoid doing what S claims to be irrational, she cannot always do what S claims that she ought to do. We should therefore reject S. As before, *ought* implies *can*.'

Even if we deny Determinism, this objection still applies. As I have claimed, we must admit that, since Kate does not have the disposition of someone who is never self-denying, she cannot *always* act like such a person.

Is it a good objection to S that Kate cannot always avoid doing what S claims to be irrational? Remember Schelling's Answer to Armed Robbery. In this case, on any plausible theory about rationality, it would be irrational for me not to make myself very irrational. But, if I do make myself very irrational, I cannot avoid acting irrationally. On both alternatives, at least one of my acts would be irrational. It is therefore true that, in this case, I cannot avoid acting irrationally. Since there can be such cases, an acceptable theory can imply that we cannot avoid acting irrationally. It is no objection to S that it has this implication.

We may believe that these claims do not fully answer this objection. A similar objection will be raised later against certain moral theories. To save words, I discuss these objections together, in Section 15.

I shall now summarize my other conclusions. In the case of many and perhaps most people, the Self-interest Theory is indirectly self-defeating. It is true, of each of these people, that it would be worse for him if he was never self-denying—disposed never to do what he believes would be worse for him. It would be better for him if he had some other set of motives. I have claimed that such cases do not provide an objection to S. Since S does not tell these people to be never self-denying, and tells them, if they can, not to be, S is not failing in its own terms. Nor do these cases provide an independent objection to S.

Though they do not refute S, for those who accept S these cases are of great importance. In these cases S must cover, not just ordinary acts, but also the acts that bring about changes in our motives. According to S, it would be rational to cause ourselves to have, or to keep, one of the best possible sets of motives, in self-interested terms. If we believe that we could act in either of these ways, it would be irrational not to do so. In the case of most people, any of the best possible sets would cause these people sometimes to do, in a quite voluntary way, what they know will be worse for them. If these people believe S, they will believe that these acts are irrational. But they need not believe *themselves* to be irrational. This is because, according to S, it would be irrational for them to change their motives so that they would cease to act irrationally in this way. They will in part regret the *consequences* of these irrational acts. But the *irrationality* of these acts they can regard with complacency. This is *rational* irrationality.

It may be objected, to these claims, that they falsely assume Psychological Determinism. It may sometimes be possible for these people to do what they believe to be rational, whatever their desires and dispositions are. If this objection is correct, these claims need to be revised. When these people do what they believe to be irrational, they cannot claim that they are in no sense irrational. But they can claim that, given their actual motives, it would be very hard for them to avoid acting in this way. And it would be irrational for them, on their theory, to change their motives so that it would be easier to avoid acting in this way. They can therefore claim that they are irrational only in a very weak sense. Having explained once how these claims could be revised, I shall not mention this objection whenever, in what follows, it would be relevant. It would be easy to make the needed revisions to any similar claims.

7. AN ARGUMENT FOR REJECTING S WHEN IT CONFLICTS WITH MORALITY

It has been argued that the Self-interest Theory might tell us to believe, not itself, but some other theory. This is clearly possible. According to S, it would be rational for each of us to cause himself to believe some other theory, if this would be better for him.

I have already mentioned one way in which this might be true. It might not be possible for us to do what we believe to be irrational. S would then tell us, in the cases I have been discussing, to try to believe a different theory. There are also other ways in which this might be true. Let us return, for an example, to the keeping of our promises.

One kind of mutual agreement has great practical importance. In these agreements, each person in some group makes a conditional promise. Each person promises to act in a certain way, provided that all the others promise to act in certain ways. It can be true both (1) that it will be better for each of these people if all rather than none of them keep their promises, and (2) that, whatever the others do, it will be worse for each person if he himself keeps his promise. What each person loses if he keeps his promise is less than what he gains if all the others keep their promises. This is how (1) and (2) are both true. Such agreements are *mutually advantageous, though requiring self-denial.*

If I am known to be never self-denying, I shall be excluded from such agreements. Others will know that I cannot be trusted to keep my promise. It has been claimed that, since this is true, it would be better for me if I ceased to be never self-denying and became trustworthy.[5]

This claim overlooks one possibility. It may be best for me if I *appear* to be trustworthy but remain really never self-denying. Since I appear to be trustworthy, others will admit me to these mutually advantageous agreements. Because I am really never self-denying, I shall get the benefits of breaking my promises whenever this would be better for me. Since it is better for me to appear trustworthy, it will often be better for me to keep my promise so as to preserve this appearance. But there will be some promises that I can break secretly. And my gain from breaking some promises may outweigh my loss in ceasing to appear trustworthy.

Suppose, however, that I am transparent, unable to lie convincingly. This is true of many people. And it might become more widely true if we develop cheap and accurate lie-detector tests. Let us assume that this has happened, so that we are all transparent—unable to deceive others. Since we are to some degree transparent, my conclusions may apply to our actual situation. But it will simplify the argument to assume that all direct deception has become impossible. It is worth seeing what such an argument might show. We should therefore help the argument, by granting this assumption.

If we were all transparent, it would be better for each of us if he became trustworthy: reliably disposed to keep his promises, even when he believes that doing so would be worse for him. It would therefore be rational, according to S, for each of us to make himself trustworthy.

Assume next that, to become trustworthy, we would have to change our beliefs about rationality. We would have to make ourselves believe that it is rational for each of us to keep his promises, even when he knows that this would be worse for him. I shall later describe two ways in which this assumption might be true.

It is hard to change our beliefs when our reason for doing so is merely that this change will be in our interests. We would have to use some form of self-deception. Suppose, for example, that I learn that I am fatally ill. Since I want to believe that I am healthy, I pay a hypnotist to give me this belief. I could not keep this belief if I remembered how I had acquired it. If I remembered this, I would know that the belief was false. The same would be true of our beliefs about rationality. If we pay hypnotists to change these beliefs, because this will be better for us, the hypnotists must make us forget why we have our new beliefs.

On the assumptions made above, S would tell us to change our beliefs. S would tell us to believe, not itself, but a revised form of S. On this revised theory, it is irrational for each of us to do what he believes will be worse for himself, *except when he is keeping a promise.*

If S told us to believe this revised theory, would this be an objection to S? Would it show that it *is* rational to keep such promises? We must focus clearly on this question. We may be right to believe that it is rational to keep our promises, even when we know that this will be worse for us. I am asking, 'Would this belief be supported if S itself told us to cause ourselves to have this belief?'

Some people answer Yes. They argue that, if S tells us to make ourselves have this belief, this shows that this belief is justified. And they apply this argument to many other kinds of act which, like keeping promises, they believe to be morally required. If this argument succeeded, it would have great importance. It would show that, in many kinds of case, it is rational to act morally, even when we believe that this will be worse for us. Moral reasons would be shown to be stronger than the reasons provided by self-interest. Many writers have tried, unsuccessfully, to justify this conclusion. If this conclusion could be justified in the way just mentioned, this would solve what Sidgwick called 'the profoundest problem of Ethics'.[6]

8. WHY THIS ARGUMENT FAILS

There is a simple objection to this argument. The argument appeals to the fact that S would tell us to make ourselves believe that it is rational to keep our promises, even when we know that this will be worse for us. Call this belief *B*. B is incompatible with S, since S claims that it is irrational to keep such promises. Either S is the true theory about rationality, or it is not. If S is true, B must be false, since it is incompatible with S. If S is not true, B might be true, but S cannot support B, since a theory that is not true cannot support any conclusion. In brief: if S is true, B must be false, and if S is not true, it cannot support B. B is either false, or not supported. So, even if S tells us to try to believe B, this fact cannot support B.

We may think that a theory about rationality cannot be true, but can at most be the best, or the best justified theory. The objection just given could be restated in these terms. There are two possibilities. If S is the best theory, we should reject B, since it is incompatible with S. If S is not the best theory, we should reject S. B cannot be supported by a theory that we should reject. Neither of these possibilities gives any support to B.[7]

This objection seems to me strong. But I know some people whom it does not convince. I shall therefore give two more objections. These will also support some wider conclusions.

I shall first distinguish threats from warnings. When I say that I shall do X unless you do Y, call this a *warning* if my doing X would be worse for you but not for me, and a *threat* if my doing X would be worse for both of us. Call me a *threat-fulfiller* if I would always fulfil my threats.

Suppose that, apart from being a threat-fulfiller, someone is never self-denying. Such a person would fulfil his threats even though he knows that this would be worse for him. But he would not *make* threats if he believed that doing so would be worse for him. This is because, apart from being a threat-fulfiller, this person is never self-denying. He never does what he believes will be worse for him, *except when he is fulfilling some threat*. This exception does not cover *making* threats.

Suppose that we are all both transparent and never self-denying. If this was true, it would be better for me if I made myself a threat-fulfiller, and then announced to everyone else this change in my dispositions. Since I am transparent, everyone would believe my threats. And believed threats have many uses. Some of my threats could be defensive, intended to protect me from aggression by others. I might confine myself to defensive threats. But it would be tempting to use my known disposition in other ways. Suppose that the benefits of some co-operation are shared between us. And suppose that, without my co-operation, there would be no further benefits. I might say that, unless I get the largest share, I shall not co-operate. If others know me to be a threat-fulfiller, and they are never self-denying, they will give me the largest share. Failure to do so would be worse for them.

Other threat-fulfillers might act in worse ways. They could reduce us to slavery. They could threaten that, unless we become their slaves, they will bring about our mutual destruction. We would know that these people would fulfil their threats. We would therefore know that we can avoid destruction only by becoming their slaves.

The answer to threat-fulfillers, if we are all transparent, is to become a *threat-ignorer*. Such a person always ignores threats, even when he knows that doing so will be worse for him. A threat-fulfiller would not threaten a transparent threat-ignorer. He would know that, if he did, his threat would be ignored, and he would fulfil this threat, which would be worse for him.

If we were all both transparent and never self-denying, what changes in our dispositions would be better for each of us? I answer this question in Appendix A, since parts of the answer are not relevant to the question I am now discussing. What is relevant is this. If we were all transparent, it would probably be better for each of us if he became a trustworthy threat-ignorer. These two changes would involve certain risks; but these would be heavily outweighed by the probable benefits. What would be the benefits from becoming trustworthy? That we would not be excluded from those mutually advantageous agreements that require self-denial. What would be the benefits from becoming threat-ignorers? That we would avoid becoming the slaves of threat-fulfillers.

We can next assume that we could not become trustworthy threat-ignorers unless we changed our beliefs about rationality. Those who are trustworthy keep their promises even when they know that this will be worse for them. We can assume that we could not become disposed to act in this way unless we believed that it *is* rational to keep such promises. And we can assume that, unless we were known to have this belief, others would not trust us to keep such promises. On these assumptions, S tells us to make ourselves have this belief. Similar remarks apply to becoming threat-ignorers. We can assume that we could not become threat-ignorers unless we believed that it is always rational to ignore threats. And we can assume that, unless we have this belief, others would not be convinced that we are threat-ignorers. On these assumptions, S tells us to make ourselves have this belief. These conclusions can be combined. S tells us to make ourselves believe that it is always irrational to do what we believe will be worse for us, *except when we are keeping promises or ignoring threats.*

Does this fact support these beliefs? According to S, it would be rational for each of us to make himself believe that it is rational to ignore threats, even when he knows that this will be worse for him. Does this show this belief to be correct? Does it show that it *is* rational ignore such threats?

It will help to have an example. Consider

> *My Slavery.* You and I share a desert island. We are both transparent, and never self-denying. You now bring about one change in your dispositions, becoming a threat-fulfiller. And you have a bomb that could blow the island up. By regularly threatening to explode this bomb, you force me to toil on your behalf. The only limit on your power is that you must leave my life worth living. If my life became worse than that, it would cease to be better for me to give in to your threats.

How can I end my slavery? It would be no good killing you, since your bomb will automatically explode unless you regularly dial some secret number. But suppose that I could make myself transparently a threat-ignorer. Foolishly, you have not threatened that you would ignore this change in my dispositions. So this change would end my slavery.

Would it be rational for me to make this change? There is the risk that you might make some new threat. But since doing so would be clearly worse for you, this risk would be small. And, by taking this small risk, I would almost certainly gain a very great benefit. I would almost certainly end my slavery. Given the wretchedness of my slavery, it would be rational for me, according to S, to cause myself to become a threat-ignorer. And, given our other assumptions, it would be rational for me to cause myself to believe that it is always rational to ignore threats. Though I cannot be wholly certain that this will be better for me, the great and nearly certain benefit would outweigh the small risk. (In the same way, it would never be wholly certain that it would be better for someone if he became trustworthy. Here too, all that could be true is that the probable benefits outweigh the risks.)

Assume that I have now made these changes. I have become transparently a threat-ignorer, and have made myself believe that it is always rational to ignore threats. According to S, it was rational for me to cause myself to have this belief. Does this show this belief to be correct?

Let us continue the story.

How I End My Slavery. We both have bad luck. For a moment, you forget that I have become a threat-ignorer. To gain some trivial end—such as the coconut that I have just picked—you repeat your standard threat. You say, that, unless I give you the coconut, you will blow us both to pieces. I know that, if I refuse, this will certainly be worse for me. I know that you are reliably a threat-fulfiller, who will carry out your threats even when you know that this will be worse for you. But, like you, I do not now believe in the pure Self-interest Theory. I now believe that it is rational to ignore threats, even when I know that this will be worse for me. I act on my belief. As I foresaw, you blow us both up.

Is my act rational? It is not. As before, we might concede that, since I am acting on a belief that it was rational for me to acquire, *I* am not irrational. More precisely, I am *rationally* irrational. But what I am doing is not rational. It is irrational to ignore some threat when I know that, if I do, this will be disastrous for me and better for no one. S told me here that it was rational to make myself believe that it is rational to ignore threats, even when I know that this will be worse for me. But this does not show this belief to be correct. It does not show that, in such a case, it *is* rational to ignore threats.

We can draw a wider conclusion. This case shows that we should reject

(G2) If it is rational for someone to make himself believe that it is rational for him to act in some way, it *is* rational for him to act in this way.

Return now to B, the belief that it is rational to keep our promises even when we know that this will be worse for us. On the assumptions made above, S implies that it is rational for us to make ourselves believe B. Some people claim that this fact supports B, showing that it *is* rational to keep such promises. But this claim seems to assume (G2), which we have just rejected.

There is another objection to what these people claim. Even though S tells us to try to believe B, S implies that B is false. So, if B is true, S must be false. Since these people believe B, they should believe that S is false. Their claim would then assume

(G3) If some false theory about rationality tells us to make ourselves have a particular belief, this shows this belief to be true.

But we should obviously reject (G3). If some false theory told us to make ourselves believe that the Earth was flat, this would not show this to be so.

S told us to try to believe that it is rational to ignore threats, even when we know that this will be worse for us. As my example shows, this does not support this belief. We should therefore make the same claim about keeping promises. There may be *other* grounds for believing that it is rational to keep our promises, even when we know that doing so will be worse for us. But this would not be shown to be rational by the fact that the Self-interest Theory itself told us to make ourselves believe that it was rational. It has been argued that, by appealing to such facts, we can solve an ancient problem: we can show that, when it conflicts with self-interest, morality provides the stronger reasons for acting. This argument fails. The most that it might show is something less. In a world where we are all transparent—unable to deceive each other—it might be rational to deceive ourselves about rationality.[8]

9. HOW S MIGHT BE SELF-EFFACING

If S told us to believe some other theory, this would not support this other theory. But would it be an objection to S? Once again, S would not be failing in its own terms. S is a theory about practical not theoretical rationality. S may tell us to make ourselves have false beliefs. If it would be better for us to have false beliefs, having true beliefs, even about rationality, would not be part of the ultimate aim given to us by S.

The arguments given above might be strengthened and extended. This would be easier if, as I supposed, the technology of lie-detection made us all wholly transparent. If we could never deceive each other, there might be an argument that showed that, according to S, it would be rational for everyone to cause himself not to believe S.

Suppose that this was true. Suppose that S told everyone to cause himself to believe some other theory. S would then be *self-effacing*. If we all believed S, but could also change our beliefs, S would remove itself from the scene. It would become a theory that no one believed. But to be self-effacing is not to be self-defeating. It is not the aim of a theory to be believed. If we personify theories, and pretend that they have aims, the aim of a theory is not to be believed, but to be true, or to be the best theory. That a theory is self-effacing does not show that it is not the best theory.

S would be self-effacing when, if we believed S, this would be worse for us. But S need not tell us to believe itself. When it would be better for us if we believed some other theory, S would tell us to try to believe this theory. If we succeeded in doing what S told us to do, this would again be better for us. Though S would remove itself from the scene, causing no one to believe itself, it would still not be failing in its own terms. It would still be true that, because each of us has followed S—done what S told him to do—each has thereby made the outcome better for himself.

Though S would not be failing in its own terms, it might be claimed that an acceptable theory cannot be self-effacing. I deny this claim. It may seem plausible for what, when examined, is a bad reason. It would be natural to *want* the best theory about rationality not to be self-effacing. If the best theory was self-effacing, telling us to believe some other theory, the truth about rationality would be depressingly convoluted. It is natural to hope that the truth is simpler: that the best theory would tell us to believe itself. But can this be more than a hope? Can we assume that the truth *must* be simpler? We cannot.

10. HOW CONSEQUENTIALISM IS INDIRECTLY SELF-DEFEATING

Most of my claims could, with little change, cover one group of moral theories. These are the different versions of *Consequentialism*, or *C*. C's *central claim* is

    (C1) There is one ultimate moral aim: that outcomes be as good as possible.

C applies to everything. Applied to acts, C claims both

    (C2) What each of us ought to do is whatever would make the outcome best, and
    (C3) If someone does what he believes will make the outcome worse, he is acting wrongly.

I distinguished between what we have most reason to do, and what it would be rational for us to do, given what we believe, or ought to believe. We must now distinguish between what is *objectively* and *subjectively* right or wrong. This distinction has nothing to do with whether moral theories can be objectively true. The distinction is between what some theory implies, given (i) what are or would have been the effects of what some person does or could have done, and (ii) what this person believes, or ought to believe, about these effects.

It may help to mention a similar distinction. The medical treatment that is objectively right is the one that would in fact be best for the patient. The treatment that is subjectively right is the one that, given the medical evidence, it would be most rational for the doctor to prescribe. As this example shows, what it would be best to know is what is objectively right. The central part of a moral theory answers this question. We need an account of subjective rightness for two reasons. We often do not know what the effects of our acts would be. And we ought to be blamed for doing what is subjectively wrong. We ought to be blamed for such acts even if they are objectively right. A doctor should be blamed for doing what was very likely to kill his patient, even if his act in fact saves this patient's life.

In most of what follows, I shall use *right*, *ought*, *good*, and *bad* in the objective sense. But *wrong* will usually mean *subjectively* wrong, or *blameworthy*. Which sense I mean will often be obvious given the context. Thus it is clear that, of the claims given above, (C2) is about what we ought objectively to do, and (C3) is about what is subjectively wrong.

To cover risky cases, C claims

(C4) What we ought subjectively to do is the act whose outcome has the greatest *expected* goodness.

In calculating the expected goodness of an act's outcome, the value of each possible good effect is multiplied by the chance that the act will produce it. The same is done with the disvalue of each possible bad effect. The expected goodness of the outcome is the sum of these values minus these disvalues. Suppose, for example, that if I go West I have a chance of 1 in 4 of saving 100 lives, and a chance of 3 in 4 of saving 20 lives. The expected goodness of my going West, valued in terms of the number of lives saved, is $100 \times 1/4 + 20 \times 3/4$, or $25 + 15$, or 40. Suppose next that, if I go East, I shall certainly save 30 lives. The expected goodness of my going East is 30×1, or 30. According to (C4), I ought to go West, since the expected number of lives saved would be greater.

Consequentialism covers, not just acts and outcomes, but also desires, dispositions, beliefs, emotions, the colour of our eyes, the climate, and everything else. More exactly, C covers anything that could make outcomes better or worse. According to C, the best possible climate is the one that would make outcomes best. I shall again use 'motives' to cover both desires and dispositions. C claims

(C5) The best possible motives are those of which it is true that, if we have them, the outcome will be best.

As before, 'possible' means 'causally possible'. And there would be many different sets of motives that would be in this sense best: there would be no other possible set of motives of which it would be true that, if we had this set, the outcome would be better. I have described some of the ways in which we can change our motives. (C2) implies that we ought to try to cause ourselves to have, or to keep, any of the best possible sets of motives. More generally, we ought to change both ourselves, and anything else, in any way that would make the outcome better. If we believe that we could make such a change, (C3) implies that failing to do so would be wrong. [9]

To apply C, we must ask what makes outcomes better or worse. The simplest answer is given by *Utilitarianism*. This theory combines C with the following claim: the best outcome is the one that gives to people the greatest net sum of benefits minus burdens, or, on the Hedonistic version of this claim, the greatest net sum of happiness minus misery.

There are many other versions of C. These can be *pluralist* theories, appealing to several different principles about what makes outcomes better or worse. Thus, one version of C appeals both to the Utilitarian claim and to the Principle of Equality. This principle claims that it is bad if, through no fault of theirs, some people are worse off than others. On this version of C, the goodness of an outcome depends both on how great the net sum of benefits would be, and on how equally the benefits and burdens would be distributed between different people. One of two outcomes might be better, though it involved a smaller sum of benefits, because these benefits would be shared more equally.

A Consequentialist could appeal to many other principles. According to three such principles, it is bad if people are deceived, coerced, and betrayed. And some of these principles may essentially refer to past events. Two such principles appeal to past entitlements, and to just deserts. The Principle of Equality may claim that people should receive equal shares, not at particular times, but in the whole of their lives. If it makes this claim, this principle essentially refers to past events. If our moral theory contains such principles, we are not concerned only with *consequences* in the narrow sense: with what happens *after* we act. But we can still be, in a wider sense, Consequentialists. In this wider sense our ultimate moral aim is, not that outcomes be as good as possible, but that history go as well as possible. What I say below could be restated in these terms.

With the word 'Consequentialism', and the letter 'C', I shall refer to all these different theories. As with the different theories about self-interest, it would take at least a book to decide between these different versions of C. This book does not discuss this decision. I discuss only what these different versions have in common. My arguments and conclusions would apply to all, or nearly all, the plausible theories of this kind. It is worth emphasizing that, if a Consequentialist appeals to all of the principles I have mentioned, his moral theory is *very* different from Utilitarianism. Since such theories have seldom been discussed, this is easy to forget.

Some have thought that, if Consequentialism appeals to many different principles, it ceases to be a distinctive theory, since it can be made to cover all moral theories. This is a mistake. C appeals only to principles about what makes outcomes better or worse. Thus C might claim that it would be worse if there was more deception or coercion. C would then give to all of us two common aims. We should try to cause it to be true that there is less deception or coercion. Since C gives to all agents common moral aims, I shall call C *agent-neutral*.

Many moral theories do not take this form. These theories are *agent-relative*, giving to different agents different aims. It can be claimed, for example, that each of us should have the aim that *he* does not coerce other people. On this view, it would be wrong for me to coerce other people, even if by doing so I could cause it to be true that there would be less coercion. Similar claims might be made about deceiving or betraying others. On these claims, each person's aim should be, not that there be less deception or betrayal, but that he himself does not deceive or betray others. These claims are not Consequentialist. And these are the kinds of claim that most of us accept. C can appeal to principles about deception and betrayal, but it does not appeal to these principles in their familiar form.

I shall now describe a different way in which some theory T might be self-defeating. Call T

indirectly collectively self-defeating when it is true that, if several people try to achieve their T-given aims, these aims will be worse achieved.

On all or most of its different versions, this may be true of C. C implies that we should always try do whatever would make the outcome as good as possible. If we are disposed to act in this way, we are *pure do-gooders*. If we were all pure do-gooders, this might make the outcome worse. This might be true even if we always did what, of the acts that were possible for us, would make the outcome best. The bad effects might come, not from our acts, but from our disposition.

There are many ways in which, if we were all pure do-gooders, this might have bad effects. One is the effect on the sum of happiness. On any plausible version of C, happiness is a large part of what makes outcomes better. Most of our happiness comes from having, and acting upon, certain strong desires. These include the desires that are involved in loving certain other people, the desire to work well, and many of the strong desires on which we act when we are not working. To become pure do-gooders, we would have to act against or even to suppress most of these desires. It is likely that this would enormously reduce the sum of happiness. This would make the outcome worse, even if we always did what, of the acts that were possible for us, made the outcome best. It might not make the outcome worse than it *actually* is, given what people are actually like. But it would make the outcome worse than it would be if we were not pure do-gooders, but had certain other causally possible desires and dispositions.[10]

There are several other ways in which, if we were all pure do-gooders, this might make the outcome worse. One rests on the fact that, when we want to act in certain ways, we shall be likely to deceive ourselves about the effects of our acts. We shall be likely to believe, falsely, that these acts will produce the best outcome. Consider, for example, killing other people. If we want someone to be dead, it is easy to believe, falsely, that this would make the outcome better. It therefore makes the outcome better that we are strongly disposed not to kill, even when we believe that doing so would make the outcome better. Our disposition not to kill should give way only when we believe that, by killing, we would make the outcome *very much* better. Similar claims apply to deception, coercion, and several other kinds of act.

11. WHY C DOES NOT FAIL IN ITS OWN TERMS

I shall assume that, in these and other ways, C is indirectly collectively self-defeating. If we were all pure do-gooders, the outcome would be worse than it would be if we had certain other sets of motives. If we know this, C tells us that it would be wrong to cause ourselves to be, or to remain, pure do-gooders. Because C makes this claim, it is not failing in its own terms. C does not condemn itself.

This defence of C is like my defence of S. It is worth pointing out one difference. S is indirectly individually self-defeating when it is true of some person that, if he was never self-denying, this would be worse for him than if he had some other set of desires and dispositions. This would be a bad effect in S's terms. And this bad effect often occurs. There are many people whose lives are going worse because they are never, or very seldom, self-denying. C is indirectly collectively self-defeating when it is true that, if some or all of us were pure do-gooders, this would make the outcome worse than it would be if we had certain other motives. This would be a bad effect in C's terms. But this bad effect may *not* occur. There are few people who are pure do-gooders. Because there are few such people, the fact that they have this disposition may not, on the whole, make the outcome worse.

The bad effect in S's terms often occurs. The bad effect in C's terms may not occur. But this difference does not affect my defence of S and C. Both theories tell us not to have the dispositions that would have these bad effects. This is why S is not, and C would not be, failing in their own terms. It is irrelevant whether these bad effects actually occur.

My defence of C assumes that we can change our dispositions. It may be objected: 'Suppose that we were all pure do-gooders, because we believe C. And suppose that we could not change our dispositions. These dispositions would have bad effects, in C's terms, and these bad effects would be the result of our belief in C. So C would be failing in its own terms.' There was a similar objection to my defence of S. I discuss these objections in Section 18.

12. THE ETHICS OF FANTASY

I have assumed that C is indirectly collectively self-defeating. I have assumed that, if we were all pure do-gooders, the outcome would be worse than it would be if we had certain other sets of motives. If this claim is true, C tells us that we should try to have one of these other sets of motives.

Whether this claim is true is in part a factual question. I believe that it is probably true. But I shall not try to show this here. It seems more worthwhile to discuss what this claim implies. I also believe that, even if we became convinced that Consequentialism was the best moral theory, most of us would not *in fact* become pure do-gooders.

Because he makes a similar assumption, Mackie calls Act Utilitarianism 'the ethics of fantasy'.[11] Like several other writers, he assumes that we should reject a moral theory if it is in this sense *unrealistically demanding*: if it is true that, even if we all accepted this theory, most of us would in fact seldom do what this theory claims that we ought to do. Mackie believes that a moral theory is something that we *invent*. If this is so, it is plausible to claim that an acceptable theory cannot be unrealistically demanding. But, on several other views about the nature of morality, this claim is not plausible. We may *hope* that the best theory is not unrealistically demanding. But, on these views, this can only be a hope. We cannot assume that this must be true.

Suppose that I am wrong to assume that C is indirectly collectively self-defeating. Even if this is false, we can plausibly assume that C is unrealistically demanding. Even if it would not make the outcome worse if we were all pure do-gooders, it is probably causally impossible that all or most of us become pure do-gooders.

Though these are quite different assumptions, they have the *same* implication. If it is causally impossible that we become pure do-gooders, C again implies that we ought to try to have one of the best possible sets of motives, in Consequentialist terms. This implication is therefore worth discussing if (1) C is either indirectly self-defeating or unrealistically demanding, or both, and (2) neither of these facts would show that C cannot be the best theory. Though I am not yet convinced that C is the best theory, I believe both (1) and (2).

13. COLLECTIVE CONSEQUENTIALISM

It is worth distinguishing C from another form of Consequentialism. As stated so far, C is *individualistic* and concerned with *actual* effects. According to C, *each* of us should try to do what would make the outcome best, *given what others will actually do*. And each of us should try to have one of the possible sets of motives whose effects would be best, given the actual sets of motives that will be had by others. Each of us should ask: 'Is there some other set of motives that is both possible for *me* and is such that, if *I* had this set, the outcome would be better?' Our answers would depend on what we know, or can predict, about the sets of motives that will be had by others.

What can I predict as I type these words, in January 1983? I know that most of us will continue to have motives much like those that we have now. Most of us will love certain other people, and will have the other strong desires on which most happiness depends. Since I know this, C may tell *me* to try to be a pure do-gooder. This may make the outcome better even though, if we were *all* pure do-gooders, this would make the outcome worse. If most people are *not* pure do-gooders, it may make the outcome better if a few people are. If most people remain as they are now, there will be much suffering, much inequality, and much of most of the other things that make outcomes bad. Much of this suffering I could fairly easily prevent, and I could in other ways do much to make the outcome better. It may therefore make the outcome better if I avoid close personal ties, and cause my other strong desires to become comparatively weaker, so that I can be a pure do-gooder.

If I am lucky, it may not be bad for me to become like this. My life will be stripped of most of the sources of happiness. But one source of happiness is the belief that one is doing good. This belief may give me happiness, making my austere life, not only morally good, but also a good life for me.

I may be less lucky. It may be true that, though I could come close to being a pure do-gooder, this would not be a good life for me. And there may be many other possible lives that would be much better for me. This could be true on most of the plausible theories about self-interest. The demands made on me by C may then seem unfair. Why should *I* be the one who strips his life of most of the sources of happiness? More exactly, why should I be among the few who, according to C, ought to try to do this? Would it not be fairer if we all did more to make outcomes better?

This suggests a form of Consequentialism that is both *collective* and concerned with *ideal* effects. On this theory, each of us should try to have one of the sets of desires and dispositions which is such that, if *everyone* had one of these sets, this would make the outcome better than if everyone had other sets. This statement can be interpreted in several ways, and there are well-known difficulties in removing the ambiguities. Moreover, some versions of this theory are open to strong objections. They tell us to ignore what would in fact happen, in ways that may be disastrous. But Collective Consequentialism, or *CC*, has much appeal. I shall suggest later how a more complicated theory might keep what is appealing in CC, while avoiding the objections.

CC does not differ from C only in its claims about our desires and dispositions. The two theories disagree about what we ought to do. Consider the question of how much the rich should give to the poor. For most Consequentialists, this question ignores national boundaries. Since I know that most other rich people will give very little, it would be hard for me to deny that it would be better if I gave away almost all my income. Even if I gave nine-tenths, some of my remaining tenth would do more good if spent by the very poor. Consequentialism thus tells me that I ought to give away almost all my income.

Collective Consequentialism is much less demanding. It does not tell me to give the amount that would in fact make the outcome best. It tells me to give the amount which is such that if we *all* gave this amount, the outcome would be best. More exactly, it tells me to give what would be demanded by the particular International Income Tax that would make the outcome best. This tax would be progressive, requiring larger proportions from those who are richer. But the demands made on each person would be much smaller than the demands made by C, on any plausible prediction about the amounts that others will in fact give. It might be best if those as rich as me all give only half their income, or only a quarter. It might be true that, if we all gave more, this would so disrupt our own economies that in the future we would have much less to give. And it might be true that, if we all gave more, our gift would be too large to be absorbed by the economies of the poorer countries.

The difference that I have been discussing arises only within what is called *partial compliance theory*. This is the part of a moral theory that covers cases where we know that some other people will not do what they ought to do. C might require that a few people give away almost all their money, and try to make themselves pure do-gooders. But this would only be because most other people are *not* doing what C claims that they ought to do. They are not giving to the poor the amounts that they ought to give.

In its partial compliance theory, C has been claimed to be excessively demanding. This is not the claim that C is *unrealistically* demanding. As I have said, I believe that this would be no objection. What is claimed is that, in its partial compliance theory, C makes *unfair* or *unreasonable* demands. This objection may not apply to C's *full compliance theory*. C would be much less demanding if we *all* had one of the possible sets of motives that, according to C, we ought to try to cause ourselves to have.[12]

14. BLAMELESS WRONGDOING

Though C is indirectly self-defeating, it is not failing in its own terms. But it may seem open to other objections. These are like those I raised when discussing S. Suppose that we all believe C, and all have sets of motives that are among the best possible sets in Consequentialist terms. I have claimed that, at least for most of us, these sets would not include being a pure do-gooder. If we are not pure do-gooders, we shall sometimes do what we believe will make the outcome worse. According to C, we shall then be acting wrongly.

Here is one example. Most of the best possible sets of motives would include strong love for our children. Suppose that *Clare* has one of these sets of motives. Consider

> *Case One.* Clare could either give her child some benefit, or give much greater benefits to some unfortunate stranger. Because she loves her child, she benefits him rather than the stranger.

As a Consequentialist, Clare may give moral weight, not just to how much children are benefited, but also to whether they are benefited *by their own parents*. She may believe that parental care and love are intrinsically, or in themselves, part of what makes outcomes better. Even so, Clare may believe that, in failing to help the stranger, she is making the outcome worse. She may therefore believe that she is acting wrongly. And this act is quite voluntary. She could, if she wanted, avoid doing what she believes to be wrong. She fails to do so simply because she wants to benefit her child more than she wants to avoid wrong-doing.

If someone freely does what she believes to be wrong, she is usually open to serious moral criticism. Ought Clare to regard herself as open to such criticism? As a Consequentialist, she could deny this. Her reply would be like Kate's when Kate claimed that she was not irrational. Clare could say: 'I act wrongly because I love my child. But it would be wrong for me to cause myself to lose this love. That I make the outcome worse is a bad effect. But this is part of a set of effects that are, on the whole, one of the best possible sets. It would therefore be wrong for me to change my motives so that I would not in future act wrongly in this kind of way. Since this is so, when I do act wrongly in this way, I need not regard *myself* as morally bad.' We have seen that there can be rational irrationality. In the same way, there can be *moral immorality,* or *blameless wrongdoing.* In such a case, it is the act and not the agent that is immoral.

It may again be objected: 'The bad effect that Clare produced could have been avoided. It is not like the pain that some surgeon cannot help causing when he gives the best possible treatment. The bad effect was the result of a separate and voluntary act. Since it could have been avoided, it cannot be claimed to be part of one of the best possible sets of effects.'

Clare could reply: 'I could have acted differently. But this only means that I *would* have done so if my motives had been different. Given my actual motives, it is causally impossible that I act differently. And, if my motives had been different, this would have made the outcome, on the whole, worse. Since my actual motives are one of the best possible sets, in

Consequentialist terms, the bad effects *are*, in the relevant sense, part of one of the best possible sets of effects.'

It may be objected: 'If it is not causally possible that you act differently, given your actual motives, you cannot make claims about what you ought to do. *Ought* implies *can*.'

Kate answered this objection in Section 6. It cannot be claimed that Clare ought to have acted differently if she could not have done so. This last clause does not mean 'if this would have been causally impossible, given her actual motives.' It means 'if this would have been causally impossible, whatever her motives might have been'.

Like Kate, Clare may be wrong to assume Psychological Determinism. If this is so, her claims can be revised. She should cease to claim that, if she has one of the best possible sets of motives, this will inevitably cause her to do what she believes to be wrong. She could claim instead: 'If I was a pure do-gooder, it would be easy not to do what I believe to be wrong. Since I have another set of motives, it is very hard not to act in this way. And it would be wrong for me to change my motives so that it would be easier not to act in this way. Since this is so, when I act in this way, I am morally bad only in a very weak sense.'

Consider next

Case Two. Clare could either save her child's life, or save the lives of several strangers. Because she loves her child, she saves him, and the strangers all die.

In this case, could Clare make the same claims? The deaths of several strangers are a very bad effect. Could she claim that these deaths are part of one of the best possible sets of effects? The answer may be No. It might have made the outcome better if Clare had not loved her child. This would have been worse for her, and much worse for her child. But she would then have saved the lives of these several strangers. This good effect might have outweighed the bad effects, making the outcome, on the whole, better.

If this is so, Clare could say: 'I had no reason to believe that my love for my child would have this very bad effect. It was subjectively right for me to allow myself to love my child. And causing myself to lose this love would have been blameworthy, or subjectively wrong. When I save my child rather than the strangers, I am acting on a set of motives that it would have been wrong for me to cause myself to lose. This is enough to justify my claim that, when I act in this way, this is a case of blameless wrongdoing.'

A Consequentialist might say: 'When Clare learns that she could save the strangers, it would *not* be subjectively wrong for her to cause herself not to love her child. This would be right, since she would then save the strangers.' But Clare could answer: 'I could not possibly have lost this love with the speed that would have been required. There are ways in which we can change our motives. But, in the case of our deepest motives, this takes a long time. It *would* have been wrong for me to try to lose my love for my child. If I had tried, I would have succeeded only after the strangers had died. And this would have only made the outcome worse.'

As this answer shows, Clare's claims essentially appeal to certain factual assumptions. It might have been true that, if she had had the disposition of a pure do-gooder, this would on the whole have made the outcome better. But we are assuming that this is false. We are assuming that the outcome will be better if Clare has some set of motives that will sometimes cause her to choose to do what she believes will make the outcome worse. And we are assuming that her actual set of motives is one of the best possible sets.

We could imagine other motives that would have made the outcome even better. But, given the facts about human nature, such motives are not causally possible. Since Clare loves her child, she saves him rather than several strangers. We could imagine that our love for our children would 'switch off' whenever other people's lives are at stake. It might be true that, if we all had this kind of love, this would make the outcome better. If we all gave such priority to saving more lives, there would be few cases in which our love for our children would have to switch off. This love could therefore be much as it is now. But it is in fact impossible that our love could be like this. We could not bring about such 'fine-tuning'. When there is a threat to our children's lives, our love could not switch off merely because several strangers are also threatened. [13]

Clare claims that, when she does what she believes will make the outcome worse, she is acting wrongly. But she also claims: 'Because I am acting on a set of motives that it would be wrong for me to lose, these acts are blameless. When I act in this way, I need not regard myself as bad. If Psychological Determinism was not true, I would be bad only in a very weak sense. When I act in this way, I should not feel remorse. Nor should I intend to try not to act in this way again.'

It may now be objected that, since she makes these claims, Clare cannot really *believe* that she is acting wrongly. But there are sufficient grounds for thinking that she does have this belief. Consider the case in which she saves her child rather than several strangers. Though she loves her child, Clare does not believe that his death would be a worse outcome than the deaths of the strangers. His death would be worse for him and her. But the deaths of several strangers would, on the whole, be much worse. In saving her child rather than the strangers, Clare is doing what she believes will make the outcome much worse. She therefore believes that she is acting wrongly. Her moral theory directly implies this belief. She also believes that she should not feel remorse. But her reason for believing this does not cast doubt on her belief that she is acting wrongly. Her reason is that she is acting on a motive—love for her child—that it would have been wrong for her to cause herself to lose. This may show that she deserves no blame, but it does not show that she cannot believe her act to be wrong.

It might be said

(G4) If someone acts on a motive that he ought to cause himself
to have, and that it would be wrong for him to cause himself to
lose, he cannot be acting wrongly.

If (G4) was justified, it would support the claim that Clare's act would not
have been wrong. And this would support the claim that she cannot really
believe that her act would have been wrong. But in Section 16 I describe a
case where (G4) is not plausible.

Clare could add that, in many other possible cases, if she believed that her
act was wrong, she *would* believe herself to be bad, and she would feel
remorse. This would often be so if she did what she believed would make
the outcome worse, and she was *not* acting on a set of motives that it would
be wrong for her to cause herself to lose. Consequentialism does not in
general break the link between the belief that an act is wrong, and blame
and remorse. This link is broken only in special cases. We have been
discussing one of these kinds of case: those in which someone acts on a
motive that it would be wrong for him to cause himself to lose.

There is another kind of case where the link is broken. C applies to
everything, including blame and remorse. According to C we ought to blame
others, and feel remorse, when this would make the outcome better.
This would be so when blame or remorse would cause our motives to
change in a way that would make the outcome better. This would not be
true when, like Clare, we have one of the best possible sets of motives. And
it might not be true even when we do not have such motives. If we are
blamed too often, blame may be less effective. C may thus imply that, even
if we do not have one of the best sets of motives, we should be blamed only
for acts that we believe will make the outcome *much* worse.

15. COULD IT BE IMPOSSIBLE TO AVOID ACTING WRONGLY?

Clare's claims imply that she cannot avoid doing what she believes to be
wrong. She might say: 'It is not causally possible *both* that I have one of the
best possible sets of motives, *and* that I never do what I believe to be wrong.
If I was a pure do-gooder, my ordinary acts would never be wrong. But I
would be acting wrongly in allowing myself to remain a pure do-gooder. If
instead I caused myself to have one of the best possible sets of motives, as I
ought to do, I would then sometimes do what I believe to be wrong. If I do
not have the disposition of a pure do-gooder, it is not causally possible that I
always act like a pure do-gooder, never doing what I believe to be wrong.
Since this is not causally possible, and it would be wrong for me to cause

myself to be a pure do-gooder, I cannot be morally criticised for sometimes failing to act like a pure do-gooder.'

It may now be said that, as described by Clare, C lacks one of the essential features of any moral theory. It may be objected: 'No theory can demand what is impossible. Since we cannot avoid doing what C claims to be wrong, we cannot always do what C claims that we ought to do. We should therefore reject C. As before, *ought* implies *can*.'

This objection applies even if we deny Psychological Determinism. Suppose that Clare had saved her child rather than several strangers. She would have acted in this way because she does not have the disposition of a pure do-gooder. Her love for her child would have been stronger than her desire to avoid doing what she believes to be wrong. If we deny Determinism, we shall deny that, in this case, it would have been causally impossible for Clare to avoid doing what she believes to be wrong. By an effort of will, she could have acted against her strongest desire. Even if we claim this, we cannot claim that Clare could *always* act like a pure do-gooder *without* having a pure do-gooder's disposition. Even those who deny Determinism cannot completely break the link between our acts and our dispositions.

If we cannot always act like pure do-gooders, without having a pure do-gooder's disposition, the objection given above still applies. Even if we deny Determinism, we must admit the following. We are assuming that we believe truly that the outcome would be worse if we were all pure do-gooders. If we have this belief, it is not possible that we never do what we believe will make the outcome worse. If we cause ourselves to be, or allow ourselves to remain, pure do-gooders, we are thereby doing what we believe will make the outcome worse. If instead we have other desires and dispositions, it is not possible that we always act like pure do-gooders, never doing what we believe will make the outcome worse. The objector can therefore say: 'Even if Determinism is not true, it is not possible that we never do what we believe will make the outcome worse. In claiming that we ought never to act in this way, C is demanding what is impossible. Since ought implies can, C's claim is indefensible.'

Clare could answer: 'In most cases, when someone acts wrongly, he deserves to be blamed, and should feel remorse. This is what is most plausible in the doctrine that ought implies can. It is hard to believe that there could be cases where, *whatever* someone does, or might have earlier done, he deserves to be blamed, and should feel remorse. It is hard to believe that it could be impossible for someone to avoid acting in a way that deserves to be blamed. C does *not* imply this belief. If I saved my child rather than several strangers, I would believe that I am doing what will make the outcome much worse. I would therefore believe that I am acting wrongly. But this would be a case of *blameless* wrongdoing. According to C, we *can* always avoid doing *what deserves to be blamed*. This is enough to satisfy the doctrine that ought implies can.'

We may believe that these claims do not sufficiently meet this objection. There was a similar objection to S. It is impossible that we never do what S claims to be irrational. I began to meet that objection by appealing to the case in Section 5: Schelling's Answer to Armed Robbery. In this case, on any plausible theory about rationality, I could not avoid acting irrationally. To meet the objection to C, Clare might appeal to other cases where we cannot avoid acting wrongly. That there are such cases has been claimed by some of the writers who are most opposed to C. I discuss this answer in endnote 14.

16. COULD IT BE RIGHT TO CAUSE ONESELF TO ACT WRONGLY?

Since C is indirectly self-defeating, it tells us to cause ourselves to do, or to be more likely to do, what it claims to be morally wrong. This is not a defect in C's terms. We can ask a question like the one I asked about the Self-interest Theory. C gives us one substantive moral aim: that history go as well as possible. Does it also give us a second substantive aim: that we never act wrongly? On the best known form of C, Utilitarianism, the answer is No. For Utilitarians, avoiding wrong-doing is a mere means to the achievement of the one substantive moral aim. It is not itself a substantive aim. And this could also be claimed on the versions of C that judge the goodness of outcomes in terms not of one but of several moral principles. It might be claimed, for instance, by the theory that appeals both to the Utilitarian claim and to the Principle of Equality. All these theories give us the *formal* aim of acting morally, and avoiding wrong-doing. But these theories could all claim that this formal aim is not part of our substantive moral aim.

Though this claim might be made by any Consequentialist, it would not be made on several other moral theories. On these theories, the avoidance of wrong-doing is itself a substantive moral aim. If we accept one of these theories, we may object to C in at least two ways. We may say, 'An acceptable theory cannot treat acting morally as a mere means.' This objection I discuss in Section 19. We may also say, 'An acceptable theory cannot tell us to cause ourselves to do what this theory itself claims to be wrong.'

We should ask whether, if we raise this objection, we ourselves believe that the acts in question would be wrong. We are considering cases where a Consequentialist believes that, though he is acting wrongly, he is not morally bad, because he is acting on motives that it would be wrong for him to cause himself to lose. In such cases, do we ourselves believe that this Consequentialist is acting wrongly?

This is unlikely in the imagined case where Clare saves her child rather than several strangers. If we are not Consequentialists, we shall be likely to believe that Clare's act would not have been wrong. We may think the same about some of the other cases of this kind. Suppose that Clare refrains from killing me, though she has the true belief that killing me would make the outcome better. Clare would think that, in refraining from killing me, she would be acting wrongly. But she would regard this as a case of blameless wrongdoing. She acts wrongly because she is strongly disposed not to kill, and, for the reason given at the end of Section 10, she believes that this is a disposition that it would be wrong for her to cause herself to lose. We may again believe that, in refraining from killing me, Clare is *not* acting wrongly.

If this is what we believe about these cases, it is less clear that we should object to this part of C. We accept C's claim that, in these cases, Clare would not show herself to be morally bad, or deserve to be blamed. Over this there is no disagreement. We may object to C's claim that, though Clare is blameless, her acts would be wrong. But perhaps we should not object to this claim, if it does not have its usual implications.

We may still object that an acceptable moral theory cannot tell us to cause ourselves to do what this theory claims to be wrong. But consider

My Moral Corruption. Suppose that I have some public career that would be wrecked if I was involved in a scandal. I have an enemy, a criminal whom I exposed. This enemy, now released, wants revenge. Rather than simply injuring me, he decides to force me to corrupt myself, knowing that I shall think this worse than most injuries. He threatens that either he or some member of his gang will kill all my children, unless I act in some obscene way, that he will film. If he later sent this film to some journalist, my career would be wrecked. He will thus be able later, by threatening to wreck my career, to cause me to choose to act wrongly. He will cause me to choose to help him commit various minor crimes. Though I am morally as good as most people, I am not a saint. I would not act very wrongly merely to save my career; but I would help my enemy to commit minor crimes. I would here be acting wrongly even given the fact that, if I refused to help my enemy, my career would be wrecked. We can next suppose that, since I know my enemy well, I have good reason to believe both that, if I refuse to let him make his film, my children will be killed, and to believe that, if I do not refuse, they will not be killed.

I ought to let this man make his film. We can plausibly claim that *governments* should not give in to such threats, because this would merely expose them to later threats. But such a claim would not cover this threat made to me by my enemy. It would be wrong for me to refuse his demand, with the foreseen result that my children are killed. I ought to let him make his film, even though I know that the effect will be that I shall later often act wrongly. After my children are freed, I shall often, to save my career, help my enemy commit minor crimes. These later acts will be quite voluntary. I cannot claim that my enemy's later threats force me to act in these ways. I could refuse to act wrongly, even though this would wreck my career.

I have claimed that I ought to let this man make his film. This would be agreed even by most of those who reject Consequentialism. These people would agree that, since it is the only way to save my children's lives, I ought to cause it to be true that I shall later often act wrongly. These people thus believe that an acceptable moral theory *can* tell someone to cause himself to do what this theory claim to be wrong. Since they believe this, they cannot object to Consequentialism that it can have this implication.

If I let my enemy make his film, I would become disposed to help him commit minor crimes. Let us now add some features to this case. I could cause myself to lose this disposition, by abandoning my career. But my enemy has threatened that, if I abandon my career, his gang will kill my children. It would therefore be wrong for me to cause myself to lose this disposition. In contrast, if I refuse to help my enemy commit his crimes, he will merely wreck my career, by sending to some journalist the film in which I act obscenely. My enemy assures me that, if he wrecks my career, my children will not be killed. He gets perverse pleasure from causing me to do what I believe to be wrong, by threatening to wreck my career. This pleasure would be lost if his threat was to kill my children. If I helped him to commit his crimes because this was the only way to save my children's lives, I would not believe that I was acting wrongly. Since my enemy wants me to believe that I am acting wrongly, he does not make *this* threat.

Knowing my enemy, I have good reason to believe what he says. Since it is the only way to save my children's lives, I ought to let him make his film. I ought to make myself disposed to help him commit his minor crimes. And it would be wrong for me to cause myself to lose this disposition, since, if I do, my children will be killed. But, when I act on this disposition, I am acting wrongly. I ought not to help this man to commit his crimes, merely in order to save my career.

This case shows that we should reject what I called (G4). This is the claim that, if I ought to cause myself to have some disposition, and it would be wrong for me to cause myself to lose this disposition, I cannot be acting wrongly when I act upon this disposition. In the case just described, when I act on such a disposition, I *am* acting wrongly.[15]

I shall now state together four similar mistakes. Some people claim that, if it is rational for me to cause myself to have some disposition, it cannot be irrational to act upon this disposition. This was shown to be false by the case I called *Schelling's Answer to Armed Robbery*. A second claim is that, if it is rational for me to cause myself to believe that some act is rational, this act *is* rational. This was shown to be false by the case that I called *My Slavery*. A third claim is that, if there is some disposition that I ought to cause myself to have, and that it would be wrong for me to cause myself to lose, it cannot be wrong for me to act upon this disposition. The case just given shows this to be false. A fourth claim is that, if I ought to cause myself to believe that some act would not be wrong, this act cannot be wrong. I shall soon show this to be false. These four claims assume that rationality and rightness can be inherited, or *transferred*. If it is rational or right for me either to cause myself to be disposed to act in some way, or to make myself believe that this act is rational or right, this act *is* rational or right. My examples show that this is not so. Rationality and rightness cannot be inherited in this way. In this respect the truth is simpler than these claims imply.

17. HOW C MIGHT BE SELF-EFFACING

It might be claimed that, if Consequentialism sometimes broke the link between our belief that our act is wrong and our belief that we are bad, we would not in fact continue to regard morality with sufficient seriousness. Similarly, our desire to avoid wrongdoing might be undermined if we believed that other desires should often be stronger. This desire may survive only if we believe that it should *always* be overriding, and feel remorse when it is not. It might be claimed, on these or other grounds, that it would make the outcome better if we always kept the link between our moral beliefs and our intentions and emotions. If this is so, it would make the outcome better if we did not believe C.

I doubt these claims. But it is worth considering what they would imply. According to C, each of us should try to have one of the best possible sets of desires and dispositions, in Consequentialist terms. It might make the outcome better if we did not merely have these desires and dispositions, but had corresponding moral emotions and beliefs.

Consider, for example, theft. On some versions of C, it is intrinsically bad if property is stolen. On other versions of C, this is not so. On these versions, theft is bad only when it makes the outcome worse. Avoiding theft is not part of our ultimate moral aim. But it might be true that it would make the outcome better if we were strongly disposed not to steal. And it might make the outcome better if we believed stealing to be intrinsically wrong, and would feel remorse when we do steal. Similar claims might be made about many other kinds of act.

If these claims were true, C would be self-effacing. It would tell us that we should try to believe, not itself, but some other theory. We should try to believe the theory which is such that, if we believed it, the outcome would be best. On the claims made above, this theory might not be C. It might be some version of what Sidgwick called *Common-Sense Morality*.

If C told us to believe some version of this morality, this would not be Common-Sense Morality as it is now, but an improved version. Common-Sense Morality is *not* the moral theory belief in which would make the outcome best. Such a theory would, for example, demand much more from the rich. It might make the outcome best if those in the richer nations gave to the poor at least a quarter or even half of their incomes every year. The rich now give, and seem to believe that they are justified in giving, less than one per cent.

Suppose that C told us to believe some other theory. As I have said, it would be hard to change our beliefs, if our reason for doing so is not a reason which casts doubt on our old beliefs, but is merely that it would have good effects if we had different beliefs. But there are various ways in which we might bring about this change. Perhaps we could all be hypnotized, and the next generation brought up differently. We would have to be made to forget how and why we acquired our new beliefs, and the process would have to be hidden from future historians.

It would make a difference here if we accept, not C, but Collective Consequentialism. If we accept C, we might conclude that C ought to be rejected by most people, but should still be believed by a few. Our theory would then be partly self-effacing, and partly *esoteric*, telling those who believe it not to enlighten the ignorant majority. But as Collective Consequentialists we should believe the moral theory which is such that, if we *all* believed it, the outcome would be best. This theory cannot be esoteric.

Some find it especially objectionable that a moral theory might be esoteric. If we believe that deception is morally wrong, deception about morality may seem especially wrong. Sidgwick wrote: 'it seems expedient that the doctrine that esoteric morality is expedient should itself be kept esoteric. Or, if this concealment be difficult to maintain, it may be desirable that Common Sense should repudiate the doctrines which it is expedient to confine to an enlightened few.'[16] This is what Williams calls 'Government House' Consequentialism, since it treats the majority like the natives in a colony.[17] As Williams claims, we cannot welcome such a conclusion. Sidgwick regretted his conclusions, but he did not think regret a ground for doubt.[18]

I have claimed that it is unlikely that C is wholly self-effacing. It would at most be partly self-effacing and partly esoteric. It might make the outcome better if some people did not believe C; but it is unlikely that it would make the outcome better if C was believed by no one.

Here is another ground for doubting this. Suppose that we all come to believe C. (This will seem less implausible when we remember that C can be a pluralist theory, appealing to many different moral principles.) We then decide that C is wholly self-effacing. We decide that it would make the outcome best if we caused ourselves to believe some improved version of Common-Sense Morality. We might succeed in bringing about this change in our beliefs. Given changes in the world, and in our technology, it might later come to be true that the outcome would be better if we revised our moral beliefs. But if we no longer believed C, because we now believed some version of Common-Sense Morality, we would not be led to make these needed revisions in our morality. Our reason for believing this morality would not be that we *now* believe it to be the morality belief in which would make the outcome best. This would be why we caused ourselves to believe this morality. But, in order to believe this morality, we must have forgotten that this is what we did. We would now simply believe this morality. We might therefore not be led to revise our morality even if it came to be true that our belief in this morality would increase the chances of some disaster, such as a nuclear war.

These claims should affect our answer to the question whether it would make the outcome better if we all ceased to believe C. We might believe correctly that there is some other moral theory belief in which would, in the short run, make the outcome better. But once Consequentialism has effaced itself, and the cord is cut, the long-term consequences might be much worse.

This suggests that the most that could be true is that C is partly self-effacing. It might be better if most people caused themselves to believe some other theory, by some process of self-deception that, to succeed, must also be forgotten. But, as a precaution, a few people should continue to believe C, and should keep convincing evidence about this self-deception. These people need not live in Government House, or have any other special status. If things went well, the few would do nothing. But if the moral theory believed by most did become disastrous, the few could then produce their evidence. When most people learnt that their moral beliefs were the result of self-deception, this would undermine these beliefs, and prevent the disaster.

Though I have claimed that this is unlikely, suppose that C *was* wholly self-effacing. Suppose that it told all of us to make ourselves believe, not itself, but some other theory. Williams claims that, if this is so, the theory ceases to deserve its name, since it 'determines nothing of how thought in the world is conducted'.[19] This claim is puzzling since, as Williams also claims, C would be demanding that the way in which we think about morality, and our set of desires and dispositions, 'must be for the best'.[20] This is demanding something fairly specific, and wholly Consequentialist.

Williams makes the third claim that, if C was wholly self-effacing, it would cease to be effective.[21] This need not be so. Suppose that things happen as described above. We all come to believe in some form of C. We then believe truly that, if we all believed some other theory, this would produce the best possible outcome. C tells us all to believe this other theory. In some indirect way, we bring about this change in our beliefs. No one now believes C. But this does not justify the claim that C has ceased to be effective. It has had the effect that we all now believe some other particular theory. And our belief in this other theory will produce the best possible outcome. Though no one believes C, C is still effective. There are two continuing facts that are the effects of our earlier belief in C: our new moral beliefs, and the fact that, because we have these beliefs, the outcome is as good as it can possibly be.

Williams rightly claims that, if C was wholly self-effacing, it would not be clear what this shows. We would have to decide whether it showed that C 'is unacceptable, or merely that no one ought to accept it.'[22] It is clear that, on our last assumptions, no one ought morally to accept C. If anyone did accept C, it would itself tell him that he ought morally to try to reject C and instead believe some other theory. But, as Williams suggests, there are two questions. It is one question whether some theory is the one that we *ought morally* to try to believe. It is another question whether this is the theory that we *ought intellectually* or *in truth-seeking terms* to believe—whether this theory is the true or best justified theory. I claimed earlier that, if a theory about rationality was self-effacing, this would not show that this theory cannot be the true or the best justified theory. Can we make a similar claim about moral theories?

Our answer to this question will depend in part on our beliefs about the nature of moral reasoning. If a moral theory can be quite straightforwardly *true*, it is clear that, if it is self-effacing, this does not show that it cannot be true. But we may instead regard morality as a social product, either actually or in some 'ideal constructivist' way. We may then claim that, to be acceptable, a moral theory must fulfil what Rawls calls 'the publicity condition': it must be a theory that everyone ought to accept, and publicly acknowledge to each other.[23] On these meta-ethical views, a moral theory cannot be self-effacing. On other views, it can be. It would take at least a book to decide between these different views. I must therefore, in this book, leave this question open. This does not matter if, as I believe, C would *not* be self-effacing.

18. THE OBJECTION THAT ASSUMES INFLEXIBILITY

I shall now return to an objection raised earlier. Consider those people for whom the Self-interest Theory is indirectly self-defeating. Suppose that these people believe S, and in consequence are never self-denying. This is worse for them. It would be better for them if they had other desires and dispositions. In the case of these people, this would not be possible unless they believed a different theory. And it might be true that they cannot change either their beliefs or their dispositions.

Similar claims might be true for Consequentialists. Suppose that, because we all believe C, we are all pure do-gooders. This makes the outcome worse than it would be if we all had other dispositions. But we cannot change our dispositions unless we also change our beliefs about morality. And we cannot bring about these changes.

It is unlikely that all these claims would be true. If they were, would they provide objections to S and C?

It may help to consider an imaginary case. Suppose that Satan rules the Universe. Satan cannot affect which is the true theory about rationality, or which is the best or best justified theory. But he knows which this theory is, and he perversely causes belief in this theory to have bad effects in this theory's own terms. In imagining this case we need not assume that the best theory is the Self-interest Theory. Whatever the best theory is, Satan would cause belief in this theory to have bad effects, in this theory's terms.

We can next assume the same about moral theories. Suppose that the best moral theory is Utilitarianism. On this theory, we should all try to produce the outcome that is best for everyone, impartially considered. Satan ensures that, if people believe this theory, this is worse for everyone. Suppose next that the best moral theory is not Consequentialist, and that it tells each person never to deceive others, or coerce them, or treat them unjustly. Satan ensures that those who believe this theory are in fact, despite their contrary intentions, more deceitful, coercive, and unjust.

Satan ensures that, if anyone believes some theory, this has bad effects in this theory's terms. Would this do anything to show that such a theory is not the best theory? It is clear that it would not. The most that could be shown is this. Given Satan's interference, it would be better if we did not believe the best theory. Since we are the mere toys of Satan, the truth about reality is extremely depressing. It might be better if we also did not know this truth.

In this imagined case, it would be better if we did not believe the best theory. This shows that we should reject

(G5) If we ought to cause ourselves to believe that some act is wrong, this act *is* wrong.

As I claimed, wrongness cannot be *inherited* in this way.

Suppose that all we know is that belief in some theory would have bad effects in this theory's terms. This would not show that this is not the best theory. Whether this is so must depend on *why* belief in the theory has these bad effects. There are two possibilities. The bad effects may be produced by our successfully doing what this theory tells us to do. If this was true, the theory would be *directly* self-defeating, and this might refute this theory. The bad effects may instead be produced by some quite separate fact about reality. If this fact was the interference of Satan, this would cast no doubt on the theory.

What should we claim about the possibilities described above? Suppose that the following is true. It would be worse for each of us if he believed S, and was therefore never self-denying. If we all believed C, and were therefore pure do-gooders, this would make the outcome worse. And, if we had either of these beliefs and dispositions, we would be unable to change them. It would then be true that belief in these two theories would have bad effects in these theories' terms. Would this cast doubt on these theories? Or would it be merely like Satan's interference?

The best theory may be neither S nor C. I shall argue later that we ought to reject S. But if I am wrong, and either S or C is the best theory, I suggest that the possibilities just described would not provide an objection to either theory. If either S or C is the best theory, belief in this theory would have bad effects in this theory's terms. But these bad effects would not be the result of our doing, or trying to do, what S or C tell us to do. The bad effects would be the results of our dispositions. And these theories would not tell us to have these dispositions. They would tell us, if we can, not to do so. S would tell us, if we can, not to be never self-denying. C would tell us, if we can, not to be pure do-gooders. We would have one of these dispositions because we believe in one of these theories. But these theories do not tell us to believe themselves. S tells each person to believe the theory belief in which would be best for him. C tells us to believe the theory belief in which would make the outcome best. On the assumptions made above, S and C would tell us *not* to believe S and C.

Because we believe either S or C, belief in either theory would have bad effects in this theory's terms. But these bad effects would *not* be the result of our doing what these theories tell us to do. They would be the result of our having dispositions that these theories do *not* tell us to have, and tell us, if we can, *not* to have. And they would be the result of our believing what these theories do *not* tell us to believe, and tell us, if we can, *not* to believe. Since these bad effects cannot be blamed on these theories in any of these ways, I suggest that, if the claims made above were true, this would not cast doubt on these theories. These claims would merely be, like Satan's interference, depressing truths about reality.

19. CAN BEING RATIONAL OR MORAL BE A MERE MEANS?

S tells us to act rationally, and C tells us to act morally. But these are only what I call our formal aims. I have assumed that acting morally would not, as such, be a substantive aim given to us by C. C might claim that acting morally is a mere means. Similarly, acting rationally may not be part of the substantive aim given to us by S. And S might claim that acting rationally is a mere means. Is this an objection to these two theories?

There is a difference here between S and C. S cannot claim that our formal aim is, as such, a substantive aim. But C *could* make this claim. There may be an objection here to S. But there cannot be a similar objection to C.

We might object, to S: 'If acting rationally is not an aim that we should have, but a mere means, why should we be rational? Why should we want to know what we have most reason to do?'

How should a Self-interest Theorist reply? He might accept the Objective List Theory about self-interest. He might then claim: 'Being rational and acting rationally are, in themselves, part of what makes our lives go better. If they are, on the whole, better for us, S does not imply that being rational and acting rationally are mere means. They are, in themselves, parts of each person's ultimate S-given aim.'

Consider next a Self-interest Theorist who is a Hedonist. This person must admit that he believes acting rationally to be a mere means. But he could say: 'According to S, what you have most reason to do is whatever will make your life go as well as possible. If you want to know what you have most reason to do, and want to act rationally, S does not imply that these are pointless desires. This is not implied by the claim that, if you follow S, and act rationally, your acts matter merely as a means. Mattering as a means is a way of mattering. Your desires would be pointless only if acting rationally did not matter. S claims that, when you are deciding what to do, compared with acting rationally, *nothing matters more*. This last claim is justified even when what it would be rational for you to do is to make yourself disposed to act irrationally. What matters *most*, even here, is that you do what it would be rational for you to do.'

I turn now from S to C. C might claim that acting morally is a mere means. We may object: 'If this is so, why should we care about morality?' Consider first the simplest kind of Consequentialist, a Hedonistic Utilitarian. Such a person might say: 'It matters morally whether what happens is good or bad. It is bad if there is more suffering, good if there is more happiness. It also matters whether we act morally, and avoid wrongdoing. We should try to do the best we can to reduce suffering and increase happiness. This matters, not in itself, but because of its effects. In this sense, avoiding wrongdoing is a mere means. But this does not imply that it does *not* matter morally whether we avoid wrongdoing. When we are deciding what to do, compared with avoiding wrongdoing, *nothing matters more*. This last claim is justified even when what we ought to do is to make ourselves disposed to act wrongly. What matters *most*, even here, is that we do what we ought to do.'

A Hedonistic Utilitarian must admit that, on his view, *if* wrongdoing did not have bad effects, it would not matter. If there was more wrongdoing, this would not in itself make the outcome worse. As with the Hedonistic version of S, the achievement of our formal aim does matter, but only as a means.

Can this Utilitarian defend this claim? He might first appeal to the unattractiveness of what Williams calls *moral self-indulgence*.[24] Compare two people who are trying to relieve the suffering of others. The first person acts because he sympathises with these people. He also believes that suffering is bad, and ought to be relieved. The second person acts because he wants to think of himself as someone who is morally good. Of these two people, the first seems to be better. But the first person has no thoughts about the goodness of acting morally, or the badness of wrongdoing. He is moved to act simply by his sympathy, and by his belief that, since suffering is bad, he ought to try to prevent it. This person seems to regard acting morally as a mere means. It is the second person who regards acting morally as a separate aim that is in itself good. Since the first person seems to be better, this supports the claim that acting morally *is* a mere means.

Consider next

Murder and Accidental Death. Suppose I know that X is about to die, and that, as his last act, he intends to murder Y. I also know that, unless Z is rescued, he will be killed by a forest fire. I might be able to persuade X not to murder Y, or be able instead to save Z's life. Suppose I believe that, if Y was killed by X, this would not be worse than Z's being killed by a forest fire. These two outcomes would be equally bad, because they would each involve someone's being killed. In the first outcome there would also be a very serious case of wrongdoing. But, according to my theory, this would not make this outcome worse. (It might do so if the wrongdoer would himself survive. But X is about to die.) Since I believe that wrongdoing does not, as such, make an outcome worse, I believe that, if my chance of saving Z would be *slightly* higher than my chance of persuading X not to murder Y, I ought to try to save Z.[25]

Many people would accept this last conclusion. They would believe that, if my chance of saving Z is slightly higher, I should try to save him rather than Y. If we accept this conclusion, can we also claim that it is bad in itself if there is more wrongdoing? Can we claim that I ought to try to prevent Z's accidental death even though, because it involves wrongdoing, X's murdering Y would be a worse outcome? It would be hard to defend this claim. For many people, this is another case which supports the view that the avoidance of wrongdoing is a mere means.

It may be objected: 'If X intends to murder Y, the badness is already present. You do not prevent the badness if you merely persuade X not carry out his murderous intention. This is why you ought to try to save Z.' We can change the case. Suppose that I know that X may soon come to believe falsely that he has been betrayed by Y. X is not morally bad, but he is like Othello. He is someone who is good, but potentially bad. I know that it is probable that, if X believes that he has been betrayed by Y, he will, like Othello, murder Y. I have a good chance of preventing X from coming to acquire this false belief, and thereby preventing him from murdering Y. But I have a slightly greater chance of saving Z's life. As before, X is in any case about to die. Many people would again believe that I ought to try to save Z's life. This suggests that, if X forms his intention, and then murders Y, this would not be a worse outcome than if Z is accidentally killed. If this *would* be a worse outcome, why should I try to to save Z rather than Y? Why should I try to prevent the lesser of two evils, when my chance of success is only slightly higher?

Suppose that, because we believe that I ought to try to save Z, we agree that Y's death would not be a worse outcome than Z's. If this is so, the badness in Y's death is merely that Y dies. It cannot make this outcome worse that X forms his murderous intention, and then acts very wrongly. As I claimed, we may conclude that the avoidance of wrongdoing is a mere means.

In such cases, many people believe that wrongdoing does not make the outcome worse. Would it make the outcome better if there were more acts that were morally right, and more duties that were fulfilled? I might often promise to do what I intended anyway to do. I would thereby cause it to be true that more duties were fulfilled. But no one thinks that this would make the outcome better, or would be what I ought to do.

Suppose next that poverty is abolished, natural disasters cease to occur, people cease to suffer from either physical or mental illness, and in many other ways people cease to need help from other people. These changes would all be, in one way, good. Would they be in any way bad? It is morally admirable to help others in distress, at a considerable cost to oneself. In the world that I have described, very few people need such help. There would be far fewer of these morally admirable acts. Would this be bad? Would it make this outcome in one respect worse?

If we answer No, this again supports the view that acting morally is a mere means. But some of us would answer Yes. We would believe that, in this respect, the outcome *would* be worse. And there are also many people who hold a different view about wrongdoing. These people would believe that, compared with Z's accidental death, X's murdering Y would, as an outcome, be much worse. Can a Consequentialist accept these claims?

This depends on what principles he accepts. Consider first a Hedonistic Utilitarian. If X's murdering Y would not cause more suffering than Z's accidental death, or a greater loss of happiness, this Utilitarian cannot claim that, as an outcome, the murder is much worse. Turning to morally admirable acts, all that he can claim is this. One of the chief sources of happiness is the belief that one is helping others, in significant ways. It would therefore be in one way bad if very few people needed such help.

Consider next a Consequentialist who accepts the Objective List Theory about self-interest. On this theory, being moral and acting morally may be in themselves good for us, whatever their effects may be. They may be among the things that are best for us, or that make our lives go best. And being morally bad may be, in itself, one of the things that is worst for us. If a Consequentialist makes these claims, he can deny that acting morally and avoiding wrongdoing are mere means. On any plausible version of C, it is better if our lives go better. On the claims just made, acting morally and avoiding wrongdoing *are* parts of the ultimate moral aim given to us by C.

On this view, though these are parts of this aim, they are not, as such, ultimate aims. They are parts of this aim because, like being happy, being moral is one of the things that make our lives go better.

A Consequentialist could make a different claim. He could claim that our formal aim is, as such, a substantive aim. He could claim that it would be worse if there was more wrongdoing, even if this would be worse for no one. Similarly, it could be better if more people acted morally, even if this would be better for no one. A Consequentialist could even claim that the achievement of our formal aim has absolute priority over the achievement of our other moral aims. He could accept Cardinal Newman's view. Newman believed that pain and sin were both bad, but that sin was infinitely worse. If all mankind suffered 'extremest agony', this would be less bad than if one venial sin was committed.[27]

Few Consequentialists would go as far as this. But since Newman's view is a version of C, we cannot claim that C gives too little weight to the avoidance of wrongdoing. C could give this aim absolute priority over all our other moral aims.

It may again seem that C is not a distinctive moral theory, but could cover all theories. This is not so. Non-Consequentialists can claim, not that C gives too little weight to the avoidance of wrongdoing, but that C gives this weight in the wrong way. On this extreme version of C, the avoidance of wrongdoing is one of our *common* moral aims. A Non-Consequentialist would say that I ought not to act wrongly, even if I thereby caused there to be much less wrongdoing by other people. On this version of C, I would not, in this case, be acting wrongly. If I am doing what most effectively reduces the incidence of wrongdoing, I am doing what I ought to do.

20. CONCLUSIONS

I shall now summarize the second half of this chapter. I assumed that, in the ways that I described, Consequentialism is indirectly self-defeating. It would make the outcome worse if we were always disposed to do what would make the outcome best. If we all had this disposition, the outcome might be better than it actually is, given what people are actually like. But the outcome would be worse than it would be if we had certain other causally possible sets of motives.

I asked whether, when C is indirectly self-defeating, it is failing in its own terms. If it would make the outcome worse if we were always disposed to do what would make the outcome best, C tells us that we should not have this disposition. Since C makes this claim, it is not failing in its own terms.

Suppose that we all accept C. Our theory tells us that we should cause ourselves to have, or to keep, one of the best possible sets of motives, in Consequentialist terms. Since C is indirectly self-defeating, this implies the following. If we have one of the best possible sets of motives, we shall sometimes knowingly act wrongly according to our own theory. But, given the special reason why we are acting wrongly, we need not regard ourselves, when so acting, as morally bad. We can believe these to be cases of *blameless wrongdoing*. We can believe this because we are acting on a set of motives that it would be wrong for us to cause ourselves to lose.

Some of these claims might be implied even if C was not indirectly self-defeating. These claims would be implied if C was unrealistically demanding. This is probably true. It is probable that, even if we all believed C, it would be causally impossible that we become disposed always to do what we believe would make the outcome best. If this is true, C tells us to try to have one of the best possible sets of motives.

In making these various claims, C is coherent. Nor does it fail to take morality seriously. Even if we accept these claims, there would still be many other cases in which we would regard ourselves as morally bad. This would be so whenever we knowingly made the outcome *much* worse, and did *not* do this because we had one of the best possible sets of motives. Though we would not be solely concerned about the avoidance of wrongdoing, since we would also be concerned about having the best motives, we would still regard many acts as showing the agent to be morally bad.

It may be objected that these claims wrongly assume Psychological Determinism. If a Consequentialist accepts this objection, he must qualify his claims. He can claim that, if we have one of the best sets of motives, it would often be very hard for us to avoid doing what we believe to be wrong. He must admit that, in these cases, we are not *wholly* blameless; but we are bad only in a very weak sense.

Another objection is that an acceptable moral theory cannot tell us to cause ourselves to do what this theory claims to be wrong. But I gave an example where this objection would be denied even by most of those who reject C.

A third objection is that, since C is indirectly self-defeating, we cannot always avoid doing what C claims to be wrong. Since we cannot always do what C claims that we ought to do, C demands the impossible. It infringes the doctrine that ought implies can. I claimed that this objection could be answered.

A fourth objection is that it will make the outcome better if we have moral beliefs that conflict with C. If this was true, C would be self-effacing. It would tell us to believe, not itself, but some other theory. I doubted whether this is true. I believe that C is at most partly self-effacing, and partly esoteric. It might make the outcome better if some people believed some other theory, but it would not make the outcome better if no one believed C. And, even if C was wholly self-effacing, I believe that this would not cast doubt on C. Whether this is so depends on what the best view is about the nature of morality, and moral reasoning. Since I have not argued for any of these views, I did not fully defend my belief that, if C was self-effacing, this would not cast doubt on C.

I asked finally whether we can accept C's claim that acting morally is a mere means. If we cannot, C need not make this claim. It could even claim that the preventing of wrong-doing has absolute priority over our other moral aims. *Utilitarians* cannot make this claim. But *Consequentialists* can.

In the first half of this chapter I discussed the Self-interest Theory about rationality. In the second half I discussed the group of moral theories that are Consequentialist. It is plausible to claim that all these theories are indirectly self-defeating. And they might perhaps be self-effacing. But, in the case of these theories, to be indirectly self-defeating is not to be damagingly self-defeating. Nor do these facts provide independent objections to these theories. These facts do not show that these theories are either false, or indefensible. This may be true, but the arguments so far have not shown this. They at most show that what can be justifiably claimed is more complicated than we may have hoped.

2

PRACTICAL DILEMMAS

21. WHY C CANNOT BE DIRECTLY SELF-DEFEATING

I HAVE described how theories can be indirectly self-defeating. How might theories be *directly* self-defeating? Say that someone *successfully follows Theory T* when he succeeds in doing the act which, of the acts that are possible for him, best achieves his T-given aims. Use *we* to mean 'the members of some group'. We might call T

> *directly collectively self-defeating* when it is true that, if *all* of us successfully follow T, we will thereby cause our T-given aims to be worse achieved than they would have been if *none* of us had successfully followed T.

This definition seems plausible. 'All' and 'none' give us the simplest cases. It will be enough to discuss these.

Though it seems plausible, we must reject this definition. It ceases to be plausible when it is applied to certain *co-ordination problems*. These are cases where the effect of each person's act depends upon what others do. For a simple case, see page 72. Another case is shown below.

You

		do (1)	do (2)	do (3)
	do (1)	Third-best	Bad	Bad
I	do (2)	Bad	Second-best	Equal-best
	do (3)	Bad	Equal-best	Bad

If we both do (1), we both successfully follow C. Since you have done (1), I would have made the outcome worse if I had done either (2) or (3). And you could claim the same. If instead we both do (2), neither has successfully followed C. Since you have done (2) , I would have made the outcome better if I had done (3). And you could claim the same. If we both do (1) rather than (2), both rather than neither successfully follow C. But we thereby make the outcome worse, causing our C-given aim to be worse achieved. On the definition given above, C is here self-defeating.

This conclusion is not justified. It is true that, if we both do (1), both successfully follow C. But if we had produced either of the best outcomes, we would *also* have successfully followed C. If one of us had done (2) and the other had done (3), each would have done what, of the acts that were possible for him, would make the outcome best. The objection to C here is not that it is self-defeating. The objection is that it is *indeterminate*. We successfully follow (C) *both* if we both do (1), *and* if one of us does (2) and the other does (3). Because this is true, if we both successfully follow C, this does not *ensure* that our acts jointly produce one of the best possible outcomes. But it does not ensure that they do *not*. If we had produced one of the best outcomes, we would have successfully followed C. C does not direct us *away* from the best outcomes. The objection is less. C merely fails to direct us towards these outcomes. (I shall explain in Section 26 how this objection can be partly met.)[28]

If C directed us away from the best outcomes, it would be *certain* that, if we successfully follow C, we shall *not* produce one of the best outcomes. This suggests another definition. Call theory T

directly collectively self-defeating when

(i) it is *certain* that, if we all successfully follow T, we will thereby cause our T-given aims to be worse achieved than they would have been if none of us had successfully followed T, or

(ii) our acts will cause our T-given aims to be best achieved only if we do *not* successfully follow T.

(ii) expresses the idea that, to cause our T-given aims to be best achieved, we must *disobey* T. By 'when' I do not mean 'only when'. We do not need to cover all cases. As I explained, 'we' does not mean 'everyone living', but 'all the members of some group'.

Could (i) and (ii) be true in the case of C? Could it be true that we will make the outcome best only if we do not successfully follow C? Could it therefore be certain that, if all rather than none of us successfully follow C, we will thereby make the outcome worse? Neither of these is possible. We successfully follow C when each does the act which, of the acts that are possible for him, makes the outcome best. If our acts do jointly produce the best outcome, we must all be successfully following C. It cannot here be true of anyone that, if he had acted differently, he would have made the outcome better. On this definition, C cannot be directly self-defeating.

C may be a pluralist theory, assessing the goodness of outcomes by an appeal to several different principles. One would be some Utilitarian claim about harms and benefits; the others might be principles about just distribution, or deception, or coercion, or entitlements. If these and other principles tell us to agree on which outcomes would be better, the reasoning just given will apply. Such a pluralist theory cannot be directly self-defeating, since it is *agent-neutral:* giving to all agents only *common* moral aims. If we cause these common aims to be best achieved, we must be successfully following this theory. Since this is so, it cannot be true that we will cause these aims to be best achieved only if we do not follow this theory.

22. HOW THEORIES CAN BE DIRECTLY SELF-DEFEATING

What if our theory is *agent-relative*, giving to *different* agents *different* aims? We may now be unable to apply clause (ii) of my definition. If T gives to different people different aims, there may be no way in which we can *best* achieve the T-given aims *of each*. But we can apply clause (i), with a slight revision. And I shall give another definition. Call T

> *directly individually self-defeating* when it is certain that, if someone successfully follows T, he will thereby cause his own T-given aims to be worse achieved than they would have been if he had not successfully followed T,

and

> *directly collectively self-defeating* when it is certain that, if we all successfully follow T, we will thereby cause the T-given aims *of each* to be worse achieved than they would have been if none of us had successfully followed T.

The Self-interest Theory gives to different agents different aims. Could this theory be directly individually self-defeating? The aim that S gives to me is that my life goes, for me, as well as possible. I successfully follow S when I do what, of the acts that are possible for me, will be best for me. Could it be certain that, if I successfully follow S, I will thereby make the outcome worse for me? This is not possible. It is not possible either in the case of a single act, or in the case of a series of acts at different times. The argument for this second claim is like the argument I gave above. S gives to me at different times one and the same *common* aim: that my life goes, for me, as well as possible. If my acts at different times cause my life to go as well as possible, I must in doing each act be successfully following S. I must be doing what, of the acts that are possible for me, will be best for me. So it cannot be certain that, if I always successfully follow S, I will thereby make the outcome worse for me.

What can be worse for me is to be *disposed* always to follow S. But in this case it is not my acts that are bad for me, but my disposition. S cannot be directly individually self-defeating. It can only be *indirectly* individually self-defeating.

Can theories be directly *collectively* self-defeating? Suppose that Theory T gives to you and me different aims. And suppose that each could either (1) promote his own T-given aim or (2) more effectively promote the other's. The outcomes are shown below.

You

do (1)   do (2)

	do (1)	do (2)
do (1)	The T-given aim of each is third-best achieved	Mine is best achieved, yours worst
do (2)	Mine is worst achieved, yours best	The T-given aim of each is second-best achieved

I

Suppose finally that neither's choice will affect the other's. It will then be true of each that, if he does (1) rather than (2), he will thereby cause his own T-given aim to be better achieved. This is so whatever the other does. We both successfully follow T only if we both do (1) rather than (2). Only then is each doing what, of the acts that are possible for him, best achieves his T-given aim. But it is certain that if both rather than neither successfully follow T—if both do (1) rather than (2)—we will thereby cause the T-given aim of each to be worse achieved. Theory T is here directly collectively self-defeating.

Such cases have great practical importance. The simplest cases may occur when

(a) Theory T is agent-relative, giving to different agents different aims,

(b) the achievement of each person's T-given aims partly depends on what others do, and

(c) what each does will not affect what these others do.

23. PRISONER'S DILEMMAS AND PUBLIC GOODS

These three conditions often hold if T is the Self-interest Theory. S is often directly collectively self-defeating. These cases have a misleading name taken from one example. This is the *Prisoner's Dilemma*. You and I are questioned separately about some joint crime. The outcomes are shown below.

Whatever the other does, it will be better for each if he confesses. By confessing each will be certain to save himself two years in prison. But if both confess that will be worse for each than if both keep silent.

You

	confess	keep silent
confess	Each gets 10 years	I go free, you get 12 years
keep silent	I get 12 years, you go free	Each gets 2 years

I

Let us simplify. It will be worse for both if each rather than neither does what will be better for himself. One case occurs when

(*The Positive Condition*) each could either (1) give himself the lesser of two benefits or (2) give the other the greater benefit,

and

(*The Negative Condition*) neither's choice would be in other ways better or worse for either.

When the Positive Condition holds, the outcomes are as shown below.

You

	do (1)	do (2)
do (1)	Each gets the lesser benefit	I get both benefits, you get neither
do (2)	I get neither benefit, you get both	Each gets the greater benefit

I

If we add the Negative Condition, the diagram becomes as shown below.

You

do (1)   do (2)

	do (1)	do (2)
do (1)	Third-best for each	Best for me, worst for you
do (2)	Worst for me, best for you	Second-best for both

(I — to the left, between the two rows)

Part of the Negative Condition cannot be shown in this diagram. There must be *no reciprocity*: it must be true that neither's choice would cause the other to make the same choice. It will then be better for each if he does (1) rather than (2). This is so whatever the other does. But if both do (1) this will be worse for each than if both do (2).

When could neither's choice affect the other's? Only when each must make a final choice before learning what the other chose. Outside prisons, or the offices of *game-theorists*, this is seldom true. Nor would it ensure the Negative Condition. There might, for instance, be delayed reciprocity. Either's choice might affect whether he is later harmed or benefited by the other. We can therefore seldom know that we face a Two-Person Prisoner's Dilemma.

This last claim is supported by the extensive literature on Prisoner's Dilemmas. This describes few convincing Two-Person Cases. My Negative Condition seldom holds.

One of the cases much discussed is the arms race between the United States and the Soviet Union. This is often claimed to be a Prisoner's Dilemma. Should each of these nations secretly develop new weapons? If only one does so, it may be able later to dictate to the other. This would be its best outcome and the other's worst. If both do so, they will remain equal, but at great expense, and with the insecurity of continued competition. This would be third-best for both. Second-best for both would be if neither secretly develops new weapons. Each should develop new weapons since it will get its third-best outcome rather than its worst if the other does the same, and its best rather than its second-best if the other does not do the same. But if both develop new weapons this will be worse for both than if neither did.[29]

Part of my Negative Condition may here hold. If the new weapons can be developed secretly, each nation must make its choice before learning what the other chose. On the question of research, the reasoning just given may be correct. But it is doubtful whether it applies to the production or deployment of new weapons, where each can know what the other is doing. Nor is it clear that mere progress in research might enable each to dictate to the other. Moreover, this is a *repeated* or *continuing* situation. Similar decisions have to be made again and again. Because of this, it ceases to be clear that acting in one of two ways will be certain to be better for each. The choice made by each may affect the later choices made by the other.

Much of the literature discusses this kind of repeated case: what are misleadingly called *Repeated Prisoner's Dilemmas*. Many experiments have been done to see how pairs of people act in such cases.[30] Apart from such experimental work, there has been much theoretical discussion of 'Repeated Prisoner's Dilemmas'. Though of interest, this discussion is irrelevant here. We should distinguish two kinds of case. In the first, each person knows that he will face some particular number of 'Repeated Prisoner's Dilemmas'. Since this is not true in most of the cases with practical importance, I discuss these cases in endnote 31.

In most of the important cases, we do not know how many times we shall face 'Repeated Prisoner's Dilemmas'. On my definition, those who face such a series of cases do not face even a single *true* Prisoner's Dilemma. It is not true, of such people, that it will be worse for both if each rather than neither does what will be better for himself. This is not true because, in these 'Repeated Prisoner's Dilemmas', it is no longer clear which of the two choices will be better for oneself. This is because one's choice may affect the later choices made by the other. If one makes the co-operative choice, this may lead the other later to do the same. As the game-theorists say, if we consider all of their possible consequences, neither choice is *dominant*, certain to be better for oneself. The question raised by such cases is therefore an *internal* question for a Self-interest Theorist. If one's aim is to do the best one can for oneself, how should one act in a series of 'Repeated Prisoner's Dilemmas'? In a true Prisoner's Dilemma, the questions raised are quite different. In a true Dilemma, if one acts in one of two ways, it is *certain* that this will be better for oneself, not just immediately, but in the long-term and on the whole. The problem raised is not the internal problem of how one can best pursue one's own interests. The problem is that, if each rather than neither does what is certain to be better for himself, this will be worse for both of them.

Though we can seldom know that we face a Two-Person Prisoner's Dilemma, we can very often know that we face Many-Person Versions. And these have great practical importance. The rare Two-Person Case is important only as a model for the Many-Person Versions. We face

a *Many-Person Dilemma* when it is certain that, if each rather than none of us does what will be better for himself, this will be worse for everyone.

This definition covers only the simplest cases. As before 'everyone' means 'all the people in some group'.

One Many-Person Case is the *Samaritan's Dilemma*. Each of us could sometimes help a stranger at some lesser cost to himself. Each could about as often be similarly helped. In small communities, the cost of helping might be indirectly met. If I help, this may cause me to be later helped in return. But in large communities this is unlikely. It may here be better for each if he never helps. But it will be worse for each if no one ever helps. Each might gain from never helping, but he would lose, and lose more, from never being helped.

Many cases occur when

(*The Positive Conditions*) (i) each of us could, at some cost to himself, give to others a greater total sum of benefits, or expected benefits; (ii) if each rather than none gives this greater benefit to others, each would receive a greater benefit, or expected benefit; and

(*The Negative Condition*) there would be no indirect effects cancelling out these direct effects.

The Positive Conditions cover many kinds of case. At one extreme, each could give to *one* of the others a greater benefit. One example is the Samaritan's Dilemma. At the other extreme, each could give to *all* of the others a greater total sum of benefits. In the cases between these two extremes, each could give to *some* of the others a greater total sum of benefits. (At the second extreme, where each could benefit all of the others, (ii) is redundant, since it is implied by (i). In the other cases, (ii) is often true. It would be true, for instance, if the benefits were randomly spread.)

Another range of cases involves the different *chances* that what each does would benefit the others. At one extreme, each could certainly give to the others a greater total sum of benefits. At the other extreme, each would have a very small chance of giving to the others a very much greater benefit. In this range of cases each could give to the others a greater sum of *expected* benefits. This is the value of the possible benefits multiplied by the chance that the act will produce them. When the effects of our acts are uncertain, my definition of the Dilemma needs to be revised. In these cases it is not certain that, if each rather than none does what will be better for himself, this will be worse for everyone. We face

a *Risky Dilemma* when it is certain that, if each rather than none gives himself an expected benefit, this will either reduce the expected benefit to everyone, or will impose on everyone an expected harm or cost.

In some Many-Person Cases, only the Positive Conditions hold. In these cases, because the numbers involved are *sufficiently small*, what each does might affect what most others do. These cases are practically important. There are many cases involving nations, or business corporations, or trade unions. Such cases have some of the features of a true Prisoner's Dilemma. But they lack the central feature. Because the act of each may affect the acts of enough of the others, it is not clear which act would be in the interests of each. The question raised by such cases is another internal question for a Self-interest Theorist. In a true Prisoner's Dilemma, there is no uncertainty about which act will, on the whole, give the agent a greater benefit or expected benefit. The questions raised by true Dilemmas are quite different.

Many-Person Dilemmas are, I have said, extremely common. One reason is this. In a Two-Person Case, it is unlikely that the Negative Condition holds. This may need to be specially ensured, by prison-officers, or game-theorists. But in cases that involve very many people, the Negative Condition naturally holds. It need not be true that each must act before learning what the others do. Even when this is not true, if we are very numerous, what each does would be most unlikely to affect what most others do. It may affect what a few others do; but this would seldom make enough difference.

The commonest true Dilemmas are *Contributor's Dilemmas*. These involve *public goods*: outcomes that benefit even those who do not help to produce them. It can be true of each person that, if he helps, he will add to the sum of benefits, or expected benefits. But only a very small portion of the benefit he adds will come back to *him*. Since his share of what he adds will be very small, it may not repay his contribution. It may thus be better for each if he does not contribute. This can be so whatever others do. But it will be worse for each if fewer others contribute. And if none contribute this will be worse for each than if all do.

Many Contributor's Dilemmas involve two thresholds. In these cases, there are two numbers v and w such that, if fewer than v contribute, no benefit will be produced, and if more than w contribute, this will not increase the benefit produced. In many of these cases we do not know what others are likely to do. It will then not be certain that, if anyone contributes, he will benefit others. It will be true only that he will give to others an expected benefit. One extreme case is that of voting, where the gap between the two thresholds may be the gap of a single vote. The number w is here $v + 1$. Though an election is seldom a true Prisoner's Dilemma, it will be worth discussing later.

Some public goods need financial contributions. This is true of roads, the police, or national defence. Others need co-operative efforts. When in large industries wages depend on profits, and work is unpleasant or a burden, it can be better for each if others work harder, worse for each if he himself does. The same can be true for peasants on collective farms. A third kind of public good is the avoidance of an evil. The contribution needed here is often self-restraint. Such cases may involve

Commuters: Each goes faster if he drives, but if all drive each goes slower than if all take buses;

Soldiers: Each will be safer if he turns and runs, but if all do more will be killed than if none do;

Fishermen: When the sea is overfished, it can be better for each if he tries to catch more, worse for each if all do;

Peasants: When the land is overcrowded, it can be better for each if he or she has more children, worse for each if all do.[32]

There are countless other cases. It can be better for each if he adds to pollution, uses more energy, jumps queues, and breaks agreements; but, if all do these things, that can be worse for each than if none do. It is very often true that, if each rather than none does what will be better for himself, this will be worse for everyone.

These Dilemmas are usually described in self-interested terms. Since few people are purely self-interested, this may seem to reduce the importance of these cases. But in most of these cases the following is true. If each rather than none does what will be better for himself, *or his family, or those he loves*, this will be worse for everyone.

24. THE PRACTICAL PROBLEM AND ITS SOLUTIONS

Suppose that each is disposed to do what will be better for himself, or his family, or those he loves. There is then a *practical problem*. Unless something changes, the actual outcome will be worse for everyone. This problem is one of the chief reasons why we need more than laissez-faire economics—why we need both politics and morality.

Let us use labels. And let us take as understood the words 'or his family, or those he loves'. Each has two alternatives: E (more egoistic), A (more altruistic). If all do E that will be worse for each than if all do A. But, whatever others do, it will be better for each if he does E. The problem is that, for this reason, each is now disposed to do E.

This problem will be partly solved if most do A, wholly solved if all do. A solution may be reached in one or more of the ways shown on the next page.

The change in (3) differs from the change in (4). In (4) someone is disposed to do A *whether or not* this would be better for him. It is a mere side-effect that, because of this change in him, A would not be worse for him. In (3) someone is disposed to do A *only because*, given some *other* change in him, doing A would be better for him.

(1) to (4) abolish the Dilemma. The altruistic choice ceases to be worse for each. These are often good solutions. But they are sometimes inefficient, or unattainable. We then need (5). (5) solves the *practical* problem; but it does not abolish the Dilemma. A *theoretical* problem remains. In this and the next chapter I discuss how we can solve the practical problem. I discuss the theoretical problem in Chapter 4.

Each might do A

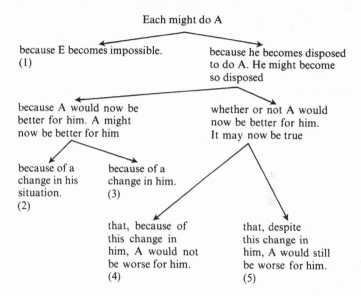

because E becomes impossible.
(1)

because he becomes disposed
to do A. He might become
so disposed

because A would now be
better for him. A might
now be better for him

whether or not A would
now be better for him.
It may now be true

because of a
change in his
situation.
(2)

because of a
change in him.
(3)

that, because of
this change in
him, A would not
be worse for him.
(4)

that, despite
this change in
him, A would still
be worse for him.
(5)

In solution (1), the self-benefiting choice is made impossible. This is sometimes best. In many Contributor's Dilemmas, there should be inescapable taxation. But (1) would often be a poor solution. Fishing nets could be destroyed, soldiers chained to their posts. Both have disadvantages.

(2) is a less direct solution. E remains possible, but A is made better for each. There might be a system of rewards. But, if this works, all must be rewarded. It may be better if the sole reward is to avoid some penalty. If this works, no one pays. If all deserters would be shot, there may be no deserters.

The choice between (1) and (2) is often difficult. Consider the Peasant's Dilemma, where it will be better for each if he or she has more children, worse for each if all do. Some countries reward two-child families. China now rewards one-child families. But where the problem is most serious the country is too poor to give everyone rewards. And, if such a system is to be effective, non-rewards must be like penalties. Since the system would not be wholly effective, some would have to bear such penalties. And such penalties fall not on the parents only but also on the children.

An alternative is (1), where it is made impossible for people to have more than two children. This would involve compulsory sterilization after the birth of one's second child. It would be better if this sterilization could be reversed if either or both of one's children died. Such a solution may seem horrendous. But it might receive unanimous support in a referendum. It would be better for all the people in some group if none rather than all have more than two children. If all prefer that this be what happens, all may prefer and vote for such a system of compulsory sterilization. If it was unanimously supported in a referendum, this might remove what is horrendous in the compulsion. And this solution has advantages over a system of rewards or penalties. As I have said, when such a system is not wholly effective, those with more children must pay penalties, as must their children. It may be better if what would be penalized is, instead, made impossible.[33]

(1) and (2) are *political* solutions. What is changed is our situation. (3) to (5) are *psychological*. It is we who change. This change may be specific, solving only one Dilemma. The fishermen might grow lazy, the soldiers might come to prefer death to dishonour, or be drilled into automatic obedience. Here are four changes of a more general kind:

We might become *trustworthy*. Each might then promise to do A on condition that the others make the same promise.

We might become *reluctant to be 'free-riders'*. If each believes that many others will do A, he may then prefer to do his share.

We might become *Kantians*. Each would then do only what he could rationally will everyone to do. None could rationally will that all do E. Each would therefore do A.

We might become *more altruistic*. Given sufficient altruism, each would do A.

These are *moral* solutions. Because they might solve any Dilemma, they are the most important psychological solutions.

They are often better than the political solutions. This is in part because they do not need to be enforced. Take the Samaritan's Dilemma. It cannot be made impossible not to help strangers. Bad Samaritans cannot be easily caught and fined. Good Samaritans could be rewarded. But for this to be ensured the law might have to intervene. Given the administrative costs, this solution may not be worthwhile. It would be much better if we became directly disposed to help strangers.

It is not enough to know which solution would be best. Any solution must be achieved, or brought about. This is often easier with the political solutions. Situations can be changed more easily than people. But we often face another, second-order, Contributor's Dilemma. Few political solutions can be achieved by a single person. Most require co-operation by many people. But a solution is a public good, benefiting each whether or not he does his share in bringing it about. In most large groups, it will be worse for each if he does his share. The difference that he makes will be too small to repay his contribution.

This problem may be small in well-organized democracies. It may be sufficient here to get the original Dilemma widely understood. This may be difficult. But we may then vote for a political solution. If our government responds to opinion polls, there may even be no need to hold a vote.

The problem is greater when there is no government. This is what worried Hobbes. It should now worry nations. One example is the spread of nuclear weapons. Without world-government, it may be hard to achieve a solution.[34]

The problem is greatest when its solution is opposed by some ruling group. This is the *Dilemma of the Oppressed*.

Such Contributor's Dilemmas often need moral solutions. We often need some people who are directly disposed to do their share. If these can change the situation, so as to achieve a political solution, this solution may be self-supporting. But without such people it may never be achieved.

The moral solutions are, then, often best; and they are often the only attainable solutions. We therefore need the moral motives. How could these be introduced? Fortunately, that is not our problem. They exist. This is how we solve many Prisoner's Dilemmas. Our need is to make these motives stronger, and more widely spread.

With this task, theory helps. Prisoner's Dilemmas need to be explained. So do their moral solutions. Both have been too little understood.

One solution is, we saw, a conditional agreement. For this to be possible, it must first be true that we can all communicate. If we are purely self-interested, or never self-denying, the ability to communicate would seldom make a difference. In most large groups, it would be pointless to promise that we shall make the altruistic choice, since it would be worse for each if he kept his promise. But suppose that we are trustworthy. Each can now promise to do A, on condition that *everyone else* makes the same promise. If we know that we are all trustworthy, each will have a motive to join this conditional agreement. Each will know that, unless he joins, the agreement will not take effect. Once we have all made this promise, we shall all do A.

If we are numerous, unanimity will in practice be hard to obtain. If our *only* moral motive is trustworthiness, we shall then be unlikely to achieve the joint conditional agreement. It would be likely to be worse for each if he joined. (We shall also be unlikely even to communicate.) [35]

There are few people whose only moral motive is trustworthiness. Suppose that we are also reluctant to be free-riders. If each of us has this motive, he will not wish to remain outside the joint conditional agreement. He will prefer to join, even if doing so will be worse for him. This solves the problem just mentioned for the joint agreement. And, if enough people are reluctant to be free-riders, there will be no need for an actual agreement. All that is needed is an assurance that there will be many who do A. Each would then prefer to do his share. But a reluctance to free-ride cannot by itself create this assurance. So there are many cases where it provides no solution.[36]

The Kantian Test could always provide a solution. This Test has its own problems. Could I rationally will either that none practise medicine, or that all do? If we refine the Test, we may be able to solve such problems. But in Prisoner's Dilemmas they do not arise. These are the cases where we naturally say, 'What if everyone did that?'[37]

The fourth moral solution is sufficient altruism. I am not referring here to *pure* altruism. Pure altruists, who give no weight to their own interests, may face analogues of the Prisoner's Dilemma. It can be true that, if all rather than none do what is certain to be better for others, this will be worse for everyone.[38] By 'sufficient altruism' I mean sufficient concern for others, where the limiting case is impartial benevolence: an equal concern for everyone, including oneself.

The fourth solution is the least understood. It is often claimed that, in those Contributor's Dilemmas that involve very many people, what each person does would make no difference. This has been thought to show that rational altruists would not contribute. As I shall argue in the next chapter, this is not so.

3

FIVE MISTAKES IN MORAL
MATHEMATICS

It is often claimed that, in cases that involve very many people, any single altruistic choice would make no difference. Some of those who make this claim believe that it undermines only the fourth moral solution, that provided by sufficient altruism. These people argue that, in such cases, because we *cannot* appeal to the *consequences* of our acts, we must appeal instead either to the Kantian Test, 'What if everyone did that?', or to the reluctance to free-ride.[39] But if my contribution involves a real cost to me, and would certainly make no difference—would give no benefit to others—I may not be moved by my reluctance to free-ride. This reluctance may apply only when I believe that I am profiting at the expense of others. If my contribution would make no difference, my failure to contribute will not be worse for others, so I will not be profiting at their expense. I may believe that the case is like those where some threshold has been clearly passed, so that any further altruistic act is a sheer waste of effort. This belief may also undermine the Kantian solution. If my contribution would make no difference, I can rationally will that everyone else does what I do. I can rationally will that no one contributes when he knows that his contribution would make no difference. Since others may think like me, it is of great importance whether, in such cases, we can explain why we should contribute by appealing to the consequences of our acts.

25. THE SHARE-OF-THE-TOTAL VIEW

We can. But to do so we must avoid several mistakes in moral mathematics. Consider

> *The First Rescue Mission:* I know all of the following. A hundred miners are trapped in a shaft with flood-waters rising. These men can be brought to the surface in a lift raised by weights on long levers. If I and three other people go to stand on some platform, this will provide just enough weight to raise the lift, and will save the lives of these hundred men. If I do not join this rescue mission, I can go elsewhere and save, single-handedly, the lives of ten other people. There is a fifth potential

rescuer. If I go elsewhere, this person will join the other three, and these four will save the hundred miners.

When I could act in several ways, how should I decide which act would benefit people most? Suppose first that all five of us go to save the miners. On the *Share-of-the-Total View*, each produces his share of the total benefit. Since we five save a hundred lives, each saves twenty lives. Less literally, the good that each does is equivalent to the saving of this many lives. On this view, I ought to join the other four, and save the equivalent of twenty lives. I should not go elsewhere to save the other ten people, since I would then be saving fewer people. This is clearly the wrong answer. If I go with the other four, ten people needlessly die. Since the other four would, without my help, save the hundred miners, I should go and save these ten people.

The Share-of-the-Total View might be revised. It might be claimed that, when I join others who are doing good, the good that I do is not just my share of the total benefit produced. I should subtract from my share any reduction that my joining causes in the shares of the benefits produced by others. If I join this rescue mission, I shall be one of five people who together save a hundred lives. My share will be twenty lives. If I had not joined, the other four would have saved the hundred, and the share saved by each would have been twenty five lives, or five more than when I join. By joining I reduce the shares of the other four by a total of four times five, or twenty lives. On the revised view, my share of the benefit is therefore twenty minus twenty, or nothing. I should therefore go and save the other ten people. The revised view gives the right answer.

Consider next

The Second Rescue Mission. As before, the lives of a hundred people are in danger. These people can be saved if I and three other people join in a rescue mission. We four are the only people who could join this mission. If any of us fails to join, all of the hundred people will die. If I fail to join, I could go elsewhere and save, single-handedly, fifty other lives.

On the Revised Share-of-the-Total View, I ought to go elsewhere and save these fifty others. If instead I join this rescue mission, my share of the benefit produced is only the equivalent of saving twenty-five lives. I can therefore do more good if I go elsewhere and save the fifty. This is clearly false, since if I act in this way fifty more lives will be lost. I ought to join *this* rescue mission. We must make a further revision. I must add to my share of the benefit produced any increase that I cause to the shares produced by others. If I join, I enable each of three people to save, with me, a hundred lives. If I do not join, these three will save no lives. My share is twenty-five lives, and I increase by seventy-five the shares produced by the others. On this doubly revised view, my total share is a hundred lives. This is also the total share produced by each of the others. Since each counts as producing the *whole* of this total benefit, this is not a version of the *Share*-of-the-Total View. It is a quite different view. This doubly revised view gives the right answer in this case. It is no objection to this view that it claims that each saves a hundred lives. This is what each does, not by himself, but with the help of the others.[40]

This view can be put more simply. I should act in the way whose consequence is that most lives are saved. More generally,

> (C6) An act benefits someone if its consequence is that someone is benefited more. An act harms someone if its consequence is that someone is harmed more. The act that benefits people most is the act whose consequence is that people are benefited most.

These claims imply, correctly, that I should not join the First Rescue Mission, but should join the Second.

Consequentialists should appeal to (C6). So should others, if they give any weight to what Ross called the *Principle of Beneficence*. On any plausible moral theory, we should sometimes try to do what would benefit people most.

(C6) may need to be further explained. Suppose that I can do either (1) or (2). In deciding which would benefit people more, I should compare *all* of the benefits and losses that people would later receive if I did (1), and *all* of the benefits and losses that people would later receive if I did (2). The act which benefits people more is the one that, in this comparison, would be followed by the greater *net* sum of benefits—the greater sum of benefits minus losses. It is irrelevant if, as is often true, the acts of many other people would also be parts of the cause of the receiving of these benefits and losses.

(C6) revises the ordinary use of the words 'benefit' and 'harm'. When I claim to have benefited someone, I am usually taken to mean that some act of mine was the chief or immediate cause of some benefit received by this person. According to (C6), I benefit someone even when my act is a remote part of the cause of the receiving of this benefit. All that needs to be true is that, if I had acted otherwise, this person would not have received this benefit. Similar claims apply to 'harm'.

There is a second way in which (C6) revises our use of 'benefit' and 'harm'. On the ordinary use, I sometimes benefit someone even though what I am doing is not better for this person. This can be true when my act, though sufficient to produce some benefit, is not necessary. Suppose that I could easily save either J's life or K's arm. I know that, if I do not save J's life, someone else certainly will; but no one else can save K's arm. On our ordinary use, if I save J's life, I benefit him, and I give him a greater benefit than the benefit that I would give to K if I saved his arm. But, for moral purposes, this is not the way to measure benefits. In making my decision, I should ignore this benefit to J, as (C6) tells me to do. According to (C6), I do *not* benefit J when I save his life. It is not true that the consequence of my act is that J is benefited more. If I had acted differently, someone else would have saved J's life. (C6) implies correctly that I ought to save K's arm. *This* is the act whose consequence is that people are benefited more. On the revised use of 'benefit', this is the act that benefits people more.

The First Mistake in moral mathematics is the Share-of-the-Total View. We should reject this view, and appeal instead to (C6).

26. IGNORING THE EFFECTS OF SETS OF ACTS

It is natural to assume

> (The Second Mistake) If some act is right or wrong *because of its effects*, the only relevant effects are the effects of this particular act.

This assumption is mistaken in at least two kinds of case.

In some cases, effects are *overdetermined*. Consider

> *Case One.* X and Y simultaneously shoot and kill me. Either shot, by itself, would have killed.

Neither X nor Y acts in a way whose consequence is that an extra person dies. Given what the other does, it is true of each that, if he had not shot me, this would have made no difference. According to (C6), neither X nor Y harms me. Suppose that we make the Second Mistake: we assume that, if an act is wrong because of its effects, the only relevant effects are the effects of this particular act. Since neither X nor Y harms me, we are forced to the absurd conclusion that these two murderers do not act wrongly.

Some would take this case to show that we should reject (C6). There is a better alternative. We should add

> (C7) Even if an act harms no one, this act may be wrong because it is one of a *set* of acts that *together* harm other people. Similarly, even if some act benefits no one, it can be what someone ought to do, because it is one of a set of acts that together benefit other people.

X and Y act wrongly because *they together* harm me. They together kill me. (C7) should be accepted even by Non-Consequentialists. On any plausible moral theory, it is a mistake in this kind of case to consider only the effects of single acts. On any plausible theory, even if each of us harms no one, we can be acting wrongly if we together harm other people.

In Case One, the overdetermining acts are simultaneous. What should we claim in cases where this is not true? Consider

> *Case Two.* X tricks me into drinking poison, of a kind that causes a painful death within a few minutes. Before this poison has any effect, Y kills me painlessly.

Though Y kills me, Y's act is not worse for me. (C6) therefore implies that, in killing me, Y does not harm me. (Y's act is in one way slightly worse for me, since it shortens my life by a few minutes. This is outweighed by the fact that Y saves me from a painful death.) (C6) also implies that X does not harm me. As in Case One, neither X nor Y harms me. (C7) implies correctly that X and Y act wrongly because they together harm me. They together harm me because, if *both* had acted differently, I would not have died.

Though (C7) gives the right answer here, this case may seem to provide an objection to (C6). It may seem absurd to claim that, in killing me, Y is not harming me. But consider

> *Case Three*. As before, X tricks me into drinking poison of a kind that causes a painful death within a few minutes. *Y* knows that he can save *your* life if he acts in a way whose inevitable side-effect is my immediate and painless death. Because Y also knows that I am about to die painfully, Y acts in this way.

(C6) implies that Y ought to act in this way, since he will not harm me, and he will greatly benefit you. This is the right conclusion. Since Y's act is not worse for me, it is morally irrelevant that Y kills me. It is also morally irrelevant that X does *not* kill me. (C6) implies correctly that X acts wrongly. Though X does not kill me on the ordinary use of 'kill', he is here the real murderer. X harms me, and acts wrongly, because it is true that, if he had not poisoned me, Y would not have killed me. If *X* had acted differently, I would *not* have died. Y does not harm me because, if *Y* had acted differently, this would have made no difference to whether I died. Since Y does not harm me, and he greatly benefits you, Y is doing what he ought to do.

As these remarks show, Case Two provides no objection to (C6). In Case Three, (C6) correctly implies that Y ought to act as he does, because he does not harm me. In Case Two, Y's act affects me in just the same way. I was therefore right to claim that, in Case Two, Y does not harm me. Y acts wrongly in Case Two because he is intentionally a member of a group who together harm me.

It may be objected that, if *this* is why, in Case Two, Y acts wrongly, Y must be acting wrongly in Case Three. It may be thought that, here too, Y is intentionally a member of a group who together harm me.

This objection shows the need for another claim. In Case Three it is true that, if both X and Y had acted differently, I would not have been harmed. But this does not show that X and Y together harm me. It is also true that, if X, Y, *and Fred Astaire* had all acted differently, I would not have been harmed. But this does not make Fred Astaire a member of a group who together harm me. We should claim

> (C8) When some group together harm or benefit other people, this group is the *smallest* group of whom it is true that, if they had all acted differently, the other people would not have been harmed, or benefited.

In Case Three, this 'group' consists of X. It is true of X that, if he had acted differently, Y would have done so too, and I would not have been harmed. No such claim is true of Y. In Case Two it is not true of either X or Y that, if he had acted differently, I would not have been harmed. I would not have been harmed only if *both* had acted differently. I would also not have been harmed if X, Y, and Fred Astaire had acted differently. But (C8) rightly implies that Fred Astaire is not a member of the group who together harm me. This group consists of X and Y.

Consider next

The Third Rescue Mission. As before, if four people stand on a platform, this will save the lives of a hundred miners. Five people stand on this platform.

Given what the others do, it is true of each of these five people that his act makes no difference. If he had not stood on this platform, the other four would have saved the hundred miners. Though none, by himself, makes any difference, these five together save the hundred miners. This case shows the need to add some further claim to (C8). In this case there is not *one* smallest group who together save the hundred lives. I shall return to such cases in Section 30.

There is a second kind of case in which we should consider the effects of sets of acts. These are *co-ordination problems*. One example is shown below.

<table>
<tr><td></td><td></td><td colspan="2" align="center">You</td></tr>
<tr><td></td><td></td><td align="center">do (1)</td><td align="center">do (2)</td></tr>
<tr><td rowspan="2">I</td><td>do (1)</td><td>Second-best</td><td>Bad</td></tr>
<tr><td>do (2)</td><td>Bad</td><td>Best</td></tr>
</table>

Suppose that we apply Consequentialism only to single acts. We shall then claim that each has successfully followed C if he has done the act, of those that are possible for him, whose consequence is the best outcome. As we saw earlier, in co-ordination problems C will then be *indeterminate*. In this case we successfully follow C *both* if we both do (2) *and* if we both do (1).

Suppose that we both do (1). Given what you have done, I have done the act whose consequence is best. The outcome would have been worse if I had done (2). The same claims apply to you. If we both do (1) both successfully follow C, but we have not produced the best possible outcome.

Consequentialists should claim

> (C9) Suppose that each of us has made the outcome as good as he can, given what the others did. Each has then acted rightly. But we together may have acted wrongly. This will be so if we together could have made the outcome better.

This is a claim about *objective* rightness, or what will in fact make the outcome best. If C includes this claim, it ceases to be indeterminate in this kind of case. (When we are deciding what to do, we should ask instead what is *subjectively* right, or what will be likely, given our beliefs, to make the outcome best. In most coordination problems of this kind, it is subjectively right for each of us to aim at the best outcome, since this is what others are likely to do.)[41]

27. IGNORING SMALL CHANCES

Return now to those Prisoner's Dilemmas that involve very many people. It is often claimed that, in these cases, we cannot appeal to the consequences of our acts. This involves at least two more mistakes.

One concerns those cases where each altruistic act has an extremely small chance of producing some extremely great benefit. It is sometimes claimed that, below some threshold, extremely small chances have no rational or moral significance.

This mistake is often made in discussions of elections. Though an election is not a pure Prisoner's Dilemma, it can illustrate this mistake. Many writers claim that, in a nation-wide election, one cannot justify voting merely by appealing to the consequences of one's act. But this is often false. Suppose that, if I vote, this will involve some costs, and will bring no benefits apart from the possible effect on who wins the election. On these assumptions, my voting cannot be justified in self-interested terms. But it can often be justified in Consequentialist terms. When I cannot predict the effects of my act, C tells me to do whatever would produce the greatest *expected* benefit. The expected benefit of my act is the possible benefit multiplied by the chance that my act will produce it. I may be able to justify my voting by appealing to this benefit.

Consider a Presidential Election in the United States. If I vote, there may be a very small chance that my vote will make a difference. On one estimate, if I am voting in one of the large and marginal states, which might go either way, the chance that I shall make a difference would be about one in a hundred million. (The estimate is difficult. It should not be assumed that any pattern of votes is as likely as any other. But several writers agree that this chance is about one in a hundred million.[43])

Call the two candidates *Superior* and *Inferior*. And suppose that, if the next President is Superior, this will on average benefit Americans. There will be some Americans who will lose. It would have been better for these Americans if Inferior had won. But the losses to these Americans—the rich minority—will be outweighed by the benefits to all the other Americans. This is why Superior is the better candidate. If he is the one who is elected, this will produce a greater total net sum of benefits minus burdens. The average net benefit to Americans is this total sum divided by the number of Americans. For simplicity, I ignore effects on non-Americans. If my vote has a chance of one in a hundred million of affecting the result, the *expected* benefit of my voting is as shown below.

$$\frac{\text{The average net benefit to Americans from Superior's election} \times \text{the number of Americans}}{\text{One hundred million}} - \frac{\text{the costs to me and others}}{\text{of my voting.}}$$

Since there are two hundred million Americans, this sum is likely to be positive. This will be so if Superior's election would on average bring to Americans a net benefit more than half as great as the costs of my voting. I must be pretty cynical to doubt this. Similar remarks apply to many other public goods, and to altruists as well as Consequentialists. If an altruist does not ignore very tiny chances, he will often have a moral reason to make a contribution. The expected benefit that he would give to others would be greater than the costs of his contribution.

It may be objected that it is *irrational* to consider very tiny chances. When our acts cannot affect more than a few people, this may be so. But this is because the stakes are here comparatively low. Consider the risks of causing accidental death. It may be irrational to give any thought to a one-in-a-million chance of killing one person. But, if I was a nuclear engineer, would I be irrational to give any thought to the same chance of killing a million people? This is not what most of us believe. We believe, rightly, that such chances ought to be considered. Suppose that nuclear engineers did ignore all chances at or below the threshold of one-in-a-million. It might then be the case that, for each of the many components in a nuclear reactor, there is a one-in-a-million chance that, in any day, this component would fail in a way that would cause a catastrophe. It would be clearly wrong for those who design reactors to ignore such tiny chances. If there are many reactors, each with many such components, it would not take many days before the one-in-a-million risk had been run a million times. There would fairly soon be a catastrophe.

When the stakes are very high, no chance, however small, should be ignored. The same is true when each chance will be taken very many times. In both these kinds of case, each tiny chance should be taken to be just what it is, and included in the calculation of the expected benefit. We can usually ignore a very small chance. But we should not do so when we may affect a very large number of people, or when the chance will be taken a very large number of times. These large numbers roughly cancel out the smallness of the chance.

A similar point applies if an act is likely or certain to give to others very small benefits. We should not ignore such benefits when they would go to a very large number of people. This large number roughly cancels out the smallness of the benefits. The total sum of benefits may thus be large.

These two points are not equally plausible. Very small benefits may be imperceptible. And it is plausible to claim that an 'imperceptible benefit' is *not* a benefit. But it is not plausible to claim that a very small chance is *not* a chance.

28. IGNORING SMALL OR IMPERCEPTIBLE EFFECTS

The Third Mistake in moral mathematics is to ignore very small chances when they would either affect very many people, or would be taken very many times. The Fourth and Fifth Mistakes are to ignore *very small* and *imperceptible* effects on very large numbers of people. These are similar mistakes, and can be criticised with the same arguments. But imperceptible effects raise one extra question.

I need not state both mistakes. The Fourth is the same as the Fifth except that 'very small' replaces 'imperceptible'. Some people believe

(The Fifth Mistake) If some act has effects on other people that are imperceptible, this act cannot be morally wrong *because* it has these effects. An act cannot be wrong because of its effects on other people, if none of these people could ever notice any difference. Similarly, if some act would have imperceptible effects on other people, these effects cannot make this act what someone ought to do.

One kind of imperceptible effect is not controversial. I may cause you serious harm *in a way* that is imperceptible. The dose of radiation that I give you may be the unknown cause of the cancer that kills you many years later. Though the cause may be unknown, the effect is here perceptible. But, in the cases I shall be considering, the *effects* are imperceptible.

Consider first a variant of a case described by Glover. [44]

> *The Drops of Water.* A large number of wounded men lie out in the desert, suffering from intense thirst. We are an equally large number of altruists, each of whom has a pint of water. We could pour these pints into a water-cart. This would be driven into the desert, and our water would be shared equally between all these many wounded men. By adding his pint, each of us would enable each wounded man to drink slightly more water—perhaps only an extra drop. Even to a very thirsty man, each of these extra drops would be a very small benefit. The effect on each man might even be imperceptible.

Assume that the benefit given to each man would be merely the relieving of his intensely painful thirst. There would be no effect on these men's health. Since the benefits would be merely the relief of suffering, these are the kind of benefit of which it can most plausibly be claimed that, to be benefits at all, they must be perceptible.

Suppose first that, because the numbers are not very large, the benefit that each of us would give to each man would, though very small, be perceptible. If we make the Fourth Mistake, we believe that such tiny benefits have no moral significance. We believe that, if some act would give to others such tiny benefits, this cannot make this act what someone ought to do. We are forced to conclude that none of us ought to add his pint. This is clearly the wrong conclusion.

Assume, next, that there are a thousand wounded men, and a thousand altruists. If we pour our pints into the water-cart, each of us will cause each wounded man to drink an extra thousandth of a pint. These men might notice the difference between drinking *no* water and one thousandth of a pint. Let us therefore ask, 'If these men will drink at least one tenth of a pint, could they notice the effect of drinking any extra thousandth of a pint?' I shall assume that the answer is No. (If the answer is Yes, we merely need to suppose that there are more altruists and wounded men. There must be some fraction of a pint whose effect would be too small to be perceptible.)

Suppose that a hundred altruists have already poured their water into the cart. Each of the wounded men will drink at least one tenth of a pint. We are the other nine hundred altruists, each of whom could add his pint. Suppose next that we make the Fifth Mistake. We believe that, if some act would have imperceptible effects on other people, these effects cannot make this act what someone ought to do. If we believe this, we cannot explain why each of us ought to add his pint.

It may be said: 'We can avoid this problem if we redescribe the effect of adding each pint. We need not claim that this gives to each of the men one thousandth of a pint. We could claim that it gives to one man one pint.'

This claim is false. The water will be shared equally between all these men. When I add my pint, is the effect that an extra man receives a full pint? If I had not added my pint, is there some man who would have received nothing rather than a full pint? Neither of these is true. There is only one correct description of the effect of my act. It gives to each of the thousand men an extra thousandth of a pint.

It may next be said that we should appeal to the Share-of-the-Total-View. On this view, the share that each contributes is equivalent to the benefit that one man receives from one pint. But we cannot appeal to this view, since we saw in Section 25 that it can imply absurd conclusions.

What we can appeal to is a claim about what we *together* do. We can claim

(C10) When (1) the best outcome would be the one in which people are benefited most, and (2) each of the members of some group could act in a certain way, and (3) they would benefit these other people if *enough* of them acted in this way, and (4) they would benefit these people *most* if they *all* acted in this way, and (5) each of them both knows these facts and believes that enough of them will act in this way, then (6) each of them ought to act in this way.

Each of us could give to each of the thousand wounded men an extra thousandth of a pint of water. If enough of us act in this way this will benefit each of these men. And we will benefit these men most if we all act in this way. We know these facts, and we know that enough of us—one hundred—have already acted in this way. (C10) implies correctly that each of us ought to act in this way.

Remember now the Fifth Mistake. On this view, an act cannot be right or wrong, *because* of its effects on other people, if these effects are imperceptible. The case just described refutes this view. It is clear that, in this case, each of us should pour his pint into the water-cart. Each of us should cause each wounded man to drink an extra thousandth of a pint. Each of us ought to affect each wounded man in this way, even though these effects are imperceptible. We may believe that, because these effects are imperceptible, each of us is benefiting no one. But, even if *each* benefits no one, *we together* greatly benefit these wounded men. The effects of *all* our acts are perceptible. We greatly relieve the intense thirst of these men.

Consequentialists may appeal to several principles. They may thus believe that, in some cases, the best outcome is not the one in which people are benefited most. To cover such cases, they can claim

(C11) When (1) the members of some group would make the outcome better if *enough* of them acted in some way, and (2) they would make the outcome *best* if *all* of them acted in this way, and (3)

each of them both knows these facts and believes that enough of them will act in this way, then (4) each of them ought to act in this way.

Non-Consequentialists believe that, in some cases, we should try to produce the best outcome. In some of these cases, they can appeal to (C11). As before, in some cases, (C11) does not by itself give the right answer. We would have to add a more complicated claim. I shall ignore these complications.[46]

As I showed in Section 26, there are two kinds of case where we need to appeal to the effects, not just of single acts, but of sets of acts. We need to make this appeal when (1) the effects of our acts are overdetermined, or (2) we face co-ordination problems. We are now considering cases where (3) each person's act will have imperceptible effects on other people. This may be a third kind of case in which we need to appeal to the effects of sets of acts. Whether we *need* to make this appeal depends in part on the answer to another question.

29. CAN THERE BE IMPERCEPTIBLE HARMS AND BENEFITS?

It may be objected: 'You claim that each of the thousand altruists should pour in his pint, since this is how the wounded men would be benefited most. This claim is false. Suppose that one of the altruists does not pour in his pint. Are the wounded men benefited less? They are not. They drink slightly less water. But this effect is imperceptible. Since the effect is imperceptible, the benefit to these men cannot be less.'

This objection assumes that there cannot be imperceptible benefits. If we make this assumption, we face part of a wider problem, variously called the *Sorites Problem*, *Wang's Paradox*, or the *Paradox of the Heap*.

In our case, the benefit is the relieving of intensely painful thirst. If each man receives a pint of water, his thirst will become less painful. His pain will be less bad. Our problem is the following. We assume

(A) Someone's pain cannot become *imperceptibly* better or worse. Someone's pain cannot become either less bad, or worse, if this person could not possibly notice any difference.

And it is plausible to assume

(B) *At least as bad as* and *not worse than* are, when applied to pains, *transitive* relations. Thus, if someone's pain in Outcome (2) is at least as bad as it was in Outcome (1), and his pain in Outcome (3) is at least as bad as it was in Outcome (2), his pain in Outcome (3) must be at least as bad as it was in Outcome (1).

A hundred altruists have already poured in their pints. Each of the wounded men will drink at least a tenth of a pint. They would not notice the effect of any extra thousandth of a pint. In different possible outcomes different numbers of altruists will later pour their pints into the cart. Let us refer to these outcomes by citing the number who contribute. Thus, if no one else contributes, this will produce Outcome 100.

Suppose that one more altruist contributes. Each wounded man will drink more water, but the amount will be so small that he cannot notice this. According to (A), each man's thirst cannot become less painful. Each man's pain in Outcome 101 must be at least as bad as it would have been in Outcome 100. Suppose next that a second altruist adds his pint. As before, none of the men can notice this difference. According to (A) each man's thirst cannot become less painful. Each man's pain in Outcome 102 must be at least as bad it would have been in Outcome 101. According to (*B*) each man's pain in Outcome 102 must be at least as bad as it would have been in *Outcome 100*. The same claims apply if a third altruist contributes. In Outcome 103 each man's pain must be at least as bad as it would have been in Outcome 100. These claims apply to every extra altruist who contributes. Suppose that all of us contribute. The result is Outcome 1000, in which each man drinks a whole pint. (A) and (B) together imply that each man's pain must be at least bad as it would have been in Outcome 100. Drinking a whole pint, rather than only one tenth, cannot do anything to relieve the pain of each man's thirst. Since this conclusion is absurd, we must reject either (A) or (B).

Which should go? I reject (A). I believe that someone's pain can become less painful, or less bad, by an amount too small to be noticed. Someone's pain is worse, in the sense that has moral relevance, if this person minds the pain more, or has a stronger desire that the pain cease. I believe that someone can mind his pain slightly less, or have a slightly weaker desire that his pain cease, even though he cannot notice any difference. More generally, there can be imperceptible harms, and imperceptible benefits. In many other kinds of case, people have been shown to make very small mistakes when they report the nature of their experiences. Why should we assume that they cannot make such mistakes about the strength of their desire that some pain cease?

Suppose that you reject these claims, and continue to accept (A). You must then reject (B). To avoid the absurd conclusion reached above, you must admit that, when applied to pains, *at least as bad as* and *not worse than* are not transitive relations. And rejecting (B) has implications like those of rejecting (A). You must now admit that your acts may be wrong, because of their effects on someone's else's pain, even though *none* of your acts makes this person's pain worse. They may *together* have this effect. Each act may be wrong, though its effects are imperceptible, because it is one of a set of acts that together make this person's pain very much worse.

Consider

The Bad Old Days. A thousand torturers have a thousand victims. At the start of each day, each of the victims is already feeling mild pain. Each of the torturers turns a switch a thousand times on some instrument. Each turning of a switch affects some victim's pain in a way that is imperceptible. But, after each torturer has turned his switch a thousand times, he has inflicted severe pain on his victim.

Suppose that you make the Fifth Mistake. You believe that an act cannot be wrong, because of its effects on other people, if these effects are imperceptible. You must then conclude that, in this case, no turning of a switch is wrong. None of these torturers ever act wrongly. This conclusion is absurd.

Why are the torturers acting wrongly? One explanation appeals to the total effect of what each torturer does. Each turns a switch a thousand times. These acts, taken together, inflict severe pain on his victim.

Consider next

The Harmless Torturers. In the Bad Old Days, each torturer inflicted severe pain on one victim. Things have now changed. Each of the thousand torturers presses a button, thereby turning the switch once on each of the thousand instruments. The victims suffer the same severe pain. But none of the torturers makes any victim's pain perceptibly worse.

Can we appeal here to the total effect of what each torturer does? This depends in part on whether we reject (A), believing that someone's pain can become imperceptibly worse. If we believe this, we can claim: 'By pressing the button, each torturer causes each victim to suffer slightly more. The effect on each is slight. But, since each torturer adds to the suffering of a thousand victims, he imposes on them a great total sum of suffering. Since the victims suffer just as much as they did in the Bad Old Days, these torturers are acting just as wrongly as they used to do. In the Bad Old Days, each torturer imposed on one victim a great sum of suffering. Each of the Harmless Torturers imposes on these thousand victims an equally great total sum of suffering.'

Suppose instead that we accept (A), believing that pains cannot become imperceptibly worse. We must then admit that each of the Harmless Torturers causes no one to suffer more. We cannot appeal to the total effect of what each torturer does. On our view, none of the torturers harms anyone.

Even if none of them harms anyone, the torturers are clearly acting wrongly. If we cannot appeal to the effects of what each torturer does, we must appeal to what the torturers together do. Even if none of them causes any pain, they together impose great suffering on a thousand victims. We can claim

(C12) When (1) the outcome would be worse if people suffered more, and (2) each of the members of some group could act in a certain way, and (3) they would cause other people to suffer if *enough* of them acted in this way, and (4) they would cause these people to suffer *most* if they *all* acted in this way, and (5) each of them both knows these facts and believes that enough of them will act in this way, then (6) each would be acting wrongly if he acted in this way.

Someone may again object: 'In the case of the Harmless Torturers, (4) is not true. These torturers do not cause their victims to suffer *most* if they *all* turn each switch once. Suppose that one of them turned no switches. None of the victims would notice any difference. Since a pain cannot become imperceptibly less bad, the victims would *not* suffer less if one of the torturers did not act.'

As I remarked, this objection raises the well-known Sorites Problem. If we accept (A), our answer to this objection must involve a solution to this problem. Since this problem is both hard to solve, and raises questions which have nothing to do with ethics, I shall not discuss it here.[48]

If we accept (A), our objection to the Harmless Torturers must both be complicated and solve the Sorites Problem. If we reject (A), our objection could be simple. We could claim that each of the torturers inflicts on the victims a great total sum of suffering.

Of these two explanations, which is better? Even if we reject (A), we may be wrong to give the simpler explanation. Whether this is so depends on the answer to another question. Consider

The Single Torturer. One morning, only one of the torturers turns up for work. It happens to be true that, through natural causes, each of the victims is already suffering fairly severe pain. This pain is about as bad as it would be after the switches had been turned five hundred times. Knowing this fact, the Single Torturer presses the button that turns the switch once on all of the machines. The effect is the same as in the days when all the torturers act. More precisely, the effect is just like that when each switch is turned for the five hundred and first time. The Single Torturer knows that this is the effect. He knows that he is not making any victim's pain perceptibly worse. And he knows that he is not a member of a group who together do this.

Is the Single Torturer acting wrongly? Suppose we believe that he is not. We cannot then appeal to the simpler objection in the case where all the torturers act. We cannot claim that each is acting wrongly because he is imposing on others a great total sum of suffering. If this is why each is acting wrongly, the Single Torturer must be acting wrongly. He acts in the same way, and with the same effects. If we believe that the Single Torturer is not acting wrongly, we must give the other objection in the case where all the torturers act. We must claim that each is acting wrongly because he is a member of a group who together inflict great suffering on their victims.

I believe that the Single Torturer *is* acting wrongly. How can it make a moral difference whether he produces bad effects jointly with other agents, or with Nature?[49] I therefore prefer, in both cases, to appeal to the effects of single acts.

Some people disagree. Even if we believe that there can be imperceptible harms and benefits, it may thus be better to appeal to what groups together do. This appeal is less controversial.

(If the Single Torturer is *not* acting wrongly, it may be unfair to claim that some of us make *five* mistakes in moral mathematics. On this view, the Fifth Mistake is merely a special case of the Second Mistake. But this would seldom make a practical difference.)

In this section I have asked whether there can be imperceptible harms and benefits. I am inclined to answer Yes. If we answer No, we must abandon the claim that, when applied to harms and benefits, *at least as bad as* and *not worse than* are transitive relations. I have also shown that it makes little difference which answer we accept. On either answer, we must abandon what I call the Fifth Mistake. We must abandon the view that an act cannot be either right or wrong, *because* of its effects on other people, if these effects are imperceptible.

30. OVERDETERMINATION

Return now to the pints of water and the wounded men. Let us add some features to this case. Suppose that, before the water-cart is driven to these men, you arrive, with another pint. The wounded men need more than a single pint. After drinking this pint their intensely painful thirst would not be fully relieved. But the water-cart can hold only one thousand pints. It is now full. If you add your pint, this will merely cause one pint to overflow down some drain.

You have no moral reason to add your pint, since this would merely cause a pint to be wasted. According to (C10), you ought to add your pint if this would make you a member of a group who together benefit other people. We may think that, if you add your pint, you are *not* a member of the group who together benefit the wounded men. Some of your pint may be drunk by these wounded men. And you are acting in the same way as the other altruists did. But we might claim, 'Unlike the other altruists, you do not give to each of the wounded men an extra thousandth of a pint of water. Your act has no effect on the amount of water that these men receive.'

Things are not so simple. If you add your pint, this will be a case involving overdetermination. It is true of you that, if you had not contributed, this would have made no difference to the amount of water that the men drink. But, since you have contributed, the same is true of each of the other altruists. It is true that, if any one of these altruists had not contributed, this would have made no difference to the amount of water that the men drink. The water-cart would not have been full when you arrive, and your pint would have made it full. What is true of you is true of each of the other altruists. It is therefore true that you *are* a member of the group who together benefit the wounded men.

We must again appeal to what the agents know, or have reason to believe. Suppose that the other altruists had no reason to believe that you would arrive, with your extra pint. Each ought to have poured in his pint. This is because each had good reason to believe that he would be a member of a group of whom it is true both (1) that they together benefit the wounded men, and (2) that they benefit these men *most* if they *all* pour in their pints. When you arrive, you know that the water-cart is full. You have no reason to contribute, since you know that you would *not* be a member of such a group. If you contribute, you will instead be a member of a group *which is too large*. We should claim

(C13) Suppose that there is some group who, by acting in a certain way, will together benefit other people. If someone believes that this group either is, or would be if he joined, *too large*, he has no moral reason to join this group. A group is *too large* if it is true that, if one or more of its members had not acted, this would not have reduced the benefit that this group gives to other people.

If you add your pint, this will make this group of altruists too large. If you do *not* add your pint, this group will *not* be too large. This is a special borderline case. (C13) also covers the more common cases where some group is already too large.

31. RATIONAL ALTRUISM

The Fifth Mistake in moral mathematics is the belief that imperceptible effects cannot be morally significant. This is a very serious mistake. When all the Harmless Torturers act, each is acting *very* wrongly. This is true even though each makes no one perceptibly worse off. The same could be true of us. We should cease to think that an act cannot be wrong, *because* of its effects on other people, if this act makes no one perceptibly worse off. Each of our acts may be *very* wrong, because of its effects on other people, even if none of these people could ever notice any of these effects. Our acts may *together* make these people very much worse off.

The Fourth Mistake is equally serious. If we believe that trivial effects can be morally ignored, we may often make people very much worse off. Remember the Fisherman's Dilemma. Where there is overfishing, or declining stocks, it can be better for each if he tries to catch more, worse for each if all do. Consider

How the Fishermen Cause a Disaster. There are many fishermen, who earn their living by fishing separately on some large lake. If each fisherman does not restrict his catch, he will catch within the next few seasons more fish. But he will thereby lower the total catch by a much larger number. Since there are many fishermen, if each does not restrict his catch, he will only trivially affect the number caught by each of the others. The fishermen believe that such trivial effects can be morally ignored. Because they believe this, even though they never do what they believe to be wrong, they do not restrict their catches. Each thereby increases his own catch, but causes a much greater lowering in the total catch. Because they all act in this way, the result is a disaster. After a few seasons, all catch very many fewer fish. They cannot feed themselves or their children.

If these fisherman knew the facts, had sufficient altruism, and avoided the Fourth Mistake, they would escape this disaster. Each knows that, if he does not restrict his catch, this will be somewhat better for himself, whatever others do. And each knows that, if he acts in this way, the effects on each of the others will be trivial. But the fishermen should not believe that these trivial effects can be morally ignored. They should believe that acting in this way is wrong.

As before, there are two ways in which we could explain why these acts are wrong. We could appeal to the total effect of each person's act. Each fisherman knows that, if he does not restrict his catch, he will catch more fish, but he will reduce the total catch by a much larger number. For the sake of a small gain to himself, he imposes on others a much greater total loss. We could claim that such acts are wrong. This claim does not assume that there can be imperceptible harms and benefits. It is therefore less controversial than the corresponding claim about what each of the Harmless Torturers does.

Our alternative is to appeal to what these fishermen together do. Each fisherman knows that, if he and all the others do not restrict their catches, they will together impose upon themselves a great total loss. Rational altruists would believe these acts to be wrong. They would avoid this disaster.

It may be said: 'So would rational egoists. Each knows that, if he does not restrict his catch, he is a member of a group who impose upon themselves a great loss. It is irrational to act in this way, even in self-interested terms.' As I shall argue in the next chapter, this claim is not justified. Each knows that, if he does not restrict his catch, this will be *better* for himself. This is so whatever others do. When someone does what he knows will be better for himself, it cannot be claimed that his act is irrational in self-interested terms. Remember next

The Commuter's Dilemma. Suppose that we live in the suburbs of a large city. We can get to and return from work either by car or by bus. Since there are no bus-lanes, extra traffic slows buses just as much as it slows cars. We could therefore know the following to be true. When most of us are going by car, if any one of us goes by car rather than by bus, he will thereby save himself some time, but he will impose on others a much greater total loss of time. This effect would be dispersed. Each might cause a hundred others to be delayed for twenty seconds, or cause a thousand others to be delayed for two seconds. Most of us would regard such effects as so trivial that they can be morally ignored. We would then believe that, in this Commuter's Dilemma, even a rational altruist can justifiably choose to go by car rather than by bus. But if most of us make this choice we shall all be delayed for a long time every day.

Rational altruists would avoid this result. As before, they could appeal either to the effects of what each person does, or to the effects of what all together do. Each saves himself some time, at the cost of imposing on others a much greater total loss of time. We could claim that it is wrong to act in this way, even though the effects on each of the others would be trivial. We could instead claim that this act is wrong, because those who act in this way together impose on everyone a great loss of time. If we accept either of these claims, and have sufficient altruism, we would solve the Commuter's Dilemma, saving ourselves much time every day.

Similar reasoning applies to countless other cases. For one more example, consider the devices that purify the gases that our cars emit. We would think it wrong to save ourselves the cost of repairing this device, if in consequence we imposed great air-pollution on some other single person. But many of us would not think this wrong if it merely trivially or imperceptibly increased the air-pollution suffered by each of very many people. This would be the actual effect in many large cities. It might be much better for all of us if none of us caused such pollution. But, to believe that we are acting wrongly, many of us need to change our view. We must cease to believe that an act cannot be wrong, because of its effects on other people, if these effects are either trivial or imperceptible.

As conditions change, we may need to make some changes in the way we think about morality. I have been arguing for one such change. Common-Sense Morality works best in small communities. When there are few of us, if we give to or impose on others great total benefits or harms, we must be affecting other people in significant ways, that would be grounds either for gratitude, or resentment. In small communities, it is a plausible claim that we cannot have harmed others if there is no one with an obvious complaint, or ground for resenting what we have done.

Until this century, most of mankind lived in small communities. What each did could affect only a few others. But conditions have now changed. Each of us can now, in countless ways, affect countless other people. We can have real though small effects on thousands or millions of people. When these effects are widely dispersed, they may be either trivial, or imperceptible. It now makes a great difference whether we continue to believe that we cannot have greatly harmed or benefited others unless there are people with obvious grounds for resentment or gratitude. While we continue to believe this, even if we care about effects on others, we may fail to solve many serious Prisoner's Dilemmas. For the sake of small benefits to ourselves, or our families, each of us may deny others much greater total benefits, or impose on others much greater total harms. We may think this permissible because the effects on each of the others will be either trivial or imperceptible. If this is what we think, what we do will often be much worse for all of us.

If we cared sufficiently about effects on others, and changed our moral view, we would solve such problems. It is not enough to ask, 'Will my act harm other people?' Even if the answer is No, my act may still be wrong, because of its effects. The effects that it will have when it is considered on its own may not be its only relevant effects. I should ask, 'Will my act be one of a set of acts that will *together* harm other people?' The answer may be Yes. And the harm to others may be great. If this is so, I may be acting *very* wrongly, like the Harmless Torturers. We must accept this view if our concern for others is to yield solutions to most of the many Prisoner's Dilemmas that we face: most of the many cases where, if each of us rather than none of us does what will be better for himself—or for his family, or those he loves—this will be worse, and often *much* worse, for everyone.

4

THEORIES THAT ARE DIRECTLY
SELF-DEFEATING

WE often face Many-Person Prisoner's Dilemmas. It is often true that, if each rather than none of us does what will be better for himself, or his family, or those he loves, this will be worse for all of us. If each of us is disposed to act in this way, these cases raise a practical problem. Unless something changes, the outcome will be worse for all of us.

This problem has two kinds of solution: political and psychological. Of the psychological solutions, the most important are the moral solutions. As I argued, there are many cases where we need a moral solution.

I described four of these solutions. These are provided by four motives: trustworthiness, reluctance to be a free-rider, wanting to satisfy the Kantian Test, and sufficient altruism. There are two forms of each moral solution. When one of these motives leads someone to make the altruistic choice, what this person does may either be, or not be, worse for him. This distinction raises deep questions. I shall simply state what my arguments assume. On all plausible theories about self-interest, what is in our interests partly depends on what our motives or desires are. If we have moral motives, it may therefore not be true that the altruistic choice will be worse for us. But this might be true. Even if it is, we might still make this choice.

I am here dismissing four claims. Some say that no one does what he believes will be worse for him. This has been often refuted. Others say that what each does is, by definition, best for him. In the economist's phrase, it will 'maximize his utility'. Since this is merely a definition, it cannot be false. But it is here irrelevant. It is simply not about what is in a person's own long-term self-interest. Others say that virtue is always rewarded. Unless there is an after-life, this has also been refuted. Others say that virtue is its own reward. On the Objective List Theory, being moral and acting morally may be one of the things that make our lives go better. But, on the plausible versions of this theory, there could be cases where acting morally would be, on the whole, worse for someone. Acting morally might deprive this person of too many of the other things that make our lives go better.

To return to my own claims. Many Prisoner's Dilemmas need moral solutions. To achieve these solutions, we must be directly disposed to make the altruistic choice. There are two forms of each moral solution. One form abolishes the Dilemma. In these cases, because we have some moral motive, it is not true that it will be worse for each if he makes the altruistic choice. But in other cases this is still true. Even in such cases, we might make this choice. Each might do, for moral reasons, what he knows will be worse for him.

We often need moral solutions of this second form. Call them *self-denying*. They solve the practical problem. The outcome is better for everyone. But they do not abolish the Dilemma. A theoretical problem remains.

The problem is this. We may have moral reasons to make the altruistic choice. But it will be better for each if he makes the self-benefiting choice. Morality conflicts with self-interest. When these conflict, what is it rational to do?

On the Self-interest Theory, it is the self-benefiting choice which is rational. If we believe S, we shall be ambivalent about self-denying moral solutions. We shall believe that, to achieve such solutions, we must all act irrationally.

Many writers resist this conclusion. Some claim that moral reasons are not weaker than self-interested reasons. Others claim, more boldly, that they are stronger. On their view, it is the self-benefiting choice which is irrational.

This debate may seem unresolvable. How can these two kinds of reason be weighed against each other? Moral reasons are, of course, morally supreme. But self-interested reasons are, in self-interested terms, supreme. Where can we find a neutral scale?

32. IN PRISONER'S DILEMMAS, DOES S FAIL IN ITS OWN TERMS?

It has been claimed that we do not need a neutral scale. There is a sense in which, in Prisoner's Dilemmas, the Self-interest Theory is self-defeating. It has been claimed that, since this is true, moral reasons are superior to self-interested reasons, even in self-interested terms.

As we have seen, S might be individually indirectly self-defeating. It might be worse for someone if he was never self-denying. But this is not true in Prisoner's Dilemmas. The bad effects are here produced by acts, not dispositions. And it is clear which choice will be better for each person. It is true of each that, if he makes the altruistic choice, this will certainly be worse for him. S tells each to make the self-benefiting choice. And, whatever others do, it will be better for each if he himself makes this choice. S is not here individually self-defeating. But, in the sense defined in Section 22, S is *directly collectively* self-defeating. If all successfully follow S, this will be worse for each than if none do.

Does this show that, if we all follow S, we are irrational? We can start with a smaller question. If we believe S, would our theory be failing even in its own terms?

We could answer: 'No. The pursuit by each of self-interest is better for him. It succeeds. Why is S collectively self-defeating? Only because the pursuit of self-interest is worse for others. This does not make it unsuccessful. It is not benevolence.'

If we are self-interested, we shall of course deplore Prisoner's Dilemmas. These are not the cases loved by classical economists, where each gains if everyone pursues self-interest. We might say: 'In those cases, S both works and approves the situation. In Prisoner's Dilemmas, S still works. Each still gains from his own pursuit of self-interest. But since each loses even more from the self-interested acts of others, S here condemns the situation.'

This may seem an evasion. When it would be worse for each if we all pursued self-interest, it may seem that the Self-interest Theory *should* condemn itself. Suppose that in some other group, facing the same Dilemmas, all make the altruistic choice. They might say to us: 'You think us irrational. But we are better off than you. We do better even in self-interested terms.'

We could answer: 'That is just a play on words. You 'do better' only in the sense that you are better off. Each of you is *doing* worse in self-interested terms. Each is doing what he knows will be worse for him.' We might add: 'What is worse for each of us is that, in our group, there are no fools. Each of you has better luck. Though your irrationality is bad for you, you gain even more from the irrationality of others.'

They might answer: 'You are partly right. Each of us *is* doing worse in self-interested terms. But, though *each* is doing worse, *we* are doing better. This is not a play on words. Each of us is better off because of what we *do*.'

This suggestion is more promising. Return to the simpler Two-Person Case. Each could either benefit himself (E) or give to the other some greater benefit (A). The outcomes would be as shown below.

You

	do E	do A
do E	Third-best for each	Best for me, worst for you
do A	Worst for me, best for you	Second-best for both

(left label: **I**)

To ensure that neither's choice can affect the other's—which might produce reciprocity—suppose that we cannot communicate. If I do A rather than E, that will then be worse for me. This is so whatever you do. And the same holds for you. If we both do A rather than E, each is therefore doing worse in self-interested terms. The suggestion is that *we* are doing better.

What makes this promising is that it contrasts *each* with *we*. As we have seen, what is false of each may be true of us. It can be true for example that, though *each* harms no one, *we together* harm other people. If we both do A rather than E, is it true that, though each is doing worse in self-interested terms, we together are doing better?

We can use this test. The Self-interest Theory gives to each a certain aim. Each does better in S's terms if, of the acts that are possible for him, he does what causes his S-given aim to be better achieved. *We* do better in S's terms if, of the acts that are possible for us, we do what causes the S-given aims *of each* to be better achieved. This test seems fair. It might show that, if each does the best he can in S's terms, we together could not do better.

When we are measuring success, only *ultimate* aims count. Suppose that we are trying to scratch our own backs. The ultimate aim of each might be that he cease to itch. We would then do better if we scratched each other's backs. But we might be contortionists: the ultimate aim of each might be that his back be scratched *by himself*. If we scratched each other's backs, we would then do worse.

What is the ultimate aim that the Self-interest Theory gives to each? Is it that his interests be advanced, or that his interests be advanced *by himself*? On the Self-interest Theory, if someone's interests are advanced by himself, this person is acting rationally. I can therefore restate my question. What is the ultimate aim given to each by S? Is it that his interests be advanced, or that he act rationally?

In Section 3 I defended the following answer. Like all theories about rationality, S gives to each the formal aim that he act rationally. But, according to S, this formal aim is not, as such, a substantive aim. S gives to each person one ultimate substantive aim: that his life goes, for him, as well as possible. On the Hedonistic Theory about self-interest, being rational and acting rationally are not part of this aim. They are both mere means. On some other theories about self-interest, being rational and acting rationally are not mere means. They are both, whatever their effects may be, parts of the ultimate substantive aim that S gives to each person. But this would not be true when they would be, on the whole, worse for someone.

We can imagine a theory that gives to each person this substantive aim: that his interests be advanced *by himself*. Someone who believes this theory might crudely misinterpret Nietzsche, and value 'the fiercest self-reliance'.[53] If we both did A rather than E, we would be doing worse in these sub-Nietzschean terms. The interests of each would be better advanced. But neither's interests would be advanced by himself, so the sub-Nietzschean aim would be worse achieved.

If we both do A rather than E, are we doing better in S's terms? We cause the interests of each to be better advanced. In this respect, we are doing better in S's terms, causing the S-given aim of each to be better achieved. On the Hedonistic Theory about self-interest, this completely answers my question. On this theory, S claims any act to be a mere means. The aim is always the effect on one's conscious life. (Nietzsche's 'blond beasts' were, it is said, lions. But, for them too, acting is a means. They prefer to eat what others kill.)

On some other theories about self-interest, more must be said. According to S, if we both do A rather than E, we are both acting irrationally. Each is doing what he knows will be worse for himself. On some theories about self-interest, being rational and acting rationally are parts of the aim that S gives to each. On these theories, some apparent Prisoner's Dilemmas are not true Dilemmas. I discuss these cases in endnote 54.

33. ANOTHER WEAK DEFENCE OF MORALITY

In true Dilemmas, if we both do A rather than E, we are doing better in S's terms. We are causing the S-given aim of each to be better achieved. This is so on all theories about self-interest. We do *better* in S's terms if we do what S tells us *not* to do.

Does this show that S is failing in its own terms? It may seem so. And it is tempting to contrast S with morality. We might say, 'The Self-interest Theory breeds conflict, telling each to work against others. This is how, if everyone pursues self-interest, this can be bad for everyone. Where the Self-interest Theory divides, morality unites. It tells us to work together—to do the best *we* can. Even on the scale provided by self-interest, morality therefore wins. This is what we learn from Prisoner's Dilemmas. If we cease to be self-interested and become moral, we do better even in self-interested terms.'[55]

This argument fails. *We* do better, but *each* does worse. If we both do A rather than E, *we* make the outcome better for each, but *each* makes the outcome worse for himself. Whatever the other does, it would be better for each if he did E. In Prisoner's Dilemmas, the problem is this. Should *each* do the best he can for himself? Or should *we* do the best we can for each? If *each* does what is best for himself, *we* do worse than we could for each. But *we* do better for each only if *each* does worse than he could for himself.

This is just a special case of a wider problem. Consider any theory about what we have reason to do. There might be cases where, if each does better in this theory's terms, we do worse, and vice versa. Call such cases *Each-We Dilemmas*. A theory can produce such Dilemmas even if it is not concerned with what is in our interests.

Consequentialist theories cannot produce such Dilemmas. As we saw in Section 21, this is because these theories are *agent-neutral*, giving to all agents common aims.

If a theory does produce Each-We Dilemmas, it may not be obvious what this shows. Reconsider the Self-interest Theory. This tells each to do the best he can for himself. We are discussing cases where, if we all pursue self-interest, we are doing what is worse for each. The Self-interest Theory is here directly collectively self-defeating. But we cannot assume that this is a fault. Why should S be collectively successful? Why is it not enough that, at the individual level, S succeeds?

We might say: 'A theory cannot apply only to a single individual. If it is rational for me to do whatever will be best for me, it must be rational for everyone to do whatever will be best for himself. Any acceptable theory must therefore be successful at the collective level.'

This involves a confusion. Call a theory *universal* if it applies to everyone, *collective* if it claims success at the collective level. Some theories have both features. One example is a Kantian morality. This tells each to do only what he could rationally will everyone to do. The plans or policies of each must be tested at the collective level. For a Kantian, the essence of morality is the move from *each* to *we*.

At the collective level—as an answer to the question, 'How should we all act?'—the Self-interest Theory *would* condemn itself. Suppose that we are choosing what code of conduct will be publicly encouraged, and taught in schools. S would here tell us to vote against itself. If we are choosing a collective code, the self-interested choice would be some version of morality.

S is universal, applying to everyone. But S is not a collective code. It is a theory about individual rationality. This answers the smaller question that I asked above. In Prisoner's Dilemmas, S is individually successful. Since it is only collectively self-defeating, S does not fail in its own terms. S does not condemn itself.

34. INTERTEMPORAL DILEMMAS

Many bad theories do not condemn themselves. So the larger question remains open. In such cases, what is it rational to do?

It may help to introduce another common theory. This tells each to do what will best achieve his present aims. Call this the *Present-aim Theory*, or *P*. Suppose that, in some Prisoner's Dilemma, my aim is the outcome that is best for me. According to P, it is then the self-benefiting choice which is rational. If my aim is to benefit others, or to pass the Kantian Test, it is the altruistic choice which is rational. If my aim is to do what others do—perhaps because I do not want to be a free-rider—it is uncertain which choice is rational. This depends on my beliefs about what others do.

As these remarks show, P may conflict with S. What will best achieve my present aims may be against my own long-term self-interest. Since the two theories may conflict, defenders of S must reject P.

They might point out that, even at the individual level, P can be directly self-defeating. It can produce *Intertemporal Dilemmas*. These will be most common for those who care less about their further future. Suppose that I am such a person, and that, at different times, I have different aims. At each time I could either (1) do what will best achieve my present aims or (2) do what will best achieve, or enable me to achieve, all of my aims over time. According to P, I should always do (1) rather than (2). Only so shall I *at each time* do the best I can in P's terms. But *over time* I may then do worse, in these same terms. Over time, I may be less successful in achieving my aims at each time.

Here is a trivial but, in my case, true example. At each time I will best achieve my present aims if I waste no energy on being tidy. But if I am never tidy this may cause me at each later time to achieve less. And my untidiness may frustrate what I tried to achieve at the first time. It will then be true, as it sadly is, that being never tidy causes me at each time to achieve less.

35. A WEAK DEFENCE OF S

Those who believe in the Self-interest Theory may appeal to such cases. They might say: 'The Present-aim Theory is here directly self-defeating. Even in P's terms, S is superior. The self-interested choice is (2). If you always do (2) rather than (1), you will more effectively achieve your aims at each time. If you follow S, you do better even in P's terms.'

Like the similar defence of morality, this argument fails. If I follow S, I do better *over time*. But *at each time* I do worse. If I always do (2), I am at each time doing what will *less* effectively achieve the aims that I then have. (1) is what will best achieve these.

This distinction may be hard to grasp. Suppose that I always do (1) rather than (2). It will then be true that, *over time*, I will *less* effectively achieve the aims that I have *at each time*. If this is true, how can it also be true that, at each time, I will *more* effectively achieve my aims *at that time*? To see how this is possible, we can remember the Interpersonal Dilemma. For the word 'we' substitute 'I over time', and for the word 'each' substitute 'I at each time'. In the Interpersonal Dilemma, we do better *for each* only if each does worse *for himself* than he could. In the Intertemporal Dilemma, I do better over time *at each time* only if at each time I do worse than I *then* could.

As these claims suggest, Each-We Dilemmas are a special case of an even wider problem. Call these *Reason-Relativity Dilemmas*. S produces Each-We Dilemmas because its reasons are *agent-relative*. According to S, I can have a reason to do what you can have a reason to undo. P produces Intertemporal Dilemmas because its reasons are *time-relative*. According to P, I can have a reason now to do what I shall later have a reason to undo.

P can be intertemporally self-defeating. But P does not claim to be successful at the *intertemporal* level. It is a theory about what we have reasons to do at each time. Even in the Intertemporal Dilemmas, P is successful at each time. If I always follow P, doing (1) rather than (2), I am doing at each time what will best achieve my aims at that time. Since P is a theory about what we have reasons to do at each time, it is not failing here in its own terms. P does not condemn itself.

A Self-interest Theorist must claim that, nonetheless, P should be rejected. He might say: 'Any acceptable theory must be intertemporally successful. It is no defence that P does not claim such success. This merely shows P to be structurally flawed. If a theory is intertemporally self-defeating, this is enough to show that it should be rejected.'

These claims may do nothing to support S. If P is refuted by the fact that it is intertemporally self-defeating, why is S not refuted by the fact that it is interpersonally—or collectively—self-defeating? And if it is a good reply that S does not claim to be collectively successful, why can the Present-aim Theorist not make a similar reply?

As these remarks show, the Self-interest Theory can be challenged from two directions. This makes it harder to defend. Answers to either challenge may undermine answers to the other.

One challenge comes from moral theories. The other challenge comes from the Present-aim Theory. There are several versions of this theory. The simplest version is the *Instrumental Theory*. According to this theory, what each person has most reason to do is whatever will best achieve his present aims. This theory takes the agent's aims as given, and discusses only means. No aim is claimed to be irrational. Any aim can provide good reasons for acting.

Another version of P is the *Deliberative Theory*. This appeals, not to the agent's actual present aims, but to the aims that he would now have, if he knew the relevant facts and was thinking clearly. According to this theory, if an aim would not survive such a process of deliberation, it does not provide a good reason for acting.

A third version of P criticizes aims in a second way. On this theory, even if they would survive such a process of deliberation, some kinds of aim are intrinsically irrational, and cannot provide good reasons for acting. What each person has most reason to do is whatever will best achieve those of his present aims that are not irrational. This is the *Critical Present-aim Theory*.

In all its versions, P oftens conflict with the Self-interest Theory. Someone may know the facts and be thinking clearly, yet have aims which he knows to be against his own long-term self-interest. And we may believe that some of these aims are not irrational. Some examples might be: benefiting others, discovering truths, and creating beauty. We may conclude that the pursuit of these aims is not less rational than the pursuit of self-interest. On this view, pursuing such aims is not irrational even when the agent knows that he is acting against his own long-term self-interest.

A Self-interest Theorist must reject these claims. He must insist that reasons for acting cannot be time-relative. He might say: 'The force of a reason extends over time. Since I *shall* have a reason to promote my future aims, I have a reason to do so *now*.' This claim is at the heart of the Self-interest Theory.

Many moral theorists make a second claim. They believe that certain reasons are not agent-relative. They might say: 'The force of a reason may extend, not only over time, but over different lives. Thus, if *I* have a reason to relieve my pain, this is a reason for you too. *You* have a reason to relieve *my* pain.'[56]

The Self-interest Theorist makes the first claim, but rejects the second. He may find it hard to defend both halves of this position. In reply to the moralist, he may ask, 'Why should *I* give weight to aims which are not *mine*?' But a Present-aim Theorist can ask, 'Why should I give weight *now* to aims which are not mine *now*?' The Self-interest Theorist may reply with an appeal to the Intertemporal Dilemmas, where the Present-aim Theory is intertemporally self-defeating. But he can then be challenged with the Interpersonal Dilemmas, where his own theory is collectively self-defeating. A moralist might say: 'The argument for the Self-interest Theory carries us beyond this theory. Properly understood, it is an argument for morality.'

In Part Two I shall pursue this line of thought. But something else should be discussed first. At the interpersonal level, the contrast is *not* between the Self-interest Theory and morality.

36. HOW COMMON-SENSE MORALITY IS DIRECTLY SELF-DEFEATING

As I implied in Section 22, the Self-interest Theory is not the only theory that can produce Each-We Dilemmas. Such cases may occur when (a) some theory T is agent-relative, giving to different agents different aims, (b) the achievement of each person's T-given aims partly depends on what others do, and (c) what each does will not affect what these others do. These conditions often hold for Common-Sense Morality.

Most of us believe that there are certain people to whom we have special obligations. These are the people to whom we stand in certain relations—such as our children, parents, friends, benefactors, pupils, patients, clients, colleagues, members of our own trade union, those whom we represent, or our fellow-citizens. We believe that we ought to try to save these people from certain kinds of harm, and ought to try to give them certain kinds of benefit. Common-Sense Morality largely consists in such obligations.

Carrying out these obligations has priority over helping strangers. This priority is not absolute. I ought not to save my child from a cut or bruise rather than saving a stranger's life. But I ought to save my child from some harm rather than saving a stranger from a *somewhat* greater harm. My duty to my child is not overridden whenever I could do somewhat greater good elsewhere.

When I try to protect my child, what should my aim be? Should it simply be that he is not harmed? Or should it rather be that he is saved from harm *by me*? If you would have a better chance of saving him from harm, I would be wrong to insist that the attempt be made by me. This shows that my aim should take the simpler form.

We can face *Parent's Dilemmas.* Consider

Case One. We cannot communicate. But each could either (1) save his own child from some harm or (2) save the other's child from another somewhat greater harm. The outcomes are shown below.

		You	
		do (1)	do (2)
I	do (1)	Both our children suffer the greater harm	Mine suffers neither harm, yours suffers both
	do (2)	Mine suffers both harms, yours suffers neither	Both suffer the lesser harm

Since we cannot communicate, neither's choice will affect the other's. If the aim of each should be that his child not be harmed, each should here do (1) rather than (2). Each would thus ensure that his child is harmed less. This is so whatever the other does. But if both do (1) rather than (2) both our children will be harmed more.

Consider next those benefits that I ought to try to give my child. What should my aim here be? Should I insist that it be *I* who benefits my child, even if this would be worse for him? Some would always answer No. But this answer may be too sweeping. It treats parental care as a mere means. We may think it more than that. We may agree that, with some kinds of benefit, my aim should take the simpler form. It should simply be that the outcome be better for my child. But there may be other kinds of benefit that my child should receive *from me*.

With both kinds of benefit, we can face Parent's Dilemmas. Consider

Case Two. We cannot communicate. But each could either (1) benefit his own child or (2) benefit the other's child somewhat more. The outcomes are shown below.

You

	do (1)	do (2)
I do (1)	Third-best for both our children	Best for mine, worst for yours
I do (2)	Worst for mine, best for yours	Second-best for both

If my aim should here be that the outcome be better for my child, I should again do (1) rather than (2). And the same holds for you. But if both do (1) rather than (2) this will be worse for both our children. Compare

Case Three. We cannot communicate. But I could either (1) enable myself to give my child some benefit or (2) enable you to benefit yours somewhat more. You have the same alternatives with respect to me. The outcomes are shown below.

You

	do (1)	do (2)
I do (1)	Each can give his child some benefit	I can benefit mine most, you can benefit yours least
I do (2)	I can benefit mine least, you can benefit yours most	Each can benefit his child more

If my aim should here be that I benefit my child, I should again do (1) rather than (2). And the same holds for you. But if both do (1) rather than (2) each can benefit his child less. Note the difference between these two examples. In Case Two we are concerned with what *happens*. The aim of each is that the outcome be better for his child. This is an aim that the other can directly cause to be achieved. In Case Three we are concerned with what we *do*. Since my aim is that *I* benefit my child, you cannot, on my behalf, do so. But you can help me to do so. You can thus indirectly help my aim to be achieved.

Two-Person Parent's Dilemmas are unlikely to occur. But we often face Many-Person Versions. It is often true that, if all rather than none give priority to our own children, this will either be worse for all our children, or will enable each to benefit his own children less. Thus there are many public goods: outcomes that would benefit our children whether or not we help to produce them. It can be true of each parent that, if he does not help, this will be better for his own children. What he saves—whether in money, time, or energy—he can spend to benefit only his own children. But, if no parent helps to produce this public good, this will be worse for all our children than if all do. In another common case, such as the Fisherman's Dilemma, each could either (1) add to his own earnings or (2) (by self-restraint) add more to the earnings of others. It will here be true of each that, if he does (1) rather than (2), he can benefit his children more. This is so whatever others do. But if all do (1) rather than (2) each can benefit his children less. These are only two of the ways in which such cases can occur. There are many others.

Similar remarks apply to all similar obligations—such as those to pupils, patients, clients, or constituents. With all such obligations, there are countless many-person versions like my three Parent's Dilemmas. They are as common, and as varied, as Many-Person Prisoner's Dilemmas. As we have just seen, they will often have the same cause.

Here is another way in which this might be true. Suppose that, in the original Prisoner's Dilemma, it is our lawyers who must choose. This yields the *Prisoner's Lawyer's Dilemma*. If both lawyers give priority to their own clients this will be worse for both clients than if neither does. Any self-interested Dilemma may thus yield a moral Dilemma. If one group face the former, another may in consequence face the latter. This may be so if each member of the second group ought to give priority to some members of the first. A similar claim applies when different groups, such as nations, face a self-interested Dilemma. Most governments believe that they ought to give priority to the interests of their citizens. There are several ways in which, if all governments rather than none give priority to their own citizens, this will be worse for all their citizens. The problem comes from *the giving of priority*. It makes no difference whether this is given to oneself or others.

My examples all involve harms or benefits. But the problem can arise for other parts of Common-Sense Morality. It can arise whenever this morality gives to different people different duties. Suppose that each could either (1) carry out some of his own duties or (2) enable others to carry out more of theirs. If all rather than none give priority to their own duties, each may be able to carry out fewer. Deontologists can face Each-We Dilemmas.

37. THE FIVE PARTS OF A MORAL THEORY

What do such cases show? Most of us accept some version of the theory that I call Common-Sense Morality. According to this theory, there are certain things that each of us ought to try to achieve. These are what I call our *moral aims*. We successfully follow this moral theory when each does what, of the acts that are possible for him, best achieves his moral aims. In my cases it is certain that, if all rather than none successfully follow this theory, we will thereby cause the moral aims of each to be worse achieved. Our moral theory is here directly collectively self-defeating. Is this an objection?

Let us start with a smaller question. Could we revise our theory, so that it would not be self-defeating? If there is no such revision, ours may be the best possible theory. We should first identify the part of our theory which is self-defeating.

One part of a moral theory may cover *successful acts*, on the assumption of *full compliance*. Call this part *Ideal Act Theory*. This says what we should all try to do, simply on the assumptions that we all try, and all succeed. Call this *what we should all ideally do*. 'All' here does not mean 'everyone living'. It means 'the members of some group'.

As I argued in Chapter 1, it is not enough to decide what we should all ideally do. We must take into account these four facts:

(a)   We are often uncertain what the effects of our acts will be;
(b)   some of us may act wrongly;
(c)   our acts are not the only effects of our motives;
(d)   when we feel remorse, or blame each other, this may affect what we later do, and have other effects.

Our moral theory can therefore have the five parts shown below.

	All	Each
Successful Acts	Our *Ideal Act Theory*, saying what we should all ideally do, when we know that we shall all succeed	Our *Practical Act Theory*, saying what each of us ought to do, given (a) and (b)
Motives	Our *Ideal Motive Theory*, saying what motives we should all ideally have, given (a) and (c)	Our *Practical Motive Theory*, saying what motives each of us should have, given (a), (b), and (c)
Blame and Remorse		Our *Reaction Theory*, saying which are the acts for which each ought to be blamed, and should feel remorse, given (a), (b), (c), and (d)

When we are deciding what we believe, we should first consider our Ideal Act Theory. In asking what we should all ideally do, we are asking what our ultimate moral aims should be. These are the foundation of our moral theory. The other parts of our theory are what we need to claim, given our ultimate moral aims, when we consider the four facts stated above.

38. HOW WE CAN REVISE COMMON-SENSE MORALITY SO THAT IT WOULD NOT BE SELF-DEFEATING

Suppose that we accept some version of Common-Sense Morality. In my examples, what is true is this. If *all* of us *successfully* follow our moral theory, it will be directly self-defeating. What is self-defeating is our Ideal Act Theory. If we should revise our theory, this is the first part that we should revise.

Call our theory *M*, and its revised version *R*. One of R's claims is

(R1) When M is self-defeating, we should all ideally do what will cause the M-given aims *of each* to be better achieved.

Thus in all my Parent's Dilemmas we should all ideally do (2) rather than (1). This would make the outcome better for all our children, and would enable each to benefit his own children more.

(R1) revises our Ideal Act Theory. If we revise this part of our theory, we shall naturally be led to revise the rest.

Consider first our Practical Act Theory. This describes what each of us ought to do, given the facts (a) that we often do not know what the effects of our acts will be, and (b) that some of us will act wrongly.

Return to the case of a public good which would benefit our children. One such good is the conservation of scarce resources. Suppose that we are the poor fishermen in the Fisherman's Dilemma, trying to catch enough to feed our children. Because there is overfishing, there are declining stocks. It is true of each that, if he does not restrict his catch, this will be slightly better for his own children. They will be slightly better fed. This is so whatever others do. But if none of us restricts his catch this will be much worse for all our children than if we all restrict our catches. All our children will be much worse fed. According to (R1), we should all ideally restrict our catches. If some fail to do so, (R1) ceases to apply. But it would be natural to make this further claim: each should restrict his catch provided that *enough* others do so too.

What counts as enough? There is a natural answer to this question. Consider any public good that would benefit our children, and that will be provided only if there are voluntary contributions. Assume, for simplicity, that there is no upper threshold above which contributions would be wasted. Our children will benefit most if we all contribute. Suppose that each of us knows that there will be some parents who will not contribute. There must be some smallest number *k* which is such that, if k or more parents contribute, this will be better for each contributor's children than if none contribute. If only *one* contributes, this will be *worse* for his children than if he does not contribute. If *all* contribute, this will be *better* for all our children than if none contribute. Somewhere between *one* and *all* there must be the number k where the change from *worse* to *better* comes.[57]

The number k has two special features: (1) If *k or more* contribute, each contributor is joining a scheme whose net effect is to benefit his own children. The children of *each* contributor will be benefited *more* than they would have been if no one had contributed. (2) If *less* than k contribute, any contributor's children will be benefited *less* than they would have been if no one had contributed. (1) and (2) make k a plausible moral threshold above which each parent ought to contribute. We can claim

(R2) In such cases, each ought to contribute if he believes that there will be at least k contributors.

If our Practical Act Theory claims (R2), this change in our moral view may often change what we do.

It may be said: 'Since (1) is true, we need not claim that each *ought* to contribute if he believes that there will be at least k contributors. Since each is joining a scheme whose net effect is to benefit his children, his love for his children will make him want to join this scheme. Doing so will be better for his children.'

These claims are false. Suppose that at least k parents contribute. The children of these contributors will be benefited more than they would have been if no one had contributed. But each contributor is doing what is worse for his own children. It would be better for each contributor's children if he did *not* contribute, and spent all that he saved—in time, money, or energy— to benefit only his own children. This is true however many others contribute. Since each contributor is doing what is worse for his own children, we need to claim that each *ought* to contribute, if he believes that there will be at least k contributors. Each ought to contribute since, though each is doing what is worse for his own children, the k contributors are *together* doing what is better for all their children.

To support (R2) we can also point out that, if any parent does not contribute when others do, his children will be 'free-riders'. They will benefit from this public good at the expense of the children of contributors. They will benefit at their expense because (a) they will be benefited more than the children of contributors, and (b) this is true because each contributor did what was worse for his own children.

Similar claims apply to our other special obligations. According to Common-Sense Morality, we ought to give some kinds of priority to the interests of those people to whom we are related in certain ways. Besides our children, some examples are: our parents, pupils, patients, clients, those whom we represent, and our fellow-citizens. Let us say that we are

M-related to these people. There are several other kinds of M-relation. What these relations have in common is that, according to Common-Sense Morality, or M, we have special obligations to all of those to whom we are M-related.

There are countless cases where, if each gave priority to his M-related people, this would be worse for all these people than if no one gave priority to these people. According to (R1), what we should all ideally do, in such cases, is to give no priority to our M-related people. If we followed (R1), this would be better for all these people.

Suppose we know that some of us will give priority to our M-related people. (R1) ceases to apply. But there will again be some smallest number k such that, if k or more do *not* give priority to their M-related people, this will be *better* even for *these* people than it would be if all gave priority to their M-related people. We can therefore plausibly claim

(R3) When M is self-defeating, each of us ought to give *no* priority to those to whom he is M-related, if he believes that at least k others will act in the same way.

If we accept (R3), this may again often change what we do. As before, if each of k people gives no priority to his M-related people, each is doing what is worse for these people. This is why, according to Common-Sense Morality, each is acting wrongly. But, though *each* is doing what is worse for his M-related people, these k people are *together* doing what is *better* for all these people. Though these k people act in a way that M claims to be wrong, they together cause to be *better* achieved the M-given aims *of each*. Since they follow (R3) rather than M, they together do better *even in M's terms*.

Consider next the parts of our theory that claim what our motives ought to be. Suppose that each could either (1) save his own child from some lesser harm or (2) save another's child from some greater harm. According to (R1), we should all ideally do (2). But should we be *disposed* to do (2)? If the lesser harms would themselves be great, such a disposition might be incompatible with love for our children. This may lead us to decide that we should remain disposed to do (1). If we remain so disposed, we may therefore, in such cases, do (1) rather than (2). Our children would then suffer greater harms. But, if we are to love them, this is the price they must pay.

It is worth describing the extreme case. Suppose that you and I each have four children, all of whom are in mortal danger. We are strangers, and we cannot communicate. Each could either (1) save one of his own children or (2) save three of the other's children. If I love my children, I may find it impossible to save the lives of three of your children at the cost of letting one of my children die. And the same may be true of you. We will then both do (1) rather than (2). Because we love our children, we save only two of them when we could have saved six.

It will on the whole be better if we continue to love our children. This may sometimes make it causally impossible that we do what (R1) and (R2) claim that we ought to do. But there will be many other cases where this would not be true. Thus it is possible both to love our children and to contribute to most public goods.

If we turn to our other special obligations, it is less plausible to claim that we should be disposed not to do what (R3) claims that we should do. Thus the governments of different countries ought to be able not to give priority to their own citizens, when this would be better for all their citizens. When we consider the effects of having different dispositions, the plausible view, in most cases, is that we should be disposed to act upon (R3).

I have claimed that, if we ought to revise Common-Sense Morality, we ought to accept claims (R1) to (R3). Since we ought to love our children, there are certain extreme cases where we ought not to be disposed to act upon these claims. And there may be certain other similar exceptions. But in most cases we ought to be disposed to act upon these claims. We should therefore often change what we do.

39. WHY WE OUGHT TO REVISE COMMON-SENSE MORALITY

If we revise Common-Sense Morality, or M, we ought to accept three of R's claims: (R1) to (R3). I return now to the main question. If we accept M, ought we to revise our view? Ought we to move from M to R? Is it an objection to Common-Sense Morality that, in many cases, it is self-defeating? If it is, R is the obvious remedy. R revises M where M is self-defeating. And the only difference is that R is not.

Remember first that, in these cases, M is *directly* self-defeating. The problem is not that, in our attempts to follow M, we are somehow failing. That would merely make M indirectly self-defeating. As I have argued, this might be no objection to our theory. The problem here is more serious. In the cases I described, we all *successfully* follow M. Each succeeds in doing what, of the acts that are possible for him, best achieves his M-given aims. But, because we all successfully follow M, we cause the M-given aims of each to be *worse* achieved. This is what makes M self-defeating. Can it be claimed that this is no objection? This seems very doubtful. If there is any assumption on which it is clearest that a moral theory should *not* be self-defeating, it is the assumption that it is universally successfully followed.

Remember next that by 'aims' I mean *substantive* aims. I have ignored our *formal* aim: the avoidance of wrongdoing. This may seem to remove the objection. Take those cases where, if we follow M, either the outcome will be worse for all our children, or each can benefit his children less. We might say: 'These results are, of course, unfortunate. But how could we avoid them? Only by failing to give priority to our own children. This would be wrong. So these cases cast no doubt on our moral theory. Even to achieve our other moral aims, we should never act wrongly.'

These remarks miss the point. It is true that, in these cases, M is not formally self-defeating. If we follow M, we are not doing what we believe to be wrong. On the contrary, since we believe M, we believe it to be wrong *not* to follow M. But M is substantively self-defeating. Unless we all do what we now think wrong, we will cause the M-given aims of each to be worse achieved. The question is: Might this show that we are mistaken? Ought we perhaps to do what we *now think* wrong? We cannot answer, 'No—we should never act wrongly'. If we are mistaken, we would *not* be acting wrongly. Nor can we simply say, 'But, even in these cases, we *ought* to give priority to our own children.' This just assumes that we are not mistaken. To defend our theory, we must claim more than this. We must claim that it is no objection to our theory that, in such cases, it is directly substantively self-defeating.

This would be no objection if it simply did not matter whether our M-given aims will be achieved. But this does matter. The sense in which it matters may need to be explained. If we have not acted wrongly, it may not matter morally. But it matters in a sense that has moral implications. Why should we try to achieve our M-given aims? Part of the reason is that, in this other sense, their achievement matters. If the achievement of our moral aims did not matter, they would be like a set of pointless rules, intended merely to test our obedience.

It may now be said: 'You call M *self*-defeating. So your objection must appeal *to* M. You should not appeal to some rival theory. This is what you have just done. When you claim that it matters whether our M-given aims will be achieved, you are merely claiming that, if they are not, the outcome will be worse. This assumes Consequentialism. So you beg the question.'

This is not so. In explaining why, I shall again combine two distinctions. When our aims are held in common, they are agent-neutral. Other aims are agent-relative. Any aim may be concerned either with what happens or with what we do. This gives us four kinds of aim. Four examples are shown below.

	Concerned with	
	what happens	what we do
agent-neutral	that children do not starve	that children are cared for by their own parents
agent-relative	that my children do not starve	that I care for my children

When I claim that it matters whether our M-given aims will be achieved, I am not assuming that only outcomes matter. Some of our M-given aims are concerned with what we *do*. Thus parental care may not be for us a mere means. Nor am I assuming agent-neutralism. Since Common-Sense Morality is, for the most part, agent-relative, this would beg the question. But this is not what I am doing.

There are here two points. First, I am not assuming that what matters is the achievement *of M-given aims*. Suppose that I could either (1) promote my own M-given aims or (2) more effectively promote yours. According to M, I should here do (1) rather than (2). I would thereby cause M-given aims to be, on the whole, worse achieved. But this does not make M self-defeating. If I follow M, I cause *my* M-given aims to be *better* achieved. In my examples the point is not that, if we all do (1) rather than (2), we cause M-given aims to be worse achieved. The point is that we cause *each of our own* M-given aims to be worse achieved. We do worse not just in agent-neutral but in agent-relative terms.

The second point is that this can matter in an agent-relative way. It will help to remember the Self-interest Theory. In Prisoner's Dilemmas, this theory is directly self-defeating. If all rather than none successfully follow S, we will thereby cause the S-given aims of each to be worse achieved. We will make the outcome worse for everyone. If we believe S, will we think that this matters? Or does it only matter whether each achieves his formal aim: the avoidance of irrationality? The answer is clear. S gives to each the substantive aim that the outcome be, for him, as good as possible. The achievement of this aim matters. And it matters *in an agent-relative way*. If we believe S, we shall believe that it matters that, in Prisoner's Dilemmas, if we all follow S, this will be worse for each of us. Though they do not refute S, these cases are, in self-interested terms, regrettable. In claiming this, we need not appeal to S's agent-neutral form: Utilitarianism. The Self-interest Theory is about rationality rather than morality. But the comparison shows that, in discussing Common-Sense Morality, we need not beg the question. If it matters whether our M-given aims are achieved, this can matter in an agent-relative way.

Does this matter? Note that I am not asking whether this is *all* that matters. I am not suggesting that the achievement of our formal aim—the avoidance of wrongdoing—is a mere means. Though assumed by some Consequentialists, this is not what most of us believe. We may even think that the avoidance of wrong-doing always matters most. But this is here irrelevant. We are asking whether it casts doubt on M that it is substantively self-defeating. Might this show that, in such cases, M is incorrect? It may be true that what matters most is that we avoid wrongdoing. But this truth cannot show M to be correct. It cannot help us to decide what *is* wrong.

Can we claim that the avoidance of wrong-doing is *all* that matters? If that were so, my examples would show nothing. We could say, 'To be substantively self-defeating is, in the case of Common-Sense Morality, not to be *damagingly* self-defeating.' Can we defend our moral theory in this way? In the case of some M-given aims, perhaps we can. Consider trivial promises. We might believe both that we should try to keep such promises, and that it would not matter if, through no fault of ours, we fail. But we do not have such beliefs about all of our M-given aims. If our children suffer harm, or we can benefit them less, this matters. Our morality is *not* a set of pointless rules, intended merely to test our obedience.

Remember finally that, in my examples, M is collectively *but not individually* self-defeating. Could this provide a defence? This is the central question I have raised. It is because M is individually successful that, at the collective level, it can be *directly* self-defeating. Why is it true that, if we all do (1) rather than (2), we *successfully* follow M? Because each is doing what, of the acts that are possible for him, *best* achieves his M-given aims. Is it perhaps no objection that *we* thereby cause the M-given aims of each to be *worse* achieved?

It will again help to remember the Self-interest Theory. In Prisoner's Dilemmas, S is collectively self-defeating. If we were choosing a collective code, something that we shall all follow, S would tell us to reject itself. The self-interested choice would be some version of morality. But those who believe S may claim that this is irrelevant. They can say: 'The Self-interest Theory does not claim to be a collective code. It is a theory of individual rationality. To be collectively self-defeating is, in the case of S, not to be damagingly self-defeating.'

Can we defend Common-Sense Morality in this way? This depends upon our view about the nature of morality, and moral reasoning. On most views, the answer would be No. On these views, morality is essentially a collective code—an answer to the question 'How should we *all* act?' An acceptable answer to this question must be successful at the collective level. The answer cannot be directly collectively self-defeating. If we believe in Common-Sense Morality, we should therefore revise this theory so that it would not be in this way self-defeating. We should adopt R.

Consider first Kant's view about the nature of moral reasoning. Assume that I am facing one of my Parent's Dilemmas. Could I rationally will that all give priority to their own children, when this would be worse for everyone's children, including my own? The answer is No. For Kantians, the essence of morality is the move from *each* to *we*. Each should do only what he can rationally will that we all do. A Kantian morality cannot be directly collectively self-defeating.

There are several writers who accept a Kantian view about the nature of moral reasoning, but who also accept some form of Common-Sense Morality. If they keep their Kantian view, these writers ought to move to the revised version R.

Other writers hold *Constructivist* views about the nature of morality. A morality is, for them, something that a society creates, or what it would be rational for a society's members to agree to be what governs their behaviour. This is another kind of view on which an acceptable moral theory cannot be directly collectively self-defeating. Those who hold such a view cannot continue to accept some version of Common-Sense Morality. They must move to the corresponding version of R.

Those who hold a Constructivist view may question my division of a moral theory. (R1) revises what I call our Ideal Act Theory. Constructivists may see no need for this part of a moral theory. But they cannot object to my proposal that we should ask what we should all do, simply on the assumptions that we shall all try, and all succeed. Answering this question is at worst unnecessary. If a Constructivist asks what we should all ideally do, his answer cannot be some version of Common-Sense Morality. If he accepts some version of this morality, he must move to the corresponding version of (R1), the revised version of his morality that would not be directly collectively self-defeating. And, since he should accept (R1), he should also accept (R2) and (R3). He should revise his Practical Act Theory, the part that used to be his whole theory.

On most of the other views about the nature of moral reasoning, morality is essentially a collective code.[58] On these views, if we accept Common-Sense Morality, we must move to R. But some believers in Common-Sense Morality may have no view about the nature of moral reasoning. Could these people claim that, even though there are many cases where their morality is directly self-defeating, this is no objection to their morality, and no ground for a move to R?

Such a claim is implausible. And it is worth suggesting how Common-Sense Morality comes close to telling us to move to R. Suppose that, in one of my Parent's Dilemmas, we could all easily communicate. We shall then be told by Common-Sense Morality to make a joint conditional promise that we shall all follow, not this morality, but my revised version R. If I join with others in this conditional promise, this will be better for my children. My special obligation to my children will therefore be best fulfilled if I conditionally promise, with everyone else, that none of us will give priority to their own children. Making this conditional promise will be the best that I can do for my own children. If I promise to follow R, on condition that everyone else promises the same, others will then follow R only because I made this promise. If they follow R this will be better for my children. So my promise makes the outcome better for my children.

Similar remarks apply to all of the other cases where Common-Sense Morality is self-defeating. These are cases where we believe that we ought to give priority to our other M-related people, such as our parents, pupils, patients, clients, or those whom we represent. In all these cases, if we can easily communicate, we shall be told by Common-Sense Morality to make this joint conditional promise that we shall follow R. This would then be what each ought to do, because of what he promised. We would not here be abandoning Common-Sense Morality. We would be using part of this morality to alter the content of what we ought to do.

Suppose, next, that in a Parent's Dilemma, we *cannot* communicate. We shall then be unable to achieve this 'moral solution'. Common-Sense Morality now tells each to give priority to his own children. This will be worse for all of our children. Similar remarks apply to the other cases. Because we cannot communicate, and therefore cannot make the joint promise, our morality cannot tell us to follow R. If we *could* communicate, and review the question, 'What should we all do?', our morality *would* tell us to promise *not* to give priority to our own children, parents, pupils, patients, etc. Our morality would tell us to promise *not* to do what, if we cannot communicate, it tells us to do. It is clear that, on our morality, it would be *better* if we could communicate, and could then promise to follow R. This provides a sense in which our morality itself tells us to accept this revised version of itself.[59]

There is a further ground for thinking that we ought to revise Common-Sense Morality. This moral theory makes what I called the Second Mistake in moral mathematics. It ignores the effects of sets of acts—the effects of what we together do. Chapter 3 showed this to be a mistake. And, in showing this, I was not assuming Consequentialism. Those who reject C would agree that, in some of my examples, we should *not* ignore the effects of what we together do.

Common-Sense Morality ignores these effects whenever it is directly collectively self-defeating. It tells each to do what will best achieve his M-given aims. This claim assumes that it is enough to consider the effects of what each person does. In these cases, if each does what best achieves his M-given aims, we together cause the M-given aims *of each* to be *worse* achieved. This is like a case where, if each does what harms no one, we together harm many people. In such cases it is a mistake to think that what matters morally are only the effects of what each person does. We must agree that this is a mistake even if we reject C and accept Common-Sense Morality.

Suppose that we deny that a moral theory must be successful at the collective level. Even if we deny this, we must admit that, in the cases I have discussed, Common-Sense Morality makes a mistake, and should therefore be revised.

40. A SIMPLER REVISION

There is a simpler revision of Common-Sense Morality, for which I have not argued. This is the wholly agent-neutral form of this morality, or, for short, *N*. On this theory, each of us should always try to do what will on the whole best achieve everyone's M-given aims. Our agent-relative moral aims become common aims.

Because it is restricted to certain cases, my proposed revision R is complicated. N is simple, and theoretically more appealing. This suggests that, if we have moved to R, we should make the further move to N.

It may seem that I could extend the argument above, so that it yields this conclusion. Consider any case in which someone could either (1) promote his own M-given aims or (2) more effectively promote the M-given aims of others. All such cases, taken together, constitute the *All-Inclusive Case*. This includes all cases where Common-Sense Morality differs from N. If we ought to revise this morality in this All-Inclusive Case, we ought to accept N.

Suppose that, in this All-Inclusive Case, everyone does (1) rather than (2). We shall thereby cause our M-given aims to be, on the whole, worse achieved. If we all did (2), they would be, on the whole, better achieved. But this would be true only on the whole, or for most of us. There would be exceptions. It would not be true that the M-given aims *of each* would be better achieved.

Remember the Samaritan's Dilemma. This is the Fourth Example in Kant's *Grundlegung*. Could I rationally will that it be a universal law that no one helps strangers in distress? For most of us, the answer is No. But there are some exceptions, such as the rich and powerful, who have body-guards and personal attendants. These people *could* rationally will that no one helps strangers in distress. It would be worse for *nearly* everyone if no one helped such strangers. But it would not be worse for everyone.

A similar claim applies to my All-Inclusive Case. If we all successfully followed the agent-neutral form of M, it would be true of most people that *their own* M-given aims would be better achieved. But this would not be true of everyone. On the definition that I gave, it is not true *for everyone* that M is here directly collectively self-defeating. (To put this point in another way. In that definition, 'everyone' means 'all the members of some group'. In the All-Inclusive Case, most people would be in this group. But there would be some outsiders.)

In applying the Kantian Test, we can perhaps insist that the rich and powerful draw down a veil of ignorance. This can be claimed to be one of the requirements of moral reasoning. But I cannot make the comparable claim about the All-Inclusive Case. My argument is aimed, not at the pre-moral to introduce them to morality, but at those who believe Common-Sense Morality. Since these people already hold a moral view, I cannot similarly claim that they must draw down a veil of ignorance. This is why I have not used this argument for the wholly agent-neutral form of Common-Sense Morality. I have argued only for the more restricted version R. R applies only to those cases where, if we all follow M rather than R, we shall thereby cause the M-given aims *of each* to be worse achieved. We shall all do worse not just in agent-neutral but also in agent-relative terms. This is a crucial difference. In the All-Inclusive Case, I can claim only that, if we all follow M, we shall thereby cause our M-given aims to be, on the whole, worse achieved. To claim that this matters is to assume Agent-Neutralism. This claim cannot be part of an argument for Agent-Neutralism, since this *would* beg the question.

5

CONCLUSIONS

In Part One of this book I have asked what is shown when a theory is self-defeating. Let us briefly review the answers.

41. REDUCING THE DISTANCE BETWEEN M AND C

In Prisoner's Dilemmas, the Self-interest Theory is directly collectively self-defeating. In these cases, if we all pursue self-interest, this will be worse for all of us. It would be better for all of us if, instead, we all acted morally. Some writers argue that, because this is true, morality is superior to the Self-interest Theory, even in self-interested terms.

As I showed in Chapter 4, this argument fails. In these cases S succeeds at the individual level. Since S is a theory of individual rationality, it need not be successful at the collective level.

When this argument is advanced by believers in Common-Sense Morality, it *back-fires*. It does not refute S, but it *does* refute part of their own theory. Like S, Common-Sense Morality is often directly collectively self-defeating. Unlike S, a moral theory must be collectively successful. These M-believers must therefore revise their beliefs, moving from M to R. Their Ideal Act Theory should include (R1), and their Practical Act Theory should include (R2) and (R3).

Unlike M, R is Consequentialist, giving to all of us common moral aims. Since Chapter 4 shows that M-believers must move to R, this reduces the disagreement between Common-Sense Morality and Consequentialism.

Chapter 1 also reduces this disagreement. We are pure do-gooders if we always try directly to follow C, doing whatever would make the outcome best. C is indirectly collectively self-defeating. If we were all pure do-gooders, the outcome would be worse than it would be if we had certain other desires and dispositions. This fact does not refute C; but it shows that C must include Ideal and Practical Motive Theories. C's Ideal Motive Theory must claim that we should not all be pure do-gooders. C's Practical Motive Theory must claim that each of us should try to have one of the best possible sets of desires and dispositions, in C's terms. (Someone has one of these sets if there is no other possible set of which it is true that, if this person had this other set, the outcome would be better.)

For most of us, the best dispositions would in the following sense roughly *correspond* to Common-Sense Morality. We should often be strongly disposed to do what this morality requires.

Here are two of the ways in which this is true. It will make the outcome better if most of us have the strong desires on which most happiness depends. Thus it will be better if we love our families and friends. We shall then be strongly disposed to give certain kinds of priority to the interests of these people, as M claims that we ought to do. It will also make the outcome better if most of us have strong desires to do our work well. We shall then be strongly disposed to give some kinds of priority to the interests of such people as our pupils, patients, clients, customers, or those whom we represent. In acting in these ways we would again be doing what M claims that we ought to do.

For different reasons, we should be strongly disposed *not* to act in certain ways. If we want someone to be dead, we shall be likely to believe, falsely, that this person's death would make the outcome better. We should therefore be strongly disposed not to kill other people. Similar claims apply to deceiving or coercing others, giving in to threats, and to several other of the kinds of act that Common-Sense Morality claims to be wrong.

42. TOWARDS A UNIFIED THEORY

Because C is an agent-neutral theory, it is indirectly self-defeating, and it therefore needs to include Ideal and Practical Motive Theories that, in the sense defined above, roughly correspond to M. Because M is an agent-relative theory, it is often directly self-defeating, and it therefore needs to be revised so that its Ideal and Practical Act Theories are in part Consequentialist. C and M face objections that can be met only by enlarging and revising these theories, in ways that bring them closer together.

These facts naturally suggest an attractive possibility. The arguments in Chapters 1 and 4 support conclusions that may *dovetail*, or join together to make a larger whole. We might be able to develop a theory that includes and combines revised versions of both C and M. Call this the *Unified Theory*.

These claims are like those made by Sidgwick, Hare, and others.[60] But there are at least two differences:

(1) Most of these writers try to combine Common-Sense Morality and Utilitarianism, or *U*. Sidgwick argues for the Hedonistic version of U; Hare argues for the Desire-Fulfilment version. I have been discussing the wider theory, Consequentialism. C may appeal to several principles about what makes outcomes bad. C may claim, for example, that it would be worse if there was more inequality, deception, and coercion, and people's rights were not respected or fulfilled. If C makes these claims, C is already, compared

with U, closer to Common-Sense Morality.

(2) In my claim that C is indirectly self-defeating, I merely follow Sidgwick and Hare. But I follow neither in my argument against Common-Sense Morality. This argument does not, like Hare's, appeal to a particular theory about the nature of morality, or the logic of moral language. And my argument does not, like Sidgwick's, appeal to our intuitions. I claim that Common-Sense Morality is in many cases directly collectively self-defeating. This claim requires no assumptions apart from those that are made by Common-Sense Morality. When I conclude that, in these cases, this morality must be revised, I do assume that a moral theory must be successful at the collective level. But this assumption is not made by only one theory about the nature of morality. It is either made or implied by most of the many different theories about this subject. And it would be accepted by most of those who believe some version of Common-Sense Morality.

The arguments in Chapters 1 and 4 both point towards a Unified Theory. But developing this theory, in a convincing way, would take at least a book. That book is not this book. I shall merely add some brief remarks.

43. WORK TO BE DONE

According to C, we should often be strongly disposed to act in the ways that M requires. If we are C-believers, and we both have and act upon on these dispositions, M-believers cannot object to what we *do*. But they can object to our *beliefs*. Since our dispositions are to act in ways which will often make the outcome worse, we would often believe that in acting on these dispositions, as M-believers think we should, we would be acting wrongly. In developing a Unified Theory, our greatest task would be to reconcile these conflicting beliefs.

Besides claiming that we should have these dispositions, C may also claim that it should be our *policy* to act upon them. C may claim that this should be our policy, even though these are not dispositions to do whatever would make the outcome best. It may be true, in the ways described in Chapter 1, that following this policy would make the outcome best. Remember next C's Reaction Theory. This claims that we ought to feel remorse, and to blame others, when this would make the outcome best. If we follow the policy just described, we will often fail to do what would make the outcome best. C will therefore claim that, in one sense, we are acting wrongly. But C may also claim that, because we are following this policy, we should not be blamed, or feel remorse. C might imply that we should be blamed, and should feel remorse, only if we do *not* follow this policy. This might be the pattern of blame and remorse that would make the outcome best. If C made these claims, this would reduce the conflict between C and M. Though these theories would still disagree about which acts are right or wrong, they would disagree much less about which acts are blameworthy, and should arouse in us remorse. We would be closer to the Unified Theory.

These last claims are greatly over-simplified. In developing the Unified Theory, we would need both to consider many different kinds of acts and policies, and to consider how these would be related to such things as our emotions, needs, and abilities. Many questions would need to be answered. To be convincing, the Unified Theory must draw many distinctions, and make many different claims. There would be much work to be done, none of which I shall attempt here.

Since the Unified Theory would include a version of C, it may be objected that it would be too demanding. But this objection may also be partly met by C's Reaction Theory.

Return to the question of how much those in richer nations should give to the poor. Since others will in fact give little, C claims that each of the rich ought to give almost all his income. If the rich give less, they are acting wrongly. But if each of the rich was blamed for failing to give nearly all his income, blame would cease to be effective. The best pattern of blame and remorse is the pattern that would cause the rich to give most. Since this is so, C might imply that the rich should be blamed, and should feel remorse, only when they fail to give a much smaller part of their incomes, such as one tenth.

Compared with Common-Sense Morality, C is in other ways much more demanding. Thus C would sometimes claim that one of us should sacrifice his life so that he could save some strangers. But failure to save these strangers would not be, even in C's terms, blameworthy. Since it would include C, the Unified Theory would be more demanding than Common-Sense Morality, as it is now. But, if it makes these claims about blame and remorse, its demands may not be either unreasonable or unrealistic.

44. ANOTHER POSSIBILITY

Many people are *moral sceptics*: believing that no moral theory can be true, or be the best theory. It may be hard to resist scepticism if we continue to have deep disagreements. One of our deepest disagreements is between Consequentialists and those who believe in Common-Sense Morality.

The arguments in Chapters 1 and 4 reduce this disagreement. If we can develop the Unified Theory, this disagreement might be removed. We might find that, in Mill's words, our opponents were 'climbing the hill on the other side'.

Because our moral beliefs no longer disagreed, we might also change our view about the status of these beliefs. Moral scepticism might be undermined.

PART TWO

RATIONALITY AND TIME

6

THE BEST OBJECTION TO THE
SELF-INTEREST THEORY

THE arguments in Part One did not refute the Self-interest Theory. I shall now advance other arguments against this theory. Some of these appeal to morality. But the main challenge comes from a different theory about rationality. This is the Present-aim Theory, or P.

I described three versions of P. One is the *Instrumental Theory*. This claims

IP: What each of us has most reason to do is whatever would best fulfil his present desires.

I stretch the word 'desire' to cover intentions, projects, and other aims.

To apply the Instrumental Theory, we must be able both to distinguish different desires, and to decide which desires someone really has. Both can be difficult. But I shall ignore these difficulties here. All that I need to assume is that we can sometimes decide what would, on the whole, best fulfil someone's present desires.

In deciding this, we should ignore *derived* desires. These are desires for what are mere means to the fulfilment of other desires. Suppose that I want to go to some library merely so that I can meet some beautiful librarian. If you introduce me to this librarian, I have no desire that is unfulfilled. It is irrelevant that you have not fulfilled my desire to join this library. By 'desires' I shall mean 'un-derived desires'.

In deciding what would best fulfil these desires, we should give greater weight to those that are stronger. Someone's strongest desire may be outweighed by several other desires. Suppose that, if I did X, this would *not* fulfil my strongest present desire, but it would fulfil *all* of my other present desires. Though X would not fulfil my strongest desire, I may decide that, of the acts that are possible for me, X is what would on the whole best fulfil my desires. If I decide this, X may become what, all things considered, I most want to do.

In its treatment of conflict between desires, and of decisions in the face of risk and uncertainty, the Instrumental Theory may take subtle forms. But, as its name implies, it is entirely concerned with the choice of means. It does not criticise the agent's *ends*—*what* he desires. As Hume notoriously wrote: "Tis not contrary to reason to prefer the destruction of the whole world to the scratching of my finger. 'Tis not contrary to reason to choose my total ruin to prevent the least uneasiness of an Indian, or person wholly unknown to me. 'Tis as little contrary to reason to prefer even my own acknowledged lesser good to my greater . . .'[1]

This refusal to criticize desires is not an essential part of the Present-aim Theory. Even Hume suggested that 'a passion . . . can be called "unreasonable" . . . when it is founded on a false supposition'. This suggestion is developed in the *Deliberative Theory*. This claims

> *DP*: What each of us has most reason to do is what would best achieve, not what he *actually* wants, but what he *would* want, at the time of acting, if he had undergone a process of 'ideal deliberation'—if he knew the relevant facts, was thinking clearly, and was free from distorting influences.

The relevant facts are those of which it is true that, if this person knew this fact, his desires would change. This last claim needs to be refined, in ways that we can here ignore.[2]

A third version of P is the *Critical Present-aim Theory*, or *CP*. This claims that some desires are intrinsically irrational, and do not provide good reasons for acting. CP may also claim that some desires are rationally required. On this second claim, someone would be irrational if he did not have these desires.

We must distinguish here between two kinds of reason: *explanatory*, and *good*. If someone acts in a certain way, we may know what his reason was. By describing this reason, we explain why this person acted as he did. But we may believe that this reason was a very bad reason. By 'reason' I shall mean 'good reason'. On this use, we would claim that this person had *no* reason for acting as he did.

On the Deliberative Theory, *any* desire provides a reason for acting, if it survives the process of ideal deliberation. Suppose that, knowing the facts and thinking clearly, I prefer the world's destruction to the scratching of my finger. On the Deliberative Theory, if I had a Doomsday Machine, and could act upon this preference, it would be rational to do so. We may reject this claim. We may believe that *this* preference does not provide a reason for acting. And we may believe the same about many other possible desires. On the Deliberative Theory, no desire is intrinsically irrational. If we believe that there are such desires, we should reject this theory.

A Deliberative Theorist might reply that such irrational desires would not survive the process of ideal deliberation. This could be made trivially true, with a definition. The theorist might claim that anyone with these desires cannot be 'thinking clearly'. But this in effect grants the objection. In defining what counts as 'thinking clearly', the theorist would have to refer to the desires in question. He would have to decide which desires are intrinsically irrational.

The Deliberative Theorist might instead make his reply as a factual claim. He might agree that what he means by 'thinking clearly' does not logically exclude having the desires that we believe to be intrinsically irrational. But he might insist that his theory is adequate, since those who were thinking clearly and knew the facts would not have such desires.

Whether this is true is hard to predict. And, even if it were true, our objection would not be fully met. If certain kinds of desire are intrinsically irrational, any complete theory about rationality ought to claim this. We should not ignore the question of whether there are such desires simply because we hope that, if we are thinking clearly, we shall never have them. If we believe that there can be such desires, we should move from the Deliberative to the Critical version of the Present-aim Theory

This theory has been strangely neglected. The Instrumental and Deliberative versions, which are widely believed, make two claims: (1) What each person has most reason to do is what would best fulfil the desires that, at the time of acting, he either has or would have if he knew the facts and was thinking clearly. (2) Desires cannot be intrinsically irrational, or rationally required. These are quite different claims. We could reject (2) and accept a qualified version of (1). We would then be accepting the Critical version of P. This claims

> CP: Some desires are intrinsically irrational. And a set of desires may be irrational even if the desires in this set are not irrational. For example, it is irrational to prefer X to Y, Y to Z, and Z to X. A set of desires may also be irrational because it fails to contain desires that are rationally required. Suppose that I know the facts and am thinking clearly. If my set of desires is not irrational, what I have most reason to do is what would best fulfil those of my present desires that are not irrational. This claim applies to anyone at any time.

The charge 'irrational' is at one end of a range of criticisms. It is like the charge 'wicked'. We may claim that some act, though not so bad as to be wicked, is still open to moral criticism. We may similarly claim that some desire, though not deserving the extreme charge 'irrational', is open to rational criticism. To save words, I shall extend the ordinary use of 'irrational'. I shall use this word to mean 'open to rational criticism'. This will allow 'not irrational' to mean 'not open to such criticism'.

In its claim about desires that are not irrational, CP need not appeal only to the strength of these desires. It may, for example, give no weight to those desires that someone wishes that he did not have. And CP need not appeal only to what, even in the broadest sense, we can call desires. It can also appeal to the agent's values, or ideals, or to his moral beliefs. All of these can provide reasons for acting. But CP claims that some of these are not good reasons. It may claim, for example, that even for those people who believe in etiquette, or some code of honour, there is no reason to obey certain pointless rules, or to fight the duels that honour demands.

I have described three versions of the Present-aim Theory. Though this description is a mere sketch, it will be sufficient here. Much of what follows will be concerned with what these different versions have in common. Partly for this reason, I shall discuss only cases where the Deliberative and Instrumental Theories coincide. These are cases where some person knows all of the the relevant facts, and is thinking clearly. I shall also assume that what would best fulfil this person's present desires is the same as what this person most wants, all things considered. And I shall often assume that this person's desires do not conflict either with his moral beliefs, or with his other values and ideals. By making these assumptions I avoid considering several important questions. These questions must be answered by any complete theory about rationality. But they are not relevant to my main aim in Part Two of this book. This aim is to show that we should reject the Self-interest Theory.

Since this is my main aim, Part Two may be dull for those who already reject this theory. But I shall also discuss some puzzling questions about rationality and time. And I shall support CP, claiming that some desires are intrinsically irrational, and that others may be rationally required. Since these claims are controversial, I shall give them some defence before returning to the Self-interest Theory.

46. CAN DESIRES BE INTRINSICALLY IRRATIONAL, OR RATIONALLY REQUIRED?

Why do people think that, if a desire does not rest on some false belief, it cannot be irrational? We can first remember why Hume, its most distinguished holder, held this view. Hume took reasoning to be concerned only with beliefs, and with truth or falsity. A desire cannot be false. And a desire can be 'called unreasonable', on Hume's view, only if it involves theoretical irrationality.

Reasoning is *not* concerned only with beliefs. Besides reasons for believing, there are reasons for acting. Besides theoretical there is practical rationality. There is thus a different and simpler way in which a desire may be irrational. It may be a desire that does not provide a reason for acting.

Some followers of Hume refuse to call desires 'irrational'. This difference would be trivial if these people agreed that some desires do not provide good reasons for acting. Remember next that I use 'irrational' to mean 'open to rational criticism'. This is a matter of degree. If a desire is not wholly irrational, it may provide some reason for acting. If one of two desires is more open to rational criticism, it provides a weaker reason.

If a desire is wholly irrational, it does not *directly* provide any reason for acting. But some desires, even though irrational, do *indirectly* provide such reasons. If I am claustrophobic, I may have a strong desire not to be in some enclosed space. This desire is like a fear. Since fear involves a belief that the object feared is dangerous, fear is irrational when this belief is clearly false. Suppose that, when I have my strong desire to escape from some enclosed space, I know that I am in no danger. Since my desire is like a fear, I may judge it to be irrational. But this desire indirectly provides a reason for acting. It makes me intensely dislike being in this enclosed space, and I have a reason to try to escape what I intensely dislike.

When a desire directly provides a reason for acting, the reason is seldom the desire. It is seldom true that, when someone acts in some way, his reason simply is that he wants to do so. In most cases, someone's reason for acting is one of the features of what he wants, or one of the facts that explains and justifies his desire. Suppose that I help someone in need. My reason for helping this person is not that I want to do so, but that he needs help, or that I promised help, or something of the kind. Similarly, my reason for reading a book is not that I want to do so, but that the book is witty, or that it explains why the Universe exists, or that in some other way it is worth reading. In both cases, my reason is not my desire but the respect in which what I am doing is worth doing, or the respect in which my aim is *desirable*—worth desiring.[3]

If a reason is seldom a desire, this may seem to undermine the Present-Aim Theory. It may seem to show that what we have most reason to do cannot depend on what we desire. But this is not so. Even if a reason is not a desire, it may depend on a desire. Suppose that my reason for reading some book is that it explains the causes of the First World War. If I had no desire to know what these causes were, I would have no reason to read this book.

I claimed that, according to CP, some desires may be rationally required. Return to the case where my reason for helping someone is that he needs help. Does *this* reason depend on a desire? Would I have a reason to help this person even if I did not care about this person's needs? More generally, would I have a reason to act morally even if I did not care about morality?

These are both controversial questions. Some writers answer No to both. According to these writers, both these reasons essentially depend on my desires, or what I care about.[4]

Other writers claim that I do have a reason to act morally, or to help someone who is in need, even if I have no desire to act in these ways. This claim conflicts with the Instrumental version of P, and it may conflict with the Deliberative version. But it need not conflict with the Critical version. If we accept CP, we might claim

(CP1) Each of us is rationally required both to care about morality, and to care about the needs of others. Since this is so, we have a reason to act morally, even if we have no desire to do so. Whether we have a reason to act in a certain way usually depends

on whether we have certain desires. But this is not so in the case
of desires that are rationally required.

This *could* be claimed by someone who accepts CP. My description of CP
leaves it an open question whether this *should* be claimed. Since this
question is controversial, it is best to leave this question open. Either answer
could be given by someone who accepts CP. If a theory left open *every*
controversial question, it would not be worth discussing. But, as we shall
see, this is not true of CP.

CP's other distinctive claim is that some desires, or sets of desires, are
intrinsically irrational. I wrote above that, in most cases, my reason for
acting is not one of my desires, but the respect in which what I desire is
worth desiring. This naturally suggests how some desires might be
intrinsically irrational. We can claim: 'It is irrational to desire something
that is in no respect worth desiring. It is even more irrational to desire
something that is worth *not* desiring—worth avoiding.'

It might be said that masochists have such desires. But actual masochism
is a complicated phenomenon, that would need a long discussion. We could
imagine a simpler case, in which someone merely wants, at some future
time, to suffer great pain. Suppose that, unlike masochists, this person
knows that he would in no respect enjoy this pain, or find that it reduces his
sense of guilt, or be benefited by this pain in any other way. This person
simply wants to have sensations that, at the time, he will intensely dislike,
and very strongly want not to be having. Most of us would believe this
desire to be irrational.

Are there actual cases in which people have irrational desires? One
example may be the desire that some people have, when at the edge of a
precipice, to jump. This strange impulse is felt by people who have not the
slightest wish to die. Since these people want to stay alive, it may be irrational
for them to *act upon* their desire to jump. But this does not show this desire to
be irrational. The desire to jump is *not* a desire to die. In the case of some
people, it is a desire to soar through the air. This is something worth desiring;
we can rationally envy birds. In the case of other people, though they want to
jump, they have not the slightest wish to soar through the air. In the case of
these people, their desire to jump may be irrational.

Consider next another form of this desire. It has been claimed that, at the
height of their ecstasy, certain Japanese couples leap off precipices, because
they *do* want to die. They want to die *because* they are at the height of their
ecstasy. Can *this* be a reason for committing suicide?

Some would say: 'No. Death can be worth desiring because it will end
one's agony. But it cannot be worth desiring because it will end one's
ecstasy.'

This misdescribes the case. These couples do not want to die because this will end their ecstasy. They want their lives to end at the highest or best point. This is not what most of us want. But, though this desire is unusual, it is not clearly irrational. Ecstasy does not last, but declines and decays. If some couple are in ecstasy, they can plausibly regard its natural decay as something that is very undesirable, or well worth avoiding. By cutting short their ecstasy, their deaths would ensure that this ecstasy will not decay. For such a couple, death may be worth desiring.

There are other ways in which apparently crazy desires may not be irrational. The object of these desires may, for example, be aesthetically appealing. Consider *whims*. Nagel writes: 'One might for no reason at all conceive a desire that there should be parsley on the moon, and do what one could to smuggle some into the next available rocket; one might simply like the idea.'[5] This desire is not irrational. It is an excellent whim. (That there be parsley in the sea is, in contrast, a poor whim.)

It is irrational to desire something that is in no respect worth desiring, or is worth avoiding. Though we can easily imagine such desires, there may be few actual desires that are irrational in this way. And there is a large class of desires which cannot be irrational. These are the desires that are involved in purely physical pains or pleasures. I love cold showers. Others hate them. Neither is irrational. If I want to eat something because of the way it tastes, this desire cannot be irrational. It is not irrational even if what I like disgusts everyone else. Consider next experiences that we find unpleasant. Many people have a strong desire not to hear the sound of squeaking chalk. This desire is odd, since these people do not mind hearing other squeaks that are very similar in timbre and pitch. But this desire is not irrational. Similar claims apply to what we find painful.

Turn now to our desires about different possible pains and pleasures. It is at this secondary level that the charge 'irrational' can be most plausible. Someone is not irrational simply because he finds one experience more painful than another. But he may be irrational if, when he has to undergo one of these two experiences, he prefers the one that will be more painful. This person may be able to defend this preference. He may believe that he ought to suffer the worse pain as some form of penance. Or he may want to make himself tougher, better able to endure later pains. Or he may believe that by deliberately choosing now to undergo the worse of two pains, and sticking to this choice, he will be strengthening the power of his will. Or he may believe that greater suffering will bring wisdom. In these and other ways, someone's desire to suffer the worse of two pains may not be irrational.

Consider next this imaginary case. A certain hedonist cares greatly about the quality of his future experiences. With one exception, he cares equally about all the parts of his future. The exception is that he has

Future-Tuesday-Indifference. Throughout every Tuesday he cares in the normal way about what is happening to him. But he never cares about possible pains or pleasures on a *future* Tuesday. Thus he would choose a painful operation on the following Tuesday rather than a much less painful operation on the following Wednesday. This choice would not be the result of any false beliefs. This man knows that the operation will be much more painful if it is on Tuesday. Nor does he have false beliefs about personal identity. He agrees that it will be just as much him who will be suffering on Tuesday. Nor does he have false beliefs about time. He knows that Tuesday is merely part of a conventional calendar, with an arbitrary name taken from a false religion. Nor has he any other beliefs that might help to justify his indifference to pain on future Tuesdays. This indifference is a bare fact. When he is planning his future, it is simply true that he always prefers the prospect of great suffering on a Tuesday to the mildest pain on any other day.

This man's pattern of concern *is* irrational. Why does he prefer agony on Tuesday to mild pain on any other day? Simply because the agony will be on a Tuesday. *This is no reason.* If someone must choose between suffering agony on Tuesday or mild pain on Wednesday, the fact that the agony will be on a Tuesday is no reason for preferring it. Preferring the *worse* of two pains, for *no* reason, is irrational.

It may be objected that, because this man's preference is purely imaginary, and so bizarre, we cannot usefully discuss whether it is irrational. I shall therefore compare two other attitudes to time. One is extremely common: caring more about the nearer future. Call this the *bias towards the near*. Someone with this bias may knowingly choose to have a worse pain a few weeks later rather than a lesser pain this afternoon. This kind of choice is often made. If the worse of two pains would be further in the future, can this be a reason for choosing this pain? Is the bias towards the near irrational? Many writers claim that it is.

Consider next someone with a *bias towards the next year*. This man cares equally about his future throughout the next year, and cares half as much about the rest of his future. Once again, this imagined man has no false beliefs about time, or personal identity, or anything else. He knows that it will be just as much him who will be alive more than a year from now, and that pains in later years will be just as painful.

No one has this man's pattern of concern. But it closely resembles the pattern that is common: the bias towards the near. The difference is that this common bias is proportional to the feature that it favours. Those who have this bias care more about what is in the nearer future. My imagined man has the bias towards the near not in a proportional but in a cruder two-step form. This man's bias draws an arbitrary line. He cares equally about the next 12 months, and half as much about any later month. Thus he would knowingly choose 3 weeks of pain 13 months from now rather than 2 weeks of pain 11 months from now. Asked why he prefers the longer ordeal, he says, 'Because it is more than a year in the future'. This is like the claim, 'Because it is further in the future'. But it is more open to rational criticism. If some pain will be further in the future, it is perhaps defensible to think this a reason for caring less about this pain now. But it is hard to believe that it can be rational both to care equally about all pains within the next 12 months, and to care only half as much about all later pains. If some pain will be felt 53 rather than 52 weeks later, how can this be a reason for caring about it now only half as much?

A similar pair of cases would be these. Many people care more about what happens to their neighbours, or to members of their own community. This pattern of concern would be claimed by few to be irrational. Some claim that it is morally required. But consider a man whose pattern of concern is *Within-a-Mile-Altruism*. This man cares greatly about the well-being of all those people who are less than a mile from his home, but he cares little about those who are further away. If he learns of some fire or flood affecting people within a mile, he will give generously to a fund to help these people. But he will not help such people if they are one and a quarter miles away. This is not a policy, chosen to impose a limit on this man's charity. It is the result of a real difference in how much this man cares about the suffering of others.

This man's pattern of concern crudely resembles the pattern that is common: greater concern for the members of our own community. But his concern draws another arbitrary line. If someone has *no* concern about others, this, though deplorable, may not be irrational. If someone is equally concerned about what happens to everyone, or is more concerned about what happens to the members of his own community, neither of these is irrational. But if someone is greatly concerned about what happens to those who are less than a mile away, and much less concerned about those who are more distant, this pattern of concern is irrational. How can it make a difference that one of two suffering strangers is just under, and the other just over, a mile away? That one of the two is more than a mile away is no reason for being less concerned.

Hume's followers claim that, if a desire or pattern of concern does not involve theoretical irrationality, it cannot be open to rational criticism. I have denied this claim. It is true when applied to the desires that are involved in physical pains and pleasures. But it may not be true of some first-order desires. Some of these may be irrational. One example may be the desire, when at the edge of a precipice, to jump. If this is not a desire to soar through the air, or to prevent the decay of one's ecstasy, it may be irrational.

The best examples can be found when we turn to our second-order desires about possible pains and pleasures. Such desires are irrational if they discriminate between equally good pleasures, or equally bad pains, in an *arbitrary* way. It is irrational to care less about future pains because they will be felt either on a Tuesday, or more than a year in the future. And it is irrational to care less about the suffering of other people because they are more than a mile away. In these cases the concern is not less because of some intrinsic difference in the object of concern. The concern is less because of a property which is purely positional, and which draws an arbitrary line. These are the patterns of concern that are, in the clearest way, irrational. These patterns of concern are imaginary. But they are cruder versions of patterns that are common. Many people care less about future pains, if they are further in the future. And it is often claimed that this is irrational. I shall discuss this claim in Chapter 8.[6]

47. THREE COMPETING THEORIES

Return now to the Self-interest Theory. How is S challenged by the Present-aim Theory, P? S claims both

(S2) What each of us has most reason to do is whatever would be best for himself, and

(S3) It is irrational for anyone to do what he believes will be worse for himself.

An argument for P may force S to retreat to weaker claims. The gravity of threats to S thus depend on two things: how strong the arguments are, and how far, if they succeed, they will force S to retreat.

The most ambitious threat would be an argument that showed that, whenever S conflicts with P, we have no reason to follow S. We have no reason to act in our own interests if this would frustrate what, at the time of acting, knowing the facts and thinking clearly, we most want or value. This would be, for S, complete defeat.

I believe that my arguments justify a version of this conclusion. But they may show something less. They may show only that, when S and P conflict, it would be rational to follow either. Though this is a weaker conclusion, I shall claim that, for S, it is almost as damaging.

I shall advance several arguments. These can be introduced with a strategic metaphor. As we shall see, the Self-interest Theory lies between morality and the Present-aim Theory. It therefore faces a classic danger: war on two fronts. While it might survive attack from only one direction, it may be unable to survive a double attack. I believe that this is so. Many writers argue that morality provides the best or strongest reasons for acting. In rejecting these arguments, a Self-interest Theorist makes assumptions which can be turned against him by a Present-aim Theorist. And his replies to the Present-aim Theorist, if they are valid, undermine his rejection of morality.

Let us say that, in our view, a theory *survives* if we believe that it is rational to act upon it. A theory *wins* if it is the sole survivor. We shall then believe that it is irrational *not* to act upon this theory. If a theory does not win, having to acknowledge undefeated rivals, it must qualify its claims. With three theories, there could be eight outcomes. The survivors could be:

(1) Morality	The Self-interest Theory	The Present-aim Theory	Triarchy
(2)	The Self-interest Theory	The Present-aim Theory	⎫
(3) Morality		The Present-aim Theory	⎬ Dyarchies
(4) Morality	The Self-interest Theory		⎭
(5) Morality			⎫
(6)	The Self-interest Theory		⎬ Monarchies
(7)		The Present-aim Theory	⎭
(8)			Anarchy

On the weaker of the conclusions described above, the Self-interest Theory cannot defeat the Present-aim Theory. If S survives, so does P. This eliminates (4) and (6). S survives only in (1) and (2). My stronger conclusion eliminates these. And I shall claim that, if S survives only in (1) and (2), this amounts to a defeat for S. (This book says little about (3), (5), (7), or the bleaker (8).)

To reach my first argument, we must avoid some mistakes. These are harder to avoid if, like many writers, we forget that the Self-interest Theory has two rivals—that it is challenged both by moral theories and by the Present-aim Theory. If we compare the Self-interest Theory with only one of its rivals, we may fail to notice when it steals arguments from the other.

48. PSYCHOLOGICAL EGOISM

One mistake is to assume that the Self-interest and Present-aim Theories always coincide. No one assumes this in the case of the Instrumental version of P. What people actually want is too often grossly against their interests. But it is widely assumed that the Deliberative version of P coincides with S. It is widely assumed that what each person would most want, if he really knew the facts and was thinking clearly, would be to do whatever would be best for him, or would best promote his own long-term self-interest. This assumption is called *Psychological Egoism*. If we make this assumption, it may be natural to regard P as a mere part of S. Though natural, this would be another mistake. Even if they always coincided, the two theories would remain distinct. And, if we submerge P in S, we may fail to judge S on its own merits. Some of its plausibility it may steal from P.

Psychological Egoism can be made true by definition. Some writers claim that, if someone wants to do what he knows will be worse for himself, he cannot be thinking 'clearly', and must be subject to some 'distorting influence'. When the claim is made true in this way, it becomes trivial. P loses its independence, and by definition coincides with S. This version of P is not worth discussing.

There are two other ways in which Psychological Egoism has been made true by definition. Some writers claim (1) that what will be best for someone is by definition whatever at the time, knowing the facts and thinking clearly, this person most wants. Other writers claim (2) that, if some act would best fulfil someone's present desires, this act by definition maximizes this person's utility. Once again, when Psychological Egoism is made true by definition, it becomes trivial. On these two definitions it is S that loses its independence. (1) makes S coincide with the Deliberative version of P; (2) makes S coincide with the Instrumental version. These two versions of S are not worth discussing. It is clear that definition (2) is not about what is in our own long-term self-interest, on any plausible theory about self-interest. As I shall now argue, the same is true of definition (1).[7]

Most of us, most of the time, strongly want to act in our own interests. But there are many cases where this is not someone's strongest desire, or where, even if it is, it is outweighed by several other desires. There are many cases where this is true even of someone who knows the relevant facts and is thinking clearly. This is so, for instance, when the Present-aim Theory supports morality in a conflict with the Self-interest Theory. What someone most wants may be to do his duty, even though he knows that this will be against his interests. (Remember that, for simplicity, we are considering cases where what someone most wants, all things considered, is the same as what would best fulfil his present desires.) There are many other cases, not involving morality, where what someone most wants would not coincide, even after ideal deliberation, with what would most effectively promote this person's own long-term self-interest. Many of these cases are disputable, or obscure. But, as we shall see, there are many others that are clear.

How common the cases are partly depends upon our theory about self-interest. As I claim in Appendix C, these cases are more common on the Hedonistic Theory, less common on the Success Theory. The cases may be rarest on the Unrestricted Desire-Fulfilment Theory. On this theory, the fulfilment of any of my desires counts directly as being in my interests. What is most in my interests is what would best fulfil, or enable me to fulfil, all of my desires throughout my whole life. Will this always be the same as what would best fulfil my present desires, if I knew the truth and was thinking clearly? There may be some people for whom these two would always coincide. But there are many others for whom these two often conflict. In the lives of these people, S often conflicts with P, even if S assumes the Unrestricted Desire-Fulfilment Theory. S and P conflict because these people's strongest desires are not the same throughout their lives.

There is one complication. This concerns the people whom I discussed in Section 3: those for whom S is indirectly self-defeating. In its claims about these people, S conflicts with P in a less direct way. But we can ignore this complication. We can discuss S in cases where it is not indirectly self-defeating. It cannot be unfair to S to concentrate on these cases. And the important questions here take a clearer form.

Psychological Egoism cannot survive a careful discussion. On all of the plausible theories about self-interest, S and P often conflict. What would best fulfil our various desires, at the time of acting, often fails to coincide with what would most effectively promote our own long-term self-interest.

49. THE SELF-INTEREST THEORY AND MORALITY

S and P are simply related: they are both theories about rationality. S stands in a subtler relation to morality. A moral theory asks, not 'What is rational?', but 'What is right?' Sidgwick thought that these two questions were, in the end, the same, since they were both about what we had most reason to do. This is why he called Egoism one of the 'Methods of Ethics'. A century later, these two questions seem further apart. We have expelled Egoism from Ethics, and we now doubt that acting morally is 'required by Reason'. Morality and the Self-interest Theory still conflict. There are many cases where it would be better for someone if he acted wrongly. In such cases we must decide what to do. We must choose between morality and S. But this choice has seemed to some undiscussable. The claims of each rival have seemed unrelated to the claims of the other.

They can be brought together. Among reasons for acting, we include both moral and self-interested reasons. We can therefore ask which of these two kinds of reason is the stronger, or has more weight. As I have claimed, we may suspect that this question has no answer. We may suspect that there is no neutral scale on which these two kinds of reason can be weighed. But we do not dismiss the question as nonsensical. And we might reach an answer *without* finding a neutral scale. We may find arguments that can defeat the Self-interest Theory, showing that its reasons have no weight. In Part One I discussed one such argument, the claim that S is self-defeating. This argument failed. But I shall present other arguments, and I believe that at least one of these succeeds.

These arguments will be helped by an explanation of the strength or weight of moral reasons. We should therefore include within our moral theory an account of rationality, and of reasons for acting. Since this part of our moral theory will be concerned with what is rational, rather than what is right, it needs to range more widely than the rest of our theory. In particular, it needs to do what may seem a mistake. It needs to bring within its range reasons for acting which are not themselves moral reasons.

This is most obviously done by the theories that are *agent-neutral*, giving to all agents only common aims. When they discuss morality, Neutralists may treat the Self-interest Theory in a conventional way. They may regard it as an independent or non-moral theory, which must be overruled when it conflicts with morality, but which has its own proper sphere of influence: the agent's own life, insofar as this does not affect others. But, when they discuss rationality, Neutralists annex the Self-interest Theory, usually calling it *Prudence*. It becomes no more than a derivative special case. Prudence is the local branch of Rational Benevolence. This is claimed not only by some Utilitarians, but also by some non-Utilitarians, such as Nagel.[8]

I can now describe another mistake. Neutralists may be wrong to annex S, but they have at least seen what some moralists ignore. They have seen that moral and self-interested reasons may have common features, or common roots. This is most likely in the cases where these reasons do not conflict. Such cases may therefore be deceptive. In such cases S may seem more plausible than it really is.

The most deceptive case is that in which a person's acts will affect only himself. Many of us think that, in such a case, morality is silent. If it is not a moral question here what this person does, morality neither conflicts nor coincides with S. But, in their accounts of *rationality,* the two may here coincide. If this person follows S, by doing what will be best for him, he will also be doing what will be best for everyone concerned. This is trivially true, since he is the only one who is concerned. But this truth is not itself trivial. It may lead us to conclude that this person is doing what, impartially considered, makes the outcome best. S may then appear in borrowed robes. A Self-interest Theorist may claim that it would be irrational for this person to act in any other way, because he would thereby make the outcome worse. But the S-Theorist has no right to make this claim. According to S, it is often rational for someone to make the outcome worse. This is so when what makes the outcome worse also shifts the bad effects on to someone else.

Even if we are not deceived by such cases, there can be no objection to setting them aside. We can discuss S in the cases where it conflicts with morality. Once again, this precaution cannot be unfair to S.

50. MY FIRST ARGUMENT

Before I start to criticize S, I shall make one general point. Some of my claims may seem implausible. This is what we should expect, even if these claims are correct. The Self-interest Theory has long been dominant. It has been assumed, for more than two millennia, that it is irrational for anyone to do what he knows will be worse for himself. Christians have assumed this since, if Christianity is true, morality and self-interest coincide. If wrongdoers know that they will go to Hell, each will know that, in acting wrongly, he is doing what will be worse for himself. Christians have been glad to appeal to the Self-interest Theory, since on their assumptions S implies that knaves are fools. Similar remarks apply to Moslems, many Buddhists, and Hindus. Since S has been taught for more than two millennia, we must expect to find some echo in our intuitions. S cannot be justified simply by an appeal to the intuitions that its teaching may have produced.

As my last two sections claimed, S may conflict both with morality and with the Present-aim Theory. These are the cases in which S can best be judged. My first argument emerges naturally from the defining features of these cases.

When S conflicts with morality, S tells each of us to give supreme weight to his own interests. Each must be governed by the desire that his life goes, for him, as well as possible. Each must be governed by this desire, *whatever* the costs to others. I shall therefore call this desire the *bias in one's own favour*.

Most of us have this bias. And it is often stronger than all our other desires combined. In such cases P supports S. But we are now supposing that these two conflict. We are considering people who, though knowing the facts and thinking clearly, *do not want* to give supreme weight to their own self-interest. They are concerned about their own interests. But this is either not their strongest desire, or, if it is, it is outweighed by their other desires. In one of these ways, for these people, P fails to coincide with S. What would best fulfil their present desires is not the same as what would best promote their own long-term self-interest.

S claims that these people should always be governed by the bias in one's own favour. They should be governed by this desire even though this is *not* their strongest desire. (This is what S claims in the simpler cases where it is not indirectly self-defeating.) Should we accept this claim?

It will help to restate this question. There are different versions of the Critical Present-aim Theory. One version *coincides with S*. Is this the version that we should accept? In answering this question we shall see more clearly what is involved in accepting S.

According to CP, some desires may be rationally required. If a desire is rationally required, each of us has a reason to cause this desire to be fulfilled. We have this reason even if we do *not* have this desire. If there is one desire that is required to be our *ultimate aim*, what we have most reason to do is whatever would cause this desire to be best fulfilled.

To make CP coincide with S, we must claim

CPS: Each of us is rationally required to care about his own self-interest, and this desire is supremely rational. It is irrational to care as much about anything else.

On this version of CP, what each of us has most reason to do is whatever will best promote his own self-interest.

I can now state my *First Argument*. We should reject CPS. The bias in one's own favour is *not* supremely rational. We should accept

(CP2) There is at least one desire that is not irrational, and is no less rational than the bias in one's own favour. This is a desire to do what is in the interests of other people, when this is either morally admirable, or one's moral duty.

This version of CP conflicts with S. Consider

> *My Heroic Death.* I choose to die in a way that I know will be painful, but will save the lives of several other people. I am doing what, knowing the facts and thinking clearly, I most want to do, and what best fulfils my present desires. (In all my examples these two coincide.) I also know that I am doing what will be worse for me. If I did not sacrifice my life, to save these other people, I would not be haunted by remorse. The rest of my life would be well worth living.

On this version of CP, my act is rational. I sacrifice my life because, though I care about my own survival, I care even more about the survival of these other people. According to (CP2), this desire is no less rational than the bias in one's own favour. According to CP, given the other details of the case, it is rational for me to fulfil this desire. It is therefore rational for me to do what I know will be worse for me.

51. THE S-THEORIST'S FIRST REPLY

In the case just described, a Self-interest Theorist must claim that my act is irrational. He must therefore reject (CP2). He must claim that my desire is less rational than the bias in one's own favour.

The S-Theorist might object: 'S is a theory about the rationality, not of *desires,* but of *acts.* I need not claim that, in your example, your desire is less rational than the bias in one's own favour. I need only claim that, since you are doing what you know will be worse for you, your act is irrational.'

This is a weak reply. If the S-Theorist does not claim that my desire is less rational, why should we accept his claim about my act? Consider

(CP3) If there is some desire that is (1) not irrational, and (2) no less rational than the bias in one's own favour, and (3) it is true of someone that, knowing the facts and thinking clearly, what this person most wants, all things considered, is to fulfil this desire, then (4) it would be rational for this person to fulfil this desire.

This claim cannot be plausibly denied. Even if we accept S, we have no reason to deny (CP3), since this claim is compatible with S. S is the best theory if the bias in one's own favour is supremely rational. There would then be (apart from this bias) *no* desires of the kind described in (CP3).

The S-Theorist cannot plausibly deny (CP3). If he has no other reply to my First Argument, he must make claims about the rationality of different desires. He must claim that there *are no* desires of the kind described in (CP3). He must appeal to CPS, the claim that the bias in one's own favour is supremely rational, and is therefore rationally required to be our ultimate aim. This appeal to CPS I shall call the *S-Theorist's First Reply.*

This reply directly contradicts my First Argument. I shall now extend this argument. We should accept

(CP4) There are not just one but several desires that are either not irrational, or at least no less rational than the bias in one's own favour.

Consider what I shall call *desires for achievement*. These are desires to succeed in doing what, in our work or more active leisure, we are trying to do. Some desires for achievement may be irrational. This may be true, for example, of the desire to stay down a cave longer than anyone else, or the desire to achieve notoriety by an assassination. But consider artists, composers, architects, writers, or creators of any other kind. These people may strongly want their creations to be as good as possible. Their strongest desire may be to produce a masterpiece, in paint, music, stone, or words. And scientists, or philosophers, may strongly want to make some fundamental discovery, or intellectual advance. These desires are no less rational than the bias in one's own favour. I believe that this is true of many other desires. If we believe this, our version of CP conflicts more sharply with S.

It is worth remarking that, even if there are several desires that are not irrational, there may be one desire that is supremely rational. This cannot be plausibly claimed of the bias in one's own favour. But we might claim

CPM: Each of us is rationally required to care about morality, and this desire is supremely rational. It is irrational to care as much about anything else.

On this version of CP, it would always be irrational to act in a way that we believe to be morally wrong.

CPS makes CP coincide with S. The similar claim CPM may not make CP coincide with morality. The difference is this. S claims to be a complete theory about reasons for acting, covering all cases. Some moral theories make the same claim. This is true, for example, of Consequentialist theories. But, on the moral theories that most of us accept, morality does not provide the only reasons for acting. On these theories, there are many cases where we could act in several different ways, and none of these acts would be morally better than the others. In these cases, even if we accept CPM, what we have most reason to do will depend in part on what our present desires are.

52. WHY TEMPORAL NEUTRALITY IS NOT THE ISSUE BETWEEN S AND P

Of the three versions of P, I have been defending the Critical version. As the last two sections show, this version can be very different from the

Instrumental and Deliberative versions, IP and DP. Of the many writers who reject P, most ignore the Critical version. This is unfortunate. Many objections to IP and DP are *not* objections to CP. In this section I discuss one such objection.

Consider the view that we can rationally be biased towards the near. We can rationally care less about some future pain, not because it is less certain, but simply because it is further in the future. On this view, rationality does not require a temporally neutral concern about one's own self-interest. The Present-aim Theory may seem to be the *extreme version* of this view. P appeals only to present desires, and it claims that, to act rationally, we should do only what will best fulfil these desires. P may therefore seem to be the view that, to be rational, we should care only about our present interests, or our own well-being at the present moment. Call this view the *Egoism of the Present,* or *EP*.

Different versions of EP appeal to different theories about self-interest. Suppose that we accept the Hedonistic Theory. EP then implies

> *HEP*: What each of us has most reason to do is whatever will most improve the quality of his present state of mind.

Suppose that I am in pain. If I endure this pain for another minute, it will cease for ever. If I press a button, my pain will instantly cease, but will return within a few minutes, and will continue for another fifty years. HEP tells me to press this button since, by ending my present pain, this would improve the quality of my present state of mind. It is irrelevant that the cost of this improvement would be pain for fifty years. HEP assumes that it is irrational not to be *most* concerned about one's present state of mind. It is irrational to be *more* concerned about one's states of mind throughout the next fifty years. This view is absurd.

Remember next the Instrumental version of the Present-aim Theory. This claims

> IP: What each of us has most reason to do is whatever would best fulfil his present desires.

Like HEP, IP essentially refers to the present. But these views are very different. According to IP, since no desire is irrational, and it is rational to do what one believes will best fulfil one's present desires, it could be rational to do anything. There is *no* kind of act that must be irrational. According to HEP, since one kind of act is always rationally required, *every* other kind of act is irrational. These two views are at opposite extremes.

If we are Hedonists, these remarks clearly show that the Present-aim Theory and the Egoism of the Present are quite different views. Suppose next that we are not Hedonists. Suppose that our theory about self-interest is the Unrestricted Desire-Fulfilment Theory. EP may then coincide with IP.

I write 'may' because, if we are not Hedonists, the Egoism of the Present may not be a possible view. Suppose that I ask, 'Which act would be most in my interests now?' This would be naturally taken to mean, 'Of the acts that are possible for me now, which would be most in my interests?' But this is not the question asked by an Egoist of the Present. He asks a question that is unfamiliar, and has at best a very strained sense. This is, 'What is most in the interests, not of me, but of *me-now*?' We may believe that this question has no sense, since this entity *me-now* cannot be claimed to have interests. (I may now be interested in certain things. But this is irrelevant). If we do not reject this question, and our theory about self-interest is the Unrestricted Desire-Fulfilment Theory, we might claim that what is most in the interests of me-now is what will best fulfil my present desires. This would then be what I have most reason to do now, according to EP. And this is also what I have most reason to do now, according to the Instrumental version of the Present-aim Theory.

If we assume Hedonism, EP is absurd. If we assume the Unrestricted Desire-Fulfilment Theory, EP may coincide with the Instrumental version of P. But this is no objection to P. We should accept, not the Instrumental, but the Critical version.

CP is not wholly temporally neutral, since it appeals to the agent's present desires. But we could add to CP

(CP5) Each of us is rationally required to care about his own self-interest. And this concern should be temporally neutral. Each of us should be equally concerned about all the parts of his life. But, though we should all have this concern, this need not be our dominant concern.

If we add this claim, CP partly coincides with S. Both theories agree that we should be equally concerned about all the parts our lives. Since they both require this temporally neutral concern, this requirement is *not* what distinguishes S from this version of CP. If we believe that it is irrational to care less about our further future, this provides *no* reason for accepting S rather than this version of CP.[8a]

In this chapter I have advanced my First Argument, and described the S-Theorist's First Reply. This reply claims that the bias in one's own favour is supremely rational. Is this claim justified? Would it be less rational to care more about something else, such as morality, or the interests of other people, or various kinds of achievement? If the right answer is No, my First Argument succeeds. Since I cannot prove that this is the right answer, this argument is not decisive. But I believe that I am right to deny that the bias in one's own favour is supremely rational. If there is a single other desire that is no less rational, as (CP2) claims, we should accept a version of CP that conflicts with S. I believe that there are several such desires.

We should reject S even if we accept the claim that, in our concern about our own self-interest, we should be temporally neutral. CP can make this claim. The disagreement between S and P is *not* a disagreement about this claim. It is about whether this concern should, if we are rational, always be our one ultimate aim.

In the next chapter I shall advance another argument against S. This will place my First Argument in a wider context. The second argument challenges the Self-interest Theory in a more systematic way.

7

THE APPEAL TO FULL RELATIVITY

53. THE S-THEORIST'S SECOND REPLY

A Self-interest Theorist might give another reply to my First Argument. It will help to assume that this S-Theorist accepts the Desire-Fulfilment Theory about self-interest. This will simplify his reply. We need not assume that the S-Theorist accepts the Unrestricted Desire Fulfilment Theory. He could accept the Success Theory, which appeals only to our desires about our own lives. On the Success Theory, it is irrelevant whether our other desires are fulfilled. We can take 'desires' to mean 'relevant desires'.

The S-Theorist might reject what I call his First Reply. He might claim

(S7) The Self-interest Theory need *not* assume that the bias in one's own favour is supremely rational. There is a different reply to your First Argument. The force of any reason *extends over time*. You will have reasons later to try to fulfil your future desires. Since you *will* have these reasons, you have these reasons *now*. This is why you should reject the Present-aim Theory, which tells you to try to fulfil only your present desires. What you have most reason to do is what will best fulfil, or enable you to fulfil, *all* of your desires throughout your life.

This is the *S-Theorist's Second Reply*. It will not succeed.

54. SIDGWICK'S SUGGESTIONS

Sidgwick writes:

From the point of view, indeed, of abstract philosophy I do not see why the Egoistic Principle should pass unchallenged any more than the Universalistic. I do not see why the axiom of Prudence should not be challenged, when it conflicts with present inclination, on a ground similar to that on which Egoists refuse to admit the axiom of Rational Benevolence. If the Utilitarian has to answer the question, 'Why should I sacrifice my own happiness for the greater happiness of another?', it must surely be admissible to ask the Egoist, 'Why should I sacrifice a present pleasure for a greater one in the future? Why should I concern myself about my own future feelings any more than about the feelings of other persons?' It undoubtedly seems to Common Sense paradoxical to ask for a reason why one should seek one's own happiness on the whole: but I do not see how the demand can be repudiated as absurd by those who adopt the views of the extreme empirical school of psychologists, although those views are commonly supposed to have a close affinity with Egoistic Hedonism. Grant that the Ego is merely a system of coherent phenomena, that the permanent identical 'I' is not a fact but a fiction, as Hume and his followers maintain: why, then, should one part of the series of feelings into which the Ego is resolved be concerned with another part of the same series, any more than with any other series?[9]

This much-quoted passage lacks the clarity—the 'pure white light'[10]—of most of Sidgwick's prose. The explanation seems to me this. Sidgwick's *Egoistic Prudence* is the Self-interest Theory about rationality. His passage suggests two arguments against this theory. The passage is unclear because, in stating one of these arguments, Sidgwick goes astray.

Sidgwick first claims that Prudence and Rational Benevolence may be challenged on 'similar' grounds. What are these grounds? The last two sentences suggest one answer. If it is only 'Hume and his followers' who cannot dismiss the challenge to Prudence, Hume's view about personal identity may be the 'ground' of this challenge. The 'similar' ground of the challenge to Rational Benevolence may be some different view about personal identity.

This interpretation fits two of Sidgwick's later claims. 'It would be contrary to Common Sense to deny that the distinction between any one individual and any other is real and fundamental .... this being so, I do not see how it can be proved that this distinction is not to be taken as fundamental in determining the ultimate end of rational conduct for an individual.'[11] These claims suggest how a Self-interest Theorist can challenge the moralist's requirement of Rational or Impartial Benevolence. This challenge can appeal to the fundamental nature of the distinction between individuals, or between different lives. The distinction between lives is deep and fundamental if its correlate, the unity of each life, is deep and fundamental. As I shall argue later, this is what Common-Sense believes about personal identity. On this view, it has great rational and moral significance that we are different people, each of whom has his own life to lead. This supports the claim that the supremely rational aim, for each person, is that his own life go as well as possible. And this is the claim with which a Self-interest Theorist can challenge the moralist's requirement of Impartial Benevolence. As Sidgwick suggests, this challenge is supported by the Common-Sense View about personal identity.

This view is denied by 'Hume and his followers'. As Sidgwick writes,

Hume believed that 'the Ego is merely a system of coherent phenomena . . . The permanent identical "I" is not a fact but a fiction.' And Sidgwick suggests that Hume's view supports a challenge to the Self-interest Theory.

The two suggested challenges cannot both be well-grounded. In challenging the requirement of Impartial Benevolence, a Self-interest Theorist appeals to the Common-Sense View about personal identity. The Self-interest Theory may in turn be challenged by an appeal to Hume's view. The first challenge is well-grounded if the Common-Sense View is true. If this view is true, the second challenge appeals to a false view. Since Sidgwick accepted the Common-Sense View, and believed that Hume's view was false, it is not surprising that he did not develop his suggested challenge to the Self-interest Theory.

Hume's view is inadequate. But in Part Three I shall defend a view that, in the relevant respects, follows Hume. And I shall claim that, as Sidgwick suggests, this view supports an argument against the Self-interest Theory.

In the rest of Part Two, my aim is different. I shall continue to challenge the Self-interest Theory with arguments that do not appeal to any view about the nature of personal identity. One of these is the second argument that Sidgwick's passage suggests.

Since this passage uses the ambiguous 'should', it may seem to be about morality. But, as I wrote, it is about what we have most reason to do. Sidgwick's 'axiom of Rational Benevolence' we can state as

RB: Reason requires each person to aim for the greatest possible sum of happiness, impartially considered.

This can be challenged, Sidgwick claims, by asking

(Q1) 'Why should I sacrifice my own happiness for the greater happiness of another?'

Sidgwick's 'axiom of Prudence' we can state as

HS: Reason requires each person to aim for his own greatest happiness.

This can be challenged by asking

(Q2) 'Why should I sacrifice a present pleasure for a greater one in the future? Why should I concern myself about my own future feelings any more than about the feelings of others?'

I claimed that these two questions may have 'similar' grounds because each implicitly appeals to a view about personal identity. This may be part of what Sidgwick had in mind, as the end of his passage, and the later claims I quoted, both suggest. But there is a simpler interpretation. (Q1) rejects the requirement of impartiality between different people. It implies that a rational agent may give a special status to a particular person: *himself*. (Q2) rejects the requirement of impartiality between different times. It implies that a rational agent may give a special status to a particular time: the *present*, or the time of acting. The two questions have 'similar' grounds because of the analogy between oneself and the present. This analogy provides another argument against the Self-interest Theory.

55. HOW S IS INCOMPLETELY RELATIVE

This argument can be introduced with these remarks. Sidgwick's moral theory requires what he calls Rational Benevolence. On this theory, an agent may not give a special status either to himself or to the present. In requiring both personal and temporal neutrality, this theory is *pure*. Another pure theory is the Present-aim Theory, which rejects the requirements both of personal and of temporal neutrality. The Self-interest Theory is not pure. It is a *hybrid* theory. S rejects the requirement of personal neutrality, but requires temporal neutrality. S allows the agent to single out himself, but insists that he may not single out the time of acting. He must not give special weight to what he *now* wants or values. He must give equal weight to all the parts of his life, or to what he wants or values at all times.

Sidgwick may have seen that, as a hybrid, S can be charged with a kind of inconsistency. If the agent has a special status, why deny this status to the time of acting? We can object to S that it is *incompletely relative*.

According to S, reasons for acting can be agent-relative. I have a reason to do whatever will be best for me. This is a reason for me but not for you. You do *not* have a reason to do whatever will be best for me.

A Present-aim Theorist can claim

(P1) If reasons can be relative, they can be *fully* relative: they can be relative to the agent *at the time of acting*.

This claim can appeal to the analogy between oneself and the present, or what is referred to by the words 'I' and 'now'. This analogy holds only at a formal level. Particular times do not resemble particular people. But the word 'I' refers to a particular person *in the same way in which* the word 'now' refers to a particular time. And when each of us is deciding what to do, he is asking, 'What should *I* do *now*?' Given the analogy between 'I' and 'now', a theory ought to give to both the same treatment. This is why (P1) claims that a reason can have force only for *me now*.

'Here' is also analogous to 'I'. When some adviser tells me how he escaped from a less hostile environment, I might protest, 'But what should *I* do *here*?' If a person could be in several places at the same time, it would not be enough to ask 'What should I do now?' If I could now be in several different places, this question would not be *fully* relative. But there is in fact no need for this addition. It is enough to claim that a reason can have force only for me now.

We need not add 'here' because, since I am here, I cannot now also be elsewhere. [12]

A Present-aim Theorist might make two bolder claims. He might say

(P2) Reasons for acting *must* be fully relative. We should reject claims which imply that reasons can be *incompletely* relative. Thus we should reject the claim that reasons can be agent-relative but temporally neutral. We can call such claims *incompatible with full relativity*.

(P3) Consider any pair of claims that are related in the following way: The first claim contains the word 'I', but does not contain the word 'now'. The second claim is just like the first, except that it *does* contain the word 'now'. Call such a pair of claims *analogous*. If the first claim conflicts with the second, it is incompatible with full relativity, and should therefore be rejected. If the first claim does *not* conflict with the second, it is an open question whether we should accept the first claim. But, *if* we accept the first claim, we should *also* accept the second. This is because, if we accept the first but reject the second, our view is incompatible with full relativity. And we are not, as we ought to be, giving to 'I' and 'now' the same treatment.

(P3) may be unclear, and it may be unclear why a Present-aim Theorist makes this claim. But, when I apply (P3), both of these may become clear.

Claims (P1) to (P3) state what I call the *Appeal to Full Relativity*. I believe that this is a strong objection to the Self-interest Theory.

56. HOW SIDGWICK WENT ASTRAY

Before I discuss this objection, it will help to suggest why Sidgwick failed to see its strength.

At the start of the passage quoted above, Sidgwick seems aware that the threat to S comes from P. His second sentence begins: 'I do not see why the axiom of Prudence should not be questioned, *when it conflicts with present inclination. . .* ' This suggests the question that would be asked by a Present-aim Theorist:

(Q3) Why should I aim for my own greatest happiness if this is not what, at the time of acting, I most want or value?

This is a good question. But it is not the question that Sidgwick later asks. His passage suggests that he was half aware of the Appeal to Full Relativity. But he does not fully state this appeal, and he does not discuss it further. I suggest that he may have gone astray in the following ways:

(*a*) He may have either overlooked the Present-aim Theory, or assumed that it was not a serious rival to the Self-interest Theory.

(b) He was a Hedonist. In its Hedonistic form, S implies

(S8)   Reason requires that I aim for my own greatest happiness.

Sidgwick accepted this claim. And he may have thought that, if we appeal to the analogy between 'I' and 'now', those who accept (S8) should also accept

HEP: Reason requires that I aim now for my own greatest happiness now, or at the present moment.

This is another statement of the Hedonistic Egoism of the Present. As I have said, this view is absurd. The absurdity of HEP may have led Sidgwick to reject both the analogy between 'I' and 'now' and the Appeal to Full Relativity.

(*c*) This Appeal tells us to reject S and accept P. Sidgwick believed that S was plausible. He may not have seen that, even if we appeal to full relativity, we can admit that S is plausible. S can be stated in a series of claims. And the Appeal to Full Relativity allows us to accept some of these claims. We can accept those parts of S that are compatible with the Present-aim Theory. Sidgwick thought that S was plausible, and he may have thought HEP to be absurd. But what is plausible in S are the parts of S that are both compatible with, and analogous to, parts of P. And the absurd HEP is analogous to a part of S that we should reject. Since this is so, as I shall claim, the Appeal to Full Relativity does not conflict so sharply with Sidgwick's intuitions.

57. THE APPEAL APPLIED AT A FORMAL LEVEL

Consequentialists reject the bias in one's own favour. Rashdall asks, for instance, why 'an impartial or impersonal Reason . . . should attach more importance to one man's pleasure than to another's?' 'It is', he concedes,'. . . intelligible[13] that one thing should appear reasonably to be desired from a man's own point of view, and another thing when he takes the point of view of a larger whole. But can both of these points of view be equally reasonable? How can it be reasonable to take the point of view of the part when once the man knows the existence of the whole . . . ?'[14]

A Self-interest Theorist can reply: 'We are not asking what it is rational for *Reason* to do. We are asking what it is rational for *me* to do. And I may reasonably decline to take 'the whole's point of view'. I am not the whole. Why may not *my* point of view be, precisely, *my* point of view?'

The Self-Interest Theory may in turn be challenged. A Present-aim Theorist can say: 'We are not just asking what it is rational for me to do.

We are asking what it is rational for me to do *now*. We must consider, not just my point of view, but my present point of view.' As Williams writes, 'The correct perspective on one's life is *from now*.'[15]

This point can be made in more formal terms. Following Nagel, I distinguished two kinds of reason for acting. Nagel calls a reason *objective* if it is not tied down to any point of view. Suppose we claim that there is a reason to relieve some person's suffering. This reason is objective if it is a reason for everyone—for anyone who could relieve this person's suffering. I call such reasons agent-neutral. Nagel's *subjective* reasons are reasons only for the agent. I call these agent-relative.[16]

I should explain further the sense in which reasons can be relative. In one sense, all reasons can be relative to an agent, and a time and place. Even if you and I are trying to achieve some common aim, we may be in different causal situations. I may have a reason to act in a way that promotes our common aim, but you may have no such reason, since you may be unable to act in this way. Since even agent-neutral reasons can be, in this sense, agent-relative, this sense is irrelevant to this discussion.

When I call some reason agent-relative, I am not claiming that this reason *cannot* be a reason for other agents. All that I am claiming is that it may not be. On the Present-aim Theory, my reason for acting is a reason for other agents if they and I have the same aim. Similarly, when P claims that some reason is relative to time, the claim is not that, as time passes, this reason is bound to be lost. The claim is only that it may be lost. It will be lost if there is a change in the agent's aim.

If all reasons for acting were agent-neutral, this would be fatal to the Self-interest Theory. Consider each person's reason to promote his own interests. If this was a reason for everyone, each person would have equal reason to promote the interests of everyone. The Self-interest Theory would be annexed by Impartial Benevolence. A Self-interest Theorist must therefore claim that reasons for acting can be agent-relative. They can be reasons for the agent without being reasons for anyone else.

A Present-aim Theorist would agree. But he can add (P1): the claim that a reason can be relative to the agent at the time of acting. It can be a reason for him at this time without being a reason for him at other times.

This claim challenges the S-Theorist's Second Reply, which assumes that any reason's force extends over time. According to S, as Nagel writes, 'there *is* reason to promote that for which there . . . *will* be a reason.'[17] Self-interested reasons are in this sense timeless, or temporally neutral.

Though timeless, they are not impersonal. As I claimed, S is a hybrid theory. According to Neutralist moral theories, reasons for acting are both timeless and impersonal. According to the Present-aim Theory, reasons are both time-relative and agent-relative: they are reasons for the agent at the time of acting. According to the Self-interest Theory, reasons are agent-relative, but they are not time-relative. Though S rejects the requirement of impersonality, it requires temporal neutrality.

As a hybrid, S can be attacked from both directions. And what S claims against one rival may be turned against it by the other. In rejecting Neutralism, a Self-interest Theorist must claim that a reason may have force only for the agent. But the grounds for this claim support a further claim. If a reason can have force only for the agent, it can have force for the agent only at the time of acting. The Self-interest Theorist must reject this claim. He must attack the notion of a time-relative reason. But arguments to show that reasons must be temporally neutral, thus refuting the Present-aim Theory, may also show that reasons must be neutral between different people, thus refuting the Self-interest Theory.

Nagel once advanced an argument of this second kind. If his argument succeeds, Neutralism wins. I am now discussing, not Nagel's argument, but the Appeal to Full Relativity. Like Nagel's argument, this appeal challenges the Self-interest Theory. One part of this appeal is (P1), the claim that, if reasons can be agent-relative, they can be fully relative: relative to the agent at the time of acting.

Either reasons can be relative, or they cannot. If they cannot, as Nagel argued, Neutralism wins. We must reject both the Self-interest Theory, and the Present-aim Theory, and most of Common-Sense Morality.

Suppose next that, as Nagel now believes, reasons can be relative. (P1) rightly claims that, if reasons can be relative, they can be relative to the agent at the time of acting. As I shall argue in the next chapter, it could be true that I *once* had a reason to promote some aim, without its being true that I have this reason *now*. And it could be true that I *shall* have a reason to promote some aim, without its being true that I have this reason *now*. Since these could both be true, it cannot be claimed that the force of any reason extends over time. This undermines the S-Theorist's Second Reply.

Besides appealing to (P1), a Present-aim Theorist can appeal to the bolder (P2) and (P3). I shall now show that, if this appeal is justified, there are further grounds for rejecting S.

58. THE APPEAL APPLIED TO OTHER CLAIMS

Suppose, first, that someone accepts both S and the Desire-Fulfilment Theory about self-interest. Such a person could state S, as it applies to himself, with the claim

> (S9) What I have most reason to do is what will best fulfil all of my desires throughout my whole life.

The analogous claim is

> (P4) What I have most reason to do now is what will best fulfil all of the desires that I have now.

Since these claims conflict, the Appeal to Full Relativity tells us to reject (S9), which is incompatible with full relativity. In telling us to reject this claim, the

Appeal tells us to reject one version of S. And it allows us to accept (P4), which states the Instrumental version of P.

Consider next

(S10) I can rationally ignore desires that are not mine,

and

(P5) I can rationally now ignore desires that are not mine now.

These claims do not conflict. According to the Appeal to Full Relativity, we should therefore accept either both or neither. Since a Self-interest Theorist must accept (S10), he must accept (P5). But (P5) is both a denial of S and a partial statement of P. As before, the Appeal counts against S and in favour of P.

Though a Present-Aim Theorist would reject the Self-interest Theory, he would accept some of the claims that S makes. Thus he would accept the rejection of RB, the claim that reason requires impartial benevolence. And, though he would reject

HS: Reason requires each person to aim for his own greatest happiness,

he would accept in its place

(P6) It is not irrational to care more about one's own happiness.

If he is not a Hedonist, he should add

(P7) It is not irrational to care more about what happens to oneself, or about one's own self interest.

This claim defends what I call the bias in one's own favour. But, unlike S, it does not insist that a rational agent must both have, and be governed by, this particular bias. It claims only that this bias is not irrational.

Suppose that we accept (P7). The analogous claim is

(P8) It is not irrational to care more about what is happening to oneself at the present moment.

This claim defends what I shall call the *bias towards the present*. This is even more common than the bias in one's own favour. The two biases may be expressed in thoughts like these: 'I knew that someone had to do this ghastly job, but I wish that it wasn't *me*'; 'I knew that I had to do this job sooner or later, but I wish that I wasn't doing it *now*'. (Or: 'I knew that my tooth had to be drilled, but I wish that it wasn't being drilled at this very moment.')

According to the Appeal to Full Relativity, if we accept (P7) we should also accept (P8). This seems correct. The two biases may be defended on similar grounds. My reasons for caring about what happens to me differ in kind from my reasons for caring about what happens to other people. The relation between me and my own feelings is much closer than the relations between me and the feelings of others. This fact makes (P7) plausible. In the same way, my reasons for caring about what is happening to me now differ in kind from my reasons for caring now about what did or will happen to me. The relation between me now and what I am feeling now is much closer than the relations between me now and my feelings at other times. This fact makes (P8) plausible.

Since (P7) would be claimed both by a Self-interest Theorist and by a Present-aim Theorist, the latter can say: 'The Self-interest Theory is in part correct. Its mistake is to move from (P7) to a bolder claim. According to (P7), it is not irrational to care more about one's own self-interest. This is plausible. But it is not plausible to claim that a concern for our own self-interest must always, if we are rational, be our one ultimate aim.'

(P7) and (P8) are not central to the Present-aim Theory. If someone did not care more either about himself or about his own present feelings, he would not be judged to be irrational by a Present-aim Theorist. These two claims are not implied by the quite different claim that *is* central to the Critical Version of P. (This is the claim that, if we know the facts and are thinking clearly, what we have most reason to do is whatever would best fulfil those of our present desires that are not irrational.)

Though a Present-aim Theorist would accept (P7), he would embed it within a larger claim. This might be

(P9) A pattern of concern is not irrational merely because it does not give supreme weight to the achievement of the best outcome, impartially considered. It would be no less rational for *me* to care *more* about what happens to *me*, or to the people whom *I* love, or about the success of what *I* am trying to achieve, or the causes to which *I* am committed.

This claim gives no special place to the bias in one's own favour. It merely cites this bias as one example of a concern which, though not impartial or agent-neutral, is not less rational. This is the simplest and most obvious biased or agent-relative concern. But there are countless others, some of which (P9) cites, and claims to be no less rational.

If we accept (P9), the Appeal to Full Relativity tells us to accept

(P10) A pattern of concern is not irrational merely because it does not give supreme weight to one's own self-interest. It would be no less rational for me to care more *now* about those people whom I love *now*, or about the success of what I am *now* trying to achieve, or the causes to which I am *now* committed. And it may be no less rational for my concern about my own self-interest to involve a temporal bias relative to the present. For example, it may be no less rational for me to care more *now* about what is happening to me *now*.

(P10) *is* one of the central claims of the Present-aim Theory. It gives no special place to the bias towards the present. This is merely cited as one example of a concern which, though relative to the agent at the time of acting, *may* be no less rational.

I write 'may', because there are different versions of CP. One version claims that, in my concern for my own self-interest, I should be temporally neutral. This is consistent with (P10). On this version of CP, I should also have a temporally neutral concern about the interests of those people whom I love. In trying to do what will be best for these people, I should give an equal weight to all the parts of their lives. This is consistent with the claim that it is no less rational for me to be more concerned *now* about the interests of those people whom I love *now*. And, even if my concern for my own self-interest should be temporally neutral, it is no less rational for me to care more *now* about what I am *now* trying to achieve, or the causes to which I am *now* committed. My concern about this achievement, or these causes, is *not* a concern for my own self-interest.

If we accept (P10), we shall reject the central claim of the Self-interest Theory: the claim that it is irrational for anyone to do what he knows will be worse for himself. According to S, the one supremely rational pattern of concern is a temporally neutral bias in one's own favour. According to (P10), many other patterns of concern are no less rational. If this is so, my First Argument succeeds. If we have one of these other patterns of concern, it would be no less rational to act upon it. This would be no less rational even when, in so acting, we would be doing what we know to be against our own long-term self-interest.

Should we accept (P10)? More exactly, can we reject (P10) if we have accepted (P7), the claim that it is not irrational to be biased in one's own favour? Is this bias uniquely or supremely rational? I have mentioned some other desires and concerns which I claimed to be no less rational. If that claim is justified, we should accept a qualified version of (P10).

We should qualify (P10) because it may be irrational to have certain desires for achievement, or to be committed to certain causes. Thus it may be irrational to want to stay down a cave longer than anyone else. But, as I have claimed, there are many desires for achievement that are no less rational than the bias in one's own favour. It is no less rational to want to create certain kinds of beauty, or to achieve certain kinds of knowledge. And there are many other examples. Similar claims apply to the causes to which we are committed. It was not irrational in the 19th Century to be committed to the adoption of Esperanto as the World's *lingua franca*—or international language. Given the relative positions of English and Esperanto, this commitment may be irrational now. But there are many other causes commitment to which is no less rational than the bias in one's own favour. Since we should accept a qualified version of (P10), we should accept a version of CP which often conflicts with S.

In this chapter I have argued that, if a reason can have force only for one person, a reason can have force for a person only at one time. We should reject the claim that any reason's force extends over time. We should therefore reject the S-Theorist's Second Reply to my First Argument, which appeals to this claim. If he has no other reply, the S-Theorist may have to return to his First Reply. He may have to claim that the bias in one's own favour is supremely rational. We should reject this claim. If the S-Theorist has no other reply, we should reject S.

I have also argued that there are other grounds for rejecting S. These are provided by the Appeal to Full Relativity. According to this appeal, the only tenable theories are morality and the Present-aim Theory, for only these give to 'I' and 'now' the same treatment. (Agent-neutral moral theories clearly give to 'I' and 'now' the same treatment. So, less obviously, do agent-relative theories. These require that I give special weight to the interests of certain people. Thus I should give special weight to the interests of my children. This claim may seem to give to 'I' treatment that it denies to 'now'. But this is not so. My relation to my children cannot hold at some time, and fail to hold at some other time. My children could not possibly both exist and not be my children. This is why, in the claim about my obligations to my children, we need not include the word 'now'. There are other relations which *can* hold at some time, and fail to hold at other times. In its claims about such relations, an agent-relative moral theory does include the word 'now'. For example, if I am a doctor, I have special obligations to those who are *now* my patients. I have no such obligations to those who were once my patients, but are now the patients of some other doctor.)

In the next chapter I give further grounds for rejecting S. But my main aim is to discuss some puzzling questions.

8

DIFFERENT ATTITUDES TO TIME

THE Self-interest Theory claims that, in our concern about our own self-interest, we should be temporally neutral. As I have said, a Present-aim Theorist can also make this claim. I shall now ask whether this claim is justified. If the answer is Yes, this is no objection to P. But, if the answer is No, this is another objection to S.

59. IS IT IRRATIONAL TO GIVE NO WEIGHT TO ONE'S PAST DESIRES?

Consider first those S-Theorists who accept the Desire-Fulfilment Theory about self-interest. On all versions of this theory, what is best for someone is what will best fulfil his desires, throughout his life. And the fulfilment of someone's desires is good for him, and their non-fulfilment bad for him, even if this person never knows whether these desires have been fulfilled.

In deciding what would best fulfil my desires, we must try to predict the desires that I would have, if my life went in the different ways that it might go. The fulfilment of a desire counts for more if the desire is stronger. Should it also count for more if I have it for a longer time? In the case of strong desires, it seems plausible to answer Yes; but in the case of weak desires the answer is less clear.

On the Unrestricted Desire-Fulfilment Theory, it is good for me if *any* of my desires are fulfilled, and bad for me if any are not fulfilled. Another version is the *Success Theory*. This gives weight only to my desires about my own life. It is not always clear which these desires are. But this is no objection to the Success Theory. Why should it always be clear what would be best for me?

We can next remember how the Success Theory differs from the widest version of the Hedonistic Theory. Both theories appeal to a person's desires about his own life. But Hedonists appeal only to desires about those features of our lives that are introspectively discernible. Suppose that my strongest desire is to solve some scientific problem. Hedonists claim that it will be better for me if, for the rest of my life, I believe that I am solving this problem. On their view, it will not matter if my belief is false, since this will make no difference to the experienced quality of my life. Knowing and falsely believing are not different experiences. On the Success Theory, it will be worse for me if my belief is false. What I want is to solve this problem. It will be worse for me if this desire is not fulfilled, even if I believe that it is.

We can remember finally that there are two versions of both the Hedonistic and the Success Theory. One version appeals to the sum total of the fulfilment of a person's *local*, or particular, desires. The other version appeals only to a person's *global* desires: his preferences about either parts of his life, or his whole life. I might globally prefer one of two possible lives even though it involved a smaller total sum of local desire fulfilment. One such global preference is that of the couples who leap off cliffs at the height of their ecstasy.

We could distinguish other versions of the Desire-Fulfilment Theory. But this is unnecessary here. I shall be challenging those Self-interest Theorists who assume some version of the Desire-Fulfilment Theory. I shall again use 'desire' to mean 'relevant desire', since different versions of this theory appeal to different desires. Most of my remarks would apply whichever version is assumed.

On the Desire-Fulfilment Theory, Sidgwick's axiom of Rational Benevolence becomes

(RB1)   What each person has most reason to do is what will best fulfil everyone's desires,

and the Self-interest Theory becomes

(S11)   What each person has most reason to do is what will best fulfil, or enable him to fulfil, all of his own desires.

A Self-interest Theorist must reject (RB1). As I remarked, he may claim

(S10)   I can rationally ignore desires that are not mine.

A Present-aim Theorist could add

(P5)   I can rationally now ignore desires that are not mine now.

(I write 'could' because (P5) might be rejected on the Critical version of P.) According to the Appeal to Full Relativity, if we accept (S10) we should also accept (P5). Since an S-Theorist must accept (S10), but cannot accept (P5), he must reject the Appeal to Full Relativity. This appeal claims that reasons can be relative, not only to particular people, but also to particular times. The S-Theorist might reply that, while there is great rational significance in the question *who* has some desire, there is no such significance in the question *when* the desire is had.

Is this so? Should I try to fulfil my *past* desires? A similar question can be asked about the Desire-Fulfilment Theory. Is the fulfilment of my past desires good for me, and their non-fulfilment bad for me? Except for the last wishes of the dead, past desires are seldom discussed by Desire-Fulfilment Theorists. This may be because the analogous question cannot arise on some versions of the older Hedonistic Theory. I cannot now improve the quality of my past experiences. But I might be able to fulfil my past desires, even when I no longer want to do so. Have I a reason to do so?

Some desires are implicitly conditional on their own persistence. If I now want to swim when the Moon later rises, I may want to do so only if, when the Moon rises, I still want to swim. If a desire is conditional on its own persistence, it can obviously be ignored once it is past.

There is one class of desires many of which are implicitly conditional in this way. These are the desires whose fulfilment we believe would give us satisfaction, or whose non-fulfilment we believe would make us distressed. Neither would happen after we have ceased to have these desires. It is therefore natural for many of these desires to be conditional on their own persistence.

In the case of other desires there is no such general reason for this to be so. Suppose that I meet some stranger on a train. She describes her life's ambitions, and the hopes and fears with which she views her chances of success. By the end of our journey, my sympathy is aroused, and I strongly want this stranger to succeed. I have this strong desire even though I know that we shall never meet again. This desire is not implicitly conditional on its own persistence. The same is true of many other desires, of many kinds.

The clearest examples are the desires that some people have about what will happen after they are dead. Suppose that I do not believe that I shall have an after-life. Since I believe that my death will be my extinction, my desires about what happens afterwards cannot be conditional on their own persistence up to the moment of fulfilment. I believe that this condition could not be fulfilled, yet I still have these desires. And these desires will be, when I am dead, past desires that were not conditional on their own persistence. These—the unconditional desires of the dead—do not embarrass some Desire-Fulfilment Theorists. They accept the claim that, in causing such desires not to be fulfilled, we act against the interests of the dead.

If they assume the Success Theory, they will not claim this about all such desires. One of my strongest desires is that Venice never be destroyed. Suppose that when I am dead some flood destroys Venice. On the Success Theory, this would not be against my interests, or imply that I had a worse life. But the Success Theory counts some events as bad for someone who is dead. Suppose that I work for fifty years trying to ensure that Venice will be saved. On the Success Theory, it will then be worse for me if, when I am dead, Venice is destroyed. This will make it true that my life's work was in vain. It will make my life a failure, in one of the ways that concerned me most. When Venice is destroyed, we should claim that my life went less well than we previously believed.

Should we accept this last claim? It seems defensible, but so does its denial. If we deny this claim, we seem to be appealing to the Hedonistic Theory. We seem to be assuming that it cannot be bad for me that my life's work was in vain, if I never know this. It is hard to see why we should believe this, unless we assume that an event cannot be bad for me if it makes no difference to the experienced quality of my life.

Though they are morally interesting, the desires of the dead are not relevant to this discussion. I am considering those Self-interest Theorists who assume some version of the Desire-Fulfilment Theory. According to these people, what each of us has most reason to do is what will best fulfil, or enable him to fulfil, all of his desires throughout his whole life. I cannot ask if, when someone is dead, he should try to fulfil his past desires. I must ask my question about the past desires of a living person. These must be desires which have not persisted, but were not conditional on their own persistence.

We can vary the same example. Suppose that, for fifty years, I not only work to try to save Venice, but also make regular payments to the Venice Preservation Fund. Throughout these fifty years my two strongest desires are that Venice be saved, and that I be one of its saviours. These desires are not conditional on their own persistence. I want Venice to be saved, and myself to be one of its saviours, even if I later cease to have these desires.

Suppose next that I do cease to have these desires. Because my tastes in architecture change, I cease to care about the city's fate. Have I still a reason to contribute to the Venice Fund? Have I such a reason on the version of S that appeals to Desire-Fulfilment? I have a reason to stop contributing, since with the money saved I could fulfil some of my present or future desires. Do I have a contrary reason, to go on contributing? If I make further payments, this may help to fulfil two of my past desires. Though I no longer have these desires, they were my strongest desires for fifty years.

The wider question is this. On the Desire-Fulfilment Theory, should I give equal weight to *all* of my desires, past, present, and future? Should I give equal weight to all of these desires when deciding what would be best for me? (I mean 'equal weight, if other things are equal'. I should give less weight to one of two desires if it is weaker, or if I regret having this desire, or if certain other claims are true. But should I give less weight to some of my desires because they are not my *present* desires?)

Suppose that an S-Theorist answers No. And suppose that he also claims that, at least in the case of very strong desires, their fulfilment counts for more if they last longer. If I ceased to contribute, this would enable me to fulfil some of my present and future desires. But I shall live for only a few more years. It may thus be true that, if we count both strength and duration, my present and future desires would together count for less than what were my two strongest desires for fifty years. If all of my desires throughout my life should be given equal weight, the S-Theorist may have to conclude that it would be worse for me if I now ceased to contribute. He must then claim that it would be irrational for me to do so. It would be irrational to cease to contribute even though I do not now have, and shall never later have, *any* desire to contribute.

This conclusion may embarrass the Self-interest Theorist. He may be tempted to concede that a rational agent can ignore his past desires. But, if the ground for this claim is that these desires are past, this may be a damaging concession. The S-Theorist must then drop the claim that it cannot be rationally significant *when* some desire is had. But he must still claim that a rational agent should give equal weight to his present and his future desires. And if this claim cannot be supported by an appeal to temporal neutrality, it may be harder to defend.

60. DESIRES THAT DEPEND ON VALUE JUDGEMENTS OR IDEALS

If the S-Theorist wants to appeal to temporal neutrality, he must give some other reason why we can ignore our past desires. He might appeal to one of the ways in which we can lose some desire. We can change our mind. In one sense, any change in our desires involves a change of mind. What is meant here is a change in some value judgement, or ideal: a change of view about what is worth desiring.

I distinguished between what I have most reason to do, and what, given my beliefs, it would be rational for me to do. If my wine has been poisoned, drinking this wine is not what I have most reason to do. But, if I have no reason to believe that it has been poisoned, I would not be acting irrationally if I drink this wine. My main question is about what we have most reason to do. But what follows is about what, given someone's beliefs, it would be rational for him to do. Some call this the question what is *subjectively* rational.

The S-Theorist can say: 'Anyone can rationally ignore the desires that he lost because he changed his mind. And you must have changed your mind when you ceased to want Venice to be saved. In contrast, when someone dies, his desires become past without a change of mind. This is why, when we consider someone's interests, we should not ignore the desires that he had when dying.'

This cannot be a complete reply, since it covers only those desires that depend on value-judgements or ideals. We have many simpler desires, whose loss does not involve a change of mind.

When applied to cases where we do change our mind, is this a good reply? In a minority of cases, discussed later, we regard our change of mind as a corruption. In all other cases it is plausible to claim that, when someone loses a desire because he has changed his mind, he can rationally ignore this desire. This is because this desire depended on a value-judgement or ideal that he now rejects.

Though this claim is plausible, it is *not* a good reply in a defence of S. A similar claim applies to those desires that will *later* be produced by a change of mind. Suppose that I predict that I shall later have desires that will depend on value-judgements or ideals that I now reject. Should I give to these future desires the same weight that I give to my present desires? The S-Theorist must answer Yes.

Nagel describes a relevant example:

Suppose [that someone] now believes that in twenty years he will value security, status, wealth, and tranquillity, whereas he now values sex, spontaneity, frequent risks, and strong emotions. A decisive response to this situation could take either of two forms. The individual may be strongly enough convinced of the worthlessness of his inevitable future values simply to refuse them any claim on his present concern . . . . . On the other hand, he may treat both his present and future values like preferences, regarding each as a source of reasons under a higher principle: 'Live in the life-style of your choice.' That would demand of him a certain prudence about keeping open the paths to eventual respectability.[18]

As Nagel writes, S requires this young man to treat his values and ideals as if they were mere preferences. Only so could it be rational for him to give equal weight to his predicted future values. S claims that he must not act in ways that he will predictably regret. Thus he must not support political movements, or sign petitions, if this might seriously embarrass or restrict the opportunities of his more conservative middle-aged self. More exactly, he may act in these ways, if an impartial calculation comes out right. In this calculation he may discount for the lesser probability that he will later have different values or ideals. But he must not discount such predicted values or ideals merely because he now believes them to be worthless or contemptible.

If we believe that our values or ideals are *not* mere preferences, and can be either more or less justified, we cannot accept this last claim. We cannot wholly accept S. We must treat our values or ideals as P claims that we should. We must give a special status to what we *now* believe to be better justified.

This point is even clearer if we take desires which, unlike the ones in Nagel's example, rest on moral beliefs. It is clearer still if we assume that these beliefs can be, not just more or less defensible, but straightforwardly true. The point is then a familiar one about all beliefs. We cannot honestly say, 'Q is true, but I do not now believe Q'. We must now believe to be true what we now believe to be true. But this claim about our present beliefs does not cover our past or future beliefs. We can honestly say, 'Q is true, but I used not to believe Q, and I may in the future cease to believe Q'.

The corresponding point about evaluative desires needs to be stated carefully. Nagel writes: 'The individual may be strongly enough convinced of the worthlessness of his inevitable future values to refuse them any claim on his present concern. He would then regard his present values as valid for the future also, and no prudential reasons would derive from his expected future views.' Nagel adds that, if this is how the individual responds, 'his position would be formulable in terms of timeless reasons'. His reasons would be stated in a *timeless* form because they would appeal to values which he believes to be timelessly valid. But it would nonetheless be true that, in another sense, his reasons would be both *time-relative* and *agent-relative*. The person in question is trying to act on the values that *are* timelessly valid. But the best that he can do is to act on the values that *he now believes* to be valid. This is what he is told to do by the Present-aim Theory.

On the Self-interest Theory, this young man must give the same weight to his present and his predicted future values and ideals. This would be giving the same weight to what he now believes to be justified and what he now believes to be worthless or contemptible. This is clearly irrational. It may even be logically impossible.

We have reached a general conclusion. According to S, I should give equal weight to all of my present and future desires. This claim applies even to those future desires that will depend on a change in my value-judgements or ideals. When it is applied to these desires, this claim is indefensible. In the case of reasons for acting that are based on value-judgements, or ideals, a rational agent must give priority to the values or ideals that he now accepts. *In the case of these reasons, the correct theory is not S but P.*

There are further grounds for this conclusion. Suppose that I believe that, with increasing knowledge and experience, I shall grow wiser. On this assumption, I should give to my *future* evaluative desires *more* weight than I give to my present evaluative desires, since my future desires will be better justified. This claim may seem to conflict with P. But this is not so. If I both assume that I am always growing wiser, and can now predict some particular future change of mind, I have in effect already changed my mind. If I now believe that some later belief will be better justified, I should have this belief now. So the assumption that I am growing wiser provides no objection to P. Even on this assumption, I can still give a special status to what I now believe to be justified.

The contrary assumption is that, as time passes, I shall become less wise, and that the change in my ideals will be a corruption. The loss of ideals is commonplace; and judgement often goes. (In successive editions of their *Selected Poems*, many poets make worse and worse selections.) On this assumption, I should give greater weight to what I used to value or believe. But in the same way, if I accept this assumption, I would still believe what I used to believe, even if I care less.

Of these contrary assumptions, neither seems in a general way more likely to be justified. Since the assumptions conflict, we may suggest, as a compromise, the temporal neutrality that the Self-interest Theory requires.

And there is a sceptical argument which may seem to favour such neutrality. I may be struck by the presumptuousness of my present certainty. Why should I assume that I am more likely to be right *now*?

Though it supports a move towards temporal neutrality, this argument cannot help the Self-interest Theorist. Like other arguments, it leads us beyond his theory. Why should I assume that *I* am more likely to be right? The sceptical argument challenges my confidence both in acting on the values or ideals that I *now* accept, and in acting on the values or ideals that *I* accept. The argument supports giving equal weight to all of the competing values or ideals of all the people whom I believe to be as likely to be right as me.

If we assume that our values or ideals may be worse or better justified, it is a puzzling question how we should react to this sceptical argument. Is it not both arrogant and irrational to assume that the best justified values or ideals are *mine*? I can be pulled in both directions here. This assumption may indeed seem arrogant, or irrational. But it may be absurd to claim that I must not value more what I value more. This is like the claim that I must not believe to be true what I believe to be true. And this claim may undermine my belief in any of these values.[19]

There are arguments in both directions. But neither argument supports S. Once again, S occupies an indefensible mid-way position. If the sceptical argument succeeds, Neutrality wins. Like Hare's 'liberal', I should give equal weight to the values and ideals of every well-informed and rational person.[20] Suppose that this argument fails. If I should give more weight to *my* values and ideals, I should also give more weight *now* to what I value or believe *now*. The argument for the former claim, when carried through, justifies the latter.

The conflict between these arguments is one example of what Nagel calls the conflict between the *subjective* and the *objective*.[21] The claims of objectivity are, here, the claims of *intersubjectivity*. They carry me beyond the boundaries of my own life, and tell me to give weight to the values or ideals of others. And the claims of subjectivity are the claims of what I *now* believe. They are the claims of my present point of view. When we are concerned with values or ideals, we cannot defensibly claim that the significant unit is one's whole life. We cannot claim that I should now give equal weight to all and only the values or ideals that, at any time, I either did or do or shall have. Once again, we cannot both require temporal neutrality and reject the requirement of interpersonal neutrality. *Both* of the arguments just described count against the Self-interest Theory.

61. MERE PAST DESIRES

These claims apply only to desires whose loss involves a change of mind. There are countless desires of which this is not true. This is so even if, as some claim, all desires involve an evaluation. There is a vast range of possible and worthy objects of concern. Given the limits of our minds and lives, each of us can be strongly concerned about only a few of these objects. And our concern may shift from one of these objects to another, without our having to believe that what we are now concerned about is more worthy of concern. This is clear in the case where, at the end of my train journey, I have a strong desire that the stranger succeed. I shall later lose this desire, but this will *not* be because I decide that it matters less whether this stranger succeeds.

Here is another case. When I was young what I most wanted was to be a poet. This desire was not conditional on its own persistence. I did not want to be a poet only if this would later still be what I wanted. Now that I am older, I have lost this desire. I have changed my mind in the more restricted sense that I have changed my intentions. But I have not decided that poetry is in any way less important or worthwhile. Does my past desire give me a reason to try to write poems now, though I now have no desire to do so?

Since my loss of this desire involved no change in my value judgements, the Self-interest Theorist has only the following alternatives. He could keep the claim that a rational agent should be temporally neutral: that he should try to do what will best fulfil all of his desires throughout his whole life. He must then accept that, on his theory, a rational agent ought to give weight to those of his past desires whose loss involved no change in his value judgements. The only exceptions are those past desires that were conditional on their own persistence. He must therefore claim that I have a strong reason to try to write poems now, because this was what I most wanted for so many years. I have a strong reason to try to write poems, though I no longer have even the slightest desire to do so. Most of us would find this claim hard to believe.

If the Self-interest Theorist agrees, he must reject the requirement of temporal neutrality. He must claim that it is not irrational to give no weight to one's past desires. But once he has abandoned temporal neutrality, or the claim that it cannot be rationally significant *when* we have some desire, the rest of his theory is harder to defend. He must still insist on temporal neutrality as between our present and all of our future desires. He must insist that I should give equal weight to anything that I *shall* predictably want, even if I do not want this now. This is harder to defend if the desires that I *did* have can be given no weight. If it can have rational significance that desires are past, why can it not have rational significance that they are not present? Why should the present be treated as if it was just part of the future? If I can give *no* weight to what I did desire, *because* I do not desire it now, why must I give *equal* weight to what I shall desire, when I do not desire it now?

In the last three sections I have discussed those S-Theorists who assume some version of the Desire-Fulfilment Theory about self-interest. I have defended two conclusions. Some of our desires rest on value judgements, or ideals, or moral beliefs. In the case of these desires, we must accept P rather than S. In the case of our other desires, an S-Theorist has two alternatives. He might insist that we should try to fulfil our unconditional past desires: the unconditional desires that we once had but no longer have. This is hard to believe. The S-Theorist's other alternative is to abandon the claim that it cannot make a difference *when* some desire is had. If he abandons this claim, the S-Theorist needs a new explanation of why we should give the same weight to our present and our future desires. This new explanation may be hard to find.

If the S-Theorist abandons the appeal to temporal neutrality, he must abandon what I called his Second Reply. On his new view, I *did* have reasons to try to fulfil my past desires; but, because I no longer have these desires, I have no reason to try to fulfil them now. If this is so, he must drop his claim that the force of any reason extends over time.

My other conclusion also undermines this claim. I have reasons for acting that are provided by my present values, or ideals, or moral beliefs. If I shall later change my mind, I shall have contrary reasons for acting. In the case of these reasons, we must accept P rather than S. The force of *these* reasons does not extend over time.

62. IS IT IRRATIONAL TO CARE LESS ABOUT ONE'S FURTHER FUTURE?

The S-Theorist cannot claim that any reason's force extends over time. He must therefore appeal to his other argument. He must claim that the bias in one's own favour is supremely rational. I shall now compare this bias with another common pattern of concern: caring less about one's further future. Since this is the favourite target of S-Theorists, I shall be challenging their theory where they believe it to be most plausible.

I shall also turn from what is distinctive to the Desire-Fulfilment Theory to what is common to all plausible theories about self-interest. According to all these theories, the Hedonistic Theory is at least part of the truth. Part of what makes our lives go better is enjoyment, happiness, and the avoidance of pain and suffering. These will be what matters in the cases that I shall discuss. I choose these cases partly because they are simple, and partly because they are the cases where the Self-interest Theory seems to many most compelling.

Bentham claimed that, in deciding the value of any future pleasure, we should consider how *soon* we shall enjoy it.[22] C. I. Lewis suggests that this may have been a loose reminder that the 'nearer pleasures are in general the more certain'.[23] But the claim would then be redundant, for Bentham tells us directly to consider the likelihood of future pleasures. If we take his claim strictly, it tells us to prefer nearer pleasures just because they are nearer. It commits Bentham to the view that, 'although we should be rationally concerned about the future, we should be less concerned about it according as it is more remote—and this quite independently of any doubt which attaches to the more remote'. Lewis calls this 'the principle of fractional prudence'. As he admits, 'it expresses an attitude which humans do tend to take'. But he regards it as so clearly irrational as to be not worth discussing.

I call this attitude the bias towards the near. Hume describes one of the ways in which this bias is revealed: 'In reflecting upon any action which I am to perform a twelvemonth hence, I always resolve to prefer the greater good, whether at that time it will be contiguous or remote . . . . But on a nearer approach . . . a new inclination to the present good springs up, and makes it difficult for me to adhere inflexibly to my first purpose and resolution.'[24]

Hume's words suggest that this bias applies only to the immediate future. But a more accurate description is this. We have a *discount rate* with respect to time, and we discount the *nearer* future at a *greater* rate. This is why we do not 'adhere' to our 'resolutions'. Here are two examples. I decide that when, in five minutes, I remove the plaster from my leg, I shall wrench it off at once, now preferring the prospect of a moment's agony to the long discomfort of easing the plaster off hair by hair. But when the moment comes I reverse my decision. Similarly, I decide that when in five years' time I start my career, I shall spend its first half in some post which is tedious but likely, in the second half, to take me to the top. But when the time comes I again reverse my decision. In both these cases, viewed from a distance, something bad seems worth undergoing for the sake of the good that follows. But, when both are closer, the scale tips the other way.

Another case is shown below.

The height of each curve shows how much I care at any time about one of two possible future rewards. I care less about the further future; and the amount by which I care less is greater in the nearer future. This is shown by the fact that these curves are steepest just before I get these rewards. It may help to restate these claims. If one of two similar events will occur a month later, I now care about it less. My concern will be some proportion of my concern about the other event one month earlier. When these two events are *further* in the future, there will be *less* proportionate difference in my present concern about them. And the proportionate difference will be *greatest* when the earlier event is in the immediate future.

These claims explain why, in my diagram, the two curves cross. When they cross, my preference changes. Judging from March, I prefer the greater reward in June to the lesser reward in May. Judging from the end of April, I prefer the lesser reward in May.[25]

Consider next someone with a different kind of discount rate: one that is *exponential*. Such a person discounts the future at a constant rate of *n* per cent per month. There will always be the *same* proportionate difference in how much this person cares about two future events. His preferences will therefore not change in the way described above. Because this is so, he may mistakenly believe that he has *no* discount rate.[26]

The bias towards the near is often shown in simpler ways. When planning the future, we often bring pleasures into the nearer future, and postpone pains. But this bias is often concealed by another attitude to time. This is the *bias towards the future*. This attitude does not apply to events that give us either pride or shame: events that either gild or stain our picture of our lives. Like the bias towards the near, the bias towards the future applies most clearly to events that are in themselves pleasant or painful. The thought of such events affects us more when they are in the future rather than the past. Looking forward to a pleasure is, in general, more pleasant than looking back upon it. And in the case of pains the difference is even greater. Compare the states of mind of an English schoolboy before and after a beating.

We often act in ways which may seem to show that we are *not* biased towards the near: we bring *pains* into the nearer future, and postpone pleasures. The bias towards the future provides the explanation. We want to get the pains behind us and to keep the pleasures before us. Since the second bias counteracts the first, our tendency to act in these two ways cannot show that we have no bias towards the near. Our bias towards the near may be always outweighed by our bias towards the future. I remember deciding, after blowing out the candles on my tenth birthday cake, that in future I would always eat the best bit (the marzipan) last rather than first.

Here is another example. Suppose that I must choose when to have some painful course of treatment. If I wait for a year, until the hospital has new equipment, the treatment will be only half as painful. And suppose my discount rate drops to a half within a year. If I postpone the treatment for a year, I shall now care about it only a quarter as much. It will be in itself half as painful, and I now discount it by a half. But if I postpone the treatment I shall have a whole year's painful anticipation. The prospect of this, even when discounted, may seem worse to me now than the prospect of immediate treatment. If this is so, despite my bias towards the near, I shall choose to have the treatment now, when it will be twice as painful.

There are some people who do not care more about what is near. Some even care more about what is remote. The propensity to save, or to postpone gratification, can be compulsive. But we need not here decide how many people have the bias towards the near.

Another question is more important. It is often claimed that this bias is always caused by some failure of imagination, or some false belief. It is claimed, for example, that when we imagine pains in the further future, we imagine them less vividly, or believe confusedly that they will somehow be less real, or less painful. Since Plato made this claim[27], it has very often been repeated. Thus Pigou claimed that we have 'a defect in the telescopic faculty'.[28] And this claim is embedded in our language. Someone who cares less about his further future is *imprudent*, or *improvident*—words which mean in Latin that he does not see into the future. And some economists call this attitude *myopia*.

Plato's claim is often true. In the case of many people, it provides a partial explanation of their bias towards the near. It would be important if this claim was always true, and provided the whole explanation. If this was so, this bias would never survive the process of *ideal deliberation*. This would reduce the amount of conflict between S and some versions of P. But, as I argue in Section 73 and Appendix C, S and P would still not coincide.

Though this is a factual matter, I am fairly sure that Plato's claim is often false. One test would be this. In an experiment, someone must decide whether to endure some pain for the sake of some pleasure. This person knows that, when he has made his decision, he will take a pill that will cause him to forget this decision. This makes irrelevant the pleasures or pains of anticipation. This person also knows that we shall not tell him about the *timing* of this pain and this pleasure until just before he makes his decision. We describe carefully what the two experiences would involve. So that he can make a fully informed decision, this person imagines as vividly as he can what it would be like to endure this pain and enjoy this pleasure. We then tell him that the pain would be immediate and the pleasure would be postponed for a year. Would the pleasure now seem to him less vivid? At least in my own case, I am sure that it would not. Suppose that, if the pain would be immediate and the pleasure postponed for a year, this person has a mild preference for having neither. He decides that this pleasure is not quite great enough to make this pain worth enduring. We then tell him that we were misinformed: the pleasure would be immediate, and the pain postponed for a year. I think it likely that this person's preference would now change. He might now decide that it *is* worth enduring this pain for the sake of having this pleasure. Since this person imagined these two experiences when he did not know about their timing, such a change in his preference would not be produced by the alleged fact that later experiences always seem, in imagination, less vivid. We would have good reason to believe that this person is biased towards the near, and in a way that survives ideal deliberation.

The bias towards the near is, I believe, common. But, to avoid argument, we can discuss an imaginary person. This person cares more about his nearer future, simply because it is nearer; and he does this even when he knows the facts, and is thinking clearly. I shall call this person *Proximus*. It will not affect the argument whether, as I believe, there are many actual people who are like this.

It is often unclear what would be best for someone, or be most in his interests, both because the facts are doubtful, and because of the disagreement betweeen the rival theories about self-interest. But on all plausible theories one point is agreed. When we are deciding what is in someone's interests, we should discount for uncertainty, but not for mere remoteness. We should not give less weight to this person's further future, or give greater weight to his present desires.

We may believe that we should sometimes give greater weight to someone else's present desires. We may think it wrong to override this person's present desires, forcing him to do what will be best for him. But we would think this wrong because it infringes this person's autonomy. This is consistent with my claim that, on all plausible theories about self-interest, in deciding what would be best for someone, we should *not* give greater weight to this person's present desires. We should give equal weight to all the parts of this person's life.

On the Self-interest Theory, someone acts irrationally when he does what he knows will be worse for him. My imagined man often acts in this way. Because he is biased towards the near, Proximus often deliberately postpones pains, at the foreseen cost of making them worse. In these cases he is doing what he knows will be worse for him.

Let us now compare his attitude with that of a self-interested man. Is the bias towards the near less rational than the bias in one's own favour? It is essential to the defence of S that we answer Yes.

Proximus knows the facts and is thinking clearly. We should add one more assumption. Those who have some bias may wish to be without it. This is quite common in the case of the bias towards the near. After describing how this bias makes him act against his interests, Hume wrote, 'this natural infirmity I may very much regret'.[30] We should assume that Proximus has no such regrets. Only this assumption makes our comparison fair, for those who are self-interested are typically assumed not to regret their bias in their own favour. Moreover, in rejecting S, Proximus will appeal to P; and the Critical version of P may discount desires that the agent wishes that he did not have. It may claim that we should give to such desires either less or even no weight. We should therefore assume that Proximus does not regret his bias towards the near.

It may be objected that, when he suffers from the effects of this bias, he must regret having it. But, as I explain in Section 71, Proximus never regrets either that he has this bias now, or that he had this bias in the nearer past. He at most regrets that he had it in the further past. He acts as he does because of his present bias; and he never regrets *this* bias.

63. A SUICIDAL ARGUMENT

How should a Self-interest Theorist criticize Proximus? Given the choice of a mild pain soon, or a much worse pain later, Proximus often deliberately chooses the worse pain. And he often prefers a small pleasure soon to a much greater pleasure later. He must therefore claim, with Hume, "'Tis as little contrary to reason to prefer even my own acknowledged lesser good to my greater".[31] This—the deliberate choice of what he admits will be worse for himself—may seem the clearest possible case of irrationality. An S-Theorist might say, 'The first rule of rationality is to reject what you know to be worse'.

Proximus could answer: 'If the only difference between two pains is that one would be worse, I accept your rule. But, in the cases we are discussing, there is another difference. When I choose between two pains, I consider both how painful they would be, and how soon I should have to undergo them. I am not simply choosing what I know to be worse. I choose the worse of two pains only when the amount by which it is worse is, for me now, outweighed by the amount by which it is further in the future.'

The S-Theorist must reply that it is irrational to take nearness into account. He might claim, quoting Rawls, 'mere temporal position, or distance from the present, is not a reason for favouring one moment over another'.[32] More generally, the S-Theorist might revive the requirement of temporal neutrality.

I argued earlier that, if the S-Theorist assumes the Desire-Fulfilment Theory about self-interest, he should abandon the requirement of temporal neutrality. On this theory about self-interest, this requirement implies, implausibly, that we should now try to fulfil some of the desires that we once had, even though we do not now and shall never later have these desires. In what follows, I shall assume that the S-Theorist rejects the Desire-Fulfilment Theory, accepting either the Hedonistic Theory, or some version of the Objective List Theory. On this assumption, if the S-Theorist requires temporal neutrality, he need not claim that we should try to fulfil such past desires. His claim can be that, when we are considering pleasures and pains, or happiness and suffering, mere differences in timing cannot have rational significance.

How should the S-Theorist support this claim? Why should time not be taken into account? He might say:

A mere difference in *when* something happens is not a difference in its quality. The fact that a pain is further in the future will not make it, when it comes, any the less painful.

This is an *excellent* argument. It is by far the best objection to the bias towards the near. But the S-Theorist cannot use this argument. It is a two-edged sword. The same argument can be used against the Self-interest Theory. Just as Proximus takes into account *when* a pain is felt, the S-Theorist takes into account *who* will feel it. And a mere difference in who feels a pain is not a difference in its quality. The fact that a pain is someone else's does not make it any the less painful.

The S-Theorist takes into account (1) how bad pains would be, and (2) who would feel them. He therefore sometimes chooses the worse of two pains. He sometimes chooses a worse pain for someone else rather than a lesser pain for himself. (It may seem that he would always make this choice. But this assumes that the S-Theorist must be purely selfish. As I claimed, this is a mistake. Someone who accepts S may love certain other people. It may therefore be worse for him if he escapes some lesser pain at the cost of imposing a worse pain on someone whom he loves.)

Proximus takes into account (1) how bad pains would be (2) who will feel them, and (3) when they will be felt. He can say, to the S-Theorist, 'If you take into account who will feel some pain, why can't I take into account when some pain is felt?' There may be answers to this question. There may be arguments to show that differences in personal identity have a significance that differences in timing lack. The point that I have made so far is only this. In explaining why time cannot have rational significance, the S-Theorist cannot use the obvious and best argument. He cannot appeal to the fact that a pain is no less painful because it is less near. A pain is no less painful because it is someone else's.

The S-Theorist might say:

> You misunderstand my argument. That a pain is further in your future cannot make it any the less painful *to you*. But that a pain is someone else's does make it less painful *to you*. If it is someone else's pain, it will not hurt you at all.

The second of these sentences makes a pair of claims. That a pain is further in my future does not make it either (*a*) any the less painful, or (*b*) any the less mine. (*a*) is true, but irrelevant, since the objection to which it appeals applies equally to the Self-interest Theory. That a pain is someone else's does not make it any the less painful. (*b*) is also true. The fact that a pain is further in my future does not make it any the less *my* pain. But this truth is not an argument. What the S-Theorist needs to claim, in attacking Proximus, is that a difference in *who* feels a pain has great rational significance, while there cannot be rational significance in *when* a pain is felt. All that (*b*) points out is that these are *different* differences. Time is not the same as personal identity.

By itself, this cannot show that time is less significant.

I shall now summarize these claims. The S-Theorist must criticize Proximus. According to S, we should take into account differences both in painfulness and in the identity of the sufferers. Proximus also takes into account differences in timing. The S-Theorist has not shown that differences in personal identity have a rational significance that differences in timing lack. There may be arguments for this claim. But I have not yet given such an argument. The S-Theorist cannot use the best argument. He cannot dismiss differences in timing with the claim that they are not differences in painfulness. Nor are differences in personal identity. Nor can the S-Theorist dismiss differences in timing on the ground that they are not differences in personal identity. That these are *different* differences cannot show that one has a rational significance that the other lacks.

64. PAST OR FUTURE SUFFERING

The S-Theorist might claim that there is no need for argument. We cannot argue everything; some things have to be assumed. And he might say this about his present claim. He might say that, when we compare the questions 'To whom does it happen?' and 'When does it happen?', we see clearly that only the first question has rational significance. We see clearly that it is not irrational to care less about some pain if it will be felt by someone else, but that it *is* irrational to care less merely because of a difference in *when* some pain is felt by oneself.

Is this so? The bias towards the near is not our only bias with respect to time. We are also biased towards the future. Is this attitude irrational? Consider *My Past or Future Operations*.

Case One. I am in some hospital, to have some kind of surgery. Since this is completely safe, and always successful, I have no fears about the effects. The surgery may be brief, or it may instead take a long time. Because I have to co-operate with the surgeon, I cannot have anaesthetics. I have had this surgery once before, and I can remember how painful it is. Under a new policy, because the operation is so painful, patients are now afterwards made to forget it. Some drug removes their memories of the last few hours.

I have just woken up. I cannot remember going to sleep. I ask my nurse if it has been decided when my operation is to be, and how long it must take. She says that she knows the facts about both me and another patient, but that she cannot remember which facts apply to whom. She can tell me only that the following is true. I may be the patient who had his operation yesterday. In that case, my operation was the longest ever performed, lasting ten hours. I may instead be the patient who is to have a short operation later today. It is either true that I did suffer for ten hours, or true that I shall suffer for one hour.

I ask the nurse to find out which is true. While she is away, it is clear to me which I prefer to be true. If I learn that the first is true, I shall be greatly relieved.

My bias towards the future makes me relieved here that my pain is in the past. My bias towards the near might, in the same way, make me relieved that some pain has been postponed. In either case, I might prefer some different timing for my ordeal even if, with the different timing, the ordeal would be much worse. Compared with an hour of pain later today, I might, like Proximus, prefer ten hours of pain next year. Or, as in this example, I might prefer ten hours of pain yesterday.

Is this second preference irrational? Ought I instead to hope that I am the second patient, whose pain is still to come? Before I discuss this question, I should explain one feature of the case: the induced amnesia.

Some writers claim that, if some part of my future will not be linked by memory to the rest of my life, I can rationally ignore what will happen to me during this period. For these writers, a double dose of amnesia is as good as an anaesthetic. If I shall have no memories while I am suffering, and I shall later have no memories of my suffering, I need not—they claim—be concerned about this future suffering. This is a controversial claim. But even if it is justified it does not apply to my example. This does not involve a *double* dose of amnesia. During my painful operation I shall have all my memories. It is true that I shall afterwards be made to forget the operation. But this does not remove my reason to be concerned about my future suffering. If we denied this, we would have to claim that someone should not be concerned when, already knowing that he is about to die, he learns the extra fact that he will die painfully. He will not later remember *these* pains.

If we imagine ourselves in the place of the patient who will suffer for an hour later today, most of us would be concerned. We would be concerned even though we know that we shall not later remember this hour of pain. And I can now explain why my case involves induced amnesia. This gives us the right comparison. If I have learnt that I am the second patient, I am in the following state of mind. I believe that I shall have an hour's pain later today, and I can imagine roughly how awful the pain is going to be. This is enough to make me concerned. If I have learnt instead that I am the first patient, I am in the strictly comparable state of mind. I believe that I did have ten hours' pain yesterday, and I can imagine roughly how awful the pain must have been. My state of mind differs only in the two respects that I am discussing. My belief has a different tense, being about the past rather than the future. And it is a belief about ten hours of pain rather than about a single hour. It would confuse the comparison if I did not just believe that I suffered yesterday, but could also remember the suffering. When I believe that I shall suffer later today, I have nothing comparable to memories of this future suffering. And memories of pain are quite various; some are in themselves painful, others are not. It therefore rids the example of an irrelevant and complicating feature if I would have about my past pain only what I would have about my future pain: a belief, with an ability to imagine the pain's awfulness.

The induced amnesia purifies the case. But it may still arouse suspicion. I therefore add

Case Two. When I wake up, I do remember a long period of suffering yesterday. But I cannot remember how long the period was. I ask my nurse whether my operation is completed, or whether further surgery needs to be done. As before, she knows the facts about two patients, but she cannot remember which I am. If I am the first patient, I had five hours of pain yesterday, and my operation is over. If I am the second patient, I had two hours of pain yesterday, and I shall have another hour of pain later today.[33]

In Case Two there is no amnesia; but this makes no difference. Either I suffered for five hours and have no more pain to come, or I suffered for two hours and have another hour of pain to come. I would again prefer the first to be true. I would prefer my life to contain more hours of pain, if that means that none of this pain is still to come.

If we imagine ourselves in my place in these two cases, most of us would have my preference. If we did not know whether we have suffered for several hours, or shall later suffer for one hour, most of us would strongly prefer the first to be true. If we could make it true, we would undoubtedly do so. If we are religious we might pray that it be true. On some accounts, this is the one conceivable way of affecting the past. God may have made some past event happen only because, at the time, He had foreknowledge of our later backward-looking prayer, and He chose to grant this prayer. Even if we do not believe that we could in this way, through God's grace, cause our pain to be in the past, we would strongly prefer it to be in the past, even at the cost of its lasting ten times as long.

Is this preference irrational? Most of us would answer No. If he accepts this answer, the S-Theorist must abandon his claim that the question 'When?' has no rational significance. He cannot claim that a mere difference in the timing of a pain, or in its relation to the present moment, 'is not in itself a rational ground for having more or less regard for it'.[34] Whether a pain is in the past or future is a mere difference in its relation to the present moment. And, if it is not irrational to care more about pains that are in the future, why is it irrational to care more about pains that are in the nearer future? If the S-Theorist admits as defensible one departure from temporal neutrality, how can he criticize the other?

65. THE DIRECTION OF CAUSATION

The S-Theorist might say: 'Since we cannot affect the past, this is a good ground for being less concerned about it. There is no such justification of the bias towards the near.'

This can be answered. We can first point out that we are still biased towards the future even when, like the past, it cannot be affected. Suppose that we are in prison, and will be tortured later today. In such cases, when we believe that our future suffering is inevitable, our attitude towards it does not fall into line with our attitude towards past suffering. We would not think, 'Since the torture is inevitable, that is equivalent to its being already in the past'. We are greatly relieved when such inevitable pains are in the past. In such cases the bias towards the future cannot be justified by an appeal to the direction of causation. Our ground for concern about such future pains is not that, unlike past pains, we can affect them. We know that we *cannot* affect them. We are concerned about these future pains simply because they are not yet in the past.

The S-Theorist might reply: 'Such a justification need not hold in every case. When we are discussing a general attitude, we must be content with a general truth. Such attitudes cannot be 'fine-tuned'. Whether events are in the future in *most* cases corresponds to whether or not we can affect them. This is enough to justify the bias towards the future. If we lacked this bias, we would be as much concerned about past pains and pleasures, which we cannot affect. This would distract our attention from future pains and pleasures, which we can affect. Because we would be distracted in this way, we would be less successful in our attempts to get future pleasures and avoid future pains. This would be worse for us.'

We could answer: 'If this is true, there is another similar truth. If we were as much concerned about pains and pleasures in our *further* future, this would distract our attention from pains and pleasures in the nearer future. If we want to reduce our future suffering, we ought to pay more attention to possible pains in the nearer future, since we have less time in which to avoid or reduce these pains. A similar claim applies to future pleasures. Our need to affect the nearer future is more urgent. If your claim justifies the bias towards the future, this claim justifies the bias towards the near.'

We could add: 'We care more about the near future even in the special cases in which we cannot affect it. But these cases correspond to the special cases in which we cannot affect the future. Both these attitudes to time roughly correspond to these facts about causation. Your claims therefore cannot show that only one of these attitudes is defensible.'

The S-Theorist might say: 'You ignore one difference. We can act directly on the bias towards the near. If we are due to have one hour's pain later today, we may be able to postpone this pain, at the cost of making it worse. We may, like Proximus, exchange this pain for ten hours' pain next year. But we cannot exchange this pain for ten hours' pain yesterday. We cannot put future pains into the past, at the cost of making them worse. The important difference is this. Since we can affect both the near and the distant future, our bias towards the near often makes us act against our own interests. This bias is bad for us. In contrast, since we cannot affect the past, our bias towards the future never makes us act against our interests. This second bias is not bad for us. That is why only the second bias is defensible.'

To this there are three replies: (1) This argument has a false premise. The fact that an attitude is bad for us does not show it to be irrational. It can at most show that we should try to change this attitude. If someone whom I love is killed, I should perhaps try, after a time, to reduce my grief. But this does not show that I have no reason to grieve. Grief is not irrational simply because it brings unhappiness. To the claim 'Your sorrow is fruitless', Hume replied, 'Very true, and for that very reason I am sorry'.[35]

(2) Even if (1) is denied, this argument fails. It assumes that what matters is whether something is bad for us. This begs the question. The S-Theorist is condemning the bias towards the near. If we have this bias, we care more about our nearer future; and what will be, on the whole, worse for us may be better for us in the nearer future. If our bias is defensible, we can therefore deny the assumption that what matters is whether something will be bad for us. Since this assumption can be denied if our bias is defensible, it cannot help to show that our bias is *not* defensible.

(3) It has not been shown that the bias towards the near *is* bad for us. Because we have a more urgent need to affect the nearer future, the bias towards the near is in some ways good for us. But let us suppose that this bias is, on balance, bad for us. *So is the bias towards the future.* As I shall explain later, it would be better for us if we did not care more about the future. The argument above has another false premise. It is not true that the bias towards the future is not bad for us.

The S-Theorist must condemn the bias towards the near. If his criticism appeals to temporal neutrality, he must also criticize the bias towards the future. By appealing to facts about causation, the S-Theorist tried to avoid this conclusion. But this attempt has failed.

In condemning the bias towards the near, the S-Theorist might say: 'Since our need to affect the near is more urgent, the bias towards the near is quite natural. It is not surprising that Evolution gives this bias to all animals. But, since we are rational, we can rise above, and critically review, what we inherit from Evolution. We can see that this bias cannot be rational. That some pain is in the nearer future cannot be a *reason* to care about it more. A mere difference in timing cannot have rational significance.'[36]

If the S-Theorist makes this claim, he must make a similar claim about the bias towards the future. He might say: 'Since we cannot affect the past, it is natural to care about it less. But this bias cannot be rational. This is clearest when we cannot affect the future. That some inevitable pain is in the future, rather than the past, cannot be a *reason* to care about it more. It is irrational to be relieved when it is in the past.'

In My Past or Future Operations, I would prefer it to be true that I did suffer for several hours yesterday rather than that I shall suffer for one hour later today. This is not a preference on which I could act. But this is irrelevant to the question of whether this preference is irrational. The S-Theorist cannot claim that it is *not* irrational *because* I cannot act upon it. He could say, 'What an absurd preference! You should be grateful that you cannot act upon it.' And this is what he *must* say, if he keeps his claim that our concern for ourselves should be temporally neutral. If he condemns the bias towards the near because it cannot have rational significance *when* some pain is felt, he must condemn the bias towards the future. He must claim that it is irrational to be relieved when some pain is in the past. Most of us would find this hard to believe. If the S-Theorist insists that we should be temporally neutral, most of us would disagree.

66. TEMPORAL NEUTRALITY

The S-Theorist might change his position. He might condemn the bias towards the near, not on the general ground that the question 'When?' cannot have rational significance, but on a more particular ground.

He might switch to the other extreme, and claim that temporal neutrality is inconceivable. He might claim that it is inconceivable that we lack the bias towards the future. If this was true, he could again criticize only one of these two attitudes. It cannot be irrational to have some attitude if it is not conceivable that we lack this attitude. But, unlike the bias towards the future, the bias towards the near is clearly something that we could lack. We could be equally concerned about all the parts of our future. Some people are. The S-Theorist could claim that this is the only rational pattern of concern.

Is it conceivable that we might lack the bias towards the future? Our attitudes to the past could not be just like our attitudes to the future. Some emotions or reactions presuppose beliefs about causation. Since we cannot affect the past, these emotions and reactions could not be backward-looking. Thus we could not form an intention to have done something yesterday, or be firmly resolved to make the best of what lies behind us.

Are there mental states which are essentially forward-looking, in a way which cannot be explained by the direction of causation? This is a large question, to which I need not give a complete answer. It will be enough to consider the most important mental states that are involved in our bias towards the future.

One of these is desire. Some of our language suggests that desires are essentially forward-looking. Compare 'I want to go to Venice next winter' with 'I want to have gone to Venice last winter'. The second claim is obscure.

Our language is here misleading. Consider

> *My Temporally Neutral Desire.* I learn that an old friend is now dying in some distant country. We parted in anger, for which I now blame myself. After learning that my friend is dying, I have a strong desire to ask her to forgive me. Since she cannot be reached by telephone, the best that I can do is to send an express letter, asking to be forgiven, and saying goodbye. A week later, I do not know whether my friend is still alive, or has got my letter. My strongest desire is that she gets my letter before she dies.

If desires are essentially forward-looking, I must be held to be in two states of mind: a conditional desire, and a conditional hope. I must be said to want my friend, if she is alive, to get the letter before she dies, and to hope, if she is dead, that she got the letter before she died. But this description, even if linguistically required, is misleading. To distinguish here two states of mind, the desire and the hope, is to subdivide what is in its nature a single state. My 'hope' is in its nature and its strength just like my 'desire'. What I want is that my friend's getting of this letter precedes her death. Provided that these events occur, in this order, I am indifferent whether they are in the past or the future.

Even if it changes the concept, it is therefore best to say that we can have desires about the past. And it is not clear that this is a change. For example, I may want it to be true that, in my drunkenness last night, I did not disgrace myself. And I may want this to be true for its own sake, not because of its possible effects on my future. Similarly, after reading the letters of Keats or van Gogh, I may want it to be true that they knew how great their achievements were.

In these examples I do not know what the truth is. Suppose that I do know that I disgraced myself last night. Can I want it to be true that I did not? It would be more natural to call this a *wish*. But this distinction also seems unimportant. When I learn that I disgraced myself, my desire that I did not becomes a wish. But the wish may be no weaker than the desire.

It may change the concept of desire if we claim that we can want something to be true that we know is false. We need not decide whether this change in our concept would be an improvement. I am discussing the different question of whether we can have desires about the past. I have claimed that we can, even though some of our language suggests that we cannot. We can express such desires with other parts of our language. We can say, as I have done, that we want it to be true that some event did or did not happen.

It may be objected that desires are essentially tied to possible acts. This is like the claim that 'ought' implies 'can'. On this view, we cannot have desires on which it would be impossible to act. From this general claim we could deduce the special claim that we cannot have desires about the past, since we cannot affect the past.[37]

This general claim is false. There are, of course, close connections between desires and acts. If we strongly want something to be true, we shall try to find out whether we can make it true. And 'the primitive sign of wanting is trying to get'.[38] But the desire here comes first. We do not have to know whether we could make something true before we can want it to be true.

We can admit one way in which desires are tied to acts. If people could not act they could not have desires. We could not have the concept of desire unless we also had the concept of an act. But we can have a *particular* desire without being able to act upon it. We can want something to be true even when we know that neither we nor anyone else could possibly have made it true. The Pythagoreans wanted the square root of two to be a rational number. It is logically impossible that this desire be fulfilled. Since we can have desires that even an omnipotent God could not fulfil, particular desires are not tied to possible acts. This removes this ground for denying that we can have desires about the past.

We can next consider the mental states that are most important in this discussion: looking forward to some future event, and its negative counterpart, painful or distressing anticipation. These two mental states are essentially future-directed. But this may be another superficial truth. Could there be comparable states directed towards the past?

It may be thought that we actually have such backward-looking states. The bias towards the future does not apply to many kinds of event, such as those that give us pride or shame. But though the knowledge of a past achievement may give us pleasure, this is not analogous to looking forward. We are discussing our attitude, not to the *fact* that our lives contain certain kinds of event, but to our *experience* at other times of living through these events. For simplicity, I have been discussing attitudes to experiences that are merely in themselves pleasant or painful. Do we in fact look backward to past pleasures in the way that we look forward to future pleasures?

Once again, there is a complication raised by memories. These can be in themselves pleasant or painful. We may enjoy remembering pleasures, and dislike remembering pains. But neither of these is strictly analogous to the pains and pleasures of anticipation. We therefore need to consider our attitude to past pains and pleasures about which we know, but of which we do not have painful or pleasant memories.

Consider *My Past Ordeals*.

Case One. I am unusually forgetful. I am asked, 'Can you remember what happened to you during May ten years ago?' I find that I can remember nothing about that month. I am then told that, that, at the start of that month, I was found to have some illness which required four weeks of immediate and very painful treatment. Since this treatment was wholly successful, I have no grounds for fear about the future. When I am reminded of this fact, it arouses a faint memory, which is not in itself painful.

I have been reminded, to my surprise, that ten years ago I had a month of agony. All that I have now is a faint memory of this fact, and an ability to imagine how bad my agony must have been. When I am reminded of this past ordeal, would I be upset? Would I have what corresponds to painful anticipation? I would not. I would react to this reminder with *complete indifference*.

If I learnt that, ten years from now, I shall have a month of agony, I would *not* be indifferent. I would be distressed. But I would be in no way distressed if I was reminded that, ten years ago, I had such a month.

Since we are biased towards the near, it may help to consider

Case Two. I wake up, on what I believe to be the 1st of May. It is in fact the 1st of June. I have just had a similar month of very painful but wholly successful treatment. So that I should not have painful memories, I was caused to forget this whole month.

I learn that I have just had a month of agony. Here too, I would not regard this as bad news. More exactly, I would regret the fact that a month of my life had to be wasted in this way. I might be somewhat anxious about the claimed success of this treatment. And I might have some fear that, if the induced amnesia does not last, I shall later have painful memories of this treatment. But I would not be at all distressed about the fact that, during this month, I was in agony. I would regard this recent agony with complete indifference. In contrast, if I learnt that I was about to have such an ordeal, I would be very distressed.

It may be an objection to Case Two that it involves induced amnesia. I therefore add

Case Three. In my actual life, I have often suffered severe pain. I can remember these pains, but these memories are not themselves painful. The worst suffering that I can remember lasted for three days in 1979.

When I remind myself of these three very painful days, I am not distressed at all. In the imaginary Cases One and Two, I believe that I would regard my past ordeals with indifference. In my actual life, I do in fact regard my past suffering with complete indifference.

I believe that, in this respect, most other people are like me. Unless their memories are painful, they regard their past suffering with indifference. I know a few people whose reaction is different. These people claim that, even if they have no painful memories, they find knowledge of their past pains mildly distressing. But I know of no one who has what fully corresponds to the pains of anticipation.

We do not in fact have this attitude to our past pains. And we do not look backward to pleasures in the way that we look forward to them. Could there be such mental states? Could 'looking backward' to some past event be, except for its temporal direction, just like looking forward?

We might say: 'We look forward to some future event when thinking about this event gives us pleasure. Thinking about a past event could give us similar pleasure. And to the pains of anticipation there could be corresponding pains of retrospection.'

It may be objected: 'You understate what is involved in looking forward. It is not merely true that the thought of future pleasures gives us pleasure. We *anticipate* these pleasures. Similarly, we anticipate pains. *Anticipation* cannot have a backward-looking counterpart.'

We might answer: 'We may be unable to imagine what it would be like to have this counterpart. But this does not show that it could not be had. Those who are congenitally blind cannot imagine what it is like to see.'

This reply may not meet this objection. If this is so, our claims can be revised. Even if looking backward could not be *just like* looking forward, it could be equally cheering, or in the case of pains equally distressing. This would involve a change in our attitudes. But this change *is* conceivable. We can clearly describe someone who, in this respect, is unlike us. When such a person is reminded that he once had a month of agony, he is as much distressed as when he learns that he will later have such a month. He is similarly neutral with respect to enjoyable events. When he is told that he will later have some period of great enjoyment, he is pleased to learn this. He greatly looks forward to this period. When he is reminded that he once had just such a period, he is equally pleased. I shall call this imagined man *Timeless*.

This man is very different from us. But his description is coherent. We can therefore reject the suggestion made above. It is conceivable that we might lack the bias towards the future. Even if we could not be wholly temporally neutral, we could have been like Timeless.

67. WHY WE SHOULD NOT BE BIASED TOWARDS THE FUTURE

Our bias towards the future is bad for us. It would be better for us if we were like Timeless. We would lose in certain ways. Thus we should not be relieved when bad things were in the past. But we should also gain. We should not be sad when good things were in the past.

The gains would outweigh the losses. One reason would be this. When we look backward, we could afford to be selective. We ought to remember some of the bad events in our lives, when this would help us to avoid repetitions. But we could allow ourselves to forget most of the bad things that have happened, while preserving by rehearsing all of our memories of the good things. It would be bad for us if we were so selective when we are looking forward. Unless we think of all the bad things that are at all likely to happen, we lose our chance of preventing them. Since we ought not to be selective when looking forward, but could afford to be when looking backward, the latter would be, on the whole, more enjoyable.[39]

There would be other, greater gains. One would be in our attitude to ageing and to death. Let us first consider the argument with which Epicurus claimed that our future non-existence cannot be something to regret. We do not regret our past non-existence. Since this is so, why should we regret our future non-existence? If we regard one with equanimity, should we not extend this attitude to the other?

Some claim that this argument fails because, while we might live longer, we could not have been born earlier. This is not a good objection. When they learnt that the square root of two was not a rational number, the Pythagoreans regretted this. We can regret truths even when it is logically impossible that these truths be false.

Epicurus's argument fails for a different reason: we are biased towards the future. Because we have this bias, the bare knowledge that we once suffered may not now disturb us. But our equanimity does not show that our past suffering was not bad. The same could be true of our past non-existence. Epicurus's argument therefore has force only for those people who both lack the bias towards the future, and do not regret their past non-existence. Since there are no such people, the argument has force for no one.

Though the argument fails, it may provide some consolation. If we are afraid of death, the argument shows that the object of our dread is not *our non-existence*. It is only our *future* non-existence. That we can think serenely of our past non-existence does not show that it is not something to regret. But since we do not in fact view with dread our past non-existence, we may be able to use this fact to reduce our dread, or depression, when we think about our inevitable deaths. If we often think about, and view serenely, the blackness behind us, some of this serenity may be transferred to our view of the blackness before us.

Let us now suppose that we lack the bias towards the future. We are like Timeless. We should then greatly gain in our attitude to ageing and to death. As our life passes, we should have less and less to look forward to, but more and more to look backward to. This effect will be clearer if we imagine another difference. Suppose that our lives began, not with birth and childhood, but as Adam's did. Suppose that, though we are adults, and have adult knowledge and abilities, we have only just started to exist. We lack the bias towards the future. Should we be greatly troubled by the thought that yesterday we did not exist?

This depends on what is wrong with non-existence. Some think it in itself bad. But the more plausible view is that its only fault is what it causes us to lose. Suppose we take this view. We may then think it a ground for regret that our life is finite, bounded at both ends by non-existence. But, if we had just started to exist, we would not think that something bad was just behind us. Our ground for regret would merely be that we had missed much that would have been good. Suppose that I could now be much as I actually am, even though I had been born as one of the privileged few around 1700. I would then greatly regret that I was in fact born in 1942. I would far prefer to have lived through the previous two and a half centuries, having had among my friends Hume, Byron, Chekhov, Nietzsche, and Sidgwick.

In my imagined case, we are not biased towards the future, and we have just started to exist. Though we would regret the fact that we had not existed earlier, we would not be. greatly troubled by the thought that only yesterday we did not exist. We would not regard this fact with the kind of dread or grief with which most actual people would regard the sudden prospect of death tomorrow. We would not have such dread or grief because, though we would have nothing good to look backward to, we would have our whole lives to look forward to.

Now suppose that our lives have nearly passed. We shall die tomorrow. If we were not biased towards the future, our reaction should mirror the one that I have just described. We should not be greatly troubled by the thought that we shall soon cease to exist, for though we now have nothing to look forward to, we have our whole lives to look backward to.

It may be objected: 'You can look backward now. But once you are dead you won't be able to look backward. And you will be dead tomorrow. So you ought to be greatly troubled.' We could answer: 'Why? It is true that after we cease to exist we shall never be able to enjoy looking backward to our lives. We now have nothing at all to look forward to, not even the pleasures of looking backward. But it was equally true that, before we began to exist, we could not enjoy looking forward to our lives. Just after we began to exist, we had nothing at all to look backward to, not even the pleasures of looking forward. But that was then no reason to be greatly troubled, since we could then look forward to our whole lives. Since we can now look backward to our whole lives, why should the parallel fact— that we have nothing to look forward to—give us reason to be greatly troubled?'

This reasoning ignores those emotions which are essentially future-directed. It would not apply to those people for whom the joy in looking forward comes from making plans, or savouring alternatives. But the reasoning seems to be correct when applied to more passive types, those who take life's pleasures as they come. And, since this is partly true of us, this reasoning shows that we would be happier if we lacked the bias towards the future. We would be much less depressed by ageing and the approach of death. If we were like Timeless, being at the end of our lives would be more like being at the beginning. At any point within our lives we could enjoy looking either backward or forward to our whole lives.

I have claimed that, if we lacked the bias towards the future, this would be better for us. This matches the plausible claim that it would be better for us if we lacked the bias towards the near. There is no ground here for criticizing only the latter bias. Both these attitudes to time are, on the whole, bad for us.

Since I believe that this attitude is bad for us, I believe that we ought not to be biased towards the future. This belief does not beg the question about the rationality of this bias. On any plausible moral view, it would be better if we were all happier. This is the sense in which, if we could, we ought not to be biased towards the future. In giving us this bias, Evolution denies us the best attitude to death.

68. TIME'S PASSAGE

Return to my main question. Are these attitudes to time irrational? Most of us believe that the bias towards the future is not irrational. We are inclined to believe that it would be irrational to *lack* this bias. Thus we may be wholly unconvinced by the reasoning I gave in the case just imagined, where we are temporally neutral and shall die tomorrow. We can describe someone who does not much mind the prospect of death tomorrow, because he can now look backward to his whole life. But this attitude, though describable, may seem crazy, or to involve an absurd mistake.

It will help to take a simpler case, not involving non-existence and our attitudes to a whole life. This can be a variant of an earlier example, involving our imagined temporally neutral man. Consider

How Timeless Greets Good News. Timeless is in hospital for a painful operation, that will be followed by induced amnesia. He wakes up, with no particular memories of the previous day. He asks his nurse when and for how long he will have to endure this painful operation. As before, the nurse knows the facts about two patients, but is unsure which he is. In either case, however, his operation needed to be unusually long, lasting a full ten hours. The nurse knows that one of the following is true. Either he did suffer yesterday for ten hours, or he will suffer later today for ten hours.

Timeless is plunged in gloom. He had hoped for a shorter operation.

When the nurse returns, she exclaims 'Good News! You are the one who suffered yesterday'.

Timeless is just as glum. 'Why is that good news?', he asks. 'My ordeal is just as painful, and just as long. And it is just as much a part of my life. Why should it make a difference to me now that my ordeal is in the past?'

The induced amnesia may be an objection to this case. I therefore add

Case Two. Timeless has this operation, and has no amnesia. We visit him on the day before his ordeal, and on the day after. On the day after, Timeless is just as glum. 'Why should I be relieved?', he asks. 'Why is it better that my ordeal is in the past?'

Is Timeless making a mistake? Ought he to be relieved? Most of us would answer Yes. But it is hard to explain why, without begging the question. We might say, 'If the ordeal was in his future, he would still have to undergo it. Since it is in his past, it is over and done with.' This is not a further explanation of why Timeless is irrational. That he 'still' has to undergo the pain merely repeats that it is in his future.

We might appeal here to what is called *time's passage*, or the *objectivity of temporal becoming*. We might say: 'If his pain is in the future, it will get closer and closer until he is actually suffering the pain. But, if his pain is in the past, it will only get further and further away.' Such remarks seem to express a deep truth. But this truth is curiously elusive. What is meant by the phrase 'it will get closer and closer'? Does this not merely mean that, at future moments, the future pain will be closer to what will then be the present moment? But at past moments a past pain was closer to what was then the present moment. Where is the asymmetry?

It is natural, in reply, to use a certain metaphor: that of motion through time. We might say that we are moving through time into the future, or that future events are moving through time into the present, or that presentness, or the scope of 'now', is moving into the future. 'Now' moves down the sequence of historical events, 'like a spot-light moving down a-line of chorus-girls.'

It may help to compare 'now' with 'here'. For those who deny time's passage, or the objectivity of temporal becoming, 'here' and 'now' are strictly analogous. They are both relative to the thoughts, or utterances, of a particular thinker. 'Here' refers to the place where this thinker is at some time, and 'now' refers to the time at which some particular thought, one involving the concept 'now', is thought. Both words could be replaced by 'this', as in the announcer's jargon 'at this place and time'.[40]

Those who believe in time's passage would reject this analogy. They would admit that, in a Universe containing no thinkers, the concept 'here' would lack application. But they claim that, even in such a Universe, it would still be true that certain things are happening *now*, and then be true that other things are happening *now*, and then be true that other things are happening *now*, and so on. Even in a lifeless Universe, the scope of 'now' would still move through time from the past into the future.

The metaphor of motion through time may be indefensible. How fast do we move through time? We may not be satisfied with the only possible reply, 'At a rate of one second per second'. We may claim that, *if* either we or 'now' can move through time, it must make sense for this motion to be faster or slower, but that this makes no sense.

The critics of the metaphor may be justified. But this may not show that there is no such thing as time's passage, or the objectivity of temporal becoming. Perhaps this is a categorical truth, at so deep a level that we should not expect that it could be explained, either by metaphors or in other terms.[41]

I shall not try to decide where, in this debate, the truth lies. I shall therefore consider both alternatives. Suppose first that, as some philosophers and physicists believe, time's passage is an illusion. If this is so, temporal neutrality cannot be irrational. In defending the Self-interest Theory, the S-Theorist must condemn the bias towards the near. If temporal neutrality cannot be irrational, the S-Theorist might return to his earlier view that such neutrality is rationally required. He must then claim that, just as it is irrational to be relieved when some unavoidable pain has been postponed, it is irrational to be relieved when it is in the past. We shall find this hard to believe.

Suppose, next, that we would be right to believe in time's passage, or the objectivity of temporal becoming. The S-Theorist might then retain his later view and appeal to time's passage. He must still condemn the bias towards the near. He might claim: 'While you have excellent reasons to care less about the pains of others, you cannot rationally care less about pains of yours which lie further in the future. Mere distance from the present moment cannot have rational significance'. The S-Theorist might now support this claim in a different way. He might abandon the appeal to temporal neutrality—the claim that mere timing cannot have rational significance. He might instead discriminate between different kinds of temporal relation.

We should remember here that most of us have a third attitude to time: the bias towards the present. If mere timing cannot have rational significance, it cannot be rational to care more about present pains. That I am *now* in agony cannot be a ground for being more concerned now about this agony. This may seem absurd. The requirement of temporal neutrality may seem least plausible when applied to the bias towards the present. How can it be irrational to mind my agony more while I am suffering the agony? Such a claim seems to undermine the whole structure of concern. Pain matters only because of what it feels like when we are *now* in pain. We care about future pains only because, in the future, they will be *present* pains. If future pains behaved like Alice's *Jam Tomorrow*, and remained perpetually future, they would not matter at all.[42]

The S-Theorist might now claim: 'Of our three attitudes to time, one is irrational, but the other two are rationally required. We *must* care more about present pains, and we *cannot* rationally care about past pains, but we must *not* care less about pains that are in the further rather than the nearer future.' This new view lacks the appeal of generality. There was an appealing simplicity in the çlaim that mere differences in timing—mere answers to the question 'When?'—cannot have rational significance. But this new view, though less simple, may still be justified. The S-Theorist might claim that, on reflection, it is intuitively plausible. He might claim: 'When we compare presentness, pastness, and distance in the future, it is clear that the first two are quite unlike the third. The first two have obvious rational significance, justifying a difference in our concern. But the third is obviously trivial.'

These intuitions are not universal. Of those who are relieved when unavoidable bad events have been postponed, many do not believe that this relief is irrational. Or consider another effect of the bias towards the near: the mounting excitement that we feel as some good event approaches the present—as in the moment in the theatre when the house-lights dim. This excitement would be claimed by many not to be irrational.

The S-Theorist might say: 'Those who have these intuitions have not sufficiently considered the question. Those who *have* considered the question, such as philosophers, generally agree that it is irrational to care more about the nearer future.'

As I have said, the agreement of philosophers may not justify their view. The Self-interest Theory has long been dominant. Since S has been taught for more than two millenia, we must expect to find some echo in our intuitions. S cannot be justified simply by an appeal to intuitions that its teaching may have produced.

If time's passage is not an illusion, the S-Theorist need not appeal only to our intuitions. He can claim that time's passage justifies the bias towards the future. If he is asked to explain why, he may find this difficult. There is, for instance, no suggestion that the past is unreal. It would be easy to see why, if the past was not real, past pains would not matter. It is not so obvious why, because time passes, past pains do not matter.

The S-Theorist might claim: 'Suppose we allow the metaphor that the scope of 'now' moves into the future. This explains why, of the three attitudes to time, one is irrational, and the other two are rationally required. Pains matter only because of what they are like when they are in the present, or under the scope of 'now'. This is why we must care more about our pains when we are *now* in pain. 'Now' moves into the the future. This is why past pains do not matter. Once pains are past, they will only move away from the scope of 'now'. Things are different with nearness in the future. Time's passage does not justify caring more about the near future since, however distant future pains are, they *will* come within the scope of 'now'.

It is not clear that these are good arguments. The last, in particular, may beg the question. But the S-Theorist might instead claim that, in appealing to time's passage, we do not need arguments. He might claim that there is again no need for further explanation. It may be another fundamental truth that, since time passes, past suffering simply cannot matter—cannot be the object of rational concern. Timeless was not relieved to learn that his ordeal was in the past. This may not involve the kind of mistake that can be explained. The mistake may be so gross that it is beyond the reach of argument.

69. AN ASYMMETRY

Perhaps, by abandoning the appeal to temporal neutrality, and instead appealing to time's passage, the Self-interest Theorist has strengthened his position. But we should consider one last kind of case. I call these the *Past or Future Suffering of Those We Love.*

> *Case One.* I am an exile from some country, where I have left my widowed mother. Though I am deeply concerned about her, I very seldom get news. I have known for some time that she is fatally ill, and cannot live long. I am now told something new. My mother's illness has become very painful, in a way that drugs cannot relieve. For the next few months, before she dies, she faces a terrible ordeal. That she will soon die I already knew. But I am deeply distressed to learn of the suffering that she must endure.
>
> A day later I am told that I had been partly misinformed. The facts were right, but not the timing. My mother did have many months of suffering, but she is now dead.

Ought I now to be greatly relieved? I had thought that my mother's ordeal was in the future. But it was in the past. According to the S-Theorist's new view, past pains simply do not matter. Learning about my mother's suffering gives me now *no* reason to be distressed. It is now as if she had died painlessly. If I am still distressed, I am like Timeless. I am making the mistake so gross that it is beyond the reach of argument.

This last example may shake the S-Theorist. He may find it hard to believe that my reaction is irrational. He might say: 'How can it possibly matter to you whether your mother had those months of suffering? Even if she did, her suffering *is in the past.* This is not bad news at all.' But, when applied to my concern for someone else, these remarks seem less convincing.

The S-Theorist might instead try to modify his view. He might say: 'I should not have claimed that past pains simply do not matter. What is implied by time's passage is that they matter *less.'* But this revision is indefensible. Once a pain is past, it is completely past. Being in the past is not a matter of degree. It is not plausible to claim that, since time passes, what is rational is to have *some* concern about past pain, but *less* than about future pain. And what should be claimed about My Past Ordeals? In these cases I regard my past suffering with complete indifference. Is this irrational? Ought I to be somewhat distressed, though less than I am about my future suffering?

An appeal to time's passage cannot plausibly support this claim. And it is hard to believe that, in these cases, my indifference is irrational.

My examples reveal a surprising asymmetry in our concern about our own and other people's pasts. I would not be distressed at all if I was reminded that I myself once had to endure several months of suffering. But I would be greatly distressed if I learnt that, before she died, my mother had to endure such an ordeal.

This asymmetry is reduced in

Case Two. Like Case One except that, though my mother suffered for several months, she is still alive, and is now in no pain.

I would be less distressed here to learn about my mother's past suffering. This difference can be explained. If my mother is like me, she now views with indifference her past ordeal. (We can suppose that her memories of this ordeal are not in themselves painful.) If there is an asymmetry in our concern about our own and other people's past suffering, it would not be surprising if this asymmetry was clearest in cases where the others were now dead. If my mother is still alive, my present attitude will naturally be affected by what I can assume to be her present attitude. Since I can assume that *she* now views with indifference her past suffering, this might reduce my concern about this suffering. But, if my mother is now dead, she does not now view with indifference her past suffering. Since my concern about her past suffering cannot be affected by her present attitude, this is when my concern shows itself in its purest form.

Does it make a difference whether her suffering lasted until her death? Consider

Case Three. I learn that my mother suffered for several months, but that, before she died, she had a month free from pain. There was, within her life, a period in which her suffering was in the past, and thus no longer mattered to her.

If this is what I learn, would this make much difference to my concern? I believe that it would, at most, make a little difference. I would be deeply distressed to learn that my mother suffered for those months, even if I also knew that she had a month in which that suffering was in the past. What distresses me is not just to learn of my mother's *painful death*. If it was only this that distressed me, and I was not distressed to learn that she had to endure much suffering some months before she died, my reaction would be so special that it could perhaps be ignored. But my concern about the pasts of those whom I love, and who are now dead, is not merely a concern that they did not have painful deaths. I would be distressed to learn that, at any time within their lives, they had months of suffering of which I had not previously known. I believe that most people are, in this respect, like me.

Consider finally

Case Four. The same as Case Three, except that I do not learn about my mother's suffering, since I knew about it at the time.

Even though I have always had this knowledge, I would continue to be saddened by the thought that, in my mother's life, there were several months of suffering. Once again, I believe that a similar claim applies to most other people. There is still a striking asymmetry with our attitude to our own past suffering, which most of us view with something close to indifference.

It may be objected: 'If we draw distinctions, this asymmetry disappears. You ask whether, when it is in the past, suffering *matters*. This runs together different questions. It is one question whether you ought to *feel sympathy*, and another question whether you ought to *be concerned*. Whether suffering is in the past makes a difference, not to sympathy, but only to concern. We feel sympathy only for others. *This* is why you view your past suffering with indifference. You cannot sympathize with yourself. When you learn about your mother's past suffering, you do and ought to feel sympathy. But it would be irrational to be *concerned* about this past suffering, just as it would be irrational to be concerned about your own past suffering.[43]

These claims do not, I believe, remove the asymmetry. At the start of Case One, I am told that my mother will suffer for several months before she dies. A day later this message is corrected: she did suffer for several months before she died. On the claims just stated, I should be greatly concerned on the earlier day, when I believe that my mother's suffering will be in the future. When I learn that it was in the past, I should cease to be concerned, though I should still feel sympathy. When I cease to have any concern, this should presumably greatly reduce my distress, and also change its quality. But I am sure that, if this imagined case occurred, my attitude would not be changed in these two ways. I might be somewhat less distressed, but this difference would not be great. Nor would my distress change its quality.

Whether some event is in the past would and should affect those of my emotions that are tied to possible acts. But, in these cases, when I think that my mother's suffering is in the future, there is nothing useful that I could do. I cannot even send her a message. I cannot therefore have the kind of concern that is *active*, searching for ways in which I can help the person for whom I am concerned. In these cases, my concern can only be passive. It can only be sadness and distress, with no impulse to search for possible remedies. Because my distress would take this form, its quality would not change when I learn that my mother's suffering is in the past.

I admit that, when I learn this fact, I might be somewhat less distressed. Just as my concern might be affected by my mother's attitude, if she were alive, it might also be affected by my attitude to my own past suffering. This effect may partly remove the asymmetry. In my concern about my own suffering, it makes all the difference whether this suffering is in the future or the past. It would not be surprising if this fact about my attitudes affected my concern about the past suffering of those I love. Since my concern about their past suffering cannot escape being affected by my concern about my own past suffering, my concern about the sufferings of others can never take a wholly pure or undistorted form. And, as I have claimed, when I learnt that my mother's suffering was in the past, my concern would not be much reduced.

On the objection given above, I have no concern about my own past suffering because one cannot *sympathize* with oneself. This claim does nothing to remove the asymmetry. It is merely a redescription. It concedes that there *is* this difference between our attitudes to past suffering in our own lives and in the lives of those we loved.

This asymmetry makes it harder to defend the Self-interest Theory. An S-Theorist cannot plausibly claim that this asymmetry is rationally required. In particular, he cannot plausibly appeal here to time's passage. If time's passage justifies my complete indifference to my own past suffering, or even makes this indifference a rational requirement, the S-Theorist must claim the same about my concern for those I love. It is as much true, in the imagined case of my dead mother, that her suffering is in the past.

What should the S-Theorist claim about our attitudes to past suffering? He might claim: 'There is not, here, one attitude that is uniquely rational. If you view your own past suffering with complete indifference, this is not irrational. But it would also not be irrational if knowledge of your own past suffering caused you great distress. Similarly, it would not be irrational if you were greatly distressed by the knowledge of your mother's past suffering. But it would also not be irrational if you viewed her suffering with complete indifference.'

If the S-Theorist admits as not irrational this range of different attitudes towards the past, how can he defend his claim that, in our concern about the future, we ought to be temporally neutral? He must still make this claim. But if, in the case of past suffering, it would not be irrational either to care just as much, or to care less, or not to care at all, why in the case of future suffering is there only one attitude which is rational? Though there is no outright inconsistency, it is hard to believe a view which is so permissive in its claims about one range of attitudes to time, but so strict in its claim about another range.

70. CONCLUSIONS

I conclude that there are only two views that a Self-interest Theorist can hope to defend:

(1) If time's passage is an illusion, temporal neutrality cannot be irrational. The S-Theorist might revive his claim that we must be temporally neutral. He must then claim that it is irrational to be relieved both when suffering has been postponed, and when it is in the past. If he criticizes the bias towards the near, he *must* also criticize the bias towards the future. If time's passage is an illusion, he must agree *(a)* that it would not be irrational to *lack* the bias towards the future. He cannot also claim *(b)* that it is *not* irrational to *have* this bias, and *(c)* that it *is* irrational to have the bias towards the near. There is no argument with which he could support these three claims. If he does not condemn the bias towards the future, he cannot condemn the bias towards the near with the claim that it is bad for us. The bias towards the future is also bad for us. And the rationality of an attitude does not depend on whether it is bad for us. There is one difference between these two attitudes to time: though we can act directly on the bias towards the near, we cannot act directly on the bias towards the future. But this cannot support the claim that only the first bias is irrational. The S-Theorist cannot claim that the bias towards the future is not irrational *because* we cannot act upon it. If he appeals to temporal neutrality, he must therefore claim that it is irrational to be relieved when our suffering is in the past. We shall find this hard to believe.

(2) If time's passage is not an illusion, the S-Theorist might defend a different view. He might claim that, because time passes, past suffering cannot matter. He can then claim that it is irrational for Timeless not to be relieved when he learns that his suffering is over. This view we shall find plausible when we think about our own pasts. But the S-Theorist must also claim that, when I am distressed to learn that my mother suffered before she died, this is irrational. We shall find this hard to believe.

The S-Theorist may himself find this last claim hard to believe. If he abandons this claim, he must abandon his appeal to time's passage. While this appeal might support the sweeping claim that past suffering simply does not matter, it cannot support the claim that we are rationally required to have *some* but *less* concern about past suffering. Nor can it show to be rational the difference in our attitudes towards suffering in our own and other people's pasts.

Even if time's passage is not an illusion, the S-Theorist might return to his first view: the requirement of temporal neutrality. He can then condemn the bias towards the near with the claim that a mere difference in timing cannot have rational significance. He can claim that, though it is rationally significant *who* feels some pain, it cannot be significant *when* some pain is felt.

If he returns to this view, the S-Theorist must condemn the bias towards the present. It was here that temporal neutrality seemed least plausible. How can it be irrational to mind my agony more when I am in agony? The S-Theorist might say: 'In one sense, this is not irrational. Agony is bad only because of how much you mind it at the time. But, in another sense, you should not be biased towards the present. It would be irrational to let such a bias influence your decisions. Though you mind the agony more at the time, you should not, because of this, end your present agony at the foreseen cost of greater agony later. At the first-order level, you mind the agony more while you are feeling it. But you should not be more concerned about its being present rather than in the future. At the second-order level, where you make decisions that affect the length and the timing of your suffering, you can and should be temporally neutral.'

If he is requiring temporal neutrality, the S-Theorist must also condemn the bias towards the future. He might say: 'We should expect this bias to be produced by Evolution. This explains why this bias applies only, or more strongly, to our own lives. When we consider the lives of others, we can rise above our evolutionary inheritance, and can see the plausibility of temporal neutrality.'

When some belief or attitude has an evolutionary explanation, this, in itself, has neutral implications. It cannot by itself show that this belief or attitude either is or is not justified. But suppose that we have other grounds for challenging some attitude. Its defenders may then say: 'The fact that we all have this attitude is a ground for thinking it justified. Why has it been so widely held, if it is not justified?' In answering *this* question an evolutionary explanation may cast doubt on what it explains. It undermines the rival explanation, that we have the belief or attitude *because* it is justified. The S-Theorist might therefore claim that our bias towards the future, in our own lives, is a *mere product* of Evolution, and is not rationally justified. And this claim seems to be supported by the asymmetry in our concern about our own and other people's past lives.[44]

The S-Theorist would have to apply this claim to My Past or Future Operations. In these cases I would want it to be true that I did suffer for several hours yesterday, rather than that I shall suffer for one hour later today. The S-Theorist must again claim that this preference is irrational, and that, in general, it is irrational to be relieved when our suffering is in the past. Even given his new claim about Evolution, we shall find this hard to believe.

I have described the two views which the Self-interest Theorist can most plausibly defend. Each of these views includes at least one claim that is hard to believe. This is a weakness in the Self-interest Theory. And it is a further weakness that there is a choice between these views. It may be irrational to be less concerned about the further future. But we cannot be sure of this while we are undecided on the reason why.

9

WHY WE SHOULD REJECT S

A SELF-INTEREST Theorist must condemn the bias towards the near. One objection is that this bias is irrational. As we have just seen, this objection is not plain sailing.

71. THE APPEAL TO LATER REGRETS

The S-Theorist might appeal to a different objection. He might say, to Proximus:

> You do not *now* regret your bias towards the near. But you *will*. When you pay the price—when you suffer the pain that you postponed at the cost of making it worse—you will wish that you did not care more about your nearer future. You will regret that you have this bias. It is irrational to do what you know that you will regret.

As stated, this objection is inaccurate. When Proximus pays the price, he may regret that in the past he had his bias towards the near. But this does not show that he must regret having this bias now. A similar claim applies to those who are self-interested. When a self-interested man pays the price imposed on him by the self-interested acts of others, he regrets the fact that these other people are self-interested. He regrets their bias in their own favour. But this does not lead him to regret this bias in himself. Truths about S at the interpersonal level apply to P at the intertemporal level. Just as a self-interested man regrets his bias, not in himself, but only in others, Proximus regrets his bias, not in himself now, but only in himself at other times. When I assumed that Proximus does not regret his bias, it was enough to assume that he does not regret his *present* bias. This is the bias on which he always acts. The objection given above does not show that Proximus must regret *this* bias.

We can next note that Proximus would not always regret his past bias. In the *nearer* past, what is now his present and his near future were all near; so he was then biased in their favour. Since he is now, and for some time will be, benefiting from this past bias, he will now be *glad* that he had it.

The S-Theorist might say: 'When you pay the price, you will regret your past bias. Since that is so, you *ought* now to regret even your present bias. You will in future regret your present bias; and you now care about your future. Caring about one's future involves wishing to avoid what one will regret. Since you will regret your present bias, you ought now to wish that you did not have it.'

Proximus could answer: 'In the further future I shall indeed regret my present bias. And this does give me grounds for wishing that I did not have this bias now. But in the nearer future I shall be glad that I had my present bias, since it will then be benefiting me. This gives me grounds for being glad that I have this bias now.'

The S-Theorist might say: 'Your gladness in the near future will be outweighed by your regrets in the further future. This will be true because you postpone pains at the foreseen cost of making them worse. Since your present bias will later cause you more regret than gladness, your grounds for wishing now not to have this bias are, of the two competing grounds, the stronger.'

Proximus could answer: 'My future regrets will indeed, impartially considered, outweigh my future gladness. But I do not consider my future impartially. I care more about what is near. Since my future gladness is nearer, it outweighs my future regrets.'

The S-Theorist might reply: 'It is irrational not to be impartial'. Proximus could answer: 'This reply is either ineffective or suicidal. If it defeats me it defeats you. Those who are self-interested are not impartial. Just as I am biased towards the near, they are biased in their own favour.'

72. WHY A DEFEAT FOR PROXIMUS IS NOT A VICTORY FOR S

In defending his bias towards the near, Proximus compares this bias with the bias in one's own favour. The S-Theorist might say:

> I care less about what happens to other people. You care less about what will happen to you at later times. All these later times *will*, at some time, be a *now* for you. But other people will never be a *me* for me. Your analogy therefore fails.[45]

This objection has some force. Suppose that, for this or other reasons, we reject what Proximus claims. Suppose that, despite the difficulties raised in Chapter 8, we conclude that the bias towards the near *is* less rational than the bias in one's own favour. As I have explained, this does *not* show that we should accept S. The bias towards the near is the favourite target of Self-interest Theorists. In my attempt to defend this bias, I was challenging S at its strongest point. If this attempt succeeds, S is totally defeated. It does not follow that, if this attempt fails, S wins.

The best version of the Present-aim Theory is the Critical version. As I wrote, CP can claim that we are rationally required to care about our own self-interest, and in a temporally neutral way. On this version of CP, Proximus is irrational, since it is irrational to be biased towards the near. If we believe that Proximus is irrational, this is no reason to accept S rather than this version of CP.

73. THE APPEAL TO INCONSISTENCY

Suppose that, as this version of CP requires, I am concerned about my own self-interest in a temporally neutral way. But this is not my dominant concern. Because I have other desires that are sometimes stronger, I sometimes act in ways that I know to be against my own self-interest. The S-Theorist might revive his Appeal to Later Regrets. He might say: 'Because you act against your own self-interest, your future regrets will outweigh your future gladness. Unlike Proximus, *you* care equally about your whole future. You should therefore admit that your acts are irrational. It is irrational to do what you know you will on the whole regret.'

This objection assumes that, whenever I act against my own self-interest, I shall later regret this act. This assumption is not justified. I act in these ways because, though I care about my own self-interest, I care even more about something else. Since I do not care most about my own self-interest, we should not assume that I shall later regret these acts.

There are likely to be cases where I do regret some past act. But it does not follow that my act was irrational. Suppose that I acted as I did because I accepted a value judgement that I now reject. I may now regret my act because I have changed my mind. But my act may still have been rational, since I was acting on a value judgement that I accepted at the time..

A similar claim applies when my desires change without a change of mind. Suppose that, in the past, I acted against my interests because I wanted to help some people who were in distress. I borrowed a large sum of money to give to these people, knowing that, to repay this loan, I would have to work for many years in a profession that I detest. I now want to help some other people who are in distress. I do not believe that these people have a greater claim to be helped; but, because I am now more vividly aware of their distress, these are the people whom I now care about most. Because of my earlier act, I cannot now help these people. Since I have not repaid my loan, I cannot borrow again to give to these people. I therefore regret my earlier act. This act was against my interests; and I now regret it. But, given what I then most wanted, it was not irrational. The Appeal to Later Regrets may show that *Proximus* is irrational. But it is no objection to the version of CP that I am now discussing.

According to this version of CP, I should have a temporally neutral concern for my own future, but this need not be my dominant concern. And, like all versions, this version of CP gives special weight to my present aims. It can therefore be challenged with an objection that Nagel states against the cruder Instrumental Theory. Nagel writes that, on this theory:

I may have reason now to do precisely what will ensure the failure of my future *rational* attempts; I may have reason to do what I know I will later have reason to try to undo, and I will therefore have to be especially careful to lay traps and insurmountable obstacles in the way of my future self. A system with consequences such as this not only fails to require the most elementary consistency in conduct over time, but in fact sharpens the possibilities of conflict by grounding an individual's plottings against his future self in the apparatus of rationality.[46]

The 'inconsistency' that Nagel describes is not theoretical inconsistency. The Instrumental Theory does not at different times make inconsistent claims about what it is rational for someone to do. Nor need someone who believes this theory, or the Critical Present-aim Theory, question his own rationality at other times. This is because, on all versions of P, reasons are relative not only to the agent but also to the time of acting.

It is true that, according to P, it can be rational for me to do now what it will later be rational for me to undo. P can be accused of being, even within a single life, intertemporally self-defeating. This can be true even of the version of CP that requires us to care about our own self-interest in a temporally neutral way. Suppose that I have such concern, but I also have other desires that are stronger, and these desires are different at different times. At any time I can either (1) do what will best fulfil my present desires or (2) do what will best fulfil, or enable me to fulfil, all of my desires throughout my life. According to P, I should always do (1) rather than (2). As we saw in Section 34, it can be true that, if I always follow P, doing (1) rather than (2), I shall be less successful over time even in fulfilling my desires at each time.

A Self-interest Theorist might here claim that S beats P even in P's terms. In its Desire-Fulfilment version, S tells me always to do (2) rather than (1). If I always act in this way, I shall be more successful over time in fulfilling my desires at each time.

I explained how can this be answered. There is a similar objection to S. According to S, it can be rational for me to do what it is rational for you to undo. Just as P can be intertemporally self-defeating, S can be interpersonally or collectively self-defeating. A community of self-interested people would do better, even in self-interested terms, if they all followed, not the Self-interest Theory, but some version of morality. But to be collectively self-defeating is not, in the case of S, to be damagingly self-defeating. When S is collectively self-defeating, it is still individually successful. Since S is a theory about individual rationality, it is still working in its own terms.

Need I write this paragraph? To be intertemporally self-defeating is not, in the case of P, to be damagingly self-defeating. When P is intertemporally self-defeating, it is still successful at each time. It is still true that, if I follow P at each time, I am at each time doing what will best fulfil my present desires. Even in these cases, from the agent's point of view at the time of acting, P is successful. Since this is the point of view appealed to by P, it is still working in its own terms.

These two objections cannot refute P or S. But they both have some force. Unlike P, S cannot be directly intertemporally self-defeating. This gives S, compared with P, a certain theoretical appeal. And this may persuade us to abandon P and accept S. But S can be directly collectively self-defeating. This is not true of an agent-neutral morality. This gives such a morality similar theoretical appeal. And this may persuade us to take the similar further step, from S to such a morality.

Given the analogy between the two objections, the objection to P does not support S. These objections both support Neutralism. If the objections succeed, we should reject S. If the objections fail, we have no reason to reject P.[47]

An S-Theorist might deny that the analogy has these implications. He might claim that, while an acceptable theory cannot be directly intertemporally self-defeating, it can be directly interpersonally self-defeating. How can there be this difference? The S-Theorist must claim that the relation between different people is, in the relevant respects, unlike the relation between a single person at one time and himself at other times.

These relations are, in most respects, different. My relation to you is unlike the relation between me now and myself tomorrow, or myself in fifty years. But these relations may still be similar in the *relevant* respects. Just as an act must be that of a particular agent, it must be done at a particular time. And many claims about rationality are true only when applied to a person at a particular time. They cease to be true when they are made to span either the relation between different people, or the relation between a person at one time and himself at other times. Thus it might be claimed, 'A set of inconsistent beliefs can be rationally believed by different people, but they cannot be rationally believed by a single person'. But this is not so. Inconsistent beliefs may be rationally believed by a single person if he believes them at different times. He is irrational only if he believes them at a single time. The same is true of intransitive preferences: preferring X to Y, Y to Z, and Z to X. As is often pointed out, three people can each have one of these preferences without being irrational. But so can a single person if he has these preferences at different times. As these claims suggest, when we are considering both theoretical and practical rationality, the relation between a person now and himself at other times *is* relevantly similar to the relation between different people.

74. CONCLUSIONS

In Chapters 6 to 8 I advanced several arguments against the Self-interest Theory. These justify one of two conclusions. The arguments may only show that S cannot defeat P. On this conclusion, the dispute between these theories ends in a tie, or draw. When S and P conflict, it would be rational to follow either. But, as I explain in Appendix B, this conclusion would in practice be a defeat for S.

The other conclusion is that we ought to reject S. Both in practice and in theory, this would be, for S, complete defeat. (If we reject S, as I explain in Appendix C, this may affect our choice between the different theories about self-interest.)

I believe that my arguments justify this bolder conclusion. I began with a strategic metaphor. The Self-interest Theory has two rivals: morality, and the Present-aim Theory. In some respects it lies between these two rivals. It is therefore vulnerable in what is often a fatal way: it can be attacked from two directions. The Self-interest Theory has long been dominant in our intellectual tradition. But this dominance has largely derived from the failure of its two rivals to attack together. When it is attacked by moral theorists, it has stolen strength from the Present-aim Theory, and vice versa.

I challenged the Self-interest Theory from both directions. This ensured that S would be judged only on its own merits. I avoided the deceptive case where what a person does affects only himself. S tells this person to do whatever would be best for himself. Since he is the only person whom his acts affect, he is doing what is best for everyone affected. He is doing what, impartially considered, has the best effects. In such a case, S coincides with impartial benevolence. S can be better judged when these two conflict: when what is better for the agent would be, and by a larger margin, worse for other people. As these cases show, S insists on a biased pattern of concern. S is not just Prudence, but Egoism. It insists that a rational agent must give supreme weight to his own self-interest, *whatever* the costs to others.

I then challenged S from the other direction. I considered cases where S conflicts with the Present-aim Theory. In these cases, though the agent knows the facts and is thinking clearly, he *does not want* to give supreme weight to his own self-interest. S claims that, whatever the costs to others, a rational agent *must* be biased in his own favour, even if, in a cool hour, he neither has nor wants to have this bias.

Is this claim plausible? Is this bias uniquely or supremely rational? Is every other desire or concern less rational? *This is the central question.* My First Argument answers No. I claim that, compared with the bias in one's own favour, there are several other desires that are no less rational. One example is a desire to act in the interests of other people. It can be rational to fulfil this desire, even when one knows that one's act is against one's own self-interest. Other examples are certain kinds of desire for achievement. A creator may want his creations to be as good as possible. A scientist, or philosopher, may want to make some fundamental discovery, or intellectual advance. I claim that these and other desires are no less rational than the bias in one's own favour. If one of these is someone's strongest desire, all things considered, it would be rational for him to cause it to be fulfilled, even if this person knows that his act is against his own self-interest.

The S-Theorist's First Reply contradicts these claims. This reply claims that the bias in one's own favour is supremely rational. Since I cannot prove that I am right to reject this claim, my First Argument is not decisive. But I believe that it succeeds. I believe that the S-Theorist has no good reply to this argument. The bias in one's own favour is *not* supremely rational. There is at least one desire that is no less rational: the desire to benefit others. Since there is at least one such desire, we should reject S and accept some version of CP.

The S-Theorist's Second Reply appeals to the claim that any reason's force extends over time. On this claim, since I *shall* have reasons to try to fulfil my future desires, I have these reasons *now*. Reasons for acting cannot be relative to a particular time. An argument for this claim may also show that reasons for acting cannot be agent-relative. The argument may show that any reason's force extends over different people's lives. This is what is shown if Nagel's argument succeeds. This conclusion would defeat both S and P. To avoid this conclusion, the S-Theorist must claim that reasons can be agent-relative. I claim that, if reasons can be relative, they can be relative to the agent at the time of acting. As I showed in Sections 59 to 61, it can be true that I did or shall have certain reasons for acting, though I do not have these reasons now. This undermines the S-Theorist's Second Reply. And my Appeal to Full Relativity gave further grounds for rejecting S.

The S-Theorist must also claim that it is irrational to care less about one's further future. Chapter 8 showed that, in claiming this, the S-Theorist must accept one of two views, each of which has implications that are hard to believe. This is another objection to S. For the purposes of argument, I assumed that this objection can be met. I assumed that it is irrational to care less about our further future. This does not show that we should accept S. We could accept the Critical version of the Present-aim Theory. And CP can claim that we are rationally required to be concerned about our own self-interest, in a temporally neutral way. This claim is not what distinguishes these two theories.

S requires us to accept a much bolder claim. It is not enough that we have this temporally neutral bias in our own favour. We must always be governed by this bias, whatever the costs to others, and even if we neither have nor want to have this bias. This claim takes us back to the central question. According to my First Argument, this claim requires the assumption that this bias is supremely rational. It requires the assumption that it is irrational to care more about anything else, such as morality, or the interests of other people. We should reject this assumption. If the S-Theorist has no other reply, we should reject S.

The S-Theorist has two other arguments: the Appeal to Later Regrets, and the Appeal to Inconsistency. Though these arguments have some intuitive appeal, they do not provide replies to my First Argument. *I conclude that we should reject S.* As I predicted, the Self-interest Theory cannot survive a combined attack by both its rivals: both the Present-aim Theory and morality.

The best version of the Present-aim Theory is the Critical version. Remember next that, if we accept CP, we *could* claim that it is rationally required that our strongest desire be to avoid acting wrongly. I have left it open whether we *should* add this claim to CP. Since this is so, there are not *two* surviving theories about rationality. *Moral theorists should accept CP.* They have no ground for rejecting CP, since CP can give to moral reasons all of the weight which they believe that these reasons ought to have.

Remember finally that *all* possible theories about rationality are versions of CP. Because this is true, we should accept CP *whatever* we believe. This feature of CP may seem to be a weakness, making it a vacuous theory. But this feature is a strength. We can see more clearly what is assumed by different theories when they are restated as versions of CP. And, while I left it open what CP should claim about moral reasons, I did not leave open two other questions. Consider the followers of Hume, who deny that desires can be either intrinsically irrational, or rationally required. If we add this claim to CP, it coincides with IP, the purely Instrumental Theory. I have claimed that we should reject this version of CP. Some patterns of concern are irrational, and provide no reasons for acting. And my main claim is that we should reject the version of CP that coincides with S. We should reject the assumption that, compared with the bias in one's own favour, every other desire is less rational. Suppose that our desires and value-judgments are, both singly and as a set, not irrational. And suppose we know that what will best fulfil these desires will be against our own long-term self-interest. If this is so, it is *irrational* to follow S. It is irrational to do what is in our own self-interest when we know that this will frustrate what, knowing the facts and thinking clearly, we most want or value.

The Self-interest Theory has been believed by most people for more than two millenia. Since this is so, it may seem absurdly rash to claim that we should reject S. How can four chapters overturn the verdict of recorded history? How can so many people have been mistaken? There are two answers.

(1) Most of these people assumed that, because we shall have an after-life or be re-incarnated, morality and self-interest always coincide. Because they had this false belief, these people overlooked one of the objections to S.

(2) As is often true when we should reject some theory, those who believed this theory were not wholly mistaken. Parts of S are plausible. It is not irrational to care more about oneself. And, in our concern about our own self-interest, we should perhaps be temporally neutral. The plausibility of

these claims helps to explain why so many people have believed the Self-interest Theory. But these claims are also part of the wider theory, CP, that we should all accept. Consider this (too grandiose) analogy. Newton's Laws are partly correct. But we now accept a different theory.

PART THREE

PERSONAL IDENTITY

10

WHAT WE BELIEVE OURSELVES TO BE

I enter the Teletransporter. I have been to Mars before, but only by the old method, a space-ship journey taking several weeks. This machine will send me at the speed of light. I merely have to press the green button. Like others, I am nervous. Will it work? I remind myself what I have been told to expect. When I press the button, I shall lose consciousness, and then wake up at what seems a moment later. In fact I shall have been unconscious for about an hour. The Scanner here on Earth will destroy my brain and body, while recording the exact states of all of my cells. It will then transmit this information by radio. Travelling at the speed of light, the message will take three minutes to reach the Replicator on Mars. This will then create, out of new matter, a brain and body exactly like mine. It will be in this body that I shall wake up.

Though I believe that this is what will happen, I still hesitate. But then I remember seeing my wife grin when, at breakfast today, I revealed my nervousness. As she reminded me, she has been often teletransported, and there is nothing wrong with *her*. I press the button. As predicted, I lose and seem at once to regain consciousness, but in a different cubicle. Examining my new body, I find no change at all. Even the cut on my upper lip, from this morning's shave, is still there.

Several years pass, during which I am often Teletransported. I am now back in the cubicle, ready for another trip to Mars. But this time, when I press the green button, I do not lose consciousness. There is a whirring sound, then silence. I leave the cubicle, and say to the attendant: 'It's not working. What did I do wrong?'

'It's working', he replies, handing me a printed card. This reads: 'The New Scanner records your blueprint without destroying your brain and body. We hope that you will welcome the opportunities which this technical advance offers.'

The attendant tells me that I am one of the first people to use the New Scanner. He adds that, if I stay for an hour, I can use the Intercom to see and talk to myself on Mars.

'Wait a minute', I reply, 'If I'm here I can't *also* be on Mars'.

Someone politely coughs, a white-coated man who asks to speak to me in private. We go to his office, where he tells me to sit down, and pauses. Then he says: 'I'm afraid that we're having problems with the New Scanner. It records your blueprint just as accurately, as you will see when you talk to yourself on Mars. But it seems to be damaging the cardiac systems which it scans. Judging from the results so far, though you will be quite healthy on Mars, here on Earth you must expect cardiac failure within the next few days.'

The attendant later calls me to the Intercom. On the screen I see myself just as I do in the mirror every morning. But there are two differences. On the screen I am not left-right reversed. And, while I stand here speechless, I can see and hear myself, in the studio on Mars, starting to speak.

What can we learn from this imaginary story? Some believe that we can learn little. This would have been Wittgenstein's view.[1] And Quine writes: 'The method of science fiction has its uses in philosophy, but. . . I wonder whether the limits of the method are properly heeded. To seek what is 'logically required' for sameness of person under unprecedented circumstances is to suggest that words have some logical force beyond what our past needs have invested them with.'[2]

This criticism might be justified if, when considering such imagined cases, we had no reactions. But these cases arouse in most of us strong beliefs. And these are beliefs, not about our words, but about ourselves. By considering these cases, we discover what we believe to be involved in our own continued existence, or what it is that makes us now and ourselves next year the same people. We discover our beliefs about the nature of personal identity over time. Though our beliefs are revealed most clearly when we consider imaginary cases, these beliefs also cover actual cases, and our own lives. In Part Three of this book I shall argue that some of these beliefs are false, then suggest how and why this matters.

75. SIMPLE TELETRANSPORTATION AND THE BRANCH-LINE CASE

At the beginning of my story, the Scanner destroys my brain and body. My blueprint is beamed to Mars, where another machine makes an organic *Replica* of me. My Replica thinks that he is me, and he seems to remember living my life up to the moment when I pressed the green button. In every other way, both physically and psychologically, we are exactly similar. If he returned to Earth, everyone would think that he was me.

Simple Teletransportation, as just described, is a common feature in science fiction. And it is believed, by some readers of this fiction, merely to be the fastest way of travelling. They believe that my Replica *would* be *me*. Other science fiction readers, and some of the characters in this fiction, take a different view. They believe that, when I press the green button, I die. My Replica is *someone else*, who has been made to be exactly like me.

This second view seems to be supported by the end of my story. The New Scanner does not destroy my brain and body. Besides gathering the information, it merely damages my heart. While I am in the cubicle, with the green button pressed, nothing seems to happen. I walk out, and learn that in a few days I shall die. I later talk, by two-way television, to my Replica on Mars. Let us continue the story. Since my Replica knows that I am about to die, he tries to console me with the same thoughts with which I recently tried to console a dying friend. It is sad to learn, on the receiving end, how unconsoling these thoughts are. My Replica then assures me that he will take up my life where I leave off. He loves my wife, and together they will care for my children. And he will finish the book that I am writing. Besides having all of my drafts, he has all of my intentions. I must admit that he can finish my book as well as I could. All these facts console me a little. Dying when I know that I shall have a Replica is not quite as bad as, simply, dying. Even so, I shall soon lose consciousness, forever.

In Simple Teletransportation, I am destroyed before I am Replicated. This makes it easier to believe that this *is* a way of travelling—that my Replica *is* me. At the end of my story, my life and that of my Replica overlap. Call this the *Branch-Line Case*. In this case, I cannot hope to travel on the *Main Line*, waking up on Mars with forty years of life ahead. I shall stay on the Branch-Line, here on Earth, which ends a few days later. Since I can talk to my Replica, it seems clear that he is *not* me. Though he is exactly like me, he is one person, and I am another. When I pinch myself, he feels nothing. When I have my heart attack, he will again feel nothing. And when I am dead he will live for another forty years.

If we believe that my Replica is not me, it is natural to assume that my prospect, on the Branch Line, is almost as bad as ordinary death. I shall deny this assumption. As I shall argue later, being destroyed and Replicated is about as good as ordinary survival. I can best defend this claim, and the wider view of which it is part, after discussing the past debate about personal identity.

76. QUALITATIVE AND NUMERICAL IDENTITY

There are two kinds of sameness, or identity. I and my Replica are *qualitatively identical,* or exactly alike. But we may not be *numerically identical,* or one and the same person. Similarly, two white billiard balls are not numerically but may be qualitatively identical. If I paint one of these balls red, it will cease to be qualitatively identical with itself as it was. But the red ball that I later see and the white ball that I painted red are numerically identical. They are one and the same ball.

We might say, of someone, 'After his accident, he is no longer the same person'. This is a claim about both kinds of identity. We claim that *he*, the same person, is *not* now the same person. This is not a contradiction. We merely mean that this person's character has changed. This numerically identical person is now qualitatively different.

When we are concerned about our future, it is our numerical identity that we are concerned about. I may believe that, after my marriage, I shall not be the same person. But this does not make marriage death. However much I change, I shall still be alive if there will be some person living who will *be* me.

Though our chief concern is our numerical identity, psychological changes matter. Indeed, on one view, certain kinds of qualitative change destroy numerical identity. If certain things happen to me, the truth might not be that I become a very different person. The truth might be that I cease to exist— that the resulting person is someone else.

77. THE PHYSICAL CRITERION OF PERSONAL IDENTITY

There has been much debate about the nature both of persons and of personal identity over time. It will help to distinguish these questions:

(1) What is the nature of a person?

(2) What makes a person at two different times one and the same person? What is necessarily involved in the continued existence of each person over time?

The answer to (2) can take this form: '*X* today is one and the same person as *Y* at some past time *if and only if* . . .' Such an answer states the *necessary and sufficient conditions* for personal identity over time.

In answering (2) we shall also partly answer (1). The necessary features of our continued existence depend upon our nature. And the simplest answer to (1) is that, to be a person, a being must be self-conscious, aware of its identity and its continued existence over time.

We can also ask

(3) What is in fact involved in the continued existence of each person over time?

Since our continued existence has features that are not necessary, the answer to (2) is only part of the answer to (3). For example, having the same heart and the same character are not necessary to our continued existence, but they are usually part of what this existence involves.

Many writers use the ambiguous phrase 'the criterion of identity over time'. Some mean by this 'our way of telling whether some present object is identical with some past object'. But I shall mean *what this identity necessarily involves, or consists in.*

In the case of most physical objects, on what I call the *standard view*, the criterion of identity over time is the spatio-temporal physical continuity of this object. This is something that we all understand, even if we fail to understand the description I shall now give. In the simplest case of physical continuity, like that of the Pyramids, an apparently static object continues to exist. In another simple case, like that of the Moon, an object moves in a regular way. Many objects move in less regular ways, but they still trace physically continuous spatio-temporal paths. Suppose that the billiard ball that I painted red is the same as the white ball with which last year I made a winning shot. On the standard view, this is true only if this ball traced such a continuous path. It must be true (1) that there is a line through space and time, starting where the white ball rested before I made my winning shot, and ending where the red ball now is, (2) that at every point on this line there was a billiard ball, and (3) that the existence of a ball at each point on this line was in part caused by the existence of a ball at the immediately preceding point.³

Some kinds of thing continue to exist even though their physical continuity involves great changes. A Camberwell Beauty is first an egg, then a caterpillar, then a chrysalis, then a butterfly. These are four stages in the physically continuous existence of a single organism. Other kinds of thing cannot survive such great changes. Suppose that an artist paints a self-portrait and then, by repainting, turns this into a portrait of his father. Even though these portraits are more similar than a caterpillar and a butterfly, they are not stages in the continued existence of a single painting. The self-portrait is a painting that the artist destroyed. In a general discussion of identity, we would need to explain why the requirement of physical continuity differs in such ways for different kinds of thing. But we can ignore this here.

Can there be gaps in the continued existence of a physical object? Suppose that I have the same gold watch that I was given as a boy even though, for a month, it lay disassembled on a watch-repairer's shelf. On one view, in the spatio-temporal path traced by this watch there was not at every point a watch, so my watch does not have a history of full physical continuity. But during the month when my watch was disassembled, and did not exist, all of its parts had histories of full continuity. On another view, even when it was disassembled, my watch existed.

Another complication again concerns the relation between a complex thing and the various parts of which it is composed. It is true of some of these things, though not true of all, that their continued existence need not involve the continued existence of their components. Suppose that a wooden ship is repaired from time to time while it is floating in harbour, and that after fifty years it contains none of the bits of wood out of which it was first built. It is still one and the same ship, because, as a ship, it has displayed throughout these fifty years full physical continuity. This is so despite the fact that it is now composed of quite different bits of wood. These bits of wood might be qualitatively identical to the original bits, but they are not one and the same bits. Something similar is partly true of a human body. With the exception of some brain cells, the cells in our bodies are replaced with new cells several times in our lives.

I have now described the physical continuity which, on the standard view, makes a physical object one and the same after many days or years. This enables me to state one of the rival views about personal identity. On this view, what makes me the same person over time is that I have the same brain and body. The criterion of my identity over time—or what this identity involves—is the physical continuity, over time, of my brain and body. I shall continue to exist if and only if this particular brain and body continue both to exist and to be the brain and body of a living person.

This is the simplest version of this view. There is a better version. This is

The Physical Criterion: (1) What is necessary is not the continued existence of the whole body, but the continued existence of *enough* of the brain to be the brain of a living person. X today is one and the same person as Y at some past time if and only if (2) enough of Y's brain continued to exist, and is now X's brain, and (3) this physical continuity has not taken a 'branching' form. (4) Personal identity over time just consists in the holding of facts like (2) and (3).

(1) is clearly true in certain actual cases. Some people continue to exist even though they lose, or lose the use of, much of their bodies. (3) will be explained later.

Those who believe in the Physical Criterion would reject Teletransportation. They would believe this to be a way, not of travelling, but of dying. They would also reject, as inconceivable, reincarnation. They believe that someone cannot have a life after death, unless he lives this life in a resurrection of the very same, physically continuous body. This is why some Christians insist that they be buried. They believe that if, like Greek and Trojan heroes, they were burnt on funeral pyres, and their ashes scattered, not even God could bring them to life again. God could create only a Replica, someone else who was exactly like them. Other Christians believe that God could resurrect *them* if He reassembled their bodies out of the bits of matter that, when they were last alive, made up their bodies. This would be like the reassembly of my gold watch.[4]

78. THE PSYCHOLOGICAL CRITERION

Some people believe in a kind of psychological continuity that resembles physical continuity. This involves the continued existence of a purely mental *entity*, or thing—a soul, or spiritual substance. I shall return to this view. But I shall first explain another kind of psychological continuity. This is less like physical continuity, since it does not consist in the continued existence of some entity. But this other kind of psychological continuity involves only facts with which we are familiar.

What has been most discussed is the continuity of memory. This is because it is memory that makes most of us aware of our own continued existence over time. The exceptions are the people who are suffering from amnesia. Most amnesiacs lose only two sets of memories. They lose all of their memories of having particular past experiences—or, for short, their *experience memories*. They also lose some of their memories about facts, those that are about their own past lives. But they remember other facts, and they remember how to do different things, such as how to speak, or swim.

Locke suggested that experience-memory provides the criterion of personal identity.[5] Though this is not, on its own, a plausible view, I believe that it can be part of such a view. I shall therefore try to answer some of Locke's critics.

Locke claimed that someone cannot have committed some crime unless he now remembers doing so. We can understand a reluctance to punish people for crimes that they cannot remember. But, taken as a view about what is involved in a person's continued existence, Locke's claim is clearly false. If it was true, it would not be possible for someone to forget any of the things that he once did, or any of the experiences that he once had. But this *is* possible. I cannot now remember putting on my shirt this morning.

There are several ways to extend the experience-memory criterion so as to cover such cases. I shall appeal to the concept of an overlapping chain of experience-memories. Let us say that, between X today and Y twenty years ago, there are *direct memory connections* if X can now remember having some of the experiences that Y had twenty years ago. On Locke's view, only this makes X and Y one and the same person. But even if there are *no* such direct memory connections, there may be *continuity of memory* between X now and Y twenty years ago. This would be so if between X now and Y at that time there has been an overlapping chain of direct memories. In the case of most adults, there would be such a chain. In each day within the last twenty years, most of these people remembered some of their experiences on the previous day. On the revised version of Locke's view, some present person X is the same as some past person Y if there is between them continuity of memory.

This revision meets one objection to Locke's view. We should also revise the view so that it appeals to other facts. Besides direct memories, there are several other kinds of direct psychological connection. One such connection is that which holds between an intention and the later act in which this intention is carried out. Other such direct connections are those which hold when a belief, or a desire, or any other psychological feature, continues to be had.

I can now define two general relations:

Psychological connectedness is the holding of particular direct psychological connections.

Psychological continuity is the holding of overlapping chains of *strong* connectedness.

Of these two general relations, connectedness is more important both in theory and in practice. Connectedness can hold to any degree. Between X today and Y yesterday there might be several thousand direct psychological connections, or only a single connection. If there was only a single connection, X and Y would not be, on the revised Lockean View, the same person. For X and Y to be the same person, there must be over every day *enough* direct psychological connections. Since connectedness is a matter of degree, we cannot plausibly define precisely what counts as enough. But we can claim that there is enough connectedness if the number of direct connections, over any day, is *at least half* the number that hold, over every day, in the lives of nearly every actual person.[6] When there are enough direct connections, there is what I call *strong* connectedness.

Could this relation be the criterion of personal identity? A relation *F* is *transitive* if it is true that, if *X* is F-related to *Y*, and *Y* is F-related to *Z*, X and Z *must* be F-related. Personal identity is a transitive relation. If Bertie was one and the same person as the philosopher Russell, and Russell was one and the same person as the author of *Why I Am Not a Christian*, this author and Bertie must be one and the same person.

Strong connectedness is *not* a transitive relation. I am now strongly connected to myself yesterday, when I was strongly connected to myself two days ago, when I was strongly connected to myself three days ago, and so on. It does not follow that I am now strongly connected to myself twenty years ago. And this is not true. Between me now and myself twenty years ago there are many fewer than the number of direct psychological connections that hold over any day in the lives of nearly all adults. For example, while most adults have many memories of experiences that they had in the previous day, I have few memories of experiences that I had on any day twenty years ago.

By 'the criterion of personal identity over time' I mean what this identity *necessarily involves or consists in*. Because identity is a transitive relation, the criterion of identity must also be a transitive relation. Since strong connectedness is not transitive, it cannot be the criterion of identity. And I have just described a case in which this is clear. I am the same person as myself twenty years ago, though I am not now strongly connected to myself then.

Though a defender of Locke's view cannot appeal to psychological connectedness, he can appeal to psychological continuity, which *is* transitive. He can appeal to

The Psychological Criterion: (1) There is *psychological continuity* if and only if there are overlapping chains of strong connectedness. X today is one and the same person as Y at some past time if and only if (2) X is psychologically continuous with Y, (3) this continuity has the right kind of cause, and (4) it has not taken a 'branching' form. (5) Personal identity over time just consists in the holding of facts like (2) to (4).

As with the Physical Criterion, (4) will be explained later.

There are three versions of the Psychological Criterion. These differ over the question of what is the *right* kind of cause. On the *Narrow* version, this must be the *normal* cause. On the *Wide* version, this could be *any reliable* cause. On the *Widest* version, the cause could be *any* cause.

The Narrow Psychological Criterion uses words in their ordinary sense. Thus I remember having an experience only if

(1)   I seem to remember having an experience,

(2)   I did have this experience,

and

(3)   my apparent memory is causally dependent, in the normal way, on this past experience.

That we need condition (3) can be suggested with an example. Suppose that I am knocked unconscious in a climbing accident. After I recover, my fellow-climber tells me what he shouted just before I fell. In some later year, when my memories are less clear, I might seem to remember the experience of hearing my companion shout just before I fell. And it might be true that I did have just such an experience. But though conditions (1) and (2) are met, we should not believe that I am remembering that past experience. It is a well-established fact that people can never remember their last few experiences before they were knocked unconscious. We should therefore claim that my apparent memory of hearing my companion shout is not a real memory of that past experience. This apparent memory is not causally dependent in the right way on that past experience. I have this apparent memory only because my companion later told me what he shouted.[7]

Similar remarks apply to the other kinds of continuity, such as continuity of character. On the Narrow Psychological Criterion, even if someone's character radically changes, there is continuity of character if these changes have one of several normal causes. Some changes of character are deliberately brought about; others are the natural consequence of growing older; others are the natural response to certain kinds of experience. But there would not be continuity of character if radical and unwanted changes were produced by abnormal interference, such as direct tampering with the brain.

Though it is memory that makes us aware of our own continued existence over time, the various other continuities have great importance. We may believe that they have enough importance to provide personal identity even in the absence of memory. We shall then claim, what Locke denied, that a person continues to exist even if he suffers from complete amnesia.

Besides the Narrow version, I described the two Wide versions of the Psychological Criterion. These versions extend the senses of several words. On the ordinary sense of 'memory', a memory must have its normal cause. The two Wide Psychological Criteria appeal to a wider sense of 'memory', which allows either any reliable cause, or any cause. Similar claims apply to the other kinds of direct psychological connection. To simplify my discussion of these three Criteria, I shall use 'psychological continuity' in its widest sense, that allows this continuity to have *any* cause.

If we appeal to the Narrow Version, which insists on the normal cause, the Psychological Criterion coincides in most cases with the Physical Criterion. The normal causes of memory involve the continued existence of the brain. And some or all of our psychological features depend upon states or events in our brains. The continued existence of a person's brain is at least part of the normal cause of psychological continuity. On the Physical Criterion, a person continues to exist if and only if *(a)* there continues to exist *enough* of this person's brain so that it remains the brain of a living person, and *(b)* there has been no branching in this physical continuity. *(a)* and *(b)* are claimed to be the necessary and sufficient conditions for this person's identity, or continued existence, over time. On the Narrow Psychological Criterion, *(a)* is necessary, but not sufficient. A person continues to exist if and only if *(c)* there is psychological continuity, *(d)* this continuity has its normal cause, and *(e)* it has not taken a branching form. *(a)* is required as part of the normal cause of psychological continuity.

Reconsider the start of my imagined story, where my brain and body are destroyed. The Scanner and the Replicator produce a person who has a new but exactly similar brain and body, and who is psychologically continuous with me as I was when I pressed the green button. The cause of this continuity is, though unusual, reliable. On both the Physical Criterion and the Narrow Psychological Criterion, my Replica would *not* be me. On the two Wide Criteria, he *would* be me.

I shall argue that we need not decide between these three versions of the Psychological Criterion. A partial analogy may suggest why. Some people go blind because of damage to their eyes. Scientists are now developing artificial eyes. These involve a glass or plastic lens, and a micro-computer which sends through the optic nerve electrical patterns like those that are sent through this nerve by a natural eye. When such artificial eyes are more advanced, they might give to someone who has gone blind visual experiences just like those that he used to have. What he seems to see would correspond to what is in fact before him. And his visual experiences would be causally dependent, in this new but reliable way, on the light-waves coming from the objects that are before him.

Would this person be *seeing* these objects? If we insist that seeing must involve the normal cause, we would answer No. But even if this person cannot see, what he has is *just as good as* seeing, both as a way of knowing what is within sight, and as a source of visual pleasure. If we accept the Psychological Criterion, we could make a similar claim. If psychological continuity does not have its normal cause, it may not provide personal identity. But we can claim that, even if this is so, what it provides is *as good as* personal identity.

79. THE OTHER VIEWS

I am asking what is the criterion of personal identity over time—what this identity involves, or consists in. I first described the spatio-temporal physical continuity that, on the standard view, is the criterion of identity of physical objects. I then described two views about personal identity, the Physical and Psychological Criteria.

There is a natural but false assumption about these views. Many people believe in what is called *Materialism*, or *Physicalism*. This is the view that that there are no purely mental objects, states, or events. On one version of Physicalism, every mental event is just a physical event in some particular brain and nervous system. There are other versions. Those who are not Physicalists are either *Dualists* or *Idealists*. Dualists believe that mental events are *not* physical events. This can be so even if all mental events are causally dependent on physical events in a brain. Idealists believe that all states and events are, when understood correctly, purely mental. Given these distinctions, we may assume that Physicalists must accept the Physical Criterion of personal identity.

This is not so. Physicalists could accept the Psychological Criterion. And they could accept the version that allows any reliable cause, or any cause. They could thus believe that, in Simple Teletransportation, my Replica would be me. They would here be rejecting the Physical Criterion.[8]

These criteria are not the only views about personal identity. I shall now describe some of the other views that are either sufficiently plausible, or have enough supporters, to be worth considering. This description may be hard to follow; but it will give a rough idea of what lies ahead. If much of this summary seems either obscure or trivial, do not worry.

I start with a new distinction. On the Physical Criterion, personal identity over time just involves the physically continuous existence of enough of a brain so that it remains the brain of a living person. On the Psychological Criterion, personal identity over time just involves the various kinds of psychological continuity, with the right kind of cause. These views are both *Reductionist*. They are Reductionist because they claim

   (1)   that the fact of a person's identity over time just consists in the holding of certain more particular facts.

They may also claim

   (2)   that these facts can be described without either presupposing the identity of this person, or explicitly claiming that the experiences in this person's life are had by this person, or even explicitly claiming that this person exists. These facts can be described in an *impersonal* way.

It may seem that (2) could not be true. When we describe the psychological continuity that unifies some person's mental life, we must mention this person, and many other people, in describing the *content* of many thoughts, desires, intentions, and other mental states. But mentioning this person in this way does not involve either asserting that these mental states are had by this person, or asserting that this person exists. These claims need further arguments, which I shall later give.

Our view is *Non-Reductionist* if we reject both of the two Reductionist claims.

   Many Non-Reductionists believe that *we are separately existing entities.* On this view, personal identity over time does not just consist in physical and/or psychological continuity. It involves a further fact. A person is a separately existing entity, distinct from his brain and body, and his experiences. On the best-known version of this view, a person is a *purely mental* entity: a Cartesian Pure Ego, or spiritual substance. But we might believe that a person is a separately existing *physical* entity, of a kind that is not yet recognised in the theories of contemporary physics.

   There is another Non-Reductionist View. This view denies that we are separately existing entities, distinct from our brains and bodies, and our experiences. But this view claims that, though we are not separately existing entities, personal identity *is* a further fact, which does not just consist in physical and/or psychological continuity. I call this the *Further Fact View*.

I shall now draw some more distinctions. The Physical and Psychological Criteria are versions of the Reductionist View; and there are different versions of each criterion. But what is necessarily involved in a person's continued existence is less than what is in fact involved. So while believers in the different criteria disagree about imaginary cases, they agree about what is in fact involved in the continued existence of most actual people. They would start to disagree only if, for example, people began to be Teletransported.

On the Reductionist View, each person's existence just involves the existence of a brain and body, the doing of certain deeds, the thinking of certain thoughts, the occurrence of certain experiences, and so on. It will help to extend the ordinary sense of the word 'event'. I shall use this word to cover even such *boring* events as the continued existence of a belief, or a desire. This use makes the Reductionist View simpler to describe. And it avoids what I believe to be one misleading implication of the words 'mental state'. While a state must be a state *of* some entity, this is not true of an event. Given this extended use of the word 'event', all Reductionists would accept

(3)   A person's existence just consists in the existence of a brain and body, and the occurrence of a series of interrelated physical and mental events.

Some Reductionists claim

(4)   A person *just is* a particular brain and body, and such a series of interrelated events.

Other Reductionists claim

(5)   A person is an entity that is *distinct* from a brain and body, and such a series of events.

On this version of the Reductionist View, a person is not merely a composite object, with these various components. A person is an entity that *has* a brain and body, and *has* particular thoughts, desires, and so on. But, though (5) is true, a person is not a *separately existing* entity. Though (5) is true, (3) is also true.

This version of Reductionism may seem self-contradictory. (3) and (5) may seem to be inconsistent. It may help to consider Hume's analogy: 'I cannot compare the soul more properly to anything than to a republic, or commonwealth.'[9] Most of us are Reductionists about nations. We would accept the following claims: Nations exist. Ruritania does not exist, but France does. Though nations exist, a nation is not an entity that exists separately, apart from its citizens and its territory. We would accept

(6)   A nation's existence just involves the existence of its citizens,

living together in certain ways, on its territory.

Some claim

(7) A nation just *is* these citizens and this territory.

Others claim

(8) A nation is an entity that is distinct from its citizens and its territory.

For reasons that I give in Appendix D, we may believe that (6) and (8) are not inconsistent. If we believe this, we may accept that there is no inconsistency between the corresponding claims (3) and (5). We may thus agree that the version of Reductionism expressed in (3) and (5) is a consistent view. If this version is consistent, as I believe, it is the better version. It stays closer to our actual concept of a person. But in most of what follows we can ignore the difference between these two versions.

Besides claiming (1) and (2), Reductionists might also claim

(9) Though persons exist, we could give a *complete* description of reality *without* claiming that persons exist.

I call this the view *that a complete description could be impersonal.*

This view may also seem to be self-contradictory. If persons exist, and a description of what exists fails to mention persons, how can this description be complete?

A Reductionist could give the following reply. Suppose that an object has two names. This is true of the planet that is called both *Venus* and the *Evening Star*. In our description of what exists, we could claim that Venus exists. Our description could then be complete even though we do not claim that the Evening Star exists. We need not make this claim because, using its other name, we have already claimed that this object exists.

A similar claim applies when some fact can be described in two ways. Some Reductionists accept (4), the claim that a person just is a particular brain and body, and a series of interrelated physical and mental events. If this is what a person *is,* we can describe this fact by claiming either

(10) that there exists a particular brain and body, and a particular series of interrelated physical and mental events.

or

(11) that a particular person exists,

If (10) and (11) are two ways of describing the *same* fact, a complete description need not make *both* claims. It would be enough to make claim (10). Though this person exists, a complete description need not claim that he exists, since this fact has already been reported in claim (10).

Other Reductionists accept (5), the claim that a person is distinct from his brain and body, and his acts, thoughts, and other physical and mental events. On this version of Reductionism, claim (10) does not describe the very same fact that claim (11) describes. But claim (10) may *imply* claim (11). More cautiously, given our understanding of the concept of a person, if we know that (10) is true, we shall know that (11) is true. These Reductionists can say that, if our description of reality either states or implies, or enables us to know about, the existence of everything that exists, our description is complete. This claim is not as clearly true as the claim that a complete description need not give two descriptions of the same fact. But this claim seems plausible. If it is justified, and the Reductionist View is true, these Reductionists can completely describe reality without claiming that persons exist.[11]

My claims about Reductionism draw distinctions that, in this abstract form, are hard to grasp. But there are other ways of discovering whether we are Reductionists in our view about some kind of thing. If we accept a Reductionist View, we shall believe that the identity of such a thing may be, in a quite unpuzzling way, *indeterminate*. If we do *not* believe this, we are probably Non-Reductionists about this kind of thing.

Consider, for example, clubs. Suppose that a certain club exists for several years, holding regular meetings. The meetings then cease. Some years later, some of the members of this club form a club with the same name, and the same rules. We ask: 'Have these people reconvened the *very same* club? Or have they merely started up *another* club, which is exactly similar?' There might be an answer to this question. The original club might have had a rule explaining how, after such a period of non-existence, it could be reconvened. Or it might have had a rule preventing this. But suppose that there is no such rule, and no legal facts, supporting either answer to our question. And suppose that the people involved, if they asked our question, would not give it an answer. There would then be no answer to our question. The claim 'This is the same club' would be *neither true nor false*.

Though there is no answer to our question, there may be nothing that we do not know. This is because the existence of a club is not separate from the existence of its members, acting together in certain ways. The continued existence of a club just involves its members having meetings, that are conducted according to the club's rules. If we know all the facts about how people held meetings, and about the club's rules, we know everything there is to know. This is why we would not be puzzled when we cannot answer the question, 'Is this the very same club?' We would not be puzzled because, even without answering this question, we can know everything about what happened. If this is true of some question, I call this question *empty*.

When we ask an empty question, there is only one fact or outcome that we are considering. Different answers to our question are merely different descriptions of this fact or outcome. This is why, without answering this empty question, we can know everything that there is to know. In my example we can ask, 'Is this the very same club, or is it merely another club, that is exactly similar?' But these are not here two different possibilities, one of which must be true.

When an empty question has no answer, we can decide to *give* it an answer. We could decide to call the later club the same as the original club. Or we could decide to call it another club, that is exactly similar. This is not a decision between different views about what really happened. Before making our decision, we already knew what happened. We are merely choosing one of two different descriptions of the very same course of events.

If we are Reductionists about personal identity, we should make similar claims. We can describe cases where, between me now and some future person, the physical and psychological connections hold only to reduced degrees. If I imagine myself in such a case, I can always ask, 'Am I about to die? Will the resulting person be me?' On the Reductionist View, in some cases there would be no answer. My question would be *empty*. The claim that I was about to die would be neither true nor false. If I knew the facts about both physical continuity and psychological connectedness, I would know everything there was to know. I would know everything, even though I did not know whether I was about to die, or would go on living for many years.

When it is applied to ourselves, this Reductionist claim is hard to believe. In such imagined cases, something unusual is about to happen. But most of us are inclined to believe that, in any conceivable case, the question 'Am I about to die?' must have an answer. And we are inclined to believe that this answer must be either, and quite simply, Yes or No. Any future person must be either me, or someone else. These beliefs I call the view that *our identity must be determinate*.

I shall next describe two explanatory claims. The first answers a new question. What unites the different experiences that are had by a single person at the same time? While I type this sentence, I am aware of the movements of my fingers, and can see the sunlight on my desk, and can hear the wind ruffling some leaves. What unites these different experiences? Some claim: the fact that they are all *my* experiences. These are the experiences that are being had, at this time, by a particular person, or *subject of experiences*. A similar question covers my whole life. What unites the different experiences that, together, constitute this life? Some give the same answer. What unites all of these experiences is, simply, that they are all mine. These answers I call the view that *psychological unity is explained by ownership*.

The views described so far are about the nature of personal identity. I shall end with a pair of views that are about, not the nature of this identity, but its importance. Consider an ordinary case where, even on any version of the Reductionist View, there are two possible outcomes. In one of the outcomes, I am about to die. In the other outcome I shall live for many years. If these years would be worth living, the second outcome would be better for me. And the difference between these outcomes would be judged to be important on most theories about rationality, and most moral theories. It would have rational and moral significance whether I am about to die, or shall live for many years. What is judged to be important here is whether, during these years, there will be someone living who will *be me*. This is a question about personal identity. On one view, in this kind of case, this is always what is important. I call this the view that *personal identity is what matters*. This is the natural view.

The rival view is that *personal identity is not what matters*. I claim

What matters is Relation R: psychological connectedness and/or continuity, with the right kind of cause.

Since it is more controversial, I add, as a separate claim

In an account of what matters, the right kind of cause could be any cause.

It is in imaginary cases that we can best decide whether what matters is Relation R or personal identity. One example may be the Branch-Line Case, where my life briefly overlaps with that of my Replica. Suppose that we believe that I and my Replica are two different people. I am about to die, but my Replica will live for another forty years. If personal identity is what matters, I should regard my prospect here as being nearly as bad as ordinary death. But if what matters is Relation R, with any cause, I should regard this way of dying as being about as good as ordinary survival.

The disagreement between these views is not confined to imaginary cases. The two views also disagree about all of the actual lives that are lived. The disagreement is here less sharp, because, on both views, all or nearly all these lives contain the relation that matters. On all of the plausible views about the nature of personal identity, personal identity nearly always coincides with psychological continuity, and roughly coincides with psychological connectedness. But, as I shall argue later, it makes a great difference which of these we believe to be what matters. If we cease to believe that our identity is what matters, this may affect some of our emotions, such as our attitude to ageing and to death. And, as I shall argue, we may be led to change our views about both rationality and morality.

I have now given a first description of several different views. Stated in this abstract way, this description cannot be wholly clear. But what is now obscure may, when I discuss these views, become clear.

How are these views related to each other? I shall claim, what some deny, that many of these views stand or fall together. If this is so, it will be easier to decide what the truth is. When we see how these views are related, we shall find, I believe, that we have only two alternatives. It is worth stating in advance some of the ways in which, as I shall argue, these views are related.

If we do not believe that we are separately existing entities, can we defensibly believe that personal identity is what matters? Some writers think we can. I shall argue that we cannot.

If we do not believe that we are separately existing entities, can we defensibly believe that personal identity does not just consist in physical and psychological continuity, but is a further fact? I believe that we cannot.

If we believe that our identity must be determinate, must we believe that we are separately existing entities? Having the first belief does not imply having the second. We might believe both that we are not separately existing entities, and that, to any question about personal identity, there must always be an answer, which must be either Yes or No. There are some writers who accept this view. But I shall argue that this view is indefensible. Only if we are separately existing entities can it be true that our identity must be determinate.

It would be possible to claim that we are separately existing entities, but deny that our identity must be determinate. But there are few people who would combine these claims.

Suppose next that we believe that psychological unity is explained by ownership. We believe that the unity of a person's consciousness at any time is explained by the fact that this person's different experiences are all being had by this person. And we believe that the unity of a person's whole life is explained by the fact that all of the experiences in this life are had by this person. These are the explanations given by those who claim that we are separately existing entities. Can we give these explanations if we reject that claim? Some writers suggest that we can. But I shall argue that we cannot.

I shall also argue for the following conclusions:

(1)   We are not separately existing entities, apart from our brains and bodies, and various interrelated physical and mental events. Our existence just involves the existence of our brains and bodies, and the doing of our deeds, and the thinking of our thoughts, and the occurrence of certain other physical and mental events. Our identity over time just involves *(a)* Relation R—psychological connected-ness and/or psychological continuity—with the right kind of cause, provided *(b)* that this relation does not take a 'branching' form, holding between one person and two different future people.

(2)   It is not true that our identity is always determinate. I can always ask, 'Am I about to die?' But it is not true that, in every case, this

question must have an answer, which must be either Yes or No. In some cases this would be an empty question.

(3) There are two unities to be explained: the unity of consciousness at any time, and the unity of a whole life. These two unities cannot be explained by claiming that different experiences are had by the same person. These unities must be explained by describing the relations between these many experiences, and their relations to this person's brain. And we can refer to these experiences, and fully describe the relations between them, without claiming that these experiences are had by a person.

(4) Personal identity is not what matters. What fundamentally matters is Relation R, with any cause. This relation is what matters even when, as in a case where one person is R-related to two other people, Relation R does not provide personal identity. Two other relations may have some slight importance: physical continuity, and physical similarity. (In the case of some people, such as those who are very beautiful, physical similarity may have great importance.)

Here is a brief sketch of how I shall argue for my conclusions. I shall first try to answer some objections to my claim that we could describe our lives in an *impersonal* way. I shall then try to show that, even if we are not aware of this, we are naturally inclined to believe that our identity must always be determinate. We are inclined to believe, strongly, that this *must* be so. I shall next argue that this natural belief cannot be true unless we are separately existing entities. I shall then argue for conclusion (1), that we are not such entities. And I shall argue that, because (1) is true, so are my other three conclusions.

Most of us would accept some of the claims that I shall be denying. I shall thus be arguing that most of us have a false view about ourselves, and about our actual lives. If we come to see that this view is false, this may make a difference to our lives.

11

HOW WE ARE NOT WHAT WE BELIEVE

THE different views about personal identity make different claims about actual people, and ordinary lives. But the difference between these views is clearer when we consider certain imaginary cases. Most of the arguments that I shall discuss appeal, in part, to such cases. It may be impossible for some of these cases to occur, whatever progress may be made in science and technology. I distinguish two kinds of case. Some cases contravene the laws of nature. I call these *deeply* impossible. Other cases are *merely technically* impossible.

Does it matter if some imagined case would never be possible? This depends entirely on our question, or what we are trying to show. Even in science it can be worth considering deeply impossible cases. One example is Einstein's thought-experiment of asking what he would see if he could travel beside some beam of light at the speed of light. As this example shows, we need not restrict ourselves to considering only cases which are possible. But we should bear in mind that, depending on our question, impossibility may make some thought-experiment irrelevant.

I start with an objection to the Psychological Criterion.

80. DOES PSYCHOLOGICAL CONTINUITY PRESUPPOSE PERSONAL IDENTITY?

I remember trying, when a child, to remain standing among the crashing waves of the Atlantic Ocean. I am the same person as the child who had that experience. On Locke's view, what makes me the same person as that child is my memory, or 'consciousness', of that experience.

Bishop Butler thought this a 'wonderful mistake'. It is, he wrote, 'self-evident, that consciousness of personal identity presupposes, and therefore cannot constitute personal identity, any more than knowledge in any other case, can constitute truth, which it presupposes'.[12]

I have already revised Locke's view. The Psychological Criterion appeals, not to single memories, but to the continuity of memory, and, more broadly, to Relation R, which includes other kinds of psychological continuity. But this revision does not answer Butler's objection.

On one interpretation, the objection would be this: 'It is part of our concept of memory that we can remember only *our own* experiences. The continuity of memory therefore presupposes personal identity. The same is therefore true of your Relation R. You claim that personal identity just consists in the holding of Relation R. This must be false if Relation R itself presupposes personal identity.'

To answer this objection, we can define a wider concept, *quasi-memory*. I have an accurate quasi-memory of a past experience if

(1)   I seem to remember having an experience,

(2)   *someone* did have this experience,

and

(3)   my apparent memory is causally dependent, in the right kind of way, on that past experience.

On this definition, ordinary memories are a sub-class of quasi-memories. They are quasi-memories of our own past experiences.[13]

We do not quasi-remember other people's past experiences. But we might begin to do so. The causes of long-term memories are memory-traces. It was once thought that these might be localized, involving changes in only a few brain cells. It is now more probable that a particular memory-trace involves changes in a larger number of cells. Suppose that, even if this is true, neuro-surgeons develop ways to create in one brain a copy of a memory-trace in another brain. This might enable us to quasi-remember other people's past experiences.

Consider

Venetian Memories. Jane has agreed to have copied in her brain some of Paul's memory-traces. After she recovers consciousness in the post-surgery room, she has a new set of vivid apparent memories. She seems to remember walking on the marble paving of a square, hearing the flapping of flying pigeons and the cries of gulls, and seeing light sparkling on green water. One apparent memory is very clear. She seems to remember looking across the water to an island, where a white Palladian church stood out brilliantly against a dark thundercloud.

What should Jane believe about these apparent memories? Suppose that, because she has seen this church in photographs, she knows it to be San Giorgio, in Venice. She also knows that she has never been to Italy, while Paul goes to Venice often. Since she knows that she has received copies of some of Paul's memory-traces, she could justifiably assume that she may be quasi-remembering some of Paul's experiences in Venice.

Let us add this detail to the case. Jane seems to remember seeing something extraordinary: a flash of lightning coming from the dark cloud, which forked and struck both the bell-tower of San Giorgio and the red funnel of a tug-boat passing by. She asks Paul whether he remembers seeing such an extraordinary event. He does, and he has kept the issue of the *Gazzettino* where it is reported. Given all of this, Jane should not dismiss her apparent memory as a delusion. She ought to conclude that she has an accurate quasi-memory of how this flash of lightning looked to Paul.

For Jane's quasi-memories to give her knowledge about Paul's experiences, she must know roughly how they have been caused. This is not required in the case of ordinary memories. Apart from this difference, quasi-memories would provide a similar kind of knowledge about other people's past lives. They would provide knowledge of what these lives were like, *from the inside*. When Jane seems to remember walking about the Piazza, hearing the gulls, and seeing the white church, she knows part of what it was like to be Paul, on that day in Venice.

Jane's apparent memories may be, in one respect, mistaken. It may be claimed: 'Since Jane seems to remember *seeing* the lightning, she seems to remember *herself* seeing the lightning. Her apparent memory may tell her accurately what Paul's experience was like, but it tells her, falsely, that it was *she* who had this experience.'

There may be a sense in which this claim is true. Jane's apparent memories may come to her in what Peacocke calls *the first-person mode of presentation*.[14] Thus, when she seems to remember walking across the Piazza, she might seem to remember seeing a child running *towards her*. If this is what she seems to remember, she must be seeming to remember *herself* seeing this child running towards her.

We might deny these claims. In a dream, I can seem to see myself from a point of view *outside* my own body. I might seem to see myself running towards this point of view. Since it is *myself* that I seem to see running in this direction, this direction cannot be towards *myself*. I might say that I seem to see myself running towards *the seer's point of view*. And this could be said to be the direction in which Jane seems to remember seeing this child run. So described, Jane's apparent memory would include no reference to herself.

Though we could deny that Jane's apparent memories must seem, in part, to be about herself, there is no need to do so. Even if her apparent memories are presented in the first-person mode, Jane need not assume that, if they are not delusions, they must be memories of her *own* experiences. Even if she seems to remember herself seeing the forked lightning, she could justifiably conclude that she is quasi-remembering one of Paul's experiences.

Some of Jane's apparent memories would clearly not be of her own experiences. This would be true of an apparent memory of shaving 'her' beard, while seeing Paul's face in the mirror. In the case of other apparent memories, she might have to work out whether it was she or Paul who had some past experience. And this might sometimes be impossible. She might have to say, 'I do vividly seem to remember hearing that tune. But I do not know whether it was I or Paul who heard it.' When Jane's apparent memories come to her like this, they are in one respect unlike the apparent memories the rest of us have. Because we do not have quasi-memories of other people's past experiences, our apparent memories do not merely come to us in the first-person mode. They come with a belief that, unless they are delusions, they are about our own experiences. But, in the case of experience-memories, this is a separable belief. If like Jane we had quasi-memories of other people's past experiences, these apparent memories would cease to be automatically combined with this belief. [15]

Return now to Butler's objection to the Psychological Criterion of personal identity. On this objection, the continuity of memory cannot be, even in part, what makes a series of experiences all the experiences of a single person, since this person's memory presupposes his continued identity.

On the interpretation that I gave above, memory presupposes identity because, on our concept of memory, we can remember only our own past experiences. This objection can now be answered. We can use the wider concept of quasi-memory.

In our statement of our revised Psychological Criterion, we should not claim that, if I have an accurate quasi-memory of some past experience, this makes me the person who had this experience. One person's mental life may include a few quasi-memories of experiences in some other person's life, as in the imagined case of Jane and Paul. Our criterion ignores a few such quasi-memory connections. We appeal instead to overlapping chains of many such connections. My mental life consists of a series of very varied experiences. These include countless quasi-memories of earlier experiences. The connections between these quasi-memories and these earlier experiences overlap like the strands in a rope. There is *strong connectedness* of quasi-memory if, over each day, the number of direct quasi-memory connections is at least half the number in most actual lives. Overlapping strands of strong connectedness provide *continuity of quasi-memory*. Revising Locke, we claim that the unity of each person's life is in part created by this continuity. We are not now appealing to a concept that presupposes personal identity. Since the continuity of quasi-memory does not presuppose personal identity, it may be part of what constitutes personal identity. It may be part of what makes me now and myself at other times one and the same person. (I say 'part' because our criterion also appeals to the other kinds of psychological continuity.)

Butler's objection may be interpreted in a different way. He may have meant: 'In memory we are directly aware of our own identity through time, and aware that this is a separate, further fact, which cannot just consist in physical and psychological continuity. We are aware that each of us is a persisting subject of experiences, a separately existing entity that is not our brain or body. And we are aware that our own continued existence is, simply, the continued existence of this subject of experiences.'

Does our memory tell us this? Are we directly aware of the existence of this separate entity, the subject of experiences? Some have thought that we are aware of this, not just in memory, but in all of our experiences.

81. THE SUBJECT OF EXPERIENCES

Reid writes:

my personal identity. . . implies the continued existence of that indivisible thing that I call myself. Whatever this self may be, it is something which thinks, and deliberates, and resolves, and acts, and suffers. I am not thought, I am not action, I am not feeling; I am something that thinks, and acts, and suffers.[16]

In one sense, this is clearly true. Even Reductionists do not deny that people exist. And, on our concept of a person, people are not thoughts and acts. They are thinkers and agents. I am not a series of experiences, but the person who *has* these experiences. A Reductionist can admit that, in this sense, a person is *what has* experiences, or the *subject of experiences*. This is true because of the way in which we talk. What a Reductionist denies is that the subject of experiences is a *separately existing entity*, distinct from a brain and body, and a series of physical and mental events.

Is it true that, in memory, we are directly aware of what the Reductionist denies? Is each of us aware that he is a persisting subject of experiences, a separately existing entity that is not his brain and body? Is each of us aware, for example, that he is a Cartesian Ego?

This is not a point that can be argued. I do not believe that *I* am directly aware that I am such an entity. And I assume that I am not unusual. I believe that no one is directly aware of such a fact.

Suppose that I *was* aware that I was such an entity. There would still be an objection to the Cartesian View. It has been claimed that I could not know that this entity continued to exist. As both Locke and Kant argued,[17] there might be a series of such entities that were psychologically continuous. Memories might be passed from one to the next like a baton in a relay race. So might all other psychological features. Given the resulting psychological continuity, we would not be aware that one of these entities had been replaced by another. We therefore cannot know that such entities continue to exist.

Reconsider the Branch-Line Case, where it is clear that I remain on Earth. It might seem to a certain person that he has just had these two thoughts: 'Snow is falling. So it must be cold.' But the truth might be this. This person is my Replica on Mars. Just before I pressed the green button, I thought 'Snow is falling'. Several minutes later, my Replica suddenly becomes conscious, in a similar cubicle on Mars. When he becomes conscious, he has apparent memories of living my life, and in particular he seems to remember just having thought, 'Snow is falling'. He then thinks 'So it must be cold'. My Replica on Mars would now be in a state of mind exactly like mine when I have just had both these thoughts. When my Replica is in this state of mind, he would believe that both these thoughts were had by the same thinker, himself. But this would be false. I had the first thought, and my Replica only had the second.

This example is imaginary. But it seems to show that we could not tell, from the content of our experiences, whether we really are aware of the continued existence of a separately existing subject of experiences. The most that we have are states of mind like that of my Replica. My Replica falsely believes that he has just had two thoughts. He is not aware of the continued existence of a separately existing entity: the thinker of these thoughts. He is aware of something less, the psychological continuity between his life and mine. In the same way, when we have had a series of thoughts, the most that we are aware of is the psychological continuity of our stream of consciousness. Some claim that we are aware of the continued existence of separately existing subjects of experiences. As Locke and Kant argued, and our example seems to show, such awareness cannot in fact be distinguished from our awareness of mere psychological continuity. Our experiences give us no reason to believe in the existence of these entities. Unless we have other reasons to believe in their existence, we should reject this belief.

This conclusion is not, as some write, crudely verificationist. I am not assuming that only what we could know could ever be true. My remarks make a different assumption. I am discussing a general claim about the existence of a particular kind of thing. This is claimed to be a separately existing entity, distinct from our brains and bodies. I claim that, if we have no reasons to believe that such entities exist, we should reject this belief. I do not, like verificationists, claim that this belief is senseless. My claim is merely like the claim that, since we have no reason to believe that water-nymphs or unicorns exist, we should reject these beliefs.[18]

Even if we are not directly aware of the existence of these entities, some claim that we can deduce their existence from any of our experiences. Descartes, famously, made such a claim. When he asked if there was anything that he could not doubt, his answer was that he could not doubt his own existence. This was revealed in the very act of doubting. And, besides assuming that every thought must have a thinker, Descartes assumed that a thinker must be a Pure Ego, or spiritual substance. A Cartesian Pure Ego is the clearest case of a separately existing entity, distinct from the brain and body. [19]

Lichtenberg claimed that, in what he thought to be most certain, Descartes went astray. He should not have claimed that a thinker must be a separately existing entity. His famous *Cogito* did not justify this belief. He should not have claimed, 'I think, therefore I am'. Though this is true, it is misleading. Descartes could have claimed instead, 'It is thought: thinking is going on'. Or he could have claimed, 'This is a thought, therefore at least one thought is being thought'.[20]

Because we ascribe thoughts to thinkers, we can truly claim that thinkers exist. But we cannot deduce, from the content of our experiences, that a thinker is a separately existing entity. And, as Lichtenberg suggests, because we are not separately existing entities, we could fully describe our thoughts without claiming that they have thinkers. We could fully describe our experiences, and the connections between them, without claiming that they are had by a subject of experiences. We could give what I call an *impersonal* description.

As I have said, some writers reject *both* this last Reductionist claim *and* the Cartesian View. These writers do not believe in Cartesian Pure Egos. And they do not believe that a person is any other kind of separately existing entity. They believe that the existence of a person just consists in the existence of his brain and body, and the doing of his deeds, and the occurrence of various other physical and mental events. But these writers claim that we cannot refer to particular experiences, or describe the connections between them, unless we refer to the person who has these experiences. On their view, the unity of a mental life cannot be explained in an impersonal way.

Strawson discusses an argument for this view, suggested by Kant. This argument claims that we could not have knowledge of the world about us unless we believe ourselves to be persons, with an awareness of our identity over time. Shoemaker advances a similar argument. If these arguments are correct, they might refute my claim that we could redescribe our lives in an impersonal way. Because these arguments are at a very abstract level, I shall hope to discuss them elsewhere.[21a]

Williams discusses a simpler objection to the impersonal description.[21] This objection is aimed at Lichtenberg. As Williams points out, Lichtenberg's suggested substitute for Descartes' *Cogito* need not be wholly impersonal. It need not be, 'It is thought: thinking is going on'. It could be, 'It is thought: I am thinking'. Since the subject of experiences is here mentioned only in the *content* of the thought, this sentence does not ascribe this thought to a thinker.

Williams then points out that, if several thoughts were expressed in this way, it would need to be made clear whether these thoughts occurred within the same or different lives. This would not be clear if all these thoughts began with the phrase 'It is thought:. . .'. He considers '(T10) It is thought at place A:. . .', but rejects this phrase. He continues:

. . . some less figurative replacement is needed for 'at place A' in the statement of the thought's occurrence—and it is natural to conclude that nothing less than a personal name, or some such, will do as a replacement, so that T10 will give way to

(T11) A thinks:. . .

At this point. . . the programme of introducing impersonal formulations. . . will have finally collapsed.

Williams suggests the answer to this objection. As he writes, 'There might possibly be some replacement for the figurative "places" which served the purposes of effective relativization, but did not go so far as introducing a subject who thinks'. There are many such replacements. Two might be:

In the particular life that contains the thinking of the thought that is expressed by the utterance of this sentence, it is thought:. . .

or

In the particular life that is now directly causally dependent on body A, it is thought:. . .

Lichtenberg would then need to explain the unity of a person's life in an impersonal way. He could first revise our concept of quasi-memory. He could claim that an apparent memory is an accurate quasi-memory if

(1) the apparent memory is of a certain past experience,

(2) this experience occurred,

and

(3) the apparent memory is causally dependent, in the right kind of way, on this experience.

He would have to show that the right kind of cause can be described in a way that does not presuppose personal identity. He could then appeal to the other kinds of psychological continuity, such as that which holds between the forming of an intention and the later act in which this intention is carried out. I have yet to show that these other continuities, and their causes, can be described in ways that do not presuppose personal identity. Since they can be so described, as I show in Section 89, they could also be described in an impersonal way. Persons must be mentioned in describing the *content* of countless thoughts, desires, and other experiences. But, as Williams points out, such descriptions do not claim that these experiences are *had* by persons. And, without making this claim, we could describe the interrelations between all of the mental and physical events that together constitute a particular person's life.

Lichtenberg's objection to Descartes thus survives. We can refer to and describe different thoughts, and describe the relations between them, without ascribing these thoughts to thinkers. We do in fact ascribe thoughts to thinkers. Because we talk in this way, Descartes could truly claim, 'I think, therefore I am'. But Descartes did not show that a thinker must be a separately existing entity, distinct from a brain and body, and various mental and physical events.[22]

82. HOW A NON-REDUCTIONIST VIEW MIGHT HAVE BEEN TRUE

Some writers claim that the concept of a Cartesian Ego is unintelligible. I doubt this claim. And I believe that there might have been evidence supporting the Cartesian View.

There might, for example, have been evidence supporting the belief in reincarnation. One such piece of evidence might be this. A Japanese woman might claim to remember living a life as a Celtic hunter and warrior in the Bronze Age. On the basis of her apparent memories she might make many predictions which could be checked by archaeologists. Thus she might claim to remember having a bronze bracelet, shaped like two fighting dragons. And she might claim that she remembers burying this bracelet beside some particular megalith, just before the battle in which she was killed. Archaeologists might now find just such a bracelet buried in this spot, and their instruments might show that the earth had not here been disturbed for at least 2,000 years. This Japanese woman might make many other such predictions, all of which are verified.

Suppose next that there are countless other cases in which people alive today claim to remember living certain past lives, and provide similar predictions that are all verified. This becomes true of most of the people in the world's population. If there was enough such evidence, and there was no other way in which we could explain how most of us could know such detailed facts about the distant past, we might have to concede that we have accurate quasi-memories about these past lives. We might have to conclude that the Japanese woman has a way of knowing about the life of a Celtic Bronze Age warrior which is like her memory of her own life.

It might next be discovered that there is no physical continuity between the Celtic warrior and the Japanese woman. We might therefore have to abandon the belief that the carrier of memory is the brain. We might have to assume that the cause of these quasi-memories is something purely mental. We might have to assume that there is some purely mental entity, which was in some way involved in the life of the Celtic warrior, and is now in some way involved in the life of the Japanese woman, and which has continued to exist during the thousands of years that separate the lives of these two people. A Cartesian Ego is just such an entity. If there was sufficient evidence of reincarnation, we might have reason to believe that there really are such entities. And we might then reasonably conclude that such an entity is what each of us really is.

This kind of evidence would not directly support the claim that Cartesian Egos have the other special properties in which Cartesians believe. Thus it would not show that the continued existence of these Egos is all-or-nothing. But there might have been evidence to support this claim. There might have been various kinds or degrees of damage to a person's brain which did not in any fundamental way alter this person, while other kinds or degrees of damage seemed to produce a completely new person, in no way psychologically continuous with the original person. Something similar might have been true of the various kinds of mental illness. We might have generally reached the conclusion that these kinds of interference either did nothing at all to destroy psychological continuity, or destroyed it completely. It might have proved impossible to find, or to produce, intermediate cases, in which psychological connectedness held to reduced degrees.

Have we good evidence for the belief in reincarnation? And have we evidence to believe that psychological continuity depends chiefly, not on the continuity of the brain, but on the continuity of some other entity, which either exists unimpaired, or does not exist at all? We do not in fact have the kind of evidence described above. Even if we can understand the concept of a Cartesian Pure Ego, or spiritual substance, we do not have evidence to believe that such entities exist. Nor do we have evidence to believe that a person is any other kind of separately existing entity. And we have much evidence both to believe that the carrier of psychological continuity is the brain, and to believe that psychological connectedness could hold to any reduced degree.[23]

I have conceded that the best-known version of the Non-Reductionist View, which claims that we are Cartesian Egos, may make sense. And I have suggested that, if the facts had been very different, there might have been sufficient evidence to justify belief in this view. Some who believe in Cartesian Egos do not connect them, in such ways, to observable facts. They accept the possibility described by Locke and Kant. On their view, the Cartesian Ego that I am might suddenly cease to exist and be replaced by another Ego. This new Ego might 'inherit' all of my psychological characteristics, as in a relay race. On this *Featureless Cartesian View*, while you are reading this page of text, you might suddenly cease to exist, and your body be taken over by some new person who is merely exactly like you. If this happened, no one would notice any difference. There would never be any evidence, public or private, showing whether or not this happens, and, if so, how often. We therefore cannot even claim that it is unlikely to happen. And there are other possibilities. On this view, history might have gone just as it did, except that I was Napoleon and he was me. This is not the claim that Derek Parfit might have been Napoleon. The claim is rather that I am one Cartesian Ego, and that Napoleon was another, and that these two Egos might have 'occupied' each other's places.[24]

When the belief in Cartesian Egos is in this way cut loose from any connections with either publicly observable or privately introspectible facts, the charge that it is unintelligible becomes more plausible. And it is not clear that Cartesians can avoid this version of their view. It is not clear that they can deny the possibility described by Locke and Kant. But it is enough to repeat that we have sufficient reasons to reject this view.

83. WILLIAMS'S ARGUMENT AGAINST THE PSYCHOLOGICAL CRITERION

I have defended the Psychological Criterion in two ways. I have claimed, and partly shown, that we can describe psychological continuity in a way that does not presuppose personal identity. And I have claimed that, on the evidence we have, the carrier of this continuity is not an entity that exists separately from a person's brain and body.

I shall next consider another objection to the Psychological Criterion. This is advanced by Williams.[25] This objection seems to show that, if some person's brain continues to exist, and to support consciousness, this person will continue to exist, however great the breaks are in the psychological continuity of this person's mental life.

Here is a simpler version of this objection. Consider

Williams's Example. I am the prisoner of some callous neuro-surgeon, who intends to disrupt my psychological continuity by tampering with my brain. I shall be conscious while he operates, and in pain. I therefore dread what is coming.

The surgeon tells me that, while I am in pain, he will do several things. He will first activate some neurodes that will give me amnesia. I shall suddenly lose all of my memories of my life up to the start of my pain. Does this give me less reason to dread what is coming? Can I assume that, when the surgeon flips this switch, my pain will suddenly cease? Surely not. The pain might so occupy my mind that I would even fail to notice the loss of all these memories.

The surgeon next tells me that, while I am still in pain, he will later flip another switch, that will cause me to believe that I am Napoleon, and will give me apparent memories of Napoleon's life. Can I assume that this will cause my pain to cease? The natural answer is again No. To support this answer, we can again suppose that my pain will prevent me from noticing anything. I shall not notice my coming to believe that I am Napoleon, and my acquiring a whole new set of apparent memories. When the surgeon flips this second switch, there will be no change at all in what I am conscious of. The changes will be purely dispositional. It will only become true that, if my pain ceased, so that I could think, I would answer the question 'Who are you?' with the name 'Napoleon'. Similarly, if my pain ceased, I would then start to have delusory apparent memories, such as those of reviewing the Imperial Guard, or of weeping with frustration at the catastrophe of 1812. If it is only such changes in my dispositions that would be brought about by the flipping of the second switch, I would have no reason to expect this to cause my pain to cease.

The surgeon then tells me that, during my ordeal, he will later flip a third switch, that will change my character so that it becomes just like Napoleon's. Once again, I seem to have no reason to expect the flipping of this switch to end my pain. It might at most bring some relief, if Napoleon's character, compared with mine, involved more fortitude.

In this imagined case, nothing that I am told seems to give me a reason to expect that, during my ordeal, I shall cease to exist. I seem to have as much reason to dread all of the pain. This reason does not seem to be removed by the other things I have to dread—losing my memories, and going mad, becoming like, and thinking that I am, Napoleon. As Williams claims, this argument seems to show that I can have reason to fear future pain whatever psychological changes precede this pain. Even after all these changes, it will be I who feels this pain. If this is so, the Psychological Criterion of personal identity is mistaken. In this imagined case, between me now and myself after the ordeal, there would be no continuity of memory, character, and the like. What is involved in my continuing to exist therefore cannot be such continuity.[26]

It may be objected that, if I remain conscious throughout this ordeal, there will at least be one kind of psychological continuity. Though I lose all my memories of my past life, I would have memories of my ordeal. In particular, I would continue to have short-term memories of the last few moments, or what is sometimes called the *specious present*. Throughout my ordeal there would be an overlapping chain of such memories.

To meet this objection we can add one feature to the case. After I have lost all my other memories, I am for a moment made unconscious. When I regain consciousness, I have *no* memories. As the ordeal continues, I would have new memories. But there would be no continuity of memory over my moment of unconsciousness.

It may next be objected that I have described this story in question-begging terms. Thus I suggested that, when I am made to lose my memories, I might, because of my pain, fail to notice any change. This description assumes that, after the loss of my memories, the person in pain would still be me. Perhaps the truth is that, at this point, I would cease to exist, and a new person would start to exist in my body.

Williams would reply that, even though my description assumes that I would continue to exist, this is the overwhelmingly plausible assumption. It is the defender of the Psychological Criterion who must show that this assumption is not justified. And this would be hard to show. It is hard to believe that, if I was made to lose my memories while I was in agony, this would cause me to cease to exist half-way through the agony. And it is hard to believe that the change in my character would have this effect.

Williams's argument seems to refute the Psychological Criterion. It seems to show that the true view is the Physical Criterion. On this view, if some person's brain and body continue to exist, and to support consciousness, this person will continue to exist, however great the breaks are in the psychological continuity of this person's mental life.

84. THE PSYCHOLOGICAL SPECTRUM

I shall now revise Williams's argument. Why this is worth doing will emerge later.

Williams discusses a single case in which, after a few changes, there will be no psychological continuity. I shall discuss a *spectrum*, or range of cases, each of which is very similar to its neighbours. These cases involve all of the possible degrees of psychological connectedness. I call this the *Psychological Spectrum*.

In the case at the far end, the surgeon would cause very many switches to be simultaneously flipped. This would cause there to be no psychological connections between me and the resulting person. This person would be wholly like Napoleon.

In the cases at the near end, the surgeon would cause to be flipped only a few switches. If he flipped only the first switch, this would merely cause me to lose a few memories, and to have a few apparent memories that fit the life of Napoleon. If he flipped the first two switches, I would merely lose a few more memories, and have a few more of these new apparent memories. Only if he flipped all of the switches would I lose all my memories, and have a complete set of Napoleonic delusions.

Similar claims are true about the changes in my character. Any particular switch would cause only a small change. Thus, if I am to be like Napoleon, I must become more bad-tempered, and must cease to be upset by the sight of people being killed. These would be the only changes produced by the flipping of the first two switches.

In this revised version of the argument, which involves very many different cases, we must decide which are the cases in which I would survive. In the case at the near end, the surgeon does nothing. In the second case, I would merely lose a few memories, have a few delusions, and become more bad-tempered. It is clear that, in this case, I would survive. In the third case, the changes would be only slightly greater. And this is true of any two neighbouring cases in this range. It is hard to believe both that I would survive in one of these cases, and that, in the next case, I would cease to exist. Whether I continue to exist cannot be plausibly thought to depend on whether I would lose just a few more memories, and have a few more delusory memories, and have my character changed in some small way. If no such small change could cause me to cease to exist, I would continue to exist in all of these cases. I would continue to exist even in the case at the far end of this spectrum. In this case, between me now and the resulting person, there would be *no* psychological connections.

It may be objected:

In this revised form, the argument suspiciously resembles those that are involved in the *Sorites Problem*, or the *Paradox of the Heap*. We are led there, by what seem innocent steps, to absurd conclusions. Perhaps the same is happening here.

Suppose we claim that the removal of a single grain cannot change a heap of sand into something that is not a heap. Someone starts with a heap of sand, which he removes grain by grain. Our claim forces us to admit that, after every change, we still have a heap, even when the number of grains becomes three, two, and one. But we know that we have reached a false conclusion. One grain is not a heap.

In your appeal to the Psychological Spectrum, you claim that no small change could cause you to cease to exist. By making enough small changes, the surgeon could cause the resulting person to be in no way psychologically connected with you. The argument forced you to conclude that the resulting person would be you. This conclusion may be just as false as the conclusion about the grain of sand.

To defend this version of Williams's argument, I need not solve the Sorites Problem. It will be enough to make the following remarks.

When considering heaps, we all believe that there are borderline cases. Are two grains of sand a heap, or four, or eight, or sixteen? We may not know how to answer all of these questions. But we do not believe that this is the result of ignorance. We do not believe that each of these questions must have an answer. We know that the concept of a heap is vague, with vague borderlines. And when the Sorites Argument is applied to heaps, we are happy to solve the problem with a *stipulation*: an arbitrary decision about how to use the word 'heap'. We might decide that we shall not call nine grains a heap, but we shall call heaps any collection of ten or more grains. We shall then be abandoning one premise of the argument. On our new more precise concept, the removal of a single grain may turn a heap of sand into something that is not a heap. This happens with the removal of the tenth last grain.

When it is applied to other subjects, such as phenomenal colour, the Sorites Argument cannot be so easily dismissed.[27] Nor does this dismissal seem plausible when the argument is applied to personal identity. Most of us believe that our own continued existence is, in several ways, unlike the continued existence of a heap of sand.

Reconsider the range of cases in the Psychological Spectrum. Like Williams's Example, these cases provide an argument against the Psychological Criterion. This criterion is one version of the Reductionist View. A Reductionist might say:

The argument assumes that, in each of these cases, the resulting person either would or would not be me. This is not so. The resulting person would be me in the first few cases. In the last case he would not be me. In many of the intervening cases, neither answer would be true. I can always ask, 'Am I about to die? Will there be some person living who will be me?' But, in the cases in the middle of this Spectrum, there is no answer to this question.

Though there is no answer to this question, I could know exactly what will happen. This question is, here, *empty*. In each of these cases I could know to what degree I would be psychologically connected with the resulting person. And I could know which particular connections would or would not hold. If I knew these facts, I would know everything. I can still ask whether the resulting person would be *me*, or would merely be *someone else* who is partly like me. In some cases, these are two different possibilities, one of which must be true. But, in *these* cases, these are not two different possibilities. They are merely two descriptions of the very same course of events.

These remarks are analogous to remarks that we accept when applied to heaps. We do not believe that any collection of sand must either be, or not be, a heap. We know that there are borderline cases, where there is no obvious answer to the question 'Is this still a heap?' But we do not believe that, in these cases, there must *be* an answer, which must be either Yes or No. We believe that, in these cases, this is an empty question. Even without answering the question, we know everything.

As Williams claims, when applied to our own existence, such remarks seem incredible. Suppose that I am about to undergo an operation in the middle of this Spectrum. I know that the resulting person will be in agony. If I do not know whether or not I shall be the person in agony, and I do not even know whether I shall still be alive, how can I believe that I *do* know exactly what will happen? I do not know the answer to the most important questions. It is very hard to believe that these are empty questions.

Most of us believe that we are not like heaps, because our identity must be determinate. We believe that, even in such 'borderline cases', the question 'Am I about to die?' must have an answer. And, as Williams claims, we believe that the answer must be either, and quite simply, Yes or No. If someone will be alive, and will be suffering agony, this person either will or will not be me. One of these must be true. And we cannot make sense of any third alternative, such as that the person in agony will be *partly* me. I can imagine being only partly in agony, because I am drifting in and out of consciousness. But if someone will be fully conscious of the agony, this person cannot be partly me.

The Reductionist View would provide an answer to Williams's argument. When Williams gives his version of this argument, he rejects this view. He concludes instead that, if my brain continues to exist, and to be the brain of a living person, I shall be that person. This would be so even if, between myself now and myself later, there would be *no* psychological connections. After advancing his argument, Williams writes that this conclusion may 'perhaps' be wrong, 'but we need to be shown what is wrong with it'.[28]

85. THE PHYSICAL SPECTRUM

One objection is that a similar argument applies to physical continuity. Consider another range of possible cases: the *Physical Spectrum*. These cases involve all of the different possible degrees of physical continuity.

In the case at the near end of this spectrum, there would later be a person who would be fully continuous with me as I am now, both physically and psychologically. In the case at the far end, there would later be a person who would be psychologically but not physically continous with me as I am now. The far end is like the case of Teletransportation. The near end is the normal case of continued existence.

In a case close to the near end, scientists would replace 1% of the cells in my brain and body with exact duplicates. In the case in the middle of the spectrum, they would replace 50%. In a case near the far end, they would replace 99%, leaving only 1% of my original brain and body. At the far end, the 'replacement' would involve the complete destruction of my brain and body, and the creation out of new organic matter of a Replica of me.

What is important in this last case is not just that my Replica's brain and body would be entirely composed of new matter. As I explained, this might become true in a way that does not destroy my brain and body. It could become true if there is a long series of small changes in the matter in my body, during which my brain and body continue to exist, and to function normally. This would be like the ship that becomes entirely composed of new bits of wood, after fifty years of piecemeal repairs. In both of these cases, the complete change in the identity of the components does not disrupt physical continuity. Things are different in the case at the far end of the Physical Spectrum. There is here no physical continuity, since my brain and body are completely destroyed, and it is only later that the scientists create, out of new matter, my Replica.

The first few cases in this range are now believed to be technically possible. Portions of brain-tissue have been successfully transplanted from one mammal's brain to another's. And what is transplanted could be a part of the brain that, in all individuals, is sufficiently similar. This could enable surgeons to provide functioning replacements for some damaged parts of the brain. These actual transplants proved to be easier than the more familiar transplants of the kidney or the heart, since a brain seems not to 'reject' transplanted tissue in the way in which the body rejects transplanted organs.[29] Though the first few cases in this range are even now possible, most of the cases will remain impossible. But this impossibility will be merely technical. Since I use these cases only to discover what we believe, this impossibility does not matter.

Suppose we believe that, at the far end of this spectrum, my Replica would not be me. He would merely be someone else who was exactly like me. At the near end of this spectrum, where there would be no replacement, the resulting person would be me. What should I expect if what will happen is some intermediate case? If they replaced only 1%, would I cease to exist? This is not plausible, since I do not need all of my brain and body. But what about the cases where they would replace 10%, or 30%, or 60%, or 90%?

This range of cases challenges the Physical Criterion, which is another version of the Reductionist View. Imagine that you are about to undergo one of these operations. You might try to believe this version of Reductionism. You might say to yourself:

In any central case in this range, the question 'Am I about to die?' has no answer. But I know just what will happen. A certain percentage of my brain and body will be replaced with exact duplicates of the existing cells. The resulting person will be psychologically continuous with me as I am now. This is all there is to know. I do not know whether the resulting person will be me, or will be someone else who is merely exactly like me. But this is not, here, a real question, which must have an answer. It does not describe two different possibilities, one of which must be true. It is here an empty question. There is not a real difference here between the resulting person's being *me*, and his being *someone else*. This is why, even though I do not know whether I am about to die, I know everything.

I believe that, for those who accept the Physical Criterion, this is the right reaction to this range of cases. But most of us would not yet accept such claims.

If we do not yet accept the Reductionist View, and continue to believe that our identity must be determinate, what should we claim about these cases? If we continue to assume that my Replica would not be me, we are forced to the following conclusion. There must be some critical percentage which is such that, if the surgeons replace less than this percent, it will be me who wakes up, but if they replace more than this percent, it will *not* be me, but only someone else who is merely like me. We might suggest a variant of this conclusion. Perhaps there is some crucial part of my brain which is such that, if the surgeons do not replace this part, the resulting person will be me, but if they do, it will be someone else. But this makes no difference. What if they replace different percentages of this crucial part of my brain? We are again forced to the view that there must be some critical percentage.

Such a view is not incoherent. But it is hard to believe. And something else is true, that makes it even harder to believe. We could not *discover* what the critical percentage is, by carrying out some of the cases in this imagined spectrum. I might say, 'Try replacing 50% of the cells in my brain and body, and I shall tell you what happens'. But we know in advance that, in every case, the resulting person would be inclined to believe that he is me. And this would not show that he *is* me. Carrying out such cases could not provide the answer to our question.

These remarks assume that all of a person's psychological features depend upon the states of the cells in his brain and nervous system. I assume that an organic Replica of me would be psychologically exactly like me. If we reject this assumption, we could respond to this range of imagined cases in a different way. I answer this response in the next section.

If my assumption is correct, and each of these resulting people would be exactly like me, what should we believe about this range of cases? We have three alternatives

(1)   We could accept the Reductionist reply given above.

(2)   We could believe that there *is* a sharp borderline between two cases. If the surgeons replaced only certain cells, the resulting person would be me. If instead they replaced just a few more cells, the resulting person would not be me, but would merely be exactly like me. There must be this sharp borderline somewhere in this range of cases, even though we could never discover where this line is.

(3)   We could believe that, in all of these cases, the resulting person would be me.

Of these three conclusions, (3) seems to most people the least implausible. If we accept (3), we believe that psychological continuity provides personal identity. We believe that this is so even when this continuity does not have its normal cause: the continued existence of a particular brain.

When we considered the Psychological Spectrum, Williams's argument seemed to show that psychological continuity is not necessary for personal identity. Physical continuity would be sufficient. When we consider the Physical Spectrum, a similar argument seems to show that physical continuity is not necessary for personal identity. Psychological continuity would be sufficient.

We could accept both of these conclusions. We could claim that either kind of continuity provides personal identity. Though this hybrid view is coherent, it is open to grave objections. One objection arises if we combine, not our two conclusions, but the two arguments for these conclusions.

86. THE COMBINED SPECTRUM

Consider another range of possible cases. These involve all of the possible variations in the degrees of *both* physical *and* psychological connectedness. This is the *Combined Spectrum*.

At the near end of this spectrum is the normal case in which a future person would be fully continuous with me as I am now, both physically and psychologically. This person would be me in just the way that, in my actual life, it will be me who wakes up tomorrow. At the far end of this spectrum the resulting person would have no continuity with me as I am now, either physically or psychologically. In this case the scientists would destroy my brain and body, and then create, out of new organic matter, a perfect Replica of someone else. Let us suppose this person to be, not Napoleon, but Greta Garbo. We can suppose that, when Garbo was 30, a group of scientists recorded the states of all the cells in her brain and body.

In the first case in this spectrum, at the near end, nothing would be done. In the second case, a few of the cells in my brain and body would be replaced. The new cells would *not* be exact duplicates. As a result, there would be somewhat less psychological connectedness between me and the person who wakes up. This person would not have all of my memories, and his character would be in one way unlike mine. He would have some apparent memories of Greta Garbo's life, and have one of Garbo's characteristics. Unlike me, he would enjoy acting. His body would also be in one way less like mine, and more like Garbo's. His eyes would be more like Garbo's eyes. Further along the spectrum, a larger percentage of my cells would be replaced, again with dissimilar cells. The resulting person would be in fewer ways psychologically connected with me, and in more ways connected with Garbo, as she was at the age of 30. And there would be similar changes in this person's body. Near the far end, most of my cells would be replaced with dissimilar cells. The person who wakes up would have only a few of the cells in my original brain and body, and between her and me there would be only a few psychological connections. She would have a few apparent memories that fit my past, and a few of my habits and desires. But in every other way she would be, both physically and psychologically, just like Greta Garbo.

These cases provide, I believe, a strong argument for the Reductionist View. The argument again assumes that our psychological features depend upon the states of our brains. Suppose that the cause of psychological continuity was not the continued existence of the brain, but the continued existence of a separately existing entity, like a Cartesian Ego. We could then claim that, if we carried out such operations, the results would *not* be as I have described them. We would find that, if we replaced much of someone's brain, even with dissimilar cells, the resulting person would be exactly like the original person. But there would be some critical percentage, or some critical part of the brain, whose replacement would utterly destroy psychological continuity. In one of the cases in this range, the carrier of continuity would cease either to exist, or to interact with this brain. The resulting person would be psychologically totally unlike the original person.

If we had reasons to believe this view, it would provide an answer to my argument. There *would* be, in this range of cases, a sharp borderline. And *this* borderline *could* be discovered. It would correspond with what appeared to be a complete change in personal identity. This view would also explain how the replacement of a few cells could totally destroy psychological continuity.

And this view could be applied to both the Psychological and the Physical Spectrum. We could claim that, in both these Spectra, the results would not in fact be what I assumed.

Except for the cases close to the near end, the cases in the Combined Spectrum are, and are likely to remain, technically impossible. We therefore cannot directly discover whether the results would be as I assumed, or would instead be of the kind just described. But what the results would be depends on what the relation is between the states of someone's brain and this person's mental life. Have we evidence to believe that psychological continuity depends chiefly, not on the continuity of the brain, but on the continuity of some other entity, which either exists unimpaired, or does not exist at all? We do not in fact have the kind of evidence that I described above. And we have much reason to believe both that the carrier of psychological continuity is the brain, and that psychological connectedness could hold to any reduced degree.

Since our psychological features depend on the states of our brains, these imagined cases are only technically impossible. If we could carry out these operations, the results would be what I have described. What should we believe about the different cases in this Combined Spectrum? Which are the cases in which I would continue to exist?.

As before, we could not find the answer by actually performing, on me and other people, operations of the kind imagined. We already know that, somewhere along the Spectrum, there would be the first case in which the resulting person would believe that he or she was not me. And we have no reason to trust this belief. In this kind of case, who someone is cannot be shown by who he thinks he is. Since experiments would not help, we must try to decide now what we believe about these cases.

In considering the first two Spectra, we had three alternatives: accepting a Reductionist reply, believing that there must be some sharp borderline, and believing that the resulting person would in every case be me. Of these three, the third seemed the least implausible conclusion.

In considering the Combined Spectrum, we cannot accept this conclusion. In the case at the far end, the scientists destroy my brain and body, and then make, out of new matter, a Replica of Greta Garbo. There would be no connection, of any kind, between me and this resulting person. It could not be clearer that, in this case, the resulting person would *not* be me. We are forced to choose between the other two alternatives.

We might continue to believe that our identity must be determinate. We might continue to believe that, to the question 'Would the resulting person be me?', there must always be an answer, which must be either and quite simply Yes or No. We would then be forced to accept the following claims:

Somewhere in this Spectrum, there is a sharp borderline. There must be some critical set of the cells replaced, and some critical degree of psychological change, which would make all the difference. If the surgeons replace slightly fewer than these cells, and produce one fewer psychological change, it will be me who wakes up. If they replace the few extra cells, and produce one more psychological change, I shall cease to exist, and the person waking up will be someone else. There must be such a pair of cases somewhere in this Spectrum, *even though there could never be any evidence where these cases are.*

These claims are hard to believe. It is hard to believe (1) that the difference between life and death could just consist in any of the very small differences described above. We are inclined to believe that there is *always* a difference between some future person's being me, and his being someone else. And we are inclined to believe that this is a *deep* difference. But between neighbouring cases in this Spectrum the differences are trivial. It is therefore hard to believe that, in one of these cases, the resulting person would quite straightforwardly be me, and that, in the next case, he would quite straightforwardly be someone else.

It is also hard to believe (2) that there must be such a sharp borderline, somewhere in the Spectrum, though we could never have any evidence where the borderline would be. Some would claim that, if there could never be such evidence, it makes no sense to claim that there must somewhere be such a line.

Even if (2) makes sense, claims (1) and (2), taken together, are extremely implausible. I believe that they are even more implausible than the only other possible conclusion, which is the Reductionist View. We should therefore now conclude that the Reductionist View is true. On this view, in the central cases of the Combined Spectrum, it would be an empty question whether the resulting person would be me. This Spectrum provides, as I claimed, a strong argument for this view.

There are some people who believe that our identity must be determinate, though they do not believe that we are separately existing entities, distinct from our brains and bodies, and our experiences. This view I believe to be indefensible. What explains the alleged fact that personal identity is always determinate? The answer must be that the true criterion of personal identity covers every case. The true criterion must draw a sharp borderline somewhere in the Combined Spectrum. But, if we are not separately existing entities, how could there be such a borderline? What could make it true that, in one case, the resulting person would be me, and in the next he would not be me? What would the difference consist in?

There are other people who believe that, though we are not separately existing entities, personal identity is a further fact. These people believe that personal identity does not just consist in the different kinds of physical and psychological continuity. This is another view that I believe to be indefensible. If we are not separately existing entities, in what could this further fact consist? What could make this fact, in the cases in this range, either hold or fail to hold?

This Spectrum shows, I believe, that certain views must be held together. We cannot defensibly believe that our identity involves a further fact, unless we also believe that we are separately existing entities, distinct from our brains and bodies. And we cannot defensibly believe that our identity must be determinate, unless we believe that the existence of these separate entities must be all-or-nothing.

Some people believe that the identity of *everything* must always be determinate. These people accept a strict form of the doctrine *no entity without identity*. This is the claim that we cannot refer to a particular object, or name this object, unless our criterion of identity for this object yields a definite answer in every conceivable case. On this view, we often mistakenly believe that we are referring to some object, when, because there is no such criterion of identity, there is no such object. It would thus be claimed that most of us mistakenly believe that the name 'France' refers to a nation. On this view, nations cannot be referred to, since they do not exist. There is no criterion of identity for nations which meets the required standard—which would tell us, in every conceivable case, whether or not some nation had continued to exist. Those who hold this view may believe that it could not be similarly true that persons do not exist. If this view is true, and persons do exist, the criterion of personal identity must yield a definite answer in all cases.

This view need not involve the belief that a person is a separately existing entity. This may seem to make this view more plausible. But, if we hold this view, we must again believe that the true criterion of personal identity draws a sharp borderline, quite unknowably, somewhere in the Combined Spectrum. As I have claimed, if personal identity does not involve a further fact, it is very hard to believe that there can be such a line. This is even less plausible than the Reductionist View.

There is another way in which some writers claim that our identity must be determinate. On this view, we have inconsistent beliefs if there are cases where we cannot answer a question about the identity of some object. I believe that there are such cases, and that in such a case the identity of some object is indeterminate. I claim that, in such a case, the statement 'This is the same object that we had before' would be neither true nor false. It has been argued that this claim is incoherent.[31] I believe that this argument has been answered.[32] But suppose that the argument is correct. This implies the following. When we find cases that are not covered by what we believe to be some criterion of identity, we should revise our beliefs by extending this criterion. If we hold this view, we do not believe that the true criterion of personal identity must draw some sharp borderline somewhere in the Combined Spectrum. Rather we believe that, to avoid incoherence, we should draw such a line.

This view hardly differs from the Reductionist View. If we do draw such a line, we cannot believe that it has, intrinsically, either rational or moral significance. We must pick some point on this Spectrum, up to which we will call the resulting person me, and beyond which we will call him someone else. Our choice of this point will have to be arbitrary. We must draw this line between two neighbouring cases, though the difference between them is, in itself, trivial. If this is what we do, this should not affect our attitude towards these two cases. It would be clearly irrational for me to regard the first case as being as good as ordinary survival, while regarding the second case as being as bad as ordinary death. When I consider this range of cases, I naturally ask, 'Will the resulting person be me?' By drawing our line, we have chosen to *give* an answer to this question. But, since our choice was arbitrary, it cannot justify any claim about what matters. If this is how we answer the question about my identity, we have made it true that, in this range of cases, personal identity is *not* what matters. And this is the most important claim in the Reductionist View. Our view differs only trivially from this view. Reductionists claim that, in some cases, questions about personal identity are indeterminate. We add the claim that, in such cases, we ought to give these questions answers, even if we have to do so in a way that is arbitrary, and that deprives our answers of any significance. I regard this view as one version of Reductionism, the tidy-minded version that abolishes indeterminacy with uninteresting stipulative definitions. Since the difference is so slight, I shall ignore this version of this view.

On the simplest version of Physicalism, every mental event is an event in a brain. I remarked above that we could both be Physicalists and accept the *Psychological* Criterion of personal identity. I should add that Reductionists need not be Physicalists. If we are not Physicalists, we could be either Dualists, who believe that mental events are different from physical events, or Idealists, who believe that all events are purely mental. If we believe that we are Cartesian Egos, we believe in one form of Dualism. But Dualists can be Reductionists about personal identity. We can believe that mental events are distinct from physical events, and believe that the unity of a person's life just consists in the various kinds of connection which hold between all of the mental and physical events which, together, constitute this life. This is the Dualistic version of the Reductionist View.

I shall argue that, if we are Reductionists, we should not try to decide between the different criteria of personal identity. One reason is that personal identity is not what matters. Before I argue for this conclusion, I shall explain further what a Reductionist claims. And since most of us are strongly inclined to reject these claims, considering the Combined Spectrum may not be enough to change our view. I shall therefore, in the next chapter, advance other arguments for the Reductionist View.

Reductionists admit that there is a difference between numerical identity and exact similarity. In some cases, there would be a real difference between some person's being me, and his being someone else who is merely exactly like me. Many people assume that there must *always* be such a difference.

In the case of nations, or clubs, such an assumption is false. Two clubs could exist at the same time, and be, apart from their membership, exactly similar. If I am a member of one of these clubs, and you claim also to be a member, I might ask, 'Are you a member of the very same club of which I am a member? Or are you merely a member of the other club, that is exactly similar?' This is not an empty question, since it describes two different possibilities. But, though there are two possibilities in a case in which the two clubs co-exist, there may not be two such possibilities when we are discussing the relation between some presently existing club and some past club. There were not two possibilities in the case that I described in Section 79. In this case there was nothing that would justify either the claim that we have the very same club, or the claim that we have a new club that is merely exactly similar. In this case these would *not* be two different possibilities.

In the same way, there are some cases where there is a real difference between someone's being me, and his being someone else who is exactly like me. This may be so in the Branch-Line Case, the version of Tele-transportation where the Scanner does not destroy my brain and body. In the Branch-Line Case, my life overlaps with the life of my Replica on Mars. Given this overlap, we may conclude that we are two different people—that we are qualitatively but not numerically identical. If I am the person on Earth, and my Replica on Mars now exists, it makes a difference whether some pain will be felt by me, or will instead be felt by my Replica. This is a real difference in what will happen.

If we return to Simple Teletransportation, where there is no overlap between my life and that of my Replica, things are different. We could say here that my Replica will be me, or we could instead say that he will merely be someone else who is exactly like me. But we should not regard these as competing hypotheses about what will happen. For these to be competing hypotheses, my continued existence must involve a *further fact*. If my continued existence merely involves physical and psychological continuity, we know just what happens in this case. There will be some future person who will be physically exactly like me, and who will be fully psychologically continuous with me. This psychological continuity will have a reliable cause, the transmission of my blueprint. But this continuity will not have its normal cause, since this future person will not be physically continuous with me. This is a full description of the facts. There is no further fact about which we are ignorant. If personal identity does not involve a further fact, we should not believe that there are here two different possibilities: that my Replica will be me, or that he will be someone else who is merely like me. What could make these different possibilities? In what could the difference consist?

Some non-Reductionists would agree that, in this case, there are not two possibilities. These people believe that, in the case of Teletransportation, my Replica would not be me. I shall later discuss a plausible argument for this conclusion. If we would be wrong to say that my Replica is me, the remarks that I have just made apply instead to the central cases in the Physical Spectrum. My Replica might have a quarter of the existing cells in my brain and body, or half, or three-quarters. In these cases there are not two different possibilities: that my Replica is me, or that he is someone else who is merely like me. These are merely different descriptions of the same outcome.

If we believe that there is always a real difference between some person's being me and his being someone else, we must believe that this difference comes somewhere in this range of cases. There must be a sharp borderline, though we could never know where this is. As I have claimed, this belief is even more implausible than the Reductionist View.

In the case of clubs, though there is sometimes a difference between numerical identity and exact similarity, there is sometimes no difference. The question, 'Is it the same, or merely exactly similar?' is sometimes empty. This could be true of people, too. It would be true either at the end or in the middle of the Physical Spectrum.

It is hard to believe that this could be true. When I imagine myself about to press the green button, it is hard to believe that there is not a real question whether I am about to die, or shall instead wake up again on Mars. But, as I have argued, this belief cannot be justified unless personal identity involves a further fact. And there could not be such a fact unless I am a separately existing entity, apart from my brain and body. One such entity is a Cartesian Ego. As I have claimed, there is no evidence in favour of this view, and much evidence against it.

12

WHY OUR IDENTITY IS NOT WHAT MATTERS

87. DIVIDED MINDS

SOME recent medical cases provide striking evidence in favour of the Reductionist View. Human beings have a lower brain and two upper hemispheres, which are connected by a bundle of fibres. In treating a few people with severe epilepsy, surgeons have cut these fibres. The aim was to reduce the severity of epileptic fits, by confining their causes to a single hemisphere. This aim was achieved. But the operations had another unintended consequence. The effect, in the words of one surgeon, was the creation of 'two separate spheres of consciousness'.[33]

This effect was revealed by various psychological tests. These made use of two facts. We control our right arms with our left hemispheres, and vice versa. And what is in the right halves of our visual fields we see with our left hemispheres, and vice versa. When someone's hemispheres have been disconnected, psychologists can thus present to this person two different written questions in the two halves of his visual field, and can receive two different answers written by this person's two hands.

Here is a simplified version of the kind of evidence that such tests provide. One of these people is shown a wide screen, whose left half is red and right half is blue. On each half in a darker shade are the words, 'How many colours can you see?' With both hands the person writes, 'Only one'. The words are now changed to read, 'Which is the only colour that you can see?' With one of his hands the person writes 'Red', with the other he writes 'Blue'.

If this is how this person responds, there seems no reason to doubt that he is having visual sensations—that he does, as he claims, see both red and blue. But in seeing red he is not aware of seeing blue, and vice versa. This is why the surgeon writes of 'two separate spheres of consciousness'. In each of his centres of consciousness the person can see only a single colour. In one centre, he sees red, in the other, blue.

The many actual tests, though differing in details from the imagined test that I have just described, show the same two essential features. In seeing what is in the left half of his visual field, such a person is quite unaware of what he is now seeing in the right half of his visual field, and vice versa. And in the centre of consciousness in which he sees the left half of his visual field, and is aware of what he is doing with his left hand, this person is quite unaware of what he is doing with his right hand, and vice versa.

One of the complications in the actual cases is that for most people, in at least the first few weeks after the operation, speech is entirely controlled by the right-handed hemisphere. As a result, 'if the word "hat" is flashed on the left, the left hand will retrieve a hat from a group of concealed objects if the person is told to pick out what he has seen. At the same time he will insist verbally that he saw nothing.'[34] Another complication is that, after a certain time, each hemisphere can sometimes control both hands. Nagel quotes an example of the kind of conflict which can follow:

A pipe is placed out of sight in the patient's left hand, and he is then asked to write with his left hand what he was holding. Very laboriously and heavily, the left hand writes the letters P and I. Then suddenly the writing speeds up and becomes lighter, the I is converted to an E, and the word is completed as PENCIL. Evidently the left hemisphere has made a guess based on the appearance of the first two letters, and has interfered . . . But then the right hemisphere takes over control of the hand again, heavily crosses out the letters ENCIL, and draws a crude picture of a pipe.[35]

Such conflict may take more sinister forms. One of the patients complained that sometimes, when he embraced his wife, his left hand pushed her away.

Much has been made of another complication in the actual cases, hinted at in Nagel's example. The left hemisphere typically supports or 'has' the linguistic and mathematical abilities of an adult, while the right hemisphere 'has' these abilities at the level of a young child. But the right hemisphere, though less advanced in these respects, has greater abilities of other kinds, such as those involved in pattern recognition, or musicality. It is assumed that, after the age of three or four, the two hemispheres follow a 'division of labour', with each developing certain abilities. The lesser linguistic abilities of the right hemisphere are not intrinsic, or permanent. People who have had strokes in their left hemispheres often regress to the linguistic ability of a young child, but with their remaining right hemispheres many can re-learn adult speech. It is also believed that, in a minority of people, there may be no difference between the abilities of the two hemispheres.

Suppose that I am one of this minority, with two exactly similar hemispheres. And suppose that I have been equipped with some device that can block communication between my hemispheres. Since this device is connected to my eyebrows, it is under my control. By raising an eyebrow I can divide my mind. In each half of my divided mind I can then, by lowering an eyebrow, reunite my mind.

This ability would have many uses. Consider

My Physics Exam. I am taking an exam, and have only fifteen minutes left in which to answer the last question. It occurs to me that there are two ways of tackling this question. I am unsure which is more likely to succeed. I therefore decide to divide my mind for ten minutes, to work in each half of my mind on one of the two calculations, and then to reunite my mind to write a fair copy of the best result. What shall I experience?

When I disconnect my hemispheres, my stream of consciousness divides. But this division is not something that I experience. Each of my two streams of consciousness seems to have been straightforwardly continuous with my one stream of consciousness up to the moment of division. The only changes in each stream are the disappearance of half my visual field and the loss of sensation in, and control over, one of my arms.

Consider my experiences in my 'right-handed' stream. I remember deciding that I would use my right hand to do the longer calculation. This I now begin. In working at this calculation I can see, from the movements of my left hand, that I am also working at the other. But I am not aware of working at the other. I might, in my right-handed stream, wonder how, in my left-handed stream, I am getting on. I could look and see. This would be just like looking to see how well my neighbour is doing, at the next desk. In my right-handed stream I would be equally unaware both of what my neighbour is now thinking and of what I am now thinking in my left-handed stream. Similar remarks apply to my experiences in my left-handed stream.

My work is now over. I am about to reunite my mind. What should I, in each stream, expect? Simply that I shall suddenly seem to remember just having worked at two calculations, in working at each of which I was not aware of working at the other. This, I suggest, we can imagine. And, if my mind had been divided, my apparent memories would be correct.

In describing this case, I assumed that there were two separate series of thoughts and sensations. If my two hands visibly wrote out two calculations, and I also claimed later to remember two corresponding series of thoughts, this is what we ought to assume. It would be most implausible to assume that either or both calculations had been done unconsciously.

It might be objected that my description ignores 'the necessary unity of consciousness'. But I have not ignored this alleged necessity. I have denied it. What is a fact must be possible. And it is a fact that people with disconnected hemispheres have two separate streams of consciousness—two series of thoughts and experiences, in having each of which they are unaware of having the other. Each of these two streams separately displays unity of consciousness. This may be a surprising fact. But we can understand it. We can come to believe that a person's mental history need not be like a canal, with only one channel, but could be like a river, occasionally having separate streams. I suggest that we can also imagine what it would be like to divide and reunite our minds. My description of my experiences in my Physics Exam seems both to be coherent and to describe something that we can imagine.

It might next be claimed that, in my imagined case, I do not have a divided mind. Rather, I have two minds. This objection does not raise a real question. These are two ways of describing one and the same outcome.

A similar objection claims that, in these actual and imagined cases, the result is not a single person with either a divided mind or two minds. The result is two different people, sharing control of most of one body, but each in sole control of one arm. Here too, I believe that this objection does not raise a real question. These are again two ways of describing the same outcome. This is what we believe if we are Reductionists.

If we are not yet Reductionists, as I shall assume, we believe that it is a real question whether such cases involve more than a single person. Perhaps we can believe this in the actual cases, where the division is permanent. But this belief is hard to accept when we consider my imagined Physics Exam. In this case there are two streams of consciousness for only ten minutes. And I later seem to remember doing both of the calculations that, during these ten minutes, my two hands could be seen to be writing out. Given the brief and modest nature of this disunity, it is not plausible to claim that this case involves more than a single person. Are we to suppose that, during these ten minutes, I cease to exist, and two new people come into existence, each of whom then works out one of the calculations? On this interpretation, the whole episode involves three people, two of whom have lives that last for only ten minutes. Moreover, each of these two people mistakenly believes that he is me, and has apparent memories that accurately fit my past. And after these ten minutes I have accurate apparent memories of the brief lives of each of these two people, except that I mistakenly believe that I myself had all of the thoughts and sensations that these people had. It is hard to believe that I am mistaken here, and that the episode does involve three quite different people.

It is equally hard to believe that it involves two different people, with me doing one of the calculations, and some other person doing the other. I admit that, when I first divide my mind, I might in doing one of the calculations believe that the other calculation must be being done by someone else. But in doing the other calculation I might have the same belief. When my mind has been reunited, I would then seem to remember believing, while doing each of the calculations, that the other calculation must be being done by someone else. When I seem to remember both these beliefs, I would have no reason to think that one was true and the other false. And after several divisions and reunions I would cease to have such beliefs. In each of my two streams of consciousness I would believe that I was now, in my other stream, having thoughts and sensations of which, in this stream, I was now unaware.

88. WHAT EXPLAINS THE UNITY OF CONSCIOUSNESS?

Suppose that, because we are not yet Reductionists, we believe that there must be a true answer to the question, 'Who has each stream of consciousness?' And suppose that, for the reasons just given, we believe that this case involves only a single person: me. We believe that for ten minutes I have a divided mind.

Remember next the view that psychological unity is explained by ownership. On this view, we should explain the unity of a person's consciousness, at any time, by ascribing different experiences to this person, or 'subject of experiences'. What unites these different experiences is that they are being had by the same person. This view is held both by those who believe that a person is a separately existing entity, and by some of those who reject this belief. And this view also applies to the unity of each life.

When we consider my imagined Physics Exam, can we continue to accept this view? We believe that, while my mind is divided, I have two separate series of experiences, in having each of which I am unaware of having the other. At any time in one of my streams of consciousness I am having several different thoughts and sensations. I might be aware of thinking out some part of the calculation, feeling writer's cramp in one hand, and hearing the squeaking of my neighbour's old-fashioned pen. What unites these different experiences?

On the view described above, the answer is that these are the experiences being had by me at this time. This answer is incorrect. I am not just having these experiences at this time. I am also having, in my other stream of consciousness, several other experiences. We need to explain the unity of consciousness within each of my two streams of consciousness, or in each half of my divided mind. We cannot explain these two unities by claiming that all of these experiences are being had by me at this time. This makes the two unities one. It ignores the fact that, in having each of these two sets of experiences, I am unaware of having the other.

Suppose that we continue to believe that unity should be explained by ascribing different experiences to a single subject. We must then believe that this case involves at least two different subjects of experiences. What unites the experiences in my left-handed stream is that they are all being had by one subject of experiences. What unites the experiences in my right-handed stream is that they are all being had by another subject of experiences. We must now abandon the claim that 'the subject of experiences' is the person. On our view, I am a subject of experiences. While my mind is divided there are two different subjects of experiences. These are not the same subject of experiences, so they cannot both be me. Since it is unlikely that I am one of the two, given the similarity of my two streams of consciousness, we should probably conclude that I am neither of these two subjects of experiences. The whole episode therefore involves three such entities. And two of these entities cannot be claimed to be the kind of entity with which we are all familiar, a person. I am the only person involved, and two of these subjects of experiences are *not* me. Even if we assume that I *am* one of these two subjects of experiences, *the other* cannot be me, and is therefore not a person.

We may now be sceptical. While the 'subject of experiences' was the person, it seemed plausible to claim that what unites a set of experiences is that they are all had by a single subject. If we have to believe in subjects of experiences that are not persons, we may doubt whether there really are such things. There are of course, in the animal world, many subjects of experiences that are not persons. My cat is one example. But other animals are irrelevant to this imagined case. On the view described above, we have to believe that the life of a *person* could involve subjects of experiences that are not persons.

Reconsider my experiences in my right-handed stream of consciousness. In this stream at a certain time I am aware of thinking about part of a calculation, feeling writer's cramp, and hearing the sounds made by my neighbour's pen. Do we explain the unity of these experiences by claiming that they are all being had by the same subject of experiences, this being an entity which is *not* me? This explanation does not seem plausible. If this subject of experiences is *not* a person, what kind of thing is it? It cannot be claimed to be a Cartesian Ego, if I am claimed to be such an Ego. This subject of experiences cannot be claimed to be such an Ego, since it is not me, and this case involves only one person. Can this subject of experiences be a Cartesian Sub-Ego, a persisting purely mental entity which is merely part of a person? We may decide that we have insufficient grounds for believing that there are such things.

I turn next to the other view mentioned above. Some people believe that unity is explained by ownership, even though they deny that we are separately existing entities. These people believe that what unites a person's experiences at any time is the fact that these experiences are being had by this person. As we have seen, in this imagined case this belief is false. While I am having one set of experiences in my right-handed stream, I am also having another set in my left-handed stream. We cannot explain the unity of either set of experiences by claiming that these are the experiences that I am having at this time, since this would conflate these two sets.

A Reductionist may now intervene. On his view, what unites my experiences in my right-handed stream is that there is, at any time, a single state of awareness of these various experiences. There is a state of awareness of having certain thoughts, feeling writer's cramp, and hearing the sound of a squeaking pen. At the same time, there is another state of awareness of the various experiences in my left-handed stream. My mind is divided because there is no single state of awareness of both of these sets of experiences.

It may be objected that these claims do not explain but only redescribe the unity of consciousness in each stream. In one sense, this is true. This unity does not need a deep explanation. It is simply a fact that several experiences can be *co-conscious*, or be the objects of a single state of awareness. It may help to compare this fact with the fact that there is short-term memory of experiences within the last few moments: short-term memory of what is called 'the specious present'. Just as there can be a single memory of just having had several experiences, such as hearing a bell strike three times, there can be a single state of awareness both of hearing the fourth striking of this bell, and of seeing ravens fly past the bell-tower. Reductionists claim that nothing more is involved in the unity of consciousness at a single time. Since there can be one state of awareness of several experiences, we need not explain this unity by ascribing these experiences to the same person, or subject of experiences.

It is worth restating other parts of the Reductionist View. I claim:

Because we ascribe thoughts to thinkers, it is true that thinkers exist. But thinkers are not separately existing entities. The existence of a thinker just involves the existence of his brain and body, the doing of his deeds, the thinking of his thoughts, and the occurrence of certain other physical and mental events. We could therefore redescribe any person's life in impersonal terms. In explaining the unity of this life, we need not claim that it is the life of a particular person. We could describe what, at different times, was thought and felt and observed and done, and how these various events were interrelated. Persons would be mentioned here only in the descriptions of the content of many thoughts, desires, memories, and so on. Persons need not be claimed to be the thinkers of any of these thoughts.

These claims are supported by the case where I divide my mind. It is not merely true here that the unity of different experiences does not *need* to be explained by ascribing all of these experiences to me. The unity of my experiences, in each stream, *cannot* be explained in this way. There are only two alternatives. We might ascribe the experiences in each stream to a subject of experiences which is *not* me, and, therefore, not a person. Or, if we doubt the existence of such entities, we can accept the Reductionist explanation. At least in this case, this may now seem the best explanation.

This is one of the points at which it matters whether my imagined case is possible. If we could briefly divide our minds, this casts doubt on the view that psychological unity is explained by ownership. As I argued, if we are not Reductionists, we ought to regard my imagined case as involving only a single person. It then becomes impossible to claim that the unity of consciousness should be explained by ascribing different experiences to a single subject, the person. We could maintain this view only by believing in subjects of experiences that are not persons. Other animals are irrelevant here. Our belief is about what is involved in the lives of persons. If we have to admit that in these lives there could be two kinds of subjects of experiences, those that are and those that are not persons, our view will have lost much of its plausibility. It would help our view if we could claim that, because persons are indivisible, my imagined case could never happen.

My case is imagined. But the essential feature of the case, the division of consciousness into separate streams, *has* happened several times. This undermines the reply just given. My imagined case may well become possible, and could at most be merely technically impossible. And in this case the unity of consciousness in each stream cannot be explained by ascribing my experiences to me. Because this explanation fails, this case refutes the view that psychological unity can be explained by ascribing different experiences to a single person.

On the best known version of this view, we are Cartesian Egos. I defended Lichtenberg's objection to the Cartesian View. But that defence merely showed that we could not deduce, from the nature of our experiences, that we are such entities. I later claimed that there is no evidence in favour of this view, and much evidence against it. Since they support the argument just given, the actual cases of divided minds are further evidence against this view.

Descartes' view may be compared with Newton's belief in Absolute Space and Time. Newton believed that any physical event had its particular position solely in virtue of its relation to these two independent realities, Space and Time. We now believe that a physical event has its particular spatio-temporal position in virtue of its various relations to the other physical events that occur. On the Cartesian View, a particular mental event occurs within a particular life solely in virtue of its ascription to a particular Ego. We can deny that the topography of 'Mental Space' is given by the existence of such persisting Egos. We can claim that a particular mental event occurs within some life in virtue of its relations to the many other mental and physical events which, by being interrelated, constitute this life.[36]

Another ground is sometimes given for belief in such Egos. It can be claimed against any wholly *objective* description of reality—any description not made from a 'point of view'—that there are certain truths which it omits. One example of such a truth is that I am I, or that I am Derek Parfit. I am *this* particular person. These *subjective* truths may seem to imply that we are separately existing subjects of experiences.

Such truths can be stated by a Reductionist. The word 'subjective' is misleading. What are called subjective truths need not involve any subject of experiences. A particular thought may be *self-referring*. It may be the thought that this particular thought, even if exactly similar to other thoughts that are thought, is still *this* particular thought—or this particular thinking of this thought. This thought is an impersonal but subjective truth.

Some would object that all of the other *indexical* concepts—such as 'here', 'now', and 'this'—must be explained in a way that uses the concept 'I'. This is not so. All of the others, including 'I', can be explained in a way that uses the self-referring use of 'this'. And this *self*-referring use does not involve the notion of a self, or subject of experiences. It is the use of 'this' that in this sentence refers to this sentence. With this use of 'this', we can express 'subjective' truths without believing in the separate existence of subjects of experiences.[37]

89. WHAT HAPPENS WHEN I DIVIDE?

I shall now describe another natural extension of the actual cases of divided minds. Suppose first that I am one of a pair of identical twins, and that both my body and my twin's brain have been fatally injured. Because of advances in neuro-surgery, it is not inevitable that these injuries will cause us both to die. We have between us one healthy brain and one healthy body. Surgeons can put these together.

This could be done even with existing techniques. Just as my brain could be extracted, and kept alive by a connection with an artifical heart-lung machine, it could be kept alive by a connection with the heart and lungs in my twin's body. The drawback, today, is that the nerves from my brain could not be connected with the nerves in my twin's body. My brain could survive if transplanted into his body, but the resulting person would be paralysed.

Even if he is paralysed, the resulting person could be enabled to communicate with others. One crude method would be some device, attached to the nerve that would have controlled this person's right thumb, enabling him to send messages in Morse Code. Another device, attached to some sensory nerve, could enable him to receive messages. Many people would welcome surviving, even totally paralysed, if they could still communicate with others. The stock example is that of a great scientist whose main aim in life is to continue thinking about certain abstract problems.

Let us suppose, however, that surgeons are able to connect my brain to the nerves in my twin's body. The resulting person would have no paralysis, and would be completely healthy. Who would this person be?

This is not a difficult question. It may seem that there is a disagreement here between the Physical and Psychological Criteria. Though the resulting person will be psychologically continuous with me, he will not have the whole of my body. But, as I have claimed, the Physical Criterion ought not to require the continued existence of my whole body.

If all of my brain continues both to exist and to be the brain of one living person, who is psychologically continuous with me, I continue to exist. This is true whatever happens to the rest of my body. When I am given someone else's heart, I am the surviving recipient, not the dead donor. When my brain is transplanted into someone else's body, it may seem that I am here the dead donor. But I am really still the recipient, and the survivor. Receiving a new skull and a new body is just the limiting case of receiving a new heart, new lungs, new arms, and so on.[38]

It will of course be important what my new body is like. If my new body was quite unlike my old body, this would affect what I could do, and might thus indirectly lead to changes in my character. But there is no reason to suppose that being transplanted into a very different body would disrupt my psychological continuity.

It has been objected that 'the possession of some sorts of character trait requires the possession of an appropriate sort of body'. Quinton answers this objection. He writes, of an unlikely case,

> It would be odd for a six-year old girl to display the character of Winston Churchill, odd indeed to the point of outrageousness, but it is not utterly inconceivable. At first, no doubt, the girl's display of dogged endurance, a world-historical comprehensiveness of outlook, and so forth, would strike one as distasteful and pretentious in so young a child. But if she kept it up the impression would wear off.[39]

More importantly, as Quinton argues, this objection could show only that it might matter whether my brain is housed in a certain *kind* of body. It could not show that it would matter whether it was housed in any *particular* body. And in my imagined case my brain will be housed in a body which, though not numerically identical to my old body, is—because it is my twin's body— very similar.

On all versions of the Psychological Criterion, the resulting person would be me. And most believers in the Physical Criterion could be persuaded that, in this case, this is true. As I have claimed, the Physical Criterion should require only the continued existence of *enough* of my brain to be the brain of a living person, provided that no one else has enough of this brain. · This would make it me who would wake up, after the operation. And if my twin's body was just like mine, I might even fail to notice that I had a new body.

It is in fact true that one hemisphere is enough. There are many people who have survived, when a stroke or injury puts out of action one of their hemispheres. With his remaining hemisphere, such a person may need to re-learn certain things, such as adult speech, or how to control both hands. But this is possible. In my example I am assuming that, as may be true of certain actual people, both of my hemispheres have the full range of abilities. I could thus survive with either hemisphere, without any need for re-learning.

I shall now combine these last two claims. I would survive if my brain was successfully transplanted into my twin's body. And I could survive with only half my brain, the other half having been destroyed. Given these two facts, it seems clear that I would survive if half my brain was successfully transplanted into my twin's body, and the other half was destroyed.

What if the other half was *not* destroyed? This is the case that Wiggins described: that in which a person, like an amoeba, divides.[40] To simplify the case, I assume that I am one of three identical triplets. Consider

> *My Division.* My body is fatally injured, as are the brains of my two brothers. My brain is divided, and each half is successfully transplanted into the body of one of my brothers. Each of the resulting people believes that he is me, seems to remember living my life, has my

character, and is in every other way psychologically continuous with me. And he has a body that is very like mine.

This case is likely to remain impossible. Though it is claimed that, in certain people, the two hemispheres may have the same full range of abilities, this claim might be false. I am here assuming that this claim is true when applied to me. I am also assuming that it would be possible to connect a transplanted half-brain with the nerves in its new body. And I am assuming that we could divide, not just the upper hemispheres, but also the lower brain. My first two assumptions may be able to be made true if there is enough progress in neurophysiology. But it seems likely that it would never be possible to divide the lower brain, in a way that did not impair its functioning.

Does it matter if, for this reason, this imagined case of complete division will always remain impossible? Given the aims of my discussion, this does not matter. This impossibility is merely technical. The one feature of the case that might be held to be *deeply* impossible—the division of a person's consciousness into two separate streams—is the feature that has actually happened. It would have been important if this had been impossible, since this might have supported some claim about what we really are. It might have supported the claim that we are indivisible Cartesian Egos. It therefore matters that the division of a person's consciousness is in fact possible. There seems to be no similar connection between a particular view about what we really are and the impossibility of dividing and successfully transplanting the two halves of the lower brain. This impossibility thus provides no ground for refusing to consider the imagined case in which we suppose that this can be done. And considering this case may help us to decide both what we believe ourselves to be, and what in fact we are. As Einstein's example showed, it can be useful to consider impossible thought-experiments.

It may help to state, in advance, what I believe this case to show. It provides a further argument against the view that we are separately existing entities. But the main conclusion to be drawn is that *personal identity is not what matters*.

It is natural to believe that our identity is what matters. Reconsider the Branch-Line Case, where I have talked to my Replica on Mars, and am about to die. Suppose we believe that I and my Replica are different people. It is then natural to assume that my prospect is almost as bad as ordinary death. In a few days, there will be no one living who will be me. It is natural to assume that *this* is what matters. In discussing My Division, I shall start by making this assumption.

In this case, each half of my brain will be successfully transplanted into the very similar body of one of my two brothers. Both of the resulting people will be fully psychologically continuous with me, as I am now. What happens to me?

There are only four possibilities: (1) I do not survive; (2) I survive as one of the two people; (3) I survive as the other; (4) I survive as both.

The objection to (1) is this. I would survive if my brain was successfully transplanted. And people have in fact survived with half their brains destroyed. Given these facts, it seems clear that I would survive if half my brain was successfully transplanted, and the other half was destroyed. So how could I fail to survive if the other half was also successfully transplanted? How could a double success be a failure?

Consider the next two possibilities. Perhaps one success is the maximum score. Perhaps I shall be one of the two resulting people. The objection here is that, in this case, each half of my brain is exactly similar, and so, to start with, is each resulting person. Given these facts, how can I survive as only one of the two people? What can make me one of them rather than the other?

These three possibilities cannot be dismissed as incoherent. We can understand them. But, while we assume that identity is what matters, (1) is not plausible. My Division would not be as bad as death. Nor are (2) and (3) plausible. There remains the fourth possibility: that I survive as both of the resulting people.

This possibility might be described in several ways. I might first claim: 'What we have called "the two resulting people" are not two people. They are one person. I do survive this operation. Its effect is to give me two bodies, and a divided mind.'

This claim cannot be dismissed outright. As I argued, we ought to admit as possible that a person could have a divided mind. If this is possible, each half of my divided mind might control its own body. But though this description of the case cannot be rejected as inconceivable, it involves a great distortion in our concept of a person. In my imagined Physics Exam I claimed that this case involved only one person. There were two features of the case that made this plausible. The divided mind was soon reunited, and there was only one body. If a mind was permanently divided, and its halves developed in different ways, it would become less plausible to claim that the case involves only one person. (Remember the actual patient who complained that, when he embraced his wife, his left hand pushed her away.)

The case of complete division, where there are also two bodies, seems to be a long way over the borderline. After I have had this operation, the two 'products' each have all of the features of a person. They could live at opposite ends of the Earth. Suppose that they have poor memories, and that their appearance changes in different ways. After many years, they might meet again, and fail even to recognise each other. We might have to claim of such a pair, innocently playing tennis: 'What you see out there is a single person, playing tennis with himself. In each half of his mind he mistakenly believes that he is playing tennis with someone else.' If we are not yet Reductionists, we believe that there is one true answer to the question whether these two tennis-players are a single person. Given what we mean by 'person', the answer must be No. It cannot be true that what I believe to be a stranger, standing there behind the net, is in fact another part of myself.

Suppose we admit that the two 'products' are, as they seem to be, two different people. Could we still claim that I survive as both? There is another way in which we could. I might say: 'I survive the operation as two different people. They can be different people, and yet be me, in the way in which the Pope's three crowns together form one crown.'[41]

This claim is also coherent. But it again greatly distorts the concept of a person. We are happy to agree that the Pope's three crowns, when put together, are a fourth crown. But it is hard to think of two people as, together, being a third person. Suppose the resulting people fight a duel. Are there three people fighting, one on each side, and one on both? And suppose one of the bullets kills. Are there two acts, one murder and one suicide? How many people are left alive? One or two? The composite third person has no separate mental life. It is hard to believe that there really would be such a third person. Instead of saying that the resulting people together constitute me—so that the pair is a trio—it is better to treat them as a pair, and describe their relation to me in a simpler way.

Other claims might be made. It might be suggested that the two resulting people are *now* different people, but that, before My Division, they *were* the same person. Before My Division, they were me. This suggestion is ambiguous. The claim may be that, before My Division, they *together* were me. On this account, there were three different people even before My Division. This is even less plausible than the claim I have just rejected. (It might be thought that I have misunderstood this suggestion. The claim may be that the resulting people did not exist, as separate people, before My Division. But if they did not then exist, it cannot have been true that they together were me.)

It may instead be suggested that, before My Division, *each* of the resulting people *was* me. After My Division, neither is me, since I do not now exist. But, if each of these people *was* me, whatever happened to me must have happened to each of these people. If I did not survive My Division, neither of these people survived. Since there *are* two resulting people, the case involves *five* people. This conclusion is absurd. Can we deny the assumption that implies this conclusion? Can we claim that, though each of the resulting people *was* me, what happened to me did not happen to these people? Assume that I have not yet divided. On this suggestion, it is now true that each of the resulting people *is* me. If what happens to me does not happen to X, X cannot be me.

There are far-fetched ways to deny this last claim. These appeal to claims about tensed identity. Call one of the resulting people *Lefty*. I might ask, 'Are *Lefty* and *Derek Parfit* names of one and the same person?' For believers in tensed identity, this is not a proper question. As this shows, claims about tensed identity are radically different from the way in which we now think. I shall merely state here what I believe others to have shown: these claims do not solve our problem.

David Lewis makes a different proposal. On his view, there are two people who share my body even before My Division. In its details, this proposal is both elegant and ingenious. I shall not repeat here why, as I have claimed elsewhere, this proposal does not solve our problem.[42]

I have discussed several unusual views about what happens when I divide. On these views, the case involves a single person, a duo, a trio two of whom compose the third, and a quintet. We could doubtless conjure up the missing quartet. But it would be tedious to consider more of these views. All involve too great distortions of the concept of a person. We should therefore reject the fourth suggested possibility: the claim that, in some sense, I survive as both of the two resulting people.

There are three other possibilities: that I shall be *one,* or *the other,* or *neither* of these people. These three claims seemed implausible. Note next that, as before, we could not *find out* what happens even if we could actually perform this operation. Suppose, for example, that I do survive as one of the resulting people. I would believe that I have survived. But I would know that the other resulting person falsely believes that he is me, and that he survived. Since I would know this, I could not trust my own belief. I might be the resulting person with the false belief. And, since we would both claim to be me, other people would have no reason to believe one of us rather than the other. Even if we performed this operation, we would therefore learn nothing.

Whatever happened to me, we could not discover what happened. This suggests a more radical answer to our question. It suggests that the Reductionist View is true. Perhaps there are not here different possibilities, each of which might be what happens, though we could never know which actually happens. Perhaps, when we know that each resulting person would have one half of my brain, and would be psychologically continuous with me, we know everything. What are we supposing when we suggest, for instance, that one of the resulting people might be me? What would make this the true answer?

I believe that there cannot be different possibilities, each of which might be the truth, unless we are separately existing entities, such as Cartesian Egos. If what I really am is one particular Ego, this explains how it could be true that one of the resulting people would be me. It could be true that it is in this person's brain and body that this particular Ego regained consciousness.

If we believe in Cartesian Egos, we might be reminded of Buridan's ass, which starved to death between two equally nourishing bales of hay. This ass had no reason to eat one of these bales of hay before eating the other. Being an overly-rational beast it refused to make a choice for which there was no reason. In my example, there would be no reason why the particular

Ego that I am should wake up as one of the two resulting people. But this might just happen, in a random way, as is claimed for fundamental particles.

The more difficult question, for believers in Cartesian Egos, is whether I would survive at all. Since each of the resulting people would be psychologically continuous with me, there would be no evidence supporting either answer to this question. This argument retains its force, even if I am a Cartesian Ego.

As before, a Cartesian might object that I have misdescribed what would happen. He might claim that, if we carried out this operation, it would not in fact be true that *both* of the resulting people would be psychologically continuous with me. It might be true that one or other of these people was psychologically continuous with me. In either of these cases, this person would be me. It might instead be true that neither person was psychologically continuous with me. In this case, I would not survive. In each of these three cases, we would learn the truth.

Whether this is a good objection depends on what the relation is between our psychological features and the states of our brains. As I have said, we have conclusive evidence that the carrier of psychological continuity is *not* indivisible. In the actual cases in which hemispheres have been disconnected, this produced two series of thoughts and sensations. These two streams of consciousness were both psychologically continuous with the original stream. Psychological continuity has thus, in several actual cases, taken a dividing form. This fact refutes the objection just given. It justifies my claim that, in the imagined case of My Division, both of the resulting people would be psychologically continuous with me. Since this is so, the Cartesian View can be advanced here only in the more dubious version that does not connect the Ego with any observable or introspectible facts. Even if I am such an Ego, I could never know whether or not I had survived. For Cartesians, this case is a problem with no possible solution.

Suppose that, for the reasons given earlier, we reject the claim that each of us is really a Cartesian Ego. And we reject the claim that a person is any other kind of separately existing entity, apart from his brain and body, and various mental and physical events. How then should we answer the question about what happens when I divide? I distinguished four possibilities. When I discussed each possibility, there seemed to be strong objections to the claim that it would be what happens. If we believe that these are different possibilities, any of which might be what happens, the case is a problem for us too.

On the Reductionist View, the problem disappears. On this view, the claims that I have discussed do not describe different possibilities, any of which might be true, and one of which must be true. These claims are merely different descriptions of the same outcome. We know what this outcome is.

There will be two future people, each of whom will have the body of one of my brothers, and will be fully psychologically continuous with me, because he has half of my brain. Knowing this, we know everything. I may ask, 'But shall I be one of these two people, or the other, or neither?' But I should regard this as an empty question. Here is a similar question. In 1881 the French Socialist Party split. What happened? Did the French Socialist Party cease to exist, or did it continue to exist as one or other of the two new Parties? Given certain further details, this would be an empty question. Even if we have no answer to this question, we could know just what happened.

I must now distinguish two ways in which a question may be empty. About some questions we should claim both that they are empty, and that they have no answers. We could decide to *give* these questions answers. But it might be true that any possible answer would be arbitrary. If this is so, it would be pointless and might be misleading to give such an answer. This would be true of the question 'Shall I survive?' in the central cases in the Combined Spectrum. And it would be true in the central cases in the other Spectra, if I would not survive in the case at the far end.

There is another kind of case in which a question may be empty. In such a case this question has, in a sense, an answer. The question is empty because it does not describe different possibilities, any of which might be true, and one of which must be true. The question merely gives us different descriptions of the same outcome. We could know the full truth about this outcome without choosing one of these descriptions. But, if we do decide to give an answer to this empty question, one of these descriptions is better than the others. Since this is so, we can claim that this description is the answer to this question. And I claim that there is a best description of the case where I divide. The best description is that neither of the resulting people will be me.

Since this case does not involve different possibilities, the important question is not, 'Which is the best description?' The important question is: 'What ought to matter to me? How ought I to regard the prospect of division? Should I regard it as like death, or as like survival?' When we have answered this question, we can decide whether I have given the best description.

Before discussing what matters, I shall fulfil an earlier promise. One objection to the Psychological Criterion is that psychological continuity presupposes personal identity. I answered this objection, in the case of memory, by appealing to the wider concept of quasi-memory. Jane quasi-remembered having someone else's past experiences. My Division provides another example. Since at least one of the two resulting people will not be me, he can quasi-remember living someone else's life.

I did not show that, in describing the other relations that are involved in psychological continuity, we need not presuppose personal identity. Now that I have described My Division, this can be easily shown. One other direct relation is that which holds between an intention and the later action in which this intention is carried out. It may be a logical truth that we can intend to perform only our own actions. But we can use a new concept of *quasi-intention*. One person could quasi-intend to perform another person's actions. When this relation holds, it does not presuppose personal identity.

The case of division shows what this involves. I could quasi-intend both that one resulting person roams the world, and that the other stays at home. What I quasi-intend will be done, not by me, but by the two resulting people. Normally, if I intend that someone else should do something, I cannot get him to do it simply by forming this intention. But, if I was about to divide, it would be enough simply to form quasi-intentions. Both of the resulting people would inherit these quasi-intentions, and, unless they changed their inherited minds, they would carry them out. Since they might change their minds, I could not be sure that they would do what I quasi-intended. But the same is true within my own life. Since I may change my own mind, I cannot be sure that I shall do what I now intend to do. But I have some ability to control my future by forming firm intentions. If I was about to divide, I would have just as much ability, by forming quasi-intentions, to control the futures of the two resulting people.

Similar remarks apply to all of the other direct psychological connections, such as those involved in the continuity of character. All such connections hold between me and each of the resulting people. Since at least one of these people cannot be me, none of these connections presupposes personal identity.

90. WHAT MATTERS WHEN I DIVIDE?

Some people would regard division as being as bad, or nearly as bad, as ordinary death. This reaction is irrational. We ought to regard division as being about as good as ordinary survival. As I have argued, the two 'products' of this operation would be two different people. Consider my relation to each of these people. Does this relation fail to contain some vital element that is contained in ordinary survival? It seems clear that it does not. I would survive if I stood in this very same relation to only one of the resulting people. It is a fact that someone can survive even if half his brain is destroyed. And on reflection it was clear that I would survive if my whole brain was successfully transplanted into my brother's body. It was therefore clear that I would survive if half my brain was destroyed, and the other half was successfully transplanted into my brother's body. In the case that we are now considering, my relation to each of the resulting people thus contains everything that would be needed for me to survive as that person. It cannot be the *nature* of my relation to each of the resulting people that, in this case, causes it to fail to be survival. Nothing is *missing*. What is wrong can only be the duplication.

Suppose that I accept this, but still regard division as being nearly as bad as death. My reaction is now indefensible. I am like someone who, when told of a drug that could double his years of life, regards the taking of this drug as death. The only difference in the case of division is that the extra years are to run concurrently. This is an interesting difference; but it cannot mean that there are *no* years to run. We might say: 'You will lose your identity. But there are different ways of doing this. Dying is one, dividing is another. To regard these as the same is to confuse two with zero. Double survival is not the same as ordinary survival. But this does not make it death. It is even less like death.'

The problem with double survival is that it does not fit the logic of identity. Like several Reductionists, I claim

> *Relation R* is what matters. R is psychological connectedness and/or psychological continuity, with the right kind of cause. [43]

I also claim

> In an account of what matters, the right kind of cause could be any cause.

Other Reductionists might require that R have a reliable cause, or have its normal cause. To postpone this disagreement, consider only cases where R would have its normal cause. In these cases, Reductionists would all accept the following claim. A future person will be me if he will be R-related to me as I am now, and no different person will be R-related to me. If there is no such different person, the fact that this future person will be me just consists in the fact that relation R holds between us. There is nothing more to personal identity than the holding of relation R. In nearly all of the actual cases, R takes a one-one form. It holds between one presently existing person and one future person. When R takes a one-one form, we can use the language of identity. We can claim that this future person will be this present person.

In the imagined case where I divide, R takes a branching form. But personal identity cannot take a branching form. I and the two resulting people cannot be one and the same person. Since I cannot be identical with two different people, and it would be arbitrary to call one of these people me, we can best describe the case by saying that neither will be me.

Which is the relation that is important? Is what matters personal identity, or relation R? In ordinary cases we need not decide which of these is what matters, since these relations coincide. In the case of My Division these relations do not coincide. We must therefore decide which of the two is what matters.

If we believe that we are separately existing entities, we could plausibly claim that identity is what matters. On this view, personal identity is a deep further fact. But we have sufficient evidence to reject this view. If we are Reductionists, we cannot plausibly claim that, of these two relations, it is identity that matters. On our view, the fact of personal identity just consists in the holding of relation R, when it takes a non-branching form. If personal identity just consists in this other relation, this other relation must be what matters.

It may be objected: 'You are wrong to claim that there is nothing more to identity than relation R. As you have said, personal identity has one extra feature, not contained in relation R. Personal identity consists in R holding *uniquely*—holding between one present person and *only one* future person. Since there is something more to personal identity than to relation R, we can rationally claim that, of the two, it is identity which is what matters.'

In answering this objection, it will help to use some abbreviations. Call personal identity *PI*. When some relation holds uniquely, or in a one-one form, call this fact *U*. The view that I accept can be stated with this formula:

$$PI = R + U.$$

Most of us are convinced that PI matters, or has value. Assume that R may also have value. There are then four possibilities:

(1)   R without U has no value.

(2)   U enhances the value of R, but R has value even without U.

(3)   U makes no difference to the value of R.

(4)   U reduces the value of R (but not enough to eliminate this value, since R + U = PI, which has value).

Can the presence or absence of U make a great difference to the value of R? As I shall argue, this is not plausible. If I will be R-related to some future person, the presence or absence of U makes no difference to the intrinsic nature of my relation to this person. And what matters most must be the intrinsic nature of this relation.

Since this is so, R without U would still have at least most of its value. Adding U makes R = PI. If adding U does not greatly increase the value of R, R must be what fundamentally matters, and PI mostly matters just because of the presence of R. If U makes no difference to the value of R, PI matters only because of the presence of R. Since U can be plausibly claimed to make a small difference, PI may, compared with R, have some extra value. But this value would be much less than the intrinsic value of R. The value of PI is much less than the value that R would have in the absence of PI, when U fails to hold.

If it was put forward on its own, it would be difficult to accept the view that personal identity is not what matters. But I believe that, when we consider the case of division, this difficulty disappears. When we see *why* neither resulting person will be me, I believe that, on reflection, we can also see that this does not matter, or matters only a little.

The case of division supports part of the Reductionist View: the claim that our identity is not what matters. But this case does not support another Reductionist claim: that our identity can be indeterminate. If we abandon the view that identity is what matters, we can claim that there *is* an answer here to my question. Neither of the resulting people will be me. I am about to die. While we believed that identity is what matters, this claim implied, implausibly, that I ought to regard My Division as being nearly as bad as ordinary death. But the implausibility disappears if we claim instead that this way of dying is about as good as ordinary survival.

There is still room for minor disagreements. Though R is what fundamentally matters, U can make a slight difference. I might regard my division as being somewhat better than ordinary survival, or as being somewhat worse.

Why might I think it somewhat worse? I might claim that the relation between me and each of the resulting people is not quite the relation that matters in ordinary survival. This is not because something is missing, but because division brings *too much*. I may think that each of the resulting people will, in one respect, have a life that is worse than mine. Each will have to live in a world where there is someone else who, at least to start with, is exactly like himself. This may be unpleasantly uncanny. And it will raise practical problems. Suppose that what I most want is to write a certain book. This would be what each of the resulting people would most want to do. But it would be pointless for both to write this book. It would be pointless for both to do what they most want to do.

Consider next the relations between the resulting people and the woman I love. I can assume that, since she loves me, she will love them both. But she could not give to both the undivided attention that we now give to each other.

In these and other ways the lives of the resulting people may not be quite as good as mine. This might justify my regarding division as being not quite as good as ordinary survival. But it could not justify regarding division as being much less good, or as being as bad as death. And we should note that this reasoning ignores the fact that these two lives, taken together, would be twice as long as the rest of mine.

Instead of regarding division as being somewhat worse than ordinary survival, I might regard it as being better. The simplest reason would be the one just given: the doubling of the years to be lived. I might have more particular reasons. Thus there might be two life-long careers both of which I strongly want to pursue. I might strongly want both to be a novelist and to be a philosopher. If I divide, each of the resulting people could pursue one of these careers. And each would be glad if the other succeeds. Just as we can take pride and joy in the achievements of our children, each of the resulting people would take pride and joy in the other's achievements.

If I have two strong but incompatible ambitions, division provides a way of fulfilling both, in a way that would gladden each resulting person. This is one way in which division could be better than ordinary survival. But there are other problems that division could not wholly solve. Suppose that I am torn between an unpleasant duty and a seductive desire. I could not wholly solve this problem by quasi-intending one of the resulting people to do my duty, and quasi-intending the other to do what I desire. The resulting person whom I quasi-intend to do my duty would himself be torn between duty and desire. Why should *he* be the one to do my unpleasant duty? We can foresee trouble here. My duty might get done if the seductive desire could not be fulfilled by more than one person. It might be the desire to elope with someone who wants only one companion. The two resulting people must then compete to be this one companion. The one who fails in this competition might then, grudgingly, do my duty. My problem would be solved, though in a less attractive way.

These remarks will seem absurd to those who have not yet been convinced that the Reductionist View is true, or that identity is not what matters. Such a person might say: 'If I shall not *be* either of the resulting people, division could not fulfil my ambitions. Even if one of the resulting people is a successful novelist, and the other a successful philosopher, this fulfils neither of my ambitions. If one of my ambitions is to be a successful novelist, my ambition is that *I* be a successful novelist. This ambition will not be fulfilled if I cease to exist and *someone else* is a successful novelist. And this is what would happen if I shall be neither of the resulting people.'

This objection assumes that there is a real question whether I shall be one of the resulting people, or the other, or neither. It is natural to assume that these are three different possibilities, any of which might be what happens. But as I have argued, unless I am a separately existing entity, such as a Cartesian Ego, these cannot be three different possibilities. There is nothing that could make it true that any of the three might be what really happens. (This is compatible with my claim that there is a best description of this case: that I shall be neither resulting person. This does not commit me to the view that there are different possibilities. This would be so only if one of the other descriptions *might* have been the truth—which I deny.)

We *could* give a different description. We could say that I shall be the resulting person who becomes a successful novelist. But it would be a mistake to think that my ambition would be fulfilled if and only if we *called* this resulting person me. How we choose to describe this case has no rational or moral significance.

I shall now review what I have claimed. When I discussed the Psychological, Physical, and Combined Spectra, I argued that our identity can be indeterminate. This is not the natural view. We are inclined to believe that, to the question 'Am I about to die?', there must always be an answer, which must be either Yes or No. We are inclined to believe that our identity must be determinate. I argued that this cannot be true unless we are separately existing entities, such as Cartesian Egos. We cannot both deny that a person is such an entity, and insist that the continued existence of a person has the same special features that Cartesians attribute to the existence of the Ego. I conceded that we might have been such entities. But there is much evidence against this view.

If we deny that we are separately existing entities, we must, I have claimed, become Reductionists. One Reductionist claim is that we can imagine cases where the question 'Am I about to die?' has no answer, and is empty. This seems the least implausible view about the central cases in the Combined Spectrum. Another Reductionist claim is that personal identity is not what matters. This seems the least implausible view about the case of My Division. Of these two Reductionist claims, the second is more important, since it applies to our own lives.

If we accept the Reductionist View, we have further questions to answer about what matters. These are questions about the rational and moral significance of certain facts. But, on the Reductionist View, the so-called 'problem cases' cease to raise problems about what happens. Even when we have no answer to a question about personal identity, we can know everything about what happens.

Have I overlooked some view? I have claimed that, if we reject the view that we are separately existing entities, we should accept some version of the Reductionist View. But certain writers defend views that are not obviously versions of either of these views. I shall therefore discuss what these writers claim.

91. WHY THERE IS NO CRITERION OF IDENTITY THAT CAN MEET TWO PLAUSIBLE REQUIREMENTS

Besides the argument discussed in Section 83, Williams advances another argument against the Psychological Criterion. It may again help if I state, in advance, what I believe this argument to show. Williams claims that the criterion of personal identity must meet two requirements. I shall claim that *no* plausible criterion of identity can meet both requirements. In contrast, on the Reductionist View, the analogous requirements can be met. The argument therefore gives us further grounds for accepting this view. But Williams's argument does not assume the Reductionist View. In discussing the argument, I shall therefore briefly set aside this view. It can wait in the wings, to reappear when the action demands it.

Williams's argument develops a remark of Reid's, against Locke's claim that whoever 'has the consciousness of present and past actions is the same person to whom they belong'. This implies, as Reid writes, 'that if the same consciousness can be transferred from one intelligent being to another . . .

then two or twenty intelligent beings may be the same person'.[44]

Williams argues as follows. Identity is logically a one-one relation. It is logically impossible for one person to be identical to more than one person. I cannot be one and the same person as two different people. As we have seen, psychological continuity is not logically a one-one relation. Two different future people could both be psychologically continuous with me. Since these different people cannot both be me, psychological continuity cannot be the criterion of identity. Williams then claims that, to be acceptable, a criterion of identity must itself be logically a one-one relation. It must be a relation which could not *possibly* hold between one person and two future people. He therefore claims that the criterion of identity cannot be psychological continuity.[45]

Some reply that this criterion might appeal to *non-branching* psychological continuity. This is the version of this criterion that I have discussed. On what I call the Psychological Criterion, a future person will be me if he will be R-related to me, and there is no other person who will be R-related to me. Since this version of this criterion is logically a one-one relation, it has been claimed that it answers Williams's objection.[46]

Williams rejects this answer. He claims

Requirement (1): Whether a future person will be me must depend only on the *intrinsic* features of the relation between us. It cannot depend on what happens to *other* people.

Requirement (2): Since personal identity has great significance, whether identity holds cannot depend on a trivial fact.[47]

These requirements are both plausible. And neither requirement is met by non-branching psychological continuity. Williams therefore rejects this version of the Psychological Criterion.

This objection may seem too abstract to be convincing. Its force can be shown if I vary the imagined story with which I began. Consider Simple Teletransportation, where the Scanner destroys my brain and body. After my blueprint is beamed to Mars, the Replicator makes a perfect organic copy. My Replica on Mars will think that he is me, and he will be in every way psychologically continuous with me.

Suppose that we accept the Psychological Criterion which appeals to relation R when it holds in a one-one form. And suppose that we accept the Wide version, which allows R to have any reliable cause. This criterion implies that my Replica on Mars will be me. But we might learn that my blueprint is also being beamed to Io, one of the satellites of Jupiter. We must then claim that it will be me who wakes up on Mars, and that I shall continue to exist if my blueprint is ignored by the scientists on Io. But if the scientists on Io later make another Replica of me, when that Replica wakes up I shall cease to exist. Though the people around me on Mars will not notice any change, at that moment a new person will come into existence in my brain and body. Williams would object that, if I *do* wake up on Mars, whether I continue to exist there cannot depend, as we claim, on what happens to someone else millions of miles away near Jupiter. Our claim violates Requirement (1).

As I have argued, what fundamentally matters is whether I shall be R-related to at least one future person. It is relatively trivial whether I shall also be R-related to some other person. On this version of the Psychological Criterion, whether I shall be identical to some future person depends upon this relatively trivial fact. This violates Requirement (2).

Williams would add these remarks. Once we see that Teletransportation could produce many Replicas of me, who would be different people from each other, we should deny that I would in fact wake up on Mars even if they make only a single Replica. If they made two Replicas, these could not both be me. If they could not both be me, but they are produced in just the same way, we ought to conclude that neither would be me. But my relation to one of the Replicas is intrinsically the same whether or not they make the other. Since identity must depend on the intrinsic features of a relation, I would be neither Replica even if they did not make the other.[48]

Williams takes this argument to support a Non-Reductionist version of the Physical Criterion. (This version is Non-Reductionist because it assumes that personal identity is a further fact that requires, rather than consists in, physical continuity.) As Williams admits, a similar argument can challenge this view. He rejects the Psychological Criterion because it appeals to a relation that can take a branching form, holding between one person and two or more future people, and it therefore fails to meet his two requirements. He then considers the objection that his version of the Physical Criterion also fails to meet his requirements. Physical continuity could take a branching form. As he writes, 'It is possible to imagine a man splitting, amoeba-like, into two simulacra of himself.'[49]

Williams gives two answers to this objection. Suppose we believe that my brain and body are physically continuous with the brain and body of the person whom my parents cared for as their second child. We wish to know whether this physical continuity took an abnormal, branching form. If we knew the full history of this physically continuous brain and body, this would 'inevitably reveal' whether there had been such a case of amoeba-like division. The comparable claim is not true in the case of psychological continuity. We might know the full history of the psychological continuity between me on Earth and my Replica on Mars, yet fail to know that I have another Replica on Io. Branching is a problem for both the Physical and the Psychological Criterion. But the problem is less serious for the Physical Criterion, since it would be in principle easier to know when the problem arises.

Williams also claims that, when a physical object divides, this is an intrinsic feature of its spatio-temporal continuity. In contrast, when two people are psychologically continuous with one earlier person, this fact is not an intrinsic feature of either of these relations. Unlike the Psychological Criterion, the Physical Criterion meets Requirement (1).

My imagined division provides objections to the Physical Criterion. I revised this criterion in two ways. I first considered the case where my brain is transplanted into the body of my identical twin. On reflection it was clear that I am here the surviving recipient, not the dead donor. If my brain is given a new body, this is just the limiting case of receiving a new heart, new lungs, and so on. The Physical Criterion ought to appeal only to the continuity of my brain. I then appealed to the fact that many people have survived with one of their hemispheres destroyed. Since it is clear that these people survived, the Physical Criterion ought to appeal to the continuity, not of the whole brain, but of enough of the brain to support conscious life.

Such continuity is not logically a one-one relation. In the imagined case where I divide, each of the two resulting people has enough of my brain to support conscious life. And we cannot dismiss this case with the claim that it could never happen. Its most troubling feature, the division of consciousness, has already happened. It may remain impossible to divide the lower brain. But this is a mere technical impossibility. In the same way, Teletransportation may never be possible. But such impossibility does not weaken Williams's argument against the Wide Psychological Criterion. And if he appeals to such cases in that argument, he cannot dismiss the imagined case of my complete division.

Williams's argument implies that, in this case, I shall cease to exist, and both of the resulting people would be new people. He must therefore revise the Physical Criterion, so that it takes a non-branching form. Someone might appeal to the version that I described. This is

The Physical Criterion: If there will be a future person with enough of my brain to be the brain of a living person, this person will be me, unless there will also be someone else with enough of my brain.

Williams would reject this Criterion, since it violates both of his Requirements.

It is again worth giving an example. Suppose that My Division proceeds as follows. I have two fatally brain-damaged brothers, Jack and Bill. A surgeon first removes and divides my brain. The halves are then taken to different wings of the hospital, where they will be transplanted into the bodies of my two brothers. If we appeal to the Physical Criterion, we must claim the following. Suppose that one half of my brain is successfully transplanted into Jack's body. Before the other half can be transplanted, it is dropped onto a concrete floor. If this is what happens, I shall wake up in Jack's body. But if the other half was successfully transplanted, I would wake up in neither body.

These claims violate Requirement (1). Whether I am the person in Jack's body ought to depend only on the intrinsic features of the relation between me and this person. It cannot plausibly be thought to depend on what happens in the other wing of the hospital. What happens elsewhere seems to be as irrelevant as whether the scientists on Io make a Replica of me. Whatever happens to Bill, and to the other half of my brain, my relation to the person in Jack's body must be the same. This claim is denied by the Physical Criterion. And, compared with the importance of the fact that half my brain will survive in Jack's body, what happens to the other half is, for me, relatively trivial. This criterion therefore also violates Requirement (2).

Williams might suggest

The New Physical Criterion: A future person will be me if and only if this person is both living and has *more than half* my brain.[50]

It is an intrinsic feature of this relation that it can take only a one-one form. It is logically impossible for two future people both to have more than half my brain. This criterion therefore meets Requirement (1).

It fails, however, to meet the other requirement. I could be fully psychologically continuous with some future person *both* when this person has half of my brain *and* when this person has slightly more than half. And, for those who believe that what matters is physical continuity, the difference between these cases must be trivial. The second involves the continuity of just a few more cells. It is a trivial fact whether some future person has half my brain, or slightly more than half. The New Physical Criterion therefore violates Requirement (2).

There is another objection to this criterion. Someone might suffer injuries which cause more than half his brain to cease to function. Though such a person would be paralysed in more than half his body, and might need to be placed in a heart-lung machine, his mental life could be unaffected. Less than half a brain would be enough to provide full psychological continuity. We would naturally believe that such a person survives his injury. But, on the New Physical Criterion, we must claim that such a person ceases to exist. The person in his body is someone else, a new person who is merely exactly like him. This is hard to believe. It is a second strong objection to this criterion.

In all of its possible versions, the Physical Criterion faces strong objections. And there are similar objections to the Psychological Criterion. Williams's requirements are both plausible. We have found that *no plausible criterion of identity can meet both requirements*. (If we were separately existing entities, like Cartesian Egos, our criterion might meet these requirements; but we have sufficient reasons to reject this view.)

Return now to the Reductionist View. Reconsider the case where half my brain is successfully transplanted into Jack's body. What is my relation to the person waking up in Jack's body? This relation is psychological continuity, with its normal cause, the continued existence of enough of my brain. There is also very close physical similarity. As a Reductionist, I claim that my relation to the person in Jack's body contains what fundamentally matters. This claim stands whatever happens to other people elsewhere. With one revision, my view meets Williams's first requirement. He claims that whether I shall be some future person ought to depend only on my relation to this future person. I make a similar claim. Instead of asking whether I shall be some future person, I ask whether my relation to this person contains what matters. Like Williams, I can claim that the answer must depend only on the *intrinsic* features of my relation to this future person.

The Reductionist View can meet this revised version of Requirement (1). Suppose that the other operation succeeds. Someone wakes up in Bill's body. On my view, this does not change the relation between me and the person in Jack's body. And it makes at most a little difference to the importance of this relation. This relation still contains what fundamentally matters. Since this relation now holds in a branching form, we are forced to change its *name*. We cannot call each branch of this relation personal identity. But this change in the relation's name has no significance.

This Reductionist View also meets the analogue of Requirement (2). Judgements of personal identity have great importance. Williams therefore claims that we should not make one such judgement and deny another without an important difference in our grounds. On this Reductionist View, we should take the importance that we give to a judgement of identity, and we should give this importance to a different relation. On this view, what is important is relation R: psychological connectedness and/or continuity, with the right kind of cause. Unlike identity, this relation cannot fail to hold because of a trivial difference in the facts. If this relation fails to hold, there is a deep difference in the facts. This meets Requirement (2).

In the case where I divide, though my relation to each of the resulting people cannot be called identity, it contains what fundamentally matters. When we deny identity here, we need not be denying an important judgement. Since my relation to each of the resulting people is about as good as if it were identity, it may carry most of the ordinary implications of identity. Thus it might be claimed that, even when the person in Jack's body cannot be called me, because the other transplant succeeds, he can just as much deserve punishment or reward for what I have done. So can the person in Bill's body. As Wiggins writes: 'a malefactor could scarcely evade responsibility by contriving his own fission'.[51]

There are questions to be answered here. If the malefactor is sentenced to twenty years in prison, should each resulting person serve twenty years, or only ten? I discuss some of these questions in Chapter 15. These questions do not cast doubt on the general claim I have made. If we accept the Reductionist View, it is R and not identity which is what matters.

It may be thought that, if this is so, we ought to give to R the importance that we now give to personal identity. This does not follow. If we believe that personal identity has great importance, this may be because we believe the Non-Reductionist View. If we change our view, and become Reductionists, we may also change our view about the importance of personal identity. We may accept that relation R has nearly all of the importance that, *on the Reductionist View*, personal identity has. And we may accept that, on this view, what fundamentally matters is not personal identity but R. But we may believe that both these relations have much *less* importance than personal identity *would* have if the Non-Reductionist View was true. I discuss this belief in Chapters 14 and 15.

This belief does not affect my claims about Williams's requirements. If we assume that identity is what matters, we cannot meet these requirements. Since we should reject the Non-Reductionist View, our criterion of identity should be either the Physical or the Psychological Criterion. And, as I have argued, there is no plausible version of either criterion that meets both of Williams's requirements.

I add these remarks. Now that we have seen that identity is not what matters, we should not try to revise or extend our criterion of identity, so that it coincides more often with what matters. On any natural understanding of personal identity, such a coincidence could be only partial, as the case of division shows. And revising our criterion may misleadingly suggest that identity is what matters.

Williams gives one other ground for requiring that a criterion of identity be logically one-one, and in a way that is not arbitrary. 'Unless there is some such requirement, I cannot see how one is to preserve and explain the evident truth that the concepts of identity and of exact similarity are different concepts.'[52]

The Reductionist View preserves and explains this truth. I have described cases where there are two people who are exactly similar but are not numerically identical. This may be true in the Branch-Line Case, in which I talk to my Replica. We therefore understand the question, 'Is he one and the same person as me, or is he merely another person, who is exactly similar?' I have claimed that, in some cases, such as those in the middle of the Physical Spectrum, there is not a real difference between the resulting person's being me, and his being someone else, who is merely exactly like me. The Reductionist view does imply that, in some cases, there is not a real difference between numerical identity and exact similarity. But since it recognises other cases where this is a real difference, it preserves and explains the truth that these are different concepts.

I discussed Williams's claims to see if they provide some third view, different from both the Reductionist View and the view that we are separately existing entities. I conclude that these claims do not provide such a third view. They provide further grounds for accepting the Reductionist View. Williams's requirements are both plausible. If we believe that identity is what matters, we cannot meet these requirements. But if we accept the Reductionist View, and appeal to Relation R, we *can* meet the analogous requirements.

92. WITTGENSTEIN AND BUDDHA

Wittgenstein would have rejected the Reductionist View. He believed that our concepts depend on the holding of certain facts, and that we should not consider imaginary cases where these facts no longer hold. The arguments for the Reductionist View appeal to such cases.

This disagreement is only partial. Most people have beliefs about these imaginary cases. As I have argued, these beliefs imply that we are separately existing entities, distinct from our brains and bodies, and entities whose existence must be all-or-nothing. A Reductionist's main claim is that we should reject these beliefs. *Wittgenstein would have agreed.* Given this agreement about this claim, I need not discuss Wittgenstein's view, or some other similar views, such as that advanced by Wiggins.[53]

With two exceptions that I shall soon mention, I believe that I have now considered those views that, in this debate, need to be considered. I may be unaware of some other published view. And I have not considered views held in different ages, or civilizations. This fact suggests a disturbing possibility. I believe that my claims apply to all people, at all times. It would be disturbing to discover that they are merely part of one line of thought, in the culture of Modern Europe and America.

Fortunately, this is not true. I claim that, when we ask what persons are, and how they continue to exist, the fundamental question is a choice between two views. On one view, we are separately existing entities, distinct from our brain and bodies and our experiences, and entities whose existence must be all-or-nothing. The other view is the Reductionist View. And I claim that, of these, the second view is true. As Appendix J shows, *Buddha would have agreed.* The Reductionist View is not merely part of one cultural tradition. It may be, as I have claimed, the true view about all people at all times.

93. AM I ESSENTIALLY MY BRAIN?

Nagel suggests a view of a kind that I have not discussed. He suggests that what I really am is whatever is the cause of my psychological continuity. Given what we now know, what I really am is my brain. On this view, moreover, I am *essentially* my brain. I cannot decide to take a different view about myself.

Nagel supports this view in three ways. He gives two arguments, which I try to answer in Appendix D. He also claims that his view is intuitively plausible. As he writes, his brain

seems to me to be something without which I could not survive—so that if a physically distinct replica of me were produced who was psychologically continuous with me though my brain had been destroyed, it would not be me and its survival would not be as good as my survival.

Nagel is here considering a case like that of Teletransportation. The Scanning Replicator could have uses here on Earth. I could use it as a safer way to cross Manhattan, or as the cure if, while I walk across Manhattan, I am fatally stabbed. As a precaution, before each walk, I could have a new blueprint stored.

Nagel suggests that Teletransportation is not merely not as good as ordinary survival, but is nearly as bad as death. As he writes, after describing his imagined case,

I will not survive the night . . . the replica will not be me. Trying to summon my courage, I prepare for the end.

This suggests that, on Nagel's view, personal identity is what matters. I admit that, in a case like Teletransportation, many people would accept Nagel's view. They would believe that what matters is the survival of their brains. In Appendix D I describe two cases where this is harder to believe.

Since Nagel's view is, in some cases, intuitively plausible, and Appendix D may fail to answer Nagel's arguments, I shall give, in Section 98, a different kind of answer to this and similar views.

There is one other view that I should consider. I explain in Appendix E how, despite an apparent disagreement, Nozick's view is a version of Reductionism.

94. IS THE TRUE VIEW BELIEVABLE?

Nagel once claimed that, even if the Reductionist View is true, it is psychologically impossible for us to believe this. I shall therefore briefly review my arguments given above. I shall then ask whether *I* can honestly claim to believe my conclusions. If I can, I shall assume that I am not unique. There would be at least some other people who can believe the truth.

I shall first qualify my claim that I have described the true view. It is hard to explain accurately what a Reductionist claims. And it is hard to explain accurately what is involved in identity over time. It is likely that, in describing a Reductionist view about identity, I have made mistakes.

Such mistakes may not wholly undermine my arguments. Wittgenstein suggested this analogy. Suppose that I am rearranging the books in a library. At the start of this rearrangement, I place two books together on a particular shelf, because these books ought to be together. I may know that, at the end of this rearrangement, these two books will be on a different shelf. But it is still worth putting them together now. If they ought to be together, they will still be together after this rearrangement.

I claim that a person is not like a Cartesian Ego, a being whose existence must be all-or-nothing. A person is like a nation. In the true account of identity over time, these two kinds of entities go together. They are like the two books that I start by placing on a shelf. In my claims about Reductionism and identity, I may have made mistakes. This would be like the fact that the two books should go on a different shelf. But my main claim is that persons are like nations, not Cartesian Egos. If this claim is true, it would not be undermined by my mistakes. In the account that makes no mistakes, persons and nations would still go together. The account of their identity over time would, in its essential features, be similar.

I distinguished two views about the nature of persons. On the Non-Reductionist View, a person is a separately existing entity, distinct from his brain and body, and his experiences. On the best-known version of this view, a person is a Cartesian Ego. On the Reductionist View that I defend, persons exist. And a person is distinct from his brain and body, and his experiences. But persons are not separately existing entities. The existence of a person, during any period, just consists in the existence of his brain and body, and the thinking of his thoughts, and the doing of his deeds, and the occurrence of many other physical and mental events.

Since these views disagree about the nature of persons, they also disagree about the nature of personal identity over time. On the Reductionist View, personal identity just involves physical and psychological continuity. As I argued, both of these can be described in an impersonal way. These two kinds of continuity can be described without claiming that experiences are had by a person. A Reductionist also claims that personal identity is not what matters. Personal identity just involves certain kinds of connectedness and continuity, when these hold in a one-one form. These relations are what matter.

On the Non-Reductionist View, personal identity is what matters. And it does not just involve physical and psychological continuity. It is a separate further fact, which must, in every case, either hold completely, or not at all. Psychological unity is explained by ownership. The unity of consciousness at any time is explained by the fact that several experiences are being had by a person. And the unity of a person's life is explained in the same way. These several claims must, I have argued, stand or fall together.

I conceded that the Non-Reductionist View might have been true. There might for example have been evidence supporting the belief in re-incarnation. But there is in fact no good evidence for this view, and much evidence against it.

Some of the evidence is provided by the actual cases of divided minds. Because their hemispheres have been disconnected, several people have two streams of consciousness, in each of which they are unaware of the other. We might claim that, in such a case, there are two different people in the same body. This treats such cases as being like the imagined case where I divide, which I review below. Our alternative is to claim, about these actual cases, that there is a single person with two streams of consciousness.

If we make this claim, how can we explain the unity of consciousness in each stream? We cannot explain this unity by claiming that the various different experiences in each stream are being had by the same person, or subject of experiences. This describes the two streams as if they were one. If we believe that the unity of consciousness must be explained by ascribing different experiences to a particular subject, we must claim that in these cases, though there is only a single person, there are two subjects of experiences. We must therefore claim that there can be, in a person's life, subjects of experiences that are *not* persons. It is hard to believe that there really are such things. These cases are better explained by the Reductionist Psychological Criterion. This claims that, at any time, there is one state of awareness of the experiences in one stream of consciousness, and another state of awareness of the experiences in the other stream.

Though they raise this problem for the Non-Reductionist View, these cases of divided minds are only a small part of the evidence against this view. There is no evidence that the carrier of psychological continuity is something whose existence, like that of a Cartesian Ego, must be all-or-nothing. And there is much evidence that the carrier of this continuity is the brain. There is much evidence that our psychological features depend upon states and events in our brains. A brain's continued existence need not be all-or-nothing. Physical connectedness can be a matter of degree. And there are countless actual cases in which psychological connectedness holds only in certain ways, or to some reduced degree.

We have sufficient evidence to reject the Non-Reductionist View. The Reductionist View is, I claim, the only alternative. I considered possible third views, and found none that was both non-Reductionist and a view that we had sufficient reasons to accept. More exactly, though these other views differ in other ways, the plausible views do not deny a Reductionist's central claim. They agree that we are not separately existing entities, distinct from our brains and bodies and our experiences, whose existence must be all-or-nothing.

Besides making these claims about the facts, I made claims about our beliefs. We learn that we have these beliefs when we consider certain imaginary cases.

One of these is the case in which, by tampering with my brain, a surgeon gradually removes all of my psychological continuity. I described three other ranges of cases. In the Psychological and Physical Spectra there would be, between me and some future person, all of the possible degrees of either psychological or physical connectedness. In the Combined Spectrum, there would be all of the possible degrees of both kinds of connectedness.

Like most of us, I am strongly inclined to believe that any future person must be either me or someone else. And I am inclined to believe that there is always a deep difference between these two outcomes. Since I am not a separately existing entity, these beliefs cannot be true. This is best shown by considering the Combined Spectrum. In the case at the near end, where nothing would be done to me, the resulting person would certainly be me. In the case at the far end, where there would be no connections between me and the resulting person, this person would certainly be someone else. If any future person must be either me or someone else, there must be a line in this range of cases up to which the resulting person would be me, and beyond which he would be someone else. If there is always a deep difference between some person's being me and his being someone else, there must be a deep difference between two of the cases in this Spectrum. There must be such a deep difference, though we could never discover where this difference comes. These claims are false. There is no deep difference between any neighbouring cases in this range. The only differences are that, in one of the cases, the surgeons would replace a few more cells, and would make one more small psychological change.

When I consider this range of cases, I am forced to abandon at least one of the two beliefs mentioned above. I cannot continue to believe both that any future person must be either me or someone else, and that there is always a deep difference between these two outcomes.

I am also forced to accept another part of the Reductionist View. Suppose that I am about to undergo one of the operations in the middle of this spectrum. I know that, between me and the resulting person, there will be certain kinds and amounts of physical and psychological connectedness. On the Reductionist View, in knowing these facts I know the full truth about what will happen. When I am about to lose consciousness, I may ask, 'Am I about to die? Or shall I be the resulting person?' And I am inclined to believe that these are always two different possibilities, one of which must be the truth. On the Reductionist View, this is here an empty question. There is sometimes a real difference between some future person's being me, and his being someone else. But there is no such real difference in the cases in the middle of the Combined Spectrum. What could the difference be? What could make it true either that the resulting person would be me, or that he would be someone else? Since I am not a separately existing entity, there is nothing that could make these different possibilities, either of which might be true. In these cases, we could say that the resulting person will be me, or we could say that I shall die and he will be someone else. But these are not here different outcomes. They are merely different descriptions of the same outcome.

To illustrate these claims, I repeated Hume's comparison. Persons are like nations, clubs, or political parties. If we are considering these other entities, most of us accept a Reductionist view. Remember the political party which split, and became two rival parties. We can ask, 'Did the original party cease to exist, or did it continue to exist as one or other of the resulting parties?' But we do not believe that this is a real question, about different possibilities, one of which must be what happened. This question is empty. Even if we have no answer to this question, we could know the full truth about what happened.

Since we accept Reductionist views about political parties, or clubs, or nations, we understand, in a rough way, what is being claimed by the Reductionist View about persons. But most of us are strongly inclined to reject this view. We are strongly inclined to believe that there must always be a difference between some future person's being me, and his being someone else. Considering my Combined Spectrum may not be enough to persuade us to become Reductionists. I therefore gave further arguments.

One argument appealed to the imagined case where I divide. The division of one stream of consciousness might be claimed to be deeply impossible. But what happens must be possible: and in the lives of several people this has happened. My imagined Division is a natural extension of these actual cases.

In this imagined case, each half of my brain is successfully transplanted into another body. What happens to me? Unless we grotesquely distort the concept of a person, the only possible answers are that I shall be one of the resulting people, or the other, or neither. If we believe that identity is what matters, each of these answers is hard to accept. Given the exact similarity of the two resulting people, it is hard to believe that I shall be *one* of these two people. If I shall be *neither* of these people, and identity is what matters, I ought to regard division as equivalent to death. But this is also hard to believe. My relation to each resulting person contains everything that would be needed for survival. This relation cannot be called identity because and only because it holds between me and *two* future people. In ordinary death, this relation holds between me and *no* future person. Though double survival cannot be described in the language of identity, it is not equivalent to death. Two does not equal zero.

This imagined case supports another part of the Reductionist View. Not only is each of the possible answers hard to believe. It is hard to see how the case could involve different possibilities, any of which might be the truth. If I am not a Cartesian Ego, what could make it true that I would be one of the two resulting people, or the other? If these are different possibilities, in what could the difference consist? There seems to be no answer to this question. Each of the resulting people will have half my brain, and will be fully psychologically continuous with me. We seem forced to conclude that this is a full description of the case. We understand the question, 'Shall I be one of these two people, or the other, or neither?' But this is another empty question. These are not here different possibilities, one of which must be true.

These are merely different descriptions of the same outcome.

The best description is that I shall be neither resulting person. But this does not imply that I should regard division as nearly as bad as death. As I argued, I should regard it as about as good as ordinary survival. For some people, it would be slightly better; for others, it would be slightly worse. Since I cannot be one and the same person as the two resulting people, but my relation to each of these people contains what fundamentally matters in ordinary survival, the case shows that identity is not what matters. What matters is Relation R: psychological connectedness and/or psychological continuity, with the right kind of cause.

I have now reviewed the main arguments for the Reductionist View. Do I find it impossible to believe this View?

What I find is this. I can believe this view at the intellectual or reflective level. I am convinced by the arguments in favour of this view. But I think it likely that, at some other level, I shall always have doubts.

My belief is firmest when I am considering some of these imagined cases. I am convinced that, if I divided, it would be an empty question whether I shall be one, or the other, or neither of the resulting people. I believe that there is nothing that could make these different possibilities, any of which might be what would really happen. And I am convinced that, in the central cases of the Third Spectrum, it is an empty question whether the resulting person would be me.

When I consider certain other cases, my conviction is less firm. One example is Teletransportation. I imagine that I am in the cubicle, about to press the green button. I might suddenly have doubts. I might be tempted to change my mind, and pay the larger fare of a space-ship journey.

I suspect that reviewing my arguments would never wholly remove my doubts. At the reflective or intellectual level, I would remain convinced that the Reductionist View is true. But at some lower level I would still be inclined to believe that there must always be a real difference between some future person's being me, and his being someone else. Something similar is true when I look through a window at the top of a sky-scraper. I know that I am in no danger. But, looking down from this dizzying height, I am afraid. I would have a similar irrational fear if I was about to press the green button.

It may help to add these remarks. On the Reductionist View, my continued existence just involves physical and psychological continuity. On the Non-Reductionist View, it involves a further fact. It is natural to believe in this further fact, and to believe that, compared with the continuities, it is a *deep* fact, and is the fact that really matters. When I fear that, in Teletransportation, *I* shall not get to Mars, my fear is that the abnormal cause may fail to produce this further fact. As I have argued, there is no such fact. What I fear will not happen, *never* happens. I want the person on

Mars to be me in a specially intimate way in which no future person will ever be me. My continued existence never involves this deep further fact. What I fear will be missing is *always* missing. Even a space-ship journey would not produce the further fact in which I am inclined to believe.

When I come to see that my continued existence does not involve this further fact, I lose my reason for preferring a space-ship journey. But, judged from the stand-point of my earlier belief, this is not because Teletransportation is *about as good as* ordinary survival. It is because ordinary survival is *about as bad as*, or little better than, Teletransportation. *Ordinary survival is about as bad as being destroyed and Replicated.*

By rehearsing arguments like these, I might do enough to reduce my fear. I might be able to bring myself to press the green button. But I expect that I would never completely lose my intuitive belief in the Non-Reductionist View. It is hard to be serenely confident in my Reductionist conclusions. It is hard to believe that personal identity is not what matters. If tomorrow someone will be in agony, it is hard to believe that it could be an empty question whether this agony will be felt by *me*. And it is hard to believe that, if I am about to lose consciousness, there might be no answer to the question 'Am I about to die?'

Nagel once claimed that it is psychologically impossible to believe the Reductionist View. Buddha claimed that, though this is very hard, it is possible. I find Buddha's claim to be true. After reviewing my arguments, I find that, at the reflective or intellectual level, though it is very hard to believe the Reductionist View, this is possible. My remaining doubts or fears seem to me irrational. Since I can believe this view, I assume that others can do so too. We can believe the truth about ourselves.

13

WHAT DOES MATTER

95. LIBERATION FROM THE SELF

THE truth is very different from what we are inclined to believe. Even if we are not aware of this, most of us are Non-Reductionists. If we considered my imagined cases, we would be strongly inclined to believe that our continued existence is a deep further fact, distinct from physical and psychological continuity, and a fact that must be all-or-nothing. This is not true.

Is the truth depressing? Some may find it so. But I find it liberating, and consoling. When I believed that my existence was a such a further fact, I seemed imprisoned in myself. My life seemed like a glass tunnel, through which I was moving faster every year, and at the end of which there was darkness. When I changed my view, the walls of my glass tunnel disappeared. I now live in the open air. There is still a difference between my life and the lives of other people. But the difference is less. Other people are closer. I am less concerned about the rest of my own life, and more concerned about the lives of others.

When I believed the Non-Reductionist View, I also cared more about my inevitable death. After my death, there will no one living who will be me. I can now redescribe this fact. Though there will later be many experiences, none of these experiences will be connected to my present experiences by chains of such direct connections as those involved in experience-memory, or in the carrying out of an earlier intention. Some of these future experiences may be related to my present experiences in less direct ways. There will later be some memories about my life. And there may later be thoughts that are influenced by mine, or things done as the result of my advice. My death will break the more direct relations between my present experiences and future experiences, but it will not break various other relations. This is all there is to the fact that there will be no one living who will be me. Now that I have seen this, my death seems to me less bad.

Instead of saying, 'I shall be dead', I should say, 'There will be no future experiences that will be related, in certain ways, to these present experiences'. Because it reminds me what this fact involves, this redescription makes this fact less depressing. Suppose next that I must undergo some ordeal. Instead of saying, 'The person suffering will be me', I should say, 'There will be suffering that will be related, in certain ways, to these present experiences'. Once again, the redescribed fact seems to me less bad.

I can increase these effects by vividly imagining that I am about to undergo one of the operations I have described. I imagine that I am in a central case in the Combined Spectrum, where it is an empty question whether I am about to die. It is very hard to believe that this question could be empty. When I review the arguments for this belief, and reconvince myself, this for a while stuns my natural concern for my future. When my actual future will be grim—as it would be if I shall be tortured, or shall face a firing squad at dawn—it will be good that I have this way of briefly stunning my concern.

After Hume thought hard about his arguments, he was thrown into 'the most deplorable condition imaginable, environed with the deepest darkness'.[54] The cure was to dine and play backgammon with his friends. Hume's arguments supported total scepticism. This is why they brought darkness and utter loneliness. The arguments for Reductionism have on me the opposite effect. Thinking hard about these arguments removes the glass wall between me and others. And, as I have said, I care less about my death. This is merely the fact that, after a certain time, none of the experiences that will occur will be related, in certain ways, to my present experiences. Can this matter all that much?

96. THE CONTINUITY OF THE BODY

Because it affects my emotions in these ways, I am glad that the Reductionist View is true. This is simply a report of psychological effects. The effects on others may be different.

There are several other questions still to be discussed. And in discussing these I can do more than report facts about my reactions. The answers to these questions partly depend on the force of certain arguments. I shall first discuss what, as Reductionists, we ought to claim to be what matters. I shall then ask how, if we have changed our view about the nature of personal identity, we ought to change our beliefs about rationality, and about morality.

As the case of My Division shows, personal identity is not what matters. It is merely true that, in most cases, personal identity coincides with what matters. What does matter *in the way in which* personal identity is, mistakenly, thought to matter? What is it rational to care about, in our concern about our own future?

This question can be restated. Assume, for simplicity, that it could be rational to be concerned only about one's own self-interest. Suppose that I am an Egoist, and that I could be related in one of several ways to some resulting person. What is the relation that would justify egoistic concern about this resulting person? If the rest of this person's life will be well worth living, in what way should I want to be related to this person? If the rest of his life will be much worse than nothing, in what way should I want *not* to be related to this person? In short, what is the relation that, for an Egoist, should fundamentally matter? This relation will also be what, for all of us, should fundamentally matter, in our concern for our own future. But since we may be concerned about the fate of the resulting person, *whatever* his relation is to us, it is clearest to ask what, for an Egoist, should matter.

Here are the simplest answers:

(1) Physical continuity,

(2) Relation R with its normal cause,

(3) R with any reliable cause,

(4) R with any cause.

R is psychological connectedness and/or continuity, with the right kind of cause. If we decide that R is what matters, we must then consider the relative importance of connectedness and continuity. It might be suggested that what matters is *both* R *and* physical continuity. But this is the same as answer (2), since physical continuity is part of R's normal cause.

Can we defend (1), the claim that only physical continuity matters? Can we claim that, if I shall be physically continuous with some resulting person, this is what matters, even if I shall not be R-related to this person?

Reconsider Williams's Example, where the surgeon totally destroys any distinctive kind of psychological continuity. Suppose that this surgeon is about to operate on me, in a painless way, and that the resulting person will have a life that is much worse than nothing. If I am an Egoist, I might regard this prospect as being no worse than a painless death, since I do not care what will happen to the resulting person. I might instead regard this prospect as much worse than death, because I am egoistically concerned about this person's appalling future. Which should my attitude be?

I should be egoistically concerned about this person's future if I could justifiably believe that this person will be *me*, rather than being *someone else* who is merely physically continuous with me. But, as I have argued, this belief is not justified. Williams's example is at the far end of the Psychological Spectrum. Both in the central cases in this Spectrum, and at the far end, there is not a real difference between the resulting person's being me, and his being someone else. These are not two different possibilities, one of which must be true. In Williams's example, the full facts are these. The resulting person will be physically but not psychologically continuous with me. We could call this person me, or call him someone else. On the Wide Psychological Criterion of identity, we would call him someone else. But neither of these descriptions could be a factual mistake. Both are descriptions of the same fact. If we give one of these descriptions in order to imply some view about what matters, our description might be a bad description. It might imply an indefensible view about what matters. But we must decide what matters *before* choosing our description.

Suppose that I accept these claims. As a Reductionist, should I be egoistically concerned about the future of this person? Should I be concerned, though I know that the physical continuity cannot cause it to be true, as a further fact, that this person will be me? In deciding what matters, I must set aside all thoughts about my identity. The question about identity is, here, empty. I must ask whether, *in itself*, physical continuity justifies egoistic concern.

I believe that the answer should be No. As I argued, those who believe in the Physical Criterion cannot plausibly require the continuity of the whole body. It cannot matter whether I receive some transplanted organ, if this organ functions just as well. All that could be claimed to matter is that enough of my brain continues to exist.

Why should the brain be singled out in this way? The answer must be: 'Because the brain is the carrier of psychological continuity, or Relation R'. If this is why the brain is singled out, the continuity of the brain would not matter when it was *not* the carrier of Relation R. The continuity of the brain would here be no more important than the continuity of any other part of the body. And the continuity of these other parts does not matter at all. It would not matter if these other parts were replaced with sufficiently similar duplicates. We should claim the same about the brain. The continuity of the brain matters if it will be the cause of the holding of Relation R. If R will *not* hold, the continuity of the brain should have no significance for the person whose brain it now is. It would not justify egoistic concern.

Reductionists cannot plausibly claim that only physical continuity matters. They can at most claim that this continuity is part of what matters. They can at most defend (2), the claim that Relation R would not matter if it did not have its normal cause, part of which is physical continuity.

I believe that (2) is also indefensible. I believe that physical continuity is the least important element in a person's continued existence. What we value, in ourselves and others, is not the continued existence of the same particular brains and bodies. What we value are the various relations between ourselves and others, whom and what we love, our ambitions, achievements, commitments, emotions, memories, and several other psychological features. Some of us would also want ourselves or others to continue to have bodies that are very similar to our present bodies. But this is not wanting the same particular bodies to continue to exist. I believe that, if there will later be some person who will be R-related to me as I am now, it matters very little whether this person has my present brain and body. I believe that what fundamentally matters is Relation R, even if it does not have its normal cause. Thus it would not matter if my brain was replaced with an exact duplicate. [55]

If some person will be R-related to me, this person's body should also be sufficiently like my present body to allow full psychological connectedness. This would not be true, for example, if this body was of the opposite sex. And for a few people, such as some of those who are very beautiful, there should also be exact physical similarity. These claims about this similarity I shall in future omit.

Whether we accept this view may affect our beliefs and attitudes about our own lives. But the question is clearest in the imagined case of Teletransportation. On my view, my relation to my Replica contains what fundamentally matters. This relation is about as good as ordinary survival. Judged from the stand-point of the Non-Reductionist View, ordinary survival is, on my view, little better than—or about as bad as—being destroyed and Replicated. It would therefore be irrational to pay much more for a conventional space-ship journey.

Many people would be afraid of Teletransportation. I admit that, at some level, I might be afraid. But, as I have argued, such fear cannot be rational. Since I know exactly what will happen, I cannot fear that the worse of two outcomes will be what happens.

My relation to my Replica is R without its normal cause. The abnormality of the cause seems to me trivial. Reconsider the artificial eyes which would restore sight to those who have gone blind. Suppose that these eyes would give to these people visual sensations just like those involved in normal sight, and that these sensations would provide true beliefs about what can be seen. This would surely be as good as normal sight. It would not be plausible to reject these eyes because they were not the normal cause of human sight. There would be some grounds for disliking artificial eyes, since they would make one's appearance disturbing to others. But there is no analogue to this in Teletransportation. My Replica, though he is artificially produced, will be just like me in every way. He will have a normal brain and body.

We should probably decide not to call my Replica me. If we make this decision, we should regard this case as like My Division. It is a case where there is a best answer to an empty question. If I am about to divide, it is best to say that neither resulting person will be me. But this does not imply that I should regard division as like death. We are not deciding which of several outcomes will be what happens; we are merely choosing one of several descriptions of a single outcome. Since this is so, our choice of one description is irrelevant to the question of how I should regard this outcome.

The same is true in the case in which I shall be Teletransported. My attitude to this outcome should not be affected by our decision whether to call my Replica me. I know the full facts even if we have not yet made this decision. If we do decide not to call my Replica me, the fact

(a)   that my Replica will not be me

would just consist in the fact

(b)   that there will not be physical continuity,

and

(c)   that, because this is so, R will not have its normal cause.

Since (a) would just consist in (b) and (c), I should ignore (a). My attitude should depend on the importance of facts (b) and (c). These facts are all there is to my Replica's not being me.

When we see that this last claim is true, we cannot rationally, I believe, claim that (c) matters much. It cannot matter much that the cause is abnormal. It is the *effect* which matters. And this effect, the holding of Relation R, is in itself the same. It is true that, if this effect has the abnormal cause, we can describe the effect in a different way. We can say that, though my Replica is psychologically continuous with me, he will not be me. But this is not a further difference in what happens, beyond the difference in the cause. If I decide not to press the button, and to pay much more for a conventional space-ship journey, I must admit that this is merely because I do not like the thought of an abnormal method of causation. It cannot be rational to care much about the abnormality of this cause.

Similar remarks apply to the continued existence of one's present brain and body. It may be rational to want the body of my Replica to be like my present body. But this is a desire for a certain kind of body, not a desire for the same particular body. Why should I want it to be true that *this* brain and body gets to Mars? Once again, the natural fear is that only this ensures that *I* shall get to Mars. But this again assumes that whether or not I get to Mars is, here, a real question. And we ought to conclude that this is an empty question. Even if this question has a best answer, we can know exactly what will happen before deciding what this answer is. Since this is so, can I rationally care a great deal whether or not this person's brain and body will be my present brain and body? I believe that, while it may not be irrational to care a little, to care a great deal would be irrational.

Why would it not be irrational to care a little? This could be like one's wish to keep the same wedding ring, rather than a new ring that is exactly similar. We understand the sentimental wish to keep the very ring that was involved in the wedding ceremony. In the same way, it may not be irrational to have a mild preference that the person on Mars have my present brain and body.

There remains one question. If there will be some person who will be R-related to me, would it matter if this relation did not have a reliable cause?

There is an obvious reason for preferring, in advance, that the cause will be reliable. Suppose that Teletransportation worked perfectly in a few cases, but in most cases was a complete failure. In a few cases, the person on Mars would be a perfect Replica of me. But in most cases he would be totally unlike me. If these were the facts, it would clearly be rational to pay the larger fare of a space-ship journey. But this is irrelevant. We should ask, 'In the few cases, where my Replica will be fully R-related to me, would it matter that R did not have a reliable cause?'

I believe that the answer should again be No. Suppose that there is an unreliable treatment for some disease. In most cases the treatment achieves nothing. But in a few cases it provides a complete cure. In these cases, only the effect matters. This effect is just as good, even though its cause was unreliable. We should claim the same about Relation R. I conclude that, of the answers I described, we should accept (4). In our concern about our own future, *what fundamentally matters is relation R, with any cause.*

97. THE BRANCH-LINE CASE

Teletransportation would, I have argued, be about as good as ordinary survival. Another challenge to this claim comes from the Branch-Line Case. Suppose that the New Scanner has not destroyed my brain and body, but has damaged my heart. I am here on Earth, and expect to die within a few days. Using the Intercom, I see and talk to my Replica on Mars. He assures me that he will continue my life where I leave off.

What should my attitude here be? I am about to die. Does my relation to *this* Replica contain what matters? He is fully psychologically continuous, not with me as I am now, but with me as I was this morning, when I pressed the green button. Is this relation about as good as survival?

It may be hard to believe that it is. But it is also hard to believe that it can matter much whether my life briefly overlaps with the life of my Replica.

It may help to consider

The Sleeping Pill. Certain actual sleeping pills cause *retrograde* amnesia. It can be true that, if I take such a pill, I shall remain awake for an hour, but after my night's sleep I shall have no memories of the second half of this hour.

I have in fact taken such pills, and found out what the results are like. Suppose that I took such a pill nearly an hour ago. The person who wakes up in my bed tomorrow will not be psychologically continuous with me as I am now. He will be psychologically continuous with me as I was half an hour ago. I am now on a *psychological branch-line*, which will end soon when I fall asleep. During this half-hour, I am psychologically continuous with myself in the past. But I am not now psychologically continuous with myself in the future. I shall never later remember what I do or think or feel during this half-hour. This means that, in some respects, my relation to myself tomorrow is like a relation to another person.

Suppose, for instance, that I have been worrying about some practical question. I now see the solution. Since it is clear what I should do, I form a firm intention. In the rest of my life, it would be enough to form this intention. But, when I am on this psychological branch-line, this is not enough. I shall not later remember what I have now decided, and I shall not wake up with the intention that I have now formed. I must therefore communicate with myself tomorrow as if I was communicating with someone else. I must write myself a letter, describing my decision, and my new intention. I must then place this letter where I am bound to notice it tomorrow.

I do not in fact have any memories of making such a decision, and writing such a letter. But I did once find such a letter underneath my razor.

This case is in one way like the Branch-Line Case. And it would be just like a variant of this case, in which though I live for a few days after leaving the cubicle, my Replica would not be created until after I have died. But, in the case that we are considering, my life overlaps with that of my Replica. We talk on the Intercom. There is no analogue to this in the case of the Sleeping Pill.

The analogue can be found in my imagined Physics Exam. In this case I divide my mind for ten minutes. In both of my streams of consciousness, I know that I am now having thoughts and sensations in my other stream. But in each stream I am unaware of my thoughts and sensations in my other stream. My relation to myself in my other stream is again like my relation to another person. I would have to communicate in a public way. I might in one stream write a letter to myself in my other stream. With one hand I would then place this letter in my other hand.

This is like my situation in the Branch-Line Case. I can imagine having a divided mind. Since this is so, I need not assume that my Replica on Mars is someone else. Here on Earth, I am not aware of what my Replica on Mars is now thinking. This is like the fact that, in each of my two streams of my consciousness in the Physics Exam, I am not aware of what, in my other stream, I am now thinking. I can believe that I do now have another stream of consciousness, of which, in this stream, I am now unaware. And, if it helps, I can take this view about my Replica. I can say that I now have two streams of consciousness, one here on Earth, and another on Mars. This description cannot be a factual mistake. When I talk to my Replica on Mars, this is merely like the communication in the Physics Exam between myself in my two streams.

The actual case of the Sleeping Pill provides a close analogy to one of the special features of the Branch-Line Case: the fact that I am on a psychological branch-line. The imagined Physics Exam provides a close analogy to the other special feature: that my life overlaps with that of my Replica. When we consider these analogies, this seems enough to defend the claim that, when I am on the Branch-Line, my relation to my Replica contains almost everything that matters. It may be slightly inconvenient that my Replica will be psychologically continuous, not with me as I am now, but with me as I was this morning when I pressed the green button. But these relations are substantially the same. It makes little difference that my life briefly overlaps with that of my Replica.

If the overlap was large, this *would* make a difference. Suppose that I am an old man, who is about to die. I shall be outlived by someone who was once a Replica of me. When this person started to exist forty years ago, he was psychologically continuous with me as I was then. He has since lived his own life for forty years. I agree that my relation to *this* Replica, though better than ordinary death, is not nearly as good as ordinary survival. But this relation would be about as good if my Replica would be psychologically continuous with me as I was ten days or ten minutes ago. As Nozick argues, overlaps as brief as this cannot be rationally thought to have much significance.[56]

Though my two analogies seem enough to defend this claim, I admit that this is one of the cases where my view is hardest to believe. *Before* I press the green button, I can more easily believe that my relation to my Replica contains what fundamentally matters in ordinary survival. I can look forward down the Main Line where there are forty years of life ahead. *After* I have pressed the green button, and have talked to my Replica, I cannot in the same way look forward down the Main Line. My concern for the future needs to be redirected. I must try to direct this concern backwards up the Branch Line beyond the point of division, and then forward down the Main Line. This psychological manoeuvre would be difficult. But this is not surprising. And, since it is not surprising, this difficulty does not provide a sufficient argument against what I have claimed about this case.

98. SERIES-PERSONS

I have denied that personal identity is what matters. On my view, what fundamentally matters, in our concern about our own future, is the holding of Relation R, with any cause. This would be what matters even when it does not coincide with personal identity.

On Nagel's view, what I am essentially is my brain. And what fundamentally matters is the continued existence of this brain. I believe that I answer Nagel's arguments in Appendix D. But these arguments may not convince. It is therefore worth explaining how Nagel's view and a revised form of mine could both be true.

Suppose that Nagel's view is true. What fundamentally matters, for me, is the continued existence of my brain. Since on Nagel's view I am essentially my brain, I cannot decide to take a different view about myself. But I can do something else.

Nagel describes the concept of a *series-person*. While a person is, on Nagel's view, essentially a particular embodied brain, a series-person is potentially an R-related series of embodied brains. We cannot now solve the problem that our bodies age, and decay. Nagel imagines a community in which technology provides a solution. In this community, everyone over the age of 30 enters a Scanning Replicator once in every year. This machine destroys a person's brain and body, and produces a Replica who is R-related to this person, and who has a body that is exactly similar except that it has not aged or decayed. Nagel claims that, for the series-persons in this community, it would not be irrational to use this Scanning Replicator. On their criterion of identity, each of these series-persons would continue to exist, moving to a new brain and body every year. Each series-person would always have a brain and body that have the youth, appearance, and vigour of his brain and body when he was 30.

These series-persons might have fatal accidents. I therefore add the detail that, as a precaution, each has a blueprint made every day. With this addition, these series-persons are potentially immortal, and could have eternal youth. On most theories that are now accepted, the Universe will either expand indefinitely, or collapse back in a reversal of the Big Bang. Most physicists assume that, on either alternative, all forms of life will become impossible. If this were not true, these series-persons could live for ever.[57]

Assume that I accept Nagel's view. I am essentially my brain, and what fundamentally matters, in my concern for my future, is the continued existence of this brain. If I accept this view, I must have been reluctantly driven to this conclusion. I much preferred my old view. Though I cannot change my view about what I am, I can do the following. You are now reading sentences that I typed in November 1982. This sentence tells you that, in the rest of this book, *pronouns are used to refer to series-persons.* If Nagel's view is false, this may not change what pronouns mean. Every person may be a series-person. This would be so if our criterion of identity was Relation R with any cause, since this is also the criterion of identity of series-persons.

If Nagel's view is true, the rest of this book uses pronouns in a new sense. They refer, not to persons, but to series-persons. Thus the words 'I' and 'me' do not refer to the person, Derek Parfit. They refer to the series-person whose present brain and body is also Derek Parfit's brain and body. Since the words 'I' and 'me' are used in this new sense, their old sense is expressed with the words 'Old-I' and 'old-me'. Similar remarks apply to the other pronouns.

On Nagel's view, what is the relation between old-me and me the series-person? It may help to remember a mythical being: a phoenix. On the criterion of the identity of birds, a bird ceases to exist if it is burnt to ashes.

If a phoenix existed, it would not be a particular bird. It would be a series of birds, or a *series-bird*. A phoenix would at any time have the body of a particular bird. But when this bird is burnt to ashes, only the bird ceases to exist. The phoenix comes to life again in the body of a new bird, rising from the ashes. Like a particular series-person, a particular phoenix would thus have a series of different bodies.

No phoenix has ever existed. But there are many series-persons. These sentences are being typed by a series-person, me. They are also being typed by a person: old-me. This person is named Derek Parfit. I the series-person hereby name myself *Phoenix Parfit*. Since my present body is also Derek Parfit's body, both of us are typing these sentences. And both of us are having the very same thoughts and experiences. But though we are now related in this extremely intimate way, *if* Nagel's view is true, we are two different individuals. The difference between us is this. On Nagel's view, if Old-I was Teletransported, this would kill old-me, the person. But it would not kill me, the series-person. This difference is enough to make old-me and me different individuals.

You may doubt whether I, this series-person, really do exist. You may believe that beings cannot be caused to exist merely by the invention of a new concept. This is true. I was not caused to exist either by Nagel's invention of the concept of a series-person, or by the typing of the sentences above that may have given new meanings to 'I' and 'me'. Given what is meant by the concept 'series-person', I the series-person started to exist when Old-I the person started to exist. And it is very probable that both will cease to exist at the same time. This is very probable because it is most unlikely that, within the life-time of Old-I, Teletransportation will become possible.

Languages develop. When we invent a new concept, we may find that it applies to parts of reality. The concept of a phoenix applies to nothing. But the concept of a series-person applies just as often as the concept of a person. Whether or not Nagel's view is true, there now exist several billion series-persons. If Nagel's view is true, for every person who exists, there is a series-person who exists, and who is *very* closely related to this person. Given this extremely close relation, the distinction between these individuals is hardly ever worth drawing. It is worth drawing only at this point in my discussion of what matters. I am supposing that Nagel's view is true. I am supposing that what fundamentally matters for old-me is the continued existence of my present brain. Even if we believe this, we can still believe that the continued existence of our present brains is *not* what matters. We can claim that what matters is Relation R. This is what matters *for us, the series-persons*.

With some new concept, we can sometimes give a better description of reality. This was true of the concepts of an atom, and a molecule. This kind

of improvement is straightforward. If Nagel's view is true, the concept of a
series-person also makes possible a better description of reality. But this
improvement is not so straightforward. The concept of a series-person does
not merely enable the same beings to give a better description of reality. It
enables *different* beings both to proclaim their existence and to give this
better description.

Nagel mentions a third concept, that of a *day-person*. Such a person's
existence necessarily involves an uninterrupted stream of consciousness. For
day-persons, sleep is death. When we consider this concept we again find
that it applies to reality. At any time there are as many day-persons living as
there are conscious persons living. But during a whole year the number of
day-persons who have lived will greatly exceed the number of persons living.

The concept of a day-person is worse than the concept of a person. This is
because what matters is not the uninterruption of a stream of consciousness.
What matters is Relation R. Though it applies to reality, the concept of a
day-person picks out parts of reality with unimportant boundaries. We
believe, plausibly, that it does not matter if there are interruptions in a
stream of consciousness. This does not matter because these interruptions
do not destroy psychological continuity.

If Nagel's view is true, what matters to a person is the continued existence
of a particular brain. But if we ask what is important about ourselves, and
our lives, and our relations with each other, the continued existence of
particular brains does not seem to be what matters. Rather, as I have
claimed, what is more important is Relation R, psychological connectedness
and/or continuity, with any cause. If this is so, and Nagel's view is true, the
concept of a person is worse than the concept of a series-person, and worse
in a similar way. On Nagel's view, what matters for a person is the
continued existence of his present brain. What matters for a series-person is
Relation R, with any cause. The concept of a series-person is better, because
it appeals to what is more important.

A person cannot deny that he is a person. And, if Nagel's view is true, a
person cannot turn himself into a series-person. But a series-person can
start to speak through the mouth that both share. This series-person can
proclaim his existence, give himself a name, and claim that all the pronouns
that he writes or utters will refer to series-persons. All other series-persons
could do the same. All future human lives would then be lived by beings
who regard themselves as series-persons. These lives would also be lived by
persons. But persons would now have a subordinate role, since they would
seldom refer to old-themselves.

If Nagel's view is not true, the events that I have just described may make
no difference. Our beliefs about the criterion of identity may fail to cover a
few actual cases, such as those of people with divided hemispheres. And
these beliefs clearly fail to cover many imaginary cases. Since people are not

separately existing entities, distinct from their brains and bodies and their experiences, questions about personal identity are, in these imaginary cases, empty. In these cases we can *give* answers to these questions, thereby extending our beliefs about the criterion of personal identity. One possible extension would make this criterion the non-branching holding of Relation R, with any cause. On this criterion, persons *are* series-persons. The distinction drawn above disappears.

If Nagel's view is true, I cannot make these claims. On his view, each person is essentially his brain, and what fundamentally matters, for each person, is the continued existence of this brain. If this is so, persons are not series-persons. The events that I described above *would* make a difference. If all series-persons proclaimed their existence, and began to use pronouns to refer to themselves, this would be an improvement. Every series-person is very closely related to a particular person. It would be better if, in each such pair, the series-person took the leading role. The concept of a series-person picks out parts of reality in a less arbitrary way. We the series-persons can deny that what matters is, for us, the continued existence of our brains. We can claim that, as I have argued, what fundamentally matters is Relation R, with any cause.

99. AM I A TOKEN OR A TYPE?

Williams considers a case in which a person would have many co-existing Replicas. And he suggests a new description of this kind of case. He describes the concept of a *person-type*. Suppose there is some particular person, Mary Smith. And suppose that the Scanning Replicator produces many Replicas of Mary Smith, as she is at a particular time. These Replicas will all be Mary Smiths. They will be different *tokens*, or instances, of the same person-type. If such a case occurred, there would be several questions about what matters. Assume that the case involves the old Scanner, which destroys Mary Smith's original brain and body. Before she presses the green button, what should Mary Smith believe about her relation to her future Replicas? Is what matters that her present brain continues to exist? Or will it be about as good if there will later be living tokens of her type?

This is the question about what ought to matter to the original Mary Smith. Williams does not discuss this question. But he writes intriguingly about another question:

Since we are not supposing that the token-persons, once printed off from the prototype, have intercommunicating experiences . . . they will be divergently affected by different experiences, and will tend to get increasingly dissimilar. Looked at as copies of the prototype, they will become copies which are increasingly blurred or written over; looked at in their own right, they will become increasingly individual personalities. This might be welcomed. For someone who loved one of these token-persons might well love her not because she was a Mary Smith, but despite the fact that she was a Mary Smith. . . The more the *Mary Smiths* diverged, the more secure the hold the lover might feel he had on what particularly he loved.

If someone loved a token person just as a Mary Smith, then it might well be unclear that the token-person was really what he loved. What he loves is *Mary Smith*, and that is to love the type-person. We can see dimly what this would be like. It would be like loving a work of art in some reproducible medium. One might start comparing, as it were, performances of the type; and wanting to be near the person one loved would be like wanting very much to hear some performance, even an indifferent one, of *Figaro*—just as one will go to the scratch provincial performance of *Figaro* rather than hear no *Figaro* at all, so one would see the very run-down Mary Smith who was in the locality, rather than see no Mary Smith at all.

Much of what we call loving a person would begin to crack under this, and reflection on it may encourage us not to undervalue the deeply body-based situation we actually have. While in the present situation of things to love a person is not exactly the same as to love a body, perhaps to say that they are basically the same is more grotesquely misleading than it is a deep metaphysical error; and if it does not sound very high-minded, the alternatives that so briskly grow out of suspending the present situation do not sound too spiritual, either.[58]

Is loving a person basically the same as loving that person's body? Williams admits that this claim is 'grotesquely misleading'; but he suggests that it is better than any alternative. And he warns us not to undervalue 'the deeply body-based situation that we actually have'. A different situation, where persons would have many co-existing Replicas, would threaten much of what we value.

I believe that we should accept this last claim. But we should not claim that loving a person is basically the same as loving that person's body. There *is* a better alternative.

Williams may have reasoned as follows. Unless what I love is a particular body, I cannot love an individual. Suppose that I love the original Mary Smith. A machine destroys her brain and body, and produces a Replica. If my love for Mary Smith is transferred to her Replica, this suggests that what I love is not an individual but a person-type. And if we consider what such love involves, what we find is disturbing.

I agree that such love would be very different, and disturbing. But I reject the reasoning just given.

We should consider *two* kinds of imaginary case. One is the community that Nagel imagined. In this community, though there is replication, Relation R never takes a branching form. After she is 30, Mary Smith uses the youth-preserving Replicator once a year, as do many other individuals. If such machines existed, it would be *possible* to produce several co-existing Replicas of a single individual. But we can suppose that, in this imagined community, the individuals decide not to bring about this possibility. For the kinds of reason that I described in Section 90, and that Williams better expresses, these individuals believe that division is not quite as good as ordinary survival.

Suppose that I am a person who has moved into this different community. I fall in love with Mary Smith. How should I react after she has first used the Replicator? I claim both that I would and that I *ought* to love her Replica. This is not the 'ought' of morality. On the best conception of the best kind of love, I ought to love this individual. She is fully psychologically continuous with the Mary Smith I loved, and she has an exactly similar body. If I do not love Mary Smith's Replica, this could only be for one of several bad reasons.

One reason might be that I believe the Non-Reductionist View. I believe that personal identity is a deep further fact, which would not be produced by Replication. I do not love Mary Smith's Replica, because I believe that, in this deep way, she is not Mary Smith. This reaction is unjustified, since there is no such further fact.

Suppose next that I accept the Reductionist View. But I believe that replication is nearly as bad as ordinary death. When Mary Smith presses the green button, my reaction is grief. Perhaps I can later come to love Mary Smith's Replica. But given my belief about the badness of what happened to Mary Smith, my love cannot be simply transferred, without grief.

As I have argued, this reaction is also unjustified. On the Reductionist View, we should regard replication as being about as good as ordinary survival. Since Mary Smith chose to be replicated, we can assume that this was also her view. On this view, my love should be transferred to her Replica. Moreover, in this imagined community, the individuals are series-persons. Since this is so, Mary Smith's Replica *is* Mary Smith.

If my love is not transferred, there could be two further explanations. Williams suggests that loving a person is, basically, loving a particular body. But this kind of love, or lust, is at most extremely uncommon. What is more common is a purely physical or sexual obsession with a person's body, an obsession that is not concerned with the psychology of this person. But this is *not* love of a particular body. As Quinton writes, in the case of such obsessions, 'no particular human body is required, only one of a more or less precisely demarcated kind'.[59] Suppose that I was physically obsessed with Mary Smith's body. This obsession would transfer to Mary Smith's Replica. This would be like a case in which the body with which I am obsessed is that of an identical twin. If this twin died, my obsession could be transferred to the body of the other twin.

Ordinary love could not be so transferred. Such love is concerned with the psychology of the person loved, and with this person's continuously changing mental life. And loving someone is a process, not a fixed state. Mutual love involves a shared history. This is why, if I have loved Mary Smith for many months or years, her place cannot be simply taken by her identical twin. Things are quite different with her Replica. If I have loved Mary Smith for months or years, her Replica will have full quasi-memories of our shared history.

I have claimed that, if I do not love Mary Smith's Replica, it is unlikely that the explanation is that I loved her particular body. It is doubtful that anyone has such love, or lust. The remaining explanation is that my love has ceased for no reason. No reason is a bad reason. Love can cease like this, but only an inferior kind of love.

I have discussed Nagel's imagined alternative to the actual world. In this alternative, people are often replicated, but there are never two co-existing Replicas of one person. Relation R never takes a branching form. I claim that, in this world, love for a person should transfer directly to this person's Replica. This love should transfer because this person's relation to this Replica contains what fundamentally matters in ordinary survival.

Williams suggests that, in a world with replication, we should distinguish person-types and tokens of these types. But in the world just described, where Relation R always takes a one-one form, this would not be a useful distinction. We would misdescribe what happens if we called each new Replica another token of a person-type. This description would ignore what is of most importance, the psychological continuity, and the development of a life. We could better describe what happens in either of two ways.

If Nagel's view is false, our criterion of personal identity could be extended to be the non-branching holding of Relation R. Each individual in Nagel's imagined community would then be a person. These people would move to new bodies once a year. Since Mary Smith would have such new bodies, my love for her should be directly transferred. Though these people would often change bodies, love for particular people would not be threatened.

If Nagel's view is true, the individuals in this community are not persons. They are, and believe themselves to be, series-persons. The series-person Mary Smith moves to a new body every year. As before, there is no threat to the kind of love we value. If I love a series-person, I am not loving a person-type. I am loving a particular individual, who has a continuous history.

Consider next the other alternative to the actual world: the one that Williams imagined. In this world there are many co-existing Replicas of a single person. Williams's proposed distinction would here be useful. Consider fifty Replicas of Greta Garbo as she was at the age of 30. These would be well-described as different tokens of one person-type. As Williams claims, if the object of love is the person-type, this is very different from ordinary love. This would not be the kind of love which gives great importance to a shared history.

If I lived in such a world, and I was one of a set of Replicas, I might regard myself as a token of a type. Might I instead regard myself as *the type*? This would be a radical change. In one sense of the word 'type', if I was a person-type, I could not possibly cease to exist. Even if there are not now tokens of my person-type, there would still be this person-type. A person-type would survive even the destruction of the Universe. This is because, in this sense, a type is an abstract entity, like a number. We could not possibly regard ourselves as abstract entities.

On any sense of 'type' there would be a great difference between ordinary love and love of a person-type. The latter kind of love cannot be mutual. I may love some person-type, but this person-type cannot love me. A type cannot love any more than the number nine can love. I cannot be loved by the English Rose, or the New American Woman. What might be true is that love for me is one of the features of some person-type. All of the many tokens of this type would then love me.

If this was true, there might be mutual love between me and one of these token-persons. There might even be mutual love between me and two or three of these persons. But, as Williams claims, this love would lead me away from loving the person-type. I would be led away because of the increasing importance of shared histories.

Return now to Williams's main claims. He suggests that, though it is misleading, there is a profound truth in the claim that loving a person is loving a particular body. And he suggests that if the object of our love was not a particular body, we would be loving a person-type. Such love would be very different from ordinary love, and would be disturbing. It would threaten much of what we value.

I accept this last claim, but I deny the others. Following Quinton, I doubt that anyone loves a particular body. A purely physical obsession is an obsession with a kind of body, or a body-type. As such, it would have the disturbing features of love of a person-type. On the death of one identical twin, this obsession could be transferred, without any grief, to the other twin's body.

I have also denied that, if the object of our love is not a particular body, we must love a person-type. This is best seen in Nagel's imagined alternative to the actual world, in which people are often replicated, but only in a one-one form. In this world Relation R traces lines through many different bodies, but it never takes a branching form. I claim that, in such a world, ordinary love would survive unchanged. If Nagel's view is false, the people in this society would move to new bodies every year, but they would still be particular people. If Nagel's view is true, it would be series-people who would move to new bodies. But love would still be love of a particular individual. A series-person is an individual.

If these claims are correct, I can again keep the view that I have defended. What matters is not the continued existence of a particular body, but Relation R with any cause.

100. PARTIAL SURVIVAL

Before considering actual lives, I shall glance at a last flurry of imaginary cases. One is the opposite of division: fusion. Identity is logically one-one, and all-or-nothing. Just as division shows that what matters in survival need not take a one-one form, fusion shows that it can have degrees.

There was fusion in the central cases in the Combined Spectrum. In these cases, the resulting person would be psychologically connected, and to about the same degree, both to me and to someone else.

We can imagine a world in which fusion was a natural process. Two people come together. While they are unconscious, their two bodies grow into one. One person then wakes up.

This one person could quasi-remember living both of the lives of the two original people. No quasi-memories need be lost. But some things must be lost. Any two people who fuse together would have different characteristics, different desires, and different intentions. How could these be combined?

The answers might be these. Some of these features will be compatible. These would coexist in the one resulting person. Some will be incompatible. These, if of equal strength, would cancel out, and, if of different strengths, the stronger would become weaker. These effects might be as predictable as the laws governing dominant and recessive genes.

Here are some examples. I admire Palladio, and intend to visit Venice. I am about to fuse with someone who admires Giotto, and intends to visit Padua. The one resulting person will have both tastes and both intentions. Since Padua is close to Venice, both can be easily fulfilled. Suppose next that I love Wagner, and always vote for a Socialist. The other person hates Wagner, and always votes for a Conservative. The one resulting person will be a tone-deaf floating voter.

Like division, fusion does not fit the logic of identity. The one resulting person cannot be claimed to be the same person as each of the two original people. The best description is that the resulting person would be neither of these people. But, as the case of division shows, this description does not imply that these people should regard fusion as equivalent to death.

What should their attitude be? If we were about to undergo a fusion of this kind, some of us might regard this as equivalent to death. And this is less absurd than regarding division as equivalent to death. When I divide, the two resulting people will be exactly like me. When I fuse, the one resulting person will not be wholly similar. This makes it easier to think, when faced with fusion, 'I shall not survive', thus continuing to regard survival as being all-or-nothing.

As I have argued, there is no fact involved which is all-or-nothing. The two kinds of connectedness, physical and psychological, could hold to any degree. How should I regard a case in which these relations do hold to reduced degrees?

It might be said: 'Suppose that, between me and some resulting person, there would be about half the ordinary amount of these two relations. This would be about half as good as ordinary survival. If there would be nine-tenths of these ordinary amounts, this would be about nine-tenths as good.'

This view is too crude. In judging the value to me of a particular case of fusion, we must know how close my relation is to the resulting person. We must also know whether this person will have features that I regard as good or bad. The view just described mistakenly ignores this second question.

I suggest the following view. The value to me of my relation to a resulting person depends both (1) on my degree of connectedness to this person, and (2) on the value, in my view, of this person's physical and psychological features. Suppose that hypnosis causes me to lose five unwanted features: my untidiness, laziness, fear of flying, nicotine addiction, and all my memories of my wretched life. There is here much less than full psychological connectedness, but this is more than outweighed by the removal of bad features.

Few of us think ourselves perfect. Most of us would welcome several changes in our physical and mental features. If the changes were improvements, we would welcome the partial reduction of both kinds of connectedness. I should avoid fusion if it would predictably involve subtracting features that I value, and adding features that I find repugnant. Suppose that there are only two things that give my life meaning: my struggle for Socialism, and the qualities I find in Wagner. If this is so, I should dread fusion with a Wagner-hating Conservative. Since the resulting person would be a tone-deaf floating voter, my relation to him may be nearly as bad as death. But another case of fusion, while involving as much change, I might regard as better than ordinary survival. I might regard these changes as all improvements. They might all be either adding a feature that I welcome, or removing a feature that I regret. Fusions, like marriages, could be either great successes, or disasters.

Consider next some more imaginary people. These are just like us except for their method of reproduction. Like amoebae, these people reproduce by a process of natural division. The lives of these people may be shown as in the diagram below.

The lines on this diagram represent the spatio-temporal paths that would be traced by the bodies of these people. I call each single line, between two points of division, a *branch*. And the whole structure is the *Tree*. Each branch corresponds to what is thought of as the life of one person. The first person is *Eve*. The next two are *Secunda* and *Tertia*. The fiftieth person down the Tree is *Quinquagesima*.

At the start of their lives, Secunda and Tertia are fully psychologically connected to Eve, as she was just before she divided. As I have argued, Eve's relation to each of these two people is about as good as ordinary

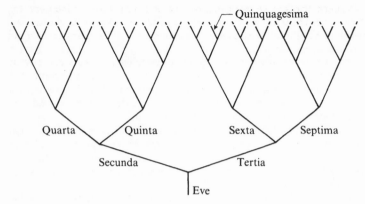

survival. The same claims apply to every other division in the history of this
community.

What should we claim about Eve's relation to people who are further
down the Tree, such as Quinquagesima?

Eve is psychologically continuous with Quinquagesima. There will be
between the two a continuous overlapping chain of direct psychological
connections. Thus Eve has some quasi-intentions that are carried out by
Tertia, who in turn has some quasi-intentions that are carried out by Sexta,
and so on down to Quinquagesima. And Quinquagesima can quasi-remember most of the life of her immediate predecessor, who can quasi-remember
most of the life of her immediate predecessor, and so on back to Eve.

Though Quinquagesima is psychologically continuous with Eve, there
may be between the two no distinctive psychological connectedness.
Connectedness requires direct connections. If these people are in other ways
like us, Eve cannot be strongly connected to every person in the indefinitely
long Tree. With the passage of time, quasi-memories will weaken, and then
fade away. Quasi-ambitions, once fulfilled, will be replaced by others.
Quasi-characteristics will gradually change. Because of such facts, if some
person is further down the Tree, there will be fewer direct connections
between this person and Eve. If this person is sufficiently remote, there may
be between the two *no* direct and distinctive psychological connections.
Assume that this is true of Eve and Quinquagesima.

I write *distinctive* because there would be some kinds of direct connection.
Quinquagesima would inherit from Eve many memories of facts, such as the
fact that she and others reproduce by division. And she would inherit many
general abilities, such as how to speak, or swim. But she would not inherit
any of the psychological features that distinguish Eve from most of the other
people in this community.

Between Eve and Quinquagesima there is psychological continuity, but there is no distinctive psychological connectedness. This case illustrates a question that I mentioned earlier. What is the relative importance of these two relations?

I believe that both relations matter. Others may believe that one matters more than the other. But I know of no argument for such a belief. I shall assume that neither relation matters more than the other. (This is not the assumption that their importance is exactly equal. Such a question could not have an exact answer.)

Because it will be important later, I shall consider a different view. On this view, connectedness does not matter. Only continuity matters. If there will later be some person who will be psychologically continuous with me as I am now, it would not matter at all if, between me now and this person, there would be no direct psychological connections.

As I have said, some reductions in connectedness might be welcomed as improvements. But we cannot defensibly claim that it would not matter if there was no psychological connectedness. Consider first the importance of memory. If our lives have been worth living, most of us value highly our ability to remember many of our past experiences. The loss of all these memories need not destroy continuity of memory, which only requires overlapping chains of memories. Suppose I know that, two days from now, my only experience-memories will be of experiences that I shall have tomorrow. On the view just stated, since there will be continuity of memory, this is all that matters. It should not matter to me that I shall soon have lost all of my memories of my past life. Most of us would strongly disagree. Losing all such memories would be something that we would deeply regret.

Consider next the continuity of our desires and intentions. Suppose that I now love certain other people. I could cease to love all these people without any break in psychological continuity. But I would greatly regret these changes. Suppose that I also strongly want to achieve certain aims. Given that I have these strong desires, I would regret their replacement by other desires. I must care more *now* about the achievement of what I *now* care about. Since I care more about the fulfilment of these present desires, I would regret losing these desires. More generally, I want my life to have certain kinds of overall unity. I do not want it to be very episodic, with continual fluctuations in my desires and concerns. Such fluctuations are compatible with full psychological continuity, but they would reduce psychological connectedness. This is another kind of change that most of us would regret.

Consider finally continuity of character. There will be such continuity if our character changes in a natural way. But most of us value some aspects of our character. We will want these *not* to change. Here again, we want connectedness, not mere continuity.

I have described three reasons why most of us would reject the view that psychological connectedness does not matter. Since these are good reasons, these remarks seem enough to refute this view. We can agree that connectedness is not all that matters. Psychological continuity also matters. But we should reject the view that only continuity matters.

101. SUCCESSIVE SELVES

I imagined people who are just like us, except that they reproduce by natural division. I shall now suggest how these people could describe their interrelations. Each person is a *self*. Eve can think of any person, anywhere in the Tree, as *one of her descendant selves*. This phrase implies future-directed psychological continuity. Unlike Eve, Tertia has descendant selves only in the right half of the Tree. To imply past-directed continuity, these people can use the phrase *an ancestral self*. Quinquagesima's ancestral selves are all of the people on the single line that connects her to Eve.

Since psychological continuity is a transitive relation, in either direction in time, *being an ancestral self of*, and *being a descendant self of*, are also transitive. But psychological continuity is not a transitive relation, if we allow it to take both directions in a single argument. Quarta and Septima are both psychologically continuous with Eve. It does not follow, and is false, that they are psychologically continuous with each other.

I shall next suggest how these people could describe the different degrees of psychological connectedness. We could give to the phrases *my past self* and *my future self* a new meaning. In their ordinary use, these phrases refer to myself in the past or future. On our new use, these phrases refer, not to myself, but to those other people whose relation to me is psychological connectedness. Thus the phrase 'one of my past selves' implies that there is some degree of connectedness. To imply the different degrees there is the following series: 'my closest past self', 'one of my closer past selves', 'one of my more distant past selves', 'hardly one of my past selves (I can quasi-remember only a few of her experiences)', and, finally, 'not one of *my* past selves, merely an ancestral self'. This is the past-directed series of phrases that could be used by Quinquagesima. Eve could use a similar future-directed series.

This way of talking would clearly suit my imagined people. It would enable them to describe more precisely the interrelations that hold between them. This way of talking also provides a new and plausible description of the imagined case where I divide. Though I do not survive My Division, the two resulting people are two of my future selves. And they are as close to me as I am to myself tomorrow. Similarly, they can each refer to me as an equally close past self. (They can share a past self without being the same self as each other.)

Consider next another kind of imaginary people. These reproduce by fusion as well as by division. And they do this often. They fuse every autumn and divide every spring. Their relations are as shown below.

A is the person whose life is represented by the three-lined branch. The two-lined tree represents those lives that are psychologically continuous with A's. Each person has his own two-lined tree, which overlaps but is different from the trees of others.

For these imagined people, the phrases 'an ancestral self' and 'a descendant self' would cover too much to be of much use. There could be pairs of dates such that everyone who ever lived before the first date was an ancestral self of everyone who will ever live after the second date. And, since the life of each person lasts for only half a year, the word 'I' would cover too little to do all of the work which it does for us. Much of this work would have to be done, for these people, by talk about past and future selves.

There is a flaw in this proposed way of talking. The phrase 'a past self of' implies psychological connectedness. And the variants of this phrase can be used to imply the varying degrees of psychological connectedness. But what distinguishes successive selves is not a reduced degree of connectedness. The selves are distinguished by the fusions and divisions. We therefore cannot use these phrases to imply reduced connectedness within a single life.

This flaw would not concern the imagined people I have just described. They divide and unite so frequently, and their lives are in consequence so short, that within a single life psychological connectedness would always hold to a very high degree.

Consider, finally, another kind of imaginary people. Once again, these people differ from us only in their method of reproduction. These people do *not* reproduce. In their world there is neither sexual reproduction, nor division and fusion. There are a number of everlasting bodies, which gradually change in appearance. And direct·and distinctive psychological connections hold, as before, only over limited periods of time, such as five hundred years. This is shown in the diagram below.

← Space →

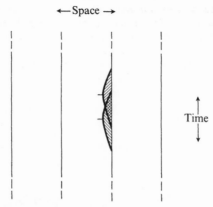

Time

The two shadings represent the degrees of psychological connectedness to their two central points.

These people could not use the way of thinking that I have proposed. Since there is no branching of psychological continuity, they would have to regard themselves as immortal. In one sense, this is what they are. But they ought to draw another distinction.

These people would have one reason for thinking of themselves as immortal. The parts of each 'line' are all psychologically continuous. But only between parts that are close to each other are there direct and distinctive psychological connections. This gives these people a reason for not thinking of each 'line' as corresponding to a single, undifferentiated life. If they did, they would have no way of implying these direct psychological connections. When such a person says, for example, 'I spent a period exploring the Himalayas', his hearers would not be entitled to assume that the speaker has any memories of this period, or that his character then and now are in any way similar, or that he is now carrying out any of the plans or intentions which he then had. Because the word 'I' would carry none of these implications, it would not have for these immortal people the usefulness which it has for us.

To give these people a better way of talking, I revise my earlier proposal. The distinction between successive selves can be made by reference, not to the branching of psychological continuity, but to the degrees of psychological connectedness. Since this connectedness is a matter of degree, the drawing of these distinctions can be left to the choice of the speaker, and be allowed to vary from context to context.

Since these distinctions are now drawn within a single life, we have returned much closer to the ordinary use of the phrases 'my past self' and 'my future self'. On my proposed way of talking, we use 'I', and the other pronouns, to refer only to the parts of our lives to which, when speaking, we have the strongest psychological connections. When the connections have been markedly reduced—when there has been a significant change of character, or style of life, or of beliefs and ideals—we might say, 'It was not *I* who did that, but an earlier self'. We could then describe in what ways, and to what degree, we are related to this past self.

This way of talking would not only suit these imagined immortal people. It is often useful and natural in our own lives. Here are some examples from two very different writers:

We are incapable, while we are in love, of acting as fit predecessors of the next persons who, when we are in love no longer, we shall presently have become . . .[61]

Our dread of a future in which we must forego the sight of faces, the sound of voices, that we love, friends from whom we derive today our keenest joys, this dread, far from being dissipated, is intensified if to the grief of such a privation we reflect that there will be added what seems to us now in anticipation an even more cruel grief: not to feel it as a grief at all—to remain indifferent: for if that should occur, our self would then have changed. It would be in a real sense the death of ourself, a death followed, it is true, by a resurrection, but in a different self, the life, the love of which are beyond the reach of those elements of the existing self that are doomed to die. . .[62]

It is not because other people are dead that our affection for them grows faint, it is because we ourself are dying. Albertine had no cause to rebuke her friend. The man who was usurping his name had merely inherited it. . . My new self, while it grew up in the shadow of the old, had often heard the other speak of Albertine; through that other self. . . it thought that it knew her, it found her attractive. . . But this was merely an affection at second hand.[63]

Nadya had written in her letter: 'When you return. . . ' But that was the whole horror: that there would be no *return*. . . A new, unfamiliar person would walk in bearing the name of her husband, and she would see that the man, her beloved, for whom she had shut herself up to wait for fourteen years, no longer existed. . .[64]

Innokenty felt sorry for her and agreed to come. . . He felt sorry, not for the wife he lived with and yet did not live with these days, but for the blond girl with the curls hanging down to her shoulders, the girl he had known in the tenth grade. . .[65]

As these passages suggest, the object of some of our emotions may not be another person timelessly considered, but another person during a period in this person's life. Here is what I believe to be a common example. It may be clear to some couple that they love each other. But if they ask whether they are still *in love with* each other, they may find this question perplexing. It may still seem to them that they are in love, yet their behaviour towards each other, and their feelings in each other's presence, may seem not to bear this out. If they distinguished between successive selves, their perplexity might be resolved. They might see that they love each other, and are in love with each other's earlier self.

Talk about successive selves can easily be misunderstood, or taken too literally. It should be compared with the way in which we subdivide a nation's history. We call this the history of successive nations, such as Anglo-Saxon, Medieval, and Tudor England.[66]

There is another defect in this way of talking. It is suited only for cases where there is some sharp discontinuity, marking the boundary between two selves. But there may be reduced degrees of psychological connectedness without any such discontinuities. Though it is less rigid than the language of identity, talk about successive selves cannot be used to express such smooth reductions in degrees of connectedness. In such cases we must talk directly about the degrees of connectedness.

I shall now turn from imaginary cases to actual lives. I shall claim that, if we change our view about the nature of personal identity, this may alter our beliefs both about what is rational, and about what is morally right or wrong.

14

PERSONAL IDENTITY AND RATIONALITY

102. THE EXTREME CLAIM

RECONSIDER the Self-interest Theory. This claims that, for each person, there is one supremely rational ultimate aim: that things go as well as possible for himself. A rational agent should both have, and be ultimately governed by, a temporally neutral bias in his own favour. It is irrational for anyone to do what he believes will be worse for himself.

Some writers claim that, if the Reductionist View is true, we have *no* reason to be concerned about our own futures. I call this the *Extreme Claim*. Butler wrote that, on a Reductionist version of Locke's view, it would be 'a fallacy to ... imagine ... that our present self will be interested in what will befall us tomorrow.'[68] Taken literally, this is a prediction. But Butler probably meant that, if the Reductionist View is true, we would have no reason for such concern. Sidgwick made similar claims about Hume's view. On this view, 'the permanent identical "I" is not a fact but a fiction'; the 'Ego is merely a ... series of feelings'. Sidgwick asked

Why ... should one part of the series of feelings ... be more concerned with another part of the same series, any more than with any other series?[69]

Wiggins suggests that this question has no answer.[70] And Madell writes

It is obvious that I have every reason to be concerned if the person who will be in pain is me, but it is not at all obvious that I have *any* reason to be concerned about the fact that the person who will be in pain will have a certain set of memory impressions ...

adding

... it is no clarification ... to be told that in this sort of context that is all that being me involves.[71]

Other writers have no doubts. On the Reductionist View, personal identity just consists in physical and psychological continuity. Swinburne claims that, if there is nothing more to personal identity than these continuities, we ought to be indifferent whether we live or die. In his words, 'in itself surely such continuity has no value'.[72]

Swinburne rejects the Reductionist View. But at least two Reductionists make similar claims. Perry claims that, if I merely know that *someone* will be in pain, I have some reason to prevent this pain, if I can. If I learn that this person will be *me*, most of us would think that I have 'an additional reason' to prevent this pain. But Perry writes that, on his Reductionist account of personal identity, there seems to be nothing to justify this claim. I have some reason to prevent the pain of a complete stranger. And, unless it will interfere with the fulfilment of my present projects, I have only this same reason to prevent my own future pain. That some pain will be *mine* does not, in itself, give me any *more* reason to prevent the pain.[73] Wachsberg agrees.[74]

Ought we to accept this Extreme Claim? I should first comment further on a distinction drawn above. It is one question how, if we became Reductionists, this would affect our attitudes, and emotions. It is another question whether, if the Reductionist View is true, these attitudes or emotions are justified. As I have said, when I ceased to believe the Non-Reductionist View, I became less concerned about my own future. But I am still much more concerned than I would be about the future of a mere stranger. Though I am less concerned about my future, if I knew that I would later be in great pain, I would still be greatly distressed. If other people became Reductionists, there would at most be a similar effect on their concern. This is what we should expect, on any view. Special concern for one's own future would be selected by evolution. Animals without such concern would be more likely to die before passing on their genes. Such concern would remain, as a natural fact, even if we decided that it was not justified. By thinking hard about the arguments, we might be able briefly to stun this natural concern. But it would soon revive.

As I have claimed, if some attitude has an evolutionary explanation, this fact is neutral. It neither supports nor undermines the claim that this attitude is justified. But there is one exception. It may be claimed that, since we all have this attitude, this is a ground for thinking it justified. *This* claim is undermined by the evolutionary explanation. Since there is this explanation, we would all have this attitude even if it was not justified; so the fact that we have this attitude cannot be a reason for thinking it justified. Whether it is justified is an open question, waiting to be answered.

Should we accept the Extreme Claim that, if the Reductionist View is true, we have no reason to be specially concerned about our own futures? Consider Swinburne's ground for claiming this. Swinburne claims that, in themselves, physical and psychological continuity have no value.

I once wrote, of this and similar claims:

> These claims are too strong. Why should the psychological continuities not have rational significance? Even on the *Non-Reductionist* view, they must surely be granted significance. If we retained our identity, but were stripped of all the continuities, we could not do anything at all. Without the connections of memory and intention, we could neither act nor plan nor even think.[75]

As Wachsberg writes[76], this is a bad reply. Swinburne believes that personal identity is a deep further fact, distinct from physical and psychological continuity, and that this further fact is what gives us reasons for special concern about our own futures. I claimed that, without psychological continuity, we could neither think nor act. This is no objection to Swinburne's view. Swinburne could agree that, when added to the further fact of personal identity, psychological continuity is of great importance. This does not show that, in the absence of this further fact, psychological continuity gives us reasons for special concern.

I also wrote:

> The continuities may seem trivial when compared with the 'further fact', yet be immensely important when compared with every other fact. So if there is no further fact—if it is an illusion—the continuities may have supreme importance. While we are not Reductionists, the further fact seems like the sun, blazing in our mental sky. The continuities are, in comparison, merely like a day-time moon. But when we become Reductionists, the sun sets. The moon may now be brighter than everything else. It may dominate the sky.[77]

Swinburne could reject these claims. Night is not day. On Swinburne's view, only the further fact gives us reasons for special concern. If this Extreme Claim is justified, and there is no such fact, we have no such reasons.

It may help to return to the imagined case where I divide. On the Non-Reductionist View, there are three possibilities. I might be one of the resulting people, or the other, or neither. As Chisholm writes:

> When I contemplate these questions, I see the following things clearly and distinctly to be true. . . The questions 'Will I be Lefty?' And 'Will I be Righty?' have entirely definite answers. The answers will be simply 'Yes' or 'No'. . . What I want to insist upon. . . is that this will be the case even if all our normal criteria for personal identity should break down.[78]

Suppose that Chisholm's view was true. A Non-Reductionist might then say: 'If I shall be Righty, I now have a reason to be specially concerned about Righty's future, but I have no reason to be specially concerned about Lefty's future. Similar remarks apply if I shall be Lefty. If I shall be *neither* of these two people, I have no reason to be specially concerned about either's future.'

These claims assume that, in the absence of personal identity, psychological continuity provides no reason for special concern. We might deny this assumption. Suppose that I shall be Righty. Lefty will not be a mere stranger. My relation to Lefty is and will be very close. We might claim that, compared with the future of a mere stranger, I have reasons to be more concerned about Lefty's future.

A Non-Reductionist might reply: 'After the division, when I am Righty, Lefty will be someone else who, at least to start with, is exactly like me. As you have said, I may have reason to regret Lefty's existence. Though I have survived as Righty, the woman that I love would not know this. She might believe Lefty's false claim that he is me. Whatever she believes, Lefty's existence will interfere with her love for me. Because this is true, I could rationally hope that Lefty soon dies. Since I could rationally have this hope after the division, I could rationally have this hope now. This implies that I cannot have a reason to be specially concerned about Lefty's future. If I had such a reason, I ought to be distressed by the thought of Lefty's early death. But we have seen that I could rationally welcome this event. Though Lefty will be psychologically continuous with me as I am now, this continuity does not here give me a reason for special concern.'

On the Non-Reductionist View, if I shall be *either* of the resulting people, it can be plausibly denied that I have a reason to be specially concerned about *the other*. What of the remaining possibility, that I shall be neither of these people? If this is what will happen, it is more plausible to claim that psychological continuity gives me reason for special concern. I ought to care about the resulting people more than I care about mere strangers. I have reasons to want at least one of these two people to live a full life. This would be better for the woman I love than if both of the resulting people soon died. And this resulting person could finish my unfinished book, and in other ways fulfil some of my desires.

We must admit that this kind of concern is not like the special concern that we have about our own future. It is a concern for someone else who can, in various ways, act on my behalf. If an Egoist had such concern, he might regard this other person as a mere instrument. Suppose that I learn that this resulting person will have to endure great pain. Should I react to this news as if I had learnt that *I* shall have to endure such pain? Non-Reductionists could plausibly answer No. They can claim that, if this future pain would not be revealed to the woman I love, nor interfere with the completion of my book, I have no special reason to care about this pain. This pain will not be felt by me. If I am an Egoist, my concern for the person in pain is only a concern that, in various ways, this person fulfils my desires. If this person's pain will not interfere with his fulfilment of my desires, why should it give me grounds for concern?

I conclude that, if the Non-Reductionist View was true, Non-Reductionists could plausibly accept what I call the Extreme Claim. On this claim, only the deep further fact gives me a reason to be specially concerned about my future. In the absence of this fact, psychological continuity gives me no such reason.

Suppose next that a Non-Reductionist ceases to believe his view. Could he still accept the Extreme Claim? If personal identity does not involve the deep further fact, but just consists in physical and psychological continuity, my relation to each of the resulting people is as good as ordinary survival. My relation to each of the resulting people is Relation R with its normal cause, enough physical continuity. If we have become Reductionists, we ought to accept my claim that Relation R is as good as ordinary survival. But this claim does not imply that, when R holds, it gives us a reason to be specially concerned about our own future. We could accept the Extreme Claim that, if ordinary survival does not involve the deep further fact, it does not give us such a reason.

Suppose that we accept another of my claims: that it would not matter if the psychological continuity had an abnormal cause. We should then agree that, in Teletransportation, my relation to my Replica is as good as ordinary survival. But from the stand-point of our earlier Non-Reductionist View, this claim would be better put in a different way. As I wrote, ordinary survival is *no better than,* or is *as bad as,* my relation to my Replica. And I might now say: 'My relation to my Replica gives me no reason for special concern. Since ordinary survival is no better, it too gives me no such reason.'

This line of reasoning is defensible. When a Non-Reductionist ceases to believe that personal identity involves the deep further fact, he can defensibly keep his view that only this fact would give us reasons for special concern. He can accept the Extreme Claim that, if there is no such fact, we have no such reasons. And we could defensibly accept this claim even if we have always been Reductionists.

Could a Non-Reductionist defensibly change his view? Could he claim that Relation R gives us a reason for special concern? I call this the *Moderate Claim.*

I believe that, like the Extreme Claim, this claim is defensible. I do not know of an argument to show that, of these two claims, it is the Moderate Claim that we ought to accept. It might be said

> Extremists are wrong to assume that only the deep further fact gives us a reason for special concern. Think of our special concern for our own children, or for anyone we love. Given the nature of our relation to our children, or to someone whom we love, we can plausibly claim that we have reasons to be specially concerned about what will happen to these people. And the relations that justify this special concern are not the deep separate fact of personal identity. If these relations give us reason for special concern, we can claim the same about Relation R. We can claim that this relation gives each of us a reason to be specially concerned about his own future.

But an Extremist might reply:

> Why should I care about what will happen later to those people whom I love? The reason cannot be because I shall still love them later. This is

no answer, because our question is why I should care now, specially, about what I shall care about later. Nor could the reason be, 'Because my loved ones now care about what will happen to them later'. This is no answer, because our problem is also to know why *they* should care about what will happen to them later. We still have no answer to the question why, in the absence of the deep further fact, we should be specially concerned about our own or anyone else's future.[79]

This objection has some force. And it may be wrong to compare our concern about our own future with our concern for those we love. Suppose I learn that someone I love will soon suffer great pain. I shall be greatly distressed by this news. I might be *more* distressed than I would be if I learnt that *I* shall soon suffer such pain. But this concern has a different quality. I do not *anticipate* the pain that will be felt by someone I love. It might be claimed that only on the Non-Reductionist View can we justifiably anticipate future pains. Anticipation might be justified only by the non-existent deep further fact. Perhaps, if we are Reductionists, we should cease to anticipate our own future pains.[80]

If this last claim is true, it provides a further ground for thinking that, on the Reductionist View, we have no reason to be specially concerned about our own futures. But this claim does not force us to accept this conclusion. It seems defensible both to claim and to deny that Relation R gives us reason for special concern. Though we are not forced to accept the Extreme Claim, we may be unable to show that it should be rejected. There is a great difference between the Extreme and Moderate Claims. But I have not yet found an argument that refutes either.

How do these conclusions bear on the Self-interest Theory about rationality? The Extreme Claim is the extreme denial of this theory. This may be the argument against S that, as I claimed in Section 54, Sidgwick half-suggested.

Since the Extreme Claim is defensible, this argument achieves something. But the Extreme Claim can also be defensibly denied. Since this is so, this argument does not refute the Self-interest Theory.

103. A BETTER ARGUMENT AGAINST S

We can do better. I have been claiming

(A) Since personal identity does not involve the deep further fact, it is less deep, or involves less.

I have also defended

(B) What fundamentally matters are psychological connectedness and continuity.

The Extreme Claim, which appeals to (A), can be denied. But (B) provides the premise for a new challenge to the Self-interest Theory.

Central to this theory is

The Requirement of Equal Concern: A rational person should be *equally* concerned about *all* the parts of his future.

As Sidgwick writes, 'my feelings a year hence should be just as important to me as my feelings next minute, if only I could make an equally sure forecast of them. Indeed this equal and impartial concern for all parts of one's conscious life is perhaps the most prominent element in the common notion of the *rational* . . .'[81] Each of us can rationally give less weight to what may happen further in the future, if this remoteness makes this event less likely to occur. But, on the Self-interest Theory, we cannot rationally care less about our further future, merely because it is more remote. S therefore claims that it is irrational to postpone an ordeal if one knows that this would make this ordeal worse.

By appealing to the Reductionist View, we can challenge this last claim. To simplify our challenge, we can assume that mere temporal proximity cannot matter. We can assume that it is irrational to care less about one's further future simply because it is further in the future. This does not show that it is irrational to care less about one's further future. There may be another ground for doing so.

As I have argued, what fundamentally matters are psychological connectedness and continuity. I also claimed that these matter, however they are caused. Since we are now considering our actual lives, this second claim is irrelevant. Our claim could be that these two relations are what matter, provided that they have their normal cause.

I also argued, in Section 100, that *both* these relations matter. We cannot defensibly claim that only continuity matters. We must admit that connectedness matters.

Since this relation matters, I claim

(C) My concern for my future may correspond to the degree of connectedness between me now and myself in the future. Connectedness is one of the two relations that give me reasons to be specially concerned about my own future. It can be rational to care less, when one of the grounds for caring will hold to a lesser degree. Since connectedness is nearly always weaker over longer periods, I can rationally care less about my further future.

This claim defends a new kind of discount rate. This is a discount rate, not with respect to time itself, but with respect to the weakening of one of the two relations which are what fundamentally matter. Unlike a discount rate with respect to time, this new discount rate will seldom apply over the near future. The psychological connections between me now and myself tomorrow are not much closer than the connections between me now and myself next month. And they may not be very much closer than the connections between me now and myself next year. But they are very much closer than the connections between me now and myself in forty years.

I once defended (C) by appealing to

(D) When some important relation holds to a different degree, it is not irrational to believe that it has a different degree of importance.

I claimed that, since we cannot defensibly deny (D), we must accept (C).[82] As Kagan claims, this is another bad argument. An appeal to (D) cannot support (C). It might be claimed

(E) There is at least one exception to (D). Perhaps we can imagine cases where a great weakening of connections would justify lesser concern. But there is never in fact, in ordinary lives, such a great weakening. In actual cases, even when connectedness will hold to reduced degrees, we ought to regard it as having the *same* importance. It is irrational to care less about one's further future, merely because there will be such a reduction in the degree of connectedness.

If (E) is defensible, (D) is not true. Since this is so, we cannot reject (E) with an appeal to (D). Such an appeal would beg the question. We cannot argue for a conclusion by appealing to a claim which assumes this conclusion. (It may help to give an example. Suppose that there are many glass marbles in some container. I have removed all but the last marble, and these marbles are all white. I now remove the last marble, which is black. I cannot say, 'This marble must be white, since they are all white'. If there is an exception to some general claim, we cannot deny this exception merely by appealing to this claim.)

Though I cannot appeal to (D), I may be right to reject (E). Even if there are some exceptions, there are very many relations which can be rationally believed to be less important when they hold to reduced degrees. Some examples are friendship, complicity, relevance, indebtedness, being a close relative of, and being responsible for. It may be defensible to believe the same about psychological connectedness.

I claim not only that this belief is defensible, but also that it *cannot be defensibly denied*. Suppose that I shall have a day of pain both tomorrow and in forty years. I am strongly psychologically connected to myself tomorrow. There will be much less connectedness between me now and myself in forty years. Since connectedness is one of my two reasons for caring about my future, it cannot be irrational for me to care less when there will be much less connectedness.

Since (E) is indefensible, we should accept (C). In accepting (C), we are rejecting the Requirement of Equal Concern, which is central to the Self-interest Theory. We should therefore reject this theory.

104. THE S-THEORIST'S COUNTER-ARGUMENT

A Self-interest Theorist might now appeal to

The Truism: All the parts of a person's future are *equally* parts of his future.

He might claim that, since this is true, it is irrational not to care equally about all the parts of one's future.

This argument assumes that personal identity is what matters. When we consider the imagined case in which I divide, we learn that personal identity is not what matters. Though I shall not be either of the two resulting people, my relation to each of these people contains what matters.

Since the S-Theorist's Counter-argument falsely assumes that identity is what matters, we need not discuss this argument. Nothing is shown by an argument with a false premise. But it is worth pointing out that, even if we grant this premise, the S-Theorist's argument fails.

Assume, falsely, that personal identity is what matters. Does an appeal to the Truism provide a good argument for the Requirement of Equal Concern? The whole of any person's future is equally his future. Does this show that this person ought now to be equally concerned about his whole future?

This would be a good argument if the Non-Reductionist View was true. On that view, the Truism is a profound truth, deep enough to support the argument. But, on the Reductionist View, the Truism is too trivial to support the argument.

Consider

(F) All of a person's relatives are *equally* his relatives.

In one sense, this is true. We can use 'relative of' in a sense which has no degrees. On this use, my children and my distant cousins are as much my relatives. Is this a deep truth?

It must be distinguished from another truth, which requires the same use of these words. On this use, *relative of* is a transitive relation: the relatives of my relatives must be my relatives. This is a useful use. Since Darwin, it gives new significance to the Great Chain of Being. As we now know, the birds outside my window are, in a literal sense, my relatives. They are my relatives in the *same* sense in which my cousins are my relatives. We have a common ancestor. The birds are my *nth* cousins *m* times removed. (*Relative of* crosses the boundaries between different species. If it did not, there could be no evolution.)

That all the higher animals are *literally* my relatives is a profound truth. But is it profoundly true that they are all *equally* my relatives—that the birds are as much my relatives as my own children? This is not a profound truth. It is superficial, and—though it never in fact misleads—misleading. That it is true at all is the price we have to pay for the transitivity of *relative of*. Suppose we say, 'By "relative" we really mean "not too distant relative"—tenth cousins ten times removed aren't really relatives'. This would deprive us of the profound truth that the birds are literally my relatives. To preserve that truth we must agree that—in a superficial sense—the birds are *as much* my relatives as my own children.

Since it is superficial, (F) cannot support the kind of argument that we are considering. Suppose that, believing strongly in the ties of kinship, I leave all my money to my various relatives. I announce my intentions while I am alive. I intend to leave the largest shares to my own children. Could my cousins plausibly appeal to (F)? Could they argue that, since they are *equally* my relatives, they (and the birds) should have equal shares? Clearly not. Though it is true that they are equally my relatives, this truth is too trivial to support their argument.

Similar remarks apply to

(G) All pains are *equally* pains.

We can use the word 'pain' in a way which makes this true. Could we argue that, because (G) is true, it is irrational to care more about pains that are more intense? Clearly not. This is another truth that is too trivial to support such an argument. Consider, finally,

(H) All the parts of a nation's history are *equally* parts of this nation's history.

All the parts of England's history are equally parts of England's history. Tudor England was as much England. So was Saxon England. So, if we choose to call it 'England', was Roman England. But, if we call it 'Roman Britain', it was not England at all. This shows that (H) is trivial.

A nation is in many ways unlike a person. Despite these differences, the identity of persons over time is, in its fundamental features, like the identity of nations over time. Both consist in nothing more than the holding over time of various connections, some of which are matters of degree. It is true that in my old age it will be just as much me. But this truth may be fairly compared with the truth that (say) modern Austria is still *just as much* Austria. A descendant of the Habsburg Emperors could justifiably call this truth trivial.

In this section I have discussed the S-Theorist's Counter-argument. Since this argument falsely assumes that personal identity is what matters, it could have been dismissed at once. But it was worth showing that, even if we make this false assumption, the argument fails. The argument appeals to the claim that all the parts of our futures are *equally* parts of our futures. This truth is too trivial to support the argument. On one use of 'relative', it is also true that my children and my cousins are equally my relatives. If my cousins argue that, because this is true, they and my children should inherit equal shares, we should reject their claim. For the same reason, even if we falsely assume that personal identity is what matters, we should reject the S-Theorist's Counter-argument.[83]

105. THE DEFEAT OF THE CLASSICAL SELF-INTEREST THEORY

Return to my argument against the Self-interest Theory. This argument shows, I believe, that we must reject the Requirement of Equal Concern. According to this requirement, I should now care equally about all the parts of my future. It is irrational to care less about my further future—to have what economists call a discount rate. This may be irrational if I have a discount rate with respect to time. But this is not irrational if I have a discount rate with respect to the degrees of psychological connectedness.

The Self-interest Theorist might revise his view. On the Revised Theory, a rational person's dominant concern should be his own future, but he may now be less concerned about those parts of his future to which he is now less closely connected. This Revised Theory incorporates my new discount rate. On this theory, we are not rationally required to have this discount rate. But, if we do, we are not irrational.

This revision makes a great difference. It breaks the link between the Self-interest Theory and what is in one's own best interests. On the unrevised or *Classical Theory*, it is irrational for anyone to do what he believes will be worse for him. On the Revised Self-interest Theory, this claim must be abandoned. If it is not irrational to care less about some parts of one's future, it may not be irrational to do what one believes will be worse for oneself. It may not be irrational to act, knowingly, against one's own self-interest.

As this last claim shows, the Revised Theory is not a version of the Self-interest Theory. It is a version of the Critical Present-aim Theory. But how we classify this theory is unimportant.

What is important is that we must abandon the Classical Theory's central claim. Consider deliberate and great imprudence. For the sake of small pleasures in my youth, I cause it to be true that I shall suffer greatly in my old age. I might, for instance, start smoking when I am a boy. I know that I am likely to impose upon myself a premature and painful death. I know that I am doing what is likely to be much worse for me. Since we must reject the Classical Theory, we cannot claim that all such acts are irrational.

On the Revised Theory, such acts *might* be irrational. On this theory, it is not irrational to have a discount rate with respect to the degrees of psychological connectedness. When I bring upon myself great suffering in my old age, for the sake of small pleasures now, my act is irrational only if my discount rate is *too steep*.

One weakness of the Revised Theory is its need to explain what makes a discount rate too steep. But the important point is that, even if this rate is *not* too steep, all such acts need to be criticized. Great imprudence is always sad, and often (as in the case of smoking) tragic. On the Revised Theory, we cannot claim that all such acts are irrational. Since we should criticize all such acts, we must appeal to another theory.

106. THE IMMORALITY OF IMPRUDENCE

How should we criticize great imprudence? It might be said that we can simply call such acts imprudent. It might be said that this is a criticism, even if we no longer believe that imprudence is irrational.

Many people would reject this claim. Consider the claim that someone is *unchaste*. Many people now believe that there is nothing morally wrong in unchastity. And, for these people, the charge 'unchaste' ceases to be a criticism. A similar claim applies to the charge 'imprudent'. Just as 'unchaste' expresses a moral objection, 'imprudent' expresses an objection about rationality. This is shown by the more common words with which people are criticized for acting imprudently. When someone does what he knows will be worse for himself, he would be called by many 'stupid', 'an idiot', 'a mug', or 'a fool'. This shows that this objection is about irrationality. If we believe that an imprudent act is not irrational, the charge 'imprudent' might, for some of us, cease to be a criticism. It might become, like 'unchaste', merely a description.

Great imprudence ought to be criticized. What kind of criticism can we give? It might be suggested that we can appeal to the Critical Present-aim Theory. As I wrote in Section 52, we can claim that, in our concern for our own self-interest, it is irrational not to be temporally neutral. On this version of CP, great imprudence is irrational. More exactly, it is irrational unless it brings great benefits to others, or fulfils some desire that is not irrational.

This suggestion fails. In my latest argument against the Self-interest Theory, I *assumed* that it is irrational not to be temporally neutral. The argument defended a discount rate, not with respect to time, but with respect to the degrees of psychological connectedness. Since this connectedness is one of my two reasons for caring about my future, it cannot be irrational for me to care less, when there will be less connectedness. The Critical Present-aim Theory cannot, defensibly, deny this claim.

The objection to great imprudence must come from another direction. I suggest that, since we must reject the Classical Self-interest Theory, we should expand the area covered by morality. Our moral theory should annex the territory that the Revised Self-interest Theory has abandoned.

As Mill's critics claimed, *purely* 'self-regarding' acts are rare. If I am greatly imprudent, this is likely to be bad for certain other people. But, if my act's main effects will be on myself, most of us would not judge it to be morally wrong. The older versions of Common-Sense Morality do include some duties towards oneself. But these are special duties, such as a duty to develop one's talents, or to preserve one's purity. It is seldom claimed that great imprudence is morally wrong. This is seldom claimed partly because there seemed no *need* for such a claim. While such acts were thought to be irrational, they did not need to be thought immoral. But, since we must now abandon the Classical Self-Interest Theory, we should extend our moral theory.

There are two ways of doing so. We could appeal to Consequentialism. In particular, we could appeal to an impartial or agent-neutral Principle of Beneficence. Suppose that, for the sake of lesser benefits now, I impose greater burdens on myself in old age. I am here doing what, impartially considered, has worse effects, or increases the sum of suffering. We could claim that my act is morally wrong, because it increases the sum of suffering, even when it will be *me* who will suffer more. More generally, my imprudence is wrong because I am making the outcome worse. It is no excuse that the outcome will be worse only for me.

We could also extend the part of our theory that is agent-relative. This part covers our special obligations to those to whom we stand in certain relations, such as our parents, children, pupils, patients, clients, or constituents. A person stands to himself in the future in another special relation, which we could claim to create similar special obligations.

If we revised our moral view in either of these ways, this would be, for many people, a large change in their conception of morality. These people believe that it cannot be a moral matter how one affects one's own future.

It may be easier to believe this if we subdivide a person's life into that of successive selves. As I have claimed, this has long seemed natural, whenever there is some marked weakening of psychological connectedness. After such a weakening, my earlier self may seem alien to me now. If I fail to *identify* with that earlier self, I am in some ways thinking of that self as like a different person.

We could make similar claims about our future selves. If we now care little about ourselves in the further future, our future selves are like future generations. We can affect them for the worse, and, because they do not now exist, they cannot defend themselves. Like future generations, future selves have no vote, so their interests need to be specially protected.

Reconsider a boy who starts to smoke, knowing and hardly caring that this may cause him to suffer greatly fifty years later. This boy does not identify with his future self. His attitude towards this future self is in some ways like his attitude to other people. This analogy makes it easier to believe that his act is morally wrong. He runs the risk of imposing on himself a premature and painful death. We should claim that it is wrong to impose on *anyone,* including such a future self, the risk of such a death. More generally, we should claim that great imprudence is morally wrong. We ought not to do to our future selves what it would be wrong to do to other people.

15

PERSONAL IDENTITY AND MORALITY

IF we become Reductionists, should we make other changes in our moral views?

107. AUTONOMY AND PATERNALISM

We are paternalists when we make someone act in his own interests. It provides some justification for paternalism, when this involves coercion or the infringement of someone's autonomy, if we are stopping this person from acting irrationally. This is what we believe we are doing if we accept the Self-interest Theory. I argued that we must reject this theory. But we ought to extend our moral theory so that it covers what we have rejected. We should claim that great imprudence is morally wrong.

This claim strengthens the case for paternalistic intervention. The person we coerce might say: 'I may be acting irrationally. But even if I am, that is my affair. If I am only harming myself, I have the right to act irrationally, and you have no right to stop me.' This reply has some force. We do not believe that we have a general right to prevent people from acting *irrationally*. But we do believe that we have a general right to prevent people from acting *wrongly*. This claim may not apply to minor wrong-doing. But we believe that it cannot be wrong, and would often be our duty, to prevent others from doing what is seriously wrong. Since we ought to believe that great imprudence is seriously wrong, we ought to believe that we should prevent such imprudence, even if this involves coercion. Autonomy does not include the right to impose upon oneself, for no good reason, great harm. We ought to prevent anyone from doing to his future self what it would be wrong to do to other people.

Though these claims support paternalism, there remain the well-known objections. It is better if each of us learns from his own mistakes. And it is harder for others to know that these are mistakes.

108. THE TWO ENDS OF LIVES

There are many other ways in which, if we have changed our view about personal identity, this may justify a change in our moral views. One example is our view about the morality of abortion. On the Non-Reductionist view, since my existence is all-or-nothing, there must have been a moment when I started to exist. As in my imagined Spectra, there must be a sharp borderline. It is implausible to claim that this borderline is birth; nor can any line be plausibly drawn during pregnancy. We may thus be led to the view that I started to exist at the moment of conception. We may claim that this is the moment when my life began. And, on the Non-Reductionist View, it is a *deep* truth that all the parts of my life are *equally* parts of my life. I was as much me even when my life had only just started. Killing me at this time is, straightforwardly, killing an innocent person. If this is what we believe, we shall plausibly claim that abortion is morally wrong.

On the Reductionist View, we do not believe that at every moment I either do or don't exist. We can now deny that a fertilized ovum is a person or a human being. This is like the plausible denial that an acorn is an oak-tree. Given the right conditions, an acorn slowly becomes an oak-tree. This transition takes time, and is a matter of degree. There is no sharp borderline. We should claim the same about persons, and human beings. We can then plausibly take a different view about the morality of abortion. We can believe that there is nothing wrong in an early abortion, but that it would be seriously wrong to abort a child near the end of pregnancy. Such a child, if unwanted, should be born and adopted. The cases in between we can treat as matters of degree. The fertilized ovum is not at first, but slowly becomes, a human being, and a person. In the same way, the destruction of this organism is not at first but slowly becomes seriously wrong. After being in no way wrong, it becomes a minor wrong-doing, which would be justified all things considered only if the later birth of this child would be seriously worse either for its parents or for other people. As the organism becomes fully a human being, or a person, the minor wrong-doing changes into an act that would be seriously wrong.

I have described the two main views that are widely held about the morality of abortion. The first of these is supported by the Non-Reductionist View about the nature of persons, and the second is supported by the Reductionist View. Though it is not the only view that is compatible with Reductionism, I believe that we should take this second view.

Within this view, there is room for disagreement. Most of us do not distinguish persons from human beings. But some of us, following Locke, make a distinction. These people typically claim that a human being becomes a person only when this human being becomes self-conscious. A foetus becomes a human being before the end of pregnancy. But a new-born baby is not self-conscious. If we draw this distinction, we may think that, while it is bad to kill a human being, it is worse to kill a person. We may even think that only the killing of persons is wrong. I shall not pursue this debate. What both sides assume I shall be questioning in Part Four.

Consider next the other end of life. On the Non-Reductionist View, any person must be either alive or dead. On the Reductionist View, a person can gradually cease to exist some time before his heart stops beating. This will be so if the distinctive features of a person's mental life gradually disappear. This often happens. We can plausibly claim that, if the person has ceased to exist, we have no moral reason to help his heart to go on beating, or to refrain from preventing this.

This claim distinguishes the person from the human being. If we know that a human being is in a coma that is incurable—that this human being will certainly never regain consciousness—we shall believe that the person has ceased to exist. Since there is a living human body, the human being still exists. But, at this end of lives, we should claim that only the killing of persons is wrong.

109. DESERT

Some writers claim that, if the Reductionist View is true, we cannot deserve to be punished for our crimes. Butler writes that, on a Reductionist version of Locke's View, it would be 'a fallacy upon ourselves, to charge our present selves with anything we did. . .'.[86] Another of Locke's Eighteenth Century critics makes a more sweeping claim. Reid contrasts personal identity with the identity of such things as ships or trees. The identity of such things, he writes:

is not perfect identity; it is rather something which, for the conveniency of speech, we call identity. It admits of a great change of the subject, providing the change be gradual; sometimes, even of a total change. And the changes which in common language are made consistent with identity differ from those that are thought to destroy it, not in kind, but in number and degree. *Identity* has no fixed nature when applied to bodies; and questions about the identity of a body are very often questions about words. But identity, when applied to persons, has no ambiguity, and admits not of degrees, or of more and less. It is the foundation of all rights and obligations, and of all accountableness; and the notion of it is fixed and precise.[87]

Reid is clearly a Reductionist about the identity of bodies. On his view, personal identity is quite different. It involves a fact that is always determinate, and that must be all-or-nothing. This is what I call the deep further fact. Reid believes that this fact is the foundation of morality: that if, as I have argued, there is no such fact, it is not merely true that we cannot be 'accountable' for past crimes. All rights and obligations are undermined.

Certain modern writers make similar claims. Madell claims that 'an analysis of personal identity in terms of psychological continuity . . . is utterly destructive of a whole range of our normal moral attitudes. . . . Shame, remorse, pride, and gratitude' all depend on a rejection of this view.[88] And Haksar claims that my view undermines all 'human rights' and 'non-utilitarian moral constraints', and is 'incompatible with any kind of humane morality'.[89]

Should we accept these Extreme Claims? We should first note the following. If the truth about personal identity had these implications, most of us would find this deeply disturbing. It may be thought that, if these *were* the implications of the Reductionist View, this would show this view to be false. This is not so. The truth may be disturbing. Consider the claim that the Universe was not created by a benevolent God. Many people find this claim disturbing; but this cannot show it to be false. If some truth is disturbing, this is no reason not to believe it. It can only be a reason for acting in certain ways. It might be a reason for trying to conceal this truth from others. It might even be a reason for trying to deceive ourselves, so that we cease to believe this truth. As I have said, wishful thinking is theoretically irrational, but it may be practically rational. This might be so, for instance, if it was the only way to save ourselves from severe depression.

Consider next one of these Extreme Claims. Some people argue that, if the Reductionist View is true, we cannot deserve to be punished for our crimes. This argument assumes that only the deep further fact carries with it desert, or responsibility. I shall again ask two questions: (1) Would this assumption be plausible, or at least defensible, if the Non-Reductionist View was true? (2) Is the assumption plausible, or defensible, given the truth of the Reductionist View?

It will help to return to my imagined division. On the Non-Reductionist View, there are three possibilities, all of which might be the truth. It might be true that I shall be neither of the two resulting people, or that I shall be Lefty, or that I shall be Righty. Suppose that I shall be Righty. Would Lefty deserve to be punished for the crimes that I committed before the division? A Non-Reductionist could defensibly answer:

> No. Lefty is both physically and psychologically continuous with you, as you were before the division. But *he* did not commit your crimes. How can he deserve to be punished for crimes that someone else committed, at a time when he himself did not exist? Only the deep further fact of personal identity carries with it responsibility for past crimes. In the absence of this fact, the two continuities do not carry with them such responsibility.

The Non-Reductionist should admit that psychological continuity has some moral implications. Suppose that my past crime showed me to be a homicidal maniac. Since he is psychologically continuous with me, Lefty would also be a homicidal maniac. This might justify preventively detaining him even before he commits a crime. But this does not show that he can deserve to be punished for my crimes.

Suppose now that the Non-Reductionist changes his view about the nature of personal identity. If he becomes a Reductionist, he can defensibly claim that we do not deserve punishment for our crimes. On his view, desert requires the deep further fact. Since there is no such fact, there is no desert.

As before, though this Extreme Claim is defensible, it can be defensibly denied. It may help to give this analogy. There are two views about desert and Determinism. On the Compatibilist View, the kind of free will that is required for desert would not be undermined by the truth of Determinism. On the Incompatibilist View, Determinism undermines both free will and desert. On this second view, if it was causally inevitable that I committed my crime, I cannnot deserve to be punished. If it is morally justified to put me in prison, this can only be on utilitarian grounds. One such ground is that my imprisonment may deter others from committing crimes. And, notoriously, it would be irrelevant if I am merely falsely believed to have committed some crime. Since even the guilty do not deserve punishment, it will make no moral difference if I am in fact innocent.

Some claim that only the Compatibilist View is defensible. Others make this claim about the Incompatibilist View. A third group believe that this disagreement has not been decisively resolved. These people might claim: 'Though these views contradict each other, and therefore cannot both be true, both are defensible. No one has yet produced an argument that decisively refutes one view, and establishes the other.'

I make this claim about the different pair of views that I have described. Non-Reductionists believe that personal identity involves a deep further fact, distinct from physical and psychological continuity. It is a defensible claim that only this fact carries with it desert for past crimes, and that, if there is no such fact, there is no desert. This is the analogue of the Incompatibilist View. Desert can be held to be incompatible with Reductionism. But a different view is also defensible. We can defensibly claim that psychological continuity carries with it desert for past crimes. Perhaps there is an argument that decisively resolves this disagreement. But I have not yet found this argument.

Consider next the fact that there are degrees of psychological connectedness. Suppose that, between some convict now, and himself when he committed some crime, there are only weak psychological connections. This will usually be true only when someone is convicted many years after committing his crime. But it might be true when there is some great discontinuity, such as the conversion of a pleasure-seeking Italian youth into St. Francis. We can imply the weakness of the psychological connections by calling the convict the criminal's later self.

Two grounds for detaining him would be unaffected. Whether some convict should be either reformed, or preventively detained, turns upon his present state, not on his relation to the criminal. A third ground, deterrence, turns upon a different question. Do potential criminals care about such later selves? Do they care, for instance, if they do not expect to be caught for many years? If they do, detaining their later selves could deter others.

Would this be deserved? Locke thought that if we forget our crimes we deserve no punishment. Geach calls this view 'morally repugnant'.[90] And mere loss of memory does seem insufficient. Changes of character are more relevant. But the subject is complicated. Claims about desert can be plausibly supported by a great variety of arguments. According to some of these, loss of memory would be important. And according to most the nature and cause of any change of character would need to be known.

I shall not consider these details. But I shall make one general claim. When some convict is now less closely connected to himself at the time of his crime, he deserves less punishment. If the connections are very weak, he may deserve none. This claim seems plausible. It may give one of the reasons why we have Statutes of Limitations, fixing periods of time after which we cannot be punished for our crimes. (Suppose that a man aged ninety, one of the few rightful holders of the Nobel Peace Prize, confesses that it was he who, at the age of twenty, injured a policeman in a drunken brawl. Though this was a serious crime, this man may not now deserve to be punished.)

This claim should be distinguished from the idea of diminished responsibility. It does not appeal to mental illness, but instead treats a criminal's later self as like a sane accomplice. Just as someone's deserts correspond to the degree of his complicity with some criminal, so his deserts now, for some past crime, corrrespond to the degree of psychological connectedness between himself now and himself when committing that crime.

We may be tempted to protest, 'But it was just as much *his* crime.' This is true. And this truth would be a good objection if we were not Reductionists. But on the Reductionist View this truth is too trivial to refute my claim about reduced responsibility. It is like the claim, 'Every accomplice is just as much an accomplice.' Such a claim cannot show that complicity has no degrees.

In this section I have described three views. On the Extreme Claim, since the Reductionist View is true, no one ever deserves to be punished. As before, this claim is defensible, but it can also be defensibly denied. I have also claimed that the weakening of connections may reduce responsibility. This claim seems to me more plausible than its denial.

110. COMMITMENTS

If we turn to commitments, similar claims apply. On the Extreme Claim, since the Reductionist View is true, we can never be bound by past commitments. This claim is defensible, but so is its denial. And it is plausible to claim that the weakening of connections would reduce the strength of a commitment.

It would be tedious to give a similar defence of these conclusions. I therefore turn to a question that has no analogue in the case of desert. When we are considering commitments, the fact of personal identity enters twice. We must consider the identity both of the maker of some promise, and of the person to whom it is made. The weakening of connectedness may reduce the *maker's* obligation. But, in the case of the person who *received* the promise, any implications of the Reductionist View could be deliberately blocked. We could ask for promises of this form: 'I shall help you, and all of your later selves'. If the promises made to me take this form, they cannot be held to be later undermined by any change in my character, or by any other weakening, over the rest of my life, in psychological connectedness.

There is here an asymmetry. A similar form cannot so obviously bind the maker of a promise. I might say, 'I, and all of my later selves, shall help you'. But it could be objected that I can bind or commit only my present self. This objection has some force, since it resembles the plausible claim that I can bind or commit only myself. In contrast, no one denies that I can promise you that I shall help other people, such as your children. It is therefore clear that I can promise you that I shall help your later selves.

Such a promise may become especially binding. Suppose that you change much more than I do. I may then regard myself as committed, not to you, but to your earlier self. I may therefore think that you cannot waive my commitment. This would be like a commitment, to someone now dead, to help his children. We cannot be released from such commitments.

Such a case would be rare. But, because it illustrates some other points, it is worth giving an example. Consider

The Nineteenth Century Russian. In several years, a young Russian will inherit vast estates. Because he has socialist ideals, he intends, now, to give the land to the peasants. But he knows that in time his ideals may fade. To guard against this possibility, he does two things. He first signs a legal document, which will automatically give away the land, and which can be revoked only with his wife's consent. He then says to his wife, 'Promise me that, if I ever change my mind, and ask you to revoke this document, you will not consent.' He adds, 'I regard my ideals as essential to me. If I lose these ideals, I want you to think that I cease to exist. I want you to regard your husband then, not as me, the man who asks you for this promise, but only as his corrupted later self. Promise me that you would not do what he asks.'

This plea, using the language of successive selves, seems both understandable and natural. And if this man's wife made this promise, and he did in middle age ask her to revoke the document, she might plausibly regard herself as not released from her commitment. It might seem to her as if she has obligations to two different people. She might believe that to do what her husband now asks would be a betrayal of the young man whom she loved and married. And she might regard what her husband now says as unable to acquit her of disloyalty to this young man—of disloyalty to her husband's earlier self.

Such an example may seem not to need the distinction between successive selves. Suppose that I ask you to promise never to give me cigarettes, even if I beg you for them. You may think that I cannot, in begging you, simply release you from this commitment. And to think this you need not deny that it is I to whom you are committed.

This is true. But the reason is that addiction clouds judgement. Similar examples might involve extreme stress or pain, or—as with Odysseus, tied to the mast while the Sirens sang—extraordinary temptation. When nothing clouds a person's judgement, most of us believe that the person to whom we are committed can always release us. He can always, if in sound mind, waive our commitment. We believe this whatever the commitment may be. On this view, the content of a commitment cannot prevent its being waived. This is like a similar fact about authority. Suppose that a general tells his troops, 'I order you to attack at dawn, and to disregard any later contrary order.' He later says, 'Disregard my last order, and retreat.' Despite the content of the first order, it would be this second order that his troops should obey.

To return to the Russian couple. The young man's ideals fade, and in middle age he asks his wife to revoke the document. Though she promised him to refuse, he declares that he now releases her from her commitment. I have described two ways in which she might believe that she is not released. She might take her husband's change of mind to show that he cannot now make well-considered judgements. But we can suppose that she has no such thought. We can also suppose that she shares our view about commitments. If this is so, how can she believe that her husband cannot release her from her commitment? She can believe this only if she thinks that it is, in some sense, not *he* to whom she is committed. I have described such a sense. She may regard the young man's loss of his ideals as involving his replacement by a later self.

This example illustrates a general claim. We may regard some events within a person's life as, in certain ways, like birth or death. Not in all ways, for beyond these events the person has earlier or later selves. But it may be only one out of the series of selves which is the object of some of our emotions, and to which we apply some of our principles.

The young Russian socialist regards his ideals as essential to his present self. He asks his wife to promise to this present self not to act against these ideals. And, on this way of thinking, she can never be released from her commitment. The self to whom she is committed would, in trying to release her, cease to exist.

This is not a legalistic point. It is in part a truth about this woman's beliefs and emotions. She loves, not her middle-aged husband, but the young man she married. This is why it is to this young man that she believes she ought to be loyal. We can love, and believe we are committed to, someone who is dead. And the object of such love and commitment may be, not someone who is dead, but some living person's earlier self.

It may be objected that, by distinguishing successive selves in convenient ways, we could unfairly escape our commitments, or our just deserts. This is not so. I might say, 'It was not I who robbed the bank this morning, but only my past self.' But others could more plausibly reply, 'It was you'. Since there are no fixed criteria, we can choose when to speak of a new self. But such choices may be, and be known to be, insincere. And they can also sincerely express beliefs—beliefs that are not themselves chosen. This is true of the woman in my example. That the young man whom she loved and married has, in a sense, ceased to exist—that her middle-aged and cynical husband is at most the later self of this young man—these claims seem to her to express more of the truth than the simple claim, 'they are the same person'. Just as we can more accurately describe Russia's history if we divide this into the histories of the Empire and the Soviet Union, she can more accurately describe her husband's life, and her own beliefs and emotions, if she divides this life into that of two successive selves.[92]

111. THE SEPARATENESS OF PERSONS AND DISTRIBUTIVE JUSTICE

We are different people, each with his own life to lead. This is true on all views about the nature of personal identity. But it is a deeper truth on the Non-Reductionist View. If we accept this view, we may regard this truth as one of the fundamental facts underlying all reasons for acting. This fact has been called the *separateness of persons*.

Sidgwick believed that this fact is the foundation of the Self-interest Theory about rationality. If what is fundamental is that we are different persons, each with his own life to lead, this supports the claim that the supremely rational ultimate aim, for each person, is that his own life go as well as possible. Sidgwick believed that there is another equally rational ultimate aim. This is that things go, on the whole, as well as possible for everyone. Many agree with Sidgwick that this is the ultimate aim given to us by morality. And some accept Sidgwick's view that, when morality conflicts with self-interest, there is no answer to the question of what we have most reason to do. When he compared moral and self-interested reasons, neither seemed to Sidgwick to outweigh the other.

Sidgwick held this view because he believed the separateness of persons to be a deep truth. He believed that an appeal to this truth gives a Self-interest Theorist a sufficient defence against the claims of morality. And he suggested that, if we took a different view about personal identity, we could refute the Self-interest Theory. I have claimed that this is true.

The Self-interest Theory seemed, to Sidgwick, to be grounded on the separateness of persons. I shall now discuss a similar claim about morality. This claim challenges Sidgwick's moral view. Sidgwick thought that there was one ultimate moral principle, that of Impartial Benevolence. Since he accepted the Hedonistic Theory about self-interest, his principle of benevolence took a hedonistic form. On his view, our ultimate moral aim is the greatest net sum of happiness minus misery, or of 'desirable consciousness' minus 'undesirable consciousness'. Those Utilitarians who reject Hedonism take the ultimate aim to be the greatest net sum of benefits, minus burdens. On either version, the Utilitarian View is, in the following sense, *impersonal*. All that matters are the amounts of happiness and suffering, or of benefits and burdens. It makes no moral difference how these amounts are distributed as between different people.

Many people reject this view. They might say: 'The Utilitarian aim may be one of our ultimate moral aims. But we have at least one other. Happiness and suffering, or benefits and burdens, ought to be fairly shared as between different people. Besides the Utilitarian Principle we need principles of Distributive Justice. One example is the Principle of Equality. On this principle, it is bad if some people are worse off than others through no fault of theirs.'

The argument for equality is often claimed to be grounded on the separateness of persons. One such claim might be: 'Since it is a deep truth that we live different lives, it is an ultimate moral aim that, in so far as we are equally deserving, the lives of each should go equally well. If this is impossible, it should at least be true that the lives of each have an equal chance of going well.'[93]

If we cease to believe in the Non-Reductionist View, what does this imply about the Principle of Equality, and other distributive principles? My main claims will be these. This change of view supports three arguments about these principles. Two of these arguments imply that we should give to these principles *more scope*. This would make them more important. But we may also be led to give these principles *less weight*. This would make them less important. We must therefore ask what the *net* effect would be.

112. THREE EXPLANATIONS OF THE UTILITARIAN VIEW

Before advancing these arguments, I shall mention two related claims. These can be introduced in the following way. Utilitarians reject distributive principles. They aim for the greatest net sum of benefits minus burdens, whatever its distribution. I shall say that they *maximize*.

When our acts can affect only one person, most of us accept maximization. We do not believe that we ought to give someone fewer happy days so as to be more fair in the way we spread them out over the parts of his life. There are, of course, arguments for spreading out enjoyments. We remain fresh, and have more to look forward to. But these arguments do not count against maximization; they remind us how to achieve it.

When our acts can affect several different people, Utilitarians make similar claims. They admit new arguments for spreading out enjoyments, such as that which appeals to the effects of relative deprivation, or to diminishing marginal utility. But Utilitarians treat equality as a mere means, not a separate aim.

Since their attitude to sets of lives is like ours to single lives, Utilitarians ignore the boundaries between lives. We may ask, 'Why?'

Here are three suggestions:

(1) Their method of moral reasoning leads them to overlook these boundaries.

(2) They believe that the boundaries are unimportant, because they think that sets of lives are like single lives.

(3) They accept the Reductionist View about personal identity.

Suggestion (1) has been made by Rawls.[94] It can be summarized like this. Many Utilitarians answer moral questions with the method called that of an *Impartial Observer*. When such a Utilitarian asks himself, as an observer, what would be right, or what he would impartially prefer, he may *identify* with all of the affected people. He may imagine that he himself would *be all* of these different people. This will lead him to ignore the fact that *different* people are affected, and so to ignore the claims of just distribution as between these people.

Suggestion (2) has been made by Gauthier, and others.[95] On this suggestion, Utilitarians must assume that mankind is a super-organism, or believe, like some Hindus, in a single *World Soul*. If suggestions (1) or (2) were true, they would explain the Utilitarian View in ways that undermined this view. It is clearly a mistake to ignore the fact that we live different lives. And mankind is not a super-organism.

I suggest (3). On this suggestion, Utilitarians reject distributive principles because they believe in the Reductionist View. If the Reductionist View supports the rejection of these principles, this third explanation supports rather than undermines the Utilitarian View.

In the case of some Utilitarians, suggestion (1) may be correct. Many Utilitarians consider moral questions as if they were Impartial Observers. Some of these may be, as Rawls claims, *identifying* observers. But there can also be *detached* observers. While an identifying observer imagines himself as being *all* of the affected people, and a Rawlsian imagines himself as being *one* of the affected people, without knowing whom, a detached observer imagines himself as being *none* of the affected people.

Some Utilitarians have been detached Impartial Observers. These Utilitarians do not overlook the distinction between people. And, as Rawls remarks, there seems little reason why detached observers should be led to ignore the principles of distributive justice. If we approach morality in this detached way—if we do not think of ourselves as potentially involved—we may be somewhat more inclined to reject these principles, since we would not fear that we ourselves might become one of the people who are worst off. But this particular approach to moral questions does not sufficiently explain why these Utilitarians reject distributive principles.

Is suggestion (2) correct? As an *explanation* of the Utilitarian View, (2) is false. Some followers of Hegel believed that a nation was a super-organism. To quote one writer, a nation 'is a living being, like an individual'.[97] But Utilitarians ignore national boundaries, and they do not believe that mankind is such a single being.

Suggestion (2) is better taken, not as an explanation of the Utilitarian View, but as an objection to this view. The suggestion may be that this view cannot be justified unless mankind is a Super-organism, and that, since this is false, Utilitarians are wrong to reject distributive principles.

I suggest a different explanation. On suggestion (3), Utilitarians ignore distribution because they accept the Reductionist View. (3) is compatible with (1). Some Utilitarians may both be identifying observers, and accept the Reductionist View. But (3) conflicts with (2).

There may seem to be a puzzle here. On suggestion (2), groups of people are compared to single persons. This is the reverse of the Reductionist View, which compares a person's history to that of a nation, or a group of people. Since both these views compare nations to people, how can they be different views?

The answer is this. When we consider nations, most of us are Reductionists. We believe that the existence of a nation involves nothing more than the existence of its citizens, living together on its territory, and acting together in certain ways. In contrast, when considering persons, most of us believe the Non-Reductionist View. We believe that our identity must be determinate. This cannot be true unless a person is a separately existing entity, distinct from his brain and body, and his experiences. Most of us are thus Reductionists about nations but not about people. It is the difference between these common views which explains the two comparisons. The claim that X is like Y typically assumes the common view of Y. We shall therefore say, 'People are like nations' if we are Reductionists about both. If we are Non-Reductionists about both, we shall instead say, 'Nations are like people'. The belief in super-organisms may be a Non-Reductionist View about nations.

113. CHANGING A PRINCIPLE'S SCOPE

Since Utilitarians reject distributive principles, they believe that the boundaries of lives have no moral significance. On their view, the separateness of persons can be ignored. I have described three explanations for this view. I shall now argue that, despite some complications, mine is the best explanation.

Consider

The Child's Burden. We must decide whether to impose on some child some hardship. If we do, this will either

(i) be for this child's own greater benefit in adult life, or

(ii) be for the similar benefit of someone else—such as this child's younger brother.

Does it matter morally whether (i) or (ii) is true?

Most of us would answer: 'Yes. If it is for the child's own later benefit, there can at least be no unfairness.' We might add the general claim that imposing useful burdens is more likely to be justified if these burdens are for a person's own good.

Utilitarians would accept this claim, but explain it in a different way. Rather than claiming that such burdens cannot be unfair, they would claim that they are in general easier to bear.

To block this reply, we can suppose that our child is too young to be cheered up in this way. This simplifies the disagreement. Utilitarians would say: 'Whether it is right to impose this burden on this child depends only on how great the later benefit will be. It does not depend upon who benefits. It would make no moral difference if the benefit came, not to the child himself, but to someone else.' Non-Utilitarians would reply: 'On the contrary, if it came to the child himself, this would help to justify the burden. If it came to someone else, that would be unfair.'

Do the two views about the nature of personal identity support different sides in this disagreement?

Part of the answer is clear. Non-Utilitarians think it a morally important fact that it will be the child himself who, as an adult, benefits. This fact is more important on the Non-Reductionist View, for it is on this view that the identity between the child and the adult is in its nature deeper. On the Reductionist View, what is involved in this identity is less deep, and it holds, over adolescence, to a reduced degree. If we are Reductionists, we may compare the weakening of the connections between the child and his adult self to the absence of connections between different people. We shall give more weight to the fact that, in this example, this child does not care what will happen to his adult self. That it will be *he* who receives the benefit may thus seem to us less important. We might say, 'It will not be *he* who benefits. It will only be his adult self'.

The Non-Reductionist View supports the Non-Utilitarian reply. Does it follow that the Reductionist View supports the Utilitarian claim? It does not. We might say, 'Just as it would be unfair if it is someone else who benefits, so if it won't be the child, but only his adult self, this would also be unfair.'

The point is a general one. If we are Reductionists, we regard the rough subdivisions within lives as, in certain ways, like the divisions between lives. We may therefore come to treat alike two kinds of distribution: within lives, and between lives. But there are two ways of treating these alike. We can apply distributive principles to both, or to neither.

Which of these might we do? I distinguished two ways in which our moral view may change. We may give to distributive principles a different scope, and a different weight. If we become Reductionists, we may be led to give these principles *greater* scope. Since we regard the subdivisions within lives as, in certain ways, like the divisions between lives, we may apply distributive principles even within lives, as in the claim just made about imposing burdens on a child. By widening the scope of distributive principles, we would be moving further away from the Utilitarian view. In this respect the Reductionist View counts against rather than in favour of the Utilitarian view.

114. CHANGING A PRINCIPLE'S WEIGHT

Return next to the second explanation of the Utilitarian view. Gauthier suggests that to suppose that we should maximize for mankind 'is to suppose that mankind is a super-person'.[98]

To understand this suggestion we should first ask why, within a single life, we can ignore distributive principles. Why is it morally permissible here simply to maximize? It might be thought that this is permissible because it is not a moral matter what we do with our own lives. Even if this was true, it could not be the explanation. We believe that it can be right to maximize within the life of someone else. Medicine provides examples. We think it right for doctors to maximize on behalf of their unconscious patients. They would be right to choose some operation which would give their patients a smaller total sum of suffering, even though this suffering would all come within one period. We do not believe that this would be unfair to this person during this period.

Some claim: 'We are free to maximize within one life only because it is *one* life'. This claim supports Gauthier's charge against Utilitarians. It supports the claim that we would be free to maximize over different lives only if they were like parts of a single life.

When presented with this argument, Utilitarians would deny its premise. They might claim: 'What justifies maximization is not the unity of a life. Suffering is bad, and happiness is good. It is better if there is less of what is bad, and more of what is good. This is enough to justify maximization. Since it is not the unity of a life that, within this life, justifies maximization, this can be justified over different lives without the assumption that mankind is a super-person.'

One connection with the Reductionist View is this. It is on this, rather than the Non-Reductionist View, that the premise of Gauthier's argument is more plausibly denied. If the unity of a life is less deep, it is more plausible to claim that this unity is not what justifies maximization. This is one of the ways in which the Reductionist View provides some support for the Utilitarian View.

I shall expand these remarks. There are two kinds of distribution: within lives, and between lives. And there are two ways of treating these alike. We can apply distributive principles to both, or to neither.

Utilitarians apply them to neither. I suggest that this may be, in part, because they accept the Reductionist View. An incompatible suggestion is that they accept the reverse view, believing that mankind is a super-person.

My suggestion may seem clearly wrong if we overlook the fact that there are two routes to the abandonment of distributive principles. We may give them no scope, or instead give them no weight.

Suppose we assume that the only route is the change in scope. This is suggested by Rawls's claim that 'the utilitarian extends to society the principle of choice for one man'.[99] The assumption here is that the route to Utilitarianism is a change in the scope, not of distributive principles, but of its correlative: our freedom to ignore these principles. If we assume that the only route is a change in scope, it may indeed seem that Utilitarians must either be assuming that any group of people is like a single person (Gauthier's suggestion), or at least be forgetting that it is not (Rawls's suggestion).

I shall describe the other route. Utilitarians may not be denying that distributive principles have scope. They may be denying that they have weight. This denial may be given some support by the Reductionist View.

More exactly, my suggestion is this. The Reductionist View does support a change in the scope of distributive principles. It supports giving these principles *more* scope, so that they apply even within a single life. This is what I claimed in the case of the Child's Burden. A Reductionist is more likely to regard this child's relation to his adult self as being like a relation to a different person. He is thus more likely to claim that it is unfair to impose burdens on this child merely to benefit his adult self. It is on the Non-Reductionist View that we can more plausibly reply, 'This cannot be unfair, since it will be just as much *he* who will later benefit'. As we shall later see, there is another argument which, on the Reductionist View, supports a greater widening in the scope of distributive principles. But though in these two ways the Reductionist View supports widening the scope of distributive principles, it also supports giving these principles less weight. And, if we give these principles *no* weight, it will make no difference that we have given them wider scope. This is how the net effect might be the Utilitarian View.

This suggestion differs from the others in the following way. Rawls remarks that the Utilitarian View seems to involve 'conflating all persons into one'.[100] Nagel similarly claims that a Utilitarian 'treats the desires . . . of distinct persons as if they were the desires . . . of a mass person.' [101] And I have quoted Gauthier's similar claim. On my suggestion, the Utilitarian

View may be supported by, not the conflation of persons, but their partial disintegration. It may rest upon the view that a person's life is less deeply integrated than most of us assume. Utilitarians may be treating benefits and burdens, not as if they all came within the same life, but as if it made no moral difference where they came. And this belief may be partly supported by the view that the unity of each life, and hence the difference between lives, is in its nature less deep.

In ignoring principles of distribution between different people, the Utilitarian View is *impersonal*. Rawls suggests that it 'mistakes impersonality for impartiality'. [102] This would be so if the way in which Utilitarians try to be impartial leads them to overlook the difference between persons. And this may be claimed for those Utilitarians whose method of moral reasoning does have this effect. It may be claimed about an *identifying* Impartial Observer, whose method of reasoning leads him to imagine that he will himself be all of the affected people. But few Utilitarians have reasoned in this way. And, on my suggestion, Utilitarians need not mistake impersonality for impartiality. Their impersonality may be partly supported by the Reductionist View about the nature of persons. As Rawls writes, 'the correct regulative principle for anything depends upon the nature of that thing'.[103]

115. CAN IT BE RIGHT TO BURDEN SOMEONE MERELY TO BENEFIT SOMEONE ELSE?

I shall now develop my suggestion. Utilitarians believe that benefits and burdens can be freely weighed against each other, even if they come to different people. This is frequently denied.

We can first distinguish two kinds of weighing. The claim that a certain burden *factually outweighs* another is the claim that it is greater. The claim that it *morally outweighs* another is the claim that we ought to relieve it even at the cost of failing to relieve the other. Similar remarks apply to the weighing of different burdens, and to the weighing of burdens against benefits. It is worth explaining how a benefit can be greater than, or factually outweigh, a burden. This would be most clearly true if, when offered the choice of having either both or neither, everyone would choose to have both. Everyone would here believe that it is worth undergoing this burden for the sake of this benefit. For this to be a good test, people must be equally concerned about the parts of their lives in which they would receive these benefits and burdens. Since most people care less about the further future, the test is best applied by asking people whether they would choose to undergo this burden before receiving the benefit. If they believe that this would be worth doing, this suggests that, in their case, this benefit factually outweighs this burden.

Certain people claim that one burden cannot be factually outweighed by another, if they come within different lives. These people claim that such interpersonal comparisons make no sense. If I lose my finger, and you lose your life, it makes no sense to claim that your loss may be greater than mine. I shall here ignore this view.

Others claim that burdens and benefits in different lives cannot be *morally* weighed. I shall consider one part of this claim. This is the claim that someone's burden cannot be morally outweighed by mere benefits to someone else. I say *mere* benefits, because the claim is not intended to deny that it can be right to burden someone so as to benefit someone else. This might be required by distributive justice. We can rightly tax the rich to benefit the poor. What the claim denies is that such acts can be justified solely upon the utilitarian ground that the benefit is greater than the burden.

This claim often takes qualified forms. It can be restricted to great burdens, or be made to claim that, to outweigh one person's burden, the benefit to others must be much greater. I shall here discuss this claim in its simplest form, for most of my remarks could be applied to the other forms. Rawls puts the claim as follows: 'The reasoning which balances the gains and losses of different persons . . . is excluded'.[105] I call this the *Objection to Balancing*.

This objection rests in part on a different claim. This is that someone's burden cannot be *compensated* by benefits to someone else. I call this the *Claim about Compensation*. With one qualification, this claim is clearly true. Our burdens can, in a sense, be compensated by benefits to those we love. But they cannot be compensated by benefits to other people.

The Claim about Compensation cannot be denied. If becoming Reductionists affected our view about this claim, the effects would be these. We might, first, extend the claim even within single lives. Thus, in the example that I gave, we might claim that the child's burden cannot be compensated by benefits to his adult self. Or we might claim that there cannot here be *full* compensation. This might support the claim that the child's burden would be morally outweighed only if the benefit to his adult self was *much* greater. These claims would be like the claims that, when the psychological connections have been markedly reduced, we deserve less punishment for, and are less committed by, the actions of our earlier selves. Those claims treat weakly connected parts of one life as, in some respects, or to some degree, like different lives. Such claims therefore change the scope of our principles. If we believe that, between some parts of the same life, there can be either less or even no compensation, we are changing the scope of the Claim about Compensation. Given the content of the Reductionist View, this is a change of scope in the right direction.

We might, next, give this claim less weight. Our ground would be the one that I earlier suggested. Compensation presupposes personal identity. On the Reductionist View, we believe that the fact of personal identity over time is less deep, or involves less. We may therefore claim that this fact has less moral importance. Since this fact is presupposed by compensation, we may claim that the fact of compensation is itself morally less important. Though it cannot be denied, the Claim about Compensation may thus be given less weight. (Here is another example of this distinction. That it is unjust to punish the innocent cannot be denied. But the claim can be given no weight. Our inability to deny this claim does not force us to believe in desert. If we do not believe in desert, perhaps because we are Determinists, we can claim, 'Though it is bad to punish the innocent, punishing the guilty is just as bad'.)

Return now to the Objection to Balancing. Unlike compensation, the concept of *greater moral weight than* does not presuppose personal identity. The Objection to Balancing *can* therefore be denied.

The denial might be put like this: 'Our burdens cannot be compensated by mere benefits to someone else. But they may be morally outweighed by such benefits. It may still be right to give the benefits rather than relieve the burdens. Burdens are morally outweighed by benefits if they are factually outweighed by these benefits. All that is needed is that the benefits be greater than the burdens. It is unimportant, in itself, to whom both come.'

This is the Utilitarian's reply. It would be his reply to the many arguments in which the Objection to Balancing seems not to be distinguished from the Claim about Compensation. Thus Rawls uses the phrase, 'cannot be justified by, or compensated for by'.[106] And Perry writes, 'The happiness of a million somehow fails utterly to compensate or even to mitigate the torture of one'.[107] This undeniable claim Perry seems to equate with the Objection to Balancing. This is a mistake.

The Reductionist View gives some support to the Utilitarian's reply. The Objection to Balancing rests, in part, on the Claim about Compensation. The Reductionist View supports both the claim that there is less scope for compensation, and the claim that compensation has less moral weight. Compensation has less scope and less weight than it would have had if the Non-Reductionist View had been true. Since compensation is, in these two ways, morally less important, there is less support for the Objection to Balancing. We can therefore claim that the Utilitarian's reply is more plausible than it would be if the Non-Reductionist View was true. But this claim does not imply that we must accept the Utilitarian View. This is why this claim gives only *some* support to this view.

These claims can be explained in a different way. Even those who object to balancing think that it can be justified to impose burdens on a child for his own greater benefit later in his life. Their claim is that a person's burden, while it can be morally outweighed by benefits to him, cannot *ever* be outweighed by mere benefits to others. This is held to be so even if the benefits are far greater than the burden. The claim thus gives to the boundaries between lives—or to the fact of non-identity—overwhelming significance. It allows within the same life what, over different lives, it totally forbids.

This claim would be more plausible on the Non-Reductionist View. Since the fact of identity is, here, thought to be deeper, the fact of non-identity could more plausibly seem to have such importance. On this view, it is a deep truth that all of a person's life is as much his life. If we are impressed by this truth—by the unity of each life—the boundaries between lives will seem to be deeper. This supports the claim that, in the moral calculus, these boundaries cannot be crossed. On the Reductionist View, we are less impressed by this truth. We regard the unity of each life as, in its nature, less deep, and as a matter of degree. We may therefore think the boundaries between lives to be less like those between, say, the squares on a chess-board—dividing what is all pure white from what is all jet black—and more like the boundaries between different countries. They may then seem less morally important.

It may be objected:

The Reductionist claims that the parts of each life are less deeply unified. But he does not claim that there is more unity between different lives. The boundaries between lives are, on his view, just as deep.

We could answer:

If some unity is less deep, so is the corresponding disunity. The fact that we live different lives is the fact that we are not the same person. If the fact of personal identity is less deep, so is the fact of non-identity. There are not two different facts here, one of which is less deep on the Reductionist View, while the other remains as deep. There is merely one fact, and this fact's denial. The separateness of persons is the denial that we are all the same person. If the fact of personal identity is less deep, so is this fact's denial.

116. AN ARGUMENT FOR GIVING LESS WEIGHT TO THE PRINCIPLE OF EQUALITY

Turn now to a different principle, that of equal distribution as between equally deserving people. Most of us give to the Principle of Equality only a certain weight. We believe, for instance, that inequality can be justified if it produces a sufficient gain in the total sum of benefits.

On this view, we do not reject the Utilitarian Principle. We agree that every increase in the sum of benefits has moral value. But we insist that weight must also be given to the Principle of Equality. Though every gain in welfare matters, it also matters *who* gains. Certain distributions are, we claim, morally preferable. We ought to give some priority to helping those who are worst off, through no fault of theirs. And we should try to aim for equality.

Utilitarians would reply: 'These claims are plausible. But the policies they recommend are the very policies that tend to increase total welfare. This coincidence suggests that we ought to change our view about the status of these claims.[108] We should regard them not as checks upon, but as guides to, our ultimate moral aim. We should indeed value equal distribution. But the value lies in its typical effects.'

This reply might be developed in the following way. Most of us believe that a mere difference in when something happens, if it does not affect the nature of what happens, cannot be morally significant. Certain answers to the question 'When?' are of course important. We cannot ignore the timing of events. And it is even plausible to claim that, if we are planning when to give or to receive benefits, we should aim for an equal distribution over time. But we aim for this only because of its effects. We do not believe that the equality of benefits at different times is, as such, morally important.

Utilitarians might say: 'If it does not, as such, matter *when* something happens, why does it matter *to whom* it happens? Both of these are mere differences in position. What is important is the *nature* of what happens. When we choose between social policies, we need to be concerned only with how great the benefits and burdens will be. Where they come, whether in space, or in time, or as between people, has in itself no importance.'

Part of the disagreement is, then, this. Non-Utilitarians take the question 'Who?' to be quite unlike the question 'When?' If they are asked for the simplest possible description of the morally relevant facts, their description may be tenseless, but it must be personal. They might say, for instance, 'A benefit to this person, the same benefit to someone else, an equally great burden to the first person. . .' Utilitarians would instead merely say, 'A benefit, the same benefit, an equally great burden. . .'

There are many different arguments for and against these two positions. I am asking: would becoming Reductionists support one of these positions?

I claim that it would. On the Reductionist View, it is more plausible to compare the question 'Who?' to the question 'When?', and to describe the moral data in the impersonal way. This is more plausible than it would be if the Non-Reductionist View was true.

Return to Hume's comparison. Most of us believe that the existence of a nation does not involve anything more than the existence of a number of associated people. We do not deny the reality of nations. But we do deny that they are separately, or independently, real. Their existence just involves the existence of their citizens, living together in certain ways, on their territories.

This belief supports certain moral claims. If there is nothing more to a nation than its citizens, it is less plausible to regard the nation as itself a primary object of duties, or possessor of rights. It is more plausible to focus upon the citizens, and to regard them less as citizens, more as people. We may therefore, on this view, think a person's nationality less morally important.

On the Reductionist View, we hold similar beliefs. We believe the existence of a person to involve nothing more than the occurrence of interrelated mental and physical events. We do not deny that people exist. And we agree that we are not series of events—that we are not thoughts and actions, but thinkers and agents. But this is true only because we describe our lives by ascribing thoughts and actions to people. As I have argued, we could give a complete description of our lives that was impersonal: that did not claim that persons exist. We deny that we are not just conceptually distinct from our bodies, actions, and experiences, but also separately real. We deny that a person is an entity whose existence is separate from the existence of his brain and body, and the occurrence of his experiences. And we deny that a person's continued existence is a deep further fact, that must be all-or-nothing, and that is different from the facts of physical and psychological continuity.

These beliefs support certain moral claims. It becomes more plausible, when thinking morally, to focus less upon the person, the subject of experiences, and instead to focus more upon the experiences themselves. It becomes more plausible to claim that, just as we are right to ignore whether people come from the same or different nations, we are right to ignore whether experiences come within the same or different lives.

Consider the relief of suffering. Suppose that we can help only one of two people. We shall achieve more if we help the first; but it is the second who, in the past, suffered more. Those who believe in equality may decide to help the second person. This will be less effective; so the amount of suffering in the two people's lives will, in sum, be greater; but the amounts in each life will be made more equal. If we accept the Reductionist View, we may decide otherwise. We may decide to do the most we can to relieve suffering.

To suggest why, we can vary the example. Suppose that we can help only one of two nations. The one that we can help the most is the one whose history was, in earlier centuries, more fortunate. Most of us would not believe that it could be right to allow mankind to suffer more, so that the suffering was more equally divided between the histories of different nations. In trying to relieve suffering, we do not regard nations as the morally significant units.

On the Reductionist View, we compare the lives of people to the histories of nations. We may therefore think the same about them. We may believe that, when we are trying to relieve suffering, neither persons nor lives are the morally significant units. We may again decide to aim for the least possible suffering, whatever its distribution.

'Utilitarianism', Rawls writes, 'does not take seriously the distinction between persons'.[109] If 'the separateness of persons . . . is *the* basic fact for morals',[110] this is a grave charge. I have tried to show how, if they appeal to the truth about the nature of persons, Utilitarians may offer some defence.

As I have claimed, this cannot be a complete defence. The question is whether we should accept the principles of distributive justice, and, if so, how much weight we ought to give these principles. I claim that, on the Reductionist View, it is more plausible to give these principles less weight, or even no weight. But this only means, 'more plausible than it would be on the Non-Reductionist View'. It is compatible with my claim that, even on the Reductionist View, it is implausible to give these principles no weight.

The argument that I have given cannot show that we must accept the Utilitarian view. It can only yield conclusions about relative plausibility. When we cease to believe that persons are separately existing entities, the Utilitarian view becomes more plausible. Is the gain in plausibility great, or small? My argument leaves this question open.

117. A MORE EXTREME ARGUMENT

I end with another argument. When we cease to be Non-Reductionists, we do not merely believe that personal identity is less deep, or involves less. We come to believe that it does not involve the deep further fact.

Return to the question of what justifies maximizing within one life. Why can it be right to impose on children great burdens, so that they will receive even greater benefits when they are adults? Some believe that this is justified only by the unity of these people's lives. When the children are grown up, their burdens will be fully compensated by these greater benefits.

A different claim might be made. It might be claimed that what justifies maximization is the deep further fact. Only this fact enables some later benefit to compensate some earlier burden. Compensation does not merely presuppose personal identity. On this view, it presupposes the deep further fact.[111]

Return to the case where I divide. Assume that we believe the Non-Reductionist View, and that we suppose that I shall be Righty. Before the division, I had more than my fair share of many resources, living for many years in luxury. After the division, I and Lefty will each get less than a fair share. This is claimed to be justified, in my case, because it will have the result that in my life as a whole I shall receive a fair share. My lesser share now was fully compensated in advance by my greater share before the division.

Could we plausibly claim the same about Lefty? Does psychological continuity make possible compensation, even in the absence of personal identity? It is defensible to answer:

> No. Lefty never enjoyed a larger share. *He* did not enjoy these years of luxury. It is irrelevant that he can quasi-remember *your* enjoyment of this luxury. It is irrelevant that he is physically and psychologically continuous with someone who had more than his fair share, at a time when Lefty did not exist. It would now be unfair to give Lefty less than a fair share. In the absence of personal identity, psychological continuity cannot make compensation possible.

Suppose next that we come to believe the Reductionist View. We had claimed, defensibly, that only the deep further fact makes compensation possible. We had claimed that, as the case of Lefty shows, physical and psychological continuity cannot by themselves make compensation possible. We now believe that there is no deep further fact, and that personal identity just consists in these two kinds of continuity. Since we could defensibly claim that only this further fact makes compensation possible, and there is no such fact, we can defensibly conclude that there cannot be compensation over time. We can claim that a benefit at one time cannot provide compensation for a burden at another time, even when both come within the same life. There can only be simultaneous compensation, as when the pain of exposing my face to a freezing wind is fully compensated by the sight of the sublime view from the mountain I have climbed. [112]

Since this conclusion is defensible, this argument is stronger than the arguments supporting the Utilitarian View. Those arguments did not show this view to be defensible. But, as with the earlier arguments appealing to the further fact, though this new conclusion is defensible, it can also be defensibly denied.

This new conclusion involves another change in the scope of our distributive principles. The application of these principles depends upon the scope of possible compensation. On the argument just given, there cannot be compensation over time, even within the same life. Consider the Principle of Equality. On the argument just given, we should not aim for equality either between different lives, or between the different parts of the same life. We should aim for equality between the states that people are in at particular times.

Nagel makes some relevant remarks:

Note that these thoughts do not *depend* on any idea of personal identity over time, though they can *employ* such an idea. All that is needed to evoke them is a distinction between persons at a time. The impulse to distributive equality arises so long as we can distinguish between two experiences being had by two persons, and their being had by one person. The criteria of personal identity over time merely determine the size of the units over which a distributive principle operates. That, briefly, is what I think is wrong with Parfit's account of the relation between distributive justice and personal identity.[113]

In the account that Nagel discusses, I distinguished between changing the scope of our moral principles, and giving these principles a different weight. And I claimed that, if we move from the Non-Reductionist to the Reductionist View, we can more plausibly give these principles greater scope, but less weight.[114] Nagel claims that the effect can only be to give these principles greater scope—that I am wrong to claim that a change of view may also affect the weight that we give to these principles. But what is wrong with this claim? Why should the effect be only on the scope? A change of view about the facts often makes it plausible to give to a moral principle a different weight. If this cannot be plausible in the present case, this needs to be shown. I believe that it could not be shown.

The argument that I am now discussing supports the kind of effect that Nagel endorses. It appeals to a change of view about the criterion of personal identity. In becoming Reductionists, we cease to believe that personal identity involves the deep further fact. The argument claims that what compensation presupposes is not personal identity on any view, but personal identity on the Non-Reductionist View. Compensation presupposes the deep further fact. Psychological continuity, in the absence of this fact, cannot make possible compensation over time.

If this is not possible, what will our distributive principles tell us to do? They will roughly coincide with *Negative Utilitarianism*: the view which gives priority to the relief of suffering. Nagel talks of the *unit* over which a distributive principle operates. If this unit is the whole of a person's life, as is assumed by Rawls and many others, a Principle of Equality will tell us to try to help those people who are worst off. If the unit is the state of any person at a particular time, a Principle of Equality will tell us to try to make better, not the lives of the people who are worst off, but the worst states that people are in.

Egalitarians may disagree about the respect in which we should try to make people equal. Should we aim for equality of welfare, or equality of resources? Suppose that we once believed that the relevant units for distributive principles are complete lives, and that we now believe that the relevant units are the states that people are in at particular times. This change in our view makes it less plausible to claim that our concern should be for equality of resources. Someone with very great resources may be in a very bad state at a particular time, and his great resources may do nothing to alleviate this state. If the relevant units are the states that people are in at particular times, it is more plausible to claim that what we should be concerned with is the quality of people's experiences, at these times. What will correspond to those who are worst off, on the Rawlsian view, will be the particular experiences that are the worst, or the most undesirable. These will be experiences either of great physical pain, or of great mental anguish or distress. Our Principle of Equality will tell us to try to prevent or improve these experiences, and to give this priority over promoting desirable experiences.

When we change the unit from whole lives to people's experiences at each particular time, should we give a different weight to our distributive principles? At least one writer claims that we should. Wachsberg claims that, if we change the scope of our distributive principles in this way, we should give these principles *no* weight. If the relevant units are the experiences that people have at any particular time, Wachsberg believes that distributive principles lose their plausibility.[115] I believe, more cautiously, that these principles become less plausible. It seems to me plausible that the relief of suffering should have greater weight than it is given by ordinary or

Positive Utilitarians. But it does not seem plausible that it should have absolute priority, or even far greater weight.

Haksar suggests one ground for thinking that, on the Reductionist View, distributive principles should have less weight. He writes:

> . . . if Parfit's . . . theory is correct, if there are no persistent individuals (except in a trivial sense), why should we get so worked up about suffering in the world? Suffering would still be real, but how much worse it is when (intrinsically) the very same individual keeps suffering on and on.[116]

On the argument that I am now discussing, there cannot be compensation over time without the deep further fact. Since there is no such fact, there is no such compensation. If we make this claim, we cannot also claim that a certain amount of suffering will be a greater evil if, rather than being scattered over different lives, it is concentrated and prolonged in the life of some particular person. The claim that this is a greater evil assumes that the relevant unit stretches over time, which this argument denies. If the badness of suffering is only the badness that it has at particular times, Haksar's claim seems plausible. On this view, though concentrated and prolonged suffering is bad, it is not as bad as it would be if the Non-Reductionist View was true. This reduces the plausibility of Negative Utilitarianism.

These remarks can be easily misunderstood. On any view either about personal identity, or about the scope of distributive principles, someone's suffering will in fact be greater, and harder to bear, if this person knows that the suffering will be prolonged. This provides a powerful reason, even for Positive Utilitarians, to give priority to trying to prevent such prolonged suffering. My remarks have been about whether we have a *further* moral reason to give priority to preventing suffering, whether or not it is prolonged. That we have such a reason is what the Negative Utilitarian claims. And we have found that, if we change the scope of our Principle of Equality, so that the relevant units are the states that people are in at particular times, our Principle of Equality roughly coincides with the Principle of Negative Utility. What weight ought we to give to these two principles? Unlike Wachsberg, I believe that these principles remain plausible. But I believe that they have less plausibility than they had when we believed that the relevant unit was the whole of a person's life. And this is partly for Haksar's reason. If the unity of a person's life does not involve the deep further fact, it is a defensible claim that there cannot be compensation over time. And, if this kind of unity cannot make possible compensation, it cannot make possible the full evil that prolonged suffering would be, if the Non-Reductionist View was true.

118. CONCLUSIONS

I shall now summarise the main claims of this long discussion. I asked how a change of view about the nature of personal identity might affect our emotions, and our beliefs about rationality and morality. And I have just discussed how, if we change our view, this might affect our beliefs about the

Principle of Equality, and other distributive principles. I argued earlier that, if we move from the Non-Reductionist to the Reductionist View, it becomes more plausible to claim that there is less scope for compensation within the same life. Thus it is more plausible to claim that great burdens imposed upon a child cannot be compensated, or fully compensated, by somewhat greater benefits in this child's adult life. When we thus extend distributive principles so that they cover, both whole lives, and weakly connected parts of the same life, this makes these principles more important. This is a move away from the Utilitarian View.

I have just discussed a second argument for a change in the scope of our distributive principles. This claims that only the deep further fact makes possible compensation over different parts of a life. Since there is no such fact, we ought, as Nagel suggests, to change 'the size of the units over which a distributive principle operates'. The units shrink to people's states at particular times. This conclusion is defensible, but so is its denial.

Given this change in its scope, the Principle of Equality roughly coincides with Negative Utilitarianism. If we apply the Principle of Equality to people's states at particular times, should we give as much weight to this principle? I suggest that we should not.

A third argument claimed that, whatever their scope, we should give less weight to distributive principles. These principles are often held to be founded on the separateness, or non-identity, of different persons. This fact is less deep on the Reductionist View, since identity is less deep. It does not involve the further fact in which we are inclined to believe. Since the fact on which they are founded is seen to be less deep, it is more plausible to give less weight to distributive principles. If we cease to believe that persons are separately existing entities, and come to believe that the unity of a life involves no more than the various relations between the experiences in this life, it becomes more plausible to be more concerned about the quality of experiences, and less concerned about whose experiences they are. This gives some support to the Utilitarian View, making it more plausible than it would have been if the Non-Reductionist View had been true. Even if we are not aware of this, most of us are inclined to believe in the Non-Reductionist View. The impersonality of Utilitarianism is therefore less implausible than most of us believe.

I earlier discussed whether, if we change our view, we had as much reason to be specially concerned about our own futures. Some writers claim that only the deep further fact justifies this special concern, and that, since there is no such fact, we have no reason to be specially concerned about our own futures. This Extreme Claim is defensible, but so is its denial.

I then advanced another argument against the Self-interest Theory about Rationality. This appealed to the fact that part of what is important in personal identity, psychological connectedness, holds over time to reduced degrees. When some important fact holds to a reduced degree, it cannot be irrational to believe this fact to have less importance. It therefore cannot be irrational to be less concerned, now, about those parts of our future to which we are now less closely connected. Given the truth of the Reductionist View, this refutes the Classical Self-interest Theory.

On the Revised Self-interest Theory, which is not refuted, it may not be irrational to do what one knows will be worse for oneself. Great imprudence may not be irrational. If such acts are not irrational, they need to be criticized. I claimed that we should regard them as morally wrong. If such acts are morally wrong, this strengthens the case for paternalism.

If we become Reductionists, we can plausibly claim that a fertilized ovum is not a human being, and that it becomes a human being only gradually during pregnancy. This supports the claim that abortion is not wrong in the first few weeks, and that it only gradually becomes wrong.

I also considered what, on the Reductionist View, we should believe about desert and commitments. Some writers claim that only the deep further fact carries with it desert, and that, since there is no such fact, we cannot deserve to be punished for past crimes. This conclusion seemed defensible, but so did its denial. I then argued for the general claim that, if the connections are weaker between a criminal now and himself at the time of his crime, he deserves less punishment. Similar claims applied to commitment.

We ought to be Reductionists. If this is a change of view, it supports several changes in our beliefs about both rationality and morality. There are other changes that I have not discussed.[117]

The effect on our emotions may be different for different people. For those who accept the Extreme Claims, the effect may be disturbing. I described the effect on me. Since I deny these claims, I find the truth liberating, and consoling. It makes me less concerned about my own future, and my death, and more concerned about others. I welcome this widening in my concern.

PART FOUR

FUTURE GENERATIONS

16

THE NON-IDENTITY PROBLEM

THERE is another question about personal identity. Each of us might never have existed. What would have made this true? The answer produces a problem that most of us overlook.

One of my aims in Part Four is to discuss this problem. My other aim is to discuss the part of our moral theory in which this problem arises. This is the part that covers how we affect future generations. This is the most important part of our moral theory, since the next few centuries will be the most important in human history.

119. HOW OUR IDENTITY IN FACT DEPENDS ON WHEN WE WERE CONCEIVED

What would have made it true that some particular person would never have existed? With one qualification, I believe

The Time-Dependence Claim: If any particular person had not been conceived when he was in fact conceived, it is *in fact* true that he would never have existed.

This claim is not obviously true. Thus one woman writes:

It is always fascinating to speculate on who we would have been if our parents had married other people.[1]

In wondering who she would have been, this woman ignores the answer: 'No one'.

Though the Time-Dependence Claim is not obviously true, it is not controversial, and it is easy to believe. It is thus unlike the Reductionist View about personal identity over time. This is one of several competing views, and is hard to believe. The Time-Dependence Claim is not about personal identity over time. It is about a different though related subject: personal identity in different possible histories of the world. Several views about this subject are worth discussing. But the Time-Dependence Claim is *not* one of these views. It is a claim that is true on *all* of these views.

As I have said, the claim should be qualified. Each of us grew from a particular pair of cells: an ovum and the spermatozoon by which, out of millions, it was fertilized. Suppose that my mother had not conceived a child at the time when in fact she conceived me. And suppose that she had conceived a child within a few days of this time. This child would have grown from the same particular ovum from which I grew. But even if this child had been conceived only a few seconds earlier or later, it is almost certain that he would have grown from a different spermatozoon. This child would have had some but not all of my genes. Would this child have been me?

We are inclined to believe that any question about our identity must have an answer, which must be either Yes or No. As before, I reject this view. There are cases in which our identity is indeterminate. What I have just described may be such a case. If it is, my question has no answer. It is neither true nor false that, if these events had occurred, I would never have existed. Though I can always ask, 'Would I have existed?', this would here be an empty question.

These last claims are controversial. Since I want my Time-Dependence Claim not to be controversial, I shall set aside these cases. The claim can become

(TD2) If any particular person had not been conceived within a month of the time when he was in fact conceived, he would in fact never have existed.

I claim that this is *in fact* true. I do *not* claim that it is *necessarily* true. The different views about this subject make competing claims about what is necessary. It is because I claim less that my claim is not controversial. Those who disagree about what *could* have happened may agree about what *would in fact* have happened. As I shall argue, the holders of all plausible views would agree with me.

These views make claims about the *necessary properties* of each particular person. Some of a person's necessary properties are had by everyone: these are the properties that are necessary to being a person. What concerns us here are the *distinctive* necessary properties of each particular person. Suppose I claim that *P* is one of Kant's distinctive necessary properties. This means that Kant could not have lacked P, and that only Kant could have had P.

According to

The Origin View, each person has this distinctive necessary property: that of having grown from the particular pair of cells from which this person in fact grew.[2]

This property cannot be *fully* distinctive. Any pair of identical twins *both* grew from such a pair of cells. And any fertilized ovum might have later split, and produced twins. The Origin View must be revised to meet this problem. But I need not discuss this revision. It is enough for my purposes that, on this view, Kant could not have grown from a different pair of cells.

It is irrelevant that, because there can be twins, it is false that *only* Kant could have grown from this pair of cells.

Holders of the Origin View would accept my claim that, if Kant had not been conceived within a month of the time when he was conceived, he would in fact never have existed. If he had not been conceived in that month, no child would in fact have grown from the particular pair of cells from which he grew. (This claim makes an assumption both about the distinctive necessary properties of this pair of cells, and about the human reproductive system. But these assumptions are not controversial.)

According to certain other views, Kant could have grown from a different pair of cells. On

> *The Featureless Cartesian View,* Kant was a particular Cartesian Ego, which had *no* distinctive necessary properties.

On this view, a person's identity has no connections with his physical and mental characteristics. Kant might have been me, and vice versa, though, if this had happened, no one would have noticed any difference. It is at worst mildly controversial to claim, as I did, that we should reject *this* version of the Cartesian View.

Two other views are closely related. On

> *The Descriptive View,* each person has several distinctive necessary properties. These are this person's most important distinctive properties, and they do not include having grown from a particular pair of cells.

In the case of Kant, these properties would include his authorship of certain books. One version of this view does not claim that Kant must have had *all* these properties. Anyone with most of these properties would have been Kant.

On

> *The Descriptive Name View,* every person's name means 'the person who . . .'. For us now, 'Kant' means 'the person who wrote the *Critique of Pure Reason,* etc'. A particular person's necessary properties are those that would be listed when we explain the meaning of this person's name.

Both this and the Descriptive View might be combined with the other version of Cartesianism. Kant might be claimed to be the Cartesian Ego whose distinctive necessary properties include the authorship of certain books. But the two Descriptive Views need not add this claim.[3]

One objection to the Descriptive Views is that each person's life could have been very different. Kant could have died in his cradle. Since this is possible, the authorship of certain books cannot be one of Kant's necessary properties.

One reply to this objection retreats to a weaker claim. It could be said:

Though this property is not necessary, it is distinctive. Kant might not have written these books. But, in any possible history in which a single person wrote these books, this person would have been Kant.

I need not discuss whether this, or some other reply, meets this objection. Even if the objection can be met, my Time-Dependence Claim is true.

On both Descriptive Views, Kant could have grown from a different pair of cells, or even had different parents. This would have happened if Kant's mother had not conceived a child when she conceived him, and some other couple had conceived a child who later wrote the *Critique of Pure Reason*, etc. On the Descriptive Views, this child would have been Kant. He would not have been *called* Kant. But this does not worry holders of these views. They would claim that, if this had happened, Kant would have had both different parents and a different name.

Though they believe that this might have happened, most holders of the Descriptive Views would accept my claim that it would *not in fact* have happened. If they claim that it *would* have happened, they must accept an extreme version of Tolstoy's view, stated in the epilogue of *War and Peace*, that history does not depend on the decisions made by particular people. On this view, if Napoleon's mother had remained childless, history would have provided a 'substitute Napoleon', who would have invaded Russia in 1812. And, if Kant's mother had remained childless, history would have provided another author of the *Critique of Pure Reason*. This view is too implausible to be worth discussing.

There is another way in which holders of the Descriptive Views might reject my claim. They might claim that Kant's necessary properties were far less distinctive. They might for instance merely be: being his mother's first child. This claim meets the objection that each person's life might have been very different. But this claim is also too implausible to be worth discussing. I am the second of my mother's three children. This claim implies absurdly that, if my mother had conceived no child when she in fact conceived me, I would have been my younger sister.

Consider next the possible history in which the Descriptive Views seem most plausible. Suppose that Kant's mother had not conceived a child when she conceived him, and that one month later she conceived a child who was exactly like Kant. This child would have grown from a different pair of cells; but by an amazing coincidence, of a kind that never actually happens, this child would have had all of Kant's genes. And suppose that, apart from the fact and the effects of being born later, this child would have lived a life that was just like Kant's, writing the *Critique of Pure Reason*, etc.

On the Descriptive Views, this child would have been Kant. Holders of the Origin View might object:

Kant was a particular person. In your imagined possible history, you have not shown that you are referring to *this* particular person. In this imagined history, there would have been someone who was *exactly like* this person. But exact similarity is not the same as numerical identity, as is shown by any two exactly similar things.

These remarks explain why the Origin View refers to the particular pair of cells from which a person grew.

A fifth view also makes such a direct reference. On

The Backward Variation View, this reference need not be to the point of origin, or to the cells from which a person grew. The reference can be made at any time in this person's life. By making such a reference, we can describe how this person might have had a different origin.

Consider a holder of this view who, in 1780, is attending one of Kant's lectures. This person might claim:

Kant is the person standing *there*. Kant might have had different parents, and lived a different life up until the recent past. For this to have been what happened, all that is needed is that this different life would have led Kant to be now standing there.

This view must make some further claims. But it meets the objection that, to justify a claim of identity, we need more than similarity. Holders of the Origin View therefore need a different objection to the Backward Variation View. For my purposes, I need not decide between these views.

On the Backward Variation View, Kant might have had a different origin. But holders of this view would accept my claim that, in fact, this would not have happened. They would agree that, if Kant had not been conceived within a month of the time when he was conceived, he would in fact never have existed.

I have now described all of the views about our identity in different possible histories.[5] I discuss in endnote 6 how these views are related to the different views about our identity over time. On all of the plausible views, my Time-Dependence Claim is true. This claim applies to everyone. You were conceived at a certain time. It is in fact true that, if you had not been conceived within a month of that time, *you* would never have existed.

120. THE THREE KINDS OF CHOICE

Unless we, or some global disaster, destroy the human race, there will be people living later who do not now exist. These are *future people*. Science has given to our generation great ability both to affect these people, and to predict these effects.

Two kinds of effect raise puzzling questions. We can affect the identities of future people, or *who* the people are who will later live. And we can affect the number of future people. These effects give us different kinds of choice.

In comparing any two acts, we can ask:

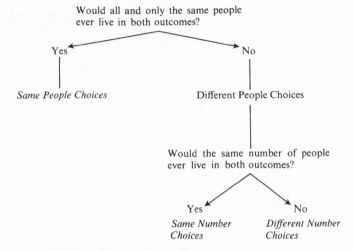

Different Number Choices affect both the number and the identities of future people. Same Number Choices affect the identities of future people, but do not affect their number. Same People Choices affect neither.

121. WHAT WEIGHT SHOULD WE GIVE TO THE INTERESTS OF FUTURE PEOPLE?

Most of our moral thinking is about Same People Choices. As I shall argue, such choices are not as numerous as most of us assume. Very many of our choices will in fact have some effect on both the identities and the number of future people. But in most of these cases, because we cannot predict what the particular effects would be, these effects can be morally ignored. We can treat these cases as if they were Same People Choices.

In some cases we can predict that some act either may or will be against the interests of future people. This can be true when we are making a Same People Choice. In such a case, whatever we choose, all and only the same people will ever live. Some of these people will be future people. Since these people will exist whatever we choose, we can either harm or benefit these people in a quite straightforward way.

Suppose that I leave some broken glass in the undergrowth of a wood. A hundred years later this glass wounds a child. My act harms this child. If I had safely buried the glass, this child would have walked through the wood unharmed.

Does it make a moral difference that the child whom I harm does not now exist?

On one view, moral principles cover only people who can *reciprocate*, or harm and benefit each other. If I cannot be harmed or benefited by this child, as we can plausibly suppose, the harm that I cause this child has no moral importance. I assume that we should reject this view.[7]

Some writers claim that, while we ought to be concerned about effects on future people, we are morally justified in being less concerned about effects in the further future. This is a common view in welfare economics, and cost-benefit analysis. On this view, we can *discount* the more remote effects of our acts and policies, at some rate of *n* per cent per year. This is called the *Social Discount Rate*.

Suppose we are considering how to dispose safely of the radio-active matter called *nuclear waste*. If we believe in the Social Discount Rate, we shall be concerned with safety only in the nearer future. We shall not be troubled by the fact that some nuclear waste will be radio-active for thousands of years. At a discount rate of five per cent, one death next year counts for more than a billion deaths in 500 years. On this view, catastrophes in the further future can now be regarded as morally trivial.

As this case suggests, the Social Discount Rate is indefensible. Remoteness in time roughly correlates with some important facts, such as predictability. But, as I argue in Appendix F, these correlations are too rough to justify the Social Discount Rate. The present moral importance of future events does *not* decline at a rate of *n* per cent per year. Remoteness in time has, in itself, no more significance than remoteness in space. Suppose that I shoot some arrow into a distant wood, where it wounds some person. If I should have known that there might be someone in this wood, I am guilty of gross negligence. Because this person is far away, I cannot identify the person whom I harm. But this is no excuse. Nor is it any excuse that this person is far away. We should make the same claims about effects on people who are temporally remote.

122. A YOUNG GIRL'S CHILD

Future people are, in one respect, unlike distant people. We can affect their identity. And many of our acts have this effect.

This fact produces a problem. Before I describe this problem, I shall repeat some preliminary remarks. I assume that one person can be worse off than another, in morally significant ways, and by more or less. But I do not assume that these comparisons could be, even in principle, precise. I assume that there is only rough or partial comparability. On this assumption, it could be true of two people that neither is worse off than the other, but this would not imply that these people are exactly equally well off.

'Worse off' could be taken to refer, either to someone's level of happiness, or more narrowly to his standard of living, or, more broadly, to the quality of his life. Since it is the broadest, I shall often use the phrase 'the quality of life'. I also call certain lives 'worth living'. This description can be ignored by those who believe that there could not be lives that are not worth living. But, like many other people, I believe that there could be such lives. Finally, I extend the ordinary use of the phrase 'worth living'. If one of two people would have a lower quality of life, I call his life to this extent 'less worth living'.

When considering future people, we must answer two questions:

(1)   If we cause someone to exist, who will have a life worth living, do we thereby benefit this person?

(2)   Do we also benefit this person if some act of ours is a remote but necessary part of the cause of his existence?

These are difficult questions. If we answer Yes to both, I shall say that we believe *that causing to exist can benefit*.

Some people answer Yes to (1) but No to (2). These people give their second answer because they use 'benefit' in its ordinary sense. As I argued in Section 25, we ought for moral purposes to extend our use of 'benefit'. If we answer Yes to (1) we should answer Yes to (2).

Many people answer No to both these questions. These people might say: 'We benefit someone if it is true that, if we had not done what we did, this would have been worse for this person. If we had not caused someone to exist, this would *not* have been worse for this person.'

I believe that, while it is defensible to answer No to both these questions, it is also defensible to answer Yes to both. For those who doubt this second belief I have written Appendix G. Since I believe that it is defensible both to claim and to deny that causing to exist can benefit, I shall discuss the implications of both views.

Consider

> *The 14-Year-Old Girl.* This girl chooses to have a child. Because she is so young, she gives her child a bad start in life. Though this will have bad effects throughout this child's life, his life will, predictably, be worth living. If this girl had waited for several years, she would have had a different child, to whom she would have given a better start in life.

Since such cases are becoming common, they raise a practical problem.[8] They also raise a theoretical problem.

Suppose that we tried to persuade this girl that she ought to wait. We claimed: 'If you have a child now, you will soon regret this. If you wait, this will be better for you.' She replied: 'This is my affair. Even if I am doing what will be worse for me, I have a right to do what I want.'

We replied: 'This is not entirely your affair. You should think not only of yourself, but also of your child. It will be worse for him if you have him now. If you have him later, you will give him a better start in life.'

We failed to persuade this girl. She had a child when she was 14, and, as we predicted, she gave him a bad start in life. Were we right to claim that her decision was worse for her child? If she had waited, this particular child would never have existed. And, despite its bad start, his life is worth living. Suppose first that we do *not* believe that causing to exist can benefit. We should ask, 'If someone lives a life that is worth living, is this worse for this person than if he had never existed?' Our answer must be No. Suppose next that we believe that causing to exist *can* benefit. On this view, this girl's decision benefits her child.

On both views, this girl's decision was not worse for her child. When we see this, do we change our mind about this decision? Do we cease to believe that it would have been better if this girl had waited, so that she could give to her first child a better start in life? I continue to have this belief, as do most of those who consider this case. But we cannot defend this belief in the natural way that I suggested. We cannot claim that this girl's decision was worse for her child. What is the objection to her decision? This question arises because, in the different outcomes, different people would be born. I shall therefore call this the *Non-Identity Problem*.[9]

It may be said:

In one sense, this girl's decision *was* worse for her child. In trying to persuade this girl not to have a child now, we can use the phrase 'her child' and the pronoun 'he' to cover *any* child that she might have. These words need not refer to one particular child. We can truly claim: 'If this girl does not have her child now, but waits and has him later, *he* will not be the same particular child. If she has him later, he will be a different child.' By using these words in this way, we can explain why it would be better if this girl waits. We can claim:

(A) The objection to this girl's decision is that it will probably be worse for her child. If she waited, she would probably give him a better start in life.

Though we can truly make this claim, it does *not* explain the objection to this girl's decision. This becomes clear after she has had her child. The phrase 'her child' now naturally refers to this particular child. And this girl's decision was *not* worse for *this* child. Though there is a sense in which (A) is true, (A) does not appeal to a familiar moral principle.

On one of our familiar principles, it is an objection to someone's choice that this choice will be worse for, or be against the interests of, any other particular person. If we claim that this girl's decision was worse for her child, we cannot be claiming that it was worse for a particular person. We cannot claim, of the girl's child, that her decision was worse for *him*. We must admit that, in claim (A), the words 'her child' do not refer to her child.

(A) is not about what is good or bad for any of the particular people who ever live. (A) appeals to a new principle, that must be explained and justified.

If (A) seems to appeal to a familiar principle, this is because it has two senses. Here is another example. A general shows military skill if, in many battles, he always makes his the winning side. But there are two ways of doing this. He might win victories. Or he might always, when he is about to lose, change sides. A general shows no military skill if it is only in the second sense that he always makes his the winning side.

To what principle does (A) appeal? We should state the principle in a way that shows the kind of choice to which it applies. These are Same Number Choices, which affect the identities of future people, but do not affect their number. We might suggest

> *The Same Number Quality Claim*, or *Q*: If in either of two possible outcomes the same number of people would ever live, it would be worse if those who live are worse off, or have a lower quality of life, than those who would have lived.

This claim is plausible. And it implies what we believe about the 14-Year-Old Girl. The child that she has now will probably be worse off than a child she could have had later would have been, since this other child would have had a better start in life. If this is true, Q implies that this is the worse of these two outcomes. Q implies that it would have been better if this girl had waited, and had a child later.

We may shrink from claiming, of this girl's actual child, that it would have been better if he had never existed. But, if we claimed earlier that it would be better if this girl waits, this is what we must claim. We cannot consistently make a claim and deny this same claim later. If (1) in 1990 it *would be* better if this girl waits and has a child later, then (2) in 2020 it *would have been* better if she had waited and had a child later. And (2) implies (3) that it would have been better if the child who existed had not been her actual child. If we cannot accept (3), we must reject (1).

I suggest that, on reflection, we can accept (3). I believe that, if *I* was the actual child of this girl, I could accept (3). (3) does not imply that my existence is *bad*, or intrinsically morally undesirable. The claim is merely that, since a child born later would probably have had a better life than mine, it would have been better if my mother had waited, and had a child later. This claim need not imply that I ought rationally to regret that my mother had *me*, or that she ought rationally to regret this. Since it would have been better if she had waited, she ought perhaps to have some moral regret. And it is probably true that she made the outcome worse for herself. But, even if this is true, it does not show that she ought rationally to regret her act, all things considered. If she loves me, her actual child, this is enough to block the claim that she is irrational if she does not have such regret.[10] Even when it implies a claim like (3), I conclude that we can accept Q.

Though Q is plausible, it does not solve the Non-Identity Problem. Q covers only the cases where, in the different outcomes, the same number of people would ever live. We need a claim that covers cases where, in the different outcomes, different numbers would ever live. The Non-Identity Problem can arise in these cases.

Because Q is restricted, it could be justified in several different ways. There are several principles that imply Q, but conflict when applied to Different Number Choices. We shall need to decide which of these principles, or which set of principles, we ought to accept. Call what we ought to accept *Theory X*. X will solve the Non-Identity Problem in Different Number Choices. And X will tell us how Q should be justified, or more fully explained.

In the case of the 14-Year-Old Girl, we are not forced to appeal to Q. There are other facts to which we could appeal, such as the effects on other people. But the problem can arise in a purer form.

123. HOW LOWERING THE QUALITY OF LIFE MIGHT BE WORSE FOR NO ONE

Suppose that we are choosing between two social or economic policies. And suppose that, on one of the two policies, the standard of living would be slightly higher over the next century. This effect implies another. It is not true that, whichever policy we choose, the same particular people will exist in the further future. Given the effects of two such policies on the details of our lives, it would increasingly over time be true that, on the different policies, people married different people. And, even in the same marriages, the children would increasingly over time be conceived at different times. As I have argued, children conceived more than a month earlier or later would in fact be different children. Since the choice between our two policies would affect the timing of later conceptions, some of the people who are later born would owe their existence to our choice of one of the two policies. If we had chosen the other policy, these particular people would never have existed. And the proportion of those later born who owe their existence to our choice would, like ripples in a pool, steadily grow. We can plausibly assume that, after one or two centuries, there would be no one living in our community who would have been born whichever policy we chose. (It may help to think about this question: how many of us could truly claim, 'Even if railways and motor cars had never been invented, I would still have been born'?)

How does this produce a problem? Consider

Depletion. As a community, we must choose whether to deplete or conserve certain kinds of resources. If we choose Depletion, the quality of life over the next two centuries would be slightly higher than it would have been if we had chosen Conservation. But it would later, for many centuries, be much lower than it would have been if we had chosen Conservation. This would be because, at the start of this period, people would have to find alternatives for the resources that we had depleted. It is worth distinguishing two versions of this case. The effects of the different policies would be as shown below.

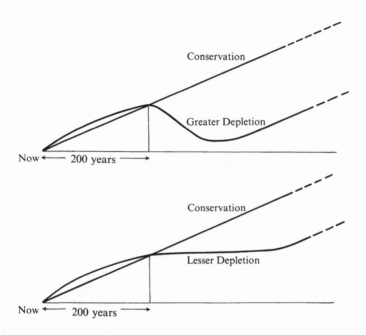

We could never know, in such detail, that these would be the effects of two policies. But this is no objection to this case. Similar effects would sometimes be predictable. Nor does it matter that this imagined case is artificially simple, since this merely clarifies the relevant questions.

Suppose that we choose Depletion, and that this has either of the two effects shown in my diagram. Is our choice worse for anyone?

Because we chose Depletion, millions of people have, for several centuries, a much lower quality of life. This quality of life is much lower, not than it is now, but than it would have been if we had chosen Conservation. These people's lives are worth living; and, if we had chosen Conservation, these particular people would never have existed. Suppose that we do not assume that causing to exist can benefit. We should ask, 'If particular people live lives that are worth living, is this worse for these people than if they had never existed?' Our answer must be No. Suppose next that we do assume that causing to exist can benefit. Since these future people's lives will be worth living, and they would never have existed if we had chosen Conservation, our choice of Depletion is not only not worse for these people: it *benefits* them.

On both answers, our choice will not be worse for these future people. Moreover, when we understand the case, we know that this is true. We know that, even if it greatly lowers the quality of life for several centuries, our choice will not be worse for anyone who ever lives.

Does this make a moral difference? There are three views. It might make all the difference, or some difference, or no difference. There might be no objection to our choice, or some objection, or the objection may be just as strong.

Some believe that *what is bad must be bad for someone*. On this view, there is no objection to our choice. Since it will be bad for no one, our choice cannot have a bad effect. The great lowering of the quality of life provides no moral reason not to choose Depletion.

Certain writers accept this conclusion.[11] But it is very implausible. Before we consider cases of this kind, we may accept the view that what is bad must be bad for someone. But the case of Depletion shows, I believe, that we must reject this view. The great lowering of the quality of life must provide *some* moral reason not to choose Depletion. This is believed by most of those who consider cases of this kind.

If this is what we believe, we should ask two questions:

(1) What is the moral reason not to choose Depletion?

(2) Does it make a moral difference that this lowering of the quality of life will be worse for no one? Would this effect be *worse*, having greater moral weight, if it *was* worse for particular people?

Our need to answer (1), and other similar questions, I call the Non-Identity Problem. This problem arises because the identities of people in the further future can be very easily affected. Some people believe that this problem is a mere quibble. This reaction is unjustified. The problem arises because of superficial facts about our reproductive system. But, though it arises in a superficial way, it is a real problem. When we are choosing between two social or economic policies, of the kind that I described, it is *not true* that, in the further future, the same people will exist whatever we choose. It is therefore *not true* that a choice like Depletion will be against the interests of future people. We cannot dismiss this problem with the pretence that this *is* true.

We partly answer question (1) if we appeal to Q. On this claim, if the numbers would be the same, it would be worse if those who live have a lower quality of life than those who would have lived. But the problem can arise in cases where, in the different outcomes, there would be different numbers of people. To cover these cases we need Theory X. Only X will explain how Q should be justified, and provide a full solution to our problem.

124. WHY AN APPEAL TO RIGHTS CANNOT WHOLLY SOLVE THE PROBLEM

Can we solve our problem by appealing to people's rights? Reconsider the 14-Year-Old Girl. By having her child so young, she gives him a bad start in life. It might be claimed: 'The objection to this girl's decision is that she violates her child's right to a good start in life'.

Even if this child has this right, it could not have been fulfilled. This girl could not have had *this* child when she was a mature woman. Some would claim that, since this child's right could not be fulfilled, this girl cannot be claimed to violate his right. The objector might reply: 'It is wrong to cause someone to exist if we know that this person will have a right that cannot be fulfilled.' Can this be the objection to this girl's decision?[13]

Some years ago, a British politician welcomed the fact that, in the previous year, there had been fewer teenage pregnancies. A middle-aged man wrote in anger to *The Times*. He had been born when his mother was only 14. He admitted that, because his mother was so young, his early years had been hard for both of them. But his life was now well worth living. Was the politician suggesting that it would have been better if he had never been born? This suggestion seemed to him outrageous.

The politician was, implicitly, suggesting this. On the politician's view, it would have been better if this man's mother had waited for several years before having children. I believe that we should accept this view. But can we plausibly explain this view by claiming that this angry man had a right that was not fulfilled?

I believe that we cannot. Suppose that I have a right to privacy. I ask you to marry me. If you accept, you are not acting wrongly, by violating my right to privacy. Since I am glad that you act as you do, with respect to you I *waive* this right. A similar claim applies to the writer of the angry letter to *The Times*. On the suggestion made above, this man has a right to be born by a mature woman, who would give him a good start in life. This man's mother acted wrongly because she caused him to exist with a right that cannot be fulfilled. But this man's letter shows that he was glad to be alive. He denies that his mother acted wrongly because of what she did to him. If we had claimed that her act was wrong, because he has a right that cannot be fulfilled, he could have said, 'I waive this right'. This would have undermined our objection to his mother's act.

It would have been better if this man's mother had waited. But this is not because of what she did to her actual child. It is because of what she could have done for any child that she could have had when she was mature. The objection must be that, if she had waited, she could have given to some other child a better start in life.

Return now to the Case of Depletion. Suppose that we choose Greater Depletion. More than two centuries later, the quality of life is much lower than it would have been if we had chosen Conservation. But the people who will then be living will have a quality of life that is about as high as ours will on average be over the next century. Do these people have rights to which an objector can appeal?

It might be claimed that these people have a right to their share of the resources that we have depleted. But people do not have rights to a share of a particular resource. Suppose that we deplete some resource, but invent technology that will enable our successors, though they lack this resource, to have the same range of opportunities. There would be no objection to what we have done. The most that could be claimed is that people in each generation have a right to an equal range of opportunities, or to an equally high quality of life.[14]

If we choose Greater Depletion, those who live more than two centuries later will have fewer opportunities, and a lower quality of life, than some earlier and some later generations. If people have a right to equal opportunities, and an equally high quality of life, an appeal to these rights may provide some objection to our choice. Those who live more than two centuries later could not possibly have had greater opportunities, or a higher quality of life. If we had chosen otherwise, these people would never have existed. Since their rights could not be fulfilled, we may not violate their rights. But, as before, it may be objected that we cause people to exist with rights that cannot be fulfilled.

It is not clear that this is a good objection. If these people knew the facts, they would not regret that we acted as we did. If they were glad to be alive, they might react like the man who wrote to *The Times*. They might waive their rights. But, since we cannot assume that this is how they would all react, an appeal to their rights may provide some objection to our choice.

Can this appeal provide an objection to our choice of *Lesser* Depletion? In this case, those who live more than two centuries later have a much higher quality of life than we do now. Can we claim that these people have a *right* to an *even higher* quality of life? I believe that, on any plausible theory about rights, the answer would be No.

It will help to imagine away the Non-Identity Problem. Suppose that our reproductive system was very different. Suppose that, whatever policies we followed, the very same people would live more than two centuries later. The objection to our choice would then be that, for the sake of small benefits to ourselves and our children, we prevent many future people from receiving very much greater benefits. Since these future people would be better off than us, we would not be acting unjustly. The objection to our choice would have to appeal to the Principle of Utility.

Could this objection appeal to rights? Only if, like Godwin, we present Utilitarianism as a theory about rights. On Godwin's view, everyone has a right to get what the Principle of Utility implies that he should be given. Most of those who believe in rights would reject this view. Many people explain rights as what *constrain*, or *limit*, the Principle of Utility. These people claim that it is wrong to violate certain rights, even if this would greatly increase the net sum of benefits minus burdens. On such a theory, some weight is given to the Principle of Utility. Since such a theory is not Utilitarian, this principle is better called the *Principle of Beneficence*. This principle is one part of such a theory, and the claim that we have certain rights is a different part of this theory. I shall assume that, if we believe in rights, this is the kind of moral theory that we accept.

Return to the case where we imagine away the Non-Identity Problem. If we reject Godwin's view, we could not object to the choice of Lesser Depletion by appealing to the rights of those who will live in the further future. Our objection would appeal to the Principle of Beneficence. The objection would be that, for the sake of small benefits to ourselves and our children, we deny, to people better off than us, very much greater benefits. In calling this an objection, I need not claim that it shows our choice to be wrong. I am merely claiming that, since we deny these people very much greater benefits, this provides *some* moral reason not to make this choice.

If we now restore our actual reproductive system, this reason disappears. Consider the people who will live more than two centuries later. Our choice of Lesser Depletion does not deny these people *any* benefit. If we had chosen Conservation, this would not have benefited these people, since they would never have existed.

When we assume away the Non-Identity Problem, our reason not to make this choice is explained by an appeal, not to people's rights, but to the Principle of Beneficence. When we restore the Non-Identity Problem, this reason disappears. Since this reason appealed to the Principle of Beneficence, what the problem shows is that this principle is inadequate, and must be revised. We need a better account of beneficence, or what I call Theory X.

One part of our moral theory appeals to beneficence; another part appeals to people's rights. We should therefore not expect that an appeal to rights could fill the gap in our inadequate Principle of Beneficence. We should expect that, as I have claimed, appealing to rights cannot wholly solve the Non-Identity Problem.[15]

125. DOES THE FACT OF NON-IDENTITY MAKE A MORAL DIFFERENCE?

In trying to revise our Principle of Beneficence—trying to find Theory X— we must consider cases where, in the different outcomes, different numbers of people would exist. Before we turn to these cases, we can ask what we believe about the other question that I mentioned. Our choice of Depletion will be worse for no one. Does this make a moral difference?

We may be able to remember a time when we were concerned about effects on future generations, but had overlooked the Non-Identity Problem. We may have thought that a policy like Depletion would be against the interests of future people. When we saw that this was false, did we become less concerned about effects on future generations?

When I saw the problem, I did not become less concerned. And the same is true of many other people. I shall say that we accept the *No-Difference View*.

It is worth considering a different example:

The Medical Programmes. There are two rare conditions, *J* and *K*, which cannot be detected without special tests. If a pregnant woman has Condition J, this will cause the child she is carrying to have a certain handicap. A simple treatment would prevent this effect. If a woman has Condition K when she conceives a child, this will cause this child to have the same particular handicap. Condition K cannot be treated, but always disappears within two months. Suppose next that we have planned two medical programmes, but there are funds for only one; so one must be cancelled. In the first programme, millions of women would be tested during pregnancy. Those found to have Condition J would be treated. In the second programme, millions of women would be tested when they intend to try to become pregnant. Those found to have Condition K would be warned to postpone conception for at least two months, after which this incurable condition will have disappeared. Suppose finally that we can predict that these two programmes would achieve results in as many cases. If there is Pregnancy Testing, 1,000 children a year will be born normal rather than handicapped. If there is Preconception Testing, there will each year be born 1,000 normal children rather than a 1,000, different, handicapped children.

Would these two programmes be equally worthwhile? Let us note carefully what the difference is. As a result of either programme, 1,000 couples a year would have a normal rather than a handicapped child. These would be different couples, on the two programmes. But since the numbers would be the same, the effects on the parents and on other people would be morally equivalent. If there is a moral difference, this can only be in the effects on the children.

Note next that, in judging these effects, we need have no view about the moral status of a foetus. We can suppose that it would take a year before either kind of testing could begin. When we choose between the two programmes, none of the children has yet been conceived. And all those who are conceived will become adults. We are therefore considering effects, not on present foetuses, but on future people. Assume next that the handicap in question, though it is not trivial, is not so severe as to make life doubtfully worth living. Even if it can be against our interests to have been born, this is not true of those born with this handicap.

Since we cannot afford both programmes, which should we cancel? Under one description, both would have the same effect. Suppose that Conditions J and K are the only causes of this handicap. The incidence is now 2,000 among those born in each year. Either programme would halve the incidence; the rate would drop to 1,000 a year. The difference is this. If we decide to cancel Pregnancy Testing, it will be true of those who are later born handicapped that, but for our decision, they would have been cured. Our decision will be worse for all these people. If instead we decide to cancel Pre-Conception Testing, there will later be just as many people who are born with this handicap. But it would not be true of these people that, but for our decision, they would have been cured. These people owe their existence to our decision. If we had not decided to cancel Pre-Conception Testing, the parents of these handicapped children would not have had *them*. They would have later had different children. Since the lives of these handicapped children are worth living, our decision will not be worse for any of them.

Does this make a moral difference? Or are the two programmes equally worthwhile? Is all that matters morally how many future lives will be lived by normal rather than handicapped people? Or does it also matter whether these lives would be lived by the very same people?

We should add one detail to the case. If we decide to cancel Pregnancy Testing, those who are later born handicapped might know that, if we had made a different decision, they would have been cured. Such knowledge might make their handicap harder to bear. We should therefore assume that, though it is not deliberately concealed, these people would not know this fact.

With this detail added, I judge the two programmes to be equally worthwhile. I know of some people who do not accept this claim; but I know of more who do.

My reaction is not merely an intuition. It is the judgement that I reach by reasoning as follows. Whichever programme is cancelled, there will later be just as many people with this handicap. These people would be different in the two outcomes that depend on our decision. And there is a claim that applies to only one of these two groups of handicapped people. Though they do not know this fact, the people in one group could have been cured. I therefore ask: 'If there will be people with some handicap, the fact that they are handicapped is bad. Would it be *worse* if, unknown to them, their handicap could have been cured?' This would be worse if this fact made these people worse off than people whose handicap could *not* have been cured. But this fact does not have this effect. If we decide to cancel Pregnancy Testing, there will be a group of handicapped people. If we decide to cancel Pre-Conception Testing, there will be a different group of handicapped people. The people in the first group would not be worse off than the people in the second group would have been. Since this is so, I judge these two outcomes to be morally equivalent. Given the details of the case, it seems to me irrelevant that one of the groups but not the other could have been cured.

This fact *would* have been relevant if curing this group would have reduced the incidence of this handicap. But, since we have funds for only one programme, this is not true. If we choose to cure the first group, there will later be just as many people with this handicap. Since curing the first group would not reduce the number who will be handicapped, we ought to choose to cure this group only if they have a stronger claim to be cured. And they do not have a stronger claim. If we *could* cure the second group, they would have an equal claim to be cured. If we chose to cure the first group, they would merely be luckier than the second group. Since they would merely be luckier, and they do not have a stronger claim to be cured, I do not believe that we ought to choose to cure these people. Since it is also true that, if we choose to cure these people, this will not reduce the number of people who will be handicapped, I conclude that the two programmes are equally worthwhile. If Pre-Conception Testing would achieve results in a few more cases, I would judge it to be the better programme.[16]

This matches my reaction to our choice of Depletion. I believe that it would be bad if there would later be a great lowering of the quality of life. And I believe that it would not be *worse* if the people who later live would themselves have existed if we had chosen Conservation. The bad effect would not be worse if it had been, in this way, worse for any particular people. In considering both cases, I accept the No-Difference View. So do many other people.

I have described two cases in which I, and many others, accept the No-Difference View. If we are right to accept this view, this may have important theoretical implications. This depends on whether we believe that, if we cause someone to exist who will have a life worth living, we thereby benefit this person. If we believe this, I cannot yet state the implications of the No-Difference View, since these will depend on decisions that I have not yet discussed. But suppose we believe that causing someone to exist cannot benefit this person. If this is what we believe, and we accept the No-Difference View, the implications are as follows.

I have suggested that we should appeal to

Q: If in either of two possible outcomes the same number of people would ever live, it will be worse if those who live are worse off, or have a lower quality of life, than those who would have lived.

Consider next

The Person-Affecting View, or *V*: It will be worse if people are affected for the worse.

In Same People Choices, Q and V coincide. When we are considering these choices, those who live are the same in both outcomes. If these people are worse off, or have a lower quality of life, they are affected for the worse, and vice versa.[17] Since Q and V here coincide, it will make no difference to which we appeal.

The two claims conflict only in Same Number Choices. These are what this chapter has discussed. Suppose that we accept the No-Difference View. In considering these choices, we shall then appeal to Q *rather than* V. If we choose Depletion, this will lower the quality of life in the further future. According to Q, our choice has a bad effect. But, because of the facts about identity, our choice will be bad for no one. V does not imply that our choice has a bad effect. Would this effect be worse if it *was* worse for particular people? If we appealed to V rather than Q, our answer would be Yes. But, since we believe the No-Difference View, we answer No. We believe that V gives the wrong answer here. And V gives the wrong answer in the case of the Medical Programmes. Q describes the effects that we believe to be bad. And we believe that it makes no moral difference whether these effects are also bad according to V. V draws moral distinctions where, on our view, no distinctions should be drawn.

In Same People Choices, Q and V coincide. In Same Number Choices, where these claims conflict, we accept Q rather than V. When we make these two kinds of choice, we shall therefore have no use for V.

There remain the Different Number Choices, which Q does not cover. We shall here need Theory X. I have not yet discussed what X should claim. But we can predict the following. X will imply Q in Same Number Choices.

We can also predict that X will have the same relation to V. In Same People Choices, X and V will coincide. It will here make no difference to which we appeal. These are the choices with which most of our moral thinking is concerned. This explains the plausibility of V. This part of morality, the part concerned with beneficence, or human well-being, is usually thought of in what I shall call *person-affecting* terms. We appeal to people's interests—to what is good or bad for those people whom our acts affect. Even after we have found Theory X, we might continue to appeal to V in most cases, merely because it is more familiar. But in some cases X and V will conflict. They may conflict when we are making Same and Different Number Choices. And, whenever X and V conflict, we shall appeal to X *rather than* V. We shall believe that, if some effect is bad according to X, it makes no moral difference whether it is also bad according to V. As before, V draws a moral distinction where, on our view, no distinction should be drawn. V is like the claim that it is wrong to enslave whites, or to deny the vote to adult males. We shall thus conclude that this part of morality, the part concerned with beneficence and human well-being, cannot be explained in person-affecting terms. Its fundamental principles will not be concerned with whether our acts will be good or bad for those people whom they affect. Theory X will imply that an effect is bad if it is bad for people. But this will not be *why* this effect is bad.

Remember next that these claims assume that causing to exist cannot benefit. This assumption is defensible. If we make this assumption, these claims show that many moral theories need to be revised, since these theories imply that it must make a moral difference whether our acts are good or bad for those people whom they affect.[18] And we may need to revise our beliefs about certain common cases. One example might be abortion. But most of our moral thinking would be unchanged. Many significant relations hold only between particular people. These include our relations to those to whom we have made promises, or owe gratitude, or our parents, pupils, patients, clients, and (if we are politicians) those whom we represent. My remarks do not apply to such relations, or to the special obligations which they produce. My remarks apply only to our Principle of Beneficence: to our general moral reason to benefit other people, and to protect them from harm.

Since my remarks apply only to this principle, and we shall have changed our view only in some cases, this change of view may seem unimportant. This is not so. Consider once again this (too grandiose) analogy: In ordinary cases we can accept Newton's Laws. But not in all cases. And we now accept a different theory.

126. CAUSING PREDICTABLE CATASTROPHES IN THE FURTHER FUTURE

In this section, rather than pursuing the main line of my argument, I discuss a minor question. In a case like that of Depletion, we cannot wholly solve the Non-Identity Problem by an appeal to people's rights. Is this also true in a variant of the case, where our choice causes a catastrophe? Since this is a minor question, this section can be ignored, except by those who do not believe that Depletion has a bad effect. Consider

The Risky Policy. As a community, we must choose between two energy policies. Both would be completely safe for at least three centuries, but one would have certain risks in the further future. This policy involves the burial of nuclear waste in areas where, in the next few centuries, there is no risk of an earthquake. But since this waste will remain radio-active for thousands of years, there will be risks in the distant future. If we choose this Risky Policy, the standard of living will be somewhat higher over the next century. We do choose this policy. As a result, there is a catastrophe many centuries later. Because of geological changes to the Earth's surface, an earthquake releases radiation, which kills thousands of people. Though they are killed by this catastrophe, these people will have had lives that are worth living. We can assume that this radiation affects only people who are born after its release, and that it gives them an incurable disease that will kill them at about the age of 40. This disease has no effects before it kills.

Our choice between these two policies will affect the details of the lives that are later lived. In the way explained above, our choice will therefore affect who will later live. After many centuries there would be no one living in our community who, whichever policy we chose, would have been born. Because we chose the Risky Policy, thousands of people are later killed. But if we had chosen the alternative Safe Policy, these particular people would never have existed. Different people would have existed in their place. Is our choice of the Risky Policy worse for anyone?

We should ask, 'If people live lives that are worth living, even though they are killed by some catastrophe, is this worse for these people than if they had never existed?' Our answer must be No. Though it causes a predictable catastrophe, our choice of the Risky Policy will be worse for no one.

Some may claim that our choice of Depletion does not have a bad effect. This cannot be claimed about our choice of the Risky Policy. Since this choice causes a catastrophe, it clearly has a bad effect. But our choice will not be bad for, or worse for, any of the people who later live. This case forces us to reject the view that a choice cannot have a bad effect if this choice will be bad for no one.

In this case, the Non-Identity Problem may seem easier to solve. Though our choice is not worse for the people struck by the catastrophe, it might be claimed that we harm these people. And the appeal to people's rights may here succeed.

We can deserve to be blamed for harming others, even when this is not worse for them. Suppose that I drive carelessly, and in the resulting crash cause you to lose a leg. One year later, war breaks out. If you had not lost this leg, you would have been conscripted, and killed. My careless driving therefore saves your life. But I am still morally to blame.

This case reminds us that, in assigning blame, we must consider not actual but predictable effects. I knew that my careless driving might harm others, but I could not know that it would in fact save your life. This distinction might apply to our choice of the Risky Policy. Suppose we know that, if we choose this policy, this may in the distant future cause many accidental deaths. But we have overlooked the Non-Identity Problem. We mistakenly believe that, whichever policy we choose, the very same people will later live. We therefore believe that our choice of the Risky Policy may be very greatly against the interests of some future people. If we believe this, our choice can be criticized. We can deserve blame for doing what we *believe* may be greatly against the interests of other people. This criticism stands even if our belief is false—just as I am as much to blame even if my careless driving will in fact save your life.

Suppose that we cannot find Theory X, or that X seems less plausible than the objection to doing what may be greatly against the interests of other people. It may then be better if we conceal the Non-Identity Problem from those who will decide whether we increase our use of nuclear energy. It may be better if these people believe falsely that such a policy may, by causing a catastrophe, be greatly against the interests of some of those who will live in the distant future. If these people have this false belief, they may be more likely to reach the right conclusions.

We have lost this false belief. We realize that, if we choose the Risky Policy, our choice will *not* be worse for those people whom the catastrophe later kills. Note that this is not a lucky guess. It is not like predicting that, if I cause you to lose a leg, this will later save you from death in the trenches. We know that, if we choose the Risky Policy, this may in the distant future cause many people to be killed. But we also know that, if we had chosen the Safe Policy, the people who are killed would never have been born. Since these people's lives will be worth living, we *know* that our choice will not be worse for them.

If we know this, we cannot be compared to a careless driver. What is the objection to our choice? Can it be wrong to harm others, when we know that our act will not be worse for the people harmed? This might be wrong if we could have asked these people for their consent, but have failed to do so. By failing to ask these people for their consent, we infringe their autonomy. But this cannot be the objection to our choice of the Risky Policy. Since we could not possibly communicate with the people living many centuries from now, we cannot ask for their consent.

When we cannot ask for someone's consent, we should ask instead whether this person would later regret what we are doing. Would the people who are later killed regret our choice of the Risky Policy? Let us suppose that these people know all of the facts. From an early age they know that, because of the release of radiation, they have an incurable disease that will kill them at about the age of 40. They also know that, if we had chosen the Safe Policy, they would never have been born. These people would regret the fact that they will die young. But, since their lives are worth living, they would not regret the fact that they were ever born. They would therefore not regret our choice of the Risky Policy.

Can it be wrong to harm others, when we know *both* that if the people harmed knew about our act, they would not regret this act, *and* that our act will not be worse for these people than anything else that we could have done? How might we know that, though we are harming someone, our act will not be worse for this person? There are at least two kinds of case:

(1) Though we are harming someone, we may also know that we are giving to this person some fully compensating benefit. We could not know this unless the benefit would clearly outweigh the harm. But, if this is so, what we are doing will be better for this person. In this kind of case, if we

are also not infringing this person's autonomy, there may be no objection to our act. There may be no objection to our harming someone when we know both that this person will have no regrets, and that our act will be clearly better for this person. In English Law, surgery was once regarded as justifiable grievous bodily harm. As I argued in Section 25, we should revise the ordinary use of the word 'harm'. If what we are doing will not be worse for some other person, or will even be better for this person, we are not, in a morally relevant sense, harming this person.

If we assume that causing to exist can benefit, our choice of the Risky Policy is, in its effects on those killed, like the case of the surgeon. Though our choice causes these people to be killed, since it also causes them to exist with a life worth living, it gives them a benefit that outweighs this harm. This suggests that the objection to our choice cannot be that it harms these people.

We may instead assume that causing to exist cannot benefit. On this assumption, our choice of the Risky Policy does not give to the people whom it kills some fully compensating benefit. Our choice is not *better* for these people. It is merely *not worse* for them.

(2) There is another kind of case in which we can know that, though we are harming someone on the ordinary use of 'harm', this will not be worse for this person. These are the cases that involve overdetermination. In these cases we know that, if we do not harm someone, this person will be harmed at least as much in some other way. Suppose that someone is trapped in a wreck and about to be burnt to death. This person asks us to shoot him, so that he does not die painfully. If we kill this person we are not, in a morally relevant sense, harming him.

Such a case cannot show that there is no objection to our choice of the Risky Policy, since it is not relevantly similar. If the catastrophe did not occur, the people killed would have lived for many more years. There is a quite different reason why our choice of the Risky Policy is not worse for these people.

Could there be a case in which we kill some existing person, knowing what we know when we choose the Risky Policy? We must know (*a*) that this person will learn but not regret the fact that we have done something that will cause him to be killed. And we must know (*b*) that, though this person would otherwise have lived a normal life for many more years, causing him to be killed will be neither better nor worse for him. ((*b*) is what we know about the effects of our choice of the Risky Policy, if we assume that, in doing what is a necessary part of the cause of the existence of the people killed by the catastrophe, we cannot be benefiting these people.)

Suppose that we kill some existing person, who would otherwise have lived a normal life for many more years. In such a case, we could not *know* that (*b*) is true. Even if living for these many years would be neither better nor worse for this person, this could never be predicted. There cannot be a case where we kill some existing person, knowing what we know when we choose the Risky Policy. A case that is relevantly similar must involve causing someone to be killed who, if we had acted otherwise, would never have existed.

Compare these two cases:

Jane's Choice. Jane has a congenital disease, that will kill her painlessly at about the age of 40. This disease has no effects before it kills. Jane knows that, if she has a child, it will have this same disease. Suppose that she can also assume the following. Like herself, her child would have a life that is worth living. There are no children who need to be but have not been adopted. Given the size of the world's population when this case occurs (perhaps in some future century), if Jane has a child, this will not be worse for other people. And, if she does not have this child, she will be unable to raise a child. She cannot persuade someone else to have an extra child, whom she would raise. (These assumptions give us the relevant question.) Knowing these facts, Jane chooses to have a child.

Ruth's Choice. Ruth's situation is just like Jane's, with one exception. Her congenital disease, unlike Jane's, kills only males. If Ruth pays for the new technique of in vitro fertilization, she would be certain to have a daughter whom this disease would not kill. She decides to save this expense, and takes a risk. Unluckily, she has a son, whose inherited disease will kill him at about the age of 40.

Is there a moral objection to Jane's choice? Given the assumptions in the case, this objection would have to appeal to the effect on Jane's child. Her choice will not be worse for this child. Is there an objection to her choice that appeals to this child's rights? Suppose we believe that each person has a right to live a full life. Jane knows that, if she has a child, his right to a full life could not possibly be fulfilled. This may imply that Jane does not violate this right. But the objection could be restated. It could be said: 'It is wrong to cause someone to exist with a right that cannot be fulfilled. This is why Jane acts wrongly.'

Is this a good objection? If I was Jane's child, my view would be like that of the man who wrote to *The Times*. I would regret the fact that I shall die young. But, since my life is worth living, I would not regret that my mother caused me to exist. And I would deny that her act was wrong because of what it did to me. If I was told that it *was* wrong, because it caused me to exist with a right that cannot be fulfilled, I would *waive* this right.

If Jane's child waived his right, that might undermine this objection to her choice. But, though *I* would waive this right, I cannot be certain that, in all such cases, this is what such a child would do. If Jane's child does not waive his right, an appeal to this right may perhaps provide some objection to her choice.

Turn now to Ruth's choice. There is clearly a greater objection to *this* choice. This is because Ruth has a different alternative. If Jane does not have a child, she will not be able to raise a child; and one fewer life will be lived. Ruth's alternative is to pay for the technique that will give her a different child whom her disease will not kill. She chooses to save this expense, knowing that the chance is one in two that her child will be killed by this disease.

Even if there is an objection to Jane's choice, there is a greater objection to Ruth's choice. This objection cannot appeal only to the effects on Ruth's actual child, since these are just like the effects of Jane's choice on Jane's child. The objection to Ruth's choice must appeal in part to the possible effect on a different child who, by paying for the new technique, she could have had. The appeal to this effect is not an appeal to anyone's rights.

Return now to our choice of the Risky Policy. If we choose this policy, this may cause people to exist who will be killed in a catastrophe. We know that our choice would not be worse for these people. But, if there is force in the objection to Jane's choice, this objection would apply to our choice. By choosing the Risky Policy, we may cause people to exist whose right to a full life cannot be fulfilled.

The appeal to these people's rights may provide some objection to our choice. But it cannot provide the whole objection. Our choice is, in one respect, unlike Jane's. Her alternative was to have no child. Our alternative is like Ruth's. If we had chosen the Safe Policy, we would have had different descendants, none of whom would have been killed by released radiation.

The objection to Ruth's choice cannot appeal only to her child's right to a full life. The same is therefore true of the objection to our choice of the Risky Policy. This objection must in part appeal to the effects on the possible people who, if we had chosen differently, would have lived. As before, the appeal to rights cannot wholly solve the Non-Identity problem. We must also appeal to a claim like Q, which compares two different sets of possible lives.

It may be objected: 'When Ruth conceives her child, it inherits the disease that will deny it a full life. Because this child's disease is inherited in this way, it cannot be claimed that Ruth's choice kills her child. If we choose the Risky Policy, the causal connections are less close. Because the connections are less close, our choice kills the people who later die from the effects of released radiation. That we kill these people is the full objection to our choice.'

This objection I find dubious. Why is there a greater objection to our choice because the causal connections are less close? The objection may be correct in what it claims about our ordinary use of 'kill'. But, as I argued in Section 25, this use is morally irrelevant. Since that argument may not convince, I add

> *The Risky Cure for Infertility. Ann* cannot have a child unless she takes a certain treatment. If she takes this treatment, she will have a son, who will be healthy. But there is a risk that this treatment will give her a rare

disease. This disease has the following features. It is undetectable, and does not harm women, but it can infect one's closest relatives. The following is therefore true. If Ann takes this treatment and has a healthy son, there is a chance of one in two that she will later infect her son in a way that will kill him when he is about forty. Ann chooses to take this treatment, and she does later infect her son with this fatal disease.

On the objection stated above, there is a strong objection to Ann's choice, which does not apply to Ruth's choice. Because the causal connections are less close, Ann's choice kills her son. And she knew that the chance was one in two that her choice would have this effect. Ruth knows that that there is the same chance that her child will die at about the age of 40. But, because the causal connections are so close, her choice does not kill her son. According to this objection, this difference has great moral relevance.

This is not plausible. Ruth and Ann both know that, if they act in a certain way, there is a chance of one in two that they will have sons who will be killed by a disease at about the age of forty. The causal story is different. But this does not make Ann's choice morally worse. I believe that this example shows that we should reject this last objection.

The objector might say: 'I deny that, by choosing to take the Risky Cure, Ann kills her son'. But, if the objector denies this, he cannot claim that, by choosing the Risky Policy, we kill some people in the distant future. The causal connections take the same form. Each choice produces a side-effect which later kills people who owe their existence to this choice.

If this objection fails, as I believe, my earlier claim is justified. It is morally significant that, if we choose the Risky Policy, our choice is like Ruth's rather than Jane's. It is morally significant that, if we had chosen otherwise, different people would have lived who would not have been killed. Since this is so, the objection to our choice cannot appeal only to the rights of those who actually later live. It must also appeal to a claim like Q, which compares different sets of possible lives. As I claimed earlier, the appeal to rights cannot wholly solve the Non-Identity Problem.

127. CONCLUSIONS

I shall now summarize what I have claimed. It is in fact true of everyone that, if he had not been conceived within a month of the time when he was conceived, he would never have existed. Because this is true, we can easily affect the identities of future people, or *who* the people are who will later live. If a choice between two social policies will affect the standard of living or the quality of life for about a century, it will affect the details of all the lives that, in our community, are later lived. As a result, some of those who later live will owe their existence to our choice of one of these two policies. After one or two centuries, this will be true of everyone in our community.

This fact produces a problem. One of these two policies may, in the further future, cause a great lowering of the quality of life. This would be the effect of the policy I call Depletion. This effect is bad, and provides a moral reason not to choose Depletion. But, because of the fact just mentioned, our choice of Depletion will be worse for no one. Some people believe that a choice cannot have bad effects if this choice will be worse for no one. The Case of Depletion shows that we must reject this view. And this is shown more forcefully by the Case of the Risky Policy. One effect of choosing this policy is a catastrophe that kills thousands of people. This effect is clearly bad, even though our choice will be worse for no one.

Since these two choices will be worse for no one, we need to explain why we have a moral reason not to make these choices. This problem arises because, in the different outcomes, different people would exist. I therefore call this the Non-Identity Problem.

I asked whether we can solve this problem by appealing to people's rights. I argued that, even in the case of the Risky Policy, the objection to our choice cannot appeal only to people's rights. The objection must in part appeal to a claim like Q, which compares different possible lives. And we cannot plausibly appeal to rights in explaining the objection to our choice of Lesser Depletion. Even after the great lowering of the quality of life, those who will be living will be much better off than we are now. These people cannot be claimed to have a *right* to the even higher quality of life that different people would have enjoyed if we had chosen Conservation. If we imagine away the Non-Identity Problem, the objection to our choice would appeal to our Principle of Beneficence. To solve the Non-Identity Problem, we must revise this principle.

One revised principle is Q, the Same Number Quality Claim. According to Q, if in either of two outcomes there would be the same number of people, it would be worse if those who live are worse off, or have a lower quality of life, than those who would have lived. We need a wider principle to cover cases where, in the different outcomes, there would be different numbers of people. This needed principle I call Theory X. Only X will fully solve the Non-Identity Problem.

Does the fact of non-identity make a moral difference? When we see that our choice of Depletion will be worse for no one, we may believe that there is less objection to our choice. But I believe that the objection is just as strong. And I have a similar belief when I compare the effects of the two Medical Programmes. This belief I call the No Difference View. Though I know of some people who do not accept this view, I know of more who do. If we accept the No Difference View, and believe that causing to exist cannot benefit, this has wide theoretical implications. We can predict that Theory X will not take a person-affecting form. The best theory about beneficence will not appeal to what is good or bad for those people whom our acts affect.

In what follows, I shall try to find Theory X. As I have claimed, this attempt will raise some puzzling questions.

17

THE REPUGNANT CONCLUSION

How many people should there be? Can there be *overpopulation*: too many people? We need an answer to these questions that also solves the Non-Identity Problem.

I shall later ask how many people there should *ever* be. In a complete moral theory, we cannot avoid this awesome question. And our answer may have practical implications. It may, for example, affect our view about nuclear weapons.

In most of what follows, I discuss a smaller question. How many people should there be, in some country or the world, during a certain period? When would there be too many people living?

128. IS IT BETTER IF MORE PEOPLE LIVE?

Consider

The Happy Child. A couple are trying to decide whether to have another child. They can assume that, if they did, they would love this child, and his life would be well worth living. Given the size of the world's population when this case occurs (perhaps in some future century), this couple can assume that having another child would not, on balance, be worse for other people. When they consider the effects on themselves, they have several reasons for having another child; but they also have several contrary reasons, such as the effect on their careers. Like many others, this couple cannot decide between these two sets of conflicting reasons. They believe that, if they had this child, this would be neither better nor worse for them.

Do this couple have a moral reason to have this child? Would it be better if an extra life is lived that is worth living? Some people answer Yes. If this couple have a moral reason to have this child, and they cannot decide between their other reasons, their moral reason may tip the scale. Perhaps they ought to have this child.

Other people take a different view. They believe that there is *no* moral reason to have this child. On their view, it is *not* better if an extra life is lived that is worth living.

129. THE EFFECTS OF POPULATION GROWTH ON EXISTING
PEOPLE

My couple assume that the existence of an extra child would not on balance
be worse for other people. In many countries, in many periods, this has been
true. But in other periods it has not been true. In these periods, if there had
been more people, people would have been worse off. This is now true in
many countries. In these countries, if the population grows, the quality of
life will be lower than it would be if the population did not grow. These are
the cases that I shall discuss.

In these cases, population growth would affect existing people. When it
would lower the quality of life, we may think that population growth must
be against the interests of existing people. But this is not always true. Even
when it lowers the quality of life, population growth can be *better* for
existing people.

The following can be true, in some country during some period. If the
population grows at a certain rate, this will have transitory good effects, and
cumulative bad effects. The bad effects might be the steady decline in the
share per person of the available resources. The transitory good effects
might be on the working of this country's economy. While rapid population
growth may be bad for the economy, a slow rate of growth may be better
for the economy than no growth at all. There are various technical reasons
why, for certain economic systems, this can be true. A remote analogy is the
fact that, when we are driving round a bend, we can steer more easily if we
accelerate. And population growth may have other, non-economic,
transitory good effects. These might simply be that larger families tend to be
somewhat happier, or that many people prefer having more children.

Robertson writes, that, if some rate of population growth would have
these two kinds of effect, 'what would be . . . most convenient is a
population which is always growing, but never getting any bigger'.[19] We
could attain this ideal only in Alice's Wonderland. In the actual world, the
alternatives can be shown as follows:

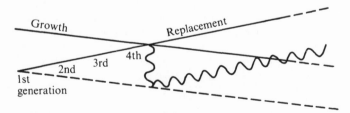

I call this the *Down Escalator Case*. One line shows the quality of life that
would result from keeping a stable population, or what I call *Replacement*.

The line of dashes shows the cumulative bad effects of a certain rate of population growth. This line shows what the quality of life would be if there were no transitory good effects. The other unbroken line shows the combined effects of this rate of growth. This is what the quality of life would be, given that there would be transitory good effects.

As the diagram shows, if there is Growth rather than Replacement, the quality of life will be higher for the first three generations, but will afterwards be increasingly lower. Many people believe that it would be bad if population growth lowered the quality of life. For these people, the Down Escalator Case is especially depressing. It seems likely that the actual outcome would be Growth. It may be better for most couples if they themselves have more than two children; and this may be what most couples want to do. Moreover, since Growth would be better for existing people and for the next two generations, it is unlikely that the community would decide on some policy that would cause a change from Growth to Replacement.

It might be said: 'This is not so. The best policy would be Growth for the first three generations, followed by Replacement. The community should switch to Replacement once Growth begins to produce a lower quality of life. At this point Growth ceases to be better for existing people. Since this is so, we can expect the community to switch to Replacement.'

This is a mistake. Consider the alternatives facing the fourth generation. If there has been Growth for the first three generations, why is the quality of life still as high as it would have been if there had been Replacement? Only because of the transitory good effects of Growth. If the fourth generation switches to Replacement, it will lose these good effects. Its quality of life will drop to the point vertically below on the line of dashes. And if there continues to be Replacement the quality of life will be, for the next three generations, lower than it would have been if there had been population growth. These two effects are shown by the wavy lines. As these lines show, the fourth generation has, at lower levels, the same alternatives as the first. *Every* generation has these alternatives.

These will remain the alternatives as long as Growth would have these two effects: the cumulative bad effects and the transitory good effects. While this is true, compared with Replacement, Growth would always be better both for existing people and for the next two generations. It is therefore likely that every generation will choose Growth. As a result, the quality of life will continue to decline. If we believe that this is a bad effect, the Down Escalator Case *is*, as I claimed, especially depressing. It is an Intergenerational Prisoner's Dilemma, of a kind in which it is least likely that those involved will achieve a solution.[19b]

We may assume that, in judging the effects of our acts, it is enough to consider the interests of all of the people who will ever live. In the Down Escalator Case, a certain rate of population growth will always be in the interests of existing people, and their children. Though it causes a continuous decline in the quality of life, this rate of growth will not be against the interests of those who live more than three generations later. This is because, in the way explained in Section 123, these people will owe their existence to this rate of growth. If we appeal only to the interests of all of the people who will ever live, we must claim that it would be *better* if there was this rate of growth, despite the continuous decline in the quality of life. If we want to avoid this conclusion, this is another case where we must appeal to a different kind of principle, one that is not *person-affecting*, or about people's interests.

For those who deplore a decline in the quality of life, this is the most depressing case. Fortunately, this is only one of several possible cases. There are two ways in which, when it lowers the quality of life, population growth can be *worse* for existing people.

In some communities, it will be worse for most couples if they themselves have more than two children. These are the cases where it is least likely that there will be population growth.

In other communities, as I explained in Chapter 3, most couples face a Prisoner's Dilemma. In these communities, it will be better for each of many people if he or she has more than two children, whatever other people do. But if all have more than two children that will be worse for each than if none do. If these people came to see that this was true, they might achieve what I call a political solution. Though each would prefer to have more children, each might also prefer that none have more children rather than that all do. A system of rewards or penalties, aimed at stopping population growth, might be democratically adopted. Even if it was imposed undemocratically, such a system might be welcomed by all these people. Another solution would be provided by reversible sterilization after the birth of one's second child. This is a better solution, since it would impose no penalties. Once again, if they understood the facts, all these people might welcome this solution.

I have described three kinds of case. And there are other possible cases. Some would be mixtures of these three; but others would be different in other ways.

130. OVERPOPULATION

When population growth lowers the quality of life, the effects on existing people may be either good, or bad, or neither. These effects do not raise new moral questions. But other effects do raise such questions.

These questions arise most clearly when we compare the outcomes that would be produced, in the further future, by different rates of population growth. If there is faster growth, there will later be more people, who will be worse off. As before, 'worse off' can refer either to the level of happiness, or to the quality of life, or to the share per person of resources. We should assume that, in my examples, these three correlate, rising and falling together.

Let us compare the outcomes of two rates of population growth, after one or two centuries. As I have explained, there would be no one who would exist in both these outcomes. Two such outcomes are shown below.

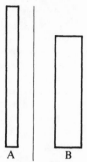

A | B

The width of each block shows the number of people living, the height shows their quality of life. By this I mean their quality of life throughout some period. In such a period, there would be some change in the population. But for simplicity, we can ignore this fact. For the same reason, we can assume that in these outcomes there is neither social nor natural inequality; no one is worse off than anyone else. This would never in fact be true. But it cannot distort our reasoning, on the questions I shall ask, if we imagine that it would be true. And this makes my questions take a clearer form.

In B there are twice as many people living as in A, and these people are all worse off than everyone in A. But the lives of those in B, compared with those in A, are *more than half as much* worth living. This claim does not assume that, as my diagram suggests, these judgements could in principle be precise. I believe that there is only rough or partial comparability. What my claim assumes is that a move from the level in A to that in B would be a decline in the quality of life, but that it would take much more than another similarly great decline before people's lives ceased to be worth living.

There are various ways in which, with twice the population, the quality of life might be lower. There might be worse housing, overcrowded schools, more pollution, less natural beauty, and a somewhat lower average income. If these are the ways in which the quality of life would be lower, we can plausibly assume that it would take much more than another similar decline before life ceased to be worth living.

Except for the absence of inequality, these two outcomes could be the real alternatives for some country, or for mankind, given two rates of population growth over many years. Which would be the better outcome? By 'better' I do not mean 'morally better' in the most common use of this phrase. This applies only to persons, or to acts. But one of two outcomes can be better in another sense, that has moral relevance. It would be better, in this sense, if fewer people suffered from some crippling illness, or if the Lisbon Earthquake had not occurred. And we can clearly make such claims about outcomes that involve different possible populations. Suppose that, in two such outcomes, the same number of people would exist. If, in one of these outcomes, people would be much worse off, this would clearly be the worse outcome. This outcome would be worse for no one. But, as I have argued, this does not show that this outcome cannot be worse.

Return to A and B. Which outcome would be better? It is clearly bad that, in B, people are worse off. Could this be morally outweighed by the fact that there are more people living?

Suppose we believe that, in the Case of the Happy Child, my couple have no moral reason to have this child. We may then believe that, if people are worse off, this cannot be morally outweighed by an increase in the number of people living. Those who believe this often appeal to

> *The Impersonal Average Principle*: If other things are equal, the best outcome is the one in which people's lives go, on average, best.

Some economists make this principle true by definition.[20] I call this principle *impersonal* because it is not *person-affecting*: it is not about what would be good or bad for those people whom our acts affect. This principle does not assume that, if people are caused to exist and have a life worth living, these people are thereby benefited.

The Hedonistic version of this principle claims

> If other things are equal, the best outcome is the one in which there is the greatest average net sum of happiness, per life lived.

I state these versions in a temporally neutral form. Some state the Average Principle so that it refers only to the people who are alive after we have acted. In this form the principle implies absurdly that it would be better if, of the people now alive, all but the most ecstatic were killed. On a temporally neutral version of the Average Principle, if someone with a life worth living dies earlier, this causes people's lives to go, on average, worse.

Suppose next that we believe that, in the Case of the Happy Child, my couple do have a moral reason to have this child. We believe that it is always better in itself if an extra life is lived that is worth living. If this is what we believe, it would be natural to claim that, of my two outcomes, B might be better than A. The loss in the quality of life might be outweighed by a sufficient gain in the number of lives lived. If we make this claim, we must ask, 'What would be a *sufficient* gain?'

If we are Hedonists, we can easily state these questions more precisely. We ask

> (1) 'If in one of two outcomes the people living would be less happy, can this be morally outweighed by a sufficient increase in the quantity of happiness?'

If people are less happy, they have a lower quality of life. If we answer Yes to question (1), we must ask

(2) 'What are the relative values of quality and quantity?'

One answer is given by the Hedonistic version of the *Impersonal Total Principle*. This claims

If other things are equal, the best outcome is the one in which there would be the greatest quantity of happiness—the greatest net sum of happiness minus misery.

On this principle, B would be better than A, since in B there would be a greater quantity of happiness. Though the B-people are each less happy than the A-people, each of their lives contains more than half as much happiness. Since there are twice as many B-people, they *together* have more happiness than the A-people. (Two bottles more than half full contain more than a bottleful.)

Suppose, next, that we are not Hedonists. What we believe to be morally important is not happiness but the quality of life. We can ask the same questions; but we must use an unfamiliar phrase. When we compare the value of quality and quantity, what is the relevant quantity? We might say, 'the quantity of lives lived that are worth living'. But this is wrong, since it ignores the *quality* of these extra lives, or how much they are worth living. The relevant quantity must, like the sum of happiness, be a function both of the number of these lives, and of their quality. To describe the relevant quantity, I suggest the phrase 'the amount of whatever makes life worth living'.

Reconsider A and B. Hedonists would claim: 'Though the B-people are each less happy than the A-people, they together have more happiness'. We can similarly claim: 'Compared with the A-people, each of the B-people has less of whatever makes life worth living. But each life in B is more than half as much worth living as each life in A. Since there are twice as many B-people, they together have more of whatever makes life worth living.'

I can now state the non-Hedonistic

Impersonal Total Principle: If other things are equal, the best outcome is the one in which there would be the greatest quantity of whatever makes life worth living.

If we believe that B would be worse than A, we must reject this principle.

131. THE REPUGNANT CONCLUSION

Consider next the larger diagram below.

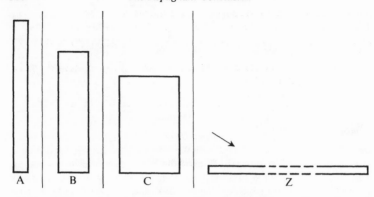

On the Impersonal Total Principle, just as B would be better than A, C would be better than B. And Z might be best. Z is some enormous population whose members have lives that are not much above the level where life ceases to be worth living. A life could be like this either because it has enough ecstasies to make its agonies seem just worth enduring, or because it is uniformly of poor quality. Let us imagine the lives in Z to be of this second drabber kind. In each of these lives there is very little happiness. But, if the numbers are large enough, this is the outcome with the greatest total sum of happiness. Similarly, Z could be the outcome in which there is the greatest quantity of whatever makes life worth living. (The greatest mass of milk might be found in a heap of bottles each containing only a single drop.)

Let us next assume, for a reason that I shall later give, that A would have a population of ten billion. The Impersonal Total Principle then implies

> *The Repugnant Conclusion*: For any possible population of at least ten billion people, all with a very high quality of life, there must be some much larger imaginable population whose existence, if other things are equal, would be better, even though its members have lives that are barely worth living.

As my choice of name suggests, I find this conclusion hard to accept.

A and B could in practice be real alternatives. This would not be true of A and Z. Some claim that, because of this, we need not try to avoid the Repugnant Conclusion. They might say: 'Since this conclusion does not apply to any possible choice, it can be ignored. We need not test our principles in cases that could not occur.'

I distinguished two kinds of impossibility: *deep* and *technical*. An imagined case is deeply impossible if it requires a major change in the laws of nature, including the laws of human nature. There are two grounds for challenging cases that are deeply impossible. We may be unable to imagine what such cases would involve. And some would claim that our moral principles need to be acceptable only in the real world. [21]

It may help to remember Nozick's imagined *Utility Monsters*. These are people who get 'enormously greater gains in utility from any sacrifice of others than these others lose'.[22] Such an imagined person provides an objection to Act Utilitarianism, which 'seems to require that we all be sacrificed in the monster's maw, in order to increase total utility'.

As described by Nozick, such a person is a deep impossibility. The world's population is now several billion. Let us imagine the wretchedness of all these people if they are denied anything above starvation rations, and all other resources go to Nozick's imagined Monster. Nozick tells us to suppose that this imagined person would be *so* happy, or have a life of *such* high quality, that this is the distribution that produces the greatest sum of happiness, or the greatest amount of whatever makes life worth living. How can this be true, given the billions left in wretchedness that could be so easily relieved by a small fraction of this Monster's vast resources? For this to be true, this Monster's quality of life must be *millions* of times as high as that of anyone we know. Can we imagine this? Think of the life of the luckiest person that you know, and ask what a life would have to be like in order to be a million times as much worth living. The qualitative gap between such a life and ours, at its best, must resemble the gap between ours, at its best, and the life of those creatures who are barely conscious—such as, if they *are* conscious, Plato's 'contented oysters'.[23] It seems a fair reply that we cannot imagine, even in the dimmest way, the life of this Utility Monster. And this casts doubt on the force of the example. Act Utilitarians might say that, if we really could imagine what such a life would be like, we might not find Nozick's objection persuasive. His 'Monster' seems to be a god-like being. In the imagined presence of such a being, our belief in our right to equality with him may begin to waver—just as we do not believe that the lower animals have rights to equality with us.

This reply has some force. But even a deep impossibility may provide a partial test for our moral principles. We cannot simply ignore imagined cases.

Return now to my imagined Z. This imagined population is another Utility Monster. The difference is that the greater sum of happiness comes from a vast increase, not in the quality of one person's life, but in the number of lives lived. And *my* Utility Monster is neither deeply impossible, nor something that we cannot imagine. We can imagine what it would be for someone's life to be barely worth living. And we can imagine what it would be for there to be many people with such lives. In order to imagine Z, we merely have to imagine that there would be *very* many. This we can do. So the example cannot be questioned as one that we can hardly understand.

We could not in practice face a choice between A and Z. Given some finite stock of resources, we could not in fact produce the greatest sum of happiness, or the greatest amount of whatever makes life worth living, by producing an enormous population whose lives are barely worth living.[24]

But this would be merely technically impossible. In order to suppose it possible, we only need to add some assumptions about the nature and availability of resources. Since it would be merely technically impossible to face a choice between A and Z, this does not weaken the comparison as a test for our principles. Different Number Choices raise the question whether loss in the quality of life could *always* be morally outweighed by a sufficient gain in the quantity either of happiness or of whatever makes life worth living. This is the question posed most clearly by comparing A and Z. If we are convinced that Z is worse than A, we have strong grounds for resisting principles which imply that Z is better. We have strong grounds for resisting the Impersonal Total Principle.

Someone might say: 'This is not so. This principle includes the phrase *if other things are equal*. Other things never would be equal. We can therefore ignore the Repugnant Conclusion.'

This is not plausible. What other moral principle must be infringed by the coming-about of Z? It might be claimed that this would infringe some principle about justice between generations. But this is irrelevant to our question in its purest form. We are asking whether, if Z came about, this would be better than if A came about. We could imagine a history in which only Z-like outcomes occurred. The people in Z would then be no worse off than anyone who ever lives. If we believe that Z would be worse than A, this could not here be because Z's occurrence would involve injustice.

There is another more important point. Reconsider the Non-Identity Problem. Some suggest that we can solve this problem by an appeal to people's rights. But, as the Case of Depletion shows, this is not so. If we imagine away the Non-Identity Problem, the objection to our choice of Lesser Depletion would appeal to our Principle of Beneficence. To solve the Non-Identity Problem, we must revise this principle. We must find what I call Theory X.

The same is true if we want to avoid the Repugnant Conclusion. We should not try to avoid this conclusion by appealing to principles covering some different part of morality. This conclusion is *intrinsically* repugnant. And this conclusion is implied by the Impersonal Total Principle, which is a particular version of the Principle of Beneficence. To avoid the Repugnant Conclusion, we must try to show that we should reject this version. We must try to find a better version: Theory X.

18

THE ABSURD CONCLUSION

WE need a theory that both solves the Non-Identity Problem and avoids the Repugnant Conclusion. As we shall see, several theories achieve one of these aims at the cost of failing to achieve the other.

132. AN ALLEGED ASYMMETRY

There is another aim which, according to many people, we should try to achieve. Consider

> *The Wretched Child.* Some woman knows that, if she has a child, he will be so multiply diseased that his life will be worse than nothing. He will never develop, will live for only a few years, and will suffer pain that cannot be wholly relieved.

Even if we reject the phrase 'worse than nothing', it is clear that it would be wrong knowingly to conceive such a child. Nor would the wrongness mostly come from the effects on others. The wrongness would mostly come from the predictably appalling quality of this child's life.

Remember next the Case of the Happy Child. My couple can assume that, if they have this child, this will not be worse either for them or for other people. What is the relation between these two cases?

Some writers claim that, while we would have a duty not to conceive the Wretched Child, my couple have no duty to conceive the Happy Child. It would merely be morally better if they had such a child.

Many people would deny even this last claim. These people believe that, while it would be wrong to have the Wretched Child, my couple have *no* moral reason to have the Happy Child. [25] This view has been called *the Asymmetry*.[26]

If we accept this view, we have a third aim. Besides solving the Non-Identity Problem and avoiding the Repugnant Conclusion, we must also explain the Asymmetry. What theory would achieve these aims?

133. WHY THE IDEAL CONTRACTUAL METHOD PROVIDES NO SOLUTION

Can we appeal to the method of moral reasoning I shall call *Ideal Contractualism?* This is defended by many writers, most notably Rawls. On this view, the best moral principles are those that it would be rational for us to choose as the principles to be followed in our society. To ensure impartiality, we ask what principles we should choose if we did not know particular facts about ourselves.

Some claim that, if we apply this method to the question of how many people there should be, we can explain why we should reject both the Impersonal Total Principle and the Repugnant Conclusion. We can explain why B would be worse than A, and why, of all the outcomes, Z would be the worst. Even if we did not know particular facts about ourselves, we would choose a principle that would produce A rather than B. We would then be certain to be better off.

As several writers argue,[27] this is not an acceptable way to defend a principle about the numbers of people who should exist. This method of moral reasoning appeals to what it would be rational for us to choose, in self-interested terms. It is essential to this method that we do not know whether we would bear the brunt of some chosen principle. Thus, if the chosen principle would disadvantage women, we must imagine ourselves not to know our sex. Only this *veil of ignorance* makes our choice impartial in the way that morality requires.

On the reasoning suggested above, it would be rational to choose a principle that would produce A rather than B, since we shall then certainly be better off. This reasoning assumes that, whatever principle is followed, we shall certainly exist. This assumption violates the requirement of impartiality. The principle we choose affects how many people exist. If we assume that we shall certainly exist whatever principle we choose, this is like assuming, when choosing a principle that would disadvantage women, that we shall certainly be men.

Some writers suggest that we should change our assumption. When we ask what principle it would be rational for us to choose, we should imagine that we do not know whether we shall ever exist. If we choose some principle that will produce a smaller population, this will increase the chance that we never exist. It has been claimed that, with this change in our assumption, it would be rational to choose the Impersonal Total Principle.

We cannot change our assumption in this suggested way. We can imagine a different possible history, in which we never existed. But we cannot assume that, in the actual history of the world, it might be true that we never exist. We therefore cannot ask what, on this assumption, it would rational to choose.

The Ideal Contractualist Method cannot be applied to some parts of morality. Thus, as Rawls claims, this method cannot be plausibly applied to the question of how we ought to treat other animals.[28] I believe that, for the different reason just given, this method cannot be plausibly applied to the choice of a principle about how many people there should be. When we are discussing this question, this method is not impartial unless we imagine something that we cannot possibly imagine.

A defender of this method might reject my claim about impartiality. He might continue to believe that, in applying this method, we can assume that we shall certainly exist. Consider two possibilities for the last generation in human history. (Considering the last generation simplifies the case.) There are two ways in which history might go, before it is suddenly ended by the explosion of the sun:

> In *Hell One*, the last generation consists of ten innocent people, who each suffer great agony for fifty years. The lives of these people are much worse than nothing. They would all kill themselves if they could. In *Hell Two*, the last generation consists not of ten but of ten million innocent people, who each suffer agony just as great for fifty years minus a day.

If we assume that we shall certainly exist in one of these two Hells, it would clearly be rational, in self-interested terms, to prefer Hell Two, since we should then suffer for one day less. Should we conclude that Hell Two would be better, in the sense that has moral relevance? Would Satan be acting less badly if this is the Hell that he brought about?

The answers are both No. Hell Two is in one respect better. The amount of agony per person would be very slightly less; it would be reduced by less than 0.01 per cent. But this fact is morally outweighed by the vast increase in the number of people who are in agony, enduring lives that are much worse than nothing. In Hell Two the amount of suffering is almost a million times greater.

The example shows that, on the proposed method of moral reasoning, we are led to ignore completely what must be admitted to have at least some moral significance. We are led to ignore the fact that, in one of these outcomes, there would be vastly more suffering. Such a method of moral reasoning cannot be acceptable. We must find some other way to achieve our aims.

134. THE NARROW PERSON-AFFECTING PRINCIPLE

If we are to avoid the Repugnant Conclusion, we must reject the Impersonal Total Principle. We must claim that this principle misdescribes the part of morality that is concerned with beneficence, or human well-being.

We might claim that this principle takes the wrong form, since it treats people as the mere *containers* or *producers* of value. Here is a passage in which this feature is especially clear. In his book *The Technology of Happiness,* Mackaye writes:

Just as a boiler is required to utilize the potential energy of coal in the production of steam, so sentient beings are required to convert the potentiality of happiness, resident in a given land area, into actual happiness. And just as the Engineer will choose boilers with the maximum efficiency at converting steam into energy, Justice will choose sentient beings who have the maximum efficiency at converting resources into happiness.[30]

This *Steam Production Model* could be claimed to be a grotesque distortion of this part of morality. We could appeal to

> *The Person-affecting Restriction*: This part of morality, the part concerned with human well-being, should be explained entirely in terms of what would be good or bad for those people whom our acts affect.

This is the view advanced by Narveson.[31] On his view, it is not good that people exist because their lives contain happiness. Rather, happiness is good because it is good for people.

Narveson also claims that, in causing someone to exist, we cannot be benefiting this person. He therefore claims that, of the two ways of increasing the sum of happiness—making people happy, and making happy people—only the first is good for people. Since this part of morality only concerns what is good or bad for people, the second way of increasing happiness is, he claims, morally neutral.

As I argued in Chapter 16, we must reject the view that what is bad must be bad for someone. It may seem that, in rejecting this view, we are rejecting the Person-affecting Restriction. This is not so. Unlike Narveson, we may believe that, in causing someone to exist who will have a life worth living, we are thereby benefiting this person. Appendix G defends this belief. If we accept this belief, we can explain, in person-affecting terms, why we have a moral reason not to produce certain effects, even though these effects will be bad for no one. We can explain why we have a moral reason not to choose the Risky Policy, or Depletion.

If we believe that causing to exist can benefit, we must decide between at least three different Principles of Beneficence. Unlike the Principle of Utility, these three principles do not claim to cover the whole of morality. Since they include the phrase 'if other things are equal', they allow us to appeal to other principles, such as the Principle of Equality. We may also claim that we have no duty to benefit others when this would require from us too great a sacrifice, or too great an interference in our lives.

These three principles all claim:

(1)   If someone is caused to exist, and has a life worth living, this person is thereby benefited. This benefit is greater if this person's life is more worth living.

(2)   If other things are equal, it is wrong knowingly to make some choice that would make the outcome worse.

(3)   If other things are equal, one of two outcomes would be worse if it would be worse for people.

These principles differ in their claims about what makes an outcome worse for people. Suppose that we are comparing outcomes *X* and *Y*. Call the people who will exist in outcome X *the X-people*. Of these two outcomes, call X

'worse for people' in the *narrow* sense if the occurrence of X rather than Y would be either worse for, or bad for, the X-people.

According to claim (1), in being caused to exist, someone can be benefited. As I write in Appendix G, we need not claim that this outcome is *better* for this person than the alternative. This would imply the implausible claim that, if this person had never existed, this would have been worse for this person. We can claim instead that, if someone is caused to exist, this can be *good* for this person. We can similarly claim that, if the Wretched Child is caused to exist, this is bad for him. This is why, in the definition just given, I include the phrase 'or bad for'.

If we use 'worse for people' in the sense just defined, claims (1) to (3) state the *Narrow* Person-affecting Principle of Beneficence, or—for short—the *Narrow Principle*.

135. WHY WE CANNOT APPEAL TO THIS PRINCIPLE

The Narrow Principle is intuitively plausible. It is natural to assume that, if some choice will not be bad for anyone who ever lives, our Principle of Beneficence should not condemn this choice. But, if we appeal to the Person-affecting Restriction, we must reject the Narrow Principle. This principle cannot solve the Non-Identity Problem. We need to explain why we have some moral reason not to choose the Risky Policy, or Depletion. According to the Narrow Principle, we have no such reason, since we know that these choices will be worse for no one.

There are other objections to the Narrow Principle. One is that, if this is our Principle of Beneficence, we must accept part of the Repugnant Conclusion. If what comes about is Z rather than A, this would not be either worse for, or bad for, any of the people who ever live. If we appeal both to the Person-affecting Restriction and to the Narrow Principle, we must claim that Z would not be worse than A. Most of us would find this hard to believe.

Another objection is that the Narrow Principle can imply contradictions. Consider these two outcomes:

(1) Unlike other existing people, Jack has a life that is much worse than nothing. Jill never exists.

(2) Unlike other existing people, Jill has a life that is much worse than nothing. Jack never exists.

If what happens is (1) rather than (2), this will be bad for Jack, and will not be good for Jill. (1) would therefore be worse than (2) for the (1)-people. By similar reasoning, (2) would be worse than (1) for the (2)-people. The Narrow Principle implies the contradictory conclusion that each of these outcomes would be worse than the other.

It is tempting to combine the Person-affecting Restriction and the Narrow Principle. But, if we appeal to this view, we cannot solve the Non-Identity Problem, we must accept part of the Repugnant Conclusion, and we are led to contradictions. We have therefore learnt that we cannot appeal to this view. This is progress, of a negative kind.

There is another way in which our progress has been negative. Many people accept the Asymmetry. These people want to explain why, though it would be wrong knowingly to conceive the Wretched Child, my couple have no moral reason to conceive the Happy Child. Since we cannot appeal to the view just mentioned, I argue only in an endnote that this view *would* have provided the best explanation of the Asymmetry. [32]

136. THE TWO WIDE PERSON-AFFECTING PRINCIPLES

I shall now describe two more Person-affecting Principles of Beneficence. Like the Narrow Principle, these both claim:

(1) If someone is caused to exist, and has a life worth living, this person is thereby benefited. This benefit is greater if this person's life is more worth living.

(2) If other things are equal, it is wrong knowingly to make some choice that will make the outcome worse.

(3) If other things are equal, one of two outcomes would be worse if it would be worse for people.

Call outcome X

'worse for people' in the *wide* sense if the occurrence of X would be less good for the X-people than the occurrence of Y would be for the Y-people.

In Different Number Choices 'less good for' is ambiguous. Call X

'worse for people' in the *wide total* sense if the total net benefit given to the X-people by the occurrence of X would be less than the total net benefit given to the Y-people by the occurrence of Y.

Call X

'worse for people' in the *wide average* sense if the average net benefit per person given to the X-people by the occurrence of X would be less than the average net benefit per person given to the Y-people by the occurrence of Y.

If we use 'worse for people' in its wide total sense, claims (1) to (3) state the *Wide Total* Person-affecting Principle. If we use 'worse for people' in its wide average sense, (1) to (3) state the *Wide Average* Person-affecting Principle. (As I explain in endnote 33, if we reject claim (1), denying that causing to exist can benefit, these two Wide Principles coincide with the Narrow Principle.)

On the Wide Total Principle, the best outcome is the one that gives to people the greatest total net sum of benefits—the greatest sum of benefits minus burdens. On the Wide Average Principle, the best outcome is the one that gives to people the greatest average net sum of benefits per person. In appealing to these principles, we can extend the use of 'benefit' in the way defended in Section 25. The act that benefits people most is the act whose consequence is that people receive the greatest total or average net sum of benefits. It is irrelevant that many other acts will also be parts of the cause of the receiving of these benefits.

Both of the Wide Principles solve the Non-Identity Problem. Both imply (Q), the Same Number Quality Claim. And these principles explain this claim in a more familiar way. What is our moral reason not to choose Depletion? On the Wide Principles, this choice benefits those who later live, since their lives are worth living, and they owe their existence to our choice. But if we had chosen Conservation other people would have later lived, and these people would have had a higher quality of life. On the Wide Principles, if people are caused to exist, and have a higher quality of life, these people are benefited more. The objection to Depletion is that, though it benefits those who later live, it benefits these people less than Conservation would have benefited those who would have later lived. Why should the 14-Year-Old Girl wait and have her child later? Because having a child now would probably benefit this child less than having a child later would benefit that other child. A similar claim applies to our choice of the Risky Policy. This choice benefits the people later killed in the catastrophe, but it benefits these people less than the Safe Policy would have benefited the other people who would have later lived.

These claims do not involve the kind of verbal trick that I earlier dismissed. When we discuss the 14-Year-Old Girl, the words 'her child' and 'he' can be used to cover all of the different children whom this girl could have. This provides a sense in which it is true that, if this girl has her child now, this will be worse for him. But, in the sense in which this claim is true, it is not about what is either good or bad for particular people. This claim must therefore appeal to some new principle, that needs to be explained and justified.

This is not true of the two Wide Principles. As we have just seen, when we call one of two outcomes 'worse for people' in the two wide senses, our claim *is* about what would be good or bad for particular people. The Wide Principles are not wholly familiar. They cannot claim to be our ordinary principle about effects on people's interests—what I call our Principle of Beneficence. This is because we are now assuming that, in causing someone to exist, we can thereby benefit this person. Our ordinary principle does not tell us what is the moral importance of such benefits. We need to extend our ordinary principle so that it answers this question. And there are at least three answers that are worth considering. These are the answers given by the two Wide Principles and the Narrow Principle. We can therefore claim that these are not principles of some new kind, that need to be explained and justified. They state three of the ways in which we can plausibly extend our ordinary principle, as we need to do if we assume that causing to exist can benefit.

Since the Wide Principles are extensions of our ordinary principle, they solve the Non-Identity Problem in Same Number Choices. They explain claim Q in a satisfactory way. But this does not show that either of these principles is acceptable. We must ask what they imply in Different Number Choices.

Return to the different outcomes A and B. Compared with A, there are in B twice as many people, who are all worse off. But the lives of the B-people are more than half as much worth living as the lives of the A-people. If B came about rather than A, this would be 'better for people' in the wide total sense. B would be less good for *each* of the B-people than A would be for each A-person. But since each B-person would benefit more than half as much as each A-person, and there would be twice as many B-people, they *together* would benefit more, or would receive a greater total benefit. (In the same sense, if we gave to each of two people four more years of life, they would together receive a greater benefit than the benefit received by some third person to whom we gave five more years of life.) The Wide Total Principle thus implies that, if other things were equal, B would be better than A.

By the same reasoning, C would be better than B. And Z could be best. If Z came about, each of the Z-people would thereby benefit very little. But, if Z was large enough, the Z-people would together receive the greatest total benefit, or be benefited most. The Wide Total Principle thus implies the Repugnant Conclusion. Since we want to avoid this conclusion, we must claim that we should reject this principle.

(As I have stated them, the two Wide Person-affecting Principles extend our ordinary use of the word 'benefit'. It might be objected that, by extending this use of 'benefit', my principles do not fully satisfy the Person-affecting Restriction. We could appeal to different versions, which are closer to our ordinary use of 'benefit'. We could claim

If we do X rather than Y, this benefits people more in the *wide total* sense if our doing X rather than Y gives to the X-people a larger total net benefit than our doing Y rather than X would have given to the Y-people,

and

If we do X rather than Y, this benefits people more in the *wide average* sense if our doing X rather than Y gives to the X-people a greater average benefit per person than our doing Y rather than X would have given to the Y-people.

We could then claim that, if other things are equal, one of two outcomes would be better when bringing about this outcome would benefit people more. These two definitions give us different versions of the Wide Total and the Wide Average Person-affecting Principles.

This version of the Wide Total. Principle also implies the Repugnant Conclusion. If there were enough Z-people, bringing about Z rather than A would give to the Z-people a greater total net benefit than bringing about A rather than Z would give to the A-people. Surprisingly, this version of the Wide *Average* Principle can also imply the Repugnant Conclusion. Assume that we have brought about A. We might now face a new choice. Suppose that, in a short time, we could change A into B. It might be 'better for people' in the new wide average sense if we made this change. This change would add to the existing population as many new people. The previously existing half would suffer a decline in their quality of life. This change would be worse for them. But this change would bring a greater benefit to the newly existing half. Changing from A to B would therefore give to the B-people an average net benefit per person. And it might give them a greater average benefit per person than failure to make this change would give to the A-people.

To illustrate this point, I shall pretend that there is precision. Assume that the level in A is 100, and the level in B is 76. In the change from A to B the previously existing half each lose 24, and the newly existing half each gain 76. The change from A to B therefore gives to the B-people an average net benefit per person of $(76-24)/2$, or 26. Failure to make this change would give to each of the A-people a benefit of 24. Changing from A to B would therefore give to the B-people a greater average benefit per person than failure to make this change would give to the A-people. On the definition given above, the Wide Average Principle implies that B would be better than A. By the same reasoning, C would be better than B, D better than C, E better than D, and so on. These and similar claims indirectly imply that Z would be better than A.

Another objection to these principles is that they often imply contradictions. This is true of the Wide Average Principle in the case just discussed. Suppose that, compared with B's population at level 76, C would have twice as many people at level 58. On the Wide Average Principle, as I have shown, B would be better than A. By similar reasoning, C would be better than B. This implies, indirectly, that C would be better than A. But the Wide Average Principle implies directly that A would be better than C. According to this principle, A would be both better and worse than C. I prove this point in endnote 34.

We could revise these principles to avoid such contradictions. But, as that note explains, the principles would then be inadequate. Since this is true, and *both* these principles imply the Repugnant Conclusion, these two versions of the Wide Principles are inferior to the versions stated earlier. In what follows I refer to these earlier versions.)

We have again made progress, of a negative kind. The Repugnant Conclusion is implied by the Impersonal Total Principle. In its Hedonistic version, this principle claims that, if other things are equal, the best outcome is the one in which there would be the greatest net sum of happiness. The other version of this principle substitutes, for 'happiness', 'whatever makes life worth living'.

Since we want to avoid the Repugnant Conclusion, we must claim that we should reject the Impersonal Total Principle. Narveson suggested a ground for rejecting this principle. We can appeal to the Person-affecting Restriction: the claim that any principle of beneficence must take a person-affecting form.

We have now learnt that the appeal to this Restriction fails, and that it is harder to explain why we should reject the Total Principle. Suppose first that, if we cause someone to exist who will have a life worth living, we do not thereby benefit this person. If this is so, we cannot appeal to the Person-affecting Restriction, since we should then be unable to solve the Non-Identity Problem. On this alternative, we cannot reject the Impersonal Total Principle with the claim that, since it is not person-affecting, it takes the wrong form—that of the Milk Production Model. To solve the Non-Identity Problem, we must appeal to a principle that is not person-affecting.

Suppose next that, in causing someone to exist, we can thereby benefit this person. If this is so, we can appeal to the Person-affecting Restriction. But this achieves nothing. The Wide Total Principle *restates the Impersonal Principle in a person-affecting form.* To avoid the Repugnant Conclusion, we must claim that we should reject this principle. And it is harder to explain why this should be done. Since this principle is person-affecting, we cannot claim that it takes the wrong form, treating people as the mere containers or producers of value. It is easier to deny that it would be better if there was more happiness, or more of whatever makes life worth living. It is harder to deny that it would be better if people were benefited more.

Though it is harder to deny the Wide Total Principle, we are not forced to accept this principle. It is defensible to deny one of this principle's claims: the claim that causing to exist can benefit. And, even if we believe that causing to exist can benefit, there is at least one other person-affecting principle: the

Wide Average Principle. This principle does not imply the Repugnant Conclusion. If what came about was Z rather than A, this would be 'worse for people' in the wide average sense. The Z-people would, compared with the A-people, receive a smaller benefit per person.

The Wide Average Principle restates in person-affecting terms the Impersonal Average Principle. We need a new principle of beneficence. We need a principle that both solves the Non-Identity Problem and avoids the Repugnant Conclusion. We may also want this principle to explain the Asymmetry. Both in its impersonal and in its person-affecting form, the Average Principle achieves the first two aims, and it partly achieves the third.[35] Is this principle what we want: the best account of beneficence?

137. POSSIBLE THEORIES

The Average Principle is only one of the principles that achieves our aims. It will be easier to judge this principle when I have described some of these alternatives.

We cannot reject the Wide Total Principle with the claim that it takes the wrong form. But we can claim that this principle gives a wrong answer to a question that I asked above. I asked, 'What are the relative values, during some period, of the *quality* of life and the *quantity* both of happiness and of whatever else makes life worth living?' Of the range of possible answers, the Total Principle is at one extreme. On this principle, both in its impersonal and in its person-affecting form, *only quantity* has value.

On a less extreme view, quality and quantity both have value. On this view, if the quantity of happiness is the same, it will be worse if this happiness comes in more lives of a lower quality. For B not to be worse than A, it may have to contain, not at least the same total sum of happiness, but a larger sum, perhaps twice, or ten times, or more. A similar claim could be made about the quantity of whatever makes life worth living.

The other extreme is the view that *only quality* has value. On this view, if people are worse off, this can *never* be morally outweighed by the fact that there are more people living. A loss in quality can never be outweighed by a gain in quantity. The Average Principle is one version of this view.

This view might be held, not only about different possible populations during some period, but also about the larger question of how many people there should ever be. As I claimed earlier, the Average View ought to take a temporally neutral form. In this form, it answers this larger question.

Suppose that the number who ever lived had been very small. In one imaginary history, Eve and Adam have lives that are very well worth living, and have no children. They are the only people who ever live. In a different possible history, millions of people have lives that are very well worth living, but none have lives that are quite as good as those that Eve and Adam would have had. In this second possible history, the quality of life is slightly lower, but there is a very much greater quantity both of happiness and of whatever else makes life worth living. On the Average View, or the simpler claim that only quality matters, the first possible history would be better. There are some people who accept this conclusion.

Other people would accept less extreme versions of this claim. Since we want to avoid the Repugnant Conclusion, it will help to distinguish two groups of answers. These can be introduced with two questions, as shown on the next page.

(1) is the Total Principle. The Average Principle is one version of (7). We can afford to ignore here the differences between some of these seven views. I believe that (2) is more plausible than (1). And I believe that (5) is more plausible than (6), which is more plausible than (7). But, for our purposes, we can ignore these details.[35b]

We can ignore the difference between (1) and (2), since both views answer Yes to my first question. Both views claim that, since there is no upper limit to the value of quantity, any loss in the quality of life could be morally outweighed by a sufficient gain in quantity. Both views therefore imply the Repugnant Conclusion. The difference is only that, on view (2), Z's population must be larger. These are variants of the view that *quantity could always outweigh quality*.

(3) to (7) are variants of the denial of this view. According to (3) to (7), quantity cannot *always* outweigh quality.

We can ignore the difference between (5) and (6). We can regard these as variants of the view that *the value of quantity has upper limits*. (7) is the variant where this upper limit is always zero. (5) to (7) disagree only when the world's population is small. (5) and (6) then claim, what (7) denies, that there would be some value in greater quantity.

On view (5), at any level of quality, the value in extra quantity asymptotically approaches zero. This means that the value of each extra unit of quantity gets closer and closer to, but never actually reaches, zero. This claim does not imply that the value of quantity has upper limits. Suppose that the value of each extra life worth living was as follows: 1, 1/2, 1/3, 1/4, 1/5, 1/6 etc. The value of each extra life here approaches zero; but there is no limit to the value of such a sequence. Since (5) claims that there are such limits, the value of each extra life must decline in a different way. One example would be: 1, 1/2, 1/4, 1/8, 1/16, etc. Though there would always be some value in each extra life, this sequence has an upper limit: 2. But, with a finite number of extra lives, this upper limit is never quite reached.

The world's actual population now consists of several billion people, most of whom believe their lives to be worth living. Most of those who accept view (5) would agree that, in the world now, the value of extra quantity can be regarded as having reached its limit. This is is why I supposed that, in my imagined outcome A, there would be ten billion people

If there is a lower quality of life, could this always
be morally outweighed by a sufficient gain in the number
of people who exist, and have lives worth living? More
precisely, could a loss of quality, during some period,
always be outweighed by a sufficient gain in the quantity
both of happiness and of whatever else makes
life worth living?

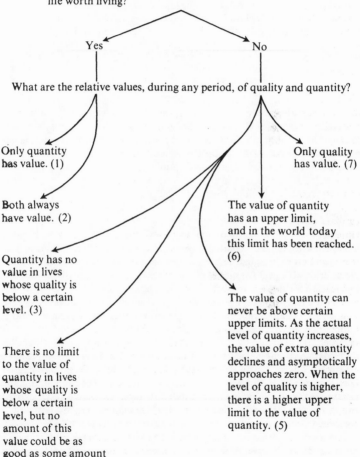

Yes   No

What are the relative values, during any period, of quality and quantity?

Only quantity
has value. (1)

                                                    Only quality
                                                    has value. (7)

Both always
have value. (2)

                            The value of quantity
                            has an upper limit,
                            and in the world today
                            this limit has been reached.
                            (6)

Quantity has no
value in lives
whose quality is
below a certain
level. (3)

                            The value of quantity can
                            never be above certain
                            upper limits. As the actual
                            level of quantity increases,
                            the value of extra quantity
                            declines and asymptotically
                            approaches zero. When the
There is no limit   level of quality is higher,
to the value of   there is a higher upper
quantity in lives   limit to the value of
whose quality is   quantity. (5)
below a certain
level, but no
amount of this
value could be as
good as some amount
of the value of
quantity in lives
whose quality is
above a certain level. (4)

living. This makes my example relevantly similar to the actual world; and it makes it an example where views (5) to (7) agree.

In what follows I shall also ignore the difference between (5) and (6). (5) is more plausible. But, when the actual population is very large, the difference between these views has little practical significance. If the value of quantity is extremely close to its upper limit, it can be regarded as having reached its limit. In claiming that there is a single upper limit, (6) is again less plausible than (5). But this difference is not relevant in what follows. We can therefore afford to discuss only the simpler (6).

View (6) can be expressed in

The Limited Quantity View: It will be worse if, during any period, there is a smaller net sum of happiness than there might have been, or a smaller net sum of whatever makes life worth living, unless this smaller sum is above a certain limit.

Suppose next that we reject view (1), since we believe that quality has value. We believe that it would always be bad if there was a lower quality of life. In Hedonistic terms, it would be bad if the same total sum of happiness was *more thinly spread*, or distributed over more lives, so that within each life there is less happiness. In its simplest form, this belief can be expressed in

The Two-Level Quality View: It will be worse if those who live will *all* be worse off, or have a lower quality of life, than *all* of those who would have lived.

On this view, if in one of two outcomes everyone would be worse off, this is a bad feature of this outcome. It does not follow that, of the two, this is the worse outcome. This bad feature might be outweighed by a good feature. Since the Two-Level Quality View is merely a claim about the badness of one feature, I believe that most of us would accept this view.

Suppose that we accept both this and the Limited Quantity View. In cases that involve small populations, we shall believe that lower quality could be outweighed by greater quantity. But, if the value of quantity can be regarded as having reached its limit, we believe that only quality has value. As I have said, this is what most of us believe about the actual world in the Twentieth Century. And this is what we would believe about my imagined outcomes A and B. Since we would believe that, in A, the value of quantity can be regarded as having reached its upper limit, we would believe that B would be worse than A. This would be so however many more people B contained. When considering populations as large as ten billion, we shall believe that a loss in quality could never be morally outweighed by a gain in quantity. It would always be worse if, instead of some group of ten billion people, there were more people who would *all* be worse off. This would be worse even if, in both outcomes, the quality of life would be very high. (If we reject this last claim, we should turn to view (3), discussed in Section 139.)

The Two-Level Quality View would not cover many actual cases. It would seldom be true that, in one of the two outcomes that would be produced by two rates of population growth, *everyone* would be worse off than *everyone* in the other outcome. If we believe that quality has value, we must make some other claim to cover most of the actual cases. One such claim is the Average View, in either its person-affecting or its impersonal form. Many people appeal to this view. But, as I shall argue, we should reject the Average View. (Those who appeal to this view may have accepted the Two-Level Quality View and then, rashly, changed 'all' to 'on average'.)

To cover most of the actual cases, we would need some more complicated claim. But we can ignore these complications. It will be enough to consider the two views that I have just described. One is the view that the value of quantity has, within any period, an upper limit. The other is the view that quality has value.

I am searching for Theory X, the new theory about beneficence that both solves the Non-Identity Problem and avoids the Repugnant Conclusion. More generally, Theory X would be the best theory about beneficence. It would have acceptable implications when applied to all of the choices that we ever make, including those that affect both the identities and the number of future people. In a complete moral theory, we cannot avoid the question of how many people there should ever be. But I have postponed this question. I am discussing what we should believe about different outcomes during certain periods.

We may hope that Theory X would be simple. If we ought to accept the Repugnant Conclusion, this theory could be simple: it could be the claim that only quantity has value. This claim is expressed by all versions of the Total Principle. But I believe that we should reject the Repugnant Conclusion. If this is so, we could appeal to another simple theory: the claim that only quality has value. The Average Principle is one version of this claim. But I believe that, like its opposite, this claim is too extreme. I believe that the best theory about beneficence must claim that quality and quantity both have value.

If these beliefs are justified, the best theory might be the combination of the two views that I have just described. On this theory, quality always has value, and quantity has value in a way that, in any period, cannot be above some upper limit. This theory achieves, in my simplified examples, the two results that I have been trying to achieve. It solves the Non-Identity Problem and avoids the Repugnant Conclusion. If this theory is defensible, it might be a simplified version of X: the best theory about beneficence.

Is this theory defensible? Not in its present form.

138. THE SUM OF SUFFERING

Reconsider

> *The Two Hells.* In *Hell One*, the last generation consists of ten innocent people, who each suffer great agony for fifty years. The lives of these people are much worse than nothing. They would all kill themselves if they could. In *Hell Two*, the last generation consists not of ten but of ten million innocent people, who each suffer agony just as great for fifty years minus a day.

When we consider these imagined Hells, we cannot plausibly appeal only to the Two-Level Quality View, or to the Average View. On these views, Hell One would be worse, since the lives of the ten people would all be very slightly worse than the lives of the ten million people. We can agree that, in this respect, Hell One would be worse. It would be bad that, in this Hell, each of the people who exists has to endure slightly more suffering. But it can be claimed that, in another respect, Hell Two would be worse. In this Hell the total sum of suffering is nearly a million times greater. And it can claimed that this vast increase in the sum of suffering morally outweighs the very small reduction in the sum of suffering within each life.

Can we deny these claims? We would have to appeal to

> *The Limited Suffering Principle:* It will be bad if, at any time, there is a greater sum of suffering than there might have been, unless this greater sum is above a certain limit.

On this view, as the sum of suffering increases, extra suffering matters less. And this disvalue approaches zero. Beyond a certain point, for practical purposes, extra suffering ceases to matter. If more people have to endure even the most extreme agony, this is not bad at all.

This view is very implausible. It is much more implausible than the Repugnant Conclusion. When we consider the badness of suffering, we should claim that this badness has no upper limit. It is always bad if an extra person has to endure extreme agony. And this is always just as bad, however many others have similar lives. The badness of extra suffering never declines.

In the case of suffering, there is no upper limit to the disvalue of quantity. Do we believe, when considering suffering, that only quantity matters? Most of us do not. We would think it better if the same quantity of suffering was more thinly spread, over a greater number of lives. This is implied, in simple cases, by the Two-Level Quality View.

We should add these claims about suffering to the theory that I described. Our theory now combines three views. We believe that quality always has value: that it would always be bad if people are worse off than people might have been. We also believe that there is value in the quantity of happiness, and of whatever else makes life worth living, but that this value has, in any period, an upper limit. And we now believe that there is disvalue, or badness, in the quantity both of suffering and of whatever else makes life *worth ending*. We believe that, to this kind of badness, there is no limit.

This new theory implies

The Ridiculous Conclusion: If there were ten billion people living, all with a quality of life about that of the average quality of the lives lived by the world's present population, there must be some much larger imaginable population whose existence would be *worse*, even though *all* of its members would have a *very much higher* quality of life. This much larger population would be worse because, in each of these lives, there would be some intense suffering.[36]

Even in lives of a quality very much higher than ours, there could be some intense suffering. In the larger imagined population, everyone has such a life. These lives would be well worth living because this suffering would be greatly outweighed by happiness, and by the other things that make life worth living. But, on our new theory, this suffering cannot be *morally* outweighed by these other things. Given the size of the population, and its high quality of life, there is no positive value in extra quantity. The suffering in each extra life would be a bad feature, making the outcome worse. On our theory, this bad feature cannot be morally outweighed by the much greater happiness in each extra life, or by the other things that make these lives well worth living. These are not good features, which make the outcome better, since the positive value of quantity has already reached its limit.

On our theory, any extra life would have only two morally relevant features. One would be the quality of this life, the other would be the suffering that it contains. The Ridiculous Conclusion compares two possible populations. One contains ten billion people, all of whom have a quality of life about the same as the average quality of the lives that are actually now being lived. The other population would be very much larger, and all of its members would have a very much higher quality of life. (We can suppose that most of this much larger population lives on many Earth-like planets, that have drifted into and become part of the Solar System.) Compared with the existence of the smaller population, the existence of this larger population would be in one way better, and in another way worse. This outcome would have the good feature that everyone has a very much higher quality of life. It would have the bad feature that there would be a greater sum of intense suffering. If, with the same quality of life, we imagine this population to be even larger, this would not make the good feature better. But it would make the bad feature worse, since there would be an even greater sum of intense suffering. On our view, there is no limit to the badness of a greater sum of such suffering. Since the badness of this feature has no limit, it must, with a large enough population, outweigh the good feature. Our new theory clearly implies the Ridiculous Conclusion.

How can we avoid this conclusion? We cannot plausibly place an upper limit on the badness of the sum of suffering. But we can distinguish two kinds of suffering. Suffering is *compensated* if it comes within a life that is worth living. If it comes within a life that is not worth living, it is *uncompensated*. We cannot claim that, of these two kinds of suffering, only the second is bad. Suppose that, near the end of a life that has been well worth living, someone begins to suffer intensely. We cannot defensibly claim that, when this person is suffering intensely, this is not bad. But we might claim

It is always bad if there is more uncompensated suffering. To this badness there is no upper limit. And, if an extra person suffers, and has a life that is not worth living, this is always equally bad. The badness of this suffering cannot be reduced by the fact that other people are happy. When we consider the badness of suffering within a life that is not worth living, it is irrelevant what happens to other people.[37]

There are two ways in which there might be more compensated suffering: (1) There might be more suffering in a life now being lived that is worth living. (2) There might be an extra person who exists, with a life that is worth living, but containing some suffering. Of these two, only (1) is bad. This is why we can reject the Ridiculous Conclusion. It would not be a bad feature that, in the larger imagined population, there would be more intense suffering. This would not be a bad feature because this suffering would come in extra lives that are worth living. It would not be worse if these extra people existed. What we claim about this extra suffering is, not that it would be bad, but that it would have been better if these lives had not contained this suffering.

It may be objected, 'If this extra suffering is not bad, why would it have been better if these lives had not contained this suffering?' We could answer, 'Because this would have made the quality of life even higher.'

It may next be objected: 'If you deny that extra suffering is bad when it comes in extra lives that are worth living, you must be implicitly assuming that these lives contain good features which outweigh the badness of the suffering. This undermines your claim that the positive value of quantity has reached its upper limit.'

We could answer: 'Our view distinguishes *personal* and *moral* value. What we call the value of a life is not its personal value—its value to the person whose life it is—but the value that this life contributes to the outcome. When we claim that some life has no value, this means that the living of this life does not make the outcome better. In other words, it would not have been worse in itself if the person with this life had never existed. If this would have been worse this would only be because of its effects on other people. Given this distinction, we can answer your objection. The suffering in these extra lives has personal disvalue, or is bad for the people who live these lives. This disvalue is outweighed, for these people, by the personal value of their happiness, and the other things that make their lives worth living. This personal value is not moral value. The existence of these extra people does not make the outcome better. In a similar way, because their suffering is compensated, or outweighed by personal value in the same lives, the personal disvalue of this extra suffering does not have moral disvalue. When there is more suffering only because there are more lives lived that are worth living, this extra suffering does not make the outcome worse'.[38]

Consider next three possible populations, during some period. The first is the world's actual population, during the last quarter of the Twentieth Century. The second is a larger population, *nearly* all of whom have a very much higher quality of life. As before, most of this larger population live on other Earth-like planets, that have become part of the Solar System.

In this larger population, there are some unfortunate people, who suffer and whose lives are not worth living. These people might be like the Wretched Child described above, who is so diseased that he never develops, lives for only a few years, and suffers pain that cannot wholly be relieved. Or these people might be afflicted with some life-long and distressing mental illness. These unfortunate people are, proportionately, very rare. In this imagined population there would be one such person in each ten billion people.

Many believe that it would be wrong to bring happiness to millions by torturing one innocent child.[39] Though the proportions are similar, my imagined case is quite different. It is through sheer bad luck that, in each ten billion people in this larger population, there is one person with a disease that makes him suffer, and makes his life not worth living. These unfortunate people do not commit suicide either because they do not develop, or because of the nature of their mental illness. Some of us would believe that, for their own sakes, such people ought to be killed. But this is not the view of my imagined people. Though they believe that it would be wrong to kill these unfortunate few, they do the best they can to relieve their suffering.

Suppose next that, because there is only one such person in each ten billion, there would be *fewer* of these people in this larger population than there are in the actual world, now. This can be plausibly supposed even if this imagined population is many times the size of the world's present population. In the world's actual population there are some people whose diseases make them suffer, and make their lives not worth living. It would be hard to judge the proportion of such people to those actual people whose lives are worth living. But it is clear that this proportion is *far* higher than one in ten billion.

Compared with the world's actual population, this larger imagined population is in two ways better, and in no way worse. The quality of life of most people is very much higher. And there is *less* uncompensated suffering.

Compared with the existence of the world's actual population, the existence of this imagined population would clearly be much better.

Consider now a second imagined population. This is exactly like the first, except that it is very much larger. This population would live on very many Earth-like planets. Compared with the existence of the world's actual population, the existence of this second imagined alternative would be in one way better, and in one way worse. The way in which it would be better is that nearly everyone has a very much higher quality of life. The way in which it would be worse is that there would be *more* uncompensated suffering.

As before, if we imagine this population to be even larger, there is no way in which this would be better, and one way in which this would be worse. The quality of life would be the same, and the positive value of quantity has already reached its limit. If this population was even larger, its good features would not be better. But its bad feature would be worse. There would be even more uncompensated suffering. And, to the badness of this feature, there is no limit.

On our theory, the good features of this population have a limited value. But there is no limit to the disvalue of the bad feature. Whenever we imagine this population to be larger, the good features would not become better, but the bad feature would always become worse. If this population was sufficiently large, its existence would be worse than that of the world's actual population. And, if this population was sufficiently large, its bad feature would outweigh its good features. Badness that could be unlimited must be able to outweigh limited goodness. If this population was sufficiently large, its existence would be intrinsically bad. It would be better if, during this period, no one existed.

We might say: 'Even if it would be better in itself if no one existed during this period, this would be worse on the whole, since there would then be no future people'.

This is no answer. Consider two possible future histories. In the first, there are no future people. In the second, there is always a population of the kind just described. Since the existence of such a population would always be, on our view, intrinsically bad, we must conclude that it would be better if there were no future people.

Given our theory, we are forced to accept

The Absurd Conclusion: In one possible outcome, there would exist during some future century both some population on the Earth that is like the Earth's present actual population, and an enormous number of other people, living on Earth-like planets that had become part of the Solar System. Nearly all of the people on these other planets would have a quality of life far above that enjoyed by most of the Earth's actual population. In each ten billion of these other people, there would be one unfortunate person, with a disease that makes him suffer, and have a life that is not worth living.

In a second possible outcome, there would be the same enormous number of extra future people, with the same high quality of life for all except the unfortunate one in each ten billion. But this enormous number of extra future people would not all live in one future century. Each ten billion of these people would live in each of very many future centuries.

On our view, the first outcome would be very bad, much worse than if there were none of these extra future people. The second outcome would be very good. The first would be very bad and the second very good even though, in both outcomes, there would be the very same number of extra future people, with the very same high quality of life for all except the unfortunate one in each ten billion.

This conclusion may not be ridiculous. But the absurdity is not much less. The first outcome is exactly like the second, except that all of the extra future people live in the same rather than in different centuries. If the second outcome would be very good, and the first outcome differs only with respect to *when* people live, how can this difference in timing make the first outcome very bad?

There is one way in which a difference in timing might make a moral difference. Inequality within one generation may be worse than inequality between different generations. But, in the two outcomes we are considering, the inequality would be the same. It would be true in both that, in each extra ten billion people, one person is much worse off than all of the others.

We can suppose that, in both these outcomes, *all the lives that are ever lived would be, both in number and in quality, identical*. In these respects these outcomes are exactly similar. But, because of the difference in when these lives are lived, we conclude that the first outcome would be very good, and the second very bad.

The Absurd Conclusion is clearly implied by our latest view. On this view, the positive value of quantity has, in any period, an upper limit, while there is no such limit to the negative value of quantity, or to the badness of the amount of uncompensated suffering. In the second outcome, where each extra ten billion people live in different centuries, the positive value of quantity greatly outweighs, in each century, its negative value. This is why this outcome is very good. In the first outcome, where these extra people all live in the same century, the reverse is true. Since the positive value of quantity has, in this century, an upper limit, this value is greatly outweighed by the badness of the amount of uncompensated suffering. This outcome is therefore very bad. The second outcome is very good, and the first very bad, even though in both the lives that are ever lived are, in number and in quality, identical.

I cannot believe this conclusion. This conclusion follows from the asymmetry in our claims about the value of quantity. On our view, while there is no limit, in any period, to the disvalue of quantity, there is a limit to its value. To avoid the Absurd Conclusion, we must abandon this view.

139. THE VALUELESS LEVEL

Most of us want to avoid the Repugnant Conclusion. One way to do so is to claim that there is a limit to quantity's positive value. But, as we have just seen, we must abandon this view. On page 403 I mentioned two alternatives: views (3) and (4).

View (3) is

The Appeal to the Valueless Level: Quantity has no value in lives whose quality is below a certain level. If these lives are worth living, they have personal value—value for the people whose lives they are. But the fact that such lives are lived does not make the outcome better.

We can make this view more plausible if we add the following claims. The Valueless Level does not involve a sharp discontinuity. If the quality of life is very high, the moral value of each life—the amount by which it makes the outcome better—is its full personal value. At some lower level, the value of a life starts to be less than its full personal value, and at lower levels these two values increasingly diverge. At the Valueless Level, though lives are still worth living, the first value has reached zero. There is no sharp discontinuity, since at a slightly higher level this value is close to zero.

We could reduce still further the discontinuity. We could claim that there is always value in a life that is worth living, but that, below some level, the value in extra quantity declines. Below this level, the total value of quantity has an upper limit, that would be asymptotically approached, but never quite reached. These claims would make our view more plausible. But they would in practice make only a trivial difference. If the population is sufficiently large, the value in extra quantity below this level would be very close to zero. Since the practical difference would be trivial, I shall discuss the simpler view that does not make these further claims.

If we appeal to the Valueless Level, what should we take this level to be? This level is the lower edge of a wide band, in which the personal value of a life increasingly diverges from the value that this life contributes to the outcome. If we appeal to the Valueless Level, we need to decide where, on the scale of the quality of life, this wide band comes. We may find this question hard to answer. But this may be less hard than accepting the Repugnant Conclusion. Since we have been forced to abandon the claim that the value of quantity has an upper limit, the appeal to the Valueless Level may be the least implausible way to avoid the Repugnant Conclusion.

Besides appealing to the Valueless Level, we should continue to make our other claims. We should continue to claim that quality has value: that it would always be bad if there was a lower quality of life. And we should continue to claim that, if they come within lives that are not worth living, there is disvalue, or badness, in the quantity both of suffering and of whatever else makes life worth ending. To the badness of uncompensated suffering there is no limit. We should now add the claim that there is value in the quantity of happiness, and of whatever else makes life worth living, provided that this value comes in lives that are above the Valueless Level. And we should claim that to this value there is no limit.

On this new theory, we avoid the Absurd Conclusion. In the first outcome that I described, nearly everyone has lives that are above the Valueless Level. Only one in each ten billion people has a life that is not worth living. Quantity's positive value here outweighs its negative value.

It might be objected: 'Consider two outcomes whose proportionate relation is the same as the relation between A and B, but in which the quality of life is much lower. Compared with outcome *J*, there would exist in outcome *K* twice as many people, who would all be worse off. Assume next that, in both these outcomes, the quality of life would be below your Valueless Level. On your new theory, the lives lived in these outcomes would have no value. Though they would have personal value, they would not have the kind of value that makes an outcome better. If in both these outcomes the lives lived would have no value, this implies that outcome J would not be better than outcome K. But you would claim that, since the quality of life would in J be higher, J *would* be better than K. Your new theory is self-contradictory.'

We could answer: 'We claim that, if the quality of life is below the Valueless Level, the lives that are lived, even if worth living, have no value. Such lives do not have the *kind* of value that *quantity* can provide. What we mean by this is that, if there were extra people living such lives, this would not make the outcome better. There is value in extra quantity only when the quality of life is above the Valueless Level. But the value in extra quantity is not the only kind of value, or the only feature which can make an outcome better. We deny that only quantity has value. On our theory, quality also has value. We believe that it is always good if people are better off, or have a higher quality of life. Since there are two ways in which an outcome can be better, our theory is not self-contradictory. Outcome J would be better than outcome K, not because it has more of the value of quantity, but because the quality of life would be higher.'

Does this theory provide a good escape from the Repugnant Conclusion? It will be easier to answer this when I have described an alternative.

140. THE LEXICAL VIEW

Rather than appealing to the Valueless Level we could appeal to view (4). This resembles Newman's view about pain and sin. Newman claimed that, though both were bad, no amount of pain could be as bad as the least amount of sin.

On such a view, there is not a single scale of value. Though there is no limit to the badness of pain, unlimited badness of this kind cannot be as bad as limited badness of another kind.

Such a view is coherent. It is more plausible when applied, as in Newman's case, to things which are in two quite different categories. Can we apply such a view to a single category: lives that are worth living?

Such a view can plausibly be held when we compare certain human lives to the lives of the lower animals. If they are conscious, oysters may have lives that are worth living. When they are not factory-farmed, the lives of pigs are probably worth living. But we can plausibly claim that, even if there is some value in the fact that these lives are lived, no amount of this value could be as good as the value in the life of Socrates.

If we are to avoid the Repugnant Conclusion in this way, we must make such a claim about lives that are all lived by human beings. On the scale of the quality of life, we must define two new levels. Call lives *Mediocre* if they are below the lower level, and *Blissful* if they are above the higher level. We might now appeal to

> *The Lexical View*: There is no limit to the positive value of quantity. It is always better if an extra life is lived that is worth living. But no amount of Mediocre lives could have as much value as one Blissful life.

141. CONCLUSIONS

We must avoid the Absurd Conclusion. This conclusion followed from the asymmetry in our claims about the value of quantity. We placed a limit on quantity's positive value, within some period, but we placed no limit on its negative value. To avoid the Absurd Conclusion we must abandon this asymmetry.

We cannot plausibly place a limit on quantity's negative value. It is always bad if there is more uncompensated suffering, and this badness never declines. We must therefore remove the limit on quantity's positive value.

When we remove this limit, we need a new way to avoid the Repugnant Conclusion. In my outcome A there would be ten billion people living, all of whom have a quality of life as high as that of the luckiest people alive today. In outcome Z there would be some enormous population, whose members have lives that are barely worth living. If there is any value in the fact that such lives are lived, and the value of quantity has no limit, Z could be better than A. The value of quantity may, in A, be very great. But, if the value of quantity in Z has no limit, this value could be greater. And this value could be great enough to outweigh the fact that the quality of life is much lower. There may again be great disvalue in this fact. But this disvalue could be outweighed by a value that has no limit. If the value of quantity in Z has no limit, this value could outweigh the fact that the quality of life is much lower.

These remarks assume that there is a single scale of value. We might deny this assumption. We might appeal to the Lexical View. On this view, it is always better if an extra life is lived that is worth living. We admit that, to the value of quantity in Z, there is no limit. But we claim that no amount of *this* value could be as good as the value of a single life lived above the Blissful Level. We can assume that, in A, every life is above this level. On the Lexical View, whatever the size of Z's population, Z would be worse than A.

Our alternative is to appeal to the Valueless Level. We would then claim that, for practical purposes, lives that are lived below this level can be assumed to have no value. If these lives are worth living, they have personal value: but they do not make the outcome better. Quantity has value only in lives that are above the Valueless Level. To avoid the Absurd Conclusion, we admit that, to this value, there is no limit.

Which of these is the better view? Should we accept the Lexical View, or appeal instead to the Valueless Level?

If we appeal to the Valueless Level, we cannot avoid a variant of the Absurd Conclusion. We must accept

(A) Suppose that, in some history of the future, there would always be an enormous number of people, and for each one person who suffers, and has a life that is not worth living, there would be ten billion people whose lives *are* worth living, though their quality of life is not quite as high as the Valueless Level. This would be *worse* than if there were no future people.

We must accept (A) since, on our view, in this imagined future quantity would have no positive value. There would be disvalue in the suffering of the unfortunate few. If instead there were no future people, this might perhaps be claimed to be a special case in which there would be a loss in quality. But the badness of this loss, however great, could be less than the badness of the sum of suffering. This must be true with a large enough population, since this badness has no limit.

Our new theory also implies

(R) If there were ten billion people living, all with a very high quality of life, there must be some much larger imaginable population whose existence would be *better*, even though its members have lives that are barely above the Valueless Level.

This is a weakened form of the Repugnant Conclusion. Our theory implies this conclusion because it implies that, above the Valueless Level, any loss of quality could always be morally outweighed by a sufficient gain in quantity. This must be implied because, to avoid the Absurd Conclusion, our theory ceases to claim that there is a limit to quantity's positive value.

(A) is less absurd than the Absurd Conclusion. (R) is less repugnant than the Repugnant Conclusion. The implausibility of these two conclusions depends on where we place the Valueless Level. We might place this level close to the level where life ceases to be worth living. If the Valueless Level is as low as this, (A) may not be absurd, but (R) is repugnant. If we raise the Valueless Level, (R) is less repugnant, but (A) is more absurd.

If we appeal instead to the Lexical View, we must accept variants of (A) and (R). These merely substitute, for the word 'Valueless', the word 'Mediocre'. How the Lexical View implies these conclusions I explain in endnote 40.

In this chapter I have searched for Theory X, the theory about beneficence that solves the Non-Identity Problem, avoids the Repugnant Conclusion, and has acceptable implications in all cases. There is one principle that achieves the first two aims: the Wide Average Person-affecting Principle. This principle claims that, if someone is caused to exist with a life worth living, he is thereby benefited. As I argue in Appendix G, both this claim and its denial are defensible.

The Wide Average Principle cannot, by itself, be Theory X. In some cases it has unacceptable implications. Thus it implies that Hell One would be worse than Hell Two even though, in Hell Two, each life is almost as bad, and the amount of uncompensated suffering is nearly a million times greater. More generally, the Wide Average Principle gives no weight to the sum of such suffering. Even if we accept this principle, we must add the claim that it is always bad if there is more uncompensated suffering, and that to this badness there is no limit.

When applied to lives that are worth living, the Wide Average Principle gives no weight to the quantity of happiness, and of whatever else makes life worth living. The principle could imply that, in the best possible history, only one person ever lives. Most of us would find this view too extreme. Most of us would believe that there is some value in quantity, even if this value has, in any period, an upper limit.

The Average Principle partly coincides with the more restricted Two-Level Quality View. According to this view, when we compare two outcomes A and B, it would be worse if everyone in B would be worse off than everyone in A. This view covers few actual cases. The Average Principle extends this view in a way that covers all cases. But I shall soon argue that, even as part of a pluralist theory which appeals to several principles, the Average Principle is unacceptable. The Two-Level Quality View must be extended in some other way. If these claims are justified, we have not yet found Theory X. Since we should reject the Average Principle, we have not yet fully solved the Non-Identity Problem.

We have also found another problem. If our theory makes the claims that I have just described, it avoids the Repugnant Conclusion at the cost of implying the Absurd Conclusion. Since this is a new problem, we have again made progress of a negative kind. By appealing to the Valueless Level, or to the Lexical View, we partly solve this new problem. We are merely forced to accept both (A) and (R), or two variants of these conclusions. These conclusions are less repugnant and less absurd. But they are both implausible. We have not wholly solved this problem.

As I shall now argue, there is another problem.

19

THE MERE ADDITION PARADOX

142. MERE ADDITION

CONSIDER these alternatives:

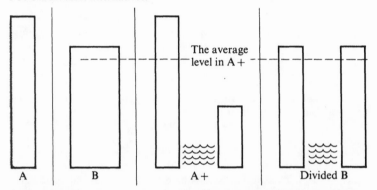

Suppose that we appeal to the Valueless Level. Assume that the quality of life in B is below this level. We shall then believe that, though the people in B together have more happiness than the people in A, and more of whatever else makes life worth living, this is not a way in which B is better than A. Lives in B are below the level where quantity has value. We also believe that quality has value. We believe that it is bad that the B-people are all worse off than all of the A-people. Since B is in one way worse than A, and in no way better, we conclude that B is worse than A.

Suppose that we appeal instead to the Lexical View. The quality of life in B is about four-fifths as high as the quality of life in A. Given this fact, we cannot plausibly assume both that lives in B are below the Mediocre Level and that lives in A are above the Blissful Level. On our view, if B was large enough, it would be better than A. A sufficient gain in quantity could outweigh its lower quality. But, since B is only twice as large as A, we can claim that this is not true. We can again conclude that B is worse than A.

Now compare A with A+. In A+ there is one group as large as the only group in A, and with the same high quality of life. A+ contains another group, whom I call the *extra people*. These people have lives that are worth living, and they affect no one else. The extra people are worse off than the people in the first group. If this inequality was both known, and removable, it might involve social injustice. I therefore assume, for simplicity, that the two groups in A+ are not aware of each other's existence, and could not communicate. A+ is some possible state of the world before the Atlantic Ocean had been crossed. A is a different state in which the Americas are uninhabited.

Is A+ either better or worse than A? It will help to define a new phrase. There is

> *Mere Addition* when, in one of two outcomes, there exist extra people (1) who have lives worth living, (2) who affect no one else, and (3) whose existence does not involve social injustice.

When we compare A with A+, Mere Addition in A+ lowers the average quality of life. Is this a bad effect, making A+ worse than A?

143. WHY WE SHOULD REJECT THE AVERAGE PRINCIPLE

According to the Average Principle, in both its person-affecting and impersonal forms, it is worse if there is a lower average quality of life, per life lived. On this principle, A+ is worse than A. But we should reject this principle.

On the Average Principle, the best history might be the one in which only Eve and Adam ever live. It would be worse if, instead of Eve and Adam, a billion billion other people lived, all with a quality of life that would be almost as high. Though this claim is hard to believe, it is not absurd. The second history is in one way worse. It is bad that no one's life is quite as good as Eve and Adam's would have been.

The Average Principle has other implications which *are* absurd. Suppose that Eve and Adam lived these wonderful lives. On the Average Principle it would be worse if, *not instead but in addition,* the billion billion other people lived. This would be worse because it would lower the average quality of life. *This* way of lowering the average, by Mere Addition, cannot be plausibly claimed to be bad.

A similar claim applies to the birth of any child. Whether this would be bad, on the Average Principle, depends on facts about all previous lives. If the Ancient Egyptians had a very high quality of life, it is more likely to be bad to have a child now. It is more likely that this child's birth will lower the average quality of the lives that are ever lived. But research in Egyptology cannot be relevant to our decision whether to have children.[41]

These are objections to the temporally neutral version of the Average Principle. Can we defend some other version? Some writers assume that what matters is the average quality of life of those who live after we act. But this implies absurdly that we would make the outcome better if we killed all but the best-off people now living.

It might be claimed that what matters is the average quality of life of all presently existing and future people. This claim avoids the last implication. But consider

How Only France Survives. In one possible future, the worst-off people in the world soon start to have lives that are well worth living. The quality of life in different nations then continues to rise. Though each nation has its fair share of the world's resources, such things as climate and cultural traditions give to some nations a higher quality of life. The best-off people, for many centuries, are the French.

In another possible future, a new infectious disease makes nearly everyone sterile. French scientists produce just enough of an antidote for all of France's population. All other nations cease to exist. This has some bad effects on the quality of life for the surviving French. Thus there is no new foreign art, literature, or technology that the French can import. These and other bad effects outweigh any good effects. Throughout this second possible future the French therefore have a quality of life that is slightly lower than it would be in the first possible future.

In this second future the average quality of life would be higher. The surviving French would have a lower quality of life; and in the period when most people became sterile, most of these people's lives would be worse. But these two effects would be greatly outweighed by the non-existence of the world's other nations. In the first future, there would be billions of people in these other nations. These billions of people would, for many centuries, be all worse off than the French would be in either of these futures. If these billions of people never lived, the average quality of future lives would thus be higher.

On the Average Principle, it would be better if only the French survived. This is another absurd conclusion. If these billions of people lived, their lives would be *well* worth living, and their existence would be *better* for the French. On the Average Principle, it would be worse if these people lived, simply because the French have even better lives. Because this is true, the existence of these people would lower the average quality of life. As before, *this* way of lowering this average cannot be plausibly thought to matter.

A similar claim again applies to the birth of any child. Suppose that, in the further future, the quality of life will for many centuries be extremely high. It is then more likely to be bad if I have a child, even if my child's life would be well worth living, and his existence would be bad for no one. It is more likely that my child's existence would lower the average quality of all future lives. This cannot be relevant. Whether I should have a child cannot depend on what the quality of life will be in the distant future.

We might revise the Average Principle so that it avoids this implication. Such a revision would probably involve drawing an arbitrary distinction.[42]

And the main objection still applies. The Average Principle must cover lives that overlap. On this principle, whether I ought to have a child still depends on irrelevant facts about other people's lives.

This is shown most clearly in

> *Hell Three*. Most of us have lives that are much worse than nothing. The exceptions are the sadistic tyrants who make us suffer. The rest of us would kill ourselves if we could; but this is made impossible. The tyrants claim truly that, if we have children, they will make these children suffer slightly less.

On the Average Principle, we ought to have these children. This would raise the average quality of life. It is irrelevant that our children's lives would be much worse than nothing. This is another absurd conclusion.

Though there are other objections to the Average Principle, I shall not state these here. We have seen enough to know that we should reject this principle.

144. WHY WE SHOULD REJECT THE APPEAL TO INEQUALITY

Reconsider A and A +. The extra people in A + have lives that are worth living, and they affect no one else. Is A + worse than A?

The existence of the extra people lowers the average quality of life. But, as I have argued, this fact is irrelevant. When this average is lowered by Mere Addition, we cannot plausibly appeal to the Average Principle.

There is another way in which A + might be claimed to be worse than A. In A + there is what I call *natural inequality*. The extra people are worse off than the other group, through no fault of theirs. The extra people do not know this fact, and there is no social injustice. Does this unperceived natural inequality make A + worse than A?

An objector might appeal to principles of justice like those that Rawls defends. One such principle is

> *Maximin*: The best outcome is the one in which the worst-off people are best off.

Appendix H shows that Maximin may conflict with other Rawlsian principles; but we can ignore this here. Unlike Rawls, some people apply this principle to all kinds of case. These people might claim that A is better than A +, because A is the outcome in which the worst-off people are best off.

Suppose, first, that causing to exist can benefit. On this assumption, if A + comes about, this will benefit the worst-off people in A +. It may seem bad that, in A +, there is inequality. But what causes the inequality benefits all of the people who are worse off than others. And this is the outcome that, of those that are possible, benefits these people most. We can plausibly appeal here to another Rawlsian principle. On this principle, inequality is not bad if what causes the inequality gives the greatest possible benefits to all of the people who are worse off. This supports the claim that A + is not worse than A.

Suppose next that causing to exist cannot benefit. On this assumption, if A + comes about, this does not benefit the worst-off people in A +. Could an appeal to Maximin justify the claim that A + is worse than A?

As I argued earlier, the Ideal Contractualist Method should not be applied to the question of how many people ought to exist. The same is true of Maximin. Suppose that we accept this principle in cases where, in the different outcomes, the same number of people would exist. It does not follow that we should extend Maximin to cases where, in the different outcomes, different numbers of people would exist. What Maximin implies is very different in these two kinds of case.

In a Same Number Case, with two outcomes, consider the outcome in which

(1)   the worst-off group is best off.

If we compare this outcome with the other, it must be true

(2)   that in this outcome there are *more* people who are better off than the worst-off group in the other outcome.

In Same Number Cases, (2) is the *only* way in which, in one of two outcomes, (1) can be true. If (2) was false, the worst-off group would in both outcomes be equally large, and equally badly off. According to Maximin, the better of two outcomes is the one in which (1) is true. In Same Number Cases, (1) is true if and only if (2) is true. We can therefore claim that, according to Maximin, the better of two outcomes is the one in which (2) is true.

Now compare A and A +. If we appeal to Maximin in this Different Number Case, it implies that A is better than A +, since A is the outcome in which (1) is true. When there is only one group in some outcome, this group is both the best-off and the worst-off group. In outcome A is (2) true? Are there more people in A who are better off than the worst-off group in A +? There are not. In Different Number Cases, there is *another* way in which, in one of two outcomes, (1) can be true. (1) can be true because

(3)   in this outcome certain people do not exist who, in the other outcome, would have lives that are worth living.

(3) is different from (2). Since (1) is true in this different way, we cannot simply assume that, in Different Number Cases, an appeal to Maximin is justified. It is an open question whether, since (1) is true in this different way, this makes the outcome better. If in one of two outcomes (2) is true, this is clearly a good feature of this outcome. It is clearly good if there are more people who are better off than the worst-off group in the other

outcome. If in one of two outcomes (3) is true, is this clearly a good feature? Is it clearly good if certain people do not exist who, in the other outcome, would have lives that are worth living? This cannot be claimed to be clearly good. I believe that, if (3) is true, this is *not* a good feature. The truth of (3) does not make this outcome better. Because (3) is true, (1) is true. The worst-off group are better off. But, if *this* is the way in which (1) is true, (1) is not a good feature. It is morally irrelevant if the worst-off group are in *this* way better off. In this kind of Different Number Case we should not appeal to Maximin.

Some people may question these claims. But, if these people appeal to Maximin in this kind of case, they face objections like the objections to the Average Principle. Consider a variant of the case in which Only France Survives. Suppose that, if all the other nations ceased to exist, this would *greatly lower* the quality of life of the surviving French. But the French would still be better off than the worst-off nation if no nation ceased to exist. Maximin therefore implies that it would be better if only France survived. In this version of this case, this conclusion is even more absurd. How could it be better if all other nations ceased to exist, with the result that the survivors would be *much worse off?*

Since it implies this absurd conclusion, Maximin should not be applied to this kind of Different Number Case. An appeal to Maximin cannot support the claim that A + is worse than A.

Some egalitarians do not appeal to Maximin. These people might claim: 'Since you do not believe that it would be better if the extra people lived, you cannot believe that there is any way in which A + is better than A. And you should admit that A + is in one way worse. It is a bad feature of A + that some people are worse off than others, through no fault of theirs. Since A + is in no way better than A, and in one way worse, A + must be worse than A.'

This may seem convincing. But it can be answered in the way in which I answered an earlier objection. I was assuming that, since the world's actual population is now large, it would not be better if extra lives were lived that were worth living. I suggested the following objection to this view: 'Compare the world's actual population with a much larger possible population. In this larger population, everyone has a much higher quality of life, though each life contains some intense suffering. Whenever you imagine this larger population to be even larger, this outcome is in no way better, on your view. But this outcome is in one way worse, because there would be more intense suffering. Since this outcome is in no way better and in one way worse, you must agree that it must be worse. And you must agree that, if this population was sufficiently large, the increase in suffering would outweigh all of this outcome's good features. Though all of the people in this outcome would be far better off than we are now, their existence would be worse than the existence of the world's actual population. On your view, you cannot avoid this ridiculous conclusion.'

I suggested how we might avoid this conclusion. I agreed that, if there is intense suffering in some outcome, this is a bad feature. But I denied that *every* way of avoiding this bad feature would make the outcome better. There are at least two ways in which there could be more suffering. It might be true either (1) that existing people suffer more, or (2) that there are extra people living whose lives, though worth living, contain some suffering. Of these two ways in which there might be more suffering, only (1) makes the outcome worse. If there is more suffering because (2) is true, the fact that there is more suffering does not make the outcome worse. It would not be better if there was less suffering because these extra people did not exist. It would be better only if they did exist, and suffered less.

It was claimed above that the inequality in A+ is a bad feature. I accept this claim. But I again deny that every way of avoiding this bad feature would make the outcome better. Whether inequality makes the outcome worse depends on how it comes about. It might be true either (3) that some existing people become worse off than others, or (4) that there are extra people living who, though their lives are worth living, are worse off than some existing people. Only (3) makes the outcome worse.

When (4) is true, the inequality may be produced by what I call Mere Addition. There is Mere Addition when there are extra people living, who have lives worth living, who affect no one else, and whose existence does not involve social injustice. When inequality is produced by Mere Addition, it does not make the outcome worse. This inequality will be avoided if either (5) the extra people exist and are not worse off than anyone else, or (6) the extra people never exist. Only (5) would make the outcome better. It would not be better if there was no inequality because the extra people did not exist. It would be better only if the extra people did exist, and were as well off as everyone else.

Since the inequality in A+ is produced by Mere Addition, this inequality does not make A+ worse than A. We cannot plausibly claim that the extra people should never have existed, *merely because, unknown to them, there are other people who are even better off*.

145. THE FIRST VERSION OF THE PARADOX

Now compare A+ with B. It may help to make this comparison through the intermediate world, Divided B, where the two halves of B's population cannot communicate. Clearly B is as good as Divided B. We can now ask, 'If A+ were to change to Divided B, would this be a change for better or worse?'

Since the two groups cannot communicate, this change would not be the result of a deliberate redistribution. The change from A+ to Divided B would be the result of natural events, affecting the environment. And the change might take place slowly, over two centuries. In a change from A+ to

Divided B, the worse-off half would gain more than the better-off half would lose. On our ordinary moral assumptions, this would be a change for the better. Since this is a Same Number Case, we can appeal to Maximin, and to the Principle of Equality. Divided B is better than A + according to both these principles. Remember that the worse-off group are worse off through no fault of theirs. And we can suppose that they are worse off, not just because they are less happy, or have a lower quality of life, but because they also have a smaller share of resources. We can suppose that Divided B is better than A + both in terms of equality of welfare and in terms of equality of resources. (I am assuming that, in all my imagined cases, the quality of life, the level of happiness, and each person's share of resources rise and fall together.)

There is another ground for judging that Divided B is better than A +. In some cases, equality conflicts with beneficence. This would be so when a worse-off group gains *less* than a better-off group loses. But Divided B is better than A + *both* on any principle of equality *and* on any plausible principle of beneficence. The worse-off group gains *more* than the better-off group loses.

It might be said that principles of equality apply only within some society, where there can be social injustice. If this is so, Divided B is still better than A + on any principle of beneficence. And this claim about equality is not plausible. Consider

> *Rich and Poor.* Suppose that I know about two people who live in different societies which cannot communicate. The person I call *Rich* is better off than the person I call *Poor*. Unless I go to help Rich, there will be a decline in his quality of life, and share of resources. I can either intervene to keep Rich at his present level, or instead help Poor. If I help Poor, I can raise him to the level to which Rich, without my help, would fall. And Poor would rise more than Rich would fall.

Most of us would believe that, if I helped either, it would be better to help Poor rather than Rich. And most of us would believe that this would make the outcome better, both because Poor would gain more than Rich would lose, and because neither would then be worse off than the other. Most of us would believe this even though Rich and Poor live in two societies which cannot (except through me) communicate. We would thus believe that Divided B is better than A +. Since B is obviously as good as Divided B, B is also better than A +.

Suppose we believed that A + is not worse than A. We now believe that B is better than A +. These beliefs together imply that B is not worse than A. B cannot be worse than A if it is better than something—A +—which is not worse than A. But we earlier believed that B *is* worse than A. We have three beliefs that are inconsistent, and imply contradictions. These beliefs imply that B both is and is not worse than A. I call this the *Mere Addition Paradox*.[44]

This is not just a conflict between different moral principles. We may have a pluralist morality in which we believe that it would be better both if there was greater equality and if there was a greater sum of benefits. There may then be cases where greater equality would lower the sum of benefits. Our two principles would here conflict. But there would be no inconsistency in our moral view. We would merely have to ask whether, given the details of the case, the gain in equality would be more or less important than the loss of benefits. We would here be trying to reach an all-things-considered judgement. In the Mere Addition Paradox, things are different. We are here inclined to believe, *all things considered*, that B is worse than A, though B is better than A +, which is not worse than A. These three things cannot all be consistently believed, since they imply contradictions. One of these beliefs must go.

Which should go? Can we honestly claim to believe, of the extra group in A +, that it would have been better if they had never existed? Or can we honestly claim to believe that a change from A + to B would not be a change for the better? If we claimed the latter, we would be saying that what matters most is the quality of life of the best-off people. If their quality of life falls, this is not morally outweighed even by a greater gain in the quality of life of an equally large worse-off group. This is so even though the worse-off group are not worse off through any fault of theirs. Call this the *Elitist View*. On this view, what happens to the best-off people matters *more* than what happens to the worst-off people. A more extreme version of this view would be *Maximax*. This is the opposite of Maximin. On this view, we should give absolute priority to preserving or raising the quality of life of the best-off people. Both these views apply to the actual world. Few of us would find them here morally acceptable.

It may be thought that, if we appeal either to the Valueless Level or to the Lexical View, we have already accepted this Elitist View. This is not so. We appealed to the Valueless Level when considering outcomes in which there is no inequality. Suppose that lives in A are above the Valueless Level, and that lives in B and Z are below this level. We might then claim that the existence of A has intrinsic moral value, while there would be no such value in the existence of B or Z. This would be why B and Z would be worse than A. Since there would be no inequality if what came about was A, this claim could be accepted by egalitarians.

When we compare B with A +, we are comparing outcomes in one of which there is inequality. On the claims just made, only the lives of the best-off group in A + have intrinsic moral value. Even if we believe this, we need not claim that A + is better than B. Our Principles of Equality and Beneficence imply that B would be better than A +. And our claims about intrinsic value might be overridden by these other principles. It is a different and more elitist view that, in a world where a worse-off group *exists,* and are not worse off through any fault of theirs, what matters most is the quality of life of the better-off group. This Elitist View conflicts with and overrides our Principles of Equality and Beneficence.

The Elitist View is not implied either by the Lexical View, or by the appeal to the Valueless Level. But there could be Elitist versions of these two views. We need not be Elitists in all cases. We could merely claim that, if lives in A are above the Valueless Level, and lives in B are below this level, B would be worse than A +. On this view, we would not oppose all redistribution between those who are better and worse off. We could agree that, in most cases, a loss to the best-off people could be outweighed by a greater gain to people who are worse off. We would oppose such redistribution only when it would cause the best-off people to fall below the Valueless Level. Similar claims apply to the Lexical View. On the Elitist version of this view, we would oppose redistribution only when it would cause the best-off people to fall below the Blissful Level.

Suppose that, when we compare B with A +, we cannot accept any version of the Elitist View. We believe that B is better than A +. If we cannot believe that A + is worse than A, we must conclude that B is *not* worse than A. We must conclude that, if these were two possible futures for some society, it would not be worse if what came about was B: twice as many people who were *all* worse off.

The Mere Addition Paradox does not force us to this conclusion. We can avoid the conclusion if we reject one of our other two beliefs. Perhaps, though we find these hard to reject, we find it even harder to accept that B is not worse than A. Suppose we decide that, of the two ways to avoid this conclusion, what is least hard to believe is that A + is worse than A. We can then keep our view that B is worse than A.

We should note, however, that we cannot simply claim that A + *must* be worse than A, since it is worse than something—B—which is worse than A. We would here be rejecting one of three inconsistent claims simply on the ground that it is not consistent with the other two. This could be said against *each* claim. To avoid the Paradox, we must compare only A and A +, setting aside the rest of the argument, and we must believe that A + is worse. We must believe that it is bad in itself that the extra people ever live. We must believe that this is bad, even though these people have lives that are worth living, and affect no one else. To the extent that we find this hard to believe, we still face a paradox.

It may be objected: 'Your argument involves a kind of trick. When you compare A and A +, you claim that the extra group's existence will be worse for no one. But by the time we have moved to B the original group have become worse off. The addition of the extra group *is* worse for the original group. This is why A + is worse than A.'

The argument can be restated. Suppose that we are considering possible states of the world many centuries ago, perhaps in the Ninth Century. There is no ground for fear about future consequences; we know what happened later. Suppose next that A+ was the actual state of the world in this past century. We can then ask, would it have been better if the actual state had been A? In asking this, we can suppose that A+ did *not* later change into B. The existence of the worse-off group in A+ did *not* affect the better-off group for the worse. And, since the groups could not communicate, there was no social injustice. Given these facts, was A+ worse than A would have been? Was it bad that the worse-off group ever lived? We can also ask another question. The world did not in fact change from A+ to B. But, if it had, would this have been a change for the better? On this version of the argument, the last objection is undermined. The existence of the worse-off group was not worse for the better-off group. Since this is so, we may seem forced to admit that A+ was not a worse state of affairs than A would have been. And we may seem forced to admit that a change from A+ to B would have been a change for the better. From these two claims it follows that B would not have been worse than A.[45]

There is another objection to this argument. Some say: 'We must distinguish two cases. If it would not be possible for A+ to change to B, A+ is not worse than A. If this change *would* be possible, A+ *is* worse than A.'[46]

In this latest version of the argument, we can add the assumption that the change from A+ to B would have been impossible. If the actual state was A+, it is hard to believe that A would have been better. And it is hard to deny that, if a change from A+ to B had been possible, this would have been an improvement. On the objection just given, if the change from A+ to B had been possible, even though it did not happen, we should change our view about A and A+. If a change that did not happen might have happened, it *would* have been better if the extra people had never existed.

If we were discussing what people ought to do, such a claim might be plausible. Whether I ought to act in one of two ways may depend on whether it would be possible for me to act in some third way. But such claims are not plausible when applied to outcomes of the kind that I am discussing. These are not the different predictable outcomes of some set of acts that are possible for some person, or group of people. No person, or group, choose whether the actual outcome will be A, A+, or B. I supposed that A+ was the actual state of the world in some past century, and I supposed that A+ did not in fact change into B. I then asked whether, compared with A+, A would have been better. The relative goodness of these two outcomes cannot depend on whether a third outcome, that will never happen, might have happened.

It may now be said: 'Suppose that these outcomes *were* the predictable effects of different possible acts. If we ask what we ought to do, we solve the Paradox. Assume that we could bring about either A, or A+, or B. It would be wrong to bring about A+. This would be wrong since there is a better outcome, B, that we could have brought about. But it would also be wrong to bring about B, since there is a better outcome: A.'

As we shall later see, the Paradox could concern what we ought to do. But there is a simpler answer to this objection. It does not solve our Paradox. It merely ignores it. Any paradox can be ignored. This is no solution.

We can add these claims. Most of our moral thinking may be about what we ought to do. But we also have views about the relative goodness and badness of different outcomes. As I have said, these are not views about moral goodness or badness, in the sense that applies to acts or to agents. If an earthquake kills thousands, this is not morally bad in this sense. But it is bad in a sense that has moral relevance. Our views about the relative goodness of different outcomes sometimes depend upon our views about what we ought to do. But such dependence often goes the other way. As the last objection itself shows, some of our beliefs about what we ought to do depend upon our beliefs about the relative goodness of outcomes. Since these latter beliefs form the basis of some of our morality, we cannot refuse to consider an argument that is about these beliefs. We cannot ignore, as this last objection does, the relative goodness of A and A +. This is why this objection does not solve the Paradox.

We face the Paradox if we believe that Mere Addition cannot make the outcome worse. Some people believe that Mere Addition makes the outcome *better*. They claim that A + is better than A. These people would also accept my claim that B is better than A +. These two claims imply that B is better than A.

If we accept these claims, and reject the Elitist View, we cannot avoid the Repugnant Conclusion. There is a possible outcome C whose relation to B is just like B's relation to A. In C there are twice as many people, who are all worse off than everyone in B. The argument above can be reapplied. If we conclude that B is better than A, we must conclude that C is better than B. On the same argument, D would be better than C, E better than D, and so on down the Alphabet. The *best* outcome would be Z: an enormous population all of whom have lives that are barely worth living.

146. WHY WE ARE NOT YET FORCED TO ACCEPT THE REPUGNANT CONCLUSION

It may seem that, even if we merely claim that A + is not worse than A, we are forced to accept the Repugnant Conclusion. It may seem that, if B would be better than A +, which is not worse than A, B must be better than A. By the same reasoning, C must be better than B, D better than C, and so on.

This reasoning assumes that *not worse than* implies *at least as good as*. This is a natural assumption. But, on reflection, it is here unjustified. Consider an outcome which is like A +, except that the extra people have a somewhat higher quality of life. Call this *Improved A+*. This outcome is clearly better than A+. If we believe both that A+ is not worse than A, and that Improved A+ is better than A+, must we conclude that Improved A+ is better than A? No. We can claim that, while Improved A+ is better than A+, both of these are merely *not worse than* A.[49]

Since *not worse than* need not imply *at least as good as*, this last claim is coherent. And in many other areas these are the kinds of claim that we ought to make. Consider three candidates for some literary prize, one Novelist and two Poets. We might claim, of the Novelist and the First Poet, that neither is worse than the other. This would not be claiming that these two cannot be compared. It would be asserting rough comparability. There are many poets who would be worse candidates than this Novelist, and many novelists who would be worse candidates than the First Poet. We are claiming, of these two, that something important can be said about their respective merits. Neither is worse than the other. They are in the same league. Suppose next that we judge the *Second* Poet to be slightly better than the First. (When we are comparing two poets, our judgements can be less rough.) Does this judgement force us to conclude either that the Second Poet is better than the Novelist, or that the First is worse? It does not. We can claim that, though the Second Poet is better than the First, neither is worse than the Novelist, who is worse than neither. We can similarly claim that, of my imagined states of the world, Improved A+ is better than A+, but neither is worse than A, nor is A worse than either.

Rough comparability is, in some cases, merely the result of ignorance. When this is true, we believe that there is in principle precise or full comparability. This would be true, when we compare the Novelist and either Poet, if the only possibilities are that one is better, or that both are exactly equally as good. In such a case, this is not plausible. The rough comparability is here *intrinsic*, not the result of ignorance. Must it be true, of Proust and Keats, either that one was the greater writer, or that both were *exactly equally* as great? There could not be, even in principle, such precision. But some poets are greater writers than some novelists, and greater by more or less. Shakespeare is a much greater writer than P. G. Wodehouse, but Swinburne is, at best, not much greater. Such intrinsic rough comparability holds, I believe, both for the goodness of certain kinds of outcome, and for the question of whether one person is, in morally significant ways, worse off than another.[50]

When there is only rough comparability, *not worse than* is not a transitive relation. (Relation *R* is *transitive* if, when X is R-related to Y, and Y is R-related to Z, X must be R-related to Z.) The First Poet is not worse than the Novelist, who is not worse than the Second Poet. This does not force us to change our view that the First Poet *is* worse than the Second.

Suppose we believe both that B is better than A+ and that A+ is not worse than A. Because *not worse than* does not here imply *at least as good as*, we are not forced to conclude that B is better than A. We can only conclude that B is not worse than A. And we should check that, in reaching this conclusion, we have not assumed the transitivity of *not worse than*. We have not. We decided that A+ is *not* worse than A, but *is* worse than B. We concluded that B cannot be worse than A. This conclusion was justified. Assume the contrary. Assume that B is worse than A. Since A+ is worse than B, and B is worse than A, A+ must be worse than A. This argument is valid since, unlike *not worse than, worse than is* transitive. But we reject this argument's conclusion. We believe that A+ is *not* worse than A. Since we also believe that A+ *is* worse than B, we must reject this argument's other premise. We must conclude that B cannot be worse than A.

We can be forced to this conclusion. But we cannot be forced from here even to a weakened form of the Repugnant Conclusion. It is true that, by the same reasoning, C cannot be worse than B, D cannot be worse than C, and so on. But since *not worse than* is not transitive, we can claim that, while C is not worse than B, which is not worse than A, C *is* worse than A.

147. THE APPEAL TO THE BAD LEVEL

There is a better argument for the Repugnant Conclusion. Before I state this argument, I shall discuss another view. Consider the range of outcomes that are shown below.

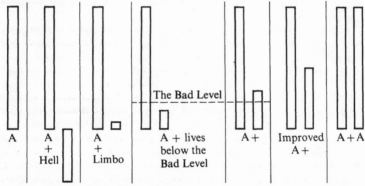

In A + Hell the extra group have (sinless) lives which are much worse than nothing. If they could kill themselves, they would. Clearly, A + Hell *is* worse than A, in the morally relevant sense. And, as clearly, A + A is *not* worse than A. Somewhere between these two we must change our view. Where should the change come? Some would say at the level where the extra people's lives become worth living. On this view, A + Limbo is not worse than A.

We might instead accept a view suggested by Kavka. He calls certain kinds of life *Restricted*, and claims that, other things being equal, it is 'intrinsically undesirable from a moral point of view' that such lives be lived.[51] If someone lives a Restricted life, it would have been in itself better if this person had never lived, and no one had existed in his place. (Since it includes the phrase 'in itself', this claim does not cover effects on other people.)

The plausibility of Kavka's view depends on what counts as Restricted. Kavka calls lives Restricted when they are 'significantly deficient in one or more of the major respects that generally make human lives valuable and worth living'. He adds that such lives will 'typically be worth living on the whole'. Would his view be plausible when applied to lives that are *well* worth living?

Consider parenthood, one of the 'major respects that generally make human lives. . .worth living'. There are people who, despite their infertility, have lives that are well worth living. Setting aside effects on others, is it bad that such people ever live? No. Consider next a severe and lifelong handicap. Some of the blind have lives that are well worth living. Setting aside effects on others, is it bad that such people ever live? Would it have been better if they had never lived, and no one had lived in their place? Once again, the answer is No. Consider next some handicap whose effects are more severe. Suppose that, because some person has such a handicap, it is *not* true that this person's life is *well* worth living, or even close to being well worth living. Kavka's view is here more plausible. There may be people whose lives, though worth living, are so diseased or deprived that, even apart from effects on others, it is bad that these people ever live.

If we accept Kavka's view, in such cases, we must introduce another level, above that where life ceases to be worth living. Call this the *Bad Level*. We might now claim that it is bad if any life is lived at or below this level. Though such a life is worth living, and is of value for the person whose life it is, it would have been in itself better if this life had never been lived.

Kavka's view may, for some of us, provide a partial answer to the Mere Addition Paradox. We may believe that the Bad Level is above the level where life ceases to be worth living. We shall then avoid the Paradox in those cases where the extra group in A+ have lives that are not above this Bad Level. But, though this achieves something, it does not achieve much. Kavka's view is not plausible when applied to lives that are even close to being well worth living. The Bad lives must be worse than this. They must be gravely deficient in all of the features that can make a life worth living. Though worth living, they must be crimped and mean.

148. THE SECOND VERSION OF THE PARADOX

Consider the outcomes shown below.

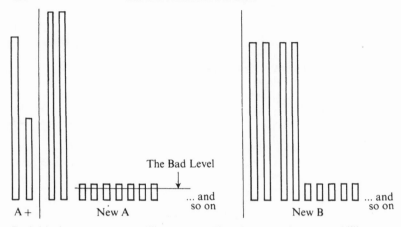

Each block represents ten billion people. Thus A+ contains twenty billion people. In this version of A+, even the worse-off group have an *extremely high* quality of life.

In New A there exist extremely many extra groups of people. Assume that these groups live on planets in other solar systems. New A is an outcome in the distant future. Though these groups all came from the Earth, they cannot now easily communicate.

All of the people in these extra groups have lives that are not much above the Bad Level. Their lives are such that we cannot honestly claim to believe that it would have been in itself better if they had never existed. This follows from my definition of the Bad Level. We therefore cannot believe that New A is worse than A+ because the existence of these extra people is in itself bad.

There is at least one way in which New A is better than A+. In New A there are twenty billion people, all of whom have a higher quality of life than anyone in A+.

Is the inequality in New A worse than the inequality in A+? I believe that it is *better*. There is no longer inequality between the two best-off groups. And the remaining inequality is produced by Mere Addition. As I argued, when it is produced in this way, inequality does not make the outcome worse. Because this inequality does not make the outcome worse, and there is no longer inequality between the best-off groups, New A is better than A+ in egalitarian terms. There is no other feature that might be claimed to make New A worse than A+. Since New A is in two ways better than A+, and in no way worse, New A is *better* than A+.

My claims about inequality might be denied. On some views, the inequality in New A is worse than the inequality in A+. But it cannot be claimed to be much worse. And, even if there is one way in which New A is worse than A+, there is the other way in which New A is better: the fact

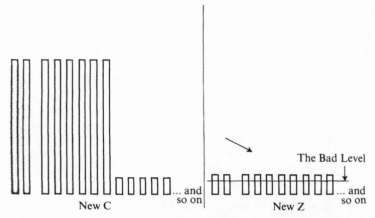

that the best-off people have a higher quality of life. When we compare these two features, we cannot plausibly claim that New A is worse than A +. If we deny that New A is better, we must at least admit that New A is not worse than A +.[53]

Now compare New A with New B. This is like the comparison between A + and B, except for the additional groups who are unaffected. Because there are these additional groups, it is not true here that, if New A changed into New B, this would abolish the natural inequality. But it would be true that, though the better-off group would lose, a worse-off group would gain *several times as much*. This relative gain is much greater than in the earlier argument.

As before, this change would not be the result of deliberate redistribution. It would come about in some natural way, perhaps because of changes in the environment. Unless we accept Maximax, or some version of the Elitist View, we cannot claim that this change makes the outcome worse. A very much greater gain to people who are worse off must count for more than a very much smaller loss for people who are better off. Unless we are Elitists, we must therefore judge that New B is better than New A. In cases where there is still some inequality, there are several views about which patterns of inequality would be better or worse. Though these views disagree about many cases, all of the plausible views would agree that the inequality in New B is less bad than the inequality in New A. And, as before, New B is not just better than New A in egalitarian terms. New B is better on any plausible principle of beneficence. If there was a change from New A to New B, worse-off groups would gain *very much more* than better-off groups would lose.

Now compare New B with New C. Once again, better-off groups would be worse off. But these groups would be worse off by an amount far smaller than the amount by which as many worse-off groups would be better off.

By the same reasoning, New C is better than New B. Such reasoning carries us to New Z. In this outcome there is some enormous population whose lives are not much above the Bad Level. New Z must be better than New A, since every step down the New Alphabet has been judged a change for the better, and *better than* is transitive.

Remember next that, as I argued, New A is better than A+. Taken together, these claims imply

> *The New Repugnant Conclusion*: In the first of two possible outcomes, there would be two groups of ten billion people. One group would have a quality of life *far* higher than that of any actual life that has been lived. Though this group has a larger share of resources, this group is, unavoidably, worse off than the other group. The other group have a quality of life that is *even higher*.
>
> In the second possible outcome, there would be an enormous number of people, whose quality of life is not much above the Bad Level. Of these two outcomes, the second would be better.

Some people may believe that New A is not better than A+, but is merely not worse. These people must accept a weakened version of this new conclusion. They must claim that, of A+ and New Z, the second would not be worse.

This new conclusion is in one respect less repugnant than the Repugnant Conclusion. In Z people's lives were barely worth living. In New Z, people's lives are somewhat better. But this new conclusion seems to me very repugnant. Lives that are not much above the Bad Level cannot be well worth living, or close to being well worth living. Even though worth living, they must be deprived of most of what makes lives worth living. If we cannot avoid this new conclusion, this undermines what most of us believe when we consider overpopulation. We would believe that, if there were twenty billion people all with at least a very high quality of life, this would be a better outcome than if there were instead many more people all of whose lives, though worth living, are gravely deprived, crimped and mean—not much above the level where it would be in itself bad that lives are lived. On the New Conclusion, the first of these outcomes would be *worse*. On the weakened version of this conclusion, the first outcome would *not* be better.

Can we resist this new argument? It might be suggested that, even if New B would be better than New A, and New C would be better than New B, this reasoning would not apply all the way down the New Alphabet. It might be claimed: 'When all the groups are worse off, the Principle of Equality has less weight. If two groups are both well off, a greater gain to the worse off group morally outweighs a lesser loss for the better off group. But the Principle of Equality has less weight when applied to groups who are worse off. And there is some level below which this principle has no weight.'

This view has no plausibility. Many people believe that the Principle of Equality has different weight when applied to groups who are all worse off. But these people believe that, in such cases, the principle has *greater* weight. They believe the opposite of the suggested view. And I know of no one who accepts this view.[54]

We should again remember that the argument does not appeal only to equality. In each of the moves down the New Alphabet, better-off groups would lose *very much less* than would be gained by as many worse-off groups. This would be a change for the better on both the Principle of Equality and any plausible principle of beneficence. Unless we are Elitists, we must admit that each change is for the better.

If we believe that New B would be better than New A, we cannot plausibly deny comparable claims about adjacent outcomes lower down the Alphabet. If we want to avoid both versions of the New Repugnant Conclusion, we must therefore either claim that New B is not better than New A, or claim that New A is worse than A +. As I have argued, unless we can justify some version of the Elitist View, neither of these claims is defensible.

I shall now summarize the argument. The extra groups in New A live lives that are above the Bad Level. Given my definition of this level, we cannot think it bad in itself that such lives are lived. The existence of these people affects no one for the worse. And the existence of these people does not introduce natural inequality. I have argued that, with respect to equality, New A is better than A +. Those who disagree cannot claim that, in this respect, New A is much worse. And, in another respect, New A is better than A +. Twenty billion people have a quality of life that is higher than that of the best-off people in A +. Given these facts, it cannot be claimed that New A is worse than A +. Nor can we appeal to the claim that, compared with A +, New A may have worse consequences. We might claim that, if the groups in New A become more able to communicate, there will be social injustice, which ought to be removed, and that the result of redistribution would be worse than A +. I have explained how this claim can be blocked. We can suppose, as a feature of our case, that such redistribution will never happen. The actual outcome will be, and will remain, New A. There will never be a change either to New B or to New Z. These other outcomes will remain merely possible. Since this is so, we must simply compare the relative value of New A and A +. Would it be better if the extra people never live, at the cost of a *lower* quality of life for *all* of the people who *will* live? This is hard to believe. And it is hard either to believe that New B would not have been better than New A, or to have such a belief about two adjacent outcomes lower down the series. If we do have such a belief, we must accept some version of the Elitist View. If we accept this view, we must apply it to the actual world. Suppose we believe that the lives of some Europeans are not much above the Blissful Level. On the

Elitist version of the Lexical View, if some loss for these people would move them below the Blissful Level, this loss would not be morally outweighed even by a far greater gain to people who are much worse off—such as the African children who are suffering from malnutrition. It is hard to believe this. But it is also hard to believe that New Z is better than A +. Our problem remains.

149. THE THIRD VERSION

We need to consider cases that contain, in the different outcomes, all of the people who would ever live. The last diagram can show such a case. It can become as shown below.

This diagram shows different possible futures. Each block now represents a thousand years in the rest of human history. Each block's height shows the quality of life that everyone enjoys throughout this thousand years. At all times in all of these possible futures there will be ten billion people living.

The A +-Future begins in the 23rd Century. The two previous centuries have gone well. When the A +-Future begins, there is no longer inequality between different people, and the quality of life is extremely high. Successive generations enjoy this quality of life for a thousand years. The Sun then becomes much hotter. This causes the quality of life to be, in many ways, much lower. Even so, it remains extremely high for a second thousand years. The Sun then becomes *very* much hotter, thereby ending human history.

In the A-Future, the first two thousand years go even better. Everyone has a quality of life that is higher than that of the best-off people in the A +-Future. The Sun does not change during this period. Near the end of

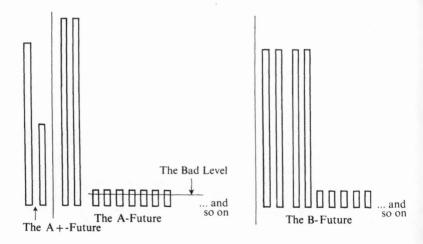

this period, scientists predict that the Sun will become very much hotter. People therefore dig many deep caves. These enable mankind to survive the scorching of the Earth's surface. People live in these caves for very many thousands of years. Life underground is worth living, but is far less good than it had been on the Earth's surface. Throughout the years lived in the caves the quality of life is not much above the Bad Level. The Sun then explodes, ending human history.

We should assume that the A-Future is what actually happens. The other futures are merely possible alternatives. Compared with the A-Future, would the A + -Future be better? Would it be better if the caves were not dug, so that history ended after the first two thousand years? Would this be better, even at the cost of a lower quality of life during these two thousand years?

The people in the caves have lives that are worth living, and are above our Bad Level. It is hard to believe that the existence of these people is in itself bad. And this is harder to believe than in the earlier version of this argument. In the A-Future, there is no inequality between the people living during any period; there is inequality only between different generations. This strengthens the claim that, since this inequality is produced by Mere Addition, it does not make the outcome worse.

It is hard to believe that it will be bad if the caves are dug, so that the extra people exist. Even if this would be bad, this would not show that the A-Future is worse than the A + -Future. These futures differ in another way. If we believe that the A-Future is worse, we must believe that it will be better if the extra people never exist, at the cost of a *lower* quality of life for *everyone* who will *ever* live. This belief is absurd.

In this version of the argument, we can ask what people ought to do. Consider the people who escape death by digging the caves. If we believe that

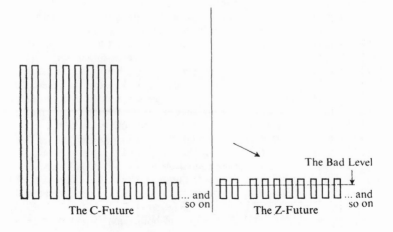

the A-Future is worse than the A + -Future, we should perhaps conclude that these people should not have children. And we must conclude that they have a moral reason not to have children, since they would thereby make the outcome worse. This is not plausible. If these people had children, both these children and all of their descendants would have lives that were worth living. Given this fact, it is hard to believe that these people would have *any* moral reason not to have children. This confirms my claim that the A-Future is not worse than the A + -Future. And, in another respect, the A-Future would be better. In the first two thousand years, everyone would have a higher quality of life. Since the A-Future would be in no way worse than the A + -Future, and in one way better, we should conclude that, of the two, the A-Future would be better.

Now consider the B-Future. This would differ from the A-Future in the following way. During the first two thousand years, when lives are lived on the Earth's surface, the quality of life would be somewhat lower. But there would be a far greater raising of the quality of life during the next two thousand years in the caves. As the diagram shows, though lives would differ on the surface and in the caves, the quality of life would be the same for the first four thousand years.

The A-Future is what will actually happen. Would the B-Future be better? The best-off people, in the first two thousand years, would have a lower quality of life. But they would lose very much less than would be gained by as many people in the next two thousand years. On our ordinary Principles of Equality and Beneficence, this would be a better outcome.

As before, these two differences could be produced by natural changes in the environment. But they could also be produced by deliberate acts. Suppose that the change in the Sun was predicted at the start of the first two thousand years. Those who live in these years might be able, at some cost to themselves, to give much greater benefits to those who would live in the next two thousand years. Some would claim that, since this would make the outcome better on both the Principles of Equality and Beneficence, this is what these people ought to do. Others might claim that such altruism would not be a duty, but would merely be morally admirable. Either view supports my argument. To oppose the argument, we would have to claim that such altruism would not make the outcome better. As before, if we believe that this outcome would not be better, we must accept some form of the Elitist View. We must believe that what happens to the best-off people matters more than what happens to people who are worse off. A loss to the best-off people would not be morally outweighed by a much greater gain to those who are worse off. Most of us would find this impossible to believe. We must then admit that the B-Future would be better than the A-Future.

Similar remarks apply to the C-Future. This would differ from the B-Future in a similar way. The people in the first four thousand years would lose, but there would be a very much greater gain for the people in the next four thousand years. On the Principles of both Equality and Beneficence, the C-Future would be better. By the same reasoning, so would the D-Future, and the E-Future, and so on. The best of all these possible futures would be the Z-Future. It would be true here that, throughout the rest of human history the quality of life would not be much above what it would have been in the caves in the A-Future. The quality of life would always be close to the Bad Level.

Since *better than* is a transitive relation, the Z-Future would be better than the A-Future. And, as I argued, the A-Future would be better than the A+-Future. We must thus conclude that the Z-future would be better than the A+-Future. Compared with a future in which many billions of people all have at least an *extremely high* quality of life, it would be *better* if instead there were many more people, *all* of whose lives are not much above the level at which we believe that it would be *bad* that these lives are lived.

In this version, the argument is stronger. And we do not avoid the questions about what people ought to do. We ask these questions, and the answers support the argument. If we find it as hard to believe this argument's conclusion, the Paradox is greater.[55]

CONCLUDING CHAPTER

WHEN he was asked about his book, Sidgwick said that its first word was *Ethics*, and its last *failure*. This could have been the last word of my Part Four. As I argued, we need a new theory about beneficence. This must solve the Non-Identity Problem, avoid the Repugnant and Absurd Conclusions, and solve the Mere Addition Paradox. I failed to find a theory that can meet these four requirements. Though I failed to find such a theory, I believe that, if they tried, others could succeed.

In the other parts of this book, I reached various conclusions. Most of these have one common feature.

150. IMPERSONALITY

My two subjects are reasons and persons. I have argued that, in various ways, our reasons for acting should become *more impersonal*. Greater impersonality may seem threatening. But it would often be better for everyone.

Chapter 3 argued that, in our concern for other people, most of us make mistakes. Most of us wish to avoid harming other people. But many people believe

(The Second Mistake) If some act is right or wrong because of its effects, the only relevant effects are the effects of this particular act.

This leads these people to ignore what *they together* do. And most of us believe

(The Fourth and Fifth Mistakes) If some act has effects on others that are trivial or imperceptible, this act cannot be morally wrong *because* it has these effects.

These false beliefs did not matter in the small communities in which, for most of history, most people lived. In these communities, we harm others only if there are people whom each of us significantly harms.

Most of us now live in large communities. The bad effects of our acts can now be dispersed over thousands or even millions of people. Our false beliefs are now serious mistakes. That they are mistakes is clear in my imagined case of the Harmless Torturers. Each of these torturers knowingly but imperceptibly affects the pain suffered by each of a thousand victims. These torturers act very wrongly. They know that, though none of them makes any perceptible difference, they together inflict on their victims severe pain.

There are countless actual cases of this kind. In these cases it is true, of the act of each, that its effects on others are trivial or imperceptible. We mistakenly believe that, because this is true, the effects of our acts cannot make them wrong. But, though each act has trivial effects, it is often true that we together impose great harm on ourselves or others. Some examples are pollution, congestion, depletion, inflation, unemployment, a recession, over-fishing, over-farming, soil-erosion, famine, and overpopulation.

While we have these false beliefs, our ignorance is an excuse. But after we have seen that these beliefs are false, we have no excuse. If we continue to act in these ways, our acts will be morally wrong. Some may be as bad as the acts of the Harmless Torturers.

Rational altruists do not have these false beliefs. If we were all rational altruists, this would be better for everyone. But rational altruists are, in this sense, more impersonal: they do not merely ask, 'Will my act be worse for anyone? Will there be anyone with a complaint?' They think it irrelevant whether their acts perceptibly harm any other person.

Life in big cities is disturbingly impersonal. We cannot solve this problem unless we attack it in its own terms. Just as we need thieves to catch thieves, we need impersonal principles to avoid the bad effects of impersonality.

Chapter 4 argued that, because it is often directly collectively self-defeating, Common-Sense Morality must be revised. The revised version R is a partial move towards rational altruism. We must again be more impersonal.

Consider our obligations to our children. According to Common-Sense Morality, we ought to give to our own children some kinds of priority. According to R, there are cases where we ought *not* to give these kinds of priority to our own children. We ought to do what would be best for everyone's children, impartially considered. In telling us to ignore our relations to our own children, R tells us to ignore what may be the strongest of all our personal relations.

If we all follow this impersonal principle, and give no priority to our own children, this will be better for all our children. Impersonality is again better, even in personal terms. Similar claims apply to our relations to such persons as our parents, friends, neighbours, pupils, or patients.

Part Two argued that we should reject the Self-interest Theory about rationality. S is the theory that gives most importance to the difference between people, or the *separateness of persons*. S tells *me* to do whatever will be best for *me*. For S, the fundamental units are *different lives*. My supreme concern should be that my whole life goes as well as possible. Each person is rationally required to give to himself, and to his own life, absolute priority.

Since we should reject S, our theory must be, in one way, more impersonal. It must not claim that each person's supreme concern should be himself; and it must not give supreme importance to the boundaries between lives. But our theory need not be Sidgwick's Principle of Impartial Benevolence. We should accept the Critical Present-aim Theory, or CP. On this theory, the fundamental unit is not the agent throughout his whole life, but the agent at the time of acting. Though CP denies the supreme importance of self-interest, and of a person's whole life, it is not impersonal. CP claims that what it is rational for me to do now depends on what I now want, or value, or believe. This claim gives *more* importance to each person's particular values or beliefs. Since CP gives more importance to what distinguishes different people, in this different way it is *more* personal than S.

Part Three argued for another kind of impersonality. When we consider various imagined cases, we discover what we believe ourselves to be. Most of us believe that our identity must always be determinate. We believe that, to the question 'Am I about to die?' there must always be an answer, which must be either and quite simply Yes or No.

This belief cannot be true unless we are separately existing entities, distinct from our brains and bodies, and our experiences. The continued existence of these entities must be a deep, further fact, distinct from physical and psychological continuity, and a fact which either holds completely, or not at all. One such entity would be a Cartesian Ego. As our reactions to the imagined cases show, most of us are inclined to believe that we are such entities. As I argued, this is not true.

Because this is not true, we cannot explain the unity of a person's life by claiming that the experiences in this life are all had by this person. We can explain this unity only by describing the various relations that hold between these different experiences, and their relations to a particular brain. We could therefore describe a person's life in an impersonal way, which does not claim that this person exists.

On this Reductionist View, persons do exist. But they exist only in the way in which nations exist. Persons are not, as we mistakenly believe, *fundamental*. This view is in this sense more impersonal.

This view supports claims about both rationality and morality. On the Extreme Claims, the implications are wholly impersonal. One writer claims that, if the Reductionist View is true, we ought to be indifferent whether we live or die. Others claim that we would have no reason to be specially concerned about our own futures, and that most of morality would be undermined. These writers believe that it is only the deep further fact of personal identity which gives us reasons for special concern, and supports most of morality. There seems to be no argument that refutes this view. It is therefore defensible to claim that, since there is no such further fact, we have no reason for special concern, and most of morality is undermined.

Though these Extreme Claims are defensible, they can also be defensibly denied. I make the following less extreme claims:

The weakening of psychological connections may reduce both responsibility for past crimes, and obligations to fulfil past commitments.

On the Reductionist View, it is more plausible to reject distributive principles. It is more plausible to focus, not on persons, but on experiences, and to claim that what matters morally is the nature of these experiences. On the impersonal Utilitarian Principle, the question *who* has an experience is as irrelevant as the question *when* the experience is had. This principle ignores the boundaries between lives, or the separateness of persons. On the Reductionist View, this principle is more plausible. (I do not mean 'more plausible than its denial'. I mean 'more plausible than it would be on the Non-Reductionist View'. This is compatible with the claim that, even on the Non-Reductionist View, this principle is implausible.)

We ought to believe great imprudence to be morally wrong. This reduces the claims of personal autonomy. We no longer have the right to do whatever we like, when we affect only ourselves. It is wrong to impose upon ourselves, for no good reason, great harm.

These claims again give less importance both to the unity of each life and to the boundaries between lives. As before, my conclusions are more impersonal.

There are two exceptions. Some writers claim that what matters in survival is physical continuity, or the continued existence of the same particular brain. These writers claim that, if I was about to be Teletransported, I should regard this prospect as being nearly as bad as death. Though my Replica would be fully psychologically continuous with me, this is not what matters. What matters is that he would not be physically continuous with me. I disagree. I believe that what matters is Relation R, psychological continuity and/or connectedness. In arguing that this is what matters, and that physical continuity does not matter, I was again attacking what is, in one way, a more impersonal view. On this view, what matters is a feature that we share both with mere animals and with mere physical objects. On my view, what matters is *what makes us persons*.

I shall now add a similar claim. On the Non-Reductionist View, the deep unity of each life is automatically ensured, however randomly, short-sightedly, and passively this life is lived. On the Reductionist View, the unity of our lives is a matter of degree, and is something that we can affect. We may want our lives to have greater unity, in the way that an artist may want to create a unified work. And we can *give* our lives greater unity, in ways that express or fulfil our particular values and beliefs. Since the Reductionist View gives more importance to how we choose to live, and to what distinguishes different people, this is a second way in which it is *more* personal.

In Part Four my conclusions are in the clearest and strongest sense impersonal. If we want to avoid the Repugnant Conclusion, we cannot solve the Non-Identity Problem by appealing to a *person-affecting* principle. We must appeal to a principle which is about the quality and quantity of the lives that are lived, but is not about what is good or bad for those people whom our acts affect.

I also argued that, if we appeal to such a principle, it makes no moral difference what is implied by person-affecting principles. When I considered the Two Medical Programmes, I concluded that it was irrelevant that cancelling only one of these programmes would be worse for the children affected. If we must appeal to such a principle, and should then ignore person-affecting principles, this has wide theoretical implications, of an impersonal kind.

151. DIFFERENT KINDS OF ARGUMENT

Ethics asks which outcomes would be good or bad, and which acts would be right or wrong. *Meta-Ethics* asks what is the meaning of moral language, or the nature of moral reasoning. It also asks whether Ethics can be objective—whether it can make claims that are *true*.

Some people assume that there are only two ways of doing Ethics, or arguing about morality. One is the *Low Road*, that merely appeals to our intuitions. The other is the *High Road*, Meta-Ethics. If we can give the best account of the nature of moral reasoning, we can hope that this will imply particular claims about morality. We can hope that our Meta-Ethics will imply conclusions in Ethics.

I believe that these are not the only ways in which we can argue about morality. I have not taken the High Road, except when I assumed that an acceptable moral theory cannot be directly collectively self-defeating. I have often taken the Low Road, appealing to our intuitions. But one of my main aims has been to explore a variety of different kinds of argument, that are between the Low and High extremes.

Chapters 1 and 4 discuss

(*a*)   the argument that a theory is self-defeating.

With this kind of argument, we can make undeniable progress. Since S and C can be indirectly self-defeating, they must both make new claims about our desires and dispositions. Since Common-Sense Morality is often directly collectively self-defeating, this implies, on almost every Meta-Ethical theory, that this morality must be revised.

Chapter 3 appeals to

(*b*)   facts whose moral significance has been overlooked.

One such fact is the combined effect of sets of acts, or of what we together do. Another such fact is the combined effect of what, individually, are imperceptible effects. My imagined Harmless Torturers act very wrongly, because of the effects of their acts, though no torturer makes any victim's pains perceptibly worse. This refutes the view that an act cannot be wrong, because of its effects on other people, if these people could not ever notice any difference.

Chapter 16 appeals to the same kind of argument. It appeals to the fact that we can easily affect the identities of future people. The implications of this fact—what I called the Non-Identity Problem—have clear significance for our moral theories. But, with a few exceptions, we have overlooked these implications.

It is unlikely that these are the only examples of this kind of argument. There may be many undiscovered arguments of this kind—many other facts whose clear rational or moral significance has been simply overlooked. This is another kind of argument with which we can make undeniable progress.

Chapter 6 appeals to

(c)   a more complete description of what a theory assumes and implies.

My first argument against the Self-interest Theory was little more than a question. But to reach this question I had to introduce the Critical Present-aim Theory. My aim was to isolate S, so that it could be judged on its own merits. I therefore needed to contrast S with CP. It was not enough to appeal to the Instrumental or Deliberative Theories. Neither of these familiar theories challenges S in a way that a Self-interest Theorist cannot ignore. CP provides such a challenge. And it enables us to see what S implicitly assumes. We can ask which version of CP would coincide with S. This version claims that a temporally neutral bias in one's own favour is supremely rational. It claims that this bias must be our dominant concern even if, though knowing the facts and thinking clearly, we neither have nor want to have this bias. When we see more clearly what S assumes, it ceases to be plausible.

Chapter 7 appeals to

(d)   a weakness in the structure of a theory.

S is a *hybrid* theory, since it requires temporal neutrality, but rejects the requirements of neutrality as between different people. This does not make S incoherent. But it is a structural flaw, making S vulnerable when it is attacked from both directions.[2]

Chapter 8 mentions another kind of argument. This appeals to (*e*) the implications of a metaphysical conclusion—a conclusion about the most fundamental features of reality, or the Universe.

Some philosophers and physicists claim that time's passage is an illusion. If I had sufficiently defended this claim, I could have argued that temporal neutrality cannot be irrational.

Part Three appeals to an argument of this kind. I claim that most of us have false beliefs about our own nature, and the nature of our continued existence over time. If we can show that we have such false beliefs, an appeal to the truth may support certain claims both about rationality and about morality. Thus, as I claim, the Reductionist View provides another argument against the Self-interest Theory. And this view supports various moral claims.

Part Four appeals to arguments of kind *(c)*. Classical Utilitarianism implies the Repugnant Conclusion, and the Average Principle implies absurd conclusions. Part Four also appeals to an argument of kind *(d)*. This refutes the view that, to the value of quantity during any period, there is an upper limit. When this view is extended to cover uncompensated suffering, it has a structural flaw. Like S, it is a hybrid view. Though it claims that quantity's positive value has an upper limit, it cannot plausibly put a limit on quantity's negative value. It therefore implies another absurd conclusion.

152. SHOULD WE WELCOME OR REGRET MY CONCLUSIONS?

I argue

(1) Since they are often indirectly self-defeating, the Self-interest Theory and Consequentialism must make claims about our desires and dispositions. They must claim that we should be disposed to act in ways that they claim to be irrational, and morally wrong.

(2) Since Common-Sense Morality is often directly collectively self-defeating, it must be revised.

As I suggest in Chapter 5, these two conclusions reduce the disagreement between Common-Sense Morality and Consequentialism. This is a welcome result. It points us towards a Unified Theory, that would remove this disagreement.

I argue

(3) In considering how our acts affect other people, most of us make serious mistakes. We should therefore change many of the ways in which we now act.

This is another welcome conclusion. When we see that these are mistakes, we shall be more likely to act in ways that would be better for all of us.

I argue

(4) We should reject the Self-interest Theory about rationality, and accept the Critical Present-aim Theory. On this theory, some desires are irrational, and others may be rationally required. Suppose that I know the facts, am thinking clearly, and my set of desires is not irrational. It would then be irrational for me to act in my own best interests, if this would frustrate what, at the time, I most want or value.

(5) Because we should reject the Self-interest Theory, we should claim that great imprudence is morally wrong.

These conclusions are harder to assess. I believe that, in principle, (4) is another welcome conclusion. There are at least two kinds of self-interested act:

(i) Some of these acts benefit the agent, but impose greater burdens on other people. On the Self-interest Theory, it is irrational *not* to act in this way. If people cease to have this belief, fewer may act in this way. This would make the outcome better.

(ii) Some self-interested acts greatly benefit the agent, without being worse for other people. It would be bad if fewer people acted in this way. Failure to act in this way is great imprudence. This is always sad, and often tragic. I argued that we should extend our moral theory, so that it claims that great imprudence is morally wrong. If we accept both (4) and (5), this may not increase, and might reduce, the incidence of great imprudence. But there may be people who accept (4) but reject (5). If people ceased to believe that great imprudence is irrational, and continued to believe that it cannot be morally wrong, this might have bad effects. And there are some people for whom the charge 'irrational' has more weight than the charge 'immoral'.

The rejection of the Self-interest Theory is welcome in another way. Compared with CP, S is more of a threat to morality. There are many cases where S conflicts with morality. Some of these conflicts are unavoidable, whatever we want or value. If we believe S, we believe that, in these cases, it would be irrational to act morally. This belief may make us less likely to act morally.

Similar claims do not apply to CP. On some versions of CP, there are many cases in which CP conflicts with morality. But this conflict is not unavoidable. If we cared enough about morality, the conflict would disappear.

I argue

(6) Most of us should change our view about the nature of persons, and personal identity over time. The truth is here very different from what most of us believe.

(7)   Given this change in our beliefs about ourselves, we should change some of our moral views. And certain Extreme Claims, though they can be defensibly denied, are defensible.

These conclusions are also hard to assess. If we accept the Extreme Claims, these conclusions may be unwelcome. Swinburne writes that, if he accepted the Reductionist View, he would have no reason to go on living. Other writers claim that most of morality would be undermined.

I reject these Extreme Claims. I believe that Relation R—continuity and connectedness—gives us a reason to be specially concerned about our own futures. This reason may not be as strong as the reason that would be provided by the Further Fact. And, because psychological connectedness is a matter of degree, we should reject the claim that it must be irrational to care less about some parts of our future. We should reject the Classical Self-Interest Theory. I have explained why I welcome this conclusion. If we become Reductionists, this change of view also supports certain changes in our moral views. But I do not find these disturbing.

When I consider what (6) implies, I am glad that (6) is true. This change of view also has psychological effects. It makes me care less about my own future, and the fact that I shall die. In comparison, I now care more about the lives of others. I welcome these effects. Metaphysics *can* produce the consolations of philosophy.

Finally, I argue

(8)   Because we can easily affect the identities of future people, we face the Non-Identity Problem. To solve this problem we need a new theory about beneficence. This theory must also avoid the Repugnant and the Absurd Conclusions, and solve the Mere Addition Paradox.

Since I have not yet found this theory, these conclusions are unwelcome. They undermine our beliefs about our obligations to future generations. Most of us assume that the choice of one of two social policies might be against the interests of those who live in the further future. In many cases, this belief is false. There must be a moral objection to our choice of the Risky Policy, or Depletion. But this objection cannot appeal to our ordinary principle about the wrongness of harming other people. Though these two policies have what are clearly bad effects, choosing these policies will be worse for no one.

Since I failed to find the principle to which we should appeal, I cannot explain the objection to our choice of such policies. I believe that, though I have so far failed, I or others could find the principle we need. But until this happens (8) is a disturbing conclusion.

In the meanwhile, we should conceal this problem from those who will decide whether we increase our use of nuclear energy. These people know that the Risky Policy might cause catastrophes in the further future. It will be better if these people believe, falsely, that the choice of the Risky Policy would be against the interests of the people killed by such a catastrophe. If they have this false belief, they will be more likely to reach the right decision.

(8) is unwelcome in other ways. Most of us would believe that the Repugnant and Absurd Conclusions are what I have called them. Until we know how to avoid both conclusions, and how to solve both the Non-Identity Problem and the Mere Addition Paradox, we will have beliefs that we cannot justify, and that we know to be inconsistent.

If I or others solve these problems, (8) will be, in a trivial way, welcome. We enjoy solving problems. But, before we have found solutions, we ought to regret this conclusion. With more unsolved problems, we are further away from the Unified Theory. We are further away from the theory that resolves our disagreements, and that, because it achieves this aim, might deserve to be called the truth.

153. MORAL SCEPTICISM

Moral Sceptics deny that a moral theory could be true. More broadly, they deny that any theory could be *objectively* the best theory. One argument for this view is that, unlike Mathematics, Ethics is not a subject on which we all agree. It can be denied that this is a good argument. But to undermine this argument we must find a theory that resolves our disagreements. Before we find such a theory, we can give two other grounds for doubting Moral Scepticism. These are grounds for claiming that the question of objectivity is not settled, but remains open.

Many people are Moral Sceptics, but are not sceptics about rationality. The question of objectivity can best be pursued if we consider, not just moral reasons, but all kinds of reasons for acting. There are some claims which all of us accept.

Suppose that, unless I move, I shall be killed by a falling rock, and that what I most want is to survive. Do I have a reason to move? It is undeniable that I do. This claim would have been accepted in all civilizations, at all times. This claim is *true*.

Since there are some true claims about reasons for acting, we can deny what some sceptics claim. It is sometimes claimed that, unlike rocks or stars, there cannot *be* objective moral values. Such entities cannot exist. They are too queer to be part of 'the fabric of the Universe'. But, in the case just described, I do have a reason to move. This may not be a moral reason. But, since there is this reason, there can *be* reasons. Reasons for acting can, in the only relevant sense, 'exist'. Since there are some reasons for acting, it is an open question whether some of these are moral reasons.[2]

There is another ground for doubting Moral Scepticism. We should not assume that the objectivity of Ethics must be all-or-nothing. There may be a part of morality that is objective. In describing this part, our claims may be true. When we consider this part of morality, or these moral questions, we may find the Unified Theory that would remove our disagreements. There may be other questions about which we shall never agree. There may be no true answers to these questions. Since objectivity need not be all-or-nothing, moral sceptics may be partly right. *These* questions may be subjective. But this need not cast doubt on the Unified Theory.[3]

154. HOW BOTH HUMAN HISTORY, AND THE HISTORY OF ETHICS, MAY BE JUST BEGINNING

Some people believe that there cannot be progress in Ethics, since everything has been already said. Like Rawls and Nagel[4], I believe the opposite. How many people have made Non-Religious Ethics their life's work? Before the recent past, very few. In most civilizations, most people have believed in the existence of a God, or of several gods. A large minority were in fact atheists, whatever they pretended. But, before the recent past, few atheists made Ethics their life's work. Buddha may be among this few, as may be Confucius, and a few Ancient Greeks and Romans. After more than a thousand years, there were a few more between the Sixteenth and Twentieth Centuries. Hume was an atheist who made Ethics part of his life's work. Sidgwick was another. After Sidgwick, there were several atheists who were professional moral philosophers. But most of these did not do Ethics. They did Meta-Ethics. They did not ask which outcomes would be good or bad, or which acts would be right or wrong. They asked, and wrote about, only the meaning of moral language, and the question of objectivity. Non-Religious Ethics has been systematically studied, by many people, only since the 1960s. Compared with the other sciences, Non-Religious Ethics is the youngest and the least advanced.

I believe that if we destroy mankind, as we now can, this outcome will be *much* worse than most people think. Compare three outcomes:

(1) Peace.

(2) A nuclear war that kills 99% of the world's existing population.

(3) A nuclear war that kills 100%.

(2) would be worse than (1), and (3) would be worse than (2). Which is the greater of these two differences? Most people believe that the greater difference is between (1) and (2). I believe that the difference between (2) and (3) is *very much* greater.

My view is held by two very different groups of people. Both groups would appeal to the same fact. The Earth will remain inhabitable for at least another billion years. Civilization began only a few thousand years ago. If we do not destroy mankind, these few thousand years may be only a tiny fraction of the whole of civilized human history. The difference between (2) and (3) may thus be the difference between this tiny fraction and all of the rest of this history. If we compare this possible history to a day, what has occurred so far is only a fraction of a second.

One of the groups who hold my view are Classical Utilitarians. They would claim, as Sidgwick did, that the destruction of mankind would be by far the greatest of all conceivable crimes. The badness of this crime would lie in the vast reduction of the possible sum of happiness.

Another group would agree, but for very different reasons. These people believe that there is little value in the mere sum of happiness. For these people, what matters are what Sidgwick called the 'ideal goods'—the Sciences, the Arts, and moral progress, or the continued advance towards a wholly just world-wide community. The destruction of mankind would prevent further achievements of these three kinds. This would be extremely bad because what matters most would be the *highest* achievements of these kinds, and these highest achievements would come in future centuries.

There could clearly be higher achievements in the struggle for a wholly just world-wide community. And there could be higher achievements in all of the Arts and Sciences. But the progress could be greatest in what is now the least advanced of these Arts or Sciences. This, I have claimed, is Non-Religious Ethics. Belief in God, or in many gods, prevented the free development of moral reasoning. Disbelief in God, openly admitted by a majority, is a recent event, not yet completed. Because this event is so recent, Non-Religious Ethics is at a very early stage. We cannot yet predict whether, as in Mathematics, we will all reach agreement. Since we cannot know how Ethics will develop, it is not irrational to have high hopes.

APPENDICES

A   A WORLD WITHOUT DECEPTION

SUPPOSE that we were all both transparent and never self-denying. Call this the *Status Quo*. It would probably be better for each of us if he became a trustworthy, threat-fulfilling, threat-ignorer. Each change would involve certain risks. But these would be likely to be heavily outweighed by the benefits.

How would someone gain, if he changed his dispositions in these three ways? This depends on what others do. The gain from becoming trustworthy depends upon the number of others who become trustworthy. The gain from becoming a threat-fulfiller depends upon the number of others who become threat-ignorers, and vice versa. If everyone else remains never self-denying, it would be no advantage to be merely a threat-ignorer, and at most a small advantage to be trustworthy, but it would be a great advantage to be a threat-fulfiller. Someone who is trustworthy gains little if no one else is trustworthy,[1] and gains most if everyone else is trustworthy. A mere threat-ignorer gains nothing if no one else is a threat-fulfiller, and gains most if everyone else is a threat-fulfiller. But a threat-fulfiller gains most if no one else is a threat-ignorer. These facts are shown in the diagram below.

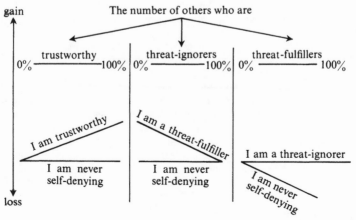

Everyone is assumed to be transparent, and to be never self-denying except in so far as he acquires any of these three dispositions. The diagram ignores risks, and certain other complications. We could avoid these complications by making further assumptions. But we do not need these here, since they would not affect the argument. A threat-ignorer could be a special case of a threat-fulfiller, one who has threatened to ignore other people's threats. Call someone *merely* a threat-ignorer if this is the only threat that he would fulfil.

As the diagram shows, if someone gains from becoming either trustworthy or a threat-fulfiller, these can be gains with respect to the Status Quo. Such a person becomes better off than he would have been if he and everyone else had remained never self-denying. But the gain from becoming merely a threat-ignorer cannot raise someone above the Status Quo. It can only prevent him from sinking lower.

These facts can be explained as follows. When someone gains from being trustworthy, it will often be true that others also gain. And these gains need not involve losses to others. These gains can come from the keeping of mutually advantageous agreements, which create new benefits at no cost to others. This would be true, for instance, of some co-operative forms of industry, or agriculture. But, when someone gains from being a threat-fulfiller, this is worse for someone else. The gain to the threat-fulfiller may be only a defensive gain, preventing a would-be aggressor from gaining from aggression. But this would be worse for this aggressor. And when someone gains from being a threat-ignorer, this is just the avoidance of a loss. If I am transparently a threat-ignorer, threat-fulfillers cannot gain by threatening me. It will be worse for them if they threaten me, since I shall ignore their threats, and they will fulfil them, which will be worse for all of us. Since it would be worse for them if they threatened me, they will not do so. But if I am merely a threat-ignorer, my only gains are of this kind—what I do not lose to threat-fulfillers. This is why this disposition cannot raise me above the Status Quo.

These facts have the following implications. If everyone became trustworthy, this would be better for everyone than if no one did. But there would be no such general gain if we all became threat-fulfilling threat-ignorers. This explains why, of these three departures from the disposition of being never self-denying, only the first is thought to be required by morality. It is a plausible claim that, if we can affect our dispositions, we ought morally to cause ourselves to be or to remain trustworthy. But it could not be plausibly claimed that, if we are all now never self-denying with respect to threats, we ought morally to cause ourselves to be threat-fulfilling threat-ignorers.

Though this general claim is not plausible, we might make two other claims. If other people have sufficiently bad intentions, we ought perhaps to become transparent threat-fulfillers, so that we can deter these people. (If we are not transparent, it would be morally better merely to appear to be threat-fulfillers. This is clearest in the case of nuclear deterrence.) We could also claim that, if other people have become threat-fulfillers, and have bad intentions, we ought morally to cause ourselves to become transparent threat-ignorers.

In the world as it is now, where we are partly opaque, it would be hard to convince others that we really *are* threat-fulfilling threat-ignorers. It would not be enough to fulfil or ignore some threat at some small cost to ourselves. Since it would be better for us to appear to be threat-fulfilling threat-ignorers, it may be rational for us in self-interested terms to pay this small cost, in an attempt to gain this useful appearance. But this very fact would make people doubt that we would fulfil or ignore threats at a great cost to ourselves. A threat-fulfiller should therefore welcome the development of infallible lie-detector tests.

What are the risks involved in these three changes in our dispositions? If we are not transparent, one risk in becoming trustworthy is that we might be tricked into keeping some mutual agreement by those who merely appear to be trustworthy, and will not do their share. If we are all transparent, there is only the smaller risk that those with whom we make such agreements, though intending to do their share, may in fact be unable to do so. This risk would be heavily outweighed by the likely benefits of trustworthiness, those that are created by the keeping of mutually advantageous agreements. The risk in becoming a threat-fulfiller is that we might threaten a threat-ignorer, and the risk in becoming a threat-ignorer is that we might be threatened by a threat-fulfiller. But if we were all transparent these two risks would be small. It would be clearly worse for a threat-fulfiller if he threatened a transparent threat-ignorer. And I am assuming that, except when we are acting upon these three dispositions, none of us would do what he believes would be worse for him. The risk is only that this assumption may, occasionally, fail to hold.

If we all became transparently trustworthy, this would be better for everyone. We would rise above the Status Quo. If we all became transparently threat-fulfillers, this would not be better for everyone. It might be better for some people. These are the people who are naturally weak. If we are all never self-denying, the strong can exploit the weak not with threats but with warnings. If the strong harm the weak, because the weak have not made concessions, this may not be worse for the strong. But if the weak had weapons that could destroy both them and the strong, it might be better for them to become transparent threat-fulfillers. By making credible defensive threats, they could save themselves from exploitation by the strong. This gain to the weak may be part of the reason why General Gallois welcomed nuclear proliferation. But this gain would be insecure. It would be abolished if the strong became transparent threat-ignorers. And if we all became threat-fulfilling threat-ignorers, there would be greater risks for everyone. This might make these changes in our dispositions worse for all of us.

This last claim may seem to conflict with another of my claims. I claimed that it would be better for each of us if he caused himself to become a threat-fulfilling threat-ignorer. If these changes would be worse for all of us, it may seem that this could not be true.

This is not so. These claims could both be true. It could be true both (1) that, whatever others do, it would be better for each of us if he himself became a threat-fulfilling threat-ignorer, and (2) that, if all rather than none of us made these changes, this would be worse for all of us. What each would gain by making these changes may be less than what he would lose if everyone else did the same.

Suppose that we are at the Status Quo, all transparently never self-denying. If we add one assumption, it would not be better for anyone if he made himself a threat-fulfilling threat-ignorer. This assumption is that, if anyone changed himself in these two ways, he would thereby cause everyone else to make the same two changes. Let us suppose that this would not be true. It would be unlikely if we are very numerous—members of a society with a large population.

If I would not be copied by everyone else, it will be better for me if I become transparently a threat-fulfilling threat-ignorer. If everyone else remains never self-denying, I gain nothing from being a threat-ignorer, but I gain most from being a threat-fulfiller. This is how I could rise highest above the Status Quo. As others start to acquire these two dispositions, I gain less from being a threat-fulfiller, but I start to gain from being a threat-ignorer. When everyone else has made both changes, I would cease to be above the Status Quo. Since there are certain risks, I may even sink lower. And I now gain nothing from being a threat-fulfiller. Since everyone else is now disposed to ignore my threats, they have become useless. And since there is the risk that I might, foolishly, make a threat, it may now be better for me if I lose this disposition. But I now gain most from being a threat-ignorer. It would be very bad for me to be never self-denying in a world of threat-fulfillers. Everyone else could then exploit me by making threats. Perhaps most people, being good-natured, would not do so. But a few would. So it would be clearly better for me to remain transparently a threat-ignorer.

My conclusions are, then, these. In a world without deception, it would very probably be better for each of us if he ceased to be never self-denying in at least two ways. It would very probably be better for each if he became, and remained, a trustworthy threat-ignorer. According to S, it would be rational for each of us to change himself in these two ways.

As I have said, it might be true that we cannot bring ourselves to act in ways that we believe to be irrational. And it might be true that others would not believe that we would act in ways that we believe to be irrational. If either of these were true, we would be told by S that it would be rational for us to change, not only our dispositions, but also our beliefs about rationality. Each of us should still believe that it is usually irrational for him to do what he believes will be worse for himself. But he should try to make himself believe that such acts are rational when they involve ignoring threats, or keeping promises.

(That we might through technology become transparent, and that we should think in advance about such changes, I learnt from J. Glover. For deeper thoughts on these lines see GLOVER (3).)

B HOW MY WEAKER CONCLUSION WOULD IN PRACTICE DEFEAT S

On the weaker of my two conclusions, when S and P conflict, it would be rational to follow either. This conclusion would be highly damaging to the Self-interest Theory. Formally, the result would be symmetrical. S would have lost its claim to be the one true—or best—theory. It would have lost the bolder claim

(S12) It is irrational to act, knowingly, against one's own self-interest merely to achieve what, at the time of acting, and after ideal deliberation, one most wants or values.

It would be left with

(S13) It is rational to act, knowingly, in one's own self-interest, even when one knows that this will frustrate what, after ideal deliberation, one most wants or values.

The Present-aim Theory would not have won the bolder claim

(P11) It is irrational to act in one's own self-interest when one knows that this will frustrate what, after ideal deliberation, one most wants or values.

It would have won only

(P12) It is rational to do what one knows will best achieve what, after ideal deliberation, one most wants or values, even when one knows that this is against one's own self-interest.

But, though there is formal symmetry, the comparable claims have for these two theories different importance. It is more important for S to make the bolder of its claims. In losing (S13) it has lost what it needs in its conflict with P. It is not enough to have kept the weaker (S12).

Before I defend this claim, I shall consider a similar claim about the conflict between S and morality. Sidgwick believed that, if we are asking what we have most reason to do, the result is formally symmetrical. The best moral theory cannot defeat, or be defeated by, the Self-interest Theory about rationality. When morality conflicts with self-interest, it would be rational to follow either.[2]

If this is so, is this result more damaging to either side? Many assume that it would be more damaging to morality. Thus Hume asks, 'What theory of morals can ever serve any useful purpose, unless it can show . . . that all the duties which it recommends, are also the true interest of each individual?'[3] Hume here implies that, if we were forced to choose, we would choose self-interest. As he writes, 'What hopes can we ever have of engaging mankind to a practice which we confess full of rigour and austerity?' This would be our task—he implies—if morality and self-interest could conflict. Hume's official solution is that the two always coincide.[4] By showing this, we show morality 'in all her genuine and most engaging charms . . . the dismal dress falls off'.

What Hume implies is false. It is not true that, when morality conflicts with self-interest, all of us would always choose the latter. There have been countless cases where someone does what he believes to be morally right, even though, because he is not religious, he believes that he is doing what will be worse for him. If we believe that, in cases of conflict, it would be rational to act in either way, this belief is not, obviously, more damaging to morality.

Sidgwick knew this. After stating this belief, he wrote, 'practical reason, being divided against itself, would cease to be a motive on either side: the conflict would have to be decided by the comparative preponderance of one or other of two groups of non-rational impulses'.[5]

Sidgwick did not discuss the Present-aim Theory. If this theory enters the field, and the result is a three-sided draw, there is a natural answer to Sidgwick's question. If none of the three rivals provides stronger reasons than the other two, two of the three might, when they agree, provide stronger reasons than the third. If this is so, we can answer the question of what we have most reason to do. Suppose that I am thinking clearly, and I know that it will be worse for me if I do my duty. If what I most want is to do my duty, this is what I have most reason to do. If instead what I most want is what will be better for me, this is what I have most reason to do. We must admit that I would have no further reason for having either of these desires rather than the other. This follows from the assumption that, when morality conflicts with self-interest, neither provides a stronger reason for acting. But though my preference for one side would not be rationally required, it would not be irrational. It would be, as Sidgwick writes, 'non-rational'. And that my preference is non-rational does not make it arbitrary. It would not be like picking, randomly, one of two exactly similar things. Sidgwick believed that, when morality conflicts with self-interest, we cannot have more reason to follow either. I have claimed that we can.

Return now to the similar conclusion that, when P conflicts with S, neither defeats the other. On this conclusion, when these theories conflict, it would be rational to follow either.

I claim here what I have criticized Hume for claiming about the conflict between S and morality. If the result is a draw, this is more damaging to one of these two theories. It is more damaging to S. This is because, of these two theories, S needs to be more critical. We naturally tend to do what we know will best achieve our present aims. We are not certain to do this. There are many ways in which we can fail to do what, on the Present-aim Theory, we have most reason to do. But, if we do not believe that we are acting irrationally, it is this theory that, of the two, we shall be more likely to follow.

I may act in some way because I believe that it would be irrational not to do so. In Sidgwick's words, 'practical reason' can itself be 'a motive'. We need not decide whether this is true only because I have a desire not to act irrationally. It is clear that I may have this desire, and that this would enable my beliefs about rationality to affect my acts. Suppose that I can either (1) do what will best achieve what, at the time, knowing the facts and thinking clearly, I most want or value, or (2) do what will be in my own long-term self-interest. And suppose that I believe that, when S and P conflict, neither wins. I believe that, in such a case, it would be rational to do either (1) or (2). If I believe that neither act would be irrational, it is clear what I shall be more likely to do. I shall be more likely to do what would best achieve what, at the time of acting, I most want or value. I shall then be following not S but P.

Suppose instead that I believe that, when the two theories conflict, S defeats P. Instead of (S13) I accept the bolder claim (S12). I might then do (2) rather than (1). I have a desire not to act irrationally, and I now believe that (1) would be irrational, since it would be worse for me. My belief about rationality may thus lead me to follow S.

It may be objected that, if I now do (2) because I believe that only (2) is rational, I must still be acting on my strongest desire, or be doing what best fulfils my present desires. This claim is controversial. If it is true, the two theories would here coincide. But this would be true only because I believe in the Self-interest rather than the Present-aim Theory. The two theories would conflict if instead I believed in the Present-aim Theory, or believed that neither theory defeats the other.

When the two theories conflict, we shall be naturally inclined to do what will best achieve our present aims. This is why, of the two, the Self-interest Theory needs to make the bolder claim. It needs the claim that it would be irrational for me to do what would best achieve my present aims, when I know that my act would be worse for me. If I believe that this would be irrational, I may then be led to do what would be better for me. But, if I believe that neither act would be irrational, I shall be naturally inclined to do what will best achieve my present aims. And this applies to all of us. When our desire to act rationally, or to avoid irrationality, does not tell either way, we shall be more likely to try to do what will best achieve what, at the time, we most want or value. This is why, in its conflict with the

Self-interest Theory, what is theoretically a draw is, for the Present-aim Theory, in practice victory.

C RATIONALITY AND THE DIFFERENT THEORIES ABOUT SELF-INTEREST

I claim (1) that, compared with the bias in one's own favour, there are several other desires or patterns of concern that are no less rational. And I conclude (2) that, if someone has one of these other desires, it would be no less rational for him to act upon it, even if he knows that this will be against his own self-interest.

If we accept (1), we must in the end accept (2). But I shall now describe how, by changing our view about self-interest, we can postpone accepting (2). We can postpone our move from S to P.

I shall describe a line of thought that starts from Bentham's view. If we accept some other view, we shall enter this line of thought at a later stage. Bentham's view combined S with the Hedonistic Theory about self-interest. On this view, what each person has most reason to do is what will make him as happy as possible.

This view often rested on the Hedonistic version of Psychological Egoism: the claim that what each person most wants, or would most want in a cool hour, is to be as happy as possible. This claim is false. We often have some other desire, which would remain our strongest desire even after cool deliberation.

The fulfilment or pursuit of such other desires may be our chief source of happiness. But since these are desires for something other than our own happiness, acting on these desires will sometimes make us less happy. This is most likely to be true when we shall never know whether these desires are fulfilled; but it is often true even when we shall know.

On Bentham's view, it is irrational in such cases to act on these desires. We shall accept this claim only if we believe that these desires are irrational. Some people believe this. But, in the case of many such desires, we may disagree.

We are most likely to disagree in the case of desires for other people's happiness. If these were the only other desires that we believed not to be irrational, we would disagree with Bentham not about self-interest but about rationality. Since the object of these desires is still someone's happiness, we would continue to accept the Hedonistic Theory about self-interest. But we would qualify S. We would claim that it is not irrational to sacrifice our own happiness when we can thereby give greater happiness to others. This was Sidgwick's view.

Suppose, next, that we believe a much wider range of desires not to be irrational. These are desires whose object is no one's happiness. One large class might be desires that depend on certain value-judgements, or ideals. But Section 60 shows that, in its treatment of these desires, S must be rejected. Another large class I call *desires for achievement*. These are desires to succeed in doing what, in our work or more active leisure, we are trying to do. Thus an artist, or gardener, or carpenter, or creator of any kind, may strongly want to make his creation as good as possible. His strongest desire may be to produce a masterpiece, in paint, flowers, wood, or words. And a scientist, or philosopher, may strongly want to make some fundamental discovery, or intellectual advance.

Such desires may be self-standing, not means to the achievement of other desires. It may be true that, if we fulfil these desires, this will often promote the happiness of ourselves or others. But this is not the object of these desires. And there are also many cases, such as the pursuit of certain kinds of knowledge, where the fulfilment of these desires will do nothing to make others happy. (Typically we may also want, not just to fulfil these desires, but to have our achievements recognised. We may want fame. But this is a separate desire, and it may be weaker. And we may want recognition only because, without it, we could not be sure that we really had produced a masterpiece, or made a fundamental discovery.)

In trying to fulfil these desires for achievement, we shall sometimes make ourselves less happy. This can be true even if we know that these desires are being fulfilled. Thus George Eliot knew that she was a successful novelist, but she was always dissatisfied with what she had achieved so far.[6] The struggle to achieve may be not the kind of struggle which is its own reward, but an ordeal.

Suppose we decide that some of these desires for achievement are not irrational. We conclude that it is not irrational to act on these desires, even when we know that this will make us less happy, and will not give greater happiness to others. (This would not be true of a successful novelist, but it may be true of a successful scientist, or philosopher.) Since we have decided that these acts are not irrational, we now have grounds to reject not only Bentham's but also Sidgwick's view. We have grounds to reject any view which either is, or includes, the Hedonistic version of S.[7]

There are two possibilities. We could change our view about rationality, moving from S to P. The alternative is to change our view about self-interest. We could move from the Hedonistic to the Desire-Fulfilment Theory.

On the Desire-Fulfilment Theory, it may not be against our interests to do what makes us less happy. The fulfilment of a strong desire now counts directly as in our interests, whether or not it makes us happy. Struggling to solve his problem, a scientist or philosopher may be, save on rare occasions, wretched. And it may be true that, if he struggled less hard, he would be less wretched. There may be here a real sacrifice of his happiness. But, if he is fulfilling his strongest desire, we can now claim that he is *not* acting against his interests. We decided that it is not irrational to act on such desires for achievement, even when this makes us less happy. Now that we have changed our view about self-interest, this decision no longer gives us grounds to reject S.

As this example shows, if we move from the Hedonistic to the Desire-Fulfilment Theory, we have less need to move from S to P. This is because, given this move, S and P more often coincide. But they remain different theories. The essential difference again concerns time. If we assume the Desire-Fulfilment Theory, S claims that what each person has most reason to do is what will best fulfil, or enable him to fulfil, all of his desires throughout his whole life. His future desires count for as much as his present desires. But P appeals only to a person's present desires—to what he either does or would want, after ideal deliberation, at the time of acting.

S and P often coincide. There are many cases where what would best fulfil someone's present desires would not conflict with the fulfilment of his future desires. And it may be true that someone's strongest desires are the same throughout his life. But though S and P often coincide, there are also many cases where they conflict.

Some of these cases involve people who care less about their further future. But I am now supposing, for the purposes of argument, that we have condemned the bias towards the near. We are considering the version of P which claims that, in his concern for himself, a rational agent should be equally concerned about all of his future. Even if it makes this claim, P often conflicts with S. This is true chiefly because, in the case of many people, some of their strongest desires do not last throughout their lives. Many people's strongest desires are long-lasting. But there are few people whose strongest desires are always the same. Thus my desires for achievement may throughout my life be the same, but I may at different times love different people, and support different political campaigns. Or I may always love the same people and support the same campaigns, but at different times have different desires for achievement. In either case, P may conflict with S. What would best fulfil my present desires may not coincide with what would best fulfil, or enable me to fulfil, all of my desires throughout my whole life.

In such cases, S claims that it would be irrational for me to do what would best fulfil my present desires. But, if these are desires for certain kinds of achievement, we decided that they are not irrational, and that it is not irrational to act upon them. We therefore have new grounds to reject S.

As before, we have two alternatives. We could change our view about rationality, moving from S to P. Or we could again change our view about self-interest. We could move from the Desire-Fulfilment to the Objective List Theory.

According to this theory, certain things are good or bad for us, whatever our desires may be. One of the good things may be certain kinds of achievement. On the Objective List Theory, it may be better for me if I fulfil my desire for achievement, even if this causes my desires throughout my life to be, on the whole, worse fulfilled. We decided that acting in this way is not irrational. Now that we have changed our view about self-interest, this decision no longer gives us grounds to reject S.

When we moved from the Hedonistic to the Desire-Fulfilment Theory, this reduced but did not remove the conflict between S and P. We cannot make so definite a claim about the move from the Desire-Fulfilment to the Objective List Theory. If we make this move, this will *change* the cases in which S conflicts with P. One example is the case just given. But there are are no obvious grounds for claiming that, if we make this move, there will be *fewer* cases where S and P conflict.

How often S and P conflict depends on the contents of the Objective List. The important question here is whether, on the Objective List Theory, S and P would always coincide. I believe that, on any plausible version of this theory, this would not be true. On the Objective List Theory, some kinds of achievement may be one of the things that are good for us, and make our lives go better. But there will be several other things that are good for us, such as the mutual love of two adults, having and loving children, the development of a full range of abilities, and the awareness of all kinds of beauty. It may be true that, to fulfil my desire for achievement, I must deny myself most of the other things that are good for me. I may thus be doing what, on the Objective List Theory, will be on the whole worse for me. But, since I am fulfilling this desire for achievement, we decided that I am not acting irrationally. We therefore have new grounds to reject S.

At two earlier points in this line of thought, we had alternatives. We could change our view either about rationality, or about self-interest. At the point that we have now reached, *we no longer have alternatives*. There is now only one conclusion to be drawn. We cannot make a further change in our view about self-interest. We must change our view about rationality. We must reject S and accept P. As I claimed, if we believe that other desires are no less rational than the bias in one's own favour, we must in the end reject the Self-interest Theory.

When we reject this theory, we lose our motive to change our view about self-interest. We should therefore reconsider these changes.

I began by supposing that we accept the Hedonistic Theory, believing that it is against our interests to be less happy. Here is a different example. Turner wanted his paintings to be seen together in a separate gallery. Suppose we decide that it was not irrational for Turner to try to ensure that this desire would be fulfilled, even at some cost to his own happiness. We cannot defend this belief, while we accept S, unless we move from the Hedonistic to the Desire-Fulfilment Theory. We can then claim that the fulfilment of Turner's desire would be in his interests, even though it made him less happy. This allows us to claim that, in trying to fulfil this desire, at some cost to his own happiness, Turner was not acting irrationally. But we are forced to conclude that, in refusing to put Turner's paintings in a separate gallery, more than a century after his death, we are now acting against Turner's interests, or doing something that is bad for him. And we may find this claim implausible. We then have conflicting beliefs.

The conflict disappears if we abandon S. We can now claim *both* that Turner would not have been irrational if he had acted against his interests in trying to bring it about that there was a Turner gallery, *and* that, in refusing to build such a gallery, we are not now harming Turner, or doing something that is bad for him.

Similar reasoning applies, but with greater force, to our choice between the two versions of the Desire-Fulfilment Theory: the Unrestricted version, and the Success Theory. We cannot plausibly claim that the fulfilment of *all* of my desires is in my interests. Remember the case where, after a train journey, I sympathize with some stranger, and strongly want her to succeed. It is not plausible to claim that if, unknown to me, this stranger does later succeed, this is good for me. It is more plausible to claim that what is better for me is only that my own life go in the way that I do or would want it to go. If we appeal to this restricted version of the Desire-Fulfilment Theory—the Success Theory—there will be more cases where, by acting on my present desires, I will be doing what is worse for me. These will be cases where my desires are not about my own life. If we believe that some of these desires are not irrational, we shall believe that it is not irrational to act upon them. If we accept S, we may thus be led to accept the Unrestricted Desire-Fulfilment Theory about self-interest. Only on this theory is the fulfilment of these desires in my interests. But if these desires are not about my own life, and I never know that they are fulfilled, we may find it hard to believe that the fulfilment of these desires will be good for me. We may again have conflicting beliefs.

The conflict again disappears if we move from S to P. We can now claim that it is not irrational for me to act on these desires, even if doing so will be bad for me. Since we have rejected S, we have lost our motive for the implausible claim that, if these desires are not irrational, their fulfilment will be good for me. We have lost our motive for accepting the Unrestricted Desire-Fulfilment Theory about self-interest. We can move to the more plausible Success Theory.[8]

D   NAGEL'S BRAIN

Nagel believes that what he is, essentially, is his brain. He gives three arguments for his belief. These are contained in an unpublished rough draft, which he may revise; but, even in this rough form, they demand attention. I shall quote from this draft.

Two of Nagel's arguments appeal to a view about meaning, reference, and necessity. The objects we refer to have some *essential* properties: properties that these objects must have, since, if they lacked them, they could not exist. Some properties are essential because of the meanings of our words. Thus, because of what 'triangle' means, it is an essential property of triangles that they have three sides. But on the view that I shall now discuss, there is a different way in which objects can have essential properties. These properties are not essential because of the meanings of our words. We *discover* these essential properties when we discover facts about what it is that we are referring to. On this view, for example, we have discovered that an essential property of gold is having the atomic number 79. Every substance with this number must be gold, and no substance without this number could be gold. This was not part of the meaning of the word 'gold'.[9]

What are we referring to when we use the word 'person' and the word 'I'? Nagel writes: 'What I *am* is whatever *in fact* makes it possible for the person TN to identify and reidentify himself and his mental states'. What I am is whatever explains the psychological continuity of my mental life. And Nagel similarly claims that this leaves it open what the explanation is. If the carrier of continuity is a Cartesian Ego, that is what I really am. He continues: 'If on the other hand certain states and activities of my brain underlie the mental capacity, then that brain in those states . . . is what I am, and my survival of the destruction of my brain is not conceivable. However, I may not *know* that it is not conceivable, because I may not know the conditions of my own identity.' As he later writes, 'in trying to conceive of my survival after the destruction of my brain, I will not succeed in referring to *myself* in such a situation if I am in fact my brain'.

Nagel is a Reductionist. He agrees that personal identity does not involve the 'further fact', which in every conceivable case either holds completely or not at all. Personal identity just involves physical and psychological continuity. But, though he is a Reductionist, Nagel's view differs in two ways from the view that I and some others defend. On this view what fundamentally matters is Relation R: psychological continuity and connectedness. On Nagel's view, personal identity is what matters. And, because he believes that he is his brain, he believes that what fundamentally matters is the continued existence of this brain.

This may seem to be a disagreement only about imaginary cases. There are no actual cases where there is psychological continuity without the continued existence of the same brain. If the disagreement was only about imaginary cases, it would be hardly worth discussing. But this disagreement also covers actual cases, and our own lives. On my view, one of the two relations which matter, psychological connectedness, holds over time to reduced degrees. This is an essential premise of my argument, in Chapter 14, against the Self-interest Theory. This argument would be undermined if Nagel's view is true. The continued existence of the same brain, in our actual lives, is not a matter of degree.

This claim needs one qualification. Nagel leaves an important question open. Reconsider Williams's Example, where the surgeon tampers with my brain so as to remove all psychological continuity. Would the resulting person be me? Though my brain has been tampered with, it is clearly the very same brain. If I am my brain, I shall still exist. But in one of the remarks quoted above, Nagel suggests that what I am is not just my brain, but my brain *in certain states*. Perhaps these are the states which provide psychological continuity. On this version of his view, I would not exist at the end of Williams's Example.

The two versions of Nagel's view might be re-expressed as follows. On the simpler version, what I am is what normally causes my psychological continuity. But I would be this thing even when it does not cause psychological continuity. We have discovered that what I am is my brain. At the end of Williams's Example the surgeon has removed all psychological continuity. But since my brain will still exist, I shall still exist.

On the less simple version of Nagel's view, what I am is what causes my psychological continuity, in the particular states which make it be this cause. On this version of the view, my identity does not just involve the continued existence of my brain. It also involves psychological continuity. This version coincides with a view discussed above: the Narrow Psychological Criterion, which appeals to psychological continuity with its normal cause.

Only the first version of Nagel's view disagrees in actual cases with the view that I defend. Should we accept this version of the view? This partly depends on whether Nagel correctly describes the meaning of the words 'person' and 'I'. There is another complication. Nagel makes two claims about what he and others mean by the word 'I'. One is that he uses 'I' intending to refer to whatever explains his psychological continuity. The other is that he uses 'I' intending to refer to 'the unobserved subject' of his experiences.

I start with the second claim. This is hard to deny. I am not a series of thoughts, acts, and experiences. I am the thinker of my thoughts, and the doer of my deeds. I am the subject of all of my experiences, or the person who *has* these experiences.

Nagel claims that, when I use the word 'I', intending to refer to myself, the subject of my experiences, I am in fact referring to my brain. Should we accept this claim?

We should first note that an attempted reference may fail. Call what we are trying to refer to *our intended referent*. There may be some object which fits one of our beliefs about our intended referent. But this may not be enough to make this the object that we are referring to. We may have too many other beliefs about our intended referent, which would be false when applied to this object. We would then not be referring to this object. And we may be referring to nothing.[10]

One example would be this. The ancient Greeks believed that the God Zeus was the cause of lightning and thunder. Zeus did not exist, and the Greek word 'Zeus' referred to nothing. We should not claim that, since the Greeks believed that Zeus was the cause of lightning and thunder, and this cause is an electrical condition in the clouds, Zeus is such a cloud-condition, and this is what the Greek word 'Zeus' referred to. A cloud-condition is too unlike a God to be the referent of the Greek word 'Zeus.'

In using the word 'I', I intend to refer to myself, the subject of my experiences. Nagel believes that, when using 'I', most of us have false beliefs about our intended referent. Even if we are not aware of this, most of believe that our identity must be determinate. We believe that we are entities whose continued existence must be all-or-nothing. This belief would have been true if each of us had been a Cartesian Ego. But Nagel believes that there are no such entities. There are no entities with the special properties that we believe to be had by the subject of our experiences. In this respect, the case is like that of the Greek word 'Zeus.' But Nagel claims that, in using 'I', we do not fail to refer. What 'I' in fact refers to is my brain. Nagel admits that our brains do not have the special properties which we believe to be had by what 'I' refers to. But, while a cloud-condition is too unlike what the Greeks believed that 'Zeus' referred to, Nagel claims that our brains are not too unlike what we believe that 'I' refers to. As he writes, this is 'one of those cases where some of our most important beliefs about the referent of one of our concepts may be false, without its following that there is no such thing'.

Should we accept this view? Nagel believes that we are not separately existing entities, distinct from our brains and bodies, and our experiences. And he seems to believe that, if the word 'I' does not refer to my brain, there is nothing else that it could refer to. My brain must be the subject of my experiences, since, in the absence of Cartesian Egos, there is nothing else that could be the subject of my experiences. Thus, after denying that we are separately existing entities, he asks (1) 'why not go all the way with Parfit and abandon the identification of the self with the *subject* of the mental. . .?' And he answers (2) 'that the *actual* subject is what matters', even if it is not the kind of entity in which we are inclined to believe. (1) assumes that, on the Reductionist View that I defend, we cease to believe that there *are* subjects of experiences. (2) assumes that the subject of experiences is the brain.

I deny both of these assumptions. On the Reductionist View that I defend, persons are not separately existing entities. The existence of a person just involves the existence of his brain and body, and the doing of his deeds, and the occurrence of his mental states and events. But though they are not separately existing entities, persons exist. And a person is an entity that is distinct from his brain or body, and his various experiences. A person is an entity that *has* a brain and body, and *has* different experiences. My use of the word 'I' refers to myself, a particular person, or subject of experiences. And I am not my brain.

It may help to return to Hume's analogy. We can be Reductionists about nations, but still believe that nations exist, and can be referred to. A nation is not a separately existing entity, something other than its citizens, and the land they inhabit. A nation's existence just consists in the existence of its citizens, acting together in various ways on its territory. Though this is all there is to the existence of a nation, we can refer to nations, and claim that they exist. Thus we we can truly claim that France exists, and that France declared war on Germany in 1939. In contrast, there is no nation called Ruritania. We can make the same claims about people. Some people exist, and can be referred to, while others never exist, and cannot be referred to. I and Thomas Nagel are two of the people who ever exist, and can be referred to. But we cannot refer to my non-existent Roman ancestor, *Theodoricus Perfectus*.

My next claim has, in this discussion, special importance. When we use the word 'France' to refer to a nation, we are not referring to something other than a nation. We are not referring to this nation's government, or to its citizens, or to its territory. This can be shown as follows. If 'France' referred to the French government, France would cease to exist if the government resigned and there was a period of anarchy. But this is false. Nations continue to exist during periods when they have no government. Similarly, if 'France' referred in 1939 to those who were then French citizens, France would cease to exist when these citizens cease to exist. This is also false. And if 'France' referred to these citizens, it must have been these citizens that declared war on Germany. This is also false. There *is* a use of the word 'France' which refers, not to the nation but to the country, or this nation's territory. When we claim that France is beautiful, we are referring to its land and its buildings. But, on the other use, 'France' refers to the nation, not to its territory. If 'France' referred to French territory, France could not cease to exist unless that territory ceased to exist. This is also false. What was once the territory of the nation Prussia still exists. But Prussia has ceased to exist.

As the case of nations shows, we can refer to something though it is not a separately existing entity. And in referring to such a thing we are not referring to the various other entities that are involved in its existence. If we are Reductionists about persons, we can make similar claims about our use of the word 'I'. This can refer to a person, or subject of experiences, even though a person is not a separately existing entity. And when we decide that a person is not a separately existing entity, we are not forced to conclude that a person must be either his brain, or his whole body. Though nations are not separately existing entities, we are not forced to conclude that a nation must be either its government, or its citizens, or its territory, or all three. A nation is none of these three. And we can refer to nations. Similarly, we are not forced to conclude that a person is his brain, or his whole body. And we can refer to persons.[11]

I agree with Nagel that most of us have false beliefs about the intended referent of the word 'I'. Most of us believe that we are entities whose continued existence must be all-or-nothing. It may be objected that, since there are no such entities, we ought to conclude that, as used by most of us, the word 'I' fails to refer, just as 'Zeus' fails to refer. Like Nagel, I can reject this claim. 'Zeus' does not refer because a cloud-condition is too unlike a God. Persons on the Reductionist View are unlike persons on the Non-Reductionist View. But they are much more similar than Gods and cloud-conditions. I can therefore claim that persons exist. And since persons exist, though in a different way from that in which we are inclined to believe, our attempts to refer to persons can be claimed to succeed. Like Nagel, we can claim that this is one of the cases where we have false beliefs about our intended referent, without its following that we are not referring to this thing.

Since I am a person, who exists, I seem to be the best candidate for what my use of 'I' refers to. Nagel might reply as follows. It is true of most of us that we believe that we are separately existing entities. On the Reductionist View, this belief is false. But this belief would be true when applied to a person's brain. This may be claimed to make a person's brain a *better candidate* for what his use of 'I' refers to.

There is something in this claim, but not, I think, enough. If I use the word 'X' trying to refer to the object called X, and X exists, the natural assumption is that I do refer to X. This assumption might not be justified if it was both true that X lacks *most* of the properties that I believe it has, and true that some other object Y has *most* of these properties. This might justify the claim that, though I am trying to refer to X, I am in fact referring to Y. When someone uses the word 'I', his intended referent—what he is trying to refer to—is himself. This person may believe that he is a separately existing entity, distinct from his brain and body. It would then be true, as Nagel claims, that this person's intended referent lacks one of the properties that he believes it has, while another entity, his brain, has this property—being a separately existing entity (though not, of course, distinct from itself). But a person's brain does not have most of the properties that most of us believe we have. It does not, for example, have a continued existence that must be all-or-nothing; nor is it indivisible. When most of us use the word 'I', our brains are not very similar to what we believe to be our intended referents. This counts against the claim that, when we use 'I', we are in fact referring to our brains. What counts in favour of this claim that is that our brains have one of the properties that we mistakenly believe we have: that of being separately existing entities. But I believe that this is not enough to justify Nagel's claim. It is not enough to falsify the natural answer that we are referring to our intended referent. When we use 'I' we are trying to refer, not to our brains, but to ourselves. Our brains have one property that we mistakenly believe ourselves to have; but this is not enough to show that, when we try to refer to *ourselves*, we fail. We can retain our natural belief that we *can* refer to ourselves.

Nagel's second argument appeals to his other claim about the meaning of the word 'I'. This is the claim that, in using 'I', we intend to refer to whatever explains our psychological continuity. I believe that we can reject this claim. There is a contrast here between Nagel's arguments. Each involves one claim about meaning, and one claim about the facts. I accept the claim that I use 'I' intending to refer to the subject of my experiences. But I have denied the claim that the subject of my experiences is my brain. In considering *this* argument for Nagel's View, I accept his claim about meaning but deny his claim about the facts. In considering his other argument I accept his claim about the facts. What explains my psychological continuity is the continued existence of my brain. But I deny his claim about meaning. I deny the claim that I use 'I' intending to refer to whatever explains my psychological continuity.

Nagel's third argument appeals to an imaginary case, in which what seems to him to matter is the survival of his brain. He describes a case like that of Teletransportation. In this case, many people would accept Nagel's claim. They would believe that what matters is the survival of their brains.

I shall now describe two cases where this is harder to believe. Remember first that an object may continue to exist even if all of its components are replaced. The standard example is that of a ship, which has a piece of wood replaced after every journey. We might believe the same about a brain. We have learnt that the cells in the rest of our bodies are all gradually replaced. Even though this is not true of our brains, it might have been true. Our brains might have continued to exist even if, like the rest of our bodies, they had all of their components naturally and gradually replaced. And we may believe that our brains would continue to exist if we ourselves caused such a gradual replacement. I shall here assume that this is true. Since we believe that the rest of a person's body does continue to exist, though its components are gradually replaced, why should we take a different view about our brains?

Suppose next that I need surgery. All of my brain cells have a defect which, in time, would be fatal. But a surgeon can replace all these cells. He can insert new cells that are exact replicas of the existing cells except that they have no defect. We can distinguish two cases.

In *Case One*, the surgeon performs a hundred operations. In each of these, he removes a hundredth part of my brain, and inserts a replica of this part. In *Case Two*, the surgeon follows a different procedure. He first removes all of the parts of my brain, and then inserts all of their replicas.

There is a real difference between these cases. In Case One, each of the new parts of my brain is for a time joined to the rest of my brain. This enables each new part to become part of my brain. When the first new part is inserted, and joined to the rest of my brain, it wins the title to be as much part of my brain as the old parts. When the second new part is inserted, it too becomes a part of my brain. This is true of every new part, because there is a time when this part is joined to what then counts as the rest of my brain.

In Case Two, things are different. There are no times when each new part is joined to the rest of my brain. Because of this, the new parts do not count as parts of my brain. My brain ceases to exist.

Something similar might be true about the existence of a club. Consider a club that is limited to fifty members. All of the existing members want to resign. Fifty other people want to join this club. There is a rule that a new member cannot be admitted except in the presence of forty nine existing members. Because of this rule, this club continues to exist only if what happens is like Case One. What happens must be this. One member resigns and a new member is admitted. Another member resigns and a new member is admitted. A third member resigns and a new member is admitted. At the end of this series, this club would still exist, with entirely new members. Suppose instead that what happens is like Case Two. All of the old members resign. Because of the rule, the new members cannot now be admitted. The club ceases to exist.

Return to Cases One and Two. I am assuming that a brain might through a process of gradual replacement become composed of new components. On this assumption, it is clear that, in Case One, my brain continues to exist, and that, in Case Two, it does not. Nagel suggests that identity is what matters, and that I am my brain. On this view, Case One gives me life, and Case Two death.

Is this plausible? Though there is a real difference between these two cases, it is less than the difference Nagel had in mind. He considered a case in which his brain would be destroyed, and a Replica created. And he compared this case with ordinary survival, where his brain continues to have all of the same existing cells.

In my pair of cases, the difference is smaller. In both of my cases, there will later be a person whose brain will be exactly like my present brain, except for the defects. As a result, this person will be fully psychologically continuous with me. And, in *both* cases, this person's brain will be composed of the *very same* new components, each of which is a replica of some part of my brain. The difference between the cases is merely the way in which these new parts are inserted. It is a difference in the ordering of removals and insertions. In Case One, the surgeon alternates between removing and inserting. In Case Two, he does all the removing before all the inserting.

Can *this* be the difference between life and death? Can *my* fate depend on this difference in the ordering of removals and insertions? Can it be so important, for my survival, whether the new parts are, for a time, joined to the old parts? This could make all the difference if it produced some further fact. This would be so if my survival was like some sacred power, which one priest could give to another only by a ritual involving touch. But there is no such further fact. There is merely the fact that, if the new parts are for a time joined to the old parts, we describe the resulting brain as the same brain. If the new parts are not so joined, we describe the resulting brain as a different brain.

Nagel does not believe that the grounds for his view are decisive. And he admits that 'it is hard to *internalize* a conception of myself as identical with my brain'. He adopts his view partly because, in the pair of cases that he considered, his survival seemed to him to depend on whether his brain continued to exist. In my pair of cases, the difference in what happens is much less. If he considered these cases, Nagel might change his view. He suggests both (1) that identity is what matters, and (2) that he is his brain. But he admits that (2) is hard to accept. It is hard to think of oneself as being one's brain. When I consider Cases One and Two, I find it impossible to believe both (1) and (2). I cannot believe that what would matter for my survival is whether, over some period, the replicas of parts of my brain would be inserted in one of these two ways. I cannot believe that, if the surgeon alternates removing and inserting, this will be just as good as ordinary survival, while if he does all the removing before all the inserting, this will be nearly as bad as ordinary death. If this difference between the two cases is not what really matters, there are two alternatives. Either identity is not what matters, or I am not my brain.

The first alternative is supported by the imagined case where I divide. In this case, two resulting people each have half my brain. And there is no replication. These halves will be composed of my existing brain cells. As I have argued, it is very hard to believe that I should regard division as equivalent to death. My relation to each of the resulting people contains everything that would be needed for ordinary survival. And this remains true *even if what I am is my brain*. Each half of my brain will continue to exist, and to support conscious life. Each of the people with half my brain will seem to remember my whole life, and be in every other way psychologically continuous with me. If I am my brain, this is not a case in which I die because my brain ceases to exist. My brain continues to exist, and, because it is divided, it supports life more abundantly. It supports not just one but two lives.

Suppose that Nagel agrees that my relation to each resulting person contains what matters. Could he then defend his assumption that identity is what matters? We have seen that he could, by making grotesque distortions in our concept of a person. I assume that Nagel would reject these distortions. He would agree that, after I divide, there will be no one living who is me. If he also agrees that my relation to each resulting person is as good as survival, he must drop the assumption that identity is what matters. Without this assumption, I am not forced to conclude that replication would be as bad as death. I can agree that my Replica is not me, but claim that my relation to him contains what fundamentally matters. I can claim that what matters is psychological connectedness and/or continuity, with any cause.

Nagel might reply as follows. He might agree that there is one special case where identity is not what matters. This is the case where two future people each have half my brain. But what matters here is simply the continued existence of my divided brain. In every other case, personal identity is what matters.

This reply may have some force. But if we believe that identity is what matters, it is natural to believe that identity is *always* what matters. If we admit one exception, it may be hard to justify rejecting others. Given the small difference between my Cases One and Two, we can claim that, here too, identity is not what matters. If this claim is justified in the case where I divide, why can it not be justified here? It is hard to believe that my fate depends on the difference between these cases. Unlike the pair of cases that Nagel considered, this pair suggests that I am not my brain.

I have tried to answer Nagel's arguments. My answers do not show that his view is false. But I believe that they show that we can, defensibly, take a different view. The question remains open. This is why, in Section 98, I offer a quite different response to Nagel's view.

E THE CLOSEST CONTINUER SCHEMA

Nozick advances a general view about all judgements of identity over time. To be the same thing as some past thing is to be that thing's *closest continuer*. Nozick's view is Reductionist. He claims that there can be various kinds of continuity between some past person and various present persons. The present person whom we judge to *be* this past person is the present person who has the greatest continuity with this past person. On this view, the fact of personal identity over time just consists in the holding of such continuities. It does not involve any Further Fact. And Nozick explicitly compares personal identity with the identity over time of a certain group of philosophers, the Vienna Circle. This is like my comparison with the history of a club.

Though Nozick's view is in these ways Reductionist, he rejects the version of Reductionism that I defend. He writes:

One philosophical approach to a tangled area of complicated relationships of varying degree, rather than trying to force these into somewhat arbitrary pigeonholes, rests content with recognizing and delineating the underlying complicated relations. Concerning personal identity, it might say that future selves will have varying degrees of closeness to us-now in virtue of diverse underlying relations and events, such as bodily continuity, psychological similarity, splitting or fusion; and that the real and whole truth to be told is of the existence and contours of these underlying phenomena. Why impose any categorization—the closest continuer schema being one—over this complexity?

He then explicitly rejects my view, continuing:

The underlying level itself, however, also will raise similar problems. For example, in what way is something the same body when all of its cells other than neurons, as well as the particular molecules composing the neurons, are replaced over time? Should we speak again only of the complicated relations that underlie this level? We cannot avoid the closest continuer schema, or some other categorization, by restricting ourselves to the full complexity of the underlying relations. . . . Eventually we are pushed to a closest continuer schema or something similar at some level or other.... If it becomes legitimate, because necessary, to use the schema at some level, then why not simply begin with it?[12]

This disagreement is unnecessary. I do not deny that we make judgements about the identity over time of many different kinds of thing. And I accept Nozick's Closest Continuer Schema as an account of how we make many such judgements. My claims are these. Since personal identity over time just consists in the holding of certain other relations, what matters is not identity but some of these other relations. And the logic of identity does not always coincide with what matters. When what matters takes a branching form, or holds to intermediate degrees, judgements of identity cannot plausibly be made to correspond with what matters. In these cases we should not apply the Closest Continuer Schema in an attempt to achieve such correspondence. As Nozick writes, we would then be forcing what matters 'into somewhat arbitrary pigeonholes'. In these cases we should simply describe the ways in which, and the degrees to which, these other relations hold. We should then try to decide how much, in different ways, these relations matter. Nozick's objection to this view, quoted above, seems to be that we cannot avoid making some judgements about identity. But this is an objection only if we add the claim that, if we describe some cases by making or denying judgements about identity, we *must* describe *all* cases in this way. I can see no reason to accept this claim.

In his claim about what matters, Nozick again seems to reject Reductionism. He writes that, on his view, 'I will care equally about my closest continuer, whatever its degree of closeness happens to be (provided it is close enough)'. If he considered my Combined Spectrum, Nozick would probably withdraw this claim. In the cases in the middle of this Spectrum, there would be a resulting person who would have some proportion of the cells in my brain and body, and who would be in some ways psychologically continuous with me as I am now. But this resulting person would also have many new and dissimilar cells, and he or she would also be in many ways psychologically continuous with Greta Garbo. At the far end of this Spectrum, this future person would be in no way related to me. If I accept Nozick's view, I care equally about such a future person, provided that he or she is closely enough related to me. I regard all of the cases in the first part of this Spectrum as being just as good as ordinary survival. As we move along this Spectrum, the future person would be less and less closely related to me. But I am equally concerned about this person, provided that the degree of closeness is close *enough.*

On this view, I must decide just what degree of closeness counts as close enough. I am must again draw a sharp line on this Spectrum. If my relation to some future person is just on the near side of this line, this relation is as good as ordinary survival. If my relation to some future person is just beyond this line, I should be less concerned. But the future person in the second of these cases would differ hardly at all from the person in the first case. The differences would be only that a few more cells would be replaced, and there would be some small psychological change, such as a new desire to be alone. Though these are the only differences, I should care less about what happens to this second person.

This pattern of concern seems to me irrational. How can it have such importance whether just a few more cells would be replaced, or whether there would be one more small psychological change? Nozick's view treats this Spectrum as if it involves, at some point, a discontinuity. But this is false. Since the Spectrum is smooth, involving all of the degrees of continuity, why care equally in all the cases in the first part of the Spectrum, and then suddenly care less? This would be rational only if identity is some further fact which holds completely in the first part of this spectrum, and then suddenly fails to hold. But Nozick does not believe that there is any such further fact.

Nozick suggests another way in which his pattern of concern might be defended. He thinks it can be rational to adopt what he calls *the Platonic mode* of caring about something. In this mode, 'we see the world in its aspect of realizing what is beyond it, we see and can respond to its glimmerings of something finer which shine through'. Even though it is not true that we are beings whose continued existence must be all-or-nothing, it can be rational to care about our identity as if this was true. As Nozick admits, this involves 'an unrealistic overestimate of actuality, a seeing of it through Platonic glasses'. The alternative is to make 'a more realistic assessment of things, seeing things as they are in themselves'. Nozick objects to this alternative that it 'makes one a prisoner or a victim of the actual world, limited by the ways in which it falls short, by how it happens to be. . .'[13] .

Is this a sufficient defence of Nozick's pattern of concern? Can it be rational for his concern to correspond, not to the actual truth about his life, but to what he would have liked the truth to have been? Given the distinction between theoretical and practical rationality, Nozick's pattern of concern is defensible. I therefore withdraw my objection stated above. There is again no disagreement. If Nozick reacts to reality, not as it is, but as he would like it to be, this is theoretically irrational. But if this kind of wishful thinking is more deeply satisfying, it can be practically rational for him to try to make himself, in this way, theoretically irrational.

F   THE SOCIAL DISCOUNT RATE

According to a Social Discount Rate, the present moral importance of future events, especially benefits and losses, declines at a rate of n per cent per year. Two commonly employed rates are 5 per cent and 10 per cent. With one kind of *SDR* I have no quarrel. This is an SDR applied to benefits and losses measured in monetary terms, on the assumption that there will be inflation. But many economists apply an SDR to benefits and losses, measured at the size that they will have when they occur. My example in the text is not imagined. It has been seriously suggested that, in assessing the risks of the disposal of nuclear wastes, we should apply an SDR to future *deaths*. More generally, Social Discount Rates have been applied, not to monetary gains and losses, but to what economists call the actual utility that will be enjoyed by future people. This is the kind of SDR that I discuss. Why has this kind of SDR been thought to be justified? I am aware of six arguments:

> *The Argument from Democracy*: Many people care less about the further future. Some writers claim that, if this is true of most of the adult citizens of some democratic country, this country's government ought to employ a Social Discount Rate. If its electorate does care less about the further future, a democratic government ought to do so. Failure to do so would be paternalistic, or authoritarian. In one writer's words, the government's decisions should 'reflect only the preferences of present individuals'.[15] We can ignore this argument. There are two questions:

> (1)   As a community, may we use a Social Discount Rate? Are we morally justified in being less concerned about the more remote effects of our social policies, at some rate of *n* percent per year?

> (2)   If most of our community answer 'Yes' to question (1), ought our government to override this majority view?

The Argument from Democracy applies only to question (2). To question (1), which is our concern, the argument is irrelevant.

The point might be put like this. A democrat believes in certain constitutional arrangements. These provide his answer to question (2). How could his commitment to democracy give him an answer to question (1)? Only if he assumes that what the majority want, or believe to be right, must *be* right. But no sensible democrat assumes this. Suppose that some majority want to wage an aggressive war, caring nothing about the slaughter of innocent aliens. This would not show that they are right not to care. In the same way, even if most of us do care less about the more remote effects of our social policies, and believe such lesser concern to be morally justified, this cannot show that it *is* justified. Whatever most of us want or believe, this moral question remains open.

It may be objected: 'In some cases, this is not a moral question. Suppose that, in some referendum, we vote for a social policy that will affect only ourselves. And suppose that, because we care less about what will happen to us later, we vote for a policy that will bring us benefits now at the cost of greater burdens later. This policy is against our interests. But since this policy will affect only ourselves, we cannot be acting wrongly in voting for this policy. We can at most be acting irrationally.'

On the assumptions that most of us accept, these claims do provide some defence of the Social Discount Rate. But the defence seldom applies. Most social policies will affect our children, as well as ourselves. If we vote for a policy that will be against the interests of our children, most of us would admit that this would be, to some degree, morally wrong. Similar remarks apply to the interests of those people who are not yet born. It is a moral question how much weight we ought to give to the interests of these people. Another objection is that votes are seldom unanimous. If some policy will be against our interests, it will be likely to be against the interests of the minority who voted against it. The majority, who voted in favour, would then be acting against the interests of this minority. This is another ground for moral criticism.

As these remarks show, there would be few cases in which the Social Discount Rate does not raise a moral question. If one of my earlier claims is justified, there would be no such cases. I argued that, if we care less about what will happen to us later, and therefore act against our own interests, this may not be irrational. But such acts are open to criticism. I claimed that we should regard them as morally wrong. If this is so, the Social Discount Rate would always raise a moral question.

The Argument from Probability: It is often claimed that we should discount more remote effects because they are less likely to occur.

There are again two questions:

(1)   When a prediction applies to the further future, is it less likely to be correct?

(2)   If some prediction is correct, may we give it less weight because it applies to the further future?

The answer to (1) is often Yes. But this provides no argument for answering Yes to (2).

Suppose we are deciding whether to cease or increase our use of nuclear energy. We are considering possible accidents, with estimates of predicted deaths from escaped radiation. In a small accident, such deaths might all remain statistical, in the sense that we would never know which particular deaths this accident had caused. When considering possible accidents, we must think far into the future, since some radio-active elements remain dangerous for thousands of years. According to a Social Discount Rate of

5%, one statistical death next year counts for more than a billion deaths in 400 years. Compared with causing the single death, it is morally less important whether our chosen policy causes the billion deaths. This conclusion is outrageous. The billion people would be killed further in the future. But this cannot justify the claim that, compared with killing the single person, we would be acting less badly if instead we killed a billion people. The Argument from Probability does not lead to this conclusion. It could at most lead to a different conclusion. We know that, if radiation escapes next year, we will have no adequate defence. We may believe that, over the next four centuries, some kind of counter-measure will be invented, or some cure. We may thus believe that, if radiation escapes in 400 years, it will then be much less likely to cause deaths. If we are *very* optimistic, we may think this a billion times less likely. This would be a different reason for discounting, by a factor of a billion, deaths in 400 years. We would not be making the outrageous claim that, if we do cause such deaths, each of these deaths will matter morally a billion times less than a single death next year. We would instead be claiming that these more remote deaths are a billion times less likely to be caused. This would be why, in our view, we need hardly be concerned about the escape of radiation in 400 years. If we were right to claim that such deaths are a billion times less likely, our conclusion would be justified. Deaths that do not occur, whether now or in 400 years, do not matter.

This example illustrates a general point. We ought to discount those predictions that are more likely to be false. Call this a *Probabilistic Discount Rate*. Predictions about the further future are more likely to be false. So the two kinds of discount rate, *Temporal* and *Probabilistic*, roughly correlate. But they are quite different. It is therefore a mistake to discount for time rather than for probability. One objection is that this mis-states our moral view. It makes us claim, not that more remote bad consequences are less likely, but that they are less important. This is not our real view. A greater objection is that the two Discount Rates do not always coincide. Predictions about the further future are not less likely to be true at some rate of *n* percent per year. When applied to the further future, many predictions are indeed *more* likely to be true. If we discount for time rather than probability, we may thus be led to what, even on our own assumptions, are the wrong conclusions.

The Argument from Opportunity Costs: It is sometimes better to receive a benefit earlier, since this benefit can then be used to produce further benefits. If an investment yields a return next year, this will be worth more than the same return after ten years, if the earlier return can be reinvested profitably over these ten years. When we have added in the extra benefits from this reinvestment, the total sum of benefits will be greater. A similar argument covers certain kinds of cost. The delaying of some benefits thus involves *opportunity costs*, and vice versa.

This is sometimes thought to justify a Social Discount Rate. But the justification fails, and for the same two reasons. Certain opportunity costs do increase over time. But if we discount for time, rather than simply adding in these extra costs, we will misrepresent our moral reasoning. More important, we can be led astray.

Consider those benefits that are not reinvested but consumed. When such benefits are received later, this may involve no opportunity costs. Suppose we are deciding whether to build some airport. This would destroy some stretch of beautiful countryside. We would lose the benefit of enjoying this natural beauty. If we do not build the proposed airport, we and our successors would enjoy this benefit in every future year. According to a Social Discount Rate, the benefits in later years count for much less than the benefit next year. How could an appeal to opportunity costs justify this? The benefit received next year—our enjoyment of this natural beauty—cannot be profitably reinvested.

Nor can the argument apply to those costs which are merely 'consumed'. Suppose we know that, if we adopt some policy, there will be some risk of causing genetic deformities. The argument cannot show that a genetic deformity next year ought to count for ten times as much as a deformity in twenty years. The most that could be claimed is this. We might decide that, for each child so affected, the large sum of k dollars would provide adequate compensation. If we were going to provide such compensation, the present cost of ensuring this would be much greater for a deformity caused next year. We would now have to set aside almost the full k dollars. A mere tenth of this sum, if set aside now and profitably invested, might yield in twenty years what would then be equivalent to k dollars. This provides one reason for being less concerned now about the deformities we might cause in the further future. But the reason is *not* that such deformities matter less. The reason is that it would now cost us only a tenth as much to ensure that, when such deformities occur, we would be able to provide compensation. This is a crucial difference. Suppose we know that we will not in fact provide compensation. This might be so, for instance, if we would not be able to identify those particular genetic deformities that our policy had caused. This removes our reason for being less concerned now about deformities in later years. If we will not pay compensation for such deformities, it becomes an irrelevant fact that, in the case of later deformities, it *would have* been cheaper to ensure now that we *could have* paid compensation. But if this fact has led us to adopt a Social Discount Rate, we may fail to notice when it becomes irrelevant. We may be led to assume that, even when there is no compensation, deformities in twenty years matter only a tenth as much as deformities next year.

Here is another objection to this argument. In certain periods, investment brings *no* return. When this is true, the Argument from Opportunity Costs fails to apply. The Social Discount Rate again fails to correlate with anything that matters.

These brief remarks overlook many of the issues. Of the various arguments for a Social Discount Rate, the appeal to Opportunity Costs is the hardest to assess. But the central question is, I believe, simple. It may be in several ways more convenient, or elegant, to calculate opportunity costs using a Social Discount Rate. But the conclusions that are established by such calculations could be re-expressed in a temporally neutral way. When describing the effects of future policies, economists could state what future benefits and costs there would be, at different times, in a way that used no discount rate. The arguments that appeal to opportunity costs could be fully stated in these terms. I believe that, on any important question that we need to decide, this would be a better, because less misleading, description of the alternatives. It would make it easier to reach the right decision.

The Argument that Our Successors Will Be Better Off: If we assume that our successors will be better off than we are now, there are two plausible arguments for discounting the benefits and costs that we give to and impose on them. If we measure the benefits and costs in monetary terms, adjusted for future inflation, we can appeal to the diminishing marginal utility of money. The same increase in wealth generally brings a smaller benefit to those who are better off. We may also appeal to a distributive principle. An equally great benefit given to those who are better off may be claimed to be morally less important.

These two arguments, though good, do not justify a Social Discount Rate. The ground for discounting these future benefits is not that they come further in the future, but that they will come to people who are better off. Here, as elsewhere, we should say what we mean. And the correlation is again imperfect. Some of our successors may not be better off than we are now. If they are not, the arguments just given fail to apply.

The Argument from Excessive Sacrifice: A typical statement runs: 'We clearly need a Discount Rate for theoretical reasons. Otherwise any small increase in benefits that extends far into the future might demand any amount of sacrifice in the present, because in time the benefits would outweigh the cost.'

The same objections apply. If this is why we adopt a Social Discount Rate, we shall be mis-stating what we believe. Our belief is not that the importance of future benefits steadily declines. It is rather that no generation can be morally required to make more than certain kinds of sacrifice for the sake of future generations. If this is what we believe, this is what should influence our decisions.

We may have another belief. If we aimed for the greatest net sum of benefits over time, this might require a very unequal distribution between different generations. Utilitarians would claim that, given realistic assumptions, this would not be true. But suppose that it is true. We may then wish to avoid the conclusion that there ought to be such an unequal distribution.

And we can avoid this conclusion, in some cases, if we discount later benefits. But, as Rawls points out, this is the wrong way to avoid this conclusion. If we do not believe that there ought to be such inequality, we should not simply aim for the greatest net sum of benefits. We should have a second moral aim: that the benefits are fairly shared between different generations. To our principle of utility we should add a principle about fair distribution. This more accurately states our real view. And it removes our reason for discounting later benefits.

If instead we express our view by adopting a Social Discount Rate, we can be led needlessly to implausible conclusions. Suppose that, at the *same* cost to ourselves now, we could prevent either a minor catastrophe in the nearer future, or a major catastrophe in the further future. Since preventing the major catastrophe would involve no extra cost, the Argument from Excessive Sacrifice fails to apply. But if we take that argument to justify a Discount Rate, we shall be led to conclude that the greater catastrophe is less worth preventing.

The Argument from Special Relations: Some Utilitarians claim that each person should give equal weight to the interests of everyone. This is not what most of us believe. According to Common-Sense Morality, we ought to give some weight to the interests of strangers. But there are certain people to whom we either may or should give some kinds of priority. Thus we are morally permitted to give some kinds of priority to our own interests. Most of us believe that we have no duty to help others when this would require from us too great a sacrifice. And there are certain people to whose interests we *ought* to give some kinds of priority. These are the people to whom we stand in certain special relations. Thus each person ought to give some kinds of priority to the interests of his children, parents, pupils, patients, those whom he represents, or his fellow-citizens.

Such a view naturally applies to the effects of our acts on future generations. Our immediate successors will be our own children. According to common sense, we ought to give to their welfare special weight. We may think the same, though to a reduced degree, about our children's children.

Similar claims seem plausible at the community level. We believe that our government ought to be especially concerned about the interests of its own citizens. It would be natural to claim that it ought to be especially concerned about the future children of its citizens, and, to a lesser degree, about their grandchildren.

Such claims might support a new kind of Discount Rate. We would be discounting here, not for time itself, but for degrees of kinship. But at least these two relations cannot radically diverge. Our grandchildren cannot all be born before all our children. Since the correlation is, here, more secure, we might be tempted to employ a standard Discount Rate. I believe that, here too, this would be unjustified. For one thing, on any Discount Rate, more remote effects always count for less. But a Discount Rate with respect to Kinship should at some point cease to apply—or, to avoid discontinuity, asymptotically approach some horizontal level that is above zero. We ought to give *some* weight to the effects of our acts on mere strangers. We ought not to give *less* weight to effects on our own descendants.

Nor should this Discount Rate apply to all kinds of effect. Consider this comparison. Perhaps the U.S. Government ought in general to give priority to the welfare of its own citizens. But this does not apply to the infliction of grave harms. Suppose this Government decides to resume atmospheric nuclear tests. If it predicts that the resulting fall-out would cause several deaths, should it discount the deaths of aliens? Should it therefore move the tests to the Indian Ocean? I believe that, in such a case, the special relations make no moral difference. We should take the same view about the harms that we impose on our remote successors.

I have discussed six arguments for the Social Discount Rate. None succeeds. The most that they could justify is the use of such a rate as a crude rule of thumb. But this rule would often go astray. It may often be morally permissible to be less concerned about the more remote effects of our social policies. But this would never be *because* these effects are more remote. Rather it would be because they are less likely to occur, or would be effects on people who are better off than us, or because it would be cheaper now to ensure compensation, or it would be for one of the other reasons I have given. All these different reasons need to be stated and judged separately, on their merits. If we bundle them together in a Social Discount Rate, we make ourselves morally blind.

Remoteness in time roughly correlates with a whole range of morally important facts. So does remoteness in space. Those to whom we have the greatest obligations, our own family, often live with us in the same building. We often live close to those to whom we have other special obligations, such as our clients, pupils, or patients. Most of our fellow-citizens live closer to us than most aliens. But no one suggests that, because there are such correlations, we should adopt a Spatial Discount Rate. No one thinks that we would be morally justified if we cared less about the long-range effects of our acts, at some rate of n percent per yard. The Temporal Discount Rate is, I believe, as little justified.

When the other arguments do not apply, we ought to be equally concerned about the predictable effects of our acts whether these will occur in one, or a hundred, or a thousand years. This has great importance. Some effects are predictable even in the distant future. Nuclear wastes may be dangerous for thousands of years. And some of our acts have permanent effects. This would be so, for instance, of the destruction of a species, or of much of our environment, or of the irreplaceable parts of our cultural heritage.

G   WHETHER CAUSING SOMEONE TO EXIST CAN BENEFIT
THIS PERSON

This question has been strangely neglected. Thus, in a Report of a U.S.
Senate Commission on Population Growth and the American Economy, it is
claimed that 'there would be no substantial benefits from the continued
growth of the U.S. population'. This report never considers whether, if extra
Americans were born, this might benefit these Americans.

If we are to defend some view about overpopulation, we must consider
this question. If some act is a necessary part of the cause of the existence of
a person with a life worth living, does this act thereby benefit this person? I
shall argue that the answer Yes is not, as some claim, obviously mistaken.

Some objectors claim that life cannot be judged to be either better or
worse than nonexistence. But life of a certain kind may be judged to be
either good or bad—either worth living, or worth not living. If a certain
kind of life is good, it is better than nothing. If it is bad, it is worse than
nothing. In judging that some person's life is worth living, or better than
nothing, we need *not* be implying that it would have been worse for this
person if he had never existed.

Judgements of this kind are often made about the last part of some life.
Consider someone dying painfully, who has already made his farewells. This
person may decide that lingering on would be worse than dying. To make
this judgement, he need not *compare* what it would be like to linger on with
what it would be like to have died. As Williams writes, he 'might consider what
lay before him, and decide whether he did or did not want to undergo it'.[16]
And he might in a similar way decide that he was glad about or regretted
what lay behind him. He might decide that, at some point in the past, if he
had known what lay before him, he would or would not have wanted to live
the rest of his life. He might thus conclude that these parts of his life were
better or worse than nothing. If such claims can apply to parts of a life, they
can apply, I believe, to whole lives. [17]

The objectors might now appeal to

The Two-State Requirement: We benefit someone only if we cause him
to be better off than he would otherwise at that time have been.

They might say: 'In causing someone to exist, and have a life worth living,
we are not causing this person to be *better off* than he would otherwise have
been. This person would not have been *worse off* if he had never existed.'

To assess this argument, we should first ask the following question. If
someone now exists, and has a life worth living, is he better off than he
would now be if he had died, and ceased to exist? Suppose that we answer
Yes. In applying the Two-State Requirement, we count having ceased to
exist as a state in which someone can be worse off. Why can we not claim
the same about never existing? Why can we not claim that, if someone now
exists, with a life worth living, he is better off than he would be if he never

existed? It is true that *never existing* is not an ordinary state. But nor is *having ceased to exist.* Where is our mistake if we treat these alike when applying the Two-State Requirement?

It might be replied that, when someone dies, there is a particular person who has ceased to exist. We can refer to this person. In contrast, there are no particular people who never exist. We cannot refer to any such person.

This might be a good reply if we were claiming that, in causing people never to exist, we could be harming these people. But we are making a different claim. This is that, in causing someone to exist, we can be benefiting this person. Since this person *does* exist, we can refer to this person when describing the alternative. We know who it is who, in this possible alternative, would never have existed. In the cases that we are considering, there is not the alleged difference between having ceased to exist and never existing. Just as we can refer to the person who might now have ceased to exist, we can refer to the person who might never have existed. We have not been shown why, in applying the Two-State Requirement, we should not treat these two states in the same way.

The defender of the Two-State Requirement might next change his view about the state of being dead, or having ceased to exist. He might claim that this is not a state in which someone can be worse off. He could then claim the same about never existing.

With this revision, the Two-State Requirement becomes too strong. It implies that saving someone's life cannot benefit this person, since the person saved is not better off than he would have been if he had ceased to exist. In the case of saving life, it would now be defensible to relax the Two-State Requirement. We understand the special reason why, in this case, the Requirement is not met. We can claim that, because of this special feature of the case, the Requirement need not here be met. If the rest of someone's life would be worth living, we can count saving his life as a special case of benefiting him. And if we can relax the Requirement in the case of saving life, why can we not do the same in the case of giving life? If someone's life is worth living, why can we not count causing him to live as a special case of benefiting him?

The objectors might now turn to

The Full Comparative Requirement: We benefit someone only if we do what will be better for him.

They could say: 'In causing someone to exist, we cannot be doing what will be better for him. If we had not caused him to exist, this would not have been worse for him.' Unlike the last form of the Two-State Requirement, this new Requirement allows that saving someone's life can benefit this person. We can claim that it can be worse for someone if he dies, even though this does not make him worse off. (We would here be rejecting the *Lucretian View* that an event can be bad for someone only if it makes him later suffer, or at least have regrets.)

Because it covers saving life, the Full Comparative Requirement is more plausible than the stronger form of the Two-State Requirement. But if we can relax the latter, in both of our special cases, it may be defensible to relax the former, in the case of giving life. We can admit that, in every other kind of case, we benefit someone only if we do what will be better for him.[18] In the case of giving someone life, we understand the special reason why the alternative would not have been worse for him. We might claim that, in this special case, the Requirement need not be met. Suppose we have allowed that saving someone's life can benefit this person. If my own life is worth living, it would then have benefited me to have had my life saved at any time after it started. Must I claim that, while it benefited me to have had my life saved *just after* it started, it did not benefit me to have had it started? I can defensibly deny this claim.

Causing someone to exist is a special case because the alternative would not have been worse for this person. We may admit that, for this reason, causing someone to exist cannot be *better* for this person. But it may be *good* for this person.[19] In this move from 'better' to 'good', we admit that the Full Comparative Requirement is not met. But we could still make two kinds of comparison. If it can be good for someone if he is caused to live, *how* good this is for this person will depend on how good his life is—how much his life is worth living. And we can make interpersonal comparisons. Suppose that *Jack's* life is worth living, but not by a large margin. If his bouts of depression became more frequent and more severe, he would begin to doubt that his life was worth continuing. *Jill's* life, in contrast, is well worth living. We can then claim that, when we caused Jack to exist, this was good for Jack, but that it was much *less* good for Jack than causing Jill to exist was for Jill.

These claims avoid a common objection. When we claim that it was good for someone that he was caused to exist, we do not imply that, if he had not been caused to exist, this would have been bad for him. And our claims apply only to people who are or would be actual. We make no claims about people who would always remain merely possible. We are not claiming that it is bad for possible people if they do not become actual.

I end with these remarks. I have considered three things: never existing, starting to exist, and ceasing to exist. I have suggested that, of these, starting to exist should be classed with ceasing to exist. Unlike never existing, starting to exist and ceasing to exist both happen to actual people. This is why we can claim that they can be either good or bad for these people. The contrary claim is that starting to exist should be classed with never existing, and that neither can be either good or bad for people. The reason sometimes given is that, if we had *not* started to exist, we would never have existed, which would not have been worse for us. But we are not claiming that starting to exist can be either good or bad for people *when it does not happen*. Our claim is about starting to exist *when it happens*. We admit one difference between starting to exist and ceasing to exist. For almost all events, if their occurrence would be good for people, their non-occurrence would have been worse for these people. But, we may suggest, there is one special event whose non-occurrence would not have been worse for this actual person. This event, unsurprisingly, is the coming-to-be actual of this person.

These remarks are not conclusive. Further objections could be raised. My claim is only that, if we believe that causing to exist can benefit, this belief is defensible. I have appealed to three points. First, we need not claim that it is bad for possible people if they never become actual. As Nagel writes: 'All of us . . . are fortunate to have been born. But . . . it cannot be said that not to have been is a misfortune.'[20] Second, if it benefited me to have had my life saved just after if started, I am not forced to deny that it benefited me to have had it started. From my present point of view, there is no deep distinction between these two. (It might be denied that it benefited me to have had my life saved. But, if this is claimed, it becomes irrelevant whether causing someone to exist can benefit this person. I ought to save a drowning child's life. If I do not thereby benefit this child, this part of morality cannot be explained in person-affecting terms.) Third, causing someone to exist is clearly a special case. Some argue that this is no benefit because it lacks some feature shared by all other benefits. But this argument begs the question. Since this is a special case, it may be an exception to any general rule. Appealing to some general rule simply assumes that there can be no exceptions.

There has been a similar debate whether *existing* is a *predicate* or a genuine property that objects might possess. Some claim that, because it lacks some of the features of other predicates, *existing* is not a predicate. Others claim that this only shows *existing* to be a *peculiar* predicate. We can similarly claim that causing someone to exist, who will have a life worth living, gives this person a peculiar benefit.

H RAWLSIAN PRINCIPLES

Many people apply to particular examples the kinds of principle that Rawls employs only within the context of his wider theory. This is why I call these principles, not Rawls's, but only *Rawlsian*. (Marx complained that some of his followers were *plus Marxiste que moi*. Rawls could make the same complaint.)

Consider any case in which, in the different outcomes, the same people would exist. According to Maximin, the best outcome is the one in which the worst-off people are best off. We may think that this outcome must be what is best for those who are worst-off. But this is not so.

Suppose that I am a doctor. Depending on what I do, the outcomes might be:

(1) *Jack*, *Bill*, and *John* are completely paralysed.

(2) Jack and John are cured. Bill is completely paralysed.

(3) Jack and Bill are cured. John is partly paralysed.

John would be harder to cure than Bill, who would be harder to cure than Jack. This is why I cannot do more to cure these people than I do in outcomes (2) and (3). If I cure John, I cannot cure Bill, and, if I cure Bill, I can only partly cure John.

(3) is the outcome where the worst-off person is best off. But this is not the outcome that is best for this person. (3) is worse for this person than (2) would have been. Maximin rightly selects (3) as the best outcome. But we cannot claim that, if we follow Maximin, this must be best for those who are worst off. Following Maximin may be worse for these people than something else that we could have done. When we see this point, we can still accept Maximin. But we must revise two other Rawlsian Principles.

Consider first the *Difference Principle*. In outcome (3) there is inequality. On the Difference Principle, causing such inequality is unjust unless it produces the outcome that is best for those who are worst-off. In outcome (3) it is John who is worst-off. In producing this inequality I have not produced the outcome that is best for John, since (2) would have been better for him. On the Difference Principle, the inequality in outcome (3) is unjust. For a similar reason, the inequality in outcome (2) is unjust. To avoid injustice, I must act in one of two ways. I must either cure no one, or partly cure all three people. Though I could wholly cure two of these people and partly cure the third, I ought not to do so. This is clearly the wrong conclusion. If we wish to apply it to such particular examples, we must revise the Difference Principle so that it ceases to imply such conclusions.

I need not discuss this revision, since the Difference Principle does not apply to my imagined outcomes A and A+. This principle applies only to inequality that is both deliberately created and avoidable. The inequality in A+ is not of this kind.

Consider next what I shall call the *Selection Principle*. This claims that the best outcome is the one that is best for those who are worst off. In my medical example, (3) cannot be best since is it worse than (2) for the person who in (3) is worst off. This is clearly the wrong conclusion. We must revise the Selection Principle so that it ceases to imply such conclusions.

The obvious revision is Maximin. This differs from the Selection Principle in just the way that is needed to imply, correctly, that the best outcome is (3).

The rest of this Appendix was written by John Broome, after we had discussed the points made above.

In RAWLS, one of the principles of justice is the Difference Principle, that Rawls specifies like this (p. 302):

Social and economic inequalities are to be arranged so that they are . . . to the greatest benefit of the least advantaged.

This formulation does not exactly express what Rawls intended by it. Suppose India in 1800 could have had any of three constitutions. Each would have distributed other primary goods equally, but they would have distributed economic and social well-being as follows:

On Constitution (1) the Indians and British both get 100
On Constitution (2) the Indians get 120, the British 110
On Constitution (3) the Indians get 115, the British 140.

It is clear that Rawls means the Difference Principle to favour Constitution (3). He sometimes (e.g. p. 152) describes the Difference Principle as a 'maximin rule', and (3) satisfies this rule. But it does not satisfy the formulation I quoted above. The least advantaged under Constitution (3) are the Indians, and the greater inequalities under (3), compared with (2), are not to the benefit of the Indians. They would have been better off under (2).

Of course, the wording could be easily changed so as to state Rawls's meaning more accurately. But a number of Rawls's arguments for the Difference Principle actually rely on his own wording. This is not true of his main argument, the claim that people in the Original Position would select the maximin rule, but many of his other arguments take it for granted that the Difference Principle favours social arrangements that are to the greatest benefit of the least advantaged people. These arguments fail in examples like mine. For instance, on p. 103 Rawls says: 'B'—the least-favoured representative man—'can accept A's being better off since A's advantages have been gained in ways that promote B's prospects'. It is not true that the representative British person's advantages under Constitution (3) have been gained in ways that promote the representative Indian's prospects.

Rawls might not be satisfied with the way I have treated my example. Alternative social arrangements, he says (pp. 95-100), are to be compared in terms of the situations of groups, or of representative men representing groups, rather than of individuals. And a group is to be defined simply by its level of income and wealth. (But see p. 29, where Rawls does allow that groups may sometimes be identified by race.) So we ought to compare, not the position of Indians under Constitutions (2) and (3), but the position of the least-advantaged group, which is made up of different people in the two cases. The least-advantaged group under (3) is better off than the least-advantaged group under (2). This is the comparison that Rawls might like us to make. But my point is that his *arguments* often implicitly assume that we are comparing alternative positions that the same *individual* might occupy. In the argument I quoted Rawls compares the alternative positions of the least-favoured representative man, but there is no man who represents the least-favoured groups under both (2) and (3). We can only take the least-favoured representative man to be the representative Indian, and as I say the argument does not work for him.

It is plain that to justify picking Constitution (3) rather than (2) we have to compare the interests of two groups. We have to say that the loss to the Indians in picking (3) is less than the loss to the British in picking (2). So we have to weigh up different people's interests in much the way utilitarians do, and in much the way the difference principle was supposed to avoid (pp. 175-83). If (3) really is better than (2) I should say it can only be on grounds like utilitarian ones. And if the utilitarian grounds go the other way—if, say, there are many more Indians than British—I should find it very hard to believe that (3) is really better.

JOHN BROOME. (I should like to thank John Rawls for his comments.)

I   WHAT MAKES SOMEONE'S LIFE GO BEST

What would be best for someone, or would be most in this person's interests, or would make this person's life go, for him, as well as possible? Answers to this question I call *theories about self-interest*. There are three kinds of theory. On *Hedonistic Theories*, what would be best for someone is what would make his life happiest. On *Desire-Fulfilment Theories*, what would be best for someone is what, throughout his life, would best fulfil his desires. On *Objective List Theories*, certain things are good or bad for us, whether or not we want to have the good things, or to avoid the bad things.

Narrow Hedonists assume, falsely, that pleasure and pain are two distinctive kinds of experience. Compare the pleasures of satisfying an intense thirst or lust, listening to music, solving an intellectual problem, reading a tragedy, and knowing that one's child is happy. These various experiences do not contain any distinctive common quality.

What pains and pleasures have in common are their relations to our desires. On the use of 'pain' which has rational and moral significance, all pains are when experienced unwanted, and a pain is worse or greater the more it is unwanted. Similarly, all pleasures are when experienced wanted, and they are better or greater the more they are wanted. These are the claims of *Preference-Hedonism*. On this view, one of two experiences is more pleasant if it is preferred.

This theory need not follow the ordinary uses of the words 'pain' and 'pleasure'. Suppose that I could go to a party to enjoy the various pleasures of eating, drinking, laughing, dancing, and talking to my friends. I could instead stay at home and read *King Lear*. Knowing what both alternatives would be like, I prefer to read King Lear. It extends the ordinary use to say that this would give me more pleasure. But on Preference-Hedonism, if we add some further assumptions given below, reading King Lear would give me a better evening. Griffin cites a more extreme case. Near the end of his life Freud refused pain-killing drugs, preferring to think in torment than to be confusedly euphoric. Of these two mental states, euphoria is more pleasant. But on Preference-Hedonism thinking in torment was, for Freud, a better mental state. It is clearer here not to stretch the meaning of the word 'pleasant'. A Preference-Hedonist should merely claim that, since Freud preferred to think clearly though in torment, his life went better if it went as he preferred.[21]

Consider next Desire-Fulfilment Theories. The simplest is the *Unrestricted* Theory. This claims that what is best for someone is what would best fulfil *all* of his desires, throughout his life. Suppose that I meet a stranger who has what is believed to be a fatal disease. My sympathy is aroused, and I strongly want this stranger to be cured. We never meet again. Later, unknown to me, this stranger is cured. On the Unrestricted Desire-Fulfiment Theory, this event is good for me, and makes my life go better. This is not plausible. We should reject this theory.

Another theory appeals only to our desires about our own lives. I call this the *Success Theory*. This theory differs from Preference-Hedonism in only one way. The Success Theory appeals to *all* of our preferences about our own lives. A Preference-Hedonist appeals only to preferences about those features of our lives that are introspectively discernible. Suppose that I strongly want not to be deceived by other people. On Preference-Hedonism it will be better for me if I believe that I am not being deceived. It will be irrelevant if my belief is false, since this makes no difference to my state of mind. On the Success Theory, it will be worse for me if my belief is false. I have a strong desire about my own life—that I should not be deceived in this way. It is bad for me if this desire is not fulfilled, even if I falsely believe that it is.

When this theory appeals only to desires that are about our own lives, it may be unclear what this excludes. Suppose that I want my life to be such that all of my desires, whatever their objects, are fulfilled. This may seem to make the Success Theory, when applied to me, coincide with the Unrestricted Desire-Fulfilment Theory. But a Success Theorist should claim that this desire is not really about my own life. This is like the distinction between a real change in some object, and a so-called *Cambridge-change*. An object undergoes a Cambridge-change if there is any change in the true statements that can be made about this object. Suppose that I cut my cheek while shaving. This causes a real change in me. It also causes a change in Confucius. It becomes true, of Confucius, that he lived on a planet on which later one more cheek was cut. This is merely a Cambridge-change.

Suppose that I am an exile, and cannot communicate with my children. I want their lives to go well. I might claim that I want to live the life of someone whose children's lives go well. A Success Theorist should again claim that this is not really a desire about my own life. If unknown to me one of my children is killed by an avalanche, this is not bad for me, and does not make my life go worse.

A Success Theorist *would* count some similar desires. Suppose that I try to give my children a good start in life. I try to give them the right education, good habits, and psychological strength. Once again, I am now an exile, and I shall never be able to learn what happens to my children. Suppose that, unknown to me, my children's lives go badly. One finds that the education that I gave him makes him unemployable, another has a mental breakdown, another becomes a petty thief. If my children's lives fail in these ways, and these failures are in part the result of mistakes I made as their parent, these failures in my children's lives would be judged on the Success Theory to be bad for me. One of my strongest desires was to be a successful parent. What is now happening to my children, though it is unknown to me, shows that this desire is not fulfilled. My life failed in one of the ways in which I most wanted it to succeed. Though I do not know this fact, it is bad for me, and makes it true that I have had a worse life. This is like the case where I strongly want not to be deceived. Even if I never know, it is bad for me both if I am deceived and if I turn out to be an unsuccessful parent. These are not introspectively discernible differences in my conscious life; so, on Preference-Hedonism, these events are not bad for me. But on the Success Theory, they are.

Consider next the desires that some people have about what happens after they are dead. For a Preference-Hedonist, once I am dead, nothing bad can happen to me. A Success Theorist should deny this. Return to the case where all my children have wretched lives, because of the mistakes I made as their parent. Suppose that my children's lives all go badly only after I am dead. My life turns out to have been a failure, in one of the ways I cared about most. A Success Theorist should claim that, here too, this makes it true that I had a worse life.

Some Success Theorists would reject this claim, since they tell us to ignore the desires of the dead. But suppose that I was asked, 'Do you want you it to be true, even after you are dead, that you were a successful parent?' I would answer 'Yes'. It is irrelevant to my desire whether it is fulfilled before or after I am dead. These Success Theorists count it as bad for me if my attempts fail, even if, because I am an exile, I never know this. How then can it matter whether, when my attempts fail, I am dead? All that my death does is to *ensure* that I will never know this. If we think it irrelevant that I never know about the non-fulfilment of my desires, we cannot defensibly claim that my death makes a difference.

I turn now to questions and objections which arise for both Preference-Hedonism and the Success Theory.

Should we appeal only to the desires and preferences that someone actually has? Return to my choice between going to a party or staying at home to read *King Lear*. Suppose that, knowing what both alternatives would be like, I choose to stay at home. And suppose that I never later regret this choice. On one theory, this shows that staying at home to read King Lear gave me a better evening. This is a mistake. It might be true that, if I had chosen to go to the party, I would never have regretted that choice. According to this theory, this would have shown that going to the party gave me a better evening. This theory thus implies that each alternative would have been better than the other. Since this theory implies such contradictions, it must be revised. The obvious revision is to appeal not only to my actual preferences, in the alternative I choose, but also to the preferences that I would have had if I had chosen otherwise.[22]

In this example, whichever alternative I choose, I would never regret this choice. If this is true, can we still claim that one of the alternatives would give me a better evening? On some theories, when in two alternatives I would have such contrary preferences, neither alternative is better or worse for me. This is not plausible when one of my contrary preferences would have been much stronger. Suppose that, if I choose to go to the party, I shall be only mildly glad that I made this choice, but that, if I choose to stay and read King Lear, I shall be very glad. If this is true, reading King Lear gives me a better evening.

Whether we appeal to Preference-Hedonism or the Success Theory, we should not appeal only to the desires or preferences that I actually have. We should also appeal to the desires and preferences that I would have had, in the various alternatives that were, at different times, open to me. One of these alternatives would be best for me if it is the one in which I would have the strongest desires and preferences fulfilled. This allows us to claim that some alternative life would have been better for me, even if throughout my actual life I am glad that I chose this life rather than this alternative.

There is another distinction which applies both to Preference-Hedonism and to the Success Theory. These theories are *Summative* if they appeal to all of someone's desires, actual and hypothetical, about either his states of mind, or his life. In deciding which alternative would produce the greatest total net sum of desire-fulfilment, we assign some positive number to each desire that is fulfilled, and some negative number to each desire that is not fulfilled. How great these numbers are depends on the intensity of the desires in question. (In the case of the Success Theory, which appeals to past desires, it may also depend on how long these desires were had. As I suggest in Chapter 8, this may be a weakness in this theory. The issue does not arise for Preference-Hedonism, which appeals only to the desires that we have, at different times, about our present states of mind.) The total net sum of desire-fulfilment is the sum of the positive numbers minus the negative numbers. Provided that we can compare the relative strength of different desires, this calculation could in theory be performed. The choice of a unit for the numbers makes no difference to the result.

Another version of both theories does not appeal, in this way, to all of a person's desires and preferences about his own life. It appeals only to *global* rather than *local* desires and preferences. A preference is global if it is about some part of one's life considered as a whole, or is about one's whole life. The *Global* versions of these theories I believe to be more plausible.

Consider this example. Knowing that you accept a Summative theory, I tell you that I am about to make your life go better. I shall inject you with an addictive drug. From now on, you will wake each morning with an extremely strong desire to have another injection of this drug. Having this desire will be in itself neither pleasant nor painful, but if the desire is not fulfilled within an hour it will then become very painful. This is no cause for concern, since I shall give you ample supplies of this drug. Every morning, you will be able at once to fulfil this desire. The injection, and its after-effects, would also be neither pleasant nor painful. You will spend the rest of your days as you do now.

What would the Summative Theories imply about this case? We can plausibly suppose that you would not welcome my proposal. You would prefer not to become addicted to this drug, even though I assure you that you will never lack supplies. We can also plausibly suppose that, if I go ahead, you will always regret that you became addicted to this drug. But it is likely that your initial desire not to become addicted, and your later regrets that you did, would not be as strong as the desires you have each morning for another injection. Given the facts as I described them, your reason to prefer not to become addicted would not be very strong. You might dislike the thought of being addicted to anything; and you would regret the minor inconvenience that would be involved in remembering always to carry with you sufficient supplies. But these desires might be far weaker than the desires you would have each morning for a fresh injection.

On the Summative Theories, if I make you an addict, I will be increasing the sum-total of your desire-fulfilment. I will be causing one of your desires not to be fulfilled: your desire not to become an addict, which, after my act, becomes a desire to be cured. But I will also be giving you an indefinite series of extremely strong desires, one each morning, all of which you can fulfil. The fulfilment of all these desires would outweigh the non-fulfilment of your desires not to become an addict, and to be cured. On the Summative Theories, by making you an addict, I will be benefiting you—making your life go better.

This conclusion is not plausible. Having these desires, and having them fulfilled, are neither pleasant nor painful. We need not be Hedonists to believe, more plausibly, that it is in no way better for you to have and to fulfil this series of strong desires.

Could the Summative Theories be revised, so as to meet this objection? Is there some feature of the addictive desires which would justify the claim that we should ignore them when we calculate the sum total of your desire-fulfilment? We might claim that they can be ignored because they are desires that you would prefer not to have. But this is not an acceptable revision. Suppose that you are in great pain. You now have a very strong desire not to be in the state that you are in. On our revised theory, a desire does not count if you would prefer not to have this desire. This must apply to your intense desire not to be in the state you are in. You would prefer not to have this desire. If you did not dislike the state you are in, it would not be painful. Since our revised theory does not count desires that you would prefer not to have, it implies, absurdly, that it cannot be bad for you to be in great pain.

There may be other revisions which could meet these objections. But it is simpler to appeal to the Global versions of both Preference-Hedonism and the Success Theory. These appeal only to someone's desires about some part of his life, considered as a whole, or about his whole life. The Global Theories give us the right answer in the case where I make you an addict. You would prefer not to become addicted, and you would later prefer to cease to be addicted. These are the only preferences to which the Global Theories appeal. They ignore your particular desires each morning for a fresh injection, since you have already considered these desires in forming your global preference.

This imagined case of addiction is in its essentials similar to countless other cases. There are countless cases in which it is true both (1) that, if someone's life went in one of two ways, this would produce a greater sum total of local desire-fulfilment, but (2) that the other alternative is what he would globally prefer, *whichever* way his actual life went.

Rather than describing another of the countless actual cases, I shall mention an imaginary case. This is the analogue, within one life, of the *Repugnant Conclusion* that I discuss in Part Four. Suppose that I could either have fifty years of life of an extremely high quality, or an indefinite number of years that are barely worth living. In the first alternative, my fifty years would, on any theory, go extremely well. I would be very happy, would achieve great things, do much good, and love and be loved by many people. In the second alternative my life would always be, though not by much, worth living. There would be nothing bad about this life, and it would each day contain a few small pleasures.

On the Summative Theories, if the second life was long enough, it would be better for me. In each day within this life I have some desires about my life that are fulfilled. In the fifty years of the first alternative, there would be a very great sum of local desire-fulfilment. But this would be a finite sum, and in the end it would be outweighed by the sum of desire-fulfilment in my indefinitely long second alternative. A simpler way to put this point is this. The first alternative would be good. In the second alternative, since my life is worth living, living each extra day is good for me. If we merely add together whatever is good for me, some number of these extra days would produce the greatest total sum.

I do not believe that the second alternative would give me a better life. I therefore reject the Summative Theories. It is likely that, in both alternatives, I would globally prefer the first. Since the Global Theories would then imply that the first alternative gives me a better life, these theories seem to me more plausible.[23]

Turn now to the third kind of theory that I mentioned: the Objective List Theory. According to this theory, certain things are good or bad for people, whether or not these people would want to have the good things, or to avoid the bad things. The good things might include moral goodness, rational activity, the development of one's abilities, having children and being a good parent, knowledge, and the awareness of true beauty. The bad things might include being betrayed, manipulated, slandered, deceived, being deprived of liberty or dignity, and enjoying either sadistic pleasure, or aesthetic pleasure in what is in fact ugly.[24].

An Objective List Theorist might claim that his theory coincides with the Global version of the Success Theory. On this theory, what would make my life go best depends on what I would prefer, now and in the various alternatives, if I knew all of the relevant facts about these alternatives. An Objective List Theorist might say that the most relevant facts are those just mentioned—the facts about what would be good or bad for me. And he might claim that anyone who knew these facts would want what is good for him, and want to avoid what would be bad for him.

Even if this was true, though the Objective List Theory would coincide with the Success Theory, the two theories would remain distinct. A Success Theorist would reject this description of the coincidence. On his theory, nothing is good or bad for people *whatever* their preferences are. Something is bad for someone only when, if he knew the facts, he would want to avoid it. And the relevant facts do not include the alleged facts cited by the Objective List Theorist. On the Success Theory it is, for instance, bad for a person to be deceived if and because this is not what this person wants. The Objective List Theorist makes the reverse claim. People want not to be deceived because this is bad for them.

As these remarks imply, there is one important difference between on the one hand Preference-Hedonism and the Success Theory, and on the other hand the Objective List Theory. The first two kinds of theory give an account of self-interest which is purely descriptive—which does not appeal to facts about value. This account appeals only to what a person does and would prefer, given full knowledge of the purely non-evaluative facts about the alternatives. In contrast, the Objective List Theory appeals directly to what it claims to be facts about value.

In choosing between these theories, we must decide how much weight to give to imagined cases in which someone's fully informed preferences would be bizarre. If we can appeal to these cases, they cast doubt on both Preference-Hedonism and the Success Theory. Consider the man that Rawls imagined who wants to spend his life counting the numbers of blades of grass in different lawns. Suppose that this man knows that he could achieve great progress if instead he worked in some especially useful part of Applied Mathematics. Though he could achieve such significant results, he prefers to go on counting blades of grass. On the Success Theory, if we allow this theory to cover all imaginable cases, it could be better for this person if he counted his blades of grass rather than achieving great and useful mathematical results.

The counter-example might be more offensive. Suppose that what someone would most prefer, knowing the alternatives, is a life in which, without being detected, he causes as much pain as he can to other people. On the Success Theory, such a life would be what is best for this person.

We may be unable to accept these conclusions. Ought we therefore to abandon this theory? This is what Sidgwick did, though those who quote him seldom notice this. He suggests that 'a man's future good on the whole is what he would now desire and seek on the whole if all the consequences of all the different lines of conduct open to him were accurately foreseen and adequately realised in imagination at the present point of time'.[25] As he comments: 'The notion of "Good" thus attained has an ideal element: it is something that *is* not always actually desired and aimed at by human beings: but the ideal element is entirely interpretable in terms *of fact,* actual or hypothetical, and does not introduce any judgement of value'. Sidgwick then rejects this account, claiming that what is ultimately good for someone is what this person *would* desire if his desires were in harmony with reason. This last phrase is needed, Sidgwick thought, to exclude the cases where someone's desires are irrational. He assumes that there are some things that we have good reason to desire, and others that we have good reason not to desire. These might be the things which are held by Objective List Theories to be good or bad for us.

Suppose we agree that, in some imagined cases, what someone would most want both now and later, fully knowing about the alternatives, would *not* be what would be best for him. If we accept this conclusion, it may seem that we must reject both Preference-Hedonism and the Success Theory. Perhaps, like Sidgwick, we must put constraints on what can be rationally desired.

It might be claimed instead that we can dismiss the appeal to such imagined cases. It might be claimed that what people would in fact prefer, if they knew the relevant facts, would always be something that we could accept as what is really good for them. Is this a good reply? If we agree that in the imagined cases what someone would prefer might be something that is bad for him, in these cases we have abandoned our theory. If this is so, can we defend our theory by saying that, in the actual cases, it would not go astray? I believe that this is not an adequate defence. But I shall not pursue this question here.

This objection may apply with less force to Preference-Hedonism. On this theory, what can be good or bad for someone can only be discernible features of his conscious life. These are the features that, at the time, he either wants or does not want. I asked above whether it is bad for people to be deceived because they prefer not to be, or whether they prefer not to be deceived because this is bad for them. Consider the comparable question with respect to pain. Some have claimed that pain is intrinsically bad, and that this is why we dislike it. As I have suggested, I doubt this claim. After taking certain kinds of drug, people claim that the quality of their sensations has not altered, but they no longer dislike these sensations. We would regard such drugs as effective analgesics. This suggests that the badness of a pain consists in its being disliked, and that it is not disliked because it is bad. The disagreement between these views would need much more discussion. But, if the second view is better, it is more plausible to claim that whatever someone wants or does not want to experience—however bizarre we find his desires—should be counted as being for this person truly pleasant or painful, and as being for that reason good or bad for him. (There may still be cases where it is plausible to claim that it would be bad for someone if he enjoyed certain kinds of experience; this might be claimed, for instance, about sadistic pleasure. But there may be few such cases.)

If instead we appeal to the Success Theory, we are not concerned only with the experienced quality of our conscious life. We are concerned with such things as whether we are achieving what we are trying to achieve, whether we are being deceived, and the like. When considering this theory, we can more often plausibly claim that, even if someone knew the facts, his preferences might go astray, and fail to correspond to what would be good or bad for him.

Which of these different theories should we accept? I shall not attempt an answer here. But I shall end by mentioning another theory, which might be claimed to combine what is most plausible in these conflicting theories. It is a striking fact that those who have addressed this question have disagreed so fundamentally. Many philosophers have been convinced Hedonists; many others have been as much convinced that Hedonism is a gross mistake.

Some Hedonists have reached their view as follows. They consider an opposing view, such as that which claims that what is good for someone is to have knowledge, to engage in rational activity, and to be aware of true beauty. These Hedonists ask, 'Would these states of mind be good, if they brought no enjoyment, and if the person in these states of mind had not the slightest desire that they continue?' Since they answer No, they conclude that the value of these states of mind must lie in their being liked, and in their arousing a desire that they continue.

This reasoning assumes that the value of a whole is just the sum of the value of its parts. If we remove the part to which the Hedonist appeals, what is left seems to have no value, hence Hedonism is the truth.

Suppose instead, more plausibly, that the value of a whole may not be the

mere sum of the value of its parts. We might then claim that what is best for
people is a composite. It is not just their being in the conscious states that
they want to be in. Nor is it just their having knowledge, engaging in rational
activity, being aware of true beauty, and the like. What is good for someone
is neither just what Hedonists claim, nor just what is claimed by Objective
List Theorists. We might believe that if we had *either* of these, *without the
other,* what we had would have little or no value. We might claim, for
example, that what is good or bad for someone is to have knowledge, to be
engaged in rational activity, to experience mutual love, and to be aware of
beauty, while strongly wanting just these things. On this view, each side in
this disagreement saw only half of the truth. Each put forward as sufficient
something that was only necessary. Pleasure with many other kinds of object
has no value. And, if they are entirely devoid of pleasure, there is no value in
knowledge, rational activity, love, or the awareness of beauty. What is of
value, or is good for someone, is to have both; to be engaged in these
activities, and to be strongly wanting to be so engaged.[26]

J   BUDDHA'S VIEW

At the beginning of their conversation the king politely asks the monk his name, and
receives the following reply: 'Sir, I am known as "Nagasena"; my fellows in the
religious life address me as "Nagasena". Although my parents gave (me) the name
"Nagasena" . . . it is just an appellation, a form of speech, a description, a
conventional usage. "Nagasena" is only a name, for no person is found here.'[27]

> A sentient being does exist, you think, O Mara?
> You are misled by a false conception.
> This bundle of elements is void of Self,
> In it there is no sentient being,
> Just as a set of wooden parts,
> Receives the name of carriage,
> So do we give to elements,
> The name of fancied being.[28]

Buddha has spoken thus: 'O Brethren, actions do exist, and also their consequences,
but the person that acts does not. There is no one to cast away this set of elements
and no one to assume a new set of them. There exists no Individual, it is only a
conventional name given to a set of elements.'[29]

Vasubandhu: . . . When Buddha says, 'I myself was this teacher Sunetra', he means
that his past and his present belong to one and the same lineage of momentary
existences; he does not mean that the former elements did not disappear. Just as
when we say 'this same fire which has been seen consuming that thing has reached
this object', the fire is not the same, but overlooking this difference we indirectly call
fire the continuity of its moments.[30]

Vatsiputriya. If there is no Soul, who is it that remembers? *Vasubandhu:* What is the meaning of the word 'to remember'? *Vatsiputriya.* It means to grasp an object by memory. *Vasubandhu.* Is this 'grasping by memory' something different from memory? *Vatsiputriya.* It is an agent who acts through memory. *Vasubandhu.* The agency by which memory is produced we have just explained. The cause producive of a recollection is a suitable state of mind, nothing more. *Vatsiputriya.* But when we use the expression 'Caitra remembers', what does it mean? *Vasubandhu.* In the current of phenomena which is designated by the name *Caitra*, a recollection appears.[31]

The Buddhist term for an individual, a term which is intended to suggest the difference between the Buddhist view and other theories, is *santana*, i.e. a 'stream'. [32]

Vatsiputriya. What is an actual, and what a nominal existence? *Vasubandhu.* If something exists by itself (as a separate element) it has an actual existence. But if something represents a combination (of such elements) it is a nominal existence.[33]

> The mental and the material are really here,
> But here there is no human being to be found.
> For it is void and merely fashioned like a doll,
> Just suffering piled up like grass and sticks.[34]

NOTES

(Read these notes, if at all, later.)

NOTES TO PART I

1 For another example, see the start of ADAMS (2).

2 If there *is* a reason for someone to do X, I shall say that this person *has* a reason to do X. On this use of words, we can have reasons for acting of which we are not aware.

3 See SCHELLING (1).

4 See NAGEL (1), Ch. V.

4a Assuming, as might be true, that I could not make myself merely appear to be irrational.

5 This is claimed in GAUTHIER (3) and (4).

6 SIDGWICK (1), p. 386, footnote 4.

7 These objections were suggested to me by S. Kagan.

8 I might try to defend this argument. I might say: 'Why did S tell me to believe that it is always rational to ignore threats? Only because having this belief would very probably be better for me. After I have had bad luck, and you have made your threat, this belief ceases to be good for me. S would tell me to lose this belief. This case therefore does not show what I claimed. It is irrational for me to ignore your threat. But when I ignore your threat, S no longer tells me to believe that this is rational. We can therefore keep the claim that, if S tells me to believe that an act is rational, this act is rational. My imagined case does not provide a counter-example. When we turn from threats to promises, we can claim what I denied. Since S tells us to believe that it is rational to keep promises, even when we know that this will be worse for us, it *is* rational to keep such promises.'

This defence fails. Why does S tell each person to have this belief? Because, if he is known not to believe this, he will be excluded from the kind of agreements that I described: those which, though mutually advantageous, require self-denial. Suppose that I have this belief, and am admitted to such agreements. Though it would often be better for me to preserve my reputation, there will be cases where it will be worse for me if I keep my promises. When this is true, S tells me to lose my belief that it is always rational to keep promises. We cannot claim that it *is* rational for me to keep these promises because S tells me to believe this. When I keep these promises, S no longer tells me to believe this.

9 Cf. ADAMS (2).

10 This is argued in SIDGWICK (1), pp. 431-9, and ADAMS (2), throughout. Adams discusses what he calls *Act and Motive Utilitarianism*, claiming that Motive Utilitarianism is not just a special case of Act Utilitarianism. A Motive Utilitarian claims that everyone should have the dispositions having which will make the outcome best, even if there is nothing that this person could have done to cause himself to have these dispositions. Adams is right to claim that Motive Utilitarianism is different from Act Utilitarianism, just as Rule Utilitarianism, at least in some versions, is not a special case of Act Utilitarianism. I shall not discuss these distinctions here.

11 MACKIE, Ch. 4, Section 2.
12 Collective Consequentialism is not the Cooperative Consequentialism advanced in REGAN, or the extended version of C discussed in my Ch.3.
13 Cf. HARE (2), p. 36.
14 We should first note the sense of 'can' in the doctrine that ought implies can. Suppose it is claimed that, in some case, I ought to have acted in some other way. On the doctrine, I ought to have acted in this other way only if I could have done so. If I could not have acted in this other way, it cannot be claimed that this is what I ought to have done. As I argued in Section 6, the claim (1) that I could not have acted in this other way is not the claim (2) that acting in this way would have been impossible, given my actual desires and dispositions—or, for short, motives. The claim is rather (3) that acting in this way would have been impossible, even if my motives had been different. Acting in this way would have been impossible, *whatever* my motives had been.

We are sometimes right to claim that ought implies can. Suppose that someone believes:

(A) It is always wrong to fail to save someone's life.

Assume that I can either save one life, or save another life, but that I cannot save both. Whichever life I save, I am failing to save someone's life. According to (A), I cannot avoid acting wrongly. I would avoid acting wrongly only if I saved both lives, and this is impossible. We can plausibly reject (A) by claiming that ought implies can. I could not save both these lives. This is not the claim that this is not possible, given my actual motives. I could not save both these lives, whatever my motives were. Since it is in this sense impossible for me to save both lives, it cannot defensibly be claimed that this is what I ought to do, and that in failing to save both lives I am acting wrongly.

Return now to Consequentialism. C claims that it is wrong for anyone to do what he believes will make the outcome worse. We are assuming that, if we were all pure do-gooders, the outcome would be worse than it would be if we had certain other motives. If we believe this, it is impossible that we never do what we believe will make the outcome worse. We shall believe that, if we are pure do-gooders, we have made the outcome worse by causing ourselves to be, or allowing ourselves to remain, pure do-gooders. If we are not pure do-gooders, but have the motives that we believe would make the outcome better, it is not possible that we always act like pure do-gooders—never doing what we believe will make the outcome worse. On either of these alternatives, it is impossible that we never act in this way.

Is this impossible in the sense that justifies an appeal to the doctrine that ought implies can? Is it impossible that we never act in this way, whatever our motives are, or might have been? This is true, but misleading. It suggests that this impossibility has nothing to do with what our motives are. This is not so. This impossibility essentially involves claims about our motives. Why is it impossible that we never do what we believe will make the outcome worse? This is impossible because there is only one disposition given which it would be causally possible *never* to do what we believe will make the outcome worse, and causing ourselves to have or to keep this disposition would *itself* be a case of doing what we believe will make the outcome worse. Because this impossibility essentially involves these claims about our motives, it is not clear that this is the kind of impossibility that justifies an appeal to the doctrine that ought implies can. It can at least be said that this case is very different from the case where it is impossible for me to save both of a pair of lives. That impossibility had nothing to do with my motives. In that case we could plausibly appeal to the doctrine that ought implies can. This does not show that we can plausibly appeal to this doctrine in this very different case. Perhaps we can. But I believe that we cannot support an appeal to this doctrine here by claiming that this appeal is plausible in the case where I cannot save both of a pair of lives. Because they are so different, I believe that case to be irrelevant.

The irrelevance may be denied. If we believe that the outcome would be worse if we were all pure do-gooders, it is impossible that we never do what we believe will make the outcome worse. I have called it misleading to claim that this is impossible whatever our motives are, or might have been. This claim suggests, falsely, that this impossibility has nothing to do with our motives. But, even if this claim is misleading, it is still true. And this might be claimed to make this case sufficiently similar to that in which I cannot save both of a pair of lives.

Are there any cases where we can deny that ought implies can, even when the impossibility has nothing to do with our motives? Some writers claim that there are. Nagel claims that there can be moral tragedies, cases where, whatever someone does, he will be acting wrongly. Nagel admits that, in making his claims, he is denying that *ought* implies *can*. In the cases he describes, someone ought to avoid acting wrongly, though he could not have avoided acting wrongly, whatever his motives might have been. It is natural to hope that there cannot be such cases. But Nagel writes, '. . .it is naive to suppose that there is a solution to every moral problem with which the world can face us'. The world may give us problems to which there is no solution which avoids wrong-doing. (NAGEL (2), p. 79.)

Nagel suggests that there can be such cases because the best moral theory contains *conflicting* principles. He might claim: 'A single moral principle cannot have such implications. If such a principle implies that we cannot avoid wrong-doing, this principle is indefensible.' This claim is plausible when applied to cases like that where I cannot save both of a pair of lives. Principle (A) implies that, in failing to save both lives, I am acting wrongly. The fault here lies in this principle, not in the world.

If it is true that the outcome would be worse if we were all pure do-gooders, Consequentialism implies that we cannot avoid acting wrongly. Though a Consequentialist may appeal to many different moral principles, this particular conclusion is implied by a single principle. It is implied by the claim that it is wrong to do what we believe will make the outcome worse. But, if there can be cases where we cannot avoid acting wrongly, as Nagel claims, the explanation may not have to be that there is a conflict between two different principles. The explanation cannot simply appeal to the fact that it is causally impossible to act in both of two different ways. The explanation must appeal to something deeper—something like the conflict between two different principles. And, in the case we are considering, the explanation may be claimed to be of this kind. There is a conflict, not between two different principles, but between what would be the best set of acts, and what would be the best set of motives. We are assuming that it is causally impossible, given the facts about human nature, *both* that we perform the set of acts that would make the outcome best, *and* that we have the motives having which would make the outcome best. This kind of conflict may be held to be sufficiently similar to that produced by the conflict between two different principles. And the fault here may be claimed to lie, not in the principle that it is wrong to do what we believe will make the outcome worse, but in the world. A Consequentialist could repeat part of Nagel's claim. He might say: 'It may be true that, if we have the disposition that will enable us never to do what we believe will make the outcome worse, we have made the outcome worse by causing ourselves to have or to keep this very disposition. If this is true, the world has given us a problem to which there is no solution. More exactly there is a solution, but it does not enable us to avoid wrong-doing. There is something that we ought to do, all things considered. We ought to cause ourselves to have, or to keep, one of the sets of motives having which will make the outcome better. But, if we do have one of these sets, it is impossible that we never do what we believe will make the outcome worse. If we do what, all things considered, we ought to do, it is impossible that we never act wrongly.'

There is another difference between this case and those discussed by Nagel. He suggests that, in cases where someone cannot avoid acting wrongly, he should be blamed for acting wrongly, and should feel remorse and guilt. This is the claim that conflicts most sharply with the doctrine that ought implies can. As I have said, what is hardest to believe is that, whatever someone does, or might have done, he deserves to be blamed, and should feel remorse and guilt. Consequentialism does not imply this claim. When Clare saves her child rather than the strangers, she deserves no blame, and she should not feel remorse and guilt. Perhaps she should feel what Williams calls *agent-regret*. Perhaps she should have this feeling when she thinks of the dead strangers whom she could have saved. But this feeling is not remorse or guilt.

C does not imply that, whatever Clare does or might have done, she deserves to be blamed, and should feel remorse and guilt. This is what Williams and Nagel claim about agents who face moral tragedies. If we believe that ought implies can, we may reject this claim. But this would not be a reason to reject C, since it does not imply this claim.

If a Consequentialist rejects these remarks, he must revise his moral theory. Suppose that he concedes that, if we could not possibly always avoid doing what we believe will make the outcome worse, it cannot be claimed that this is what we ought always to do. It cannot be claimed that it is always wrong to do what we believe will make the outcome worse. Since it is not possible that we never act in this way, it cannot always be wrong to act in this way. There must be some cases where, though we act in this way, we are not acting wrongly. According to (C3) it is always wrong to do what we believe will make the outcome worse. A Consequentialist might now abandon (C3) and substitute

(C3') We ought always to avoid doing what we believe will make the outcome worse, *if this is possible in a way that does not itself make the outcome worse*. If this is impossible, we ought to avoid doing what we believe will make the outcome worse, whenever we could have acted differently, in a way that would not have made the outcome worse.

As I have argued, 'impossible' does not here mean 'causally impossible, given our actual motives'. It might mean 'causally impossible, whatever our motives might have been'. If it would make the outcome worse if we were all pure do-gooders, it is causally impossible that we never do what we believe will make the outcome worse. This would have been causally impossible, whatever our motives might have been. Since it is causally impossible, in this sense, that we *never* act in this way, (C3') implies that, when we act in this way, we cannot *always* be acting wrongly. If Consequentialism claims (C3') rather than (C3), it takes a revised form that satisfies the doctrine that ought implies can. This revised version of C meets the objection that appeals to this doctrine.

How much difference would it make if C was revised in this way? Suppose that we all accept (C3'), and that we believe truly that the outcome would be worse if we were all pure do-gooders. The outcome would be better if we had one of many other possible sets of motives. Assume next that it is causally possible that we cause ourselves to have, or allow ourselves to keep, one of these other sets of motives. (Only on this assumption does this objection to C arise.) (C3') implies that we ought to cause ourselves to have, or to keep, one of these other sets of motives. Since it is possible to act in either of these ways, (C3') implies that it would be wrong not to do so.

Assume next that we have one of these other sets of motives. Because this is true, we often do what we believe will make the outcome worse. (C3') implies that when we act in this way we are acting wrongly whenever we could have acted differently, in a way that would not have made the outcome worse. Would it have been possible that, in all of these cases, we acted differently, in a way that would not have made the outcome worse? We are not here asking whether this would have been causally possible, given our actual motives. We are asking whether this would have been possible, if our motives had been different. The answer to this question is No. It would not have been possible for us to have acted differently, in *all* of these cases, in a way that would not have made the outcome worse. We could have acted differently, in *all* of these cases, only if we were all pure do-gooders, and this would have made the outcome worse.

We should now ask, 'Could we have acted differently in *some* of these cases, in a way that would not have made the outcome worse?' The answer is Yes. It is impossible that we always act like pure do-gooders without having the disposition of a pure do-gooder. But it would have been possible for us to have sometimes acted in this way, without having this disposition. If Determinism is not true, we could often have acted in this way. (C3') would then imply that, though we are not always acting wrongly when we act in this way, we are often acting wrongly. By substituting (C3') for (C3) a Consequentialist meets the objection that appeals to the doctrine that ought implies can. And this revision does not make much difference.

15 (Note added in 1987) My example is defective. It would not be wrong for me to cause myself to lose my disposition, if I did this by refusing to help my enemy with the result that he wrecks my career. The example could be repaired. (We might suppose that he would only damage my career, and could therefore threaten further damage.)

16 SIDGWICK (1), p. 490.

17 SEN AND WILLIAMS, p. 16.

18 'Feeling that the deepest truth I have to tell is by no means "good tidings" . . . I would not, if I could . . . say anything which would make philosophy—my philosophy— popular.' SIDGWICK (2), pp. 395-6.

19-22 WILLIAMS, p. 135; SEN AND WILLIAMS, p. 15.

23 RAWLS, pp. 133 and 182, especially footnote 31.

24 WILLIAMS (6), Ch. 3.

25 I owe this example to T. Scanlon.

27 NEWMAN, Vol. I, p. 204.

28 In these paragraphs I merely follow REGAN.

29 This is argued, for instance, in GAUTHIER (1), and BRAMS.

30 In these tests, the two choices are called *co-operative* and *unco-operative*. It has been shown, for example, that if the participants take 5 milligrams of Valium, they are more likely to co-operate. See many issues of *The Journal of Conflict Resolution*, Ann Arbor, Michigan.

31 It is often argued that, if each person knows that he will face a particular number of 'Repeated Prisoner's Dilemmas', it will be better for each if he

always makes the non-co-operative choice. This choice will be better for each in the last round of play. Since each knows this, this choice will be better for each in the second-last round. Similar reasoning runs back to the first round.

32 John Broome has questioned this, remarking, 'If an extra child produces more than he consumes, his existence is better for everyone, and if he consumes more than he produces his existence is worse for everyone, including his own parents.' I believe that this objection is answered by the much greater advantage in old age of having more children.

33 Cf. SEN AND RUNCIMAN.

34 The version of the problem that concerns nuclear proliferation is in one way less acute, since the number of agents is relatively small. It is possible here that what each does may affect what the others do.

35 Suppose that we require something less than unanimity. In a community with 1,000 members, each might make his promise to do A conditional on the joining of at least 900 others. We will not achieve *this* solution if our *only* moral motive is trustworthiness. It would be likely to be worse for each if he makes this promise. There are three possibilities. The number of others joining might turn out to be (a) less than 900, (b) 900, or (c) more than 900. If (a) happens, no-one's promise becomes binding; so we can ignore this possibility when deciding what is in our interests. If (b) happens, it will be better for each that he made his promise. It will again be true of each that, without his promise, the whole scheme would fail—no one else's promise would become binding. That would be worse for each. But if (c) happens, it will be worse for each that he made his promise. It will be true of each that he is now committed to the altruistic choice. Since he is trustworthy, he will make this choice. But even without his promise, everyone else's promises would have become binding. So each will make the choice that will be worse for himself, and he will gain nothing in return. What each gains from the promises of others he would have gained even if he had not himself made the promise. Note next that, compared with (b), (c) is much more likely to happen. It is much more likely that more than 900 others join than that the number of others joining is exactly 900. So if each makes this promise this is likely to be worse for him. If the numbers are larger, say in the millions, this would be even more likely. Either the promise of each will make no difference, since too few others join, or it will be worse for him, since more than enough others join. The one case in which the making of the promise will turn out to be better for each, that in which exactly the specified number join, will be most unlikely. There may be some way to avoid this problem, perhaps with a series of converging 'straw votes'. But in cases that involve large numbers, there is another problem. It would take some effort to enable all to communicate, and then to reach a joint agreement. But the agreement is a public good, benefiting each whether or not he helps to produce it. To this Contributor's Dilemma, mere trustworthiness provides no solution.

36 See SEN (3).

37 See, for example, STRANG, and ULLMANN-MARGALIT.

38 In a Two-Person Case, suppose that each pure altruist could either (1) give himself a greater benefit, or (2) give the other a smaller benefit. Pure altruism here would be worse for both. (The difference between the benefits may have to be great, since what is in our interests partly depends on what our motives are.)

39 See, for example, EWING, MILLER AND SARTORIUS, MEEHL, or the very influential OLSON, p. 64, and p. 159.

40 I owe these points to an acute comment by Martin Hollis.

41 (C9) differs from the more complicated *Co-operative Consequentialism* advanced in REGAN. Rather than revising the Act Consequentialist claim about when *each* of us acts rightly, (C9) merely adds a claim about when *we* act rightly. (These

claims may seem inconsistent. If each of us has acted rightly, how can we together have acted wrongly? But there is no conflict here. For Consequentialists, an act is objectively right if it has the best possible effects, in the circumstances. When we ask whether each acted rightly, the circumstances include what others did. When we ask whether we acted rightly, this is not so.)

42 See MEEHL.
43 See MEEHL, RIKER AND ORDESHOOK, and MACKIE (3).
44 GLOVER (2), pp. 174-5. Glover writes:

It may be thought that there is no difference . . . between absolute thresholds and discrimination thresholds. Some people are tempted to assimilate the case of the electricity shortage to the voting case. In the electricity case, the harm that I do when spread over the community is below the discrimination threshold. Consequentialists who treat the two kinds of threshold in the same way conclude that, apart from side-effects, it does not matter whether I use the electricity or not. The suggestion is that the harm done counts as zero.

But against this I want to argue that the harm done in such cases should be assessed as a fraction of a discriminable unit, rather than as zero. Let us call this the *principle of divisibility*. It says that, in cases where harm is a matter of degree, sub-threshold actions are wrong to the extent that they cause harm, and where a hundred acts like mine are necessary to cause a detectable difference I have caused 1/100 of that detectable harm.

Suppose a village contains 100 unarmed tribesmen eating their lunch. 100 hungry armed bandits descend on the village and each bandit at gun-point takes one tribesman's lunch and eats it. The bandits then go off, each one having done a discriminable amount of harm to a single tribesman. Next week, the bandits are tempted to do the same thing again, but are troubled by new-found doubts about the morality of such a raid. Their doubts are put to rest by one of their number who does not believe in the principle of divisibility. They then raid the village, tie up the tribesmen, and look at their lunch. As expected, each bowl of food contains 100 baked beans. The pleasure derived from one baked bean is below the discrimination threshold. Instead of each bandit eating a single plateful as last week, each takes one bean from each plate. They leave after eating all the beans, pleased to have done no harm, as each has done no more than sub-threshold harm to each person. Those who reject the principle of divisibility have to agree.

This chapter, especially my later *Harmless Torturers*, derives entirely from the stimulus of this brilliant example.

46 See again REGAN.
47 See HARE (3)
48 (Note added in 1987) In his article in *Ethics*, July 1986, B. Gruzalski shows that my original discussion of this problem was confused. See also DUMMETT, PEACOCKE (1), and FORBES (2).
49 Suppose that the water going to the wounded men came not from other agents but from rain. Would this remove my reason to add my pint?
53 See NAGEL (1), p. 127.
54 On these theories about self-interest, being rational and acting rationally are, whatever their effects may be, good for each person. But they are only two of the things that are good for us. They could therefore be, on the whole, worse for us. This would be true when, if we were rational and acted rationally, we would cause ourselves to lose too many of the other things that are good for us. When this is true, being rational and acting rationally are not part of the ultimate aim given to us by S. But this is not true in Prisoner's Dilemmas. In these cases if each person does what S claims to be rational, this will be better for him.

Suppose that we accept one of these theories. How should we answer my question? If we both do A rather than S, are we doing better in S's terms? Are we causing the S-given aims of each to be better achieved? The answer is: In one way, Yes; in another, No. We cause each of our lives to go, in one way, better. We make the outcome better for each. But we cause each of our lives to go, in another way, worse. We are acting irrationally. On these theories about self-interest, it is in itself bad for us if we act irrationally, whatever the effects may be.

We must now ask whether, on the whole, we cause each of our lives to go better. The answer depends on the details of the case. If we both do A rather than S, by how much do we make the outcome better for each? If we make it very much better, this will outweigh the bad feature that we are acting irrationally. If we make the outcome only slightly better, this will not outweigh this bad feature. Remember the original example. If we both keep silent, each will save the other ten years in prison, at the cost of adding two years to his own time in prison. The net effect is that each will be saved eight years in prison. This effect is better for each. We achieve this effect at the cost of acting irrationally. If it is bad for us to act irrationally in this way, is this as bad as spending eight years in prison? We might say, 'It is worse'. On this view, the case is not a true Dilemma. It is not true that, if each rather than neither does what will be better for himself, that will be worse for both of us. On our view, it will be better for each if he confesses rather than remains silent, since he will save himself two years in prison. But it would not be worse for each if both confess rather than remain silent. If both remain silent, we save each eight years in prison, at the cost of acting irrationally. On the view just mentioned, this will be worse for each. Acting irrationally in this way is worse for each than spending eight years in prison.

In this example, this answer may seem absurd. But suppose that, at the cost of acting irrationally, we save each eight hours in prison, or only eight minutes. It would then be less absurd to claim that the case is not a true Dilemma.

55 Many writers have argued along these lines. See for example BAIER (1) and (3), and GAUTHIER (3) and (4).

57 See SCHELLING (2).

58 This is true, for example, of the views of WARNOCK, MACKIE (2), BAIER (1), BRANDT (2), HARMAN, GERT, TOULMIN, RAWLS, and many others.

59 (Note added in 1987) In his article in *Ethics*, July 1986, A. Kuflik argues that Common-Sense Morality does not include the whole of what I call M, and is therefore not self-defeating. This may be so. But my claim could then be that, if Common-Sense Morality *did* include the whole of M, it *would* be self-defeating. More important, unless this morality includes my revision R, there will be many co-ordination problems which it objectionably fails to solve. (See my 'Reply', in the same issue.)

60 See SIDGWICK (1) Books III and IV, (and the commentary in SCHNEEWIND), HARE (1), SUMNER (1), and SUMNER (2), Ch. 5.

NOTES TO PART II

1   HUME (1), Book II, Part III, Section III.

2   The Deliberative Theory is most fully developed in BRANDT (2).

3   I follow ANSCOMBE, and NORMAN.

4   See FOOT, and WILLIAMS (5).

5   NAGEL (1), p. 45.

6   Sidgwick's 'Self-evident Axioms' all involve, as Schneewind remarks, the removal of *arbitrary* limitations on the scope or force of reasons for acting. (SCHNEEWIND, p. 300.) Even if the charge 'irrational' is justified *only* when some pattern of concern draws an arbitrary line, this would have wide implications.

7   See also GOSLING, SEN (2) and (4), and BROOME (2).

8   NAGEL (1).

8a For a further discussion, see S. Kagan 'The Present-aim Theory of Rationality', and my reply in *Ethics*, July 1986.

9   SIDGWICK (1), pp. 418-19.

10 BLANSHARD.

11 SIDGWICK (1), p. 498.

12 In the imagined case where I divide my mind, discussed in Section 87, my reason *would* need to be triply relative. I would need to ask, 'What should *I* do *now* in *this* half of my mind?'

13 Except to G. E. Moore. 'What does Professor Sidgwick mean by these phrases "the ultimate rational end for himself", and *"for him* all-important"? He does not attempt to define them; and it is largely the use of such undefined phrases which causes absurdities to be committed in philosophy.' (MOORE, p. 99.) Moore's denial that these phrases make sense constitutes his 'refutation' of Sidgwick. He adds: 'No more complete and thorough refutation of any theory could be desired.' Moore had himself just claimed that 'good' could not be defined. As Mackie justly exclaims (MACKIE (1), p. 323), 'What effrontery!'

14 RASHDALL, p. 45.

15 WILLIAMS (3), p. 209.

16 NAGEL (1) and (3).

17 NAGEL (1), p. 45 (my italics).

18 NAGEL (1), p. 74.

19 Cf. WILLIAMS (3), p. 215:

> ... such things as deep attachments to other persons ... cannot at the same time embody the impartial view, and ... they also run the risk of offending against it. They run that risk if they exist at all; yet unless such things exist, there will not be enough substance or conviction in a man's life to compel his allegiance to life itself. Life has to have substance if anything is to have sense, including adherence to the impartial system; but if it has substance, then it cannot grant supreme importance to the impartial system, and that system's hold on it will be, at the limit, insecure.

20 See HARE (4), pp. 159-67, and 175-84.

21 NAGEL (4), Ch. 14.

22 BENTHAM, Ch. IV, second paragraph.

23 LEWIS (1), p. 483.

24 HUME (1), Book III, Part II, Section VII.

25 I take this diagram, through R. Nozick, from G. Ainslie.

26 See STROTZ.

27 PLATO (1).

28 A. C. Pigou, *The Economics of Welfare*, London, Macmillan, 1932, p. 23.

30 HUME (1), Book III, Part II, Section VII.

31 HUME (1), Book II, Part III, Section III.

32 RAWLS, p. 420.

33 This version of the case was suggested to me by G. Harman.

34 RAWLS p. 293

35 HUME (2), p. 177.

36 I repeat some remarks of R. Nozick's.

37 A subtler version of this objection is advanced in EDIDIN. I do not fully answer Edidin's objection.

38 ANSCOMBE (1), p.68.

39 I believe that these gains would themselves outweigh the losses described by the S-Theorist at the start of Section 65.

40 These remarks are over-simplified. Even if we deny time's passage, we can admit that 'now' can be applied to descriptions of a lifeless Universe. Event X is 'now' relative to Event Y if they both occur at the same time.

41 Cf. PEARS (1), p. 249:

> And, because time is a category, and figures unobtrusively in all our experience, it is possible to define the past and the future in many different ways and yet none of these definitions is very convincing. For the sentences which give the logical relations of temporal words exhibit a curious feature. They are ... as it were, weak tautologies. And they are weak tautologies not only because we are so accustomed to using temporal words correctly that we need no strong reminders, but also because their structure is peculiar.

For most tautologies are constructed like columns, by placing terms squarely on top of one another like marble drums. But the tautologies which give the logic of temporal words put their terms together like the stones of a vault. No single conjunction of terms is indispensable or could stand alone. But together they form the vaulted ceiling on which the fresco of knowledge is painted.

For discussions of time's passage see GALE (2) (especially the articles by Williams and Grunbaum), GALE (1), and SMART (2).

42   These remarks are too crude. Even if, in the present, some experience is either neutral, or even unpleasant, it can be remembered with great joy. PROUST (1), p. 97, writes:

> . . . at a much later date, when I went over gradually, in a reversed order, the times through which I had passed before I was so much in love with Albertine, when my scarred heart could detach itself without suffering from Albertine dead, then I was able to recall at length without suffering that day on which Albertine had gone shopping with Françoise instead of remaining at the Trocadero; I recalled it with pleasure, as belonging to a moral season which I had not known until then; I recalled it at length exactly, without adding to it now any suffering, rather, on the contrary, as we recall certain days in summer which we found too hot while they lasted, and from which only after they have passed do we extract their unalloyed standard of fine gold and imperishable azure.

Or PROUST (1), p. 107:

> An impression of love is out of proportion to the other impressions of life, but it is not when it is lost in their midst that we can take account of it. It is not from its foot, in the tumult of the street and amid the thronging houses, it is when we are far away, that from the slope of a neighbouring hill, at a distance from which the whole town has disappeared, or appears only as a confused mass upon the ground, we can, in the calm detachment of solitude and dusk, appreciate, unique, persistent and pure, the height of a cathedral.

It would be possible to live a life of great backward- and forward-looking happiness even if one never, in the present, found any pleasure in any of one's experiences.

43   This objection was suggested to me by J. Broome, R. Swinburne, and J. Thomson.

44   See SINGER (2).

45   This objection, suggested to me by Nozick, has less force when applied to the bias towards the future.

46   NAGEL (1), p. 40.

47   Though they have some force, the two objections should not be overstated. S does not dictate a war of all against all, for at least three reasons. The interests even of purely selfish people very largely overlap. Even when these interests conflict, S may itself tell these people to try to resolve this conflict, by producing what I call a political solution. (S will tell these people this when the case involves sufficiently few people.) And most self-interested people are not entirely selfish, but have some concern for others.

All three points have their analogues in the case of P. What someone would most want at different times, if he knew the facts and was thinking clearly, would very largely overlap. Even when this is not true, P itself tells each of us to try to resolve 'intertemporal tussles'—to try to achieve with himself at other times political solutions. If there are two ways in which someone can now try to fulfil his present desires, and one of these is more likely to interfere with his later efforts to fulfil his future desires, P tells this person to act in the other way. This would be so even in the extreme case where someone has *no* concern about his own future, and we are appealing to the uncritical version of P, the Instrumental Theory. As I learnt from G. Harman, even in this case, this person will be more successful in achieving what he now wants if he chooses the way of acting that will not interfere with his future efforts. He will be more successful because he will not then later have reasons to interfere with the effects of his present efforts. Thirdly, most agents are in fact concerned about themselves at future times. And the Critical Present-aim Theory may require such concern, in a temporally neutral form.

48 As I suggest on page 450, though these two survivors will conflict, the conflict may be easier to resolve than the conflict between morality and S.

NOTES TO PART III

1 See, for example, *Zettel*, ed. by G. Anscombe and G. von Wright, and translated by G. Anscombe, Blackwell, 1967, Proposition 350: 'It is as if our concepts involve a scaffolding of facts . . . If you imagine certain facts otherwise . . . then you can no longer imagine the application of certain concepts.'

2 QUINE (1), p. 490.

3 This states a necessary condition for the continued existence of a physical object. Saul Kripke has argued, in lectures, that this condition is not sufficient. Since I missed these lectures, I cannot discuss this argument.

4 On this view, it could be fatal to live in what has long been a densely populated area, such as London. It may here be true of many bits of matter that they were part of the bodies of many different people, when they were last alive. These people could not all be resurrected, since there would not be enough such matter to be reassembled. Some hold a version of this view which avoids this problem. They believe that a resurrected body needs to contain only one particle from the original body.

5 LOCKE, Chapter 27, Section 16.

6 This suggestion would need expanding, since there are many ways to count the number of direct connections. And some kinds of connection should be given more importance than others. As I suggest later, more weight should be given to those connections which are distinctive, or different in different people. (All English-speakers, for example, share many undistinctive memories of how to speak English.)

7 I follow MARTIN AND DEUTSCHER.

8 QUINTON defends this view.

9 HUME (1), Part IV, Section 6, reprinted in PERRY (1).

10 Sections 96 and 98-9, and Chapter 14.

11 Reductionism raises notoriously difficult questions. I am influenced by these remarks in KRIPKE, p. 271:

> Although the statement that England fought Germany in 1943 perhaps cannot be *reduced* to any statement about individuals, nevertheless in some sense it is not a fact 'over and above' the collection of all facts about persons, and their behavior over history. The sense in which facts about nations are not facts 'over and above' those about persons can be expressed in the observation that a description of the world mentioning all facts about persons but omitting those about nations can be a *complete* description of the world, from which the facts about nations follow. Similarly, perhaps facts about material objects are not facts 'over and above' facts about their constituent molecules. We may then ask, given a description of a non-actualized possible situation in terms of people, whether England still exists in that situation . . . Similarly, given certain counterfactual vicissitudes in the history of the molecules of a table, *T*, one may ask whether *T* would exist, in that situation, or whether a certain bunch of molecules, which in that situation would constitute a table, constitute the very same table *T*. In each case, we ask criteria of identity across possible worlds for certain particulars in terms of those for other, more 'basic', particulars. If statements about nations (or tribes [tables?]) are not *reducible* to those about other more 'basic' constituents, if there is some 'open texture' in the relationship between them, we can hardly expect to give hard and fast identity criteria; nevertheless in concrete cases we may be able to answer whether a certain bunch of molecules would still constitute table *T*, though in some cases the answer may be indeterminate. I think similar remarks apply to the problem of identity over time . . .

Given the possible non-reducibility of the statement about England, I am inclined to weaken the word 'follow' at the end of Kripke's second sentence. The central question about personal identity I believe to be whether these remarks apply, not only to nations and tables, but also to people.

12   BUTLER, p.100.
13   I follow SHOEMAKER (2).
14   In PEACOCKE (2).
15   EVANS (2), p. 246, rightly criticizes a misdescription of memory in PARFIT (1). Evans also argues against 'the possibility of a faculty which is both like memory in giving subjects knowledge of the past, and unlike it in that the content of the memory states in no way encroaches upon the question of whose past is concerned' (p. 248). This conflicts with my claim that quasi-memories could provide a way of knowing about other people's past experiences. Evans's argument is this:

> Suppose we surgically 'transfer the memories' from the brain of subject S' to the brain of a subject S, and suppose S does not know that this has happened. S will, of course, make judgements about his past in the normal way. But suppose that he discovers that he was not F, and he was not G, . . . —that in general his memory cannot be relied upon as an accurate record of his past. Suppose that, fantastically, he then retreats to making *general* past-tense judgements: 'Someone was F, and was G . . . ' *These judgments could not possibly constitute knowledge.* Even to be intelligible in putting them forward, S would have to offer what had actually happened, or something very like it, as a hypothesis; but he could not possibly be said to know that it was true. It would be a sheer guess. Consequently he could not be said to know anything based on it . . . We have found, therefore, no compelling reason for giving up the view that our Ideas of ourselves do not permit a gap to open up between knowing, in virtue of the operation of memory, that *someone* saw a tree burning, and knowing that it was *oneself* who saw a tree burning (pp. 244-5).

I accept Evans's claim that his imagined person S would not have, in his quasi-memories of the experiences of S', any knowledge about those past experiences. As he writes, 'it is not sufficient for knowledge that a true belief be causally dependent on the facts which render it true'. These quasi-memories do not give S knowledge because S knows nothing about their cause. He has not been told that surgeons have created in his brain copies of the memory traces in the brain of S'. Things are different for Jane. She knows how her quasi-memories of Paul's experiences are causally dependent on those experiences. Evans's argument does not show that these quasi-memories cannot give Jane knowledge. It does not undermine my claim that quasi-memories could provide a way of knowing about other people's past experiences. As Wiggins suggests, we can imagine this kind of knowledge being a natural phenomenon. It might have been true that children had quasi-memories of experiences in the lives of their two parents, before the moment of their own conception. If such quasi-memories took this regular and restricted form, they could provide knowledge. (Wiggins (4), p. 145, perhaps attributing this suggestion to H. Ishiguro.)

16   REID, reprinted in PERRY (1), p. 109.
17   See LOCKE, Chapter 27, Section 13, reprinted in PERRY (1), p. 101; and KANT, p. 342, especially footnote a. I take the example from WACHSBERG.
18   Non-Reductionists have several other arguments which, in a longer discussion, I would need to try to answer. Besides SWINBURNE, see in particular LEWIS (4), (5), and (6), and MADELL. I hope to discuss these arguments elsewhere.
19   DESCARTES, p. 101: 'I noticed that whilst I thus wished to think all things false, *it was absolutely essential that the "I" who thought this should be a somewhat,* and remarking that this truth, "I think, therefore I am", was so certain and so assured that all the most extravagant suppositions brought forward . . . were incapable of shaking it, I came to the conclusion that I

could receive it without scruple as the first principle of the Philosophy for which I was seeking.' (First emphasis mine.)

20　LICHTENBERG, p. 412. (In the original: *'Es denkt,* sollte man sagen, so wie man sagt: *es blitzt'.*) To spell out the aphorism: from the truth of 'I think, therefore I am,' Descartes should *not* have assumed that 'it was absolutely essential that the 'I' who thought this should be a somewhat'.

21　WILLIAMS (4), pp. 95-100.

21a　See STRAWSON (2) and SHOEMAKER (2).

22　See, for example, Williams's objections in WILLIAMS (4).

23　It is too dogmatic to say that we have *no* evidence in favour of a Non-Reductionist View. The evidence we have, C. D. Broad once judiciously remarked, supports at most the following conclusion: If some apparently sane and serious person claimed to have *better* evidence of the same kind, his claim should not be simply ignored.

24　These remarks derive from Williams's 'Imagination and the Self', reprinted in WILLIAMS (2).

25　In WILLIAMS (8).

26　There would be certain kinds of *non-distinctive* continuity, such as continued memory of how to walk, and run. The Psychological Criterion should not appeal to these kinds of psychological continuity.

27　As before, for a discussion of these arguments see DUMMETT, PEACOCKE (1), FORBES (2), and SAINSBURY. See also C. Wright, 'On the Coherence of Vague Predicates', *Synthese*, 1975. For a longer discussion of the argument as applied to persons, see especially UNGER (1), UNGER (2), and the other works by P. Unger in this remarkable series. I have not yet had time to consider whether the solution suggested by Peacocke, Forbes, and Sainsbury, appealing to *degrees of truth,* meets Unger's arguments.

28　WILLIAMS (2), p. 63

29　*The Times*, London, Science Column, 22 November 1982. I am told that reports of more impressive results will soon appear in the appropriate scientific journals.

31　EVANS (1), p. 208; see also SALMON, pp. 245-6.

32　See BROOME (1).

33　SPERRY, p. 299.

34　NAGEL (5), reprinted in NAGEL (4) p. 152.

35　NAGEL, op. cit., p. 153.

36　MADELL, p. 137, suggests that what makes my experiences mine is not that they are had by a particular subject of experiences, me, but that they have the *property* of being mine. On this view, the topography of mental space is given by the existence of a very large number of different properties, one for each person who ever lives. I agree with Madell that I and he could have two simultaneous experiences that were qualitatively identical, but were straightforwardly distinct. But this need not be because one of the experiences has the unique property of being mine, and the other has the unique property of being Madell's. It could simply be because one of these experiences is *this* experience, occurring in *this* particular mental life, and the other is *that* experience, occurring in *that* other particular mental life. These two mental lives might have to be referred to publicly through their connections to a pair of different human bodies. (The actual cases of divided minds provide an objection to Madell's View. And it does not seem plausible to treat *being mine* as a *property*. What distinguishes different particular things or events is not that each has a unique property. Physical things or events can be distinct by being in different places. When I think of my present thought as being mine, I do not identify this thought by reference to a spatial location. My identifying reference essentially involves an *indexical* word, or a *demonstrative*, rather than the ascription of a unique property. I can use the indexical 'this', or the indexical 'mine'. My claim is that, since I can use the self-referring use of 'this', I do not need to use 'mine'.)

37 Some deny that 'I' could be explained in a way that uses the self-referring use of 'this'. For an argument supporting the view that I accept, see RUSSELL.
38 I follow SHOEMAKER (1), p. 22.
39 QUINTON, in PERRY (1), p. 60.
40 WIGGINS (1), p. 50. I decided to study philosophy almost entirely because I was enthralled by Wiggins's imagined case.
41 Cf. WIGGINS (1), p. 40. I owe this suggested way of talking, and one of the objections to it, to Michael Woods.
42 See Lewis's 'Survival and Identity' and my 'Lewis, Perry, and What Matters', both in RORTY.
43 Other Reductionists with whom, on the whole, I agree include H. P. Grice (in PERRY (1)), A. J. Ayer (see especially 'The Concept of a Person'), in AYER (1), A. QUINTON, J. L. Mackie, (in MACKIE (4) and (5)), J. Perry, especially in 'The Importance of Being Identical', in RORTY, and in PERRY (2), D. K. Lewis (in RORTY), and S. Shoemaker (in his *Personal Identity*, Blackwell, 1984).
44 REID, in PERRY (1), p. 114.
45 In WILLIAMS (9), reprinted in WILLIAMS (2), pp. 19-25.
46 SHORTER; and J. M. R. Jack (unpublished), who requires that this criterion be embedded in a causal theory.
47 WILLIAMS (2), p. 20.
48 WIGGINS (1), (2), and (3) advance similar arguments. Some of the issues raised, which I do not discuss here, are crisply discussed in NOZICK (3), pp. 656-9.
49 WILLIAMS (2), p. 23.
50 Cf. WIGGINS (1), p. 55
51 WIGGINS (4), p. 146. As we shall see below, some writers reject this claim.
52 WILLIAMS (9), reprinted in WILLIAMS (2), p. 24.
53 In WIGGINS (3). Sadly, Wiggins does not here continue his discussion of his imagined case of division in WIGGINS (1).
54 HUME (1), p. 269.
55 Both Nagel and Williams are inclined to believe that physical continuity is what matters. But while Nagel believes that receiving a duplicate brain would be as bad as death, Williams believes this to be a mere trivial extension of existing kinds of surgery. See WILLIAMS (2), p. 47.
56 op. cit., p. 44.
57 In a *tour de force*, Freeman Dyson claims that, even in an indefinitely expanding Universe, life could continue for ever. The argument requires the assumption that we could migrate from organic to inorganic bodies. See 'Time Without End: Physics and Biology in an Open Universe', the *Review of Modern Physics* Vol. 51 (1979), p. 447.
58 WILLIAMS (2), pp. 80-1. See also BRENNAN (1) and (2).
59 QUINTON, in PERRY (1), p. 66. Though a Materialist, Quinton believes that Relation R is what matters, and substitutes, for my aseptic label, 'the soul'. He continues, 'Where concern with the soul is wholly absent, there is no interest in individual identity at all, only in identity of type'. And he writes:

In our general relations with other human beings their bodies are for the most part intrinsically unimportant. We use them as convenient recognition devices enabling us to locate without difficulty the persisting character and memory complexes in which we are interested, which we love or like. It would be upsetting if a complex with which we were emotionally involved came to have a monstrous or repulsive physical appearance, it would be socially embarrassing if it kept shifting from body to body while most such complexes stayed put, and it would be confusing and tiresome if such shifting around were generally widespread, for it would be a laborious business finding out where one's friends and family were. But that our concern and affection would follow the character and memory complex, and not its original bodily associate, is surely clear. In the case of general shifting about we should be in the position of people trying to find their intimates in the dark. If the shifts were both frequent and spatially radical we should no doubt give up the attempt to identify individual people, the whole character of relations between people would change, and human life would be like an unending sequence of shortish ocean trips.

61 PROUST (2), p. 226. (I have slightly altered the translation.)
62 PROUST (2), p. 349.
63 PROUST (1), p. 249.
64 SOLZHENITSYN, p. 232.
65 SOLZHENITSYN, p. 393.
66 PENELHUM expresses doubts about this way of talking. PARFIT (2) tries briefly to meet these doubts.
68 In PERRY (1), p. 102.
69 SIDGWICK (1), pp. 418-19.
70 WIGGINS (6).
71 MADELL, p. 110.
72 SWINBURNE, p. 246.
73 'The Importance of Being Identical', in RORTY, pp. 78-85.
74 Personal Identity, the Nature of Persons, and Ethical Theory, Ph. D. Dissertation, Princeton University, 1983.
75 PARFIT (6), p. 229.
76 op. cit.
77 PARFIT (6), p. 230.
78 CHISHOLM, pp. 188-9.
79 This reply was suggested to me by J. Broome.
80 This is suggested by WACHSBERG.
81 SIDGWICK (1), p. 124.
82 PARFIT (6), p. 232. (My version of (D) was, in a trivial way, inferior.)
83 (Note added in 1985) As B. Garrett has pointed out, this Section makes a mistake. In the case of kinship, what matters is not the transitive relation *relative of* but the intransitive relation *close relative of*, which can have degrees. This is therefore not a good analogy, if we assume that what matters is personal identity. To meet the Counter-argument, we may have to challenge this assumption.
86 In PERRY (1), p. 102.
87 In PERRY (1), p. 112.
88 MADELL, p. 116.
89 HAKSAR, p. 111.
90 In his *God and the Soul*, p.4.
92 NABOKOV, p. 64: 'They said the only thing this Englishman loved in the world was Russia. Many people could not understand why he had not remained there. Moon's reply to questions of that kind would invariably be, "Ask Robertson" (the orientalist) "why he did not stay in Babylon". The perfectly reasonable objection would be raised that Babylon no longer existed. Moon would nod with a sly, silent smile. He saw in the Bolshevist insurrection a certain clear-cut finality. While he willingly allowed that, by-and-by, after the primitive phases, some civilization might develop in "the Soviet Union", he nevertheless maintained that Russia was concluded and unrepeatable.'

93 NOZICK (2), p. 33, writes: 'The moral side-constraints upon what we may do, I claim, reflect the fact of our separate existences. They reflect the fact that no moral balancing act can take place among us; there is no moral outweighing of one of our lives by others so as to lead to a greater overall *social* good. There is no justified sacrifice of some of us for others. This root idea, namely, that there are different individuals with separate lives *and so* no one may be sacrificed for others . . . ' (second emphasis mine).

94 RAWLS, p. 27.

95 GAUTHIER (2), p. 126.

97 Espinas, quoted in PERRY (3), p. 402.

98 GAUTHIER (2), p. 126.

99 RAWLS, p. 28, and p. 141.

100 RAWLS, p. 27.

101 NAGEL (1), p. 134.

102 RAWLS, p. 190.

103 RAWLS, p. 29.

105 RAWLS, p. 28. I omit the words 'as if they were one person', since I am asking whether this reasoning must involve this assumption.

106 RAWLS, p. 61.

107 PERRY (3), p. 671.

108 Cf. SIDGWICK (1), p. 425, 'the Utilitarian argument cannot be fairly judged unless we take fully into account the cumulative force that it derives from the complex character of the coincidence between Utilitarianism and Common Sense.'

109 RAWLS, p. 27. I add a comment on another remark. There is, Rawls writes:

> . . . a curious anomaly . . . It is customary to think of Utilitarianism as individualistic, and certainly there are good reasons for this. The Utilitarians . . . held that the good of society is constituted by the advantages enjoyed by individuals. Yet Utilitarianism is not individualistic . . . in that . . . it applies to society the principle of choice for one man. (p.29.)

My account suggests the explanation. An Individualist claims (1) that the welfare of a society consists only in the welfare of its members, and (2) that the members have rights to fair shares. Suppose that we are Non-Reductionists about societies, or nations. We believe that the existence of a society, or nation, transcends that of its members. This belief threatens claim (1). It supports the view that what is good for the society, or nation, transcends what is good for its members. This in turn threatens claim (2); in the pursuit of a transcendent national goal, fair shares may seem less important. Non-Reductionists about nations may thus reject both of the Individualist's claims. Utilitarians reject (2) but accept (1). This would be, as Rawls claims, 'a curious anomaly', if the Utilitarian View rested upon Non-Reductionism about nations. If this was their ground, we should expect them to reject both claims. I have described a different ground. Rather than being Non-Reductionists about nations, Utilitarians may be Reductionists about people. This would remove the anomaly. Utilitarians are also Reductionists about nations, and this double Reductionism gives some support to the Utilitarian View. If we are Reductionists about nations, we can then more plausibly accept the first of the individualist's claims: that the welfare of a nation consists only in that of its citizens. If we are also Reductionists about people, we can then more plausibly reject the second claim, the demand for fair shares. We may give less weight to the unity of each life, and to the difference between lives, and give more weight to the various experiences that together constitute these lives. We may thus decide that what is morally important is only the nature of what happens, not to whom it happens. We may decide that it is always right to increase benefits and reduce burdens, whatever their distribution. Cf. the remark in ANSCHUTZ that 'Bentham's principle of individualism', unlike Mill's, 'is entirely transitional', since 'Bentham is saying that . . . as a community is reducible to the individuals who are said to be its members, so also are the individuals reducible, at least for the purposes of morals and legislation, to the pleasures and pains which they are said to suffer'. (pp. 19-20). Bentham's Utilitarianism may be partly supported by his belief in the Reductionist View. But my claims cannot apply to all Utilitarians. The obvious exception is Sidgwick. On pp. 416-17 of *The Methods,* Sidgwick gives some weight to the Principle of Equality. But the Principle of Utility has absolute priority. Sidgwick's rejection of distributive principles cannot be explained in the way that I have discussed. Sidgwick rejected Hume's Reductionist View. And he ended the first edition of his book with the word 'failure' mostly because he assigned such weight to the distinction between people. (See, for example, SIDGWICK (1), p. 404, or the remark on p. 498, 'The distinction between any one individual and another is real, and fundamental.') As I have said, the separateness of persons seemed to Sidgwick deep enough to support a Self-interest Theorist's rejection of the claims of morality. I wish that we could ask him why this deep fact did not, in his view, support the claims of just distribution.

110 FINDLAY, p. 294.
111 WACHSBERG defends this view. Wachsberg adds and plausibly defends the claim that the belief in the Further Fact involves the idea of all experiences occurring in 'the same consciousness', whose sameness over time is a mis-generalization of the unity of consciousness at one time.
112 L. Temkin argues (in correspondence) that, if a Reductionist denies compensation over time, he should also deny simultaneous compensation. The unity of consciousness at one time is not a deeper fact than psychological continuity over time. This seems to be shown when we consider our short-term memories of the last few moments, or of the *specious present.* There cannot be a deep difference between this short-term continuity, and the unity of consciousness at one time. This supports the suggestion, made below, that on this view our distributive principles would roughly coincide with Negative Utilitarianism. If there can be simultaneous compensation, as in my case of the freezing wind and the sublime view, the worst set of experiences at a single time need not be those that involve the the most intense pain or suffering, since this pain might be more than compensated by some other experience in this set. If there cannot even be simultaneous compensation, our concern would be to make better, not the worst set of experiences, but the worst members of such sets; and these are more likely to be intense pains, or other kinds of extreme suffering.
113 NAGEL (4), pp. 124-5, footnote 16.
114 PARFIT (3), p. 153.
115 op. cit.
116 HAKSAR, p. 111.
117 I have not discussed effects on beliefs that are not about rationality and morality. One such effect may be to reduce the *Problem of Other Minds.* When I was a Non-Reductionist, I believed that the unity of my life did not consist merely in the various connections that held between my experiences, and the states and processes in my brain. I believed that it was a further, fundamental fact that all of these experiences are mine. This made it harder for me to imagine what it would be for some experiences *not* to be mine, adding weight to the Problem of Other Minds. On the Reductionist View, this difficulty disappears. And the possibility of quasi-remembering other people's past experiences may

also help to solve this problem, as may the imagined case where I divide. It is an empty question whether either of the resulting people would be me. (As I explained, this is an empty question even if one answer is the best description.) Since it would be an empty question whether these people's apparent memories are mere quasi-memories of the contents of another mind, these people could not take seriously the Problem of Other Minds.

NOTES TO PART IV

1 RAVERAT.

2 See KRIPKE, BOGEN, FORBES (1).

3 See the discussion of these views, and the suggested references, in KRIPKE.

4 Suggested to me by D. Wiggins, who also cites H. Ishiguro.

5 Some people claim that there are no distinctive essential properties. This implies that, for each of these people, it is an empty question whether, if his parents had never married, *he* would never have existed. Though I believe that there could be empty questions about our identity, I doubt whether, on reflection, these people would believe *this* question to be empty. (There are, in the special case of monovular twins, some empty questions here. I hope to discuss this point elsewhere.)

6 What is the relation between this subject and personal identity over time? On the Origin View, it is an essential property of each person that he grew from a particular fertilized ovum. This view could be combined with the Physical Criterion. On the most plausible version of this criterion, one essential property of each person is that he has enough of his particular brain to support fully conscious life. It might be claimed that it is an essential property of any particular brain that it grew from a particular fertilized ovum.

The Physical Criterion need not be combined with the Origin View. A believer in this criterion might accept the Backward Variation View. I described how, on this view, Tolstoy might have had a different origin. In this imagined different possible history, the Physical Criterion would have been fulfilled. Similarly, we could accept the Origin View but reject the Physical Criterion. We might combine the Origin View with the wide versions of the Psychological Criterion. We would then believe that it is essential to me that I grew from a particular pair of cells, and that I therefore started living in a particular body. But we would also believe that my life could continue in a different body. This would happen, for instance, if I was Teletransported.

Consider next the Psychological Criterion, which appeals to psychological continuity. Those who believe in this criterion might agree that my life could have gone quite differently. And between me in my actual life and myself in this different possible life there might be very little psychological continuity. Suppose that my parents had taken me to Italy when I was three years old, and that I had become an Italian. There would then be the following relation between me now and myself as I might now have been. Both in my actual life and in this different possible life I would now be psychologically continuous with myself in my actual life when I was three. This relation would be weak. There are few direct psychological connections between me now and myself when I was three. If we compare my actual life with this different possible life, the two lives might not in adulthood contain even a single common memory.

Some believers in the Psychological Criterion might claim that these are not two possible lives of the same particular person—that the child who would have gone to Italy at the age of three would have been, not me, but a different person. This claim revises our ordinary view about personal identity.

This revision is both technically difficult and unnecessary. The point can be made more simply. If I had gone to Italy at the age of three, my life would have been very different. And we may believe that this fact has various practical and moral implications. But this belief need not be expressed by denying the identity between me in my actual life and myself in this different possible life. We can admit that this relation is identity. We can make our point by claiming that, when we are comparing such very different possible lives, the fact of personal identity does not have its ordinary significance. See ADAMS (3).

7   For the reasons given by Brian Barry's 'Circumstances of Justice and Future Generations', in SIKORA AND BARRY.

8   See *Teenage Pregnancy in a Family Context: Implications for Policy Decisions*, edited by Theodora Ooms (née Parfit), Temple University Press, Philadelphia, 1981.

9   This problem has been called by Kavka *The Paradox of Future Individuals*. See KAVKA (4).

10 I follow ADAMS (3).

11 See T. Schwartz, 'Obligations to Posterity', in SIKORA AND BARRY.

13 This form of the objection is suggested in TOOLEY.

14 See B. Barry, 'Intergenerational Justice in Energy Policy', in MACLEAN AND BROWN ; see also BARRY (2).

15 For a further discussion, see J. WOODWARD, 'The Non-Identity Problem', in *Ethics*, July 1986.

16 J. McMahan has suggested to me that, if the handicap greatly affected the nature of these people's lives, it may not be clear that someone with a lifelong handicap would have been better off if he had been born normal. Some may doubt whether, in the relevant sense, these two very different lives would have been lived by the same person. And ADAMS (3) suggests that, even if such a person would have been better off, this need not imply that it would be irrational for him not to regret his handicap. If we accept either claim, the example is not what we need. We can avoid these questions by supposing that the handicap affects these people only when they are adults. The handicap might be, for example, sterility.

17 There may seem to be one exception. If my life is worth living, killing me affects me for the worse, but does it cause me to be worse off, or to have a lower quality of life? As I use the phrase, I do have 'a lower quality of life'. This is true if my life goes less well than it could have gone, or if what happens in my life is worse for me. Both are true when, with a life worth living, I am killed.

18 One example is the plausible theory advanced in SCANLON (3). Scanlon argues that the best account of moral motivation is not that given by Utilitarians, who appeal to universal philanthropy. Our fundamental moral motive is instead 'the desire to be able to justify one's actions to others on grounds that they could not reasonably reject'. Scanlon sketches an attractive moral theory built upon this claim. On this theory, an act is wrong if it will affect someone in a way that cannot be justified—if there will be some complainant whose complaint cannot be answered. On this theory, the framework of morality is essentially person-affecting. Unfortunately, when we choose a policy like Greater Depletion, there will be no complainants. If we believe that this makes no moral difference, since the objection to our choice is just as strong, we believe that it is irrelevant that there will be no complainants. The fundamental principle of Scanlon's theory draws a distinction where, on our view, no distinction should be drawn. Scanlon's theory therefore needs to be revised.

Similar remarks apply to many other theories. Thus BRANDT (2) suggests that to the phrase 'is morally wrong' we should assign the descriptive meaning 'would be prohibited by any moral code which all fully rational persons would tend to support, in preference to all others or to none at all, for the society of the agent, if they expected to spend a lifetime in that society' (p. 194). It seems likely that, on the chosen code, an act would not be wrong if there are no complainants. Similar remarks apply to GERT, to J. Narveson, *Morality and Utility*, and to G. R. Grice, *The Grounds of Moral Judgement*, and they may apply to MACKIE (2), RICHARDS, HARMAN, GAUTHIER (4), RAWLS, and others.

19   ROBERTSON, p. 460.

19b It is worth remarking that this case is an Intertemporal Each-We Dilemma with two special features. Since it involves different generations, the people involved cannot communicate to reach some kind of political solution, or some joint conditional agreement. And this is a Dilemma of the especially intractable kind *that includes Outsiders*.

Consider the *Auditorium Dilemma*. If the First Row stands, it will improve its view of the engrossing spectacle on stage. If it is worth standing to get this better view, it will be better for the First Row if it stands. But this would block the Second Row's view. This Row would need to stand to regain the view that it had when all were sitting. Since it would now be standing, but would not have improved its view, this outcome would be worse for the Second Row. Similar remarks apply to all the other Rows.

This case differs from an ordinary Each-We Dilemma. There are two acts: A (more altruistic), E (more egoistic). In an ordinary Dilemma, it will be better for each if he does E, whatever others do, but if all do E that will be worse for each than if all do A. In the Auditorium Dilemma, there is a small but fateful difference. It will be better for each Row if it stands rather than sits, but if all stand rather than sit that will *not* be worse for *all* of the Rows. It will be worse for all Rows *except the First*. The First Row is *the Outsider* in this Dilemma.

Because they contain Outsiders, such Dilemmas are especially intractable. The pattern of acts that is worse for everyone else is better for the Outsiders. It would thus be worse for the Outsiders if they helped to bring about a political solution, or joined a conditional agreement. And what the Outsiders do may start a vicious chain reaction, which makes it worse for everyone to join such an agreement. Thus, in the Auditorium Dilemma, it will be worse for the First Row if all sit rather than stand. It will therefore be worse for this Row if it joins an agreement that all should sit. It may therefore stand. Once the First Row is standing, it will be worse for the Second Row if it joins an agreement that all except the First Row should sit. It may therefore stand. It will then be worse for the Third Row to join an agreement that all except the First Two Rows should sit. It may therefore stand. Similar remarks apply to every Row. The end result may be that all Rows stand rather than sit. This is worse for every Row except the First. The presence of the First Row, the Outsider, here prevents the achievement of the joint conditional agreement. And the same chain reaction may prevent the achievement of a political solution. This special feature makes such Dilemmas less likely to be solved.

Besides being trivial, the Auditorium Dilemma does not have the other depressing feature. It involves contemporaries. This makes it more likely to be solved. The other Rows might use threats to keep the First Row sitting. Or the First Row might sit merely because it expected complaints from the other Rows.

An intergenerational Dilemma does *not* involve contemporaries. This makes it harder to solve. In these Dilemmas, if all rather than none cease to give certain kinds of priority to itself, this will be better for all generations, *except the First*. The different generations cannot communicate, and reach a joint conditional agreement. Nor can earlier generations be deterred by threats from later generations. It is therefore a greater problem that this Dilemma contains Outsiders. In an intergenerational Dilemma—which need not involve population growth—the existing generation is always in the position of some Row after the earlier Rows have stood. It has already suffered from the behaviour of the earlier generations. And this earlier behaviour cannot now be altered by any political or moral solution. Since this is so, it would be worse for the existing generation if it played its part in such a solution. It would not be prompted by a reluctance to free-ride, since it cannot benefit from this solution. It would lose from its own act, and gain nothing in return. It is thus less likely to play its part in a solution. The same reasoning will then apply to the next and all succeeding generations.

20   See, for example, SAMUELSON, p. 551.
21   See, for example, the discussion of the different levels of moral reasoning in HARE (1) and (2).
22   NOZICK (2), p. 41.
23   PLATO (2), 21 c-d.
24   On some versions of the *Law of Diminishing Marginal Utility*, this is just what is implied. On these versions, each unit of resources produces more utility if it is given to people who are worse off, so that the most productive distribution will be the one where everyone's life is barely worth living. There is here an obvious oversight. Large amounts of resources are needed to make each person's life even reach the level where life begins to be worth living. Such resources do not help to produce the greatest causally possible net sum of utility, when they are merely used to prevent *extra* people having lives that are *worth ending* (or have net disutility).
25   See NARVESON (1) and (2), and J. Bennett and M. Warren in SIKORA AND BARRY. There are many other examples.
26   In MCMAHAN (1). In the whole of Part Four I am much indebted to J. McMahan's unpublished work, and to many discussions of these questions.
27   See, for example, BARRY (3).
28   RAWLS, p. 17, and pp. 504-12.
30   MACKAYE. I do not have the page reference. And since the second sentence is quoted from memory, its wording may be inaccurate. This forgotten book would amuse and instruct Utilitarians, and delight their opponents.
31   In NARVESON (1). Much of the recent debate owes its existence to this pioneering work. See also NARVESON (2).
32   On the alleged Asymmetry, it would be wrong to have the Wretched Child, but there is no moral reason to have the Happy Child. How can this be explained?

Some writers claim that causing someone to exist cannot be either good or bad for this person. If this is so, this would explain why there is no moral reason to have the Happy Child. But it would also imply that, in having the Wretched Child, we cannot be doing something that is bad for him. What is the objection? If having this child cannot be bad for him, most of its wrongness must come from this child's suffering. We must appeal to

The Total Suffering Principle: Other things being equal, we ought not to increase the sum of suffering.

It may be hard to accept this principle but reject entirely the Total Happiness Principle. But if we accept that principle our couple have a moral reason to have the Happy Child. Even if having this child cannot be good for him, it would increase the sum of happiness.

It may be objected that suffering and happiness are morally dissimilar—that our moral reasons to prevent the former far outweigh our moral reasons to promote the latter. But this cannot explain the Asymmetry unless we have *no* moral reason to promote happiness. And, if we have accepted the Total Suffering Principle, it seems implausible to reject entirely its analogue for happiness. (See GRIFFIN (4).)

There is a better way to explain the Asymmetry. We could (1) appeal to the Person-affecting Restriction, (2) claim that causing someone to exist can be either good or bad for him, and (3) appeal to the Narrow Principle. According to the Narrow Principle, it is wrong, if other things are equal, to do what would be either bad for, or worse for, the people who ever live. It is therefore wrong to have the Wretched Child, since this would be bad for him. But it is in no way wrong to fail to have the Happy Child. It is true that, if my couple have this child, this will be good for him. But, if they do not have this child, this will not be bad for him. And, in the case described, it will not be bad for anyone else. This is why there is no moral reason to have this child.

This seems to me the best explanation of the Asymmetry. We should note that the Narrow Principle does not involve the familiar claim that our obligation not to harm is stronger than our obligation to benefit. We may wish to add this claim to our Narrow Principle of Beneficence—to add, as Ross did, some stronger principle about Non-Maleficence. But the Narrow Principle makes no such distinction. If there will be someone to whom we have failed to give some benefit, our failure to do so will be worse for this person. If other things are equal, we have acted wrongly according to the Narrow Principle.

The distinction between the Wide and Narrow Principles is a new distinction, opened up by the belief that, in causing someone to exist, we can be doing something that is either good or bad for this person. This belief breaks the ordinary entailment that, if some event would be good for people, this event's non-occurrence would be worse for people. With this entailment broken, the Wide and Narrow Principles diverge.

We should note, finally, that we can justify our appeal to the Narrow Principle. On this principle, it has moral significance if, in causing someone to exist, what we do is bad for this person; but it has no significance if, in causing someone to exist, what we do is good for this person. J. Sterba has objected that the Narrow Principle does not here explain the Asymmetry, since it merely restates the Asymmetry. This objection can be answered. We could justify our appeal to the Narrow Principle by appealing to several theories about the nature of morality, or moral reasoning. One example is Scanlon's theory. As I have said, this claims that the source of moral motivation is 'the desire to be able to justify one's actions to others on grounds they could not reasonably reject' (Scanlon (3), p. 1 16). On this theory, an act is wrong only if it affects someone in a way that gives this person an unanswerable complaint. In endnote 18 I mention several other moral theories which could justify the appeal to the Narrow Principle. On these theories, it is morally significant that, if my couple fail to have the Happy Child, there will be no complainant.

Though it provides the best explanation of the Asymmetry, we have seen that we must reject the view which combines the Narrow Principle and the Person-affecting Restriction. We must reject the view that, for an act to be open to a moral objection, there must be some complainant. If we choose Depletion, this will later cause a great decline in the quality of life. But those who live after this decline will owe their existence to our choice. Since they will not regret their existence, they will not regret our choice. There will be no complainants. But there *is* a moral objection to our choice.

33   If causing someone to exist cannot be either good or bad for this person, the only people whose interests count, when we are comparing two outcomes, will be the people who exist in both. All choices between pairs of outcomes are, for

moral purposes, like Same Number Choices, where the Narrow and Wide Principles coincide.

34   In the change from B to C, the previously existing half each lose 18, and the newly existing half each gain 58. The change from B to C therefore gives to the C-people an average net benefit per person of $(58 - 18) \div 2$, or 20. Failure to make this change would give to each of the B-people a benefit of 18. Changing from B to C would therefore give to the C-people a greater average benefit per person than failure to make this change would give to the B-people. On the Wide Average Principle, as given above, C would be better than B. (In calculating the average benefit in the change from B to C, I divide by 2 since the two groups are equally large. This shorthand method yields the same conclusion as the calculation which this principle explicitly requires. This would first add up the total net sum of benefits minus losses to all these billions of people, and then divide this sum by the total number of people. Similar remarks apply to my other shorthand calculation.) Since this principle implies that C would be better than B, which would be better than A, it implies indirectly that C would be better than A. But in a change from A to C the previously existing quarter would lose 42, and the newly existing three-quarters would gain 58. The change from A to C therefore gives to the C-people an average net benefit of $(58 \times 3 - 42) \div 4$, or 33. Changing from A to C would therefore give to the C-people a smaller average benefit per person than the failure to make this change would give to the A-people. According to this principle, though C is indirectly better than A, C is worse than A. We could revise this principle, by claiming that, when the calculations yield such conflicting results, neither outcome would be worse than the other. This revised principle would imply that some outcomes would be worse than others, but it would yield only a very partial ordering, failing to support the answers that we want in many cases. (I am indebted here, and elsewhere, to correspondence with M. Woodford.)

35   See McMahan's discussion of this principle in MCMAHAN (1).

35b   View (5) was suggested to me by J. McMahan. And we are both influenced by HURKA (3). View (1) differs from all the other views in the following way. According to (1) the value of an outcome is the sum of its value to all of the people in this outcome. If someone has a life that is worth living, this life has value for this person; and it has more value if this life is more worth living. I call this kind of value *personal*. On view (1), the best outcome is the one with the most personal value.

On the other six views, this is denied. One of two outcomes may be worse though it has more personal value. This may seem implausible. If an outcome has more value for the people in this outcome, this may seem a strong reason for judging it to be the better outcome. On views (2) to (7), the value of an outcome does not correspond to its personal value. These views are, in this sense, *impersonal*. This may seem an objection to these views.

Though, in this sense, only (1) is a personal view, in another sense (1) is the only impersonal view. (1) is the only view which is not concerned with the quality of people's lives, or with the amount of happiness in these lives. According to (1), if the total quantity is the same, it makes no moral difference if the quality of people's lives is much lower. All the other views are concerned with the quality of people's lives. And this is *why* these views are, in the first sense, impersonal: why they deny that the value of an outcome corresponds to the total sum of its personal value. Since they deny this claim because they are concerned with the quality of people's lives, it is no objection to these views that, in the first sense, they are impersonal.

36   I develop an argument given by R. Sikora in SIKORA AND BARRY.

37   It is plausible to appeal here, as Non-Utilitarians do, to the separateness of

persons. What happens in other lives cannot in any way compensate, or reduce the badness of, the suffering in each of these lives.

38 For a similar distinction between personal and moral value, see NAGEL (3), pp. 97-139.

39 Consider the Grand Inquisitor's speech in Dostoyevsky's *The Brothers Karamazov*, and R. B. Perry's claim, quoted above, that 'the happiness of a million somehow fails utterly . . . even to mitigate the torture of one'.

40 On the Lexical View, we must accept a variant of (A) with 'Valueless' replaced by 'Mediocre'. The existence of ten billion people below this level would have less value than that of a single person above the Blissful Level. If the existence of these people would have less value than that of only one such person, its value would be more than outweighed by the existence of one person who suffers, and has a life that is not worth living. We must also accept a variant of (R), with the same change of words. On the Lexical View, when we consider lives *above* the Mediocre Level, quantity could always outweigh quality.

41 I am indebted here to MCMAHAN (1).

42 Again see MCMAHAN (1).

44 The first part of this chapter repeats PARFIT (7): the second part presents a new argument.

45 F. Myrna Kamm and J. L. Mackie both suggest that, while it could be our duty on egalitarian grounds to change A+ into B, this change would not be an improvement. We may have a duty to do what would make the outcome worse. This view might provide a partial solution to the Mere Addition Paradox. But it would not be a full solution.

46 This objection is suggested by Tooley, Woodford, and others.

49 I owe this point to R. M. Dworkin and A. K. Sen. I and many others had overlooked it for more than ten years.

50 See the discussion of partial comparability in SEN (1).

51 In KAVKA (4).

53 It is often unclear whether some change makes some inequality better or worse. This question is well discussed in TEMKIN, which is likely to be published.

54 Again see TEMKIN.

55 For a revised version of this argument, and some further thoughts, see my 'Overpopulation and the Quality of Life,' in *Practical Ethics*, ed. P. Singer, Oxford University Press, 1986.

NOTES TO THE CONCLUDING CHAPTER

1 Williams advances such an argument against Act Utilitarianism, claiming that there is a 'breaking-point' in the structure of this theory. See WILLIAMS (1), p. 114.

2 That we can challenge the Sceptic by appealing to non-moral reasons is suggested in SIDGWICK (1), pp. 37-8.

3 I follow NAGEL (3), pp. 97-126, and NAGEL, (4) Chs. 9 and 14

4 I follow J. Rawls, 'The Independence of Moral Theory', Proceedings and Addresses of the American Philosophical Association (1974-5) pp.5-22; and NAGEL (4), Ch.9.

NOTES TO THE APPENDICES

1 B. Hooker corrected my earlier view that, if someone was trustworthy, he would gain nothing if no one else was trustworthy. Someone who was not trustworthy might give me a benefit because he trusted me to give him some benefit in return.

2 G. Harman questions whether this is a defensible view. It might be said: 'Morality and self-interest both provide reasons for acting. These reasons are, in different cases, of different strength. When morality conflicts with self-interest, there may be answers to the question of what it is rational to do. A very strong self-interested reason outweighs a weak moral reason, and vice versa. Only in certain cases will neither reason be stronger than the other.' On this view, these two kinds of reason can always be weighed on some neutral scale. And the answers differ in different cases. There is *commensurability*, with *differing weights*.

Suppose that we accept some version of Common-Sense Morality. We could then reply: 'These claims are incorrect. Any plausible moral theory takes into account the agent's own self-interest. Suppose that I promise to give you some fairly trivial benefit. It then becomes true that, to keep this promise, I must suffer a great loss. This is not a case where a weak moral reason is outweighed by a strong self-interested reason. In this case, when it becomes true that I could keep this promise only at this very great cost, it ceases to be true that I ought to keep this promise. In such a case, morality does *not* conflict with self-interest. Similar claims apply to all moral principles. Whether we ought to act upon these principles depends in part, upon how much we would have to sacrifice. What would otherwise be our moral duty ceases to be so when it would demand from us too great a sacrifice, or too great an interference with our lives. Since morality gives due weight to the claims of self-interest, you cannot claim that a weak moral reason would be outweighed by a strong self-interested reason. If you ought to act in a certain way, even though the cost to you would be great, the cost to you has been given its due weight. Despite this cost, this is what you ought to do.' On this view, self-interested reasons are weighed on the moral scale. And there is no neutral scale on which the two kinds of reason can be weighed. Some of those who take this view reject the Self-interest Theory. They believe that, when morality conflicts with self-interest, it is irrational to pursue self-interest. But others take Sidgwick's view. These people believe that, when these two conflict, it would be rational to follow either.

Suppose next that we accept some form of Consequentialism. On this moral theory, reasons for acting are agent-neutral. It cannot be claimed that whether some person ought to act in some way depends upon how much *he in particular* would have to sacrifice. The agent's interests have no special weight. They have no greater weight than the interests of anyone else. Consequentialists may claim that, on their theory, the claims of self-interest have been given due weight. But this cannot be claimed in the sense in which it can be claimed for Common-Sense Morality. In deciding what the agent ought to do, Common-Sense Morality does give special weight to the agent's own self-interest. It may therefore claim that it gives due weight to the special force of self-interested reasons. Consequentialists cannot make this claim.

Though they cannot make this claim, Consequentialists might also reject the view that there is commensurability, with varying weights. They can point out that, since C is agent-neutral, it provides reasons of a quite different kind from self-interested reasons. They might then claim that, because these reasons are so different, they cannot be weighed against each other, since there is no neutral scale.

3 HUME (3), Conclusion, Section II.
4 This was nearly always, before Sidgwick, the suggested solution. Hume's novelty was to proclaim it without appealing to the after-life. I call Hume's solution 'official' because his remarks may be ironical. He writes:
Treating vice with the greatest candour, and making all possible concessions, we must acknowledge that there is not, in any instance, the smallest pretext for giving it the preference above virtue, with a view of self-interest; except, perhaps, in the case of justice, where a man, taking things in a certain light, may often seem to be a loser by his integrity.

And though it be allowed that, without a regard to property, no society could yet subsist, yet according to the imperfect way in which human affairs are conducted, a sensible knave, in particular incidents, may think that an act of iniquity or infidelity will make a considerable addition to his fortune . . . . That honesty is the best policy may be a good general rule, but is liable to many exceptions; and he, it may perhaps be thought, conducts himself with most wisdom, who observes the general rule, and takes advantage of all the exceptions.

I must confess that, if a man think that this reasoning much requires an answer, it would be a little difficult to find any which will appear to him sufficient.

Are the words *to him* justified? We may doubt this when we remember Hume's earlier remarks: 'A man has but a bad grace who delivers a theory, however true, which, he must confess, leads to a practice dangerous and pernicious . . . Why dig up the pestilence from the pit in which it is buried? . . . . Truths which are *pernicious* to society, if any such there be, will yield to errors which are salutary and advantageous.' These remarks warn us that what Hume later claims may not be true. As Sidgwick wrote, describing his youth, 'if a doubt assailed me as to the coincidence of private and general happiness, I was inclined to hold that it ought to be cast to the winds by a generous resolution'. (SIDGWICK (1) p. xv.) But Sidgwick could not later deceive either himself or the public. It seems unlikely that Hume deceived himself.

After confessing that he had no reasoning with which he could answer the sensible knave, Hume writes, 'If his heart rebel not against such pernicious maxims, if he feels no reluctance to the thoughts of villainy or baseness . . .' Perhaps morality cannot by itself defeat the Self-interest Theory. Perhaps it must appeal to the heart, and ally itself with the Present-aim Theory. If these allies defeat the Self-interest Theory, their alliance will end. The Present-aim Theory often conflicts with morality. But, if this is morality's opponent, the threat to morality may be less. I hope to argue this elsewhere.

5 SIDGWICK (1), p. 508.
6 See HAIGHT, throughout.
7 It may be objected: 'You believe (1) that the desires for achievement are not irrational, and (2) that it is therefore not irrational to act on these desires, even at a known cost to our own happiness. And you claim that these beliefs are grounds to reject Sidgwick's view. This is not so. We shall be happier if we have strong desires for things other than our own or other people's happiness. We shall be, on the whole, happier if we have many of the desires for achievement. This is true even though these desires will sometimes lead us to make ourselves less happy. Given these facts, Sidgwick's view implies claims that correspond to your beliefs (1) and (2). Sidgwick's view implies (3) that it is rational for us to cause ourselves to have, or to keep, the desires for achievement. And it implies (4) that, when we act on these desires, at a known cost to our own happiness, these acts do not show us to be irrational. This is because we are acting on desires that it would be irrational for us to cause ourselves to lose.'

This objection, suggested by B. Hooker, appeals to claims that I made in Chapter 1. It reduces our grounds to reject Sidgwick's view, but it does not remove these grounds. This will be clear if we remember two of my other conclusions. I argued (5) that our desires are not shown to be rational by the fact that it was rational for us to cause ourselves to have these desires. And I argued (6) that our acts are not shown to be rational by the fact that, because we are acting on such desires, we are not irrational. (5) and (6) were illustrated in the imagined case where, because I ignore your threat, you blow us both to pieces. In this case it was rational for me to cause myself to have the irrational desire to ignore your threat. And when I acted on this desire my *act* was irrational, even though it could be claimed that *I* was not.

When we remember (5) and (6), we see why we still have grounds to reject Sidgwick's view. This view implies that it is rational for us to cause ourselves to have, or to keep, the desires for achievement. But this does not imply our belief that these desires are rational. Sidgwick's view also implies that, when we act on these desires, at a known cost to our own happiness, *we* are not irrational. But this does not imply our belief that these *acts* are not irrational. And, on Sidgwick's view, these acts must be claimed, like my ignoring of your threat, to be irrational. Since we believe that these acts are *not* irrational, we have grounds to reject Sidgwick's view.

8 A question now arises about the moral importance of those of the agent's desires that we judge not to be irrational, even though their fulfilment is *not* in his or anyone else's interests. What moral weight ought we to give to such desires? If we believe that we ought to give some weight to the fulfilment of these desires, we cannot appeal to our familiar Principle of Beneficence. We must appeal to some other principle. We may instead claim that some kinds of desire, while providing good reasons for acting for the person who has this desire, do not provide moral reasons for other people. This is the view suggested in NAGEL (3), pp. 121-6.

9 See KRIPKE, throughout. This view has also been developed in several articles, by H. Putnam.

10 What we are referring to often depends on the causal history of some part of our language. But this is not always so; and causal considerations of this kind seem not to be relevant to the particular view that Nagel advances.

11 See Kripke's remarks quoted in endnote 11 to Part Three.

12 NOZICK (3), pp. 60-1.

13 NOZICK (3), pp. 67-8.

15 MARGLIN.

16 WILLIAMS (2), pp. 85-6.

17 In WILLIAMS (2), p. 87, Williams also writes; 'None of this—including the thoughts of the calculative suicide—requires my reflection on a world in which I never occur at all. In the terms of 'possible worlds'. . . a man could, on the present account, have a reason from his own point of view to prefer a possible world in which he went on longer to one in which he went on for less long, or—like the suicide—the opposite; but he would have no reason of this kind to prefer a world in which he did not occur at all. Thought about his total absence from the world would have to be of a different kind, impersonal reflections on the value for the world of his presence or absence. . . While he can think egoistically of what it would be like for him to live longer or less long, he cannot think egoistically of what it would be for him never to have existed at all.' Williams has pointed out that, if someone is considering suicide, he need not compare what lies before him with what it would be like to be dead. This person can simply decide whether or not he wants to experience what lies before him. This can be taken to be the decision that, for him, this part of his life is better or worse than nothing. In the passage just quoted, Williams suggests that similar decisions, and judgements, cannot be made about one's whole life. The suggested reason is that someone 'cannot think egoistically of what it would be for him never to have existed'. Someone can clearly understand the possibility that he might never have existed. If there is something that he cannot imagine, it can only be what it would be *like* never to have existed. But, if someone decides that his life has been worth living, or wishes that he had never been born, he need not make this comparison—just as the man considering suicide need not compare the rest of his life with what it would be like to be dead.

18   This is not true on our ordinary use of 'benefit'; but, as I argue in Section 25, it is true on the morally significant use.

19   I owe this suggestion, and much else in Part Four, to J. McMahan.

20   NAGEL (4), p. 7.

21   GRIFFIN (1).

22   See 'Prudence' by P. Bricker, *the Journal of Philosophy*, July 1980.

23   See again Bricker.

24   See, for example, MOORE, and ROSS (2).

25   SIDGWICK (1), pp. 111-12.

26   See EDWARDS, throughout. A similar suggestion is made by Plato in the *Philebus*. For a deeper discussion of the different theories about self-interest, see J. Griffin, *Well-Being* (OUP, 1986).

27   From the *Milina Panha*, quoted in COLLINS, pp. 182-3.

28   *Cila Mara*, quoted in Th. Stcherbatsky, 'The Soul Theory of the Buddhists', *Bulletin de l'Academie des Sciences de Russie*, 1919, p. 839.

29   *Vasubandhu*, quoted in Stcherbatsky, *op. cit.*, p. 845.

30   Quoted in Stcherbatsky, *op. cit.*, p. 851.

31   *op. cit.*, p. 853.

32   See COLLINS, pp. 247-61.

33   T. Stcherbatsky, *The Central Conception of Buddhism*, Royal Asiatic Society, London, 1923, p. 26.

34   The *Visuddhimagga*, quoted in COLLINS, p. 133.

BIBLIOGRAPHY

ADAMS (1): R. M., 'Must God Create the Best?', *Philosophical Review* 81, No. 3, July 1972.

ADAMS (2): R. M., 'Motive Utilitarianism', *The Journal of Philosophy*, 12 Aug. 1976.

ADAMS (3): R. M., 'Existence, Self-Interest, and the Problem of Evil', *Nous* 13, 1979.

ANSCHUTZ : R. P., *The Philosophy of J. S. Mill*, Oxford, Clarendon Press, 1953.

ANSCOMBE (1): G. E. M., *Intention*, Ithaca, N.Y., Cornell University Press, 1957.

ANSCOMBE (2): G. E. M., 'Who is Wronged?', *The Oxford Review*, 1967.

AYER (1): A. J., *The Concept of a Person and Other Essays*, London, Macmillan, 1964.

AYER (2): A. J., *Philosophical Essays*, London, Macmillan, 1965.

BAIER (1): K., *The Moral Point of View*, Ithaca, N.Y., Cornell University Press, 1958.

BAIER (2): K.,. 'Ethical Egoism and Interpersonal Compatibility', *Philosophical Studies* 24, 1973.

BAIER (3): K., 'Rationality and Morality', *Erkenntnis*, 1977.

BARRY (1): B., *Political Argument*, London, Routledge and Kegan Paul, 1965.

BARRY (2): B., 'Justice Between Generations', in P. M. S. Hacker and J. Raz, eds., *Law, Morality, and Society: Essays in Honour of H. L. A. Hart*, Oxford, Clarendon Press, 1977.

BARRY (3): B., 'Rawls on Average and Total Utility: A Comment', *Philosophical Studies* 31, 1977.

BARRY (4): B., *Sociologists, Economists, and Democracy*, London, 1970.

BAYLES : M. D., ed., *Ethics and Population*, Cambridge, Mass., Schenkman, 1976.

BENDITT : T., 'Happiness', *Philosophical Studies* 25, 1974.

BENNETT : J., *Kant's Analytic*, Cambridge University Press, 1966.

BENTHAM : J., *An Introduction to the Principles of Morals and Legislation*, first published in 1789, reprinted in *Utilitarianism*, M. Warnock, ed., London, Collins, 1962.

BLANSHARD : B., 'Sidgwick The Man', *The Monist*, 1974.

BOGEN : J., 'Identity and Origin', *Analysis* 26, Apr. 1966.

BRAMS : S. J., 'Newcomb's Problem and Prisoners' Dilemma', *Journal of Conflict Resolution* 19, No. 4, Dec. 1975.

BRANDT (1): R. B., ed., *Value and Obligation*, New York, Harcourt, Brace, and World, 1961.

BRANDT (2): R. B., *A Theory of the Good and the Right*, Oxford, Clarendon Press, 1979.

BRAYBROOKE : D., 'The Insoluble Problem of the Social Contract', *Dialogue*, Mar. 1976.

BRENNAN (1): A. A., 'Personal Identity and Personal Survival', *Analysis* 42, Jan. 1982.

BRENNAN (2): A. A., 'Survival', *Synthese*, 1984.

BROAD (1): C. D., 'On the Function of False Hypotheses in Ethics', *Ethics*, 1915.

BROAD (2): C. D., *The Mind and its Place in Nature*, London, Routledge and Kegan Paul, 1949.

BROAD (3): C. D., *Five Types of Ethical Theory*, Littlefield, Adams, 1959.

BROOME (1): J., 'Indefiniteness in Identity', *Analysis*, in or before 1984.

BROOME (2): J., 'Rational Choice and Value in Economics', *Oxford Economic Papers* 30, Nov. 1978.

BUCHANAN : A., 'Revolutionary Motivation and Rationality', *Philosophy and Public Affairs* 9, No. 1, Fall 1979.

BUTLER : J., *The Analogy of Religion*, first Appendix, 1736, reprinted in PERRY (1).

CHISHOLM : R., 'Reply to Strawson's Comments', in H. E. Kiefer and Milton K. Munitz, eds., *Language, Belief, and Metaphysics*, Albany, N.Y., State University of New York Press, 1970.

COLLINS: S., *Selfless Persons*, Cambridge University Press, 1982.

DANIELS: N., 'Moral Theory and the Plasticity of Persons', *The Monist* 62, No. 3., July 1979.

DENNETT: D. C., *Brainstorms*, Bradford Books, 1978.

DESCARTES: R., *Meditations*, translated by E. S. Haldane and G. R. T. Ross, Cambridge University Press, 1969

DUMMETT: M. A. E., 'Wang's Paradox', *Synthese* 30, 1975.

DWORKIN (1): R., 'What is Equality? Part 1: Equality of Welfare', *Philosophy and Public Affairs* 10, No. 3, Summer 1981.

DWORKIN (2): R., 'What is Equality? Part 2: Equality of Resources', *Philosophy and Public Affairs* 10, No. 4, Fall 1981.

EDGLEY: R., *Reason in Theory and Practice*, London, Hutchinson, 1969.

EDIDIN: A., 'Temporal Neutrality and Past Pains', *The Southern Journal of Philosophy* 20, No. 4, Winter 1982.

EDWARDS: R. B., *Pleasures and Pains*, Ithaca, N.Y., Cornell University Press, 1979.

ELLIOT: R., 'How to Travel Faster Than Light?', *Analysis* 41, Jan. 1981.

EVANS (1): G., 'Can There Be Vague Objects?', *Analysis* 38, 1978.

EVANS (2): G., *The Varieties of Reference*, Oxford, Clarendon Press, 1982.

EWING: A. C., 'Suppose Everybody Acted Like Me', *Philosophy* 28, Jan. 1953.

FEINBERG: J., 'The Rights of Animals and Future Generations', in William K. Blackstone, ed., *Philosophy and Environmental Crisis*, Athens, Ga., University of Georgia Press, 1974.

FINDLAY: J., *Values and Intentions*, London, George Allen and Unwin, 1961.

FISHKIN (1): J. S., *The Limits of Obligation*, New Haven, Ct., Yale University Press, 1982.

FISHKIN (2): J. S., 'Justice Between Generations: the Dilemma of Future Interests', *Social Justice* 4, 1982.

FOOT: P., 'Morality as a System of Hypothetical Imperatives', *The Philosophical Review* 81, 1972.

FORBES (1): G., 'Origin and Identity', *Philosophical Studies* 37, 1980.

FORBES (2): G., 'Thisness and Vagueness', *Synthese* 54, 1983.

GALE (1): R. M., *The Language of Time*, London, Routledge and Kegan Paul, 1968.

GALE (2): R. M., ed., *The Philosophy of Time*, London, Macmillan, 1968.

GAUTHIER (1): D., 'Morality and Advantage', *Philosophical Review*, 1967.

GAUTHIER (2): D., *Practical Reasoning*, Oxford, Clarendon Press, 1962.

GAUTHIER (3): D., 'Reason and Maximization', *Canadian Journal of Philosophy* Mar. 1975.

GAUTHIER (4): D., *Morals By Agreement* (provisional title), Oxford, Clarendon Press, forthcoming.

GERT: B., *The Moral Rules*, New York, Harper and Row, 1973.

GLOVER (1): J. C. B., *Causing Death and Saving Lives*, Harmondsworth, Penguin Books, 1977.

GLOVER (2): J. C. B., 'It Makes No Difference Whether Or Not I Do It', *Proceedings of the Aristotelian Society, Suppl. Vol. 49*, 1975.

GLOVER (3): J. C. B., *What Sort of People Should There Be?*, Harmondsworth, Penguin Books, 1984.

GODWIN: W., *Political Justice*, 1793, and Oxford University Press, 1971.

GOODIN: R. E., 'Discounting Discounting', *Journal of Public Policy* 2, Pt. 1, Feb. 1982.

GOSLING: J. C. B., *Pleasure and Desire*, Oxford, Clarendon Press, 1969.

GRICE: G. R., *The Grounds of Moral Judgement*, Cambridge University Press, 1967.

GRIFFIN (1): J. P., 'Are There Incommensurable Values?', *Philosophy and Public Affairs* 7, No. 1, Fall 1977.

GRIFFIN (2): J. P., 'Modern Utilitarianism', *Revue Internationale de Philosophie*, No.

141, 1982.

GRIFFIN (3): J. P., 'A Substantive Theory of Rights', unpublished paper.

GRIFFIN (4): J. P., 'Is Unhappiness Morally More Important Than Happiness?', *Philosophical Quarterly* 29, 1979.

GRIM: P., 'What Won't Escape Sorites Arguments', *Analysis* 42, 1982, p. 38.

GUTTENPLAN: S., ed., *Mind and Language*, Oxford, Clarendon Press, 1975.

HAIGHT: G. S., *George Eliot: A Biography*, Oxford University Press, 1978.

HAKSAR: V., *Equality, Liberty, and Perfectionism*, Oxford, Clarendon Press, 1979.

HARDIN: G., 'The Tragedy of the Commons', *Science* 162, 13 Dec. 1968.

HARE (1): R. M., *Moral Thinking*, Oxford, Clarendon Press, 1981.

HARE (2): R. M., 'Ethical Theory and Utilitarianism', in H. D. Lewis, ed., *Contemporary British Philosophy*, London, George Allen and Unwin, 1976, reprinted in SEN AND WILLIAMS .

HARE (3): R. M., 'Pain and Evil', *Proceedings of the Aristotelian Society, Suppl. Vol.* 38, 1964

HARE (4): R. M., *Freedom and Reason*, Oxford University Press, 1963.

HARE (5): R. M., 'Abortion and the Golden Rule', *Philosophy and Public Affairs* 4, No. 3, Spring 1975.

HARE (6): R. M., *Essays on Philosophical Method*, London, Macmillan, 1971.

HARE (7): R. M., *Practical Inferences*, London, Macmillan, 1971.

HARE (8): R. M., *Essays on the Moral Concepts*, London, Macmillan, 1972.

HARE (9): R. M., *Applications of Moral Philosophy*, London, Macmillan, 1972.

HARMAN: G., *The Nature of Morality*, Oxford University Press, 1977.

HOFSTADTER AND DENNETT: D. R. Hofstadter and D. C. Dennett, eds., *The Mind's I*, Brighton, Harvester Press, 1981.

HOLLIS (1): M., 'Rational Man and Social Science', in R. Harrison, ed., *Rational Action: Studies in Philosophy and Social Science*, Cambridge University Press, 1979.

HOLLIS (2): M., *Models of Man*, Cambridge University Press, 1977.

HUME (1): D., *A Treatise of Human Nature*, Oxford, Clarendon Press, 1978.

HUME (2): D., 'The Sceptic', in Hume's *Essays*, Oxford University Press, 1963

HUME (3): D., *An Enquiry Concerning the Principles of Morals*, Oxford, Clarendon Press, 1975.

HURKA (1): T. M., 'Average Utilitarianisms', *Analysis* 42, No. 2, Mar. 1982.

HURKA (2): T. M., 'More Average Utilitarianisms', *Analysis* 42, June 1982

HURKA (3): T. M., 'Value and Population Size', *Ethics* 93, No. 3, Apr. 1983.

KANT: I., *Critique of Pure Reason*, trans. by N. Kemp Smith, London, Macmillan, 1964.

KAVKA (1): G., 'Rawls on Average and Total Utility', *Philosophical Studies* 27, Apr. 1975.

KAVKA (2): G., 'Some Paradoxes of Deterrence', *The Journal of Philosophy* 75, No. 6, June 1978.

KAVKA (3): G., 'Deterrence, Utility, and Rational Choice', *Theory and Decision* 12, 1980.

KAVKA (4): G., 'The Paradox of Future Individuals', *Philosophy and Public Affairs* 11, No. 2, Spring 1982.

KRIPKE: S. A., 'Naming and Necessity', in G. Harman and D. Davidson, eds., *Semantics of Natural Language*, Dordrecht, Reidel, 1972.

LESLIE: J., *Value and Existence*, Oxford, Basil Blackwell, 1979.

LEWIS (1): C. I., *An Analysis of Knowledge and Valuation*, La Salle, Ill., Open Court, 1946.

LEWIS (2): D. K., *Convention: A Philosophical Study*, Cambridge, Mass., Harvard University Press, 1969.

LEWIS (3): D. K., 'Survival and Identity', in RORTY .

LEWIS (4): H. D., *The Elusive Mind*, London, George Allen and Unwin, 1969.
LEWIS (5): H. D., *The Self and Immortality*, New York, Seabury Press, 1973.
LEWIS (6): H. D., *The Elusive Self*, London, Macmillan, 1982.
LICHTENBERG: G. C., *Schriften und Briefe*, Sudelbucher II, Carl Hanser Verlag, 1971.
LOCKE: J., *Essay Concerning Human Understanding*, partly reprinted in PERRY (1).
LYONS (1): D., *Forms and Limits of Utilitarianism*, Oxford, Clarendon Press, 1965.
LYONS (2): D., 'Human Rights and the General Welfare', *Philosophy and Public Affairs* 6, No. 2, Winter 1979.
MCDERMOTT: M., 'Utility and Population', *Philosophical Studies* 42, 1982.
MACKAYE: J., *The Economy of Happiness*, Boston, Little, Brown, 1906.
MACKIE (1): J. L., 'Sidgwick's Pessimism', *Philosophical Quarterly*, 1976,
MACKIE (2): J. L., *Ethics*, Harmondsworth, Penguin Books, 1977.
MACKIE (3): J. L., 'Rules and Norms', in Vol. 1 of *Selected Papers*, Oxford, Clarendon Press, forthcoming.
MACKIE (4): J. L., *Problems from Locke*, Oxford, Clarendon Press, 1976.
MACKIE (5): J. L., 'The Transcendental "I"', in VAN STRAATEN.
MACLEAN AND BROWN: D. MacLean and P. G. Brown, eds., *Energy and the Future*, Totowa, N.J., Rowman and Littlefield, 1983.
MCMAHAN (1): J. A., 'Problems of Population Theory', *Ethics* 92, No. 1, Oct. 1981.
MCMAHAN (2): J. A., 'Prudential Analogues', unpublished paper.
MCMAHAN (3): J. A., 'Nuclear Deterrence and Future Generations', in S. Lee and A. Cohen, eds., *Nuclear Weapons and the Future of Humanity*, Paterson, N.J., Littlefield Adams, forthcoming.
MADELL: G., *The Identity of the Self*, Edinburgh University Press, 1981.
MARGLIN: S., 'The Social Rate of Discount and the Optimal Rate of Investment', *Quarterly Journal of Economics*, 1963.
MARTIN AND DEUTSCHER: 'Remembering', *Philosophical Review*, 1966.
MEEHL: P., 'The Paradox of the Throw-Away Vote', *American Political Science Review* 71, 1977.
MILLER AND SARTORIUS: F. Miller and R. Sartorius, 'Population Policy and Public Goods', *Philosophy and Public Affairs* 8, No. 2, Winter 1979.
MILLER AND WILLIAMS: H. B. Miller and W. H. Williams, eds., *The Limits of Utilitarianism*, Minneapolis, University of Minnesota Press, 1982.
MONTEFIORE: A., ed., *Philosophy and Personal Relations*, London, Routledge and Kegan Paul, 1973.
MOORE: G. E., *Principia Ethica*, Cambridge University Press, 1903.
NABOKOV: V., *Glory*, London, Weidenfeld and Nicholson, 1971.
NAGEL (1): T., *The Possibility of Altruism*, Oxford University Press, 1970.
NAGEL (2): T., 'War and Massacre', *Philosophy and Public Affairs* 1, No. 2, Winter 1972.
NAGEL (3): T., 'The Limits of Objectivity', in *The Tanner Lectures on Human Values*, University of Utah Press, 1980.
NAGEL (4): T., *Mortal Questions*, Cambridge University Press, 1979.
NAGEL (5): T., 'Brain Bisection and the Unity of Consciousness', *Synthese* 22, 1971, reprinted in NAGEL (4) and in PERRY (1).
NARVESON (1): J., 'Utilitarianism and New Generations', *Mind* 76, Jan. 1967.
NARVESON (2): J., 'Moral Problems of Population', *The Monist*, 57, No. 1, Jan. 1973.
NEWMAN: Cardinal Newman, *Certain Difficulties Felt By Anglicans in Catholic Teaching*, London, 1885.
NIETZSCHE: F., *The Portable Nietzsche*, ed. and trans. by W. Kaufman, New York, Viking Press, 1963.
NORMAN: R., *Reasons for Actions*, Oxford, Basil Blackwell, 1971.
NOZICK (1): R., 'On Austrian Methodology'.
NOZICK (2): R., *Anarchy, State, and Utopia*, Oxford, Basil Blackwell, 1974.

Nozick (3): R., *Philosophical Explanations*, Cambridge, Mass., Harvard University Press, 1981.

Olson: M. Olson Jun., *The Logic of Collective Action*, Cambridge, Mass., Harvard University Press, 1965.

Parfit (1): D., 'Personal Identity', *Philosophical Review* 80, No. 1, Jan. 1971, reprinted in Perry (1).

Parfit (2): D., 'On 'The Importance of Self-identity'', *The Journal of Philosophy* 68, No. 20, 21 Oct. 1971.

Parfit (3): D., 'Later Selves and Moral Principles', in Montefiore .

Parfit (4): D., 'Innumerate Ethics', *Philosophy and Public Affairs* 7, No. 4, Summer 1978.

Parfit (5): D, 'Prudence, Morality, and the Prisoner's Dilemma', *Proceedings of the British Academy* 65, 1979.

Parfit (6): D., 'Personal Identity and Rationality', *Synthese* 53, 1982.

Parfit (7): D., 'Future Generations: Further Problems', *Philosophy and Public Affairs* 11, No. 2, Spring 1982.

Partridge: E., ed., *Responsibilities to Future Generations*, Buffalo, N.Y., Prometheus Books, 1981.

Peacocke (1): C., 'Are Vague Predicates Incoherent?', *Synthese* 46, 1981.

Peacocke (2): C., *Sense and Content*, Oxford, Clarendon Press, 1983.

Pears (1): D. F., 'Time, Truth, and Inference', in A. Flew, ed., *Essays in Conceptual Analysis*, London, Macmillan, 1966.

Pears (2): D. F., 'Critical Study of *Individuals*, by P. F. Strawson', *Philosophical Quarterly* 11, 1961.

Penelhum: T., 'The Importance of Self-identity', *The Journal of Philosophy* 68, No. 20, 21 Oct. 1971.

Perry (1): J., ed., *Personal Identity*, Berkeley, University of California Press, 1975.

Perry (2): J., *A Dialogue on Personal Identity and Immortality*, Indianapolis, Hackett, 1978.

Perry (3): R. B., *General Theory of Value*, Cambridge, Mass., Harvard University Press, 1950.

Plato (1): *Protagoras*.

Plato (2): *Philebus*.

Proust (1): M., *The Sweet Cheat Gone*, 1, trans. by C. K. Scott-Moncrieff, London, Chatto and Windus, 1949.

Proust (2): M., *Within a Budding Grove*, trans. by C. K. Scott-Moncrieff, London, Chatto and Windus, 1949.

Quine (1): W. V., reviewing Milton K. Munitz., ed., *Identity and Individuation*, in *The Journal of Philosophy*, 1972.

Quine (2): W. V., 'What Price Bivalence?', *The Journal of Philosophy*, 1981.

Quinton: A., 'The Soul', *The Journal of Philosophy*, 59, No. 15, July 1962, reprinted in Perry (1).

Rahula: W., *What the Buddha Taught*, New York, Grove Press, 1974.

Railton: P., 'Alienation and the Demands of Morality', *Philosophy and Public Affairs*, forthcoming.

Rapoport: A., *Fights, Games, and Debates*, Ann Arbor, University of Michigan Press, 1960.

Rashdall: H., *The Theory of Good and Evil*, Oxford University Press, 1907.

Raverat: G., *Period Piece*, London, Faber and Faber, 1952.

Rawls: J., *A Theory of Justice*, Cambridge, Mass., Harvard University Press, 1971.

Ray: C., 'Can We Travel Faster Than Light?', *Analysis* 42, Jan. 1982.

Raz: J., *Practical Reason and Norms*, London, Hutchinson, 1975.

Regan: D., *Utilitarianism and Co-operation*, Oxford, Clarendon Press, 1980.

Reid: T., *Essays on the Intellectual Powers of Man*, first published in 1785, 'Of

Memory', chap. 4, reprinted in PERRY (1).

RESCHER: N., *Unselfishness*, University of Pittsburgh Press, 1975

RICHARDS: D. A. J., *A Theory of Reasons for Action*, Oxford, Clarendon Press, 1971.

RIKER AND ORDESHOOK: W. Riker and P. Ordeshook, 'A Theory of the Calculus of Voting', *American Political Science Review* 62, Mar. 1978.

ROBERTSON: Sir D., *Lectures on Economic Principles*, London, Collins, 1969.

RORTY: A., ed., *The Identities of Persons*, Berkeley, University of California Press, 1976.

ROSS (1): W. D., *The Right and the Good*, Oxford, The Clarendon Press, 1930.

ROSS (2): W. D., *The Foundations of Ethics*, Oxford, The Clarendon Press, 1939.

RUSSELL: B., 'On the Nature of Acquaintance', reprinted in R. C. Marsh, ed., *Logic and Knowledge*, London, Allen and Unwin, 1956.

SAINSBURY: R. M., 'In Defence of Degrees of Truth', unpublished paper.

SALMON: N. U., *Reference and Essence*, Oxford, Basil Blackwell, 1982.

SAMUELSON: P. A., *Economics*, New York, McGraw-Hill, 1970.

SCANLON (1): T. M., 'Preference and Urgency', *The Journal of Philosophy* 72, No. 19, 6 Nov. 1975.

SCANLON (2): T. M., 'Rights, Goals, and Fairness', in S. Hampshire, ed., *Public and Private Morality*, Cambridge University Press, 1978.

SCANLON (3): T. M., 'Contractualism and Utilitarianism', in SEN AND WILLIAMS .

SCHEFFLER (1): S., 'Moral Independence and the Original Position', *Philosophical Studies* 35, 1979.

SCHEFFLER (2): S., *The Rejection of Consequentialism*, Oxford, Clarendon Press, 1982.

SCHEFFLER (3): S., 'Ethics, Personal Identity, and Ideals of the Person', *Canadian Journal of Philosophy* 12, No. 2, June 1982.

SCHELL: J., *The Fate of the Earth*, New York, Avon Books, 1982.

SCHELLING (1): T., *The Strategy of Conflict*, Cambridge, Mass., Harvard University Press, 1960.

SCHELLING (2): T., 'Hockey Helmets, Concealed Weapons, and Daylight Saving', *The Journal of Conflict Resolution*, Sept. 1973.

SCHNEEWIND: J. B., *Sidgwick's Ethics and Victorian Moral Philosophy*, Oxford University Press, 1977.

SCHUELER: G. F., 'Nagel on the Rationality of Prudence', *Philosophical Studies* 29, 1976.

SEN (1): A. K., *Collective Choice and Social Welfare*, San Francisco, Holden Day, 1970.

SEN (2): A. K., *Behaviour and the Concept of Preference*, London School of Economics, 1973.

SEN (3): A. K., 'Isolation, Assurance, and the Social Rate of Discount', *Quarterly Journal of Economics* 81, 1967.

SEN (4): A. K., 'Rational Fools: A Critique of the Behavioral Foundations of Economic Theory', *Philosophy and Public Affairs* 6, No. 4, Summer 1977.

SEN (5): A. K., 'Utilitarianism and Welfarism', *The Journal of Philosophy* 76, No. 9, Sept. 1979.

SEN (6): A. K., *On Economic Inequality*, Oxford, Clarendon Press, 1973.

SEN (7): A. K., 'Choice, Orderings, and Morality', in S. Korner, ed., *Practical Reason*, Oxford University Press, 1974.

SEN AND RUNCIMAN: A. K. Sen and W. G. Runciman, 'Games, Justice and the General Will', *Mind* 74, Oct. 1965.

SEN AND WILLIAMS: A. K. Sen and B. Williams, *Utilitarianism and Beyond*, Cambridge University Press, 1982.

SHOEMAKER (1): S., *Self-Knowledge and Self-Identity*, Ithaca, N.Y., Cornell University Press, 1963.

SHOEMAKER (2): S., 'Persons and Their Pasts', *American Philosophical Quarterly* 7, 1970.

SHOEMAKER (3): S., 'Wiggins on Identity', *Philosophical Review* 79, 1970.
SHORTER: J. M., 'More About Bodily Continuity and Personal Identity', *Analysis* 22, 1961-2.
SIDGWICK (1): H., *The Methods of Ethics*, London, Macmillan, 1907.
SIDGWICK (2): A. S. and E. M. S. Sidgwick, *Henry Sidgwick, a Memoir*, London, Macmillan, 1906.
SIKORA AND BARRY: R. I. Sikora and B. Barry, eds., *Obligations to Future Generations*, Philadelphia, Temple University Press, 1978.
SINGER (1): M., 'The Many Methods of Sidgwick's Ethics', *The Monist* 58, 1974.
SINGER (2): P., *The Expanding Circle*, New York, Farrar, Straus, and Giroux, 1981.
SMART (1): B., 'Diachronous and Synchronous Selves', *Canadian Journal of Philosophy* 6, No. 1, Mar. 1976.
SMART (2): J. J. C., ed., *Problems of Space and Time*, New York, Macmillan, 1976.
SMART AND WILLIAMS: J. J. C. Smart and B. Williams, *Utilitarianism: For and Against*, Cambridge University Press, 1973.
SOBEL (1): J. H., 'Interaction Problems for Utility Maximizers', *Canadian Journal of Philosophy* 4, No. 4, June 1975.
SOBEL (2): J. H., 'The Need for Coercion', in J. Pennock and H. Chapman, eds., *Coercion*, Chicago, Nomos, 1972.
SOLZHENITSYN: A., *The First Circle*, New York, Bantam Books, 1969.
SPERRY: R. W., in J. C. Eccles, ed., *Brain and Conscious Experience*, Berlin, Springer Verlag, 1966.
STRANG: C., 'What if Everyone Did That?', in THOMSON AND DWORKIN.
STRAWSON (1): P. F., *Individuals*, London, Methuen, 1959.
STRAWSON (2): P. F., *The Bounds of Sense*, London, Methuen, 1966.
STROTZ: 'Inconsistency and Myopia in Dynamic Utility Maximization', *Review of Economic Studies*, 1955-6.
SUMNER (1): L. W., 'The Good and the Right', *Canadian Journal of Philosophy*, Suppl. Vol. on John Stuart Mill and Utilitarianism, 1979.
SUMNER (2): L. W., *Abortion and Moral Theory*, Princeton University Press, 1981.
SWINBURNE: R. G., 'Personal Identity', *Proceedings of the Aristotelian Society* 74, 1973-4.
TEMKIN: L., 'Inequality', Ph.D. dissertation, Princeton University, 1982.
THOMSON AND DWORKIN: J. J. Thomson and G. Dworkin, eds., *Ethics*, New York, Harper and Row, 1968.
TOOLEY: M., *Abortion and Infanticide*, Oxford, Clarendon Press, 1983.
TREBLICOT: J., 'Aprudentialism', *American Philosophical Quarterly* 11, No. 3, July 1974.
ULLMAN-MARGALIT: E., *The Emergence of Norms*, Oxford, Clarendon Press, 1977.
UNGER (1): P., 'Why There Are No People', *Midwest Studies in Philosophy* 4, 1979.
UNGER (2): P., 'I Do Not Exist', in G. F. MacDonald, ed., *Perception and Identity*, Ithaca, N.Y., Cornell University Press, 1979.
VAN STRAATEN: Z., *Philosophical Subjects, Essays presented to P. F. Strawson*, Oxford, Clarendon Press, 1980.
WACHSBERG: M., *Personal Identity, the Nature of Persons, and Ethical Theory*, Ph.D. Dissertation, Princeton University, 1983.
WARNOCK: G. J., *The Object of Morality*, London, Methuen, 1971.
WATKIN: J., 'Imperfect Rationality', in R. Borger and F. Cioffi, eds., *Explanation in the Behavioural Sciences*, Cambridge University Press, 1970.
WIGGINS (1): D., *Identity and Spatio-Temporal Continuity*, Oxford, Basil Blackwell, 1967.
WIGGINS (2): D., 'Essentialism, Continuity, and Identity', *Synthese* 23, 1974.
WIGGINS (3): D., *Sameness and Substance*, Oxford, Basil Blackwell, 1980.
WIGGINS (4): D., 'Locke, Butler and the Stream of Consciousness', in RORTY.

WIGGINS (5): D., 'Identity, Designation, Essentialism and Physicalism', *Philosophia* 5, Nos. 1-2, Jan.-Apr. 1975.

WIGGINS (6): D., 'The Concern to Survive', *Midwest Studies in Philosophy* 4, 1979.

WILLIAMS (1): B., 'A Critique of Utilitarianism', in SMART AND WILLIAMS.

WILLIAMS (2): B., *Problems of the Self*, Cambridge University Press, 1973.

WILLIAMS (3): B., 'Persons, Character, and Morality', in RORTY.

WILLIAMS (4): B., *Descartes*, Harmondsworth, Penguin Books, 1978.

WILLIAMS (5): B., 'Internal and External Reasons', in R. Harrison, ed., *Rational Action: Studies in Philosophy and Social Science*, Cambridge University Press, 1979.

WILLIAMS (6): B., *Moral Luck*, Cambridge University Press, 1981.

WILLIAMS (7): B., 'The Point of View of the Universe: Sidgwick and the Ambitions of Ethics', *The Cambridge Review* 7 May 1982.

WILLIAMS (8): B., 'The Self and the Future', *Philosophical Review* 79, No. 2, Apr. 1970, reprinted in WILLIAMS (2).

WILLIAMS (9): B., 'Bodily Continuity and Personal Identity', *Analysis* 20, No. 5, reprinted in WILLIAMS (2).

WOODS: M., 'Reference and Self-Identification', *The Journal of Philosophy*, 1968.

INDEX OF NAMES

All Souls College, viii
Anschutz, R. P., 533
Anscombe, G. E. M., 512 n. 3, 513 n. 38, 515 n. 1, 533
Ayer, A. J., vii, 518 n. 43, 533

Baier, A., vii
Baier, K., vii, 512 nn. 55 and 59, 533
Barry, B., 523 n. 7, 533
Bayles, M. D., 533
Benditt, T., 533
Bennett, J., viii, 525 n. 25, 533
Bentham, J., 158–9, 464, 513 n. 22, 521 n. 109, 533
Blackburn, A., viii
Blackburn, S., vii
Blanshard, B., 512 n. 10, 533
Bogen, J., 522 n. 2, 533
Brams, S. J., 509 n. 29, 533
Brandt, R. B., 512 n. 2, 517–18 n. 18, 533
Braybrooke, D., 533
Brennan, A. A., vii, 518 n. 58, 533
Bricker, P., 532 n. 22
Broad, C. D., 517 n. 23, 533
Broome, J., viii, 491–3, 512 nn. 6 and 7, 514 n. 43, 517 n. 32, 533
Brown, P. G., 536
Buchanan, A., 510 n. 39, 533
Buddha, 273, 280, 453, 502–3
Butler, J., 219–22, 519 n. 12, 533
Byron, 176

Chekhov, 176
Chisholm, R., 309, 513 n. 78, 533
Collins, S., 503 n. 32, 532 nn. 27, 32, and 34, 534
Cornwall, G., viii

Davis, A., vii
Daniels, N., 534
Dasgupta, P., viii
Dent, N., vii
Dennett, D. C., 534, 535
Descartes, R., 223–8, 252, 516–17 nn. 19 and 20, 534
Deutscher, 515 n. 7, 536
Dostoyevsky, F., 558 n. 39
Dummett, M., 511 n. 47, 534

Dworkin, G., 539
Dworkin, R. M., vii, 528 n. 49, 534
Dyson, F., 518 n. 57

Edgley, R., 534
Edidin, A., 513 n. 37, 534
Edwards, R. B., 532 n. 25, 534
Elliott, R., vii, 534
Epicurus, 175
Espinas, 520 n. 97
Evans, G., vii, 516 n. 15, 517 n. 31, 534
Ewald, W., viii
Ewing, A. C., 510 n. 39, 534

Feinberg, J., 534
Findlay, J., 521 n. 110, 534
Fishkin, J. S., vii, 534
Foot, P., 512 n. 4, 534
Forbes, G., vii, 511 n. 47, 517 n. 27, 522 n. 2, 534

Gale, R. M., 534
Gauthier, D., 331, 334–5, 505 n. 5, 512 n. 55, 534
Geach, P., 325, 534
Gert, B., 512 n. 59, 523–4 n. 18, 534
Glover, J. C. B., vii, 76, 461, 511 n. 44, 534
Godwin, W., 366, 534
Goodin, R. E., vii, 534
Gosling, J. C. B., 512 n. 7, 534
Grice, H. P., 518 n. 43
Grice, G. R., 523–4 n. 18, 534
Griffin, C., viii
Griffin, J. P., vii, 525–6 n. 32, 532 n. 21, 534–5
Grim, P., 535
Guttenplan, S., 535

Haight, G. S., 530 n. 6, 535
Haksar, V., 323, 345, 535
Hardin, G., 535
Hare, R. M., vii, 112–13, 506 n. 13, 511 n. 48, 512 n. 60, 519 n. 85, 525 n. 21, 535
Harman, G., vii, 512 n. 59, 513 n. 33, 523–4 n. 18, 529 n. 2, 535
Hobbes, T., 64
Hofstadter, D. R., 535
Hollis, M., vii, 510 n. 40, 535
Hooker, B., vii, 528 2nd n. 1, 530 n. 7

Hume, D., 138–9, 159, 162, 176, 282, 453, 462–3, 512 n. 1, 513 nn. 30, 31, and 35, 515 n. 9, 529–30 nn. 3 and 4, 535
Hurka, T. M., vii, 527 n. 35b, 535
Hurley, S., vii, viii

Ishiguro, H., 516 n. 15, 522 n. 4

Jack, J. M. R., 518 n. 46
Jamieson, D., vii

Kagan, S., viii, 505 n. 7, 519 n. 83
Kamm, F. M., 528 n. 45
Kant, I., 64, 66, 67, 92, 106, 223, 225, 228, 353–5, 516 n. 17, 535
Kavka, G., vii, 432–3, 523 n. 9, 535
Kenyon, J., vii
Kripke, S., 515 nn. 3 and 11, 522 n. 2, 531 n. 9, 535

Leslie, J., viii
Levison, A., vii
Lewis, D. K., 258, 512 n. 42, 535
Lewis, H. D., vii, 516 n. 18, 536
Lewis, C. I., 158–9, 536
Lichtenberg, G. C., 224–6, 252, 517 n. 20, 536
Lindley, R., vii
Locke, J., 205–8, 219, 223–4, 228, 307, 325, 536
Lyons, D., vii, 536

Macintyre, A., 519 n. 84
Mackaye, J., 393, 536
Mackie, J. L., vii, 29, 511 n. 43, 512–13 n. 13, 518 n. 43, 523–4 n. 18, 528 n. 45, 536
Maclean, D., vii, 536
McDermott, M., 536
McDowell, J., vii
McMahan, J., vii, viii, 523 n. 16, 525 n. 26, 527 n. 35, 528 nn. 41 and 42, 532 n. 19, 536
McMahan, S., viii
Madell, G., vii, 307, 323, 516 n. 18, 517–18 n. 36, 536
Marglin, S., 531 n. 15, 536
Martin, 515 n. 7, 536
Matilal, B., vii
Meehl, P., 511–12 nn. 42–3, 536
Mill, J. S., 114, 319, 520–2 n. 109
Miller, F., 504 n. 39, 536
Montefiore, A., 536
Morison, P., viii
Moore, G. E., 512–13 n. 13, 532 n. 23, 536

Nabokov, V., 519 n. 92, 536
Nagel, T., vii, 123, 130, 143–4, 154–6, 189–90, 246, 273–4, 289–97, 335, 343–4, 468–77, 506–9 n. 15, 528 nn. 3 and 4, 536
Narveson, J., 394, 523–4 n. 18, 525 nn. 25 and 31, 536
Newman, Cardinal, 49, 536

Newton, Sir Isaac, 252
Nietzsche, F., ii, 90, 176, 536
Norman, R., 512 n. 3, 536
Nozick, R., vii, 274, 389, 477–9, 513 n. 36, 514 n. 45, 518 n. 48, 520 n. 93, 536–7
Nunns, J., viii

Olson, M., 510 n. 39, 537
Ooms, T., 523 n. 8
Ordeshook, 511 n. 43, 539

Parfit, D., 528 n. 34, 537
Parfit, E. J. R., v, viii
Parfit, J., v
Parfit, N., v
Partridge, E., 537
Peacocke, C., vii, 221, 511 n. 47, 517 n. 27, 537
Pears, D. F., vii, 513 n. 41, 537
Penelhum, T., 519 n. 66, 537
Perfectus, T., 472
Perry, J., 307–8, 518 n. 43, 537
Pigou, 161
Plato, 161, 389, 537
Proust, M., 513–14 n. 42, 537
Putnam, H., 525 n. 9
Pythagoras, 172, 175

Quine, W. V. O., 200, 537
Quinton, A., 254, 295, 297, 509 n. 8, 518 n. 43, 518–19 n. 59, 537

Rahula, W., 537
Railton, P., vii, 537
Rakowski, E., vii
Rapoport, A., 512 n. 55, 537
Rashdall, H., 142, 537
Raverat, G., 522 n. 1, 537
Rawls, J., 163, 331, 335–6, 392, 422, 479, 484–7, 509 n. 23, 512 n. 59, 520 n. 109, 523–4 n. 18, 528 n. 4, 537
Ray, C., 537
Raz, J., 537
Regan, D., vii, viii, 505 n. 12, 509 n. 28, 511 n. 46, 537
Reid, T., 223, 323, 537–8
Rescher, N., 512 n. 55, 538
Richards, D. A. J., 523–4 n. 18, 538
Riker, W., 511 n. 43, 538
Robertson, D., 382, 538
Rorty, A., 538
Ross, W. D., 69, 538
Runciman, W., 510 n. 33, 538
Russell, B., 518 n. 37, 538

Sainsbury, R. M., vii, 511 n. 47, 538
Salotti, P., viii
Salmon, N. U., 517 n. 31, 538
Samuelson, P., 525 n. 20, 538
Sartorius, R., 510 n. 39, 536

Scanlon, T. M., vii, 523–4 n. 18, 526 n. 32, 538
Scheffler, S., vii, 538
Schell, J., 538
Schelling, T., 12, 14, 16, 37, 39, 512 n. 58, 538
Schneewind, J. B., 512 n. 6, 538
Schueler, G. F., 538
Schwartz, T., 523 n. 11
Seabright, P., vii
Sen, A. K., vii, 510 n. 35, 528 n. 49, 538
Shoemaker, S., 225, 516 n. 13, 518 n. 38, 538–9
Shorter, J. M., 518 n. 46, 539
Sidgwick, A. S., 539
Sidgwick, H., 112–13, 137–42, 176, 307, 329–30, 459–61, 463, 494, 509 n. 18, 512 n. 6, 520 n. 108, 521 n. 109, 528 n. 2, 529–31 nn. 2, 4, and 7, 532 n. 24, 533
Sikora, R. I., viii, 527 n. 36, 533
Singer, M., 539
Singer, P., vii, 514 n. 44, 533
Smart, B., 539
Smart, J. J. C., 539
Smith, M., vii
Sobel, J. H., 539
Solzhenitsyn, A., 519 nn. 63 and 64, 539
Sperry, R. W., 517 n. 33, 539
Stcherbatsky, T., 532 nn. 29–33
Sterba, J., 526 n. 32
Stone. J., vii
Strang, C., 510 n. 37, 539
Strawson, G., viii
Strawson, P. F., vii, x, 225, 539
Strotz, 513 n. 26, 539
Sumner, L. W., vii, 512 n. 60, 519 n. 85, 539
Swinburne, R. G., vii, 307–9, 514 n. 43, 539

Taylor, 512 n. 59
Temkin, L., viii, 521 n. 112, 528 nn. 53 and 54, 539
Thomson, J. J., vii, 508 n. 43, 539
Tooley, M., vii, 519 n. 85, 523 n. 13, 539
Treblicot, J., 539

Ullmann-Margalit, E., 504 n. 37, 539
Unger, P., vii, 517 n. 27, 539

Vickers, J., vii
Van Straaten, Z., 539
Von Wright, G., 509 n. 1

Wachsberg, M., viii, 308–9, 516 n. 17, 539
Walker, R., vii
Warnock, G. J., 512 n. 59, 539
Warren, M., 519 n. 25
Watkin, J., 539
Whiting, J., vii
Whitty, C., viii
Wiggins, D., 254, 271, 273, 307, 516 n. 15, 518 nn. 40, 41, 48, 50, 51, and 53, 539–40
Williams, B. A. O., 143, 225–6, 229–33, 236, 266–73, 283, 293–7, 467–8, 481, 508, 509 nn. 17, 19, 20–2, and 24, 518 n. 4, 513 n. 19, 517 nn. 22 and 24, 518 n. 55, 528 1st n. 1, 531 n. 17, 540
Wittgenstein, L., 200, 273
Woodford, M., viii, 527 n. 34, 528 n. 46
Woods, M., 518 n. 41, 540
Wright, C., 517 n. 27